Keywords for American Cultural Studies

Keywords for American Cultural Studies

SECOND EDITION

Edited by Bruce Burgett *and* Glenn Hendler

NEW YORK UNIVERSITY PRESS   New York *and* London

NEW YORK UNIVERSITY PRESS
New York and London
www.nyupress.org

References to Internet websites (URLs) were accurate at the time
of writing. Neither the author nor New York University Press is
responsible for URLs that may have expired or changed since the
manuscript was prepared.

Library of Congress Cataloging-in-Publication Data
Keywords for American cultural studies / edited by Bruce Burgett and
Glenn Hendler. — Second edition.
pages cm   Includes bibliographical references.
ISBN 978-0-8147-2531-3 (hardback) — ISBN 978-0-8147-0801-9 (pb)
1. Vocabulary. 2. United States—Civilization. 3. Social structure—
Terminology. 4. Culture—Terminology. I. Burgett, Bruce, 1963–
editor. II. Hendler, Glenn, 1962– editor.
PE1449.K49   2014
428.1—dc23   2014024855

New York University Press books are printed on acid-free paper, and
their binding materials are chosen for strength and durability. We
strive to use environmentally responsible suppliers and materials to
the greatest extent possible in publishing our books.

Manufactured in the United States of America

10 9 8 7 6 5 4 3 2 1

Also available as an ebook

Contents

The following essays are available online at keywords.nyupress.org:

Acknowledgments

Writing the acknowledgments for a publication such as this one is a daunting task, particularly when the friendships and collaborations that have made it possible span many years and cover the production of two volumes, one of which is print and digital. We should begin, of course, by listing the names of our contributors. All of them have produced marvelous intellectual work, after enduring what must have seemed endless requests for revision. We thank them all for putting up with us, and many of them for putting up with us twice.

The idea for this publication emerged, developed, and was tested through interactions with a series of collaborators, interlocutors, and audiences, including the American Cultures workshop at the University of Chicago; the Americanist Workshop at the University of Notre Dame; the Columbia American Studies Seminar; the Simpson Center for the Humanities at the University of Washington; the Clinton Institute at University College Dublin; the Futures of American Studies Institute at Dartmouth College; the Cultural Studies Now Conference at the University of East London; the Mobility Shifts Learning Summit at the New School for Social Research; the Graduate Center at the City University of New York; Evergreen State College; St. John's University; the University of Wisconsin–Milwaukee; Yale University; and the annual conferences of the American Studies Association, the Cultural Studies Association, and the Modern Language Association, among others.

Thanks to everyone who participated in and attended those events and specifically to Carla Peterson and Sandy Zagarell for sharing their concept early on for a keywords conference panel, to Chandan Reddy and Nikhil Singh for offering advice at various points along the way, and to Kathy Woodward for being a catalyst for the digital aspects of the publication. We also want to thank the University of Notre Dame's Institute for Scholarship in the Liberal Arts for its support of the first edition of *Keywords for American Cultural Studies*. Generous support for the development of the second edition and, especially, its digital components was provided by the Simpson Center for the Humanities at the University of Washington and by the Graduate School of Arts and Sciences, Instructional Technology and Academic Computing, the Office of Research, and the Deans of Arts and Sciences at Fordham University.

One thing those institutions funded was the labor of a series of brilliant and efficient graduate students. Brooke Cameron was absolutely central to the production of the first edition, working tirelessly to correspond with contributors, to maintain files on all of the essays, to check and recheck bibliographical citations, and to generate an increasingly baroque spreadsheet of deadlines, revisions, and addresses. Liz Porter and then Julia Cosacchi played similar roles in the second edition, tracking a dizzying array of citations across more than ninety essays and putting them in their proper places. Deborah Kimmey was critical to the launch of the first iteration of the *Keywords* website, including the management of the Keywords Collaboratory at the University of Washington. It would not have happened without her. Elizabeth Cornell followed ably in

Deborah's place when the Collaboratory moved from the University of Washington to Fordham University and has been equally central to its subsequent success and further development.

Eric Zinner deserves credit for looking at lists of words and names and seeing the idea not for one or two publications but for an entire enterprise. His keyword has to be *branding*. Thanks to Garbo, whose keyword was *squirrel*; to Miriam, whose keyword is *skill*; to Nina, whose keyword is *mood ring*; and to Ezra, whose keyword is *David Bowie*. Thanks, finally, to our readers and users, past and future, who treat the *Keywords for American Cultural Studies* not as summative of work completed but as generative of future projects. You are the reason we undertook it.

* * *

We dedicate this edition of *Keywords* to the memory of three important scholars who worked in American studies and cultural studies, all of whom passed away in the months before this publication went to press. Rosemary Marangoly George's contributions to postcolonial studies, especially in *The Politics of Home* and *Burning Down the House*, were the reason we asked her to write on *domesticity*; we mourn her passing in October 2013. The ideas that José Estaban Muñoz developed in *Disidentifications* and *Cruising Utopia*, along with his larger body of work in performance studies and queer theory, reverberate through many of the essays in this volume, even though he could not complete the essay he was working on when he passed away in late 2013. And one of the giants of cultural studies, Stuart Hall, died in early February 2014. His influence on this publication is a testament to the ongoing power of his scholarship. We hope that *Keywords for American Cultural Studies* carries on the intellectual tradition of these three scholars.

Keywords

An Introduction

Bruce Burgett and Glenn Hendler

I. What Is a Keyword?

In contemporary usage, the term "keyword" generally refers to a type of data or metadata. The *Oxford English Dictionary*'s primary definition is "a word serving as a key to a cipher or code," one that provides "a solution or explanation" or one that is "of particular importance or significance." Dating from the mid-eighteenth century, these usages represent keywords as data that unlock mysteries. The *OED*'s second definition is a term "chosen to indicate or represent the content of a larger text or record" in an "index, catalogue, or database." Dating from the early nineteenth century, this usage represents keywords as tools for information retrieval within various archiving systems. This second meaning points toward the most familiar usage of the term today. Keywords are forms of metadata that authors, librarians, book indexers, concordance makers, web designers, and database builders add to a print or digital text to guide users to significant clusters of meaning. The interactive information ecologies of "Web 2.0" extend this usage in interesting ways. They enable consumers of information to produce their own metadata, which can then be visualized as keyword clouds or tag clouds. Metadata becomes a user-centered and interactive means of organizing, customizing, and sharing data.

When you look up a term in *Keywords for American Cultural Studies*, you will find that these definitions are both resonant and limited. The essays you will encounter synthesize a great deal of information about the historical and contemporary meanings of terms that structure the fields of American studies and cultural studies. By discussing how the meanings of those terms have developed over time, they may unlock some mysteries and crack a few codes. In this sense, the essays help readers to understand the concepts they encounter and to chart relations among them. But *Keywords for American Cultural Studies* is not a reference guide written for novices by academic cryptologists revealing the secrets of American studies and cultural studies. Nor is it an effort to set or fix the meanings of words on the basis of past usage, as a dictionary might. While many of the essays open by referring, as we do here, to usage histories archived in dictionaries such as the *OED*, they do so not to anchor the meanings of words in their past deployments but to remind readers that words change their meanings over time and across space. They then explore and explain the social and historical contexts of those usages, trace the genealogy of debates over key terms that have structured the fields of American studies and cultural studies, and speculate about the ongoing significance of those debates. As a whole, *Keywords for American Cultural Studies* aims to map the fissures and fault lines of the past, present, and future, treating the terms within it as sites of unresolved conflict and contestation.

II. Where Does *Keywords for American Cultural Studies* Come From?

The understanding of keywords central to this publication—both the print book and the digital site—is rooted in the writings of the British cultural studies scholar Raymond Williams. Upon his return from World War II, Williams became interested in how the meanings of certain words, which he only later called "keywords," seemed to have shifted during his absence. Two books that were to hold great importance for the emerging field of cultural studies resulted from this experiential insight. The first, *Culture and Society, 1780–1950* (1958), traced a genealogy of the complex and contradictory mid-twentieth-century usages of the word "culture" through nearly two centuries of writings by British intellectuals concerned with the antagonistic relations between political democracy and capitalist industrialization. The second, *Keywords: A Vocabulary of Culture and Society* (1976), collected 134 short essays (151 in the 1983 revised edition), all of which gloss shifts over the same two centuries in the meanings of terms ranging from "behavior" and "charity" to "sensibility" and "work." As Williams explained in his introduction to the first edition of *Keywords*, he wrote these short essays in his spare moments and originally conceived of them as an appendix to *Culture and Society*. Only later did he develop them into a separate publication, as their sum grew in scope and complexity and as he began to understand and articulate the methodological stakes of the project he had undertaken. *Keywords* is, Williams insisted, "not a dictionary or glossary of a particular academic subject. It is not a series of footnotes to dictionary histories or definitions of a number of words. It is, rather, the record of an inquiry into a *vocabulary*" (15).

"Vocabulary" is in many ways the unacknowledged keyword of Williams's introduction. His use of that term can help us to explain how *Keywords for American Cultural Studies* works and to clarify how it differs from more conventional reference books. Williams deployed the term in order to distinguish his project not only from those of dictionary editors and glossary makers but also from the research and writings of academic philologists and linguists, who examine the formal and structural components of language systems and their evolution. In contrast, Williams focused his keyword essays on what he called "historical semantics" (1976, 23), emphasizing the ways in which meanings are made and altered over time through contestations among the usages of diverse social groups and movements. "What can be done in dictionaries," Williams wrote, "is necessarily limited by their proper universality and by the long time-scale of revision which that, among other factors, imposes. The present inquiry, being more limited—not a dictionary, but a vocabulary—is more flexible" (26). This underlining of the flexibility of a "vocabulary"—as opposed to the universality of a "dictionary"—points to Williams's general premise that language systems develop and change in relation to local and practical usages. Dictionaries, glossaries, and other reference books rely on experts and reproduce a discourse of expertise by downplaying the creative and unpredictable aspects of interactive and idiosyncratic forms of meaning making. Vocabularies provide a counterpoint to this reliance on experts and expertise. They treat knowledge as a process that is responsive to the diverse constituencies that use and revise the meanings of the keywords that shape our understandings of the present, the future, and the past. To return to our opening conceit, they think about keywords as metadata produced socially and historically in relation to specific communities of users and emerging forms of practice.

Keywords for American Cultural Studies shares a number of these fundamental premises with Williams's volume, as well as its other successors (Bennett, Grossberg, and Morris 2005) and the various *Keywords* volumes published by NYU Press (Nel and Paul 2011; Schlund-Vials, Vo, and Wong, forthcoming; Adams, Reiss, and Serlin, forthcoming; Adamson, Gleason, and Pellow, forthcoming). It provides an accessible and readable introduction to some of the central terms and debates that shape the study of culture and society today. It circles around the keyword "culture" in the same way Williams's two volumes did as they explored that central term's interactions with neighboring concepts such as art, industry, class, and democracy. And it insists that our understanding of these terms and the interactions among them can be enhanced—rather than settled or shut down—by a heightened awareness of their historical genealogies and the conflicts embedded in differing and even contradictory uses of those terms. At the same time, there are several aspects of *Keywords for American Cultural Studies* that distinguish it from Williams's *Keywords*. Most obviously, it is a collaborative enterprise involving more than ninety authors working across a range of disciplinary and interdisciplinary fields that overlap with—but seldom map neatly onto—either American studies or cultural studies. Most importantly, its exploration of culture and society is explicitly linked to a nation (the United States) or, at times, a geography (the Americas).

The keyword "America" is thus essential to our project in two ways. First, the term in all of its mutations—"American," "Americas," "Americanization," "Americanist"—has to be defined in relation to what Williams called "particular formations of meaning" (1976/1983, 15). "America," in other words, is a category with particularizing effects that are as central to how we think about the possibilities and limitations of the field of American studies as the universalizing term "culture" is to our understanding of the shape of the field of cultural studies. Second, contemporary disagreements over the category's field-defining function point toward a wide range of debates related to what is now commonly called the postnational or transnational turn in American studies. Just as the universalizing referents of Williams's own project have been troubled by subsequent work in cultural studies that has rendered

explicit his tendency to assume a narrowly "British" (largely white, working-class) readership and archive for that project (Gilroy 1987), the category "America" has been troubled within American studies in part through the field's interactions with cultural studies, though more pressingly by its engagements with new "formations of meaning" emerging from shifting patterns of migration and immigration, existing and evolving diasporic communities, and the neoliberal cultural and economic phenomena associated with financialization and globalization. The fact that twelve of the words in this last sentence—"culture," "white," "class," "America," "migration," "immigration," "diaspora," "community," "economy," "neoliberal," "finance," and "globalization"—are titles of essays in *Keywords for American Cultural Studies* indicates how rich and complex this research has become.

In our editorial conversations with our contributors, we have attempted to draw out this richness and complexity by insisting—as Kirsten Silva Gruesz does in her essay on "America"—that authors specify when they are talking about "America" and when they are talking about the "United States." It is an editorial decision that has produced some useful results. Nearly all of the essays reach across U.S. national borders to track usages of terms such as "America," "South," and "West" and across disciplinary formations such as political philosophy and social theory, where terms ranging from "neoliberalism" and "politics" to "secularism" and "religion" may be inflected in particular ways in the United States but cannot be subsumed under either an "American" or an "Americanist" rubric. Similarly, terms that might from one perspective be viewed as a subset of American studies (or cultural studies focused on the United States) are consistently shown to have transnational histories and future trajectories. Essays on "African," "Asian," "mestizo/a," "Latin@," "indigenous," "Indian," "coolie," "black," and "white" all map cultural formations and develop lines of inquiry that are neither exclusive to the United States nor exhausted by U.S.-based versions of ethnic studies. Transnational understandings of keywords such as "diaspora," "migration," "immigration," "youth," and "naturalization" similarly push us to reimagine the political geographies of the United States, as well as the nation-based intellectual geographies of the institutions that study it. And they indicate the involvement of our contributors in a wide variety of critical interdisciplinarities, ranging from queer studies to indigenous studies to community studies.

A final difference between the two projects is evident in the fact nearly all of our contributors have followed our editorial lead by referring in their essays to American studies and cultural studies as two separate fields of inquiry, even as our title seems to name just one: American cultural studies. The point of this analytic separation is to stage an ongoing encounter between the two fields. That encounter is not new, of course, and critical engagement with the usage history of key terms ranging from "pastoralism" (L. Marx 1964/2000) to "gay" (Chauncey 1994) to "racism" (Fields and Fields 2012) has been as central to American studies as it has been to cultural studies. As Michael Denning (2004) observes, the reasons for this parallel development are complex. Both American studies and cultural studies emerged in the 1940s, '50s, and '60s as critical responses to reductionist versions of literary formalism and Marxist materialism, and both advocated for cultural criticism as a means of reconstructing a usable past oriented toward a more democratic and socially just future. Yet the two fields also evolved differently, with cultural studies taking on the question "What is culture?" while American studies focused on the question "What is American?" Denning suggests that

the first question proved more useful than the second since it opened inquiry onto a wider range of cultural forms and forms of political action. Since Denning drew this conclusion in the mid-1980s, the field of American studies itself has turned toward those modes of inquiry, partly as a result of its encounter with work in cultural studies on questions of region, migration, and diaspora but also due to the engagement of both fields with other forms of intersectional analysis, including work produced in the new interdisciplinary formations that emerged from the social movements of the 1960s and have evolved significantly since then, such as ethnic studies, postcolonial studies, disability studies, working-class studies, and women, gender, and sexuality studies.

III. What Does *Keywords for American Cultural Studies* Do?

Keywords for American Cultural Studies provides readers with a map of the shifting terrain created by several decades of work located at the intersections of American studies, cultural studies, and other emergent interdisciplinary fields. A rigorous encounter with these relatively new intellectual and institutional formations requires recognition of one of their central lessons: all forms of inquiry and sites of institutionalization, including academic departments, conferences, and journals, police their boundaries by leaving something—and often someone—out of the analytical frame. This boundedness is not simply a result of the limitations of time and space. Exploring its causes is central to the core methodology of those fields, all of which stress the importance of reflexivity with respect to the social and political commitments of readers, interpreters, and researchers, as well as their temporal and spatial positionalities. For this reason, it is critical to understand *Keywords for American Cultural Studies* not only as a map of contemporary scholarship or lexicon of critical terms but also as a methodological provocation to think about inquiry in ways that are self-reflexive, open-ended, and future oriented. All of the essays frame and pursue research questions that are situated responses to shifts in contemporary political, social, and institutional life. We want to provoke our readers to do the same by encouraging them to think critically and creatively about how knowledge about "America" and its "cultures" has been, is, and should be made. *Keywords for American Cultural Studies* is, in this sense, both a guide to some of the best existing research in and across the fields it maps and an argument for maintaining and enhancing a commitment to critical and interdisciplinary approaches to the future evolution of those fields.

In *Keywords*, Williams demonstrated his commitment to a self-reflexive and future-oriented approach to inquiry by including several blank pages at the end of his book. These pages were intended, as he put it, "not only for the convenience of making notes, but as a sign that the inquiry remains open, and that the author will welcome all amendments, corrections, and additions" (26). We share this desire to mark the boundedness— and openness—of the inquiry, though readers will find no blank pages at the back of *Keywords for American Cultural Studies*. Instead, we want to underscore the obvious point that many keywords of American studies and cultural studies do not appear here. Take as an example the keyword "individual." A reader who in high school was exposed to the old saw that "American" (read: U.S.) culture is characterized by an ideology of "individualism" might at first be dismayed to find no essay on that term. But that reader might then look for—or be guided to—terms closely related to the concept of individuality: most clearly "subject" and "identity" but also "interiority" and "body." From there, he or she could move either to keywords that qualify and constitute individuality, such as "race,"

"ethnicity," "gender," "sex," "normal," and "disability," or to keywords that name places and concepts within which "individualism" is contested and constructed, such as "family," "religion," "corporation," "state," and "city." This line of inquiry could then bring the reader to "public" and "community" for broader framings of the missing essay on "individual." And he or she might even end up reading the essay on "society," recognizing that individualism is always in tension with social norms. At this point, the reader would have a much more nuanced understanding of what other keywords and concepts are necessary to map the relationship between "individual" and "society."

We imagine that this hypothetical example will strike some readers as persuasive, while others will remain skeptical of our editorial choices. In relation to both groups, we want to echo Williams by extending an invitation to our readers to become collaborators in keywords projects that extend beyond the essays in *Keywords for American Cultural Studies*. We ask you to revise, reject, and respond to the essays that do— and do not—appear in this publication, to create new clusters of meaning among them, and to develop deeper and richer discussions of what a given term does and can mean when used in specific local and global contexts. To this end, we offer the following, necessarily incomplete list of words about which we, as coeditors of *Keywords for American Cultural Studies*, would like to hear and read more: activism, age, agency, alien, anarchy, Arab, archive, art, book, bureaucracy, canon, celebrity, character, child, Christian, commodity, consent, conservative, country, creativity, creole, debt, depression, derivative, desire, development, disciplinary, education, elite, equality, European, evolution, experience, expert, fascism, feminine, fiction, folk, friendship, hegemony, heritage, heterosexual, history, homosexual, human, imagination, individual, intellectual, Jewish, justice, liberty, literacy, local, masculine, management, manufacture, minority, mission, multicultural, Muslim, native, nature, opinion, oratory, patriotism, performativity, place, pleasure, pluralism, policy, popular, poverty, pragmatism, print, psychology, radical, reality, representation, republicanism, reservation, resistance, revolution, rights, romance, security, segregation, settler, socialism, sodomy, sovereignty, subaltern, text, theory, tourism, tradition, transgender, translation, trauma, university, utopia, virtual, virtue, wealth, welfare, work.

This already too-long list could go on for pages, and even then it would be easy to conjure other possibilities. Whether keywords projects take the form of classroom assignments, research and working groups, edited volumes, or public forums, they must remain open to further elaboration and amendment not simply due to dynamics of inclusion and exclusion or limitations of time and space. Rather, their incompletion is methodologically central to any self-reflexive and future-oriented understanding of how research is conducted and how knowledge is made, both inside and outside academic settings. Claiming the ability to map complex fields of knowledge while also maintaining a critical approach to how the questions and problems that constitute those fields are—and should be—framed requires both intellectual modesty and an openness to further collaboration. One useful response to this modesty and openness may be a critique of what is included in and excluded from this publication. We welcome this response, and we also want to encourage all of our readers to take this response a step further by making something new, whether that new thing is as minor as a conversation or classroom assignment or as major as an edited volume, digital archive, or public initiative. The true measure of the success of *Keywords for American Cultural Studies* will be its ability

to clear conceptual space for these future projects, as readers, scholars, teachers, and students develop new and challenging research questions in dialogue with others who may not quite share a common vocabulary but who do know something about where conflicts and debates over meaning come from, why they matter, and how they might matter differently in the future. We look forward to reading and hearing about the results of these inquiries.

IV. Why Is *Keywords for American Cultural Studies* a Print-Digital Hybrid?

When we published the first edition of *Keywords for American Cultural Studies*, we knew that our gestures toward creative response and open-ended inquiry would be empty if we did not follow through on them. This knowledge led us to design, with the generous and generative assistance of Deborah Kimmey, a digital supplement to the print book where readers could work individually or collaboratively to create new keyword essays. The Keywords Collaboratory—which was later administered and developed further by Elizabeth Cornell—was our Web 2.0 version of Williams's blank pages. It was an experiment designed to supplement the print volume by catalyzing collaboration and publishing responses to the essays the book did and did not contain. As we discuss in our "Note on Classroom Use," the experiment worked, at least in some college classrooms where students collaborated on a variety of assignments that asked them either to supplement existing essays or to create new ones. Like our authors, students developed different approaches to the keywords they had been assigned. Some of the essays in the book and some of the responses to course assignments are explicitly argumentative and polemical, while others are more descriptive and ecumenical. A few are willfully idiosyncratic, and several hint at implicit disagreements among their authors. Yet across all of this work, the reader will find scholarly writing that models critical and creative thinking and authors who simultaneously analyze and evince the ways in which keywords are, as Williams put it, both "binding words in certain activities and their interpretation" and "indicative words in certain forms of thought" (1976, 15).

In our planning for the current edition of *Keywords for American Cultural Studies*, we extended this experiment by talking about the publication as a "print-digital hybrid," a term we used with NYU Press even before we knew exactly what it would mean. This commitment resulted in the current publication, with sixty-four essays appearing in the print volume and another thirty-three on the digital site. Three of the essays—on "digital," "media," and "technology"—form a thematic cluster that appears in print and on the site. When linked to the print book, the site provides four opportunities that the print book could not: it enables us to publish more essays without expanding the physical volume beyond a manageable and affordable size; it allows for a broader circulation of the essays that appear on the site; it enables an interactive indexing of all of the essays in the publication; and it opens the possibility of multimodal composition and postpublication response. Most important, though, the site allows users to supplement and expand on the existing essays in ways that print books preclude. Readers and users can work individually or collaboratively to assemble and publish responses and additions to what we offer in *Keywords for American Cultural Studies*. Readers interested in these possibilities—especially instructors of courses—should consult our "Note on Classroom Use" for ideas about how to get started.

Note on Classroom Use

We emphasize in "Keywords: An Introduction" that one of the primary aims of *Keywords for American Cultural Studies* is to provoke readers to engage in self-reflexive, open-ended, and future-oriented forms of inquiry as they conduct research on and make claims about "America" and its various "cultures." We want our readers to respond to the online and print essays by revising them or adding to them and, in doing so, supplementing the collective argument of the whole. In order to make good on this desire, we built a website (http://keywords.nyupress.org) as a complement to the first print version of *Keywords for American Cultural Studies* in 2007. This site included an interactive forum, which we called the "Keywords Collaboratory," where readers could work individually or collaboratively to create new keywords essays. Between 2007 and 2014, over five hundred readers used the site to that end, with the vast majority of those uses taking place in the context of college courses in which all or parts of *Keywords for American Cultural Studies* were assigned. These courses included first-year writing sections, large undergraduate lectures, small upper-division seminars, and advanced graduate courses. They focused on topics ranging from American studies and cultural studies research methodologies to gender and ethnic studies to video-game studies. Our goal in this "Note on Classroom Use" is to catalyze further experimentation on the site, now that *Keywords for American Cultural Studies* is a fully print-digital publication. To this end, we focus on classroom use of the print book and digital site, though we also welcome other possibilities, including revisions and additions produced by individuals and collectives located inside or outside higher education.

Syllabi and assignments from courses that have used *Keywords for American Cultural Studies* are available on the website, as are selected essays, published there after being edited and reviewed by us. We have learned from this emerging archive that keyword essays can play many different roles in courses. It is possible to assign them to provide background for other materials that students are reading or research that they are undertaking, though this approach tends to be successful only with advanced students who are prepared to digest the critical debates they encounter. In discussions with instructors who have used *Keywords for American Cultural Studies* in introductory or survey courses, we have consistently heard that it is important to *teach* the essays by providing some time in class to unpack them, rather than simply assigning them and assuming their immediate legibility. The reason for this caution is not that the essays are particularly dense or jargon laden. Rather, instructors have found that students need to learn how to approach a keyword essay, to understand it as a specific genre of writing and mode of inquiry. If this preparatory work is not done, the risk is that students will misread the individual essays and the publication as a whole as a reference guide whose aim is to define or fix the meanings of terms. If they adopt this approach, they will be frustrated, largely because the essays quite deliberately take a more critical, self-reflexive, and speculative stance in relation to their objects of inquiry. We wrote "Keywords: An Introduction," in part, to provide a resource for instructors who want to teach *Keywords for American Cultural Studies* as a methodology, not just a mapping of clusters of important concepts and terms.

Other instructors have moved beyond using *Keywords for American Cultural Studies* as a map of the fields it surveys or a primer in critical methodologies. With great success, they have asked students to produce keywords projects of their own, accepting the invitation we offer to our readers to respond to the publication by producing new knowledge themselves. Some assignments ask students to revise or supplement published keyword essays; others invite them to create essays about terms not included there. Both types of assignments have often begun from a version of the prompts we asked our authors to use in constructing their essays:

- What kinds of critical projects does your keyword enable?
- What are the critical genealogies of the term, and how do these genealogies affect its use today?
- Are there ways of thinking that are occluded or obstructed by the use of this term?
- What other keywords constellate around it?

These prompts were intended to spur our contributors to map the contemporary critical terrain as they see it developing through their keyword. They can serve a similar purpose in relation to student work, so long as students understand that their compositions will be more limited in scope than those published in *Keywords for American Cultural Studies* and will draw on significantly different (and usually smaller) archives. Our contributors work primarily with historical and contemporary research in American studies, cultural studies, and related fields. For students assigned to compose a keyword essay, the primary archive is often materials encountered in their particular course. Since the meanings and connotations of keywords are never settled and depend significantly on the local context in which they are used, students can write original essays based on these types of materials. They can produce

essays on terms that may not be keywords for the broader field but are crucial sites of debate and conflict within the scope of an individual course's subject matter.

Instructors have taken a wide range of approaches to assigning students to compose a keyword essay, but most have broken the process into two stages:

1. *Archiving usages of a particular keyword.* Many assignments begin by asking students to archive usages of their keyword. Archiving can involve simply copying or typing out every sentence students read that uses their keyword, though the archive need not be textual. It can also involve images and sound, conversations overheard on the street, or exchanges on a bus. Depending on the course, the process of archiving can build core skills in close reading, participant-observation, and other forms of data gathering. These processes usefully focus on the nuances of language and inflection in students' readings and interactions but can also reveal the tensions and contradictions in that language, underscoring the crucial point that keywords are sites of contestation. It can be useful to ask students to keep a usage log in which they record the spatial and temporal location of a specific use of the term.

2. *Composing a keyword essay.* This portion of the assignment typically asks students to tell a story about the various usages they have logged of their keyword. From reading essays in *Keywords for American Cultural Studies*, students should already know that it is rarely possible to produce a linear narrative about a complex term; the effort to do so themselves underscores this point. Especially in an interdisciplinary context in which students are asked to make sense of an array of materials that use different vocabularies and methodologies, the effort to bring together the varying usages of a single keyword can make the content of the course clearer and more coherent. Ethnographic assignments can serve a similar function by

asking students to attend to the contexts of specific usages. Depending on the context and objectives of any given course, these types of assignments can be completed either individually or collaboratively and may involve written, visual, or multimodal composition strategies.

While instructors have structured their assignments in a variety of ways to suit their specific course goals, we do provide a location on the digital site that is designed to catalyze these sorts of activities: the "Keywords Collaboratory." Dozens of courses have used the Collaboratory, allowing students to grasp and internalize the intellectual and theoretical points implicit in a keywords project. Sometimes students have been divided into small working groups of three to five, each focused on a different keyword that runs through or is central to the course. Sometimes an entire course or seminar has worked together on a single keyword. In each case, the students need to be taught to collaborate both on the ideas and on the mechanics of the essay composition, whether it is written, audio, visual, or some combination of the three. This approach tends to jolt students out of the idea that writing and composition *has* to be the solitary and individualistic activity typical of college classrooms, especially in the humanities and humanistic social sciences. The Collaboratory is, in this sense, an illustration of a point made by some of the most ardent advocates for the digital humanities: digital work tends to push scholars in the cultural disciplines toward more collaborative research methodologies and composition practices. It also makes clear one point that college instructors labor to teach: the audience for classroom assignments is not limited to the person who is assessing those assignments. The Collaboratory teaches this lesson since it is open to the broader public, not only to the students in the course but also to anyone who wanders onto the site. Instructors using the Collaboratory have found that an

orientation toward a larger public encourages students to think more carefully and, often, more ambitiously about their writing and composition choices.

We urge instructors to go to keywords.nyupress. org to look over the technological options, sample assignments, and syllabi provided by instructors who have used *Keywords for American Cultural Studies* in the past and to consider adapting them or inventing new assignments. If you devise your own, you will find on the site a way of sharing it with others, along with tips about what worked and what did not. The site is meant to promote collaboration not just between students in a single course but also among instructors. We urge you to experiment with using the Collaboratory to link students and courses across two or more institutions by developing assignments through which they can work together on the same keyword or keywords. In any one of these contexts, your own students can learn more effectively by contributing to the production and dissemination of knowledge at the core of research and scholarship.

1

Affect

Ann Cvetkovich

"Affect" names a conceptual problem as much as a tangible thing. As such, it is best understood as an umbrella term that includes related, and more familiar, words such as "feeling" and "emotion," as well as efforts to make distinctions among them. The *Oxford English Dictionary* (*OED*) traces the history of the term to the seventeenth century, aligning it with "desire" or "passion" and opposing it to "reason." Further specifying that "affect" is both a "mental" and a "bodily" disposition, the *OED* sets in place a persistent ambiguity that challenges distinctions between mind and body. More technical uses of the term emerge from mid-twentieth-century scientific psychology, where "affect" designates sensory processes or experiences prior to cognition and distinguishes such sensations from the cognitive processes that produce emotions (Damasio 1994). Because affect, emotions, and feelings stand at the intersection of mind and body, cognition and sensation, and conscious and unconscious or autonomic processes, it is not easy to identify the material basis for their social and historical construction, which includes parts of the body (nerves, brains, or guts) as well as environments and transpersonal relations.

As the recent declaration of an "affective turn" in American studies and cultural studies suggests (Clough and Halley 2007; Gregg and Seigworth 2010), the current prominence of "affect" as a keyword represents the convergence of many strands of thinking. Foundational for both fields are French theorist Michel Foucault's histories of the social construction of categories such as body, gender, and sex that seem like natural phenomena. These categories form the basis for modern notions of subjectivity and power that conceive of the self as possessing a depth or interiority evident in the supposed natural truth of feelings (Foucault 1976/1990). Following this line of research, the affective turn takes up debates about the construction of binary oppositions between reason and emotion and the reversal of hierarchies that subordinate emotion to reason as part of a mind/body split often associated with the seventeenth-century philosopher René Descartes. In the Cartesian worldview, passions, instincts, and feelings are unruly and uncontrollable, requiring subordination to the rational control of reason and the mind—a hierarchical ordering that has sometimes led to a romantic embrace of their subversive power. In response to such reversals, Foucault's critique of the idea that freedom of expression and resistance to repression constitutes political liberation has inspired cautionary accounts of the politics of affect. Efforts to historicize subjectivity and to conceive of the self in non-Cartesian terms have required new conceptions of affect, emotion, and feeling. Indeed, the use of the term "affect" rather than "feeling" or "emotion" arguably stems from the desire to find a more neutral word, given the strong vernacular associations of "feeling" and "emotion" with irrationality.

Within cultural studies, the project of accounting for social life and political economy through everyday and sensory experiences, including feelings, has an extensive history. Affect, emotion, and feeling have been central to long-standing efforts to combine Marxism and psychoanalysis and to theorize the relations between the psychic and the social, the private and the public. Psychoanalysis has used "affect" and related categories as part of a vocabulary for drives, unconscious processes, and the psychic energies created by both internal and external stimuli. The term "affect" is also present in social and cultural theories that seek alternatives to psychoanalytic models, such as Eve Sedgwick's use of Sylvan Tompkins, who describes nine affects that link outward behavior with mental and physical states (Sedgwick and Frank 1995; Sedgwick 2003). Whether drawing on psychoanalysis or on its alternatives, accounts of psychic life and felt experience have been important to cultural studies in its efforts to explain the social and political uses of feeling (including the divide between reason and emotion) and to negotiate differences of scale between the local and the global, the intimate and the collective. Raymond Williams's elusively suggestive term "structure of feeling" (1977/1997, 128–35) is a good example of the use of the vocabulary of feeling to describe how social conditions are manifest in everyday life and how felt experience can be the foundation for emergent social formations. Rather than being attached to one theoretical school or discipline, "affect" has named multiple projects and agendas, including broad inquiry into the public life of feelings. Following Williams, the vernacular term "feeling" remains a useful way to signify these projects, which extend beyond the question of specifying what affects are.

Though the affective turn has conceptual roots in Marxism and psychoanalysis, it has also been significantly catalyzed by feminist critiques of the gendering of dichotomies between reason and emotion, which made their way into the academy from popular culture and political movements. The 1970s feminist cultures of consciousness raising reversed the disparaging association of femininity with feeling and, in a version of the discourse of sexual revolution, celebrated emotional expression as a source of feminine power associated with social and political liberation (Sarachild 1978; Lorde 1984b). Subsequent generations of scholarship in feminist cultural studies have been more skeptical about an easy reversal of the reason/

emotion binary, the often essentializing assumption that women are more emotional or nurturing than men, and claims for affective expression's liberatory possibilities. Instead, this scholarship has provided rich and nuanced histories of the centrality of feeling to the relations between private and public spheres and especially of how the intimate life of romance, the family, and the domestic sphere serves as the foundation for social relations of power (Davidson and Hatcher 2002). In the field of American studies, scholarship on categories such as sentimentality, sensationalism, sympathy, melodrama, and the gothic has shown how cultural genres, especially fiction, produce social effects through mobilizing feeling (Tompkins 1985; S. Samuels 1992; Cvetkovich 1992; Halberstam 1995). Attention to affect is the culmination of several decades of feminist scholarship on clusters of related terms such as "domesticity," "family," and "marriage," as well as on the historical continuities that link women's popular genres, such as domestic and sentimental novels, theatrical melodrama, and women's film (L. Williams 2002; Berlant 2008).

The far-reaching impact of feminist approaches to feeling and politics, including their relevance to histories of racism and colonialism, is exemplified by scholarship on the sentimental politics of abolition in texts such as Harriet Beecher Stowe's *Uncle Tom's Cabin* (1852/1981), nineteenth-century slave narratives, and contemporary neo-slave narratives. Stowe uses representations of slave mothers separated from their children and innocent slaves being beaten to generate appeals to universal feeling as the marker of the humanity of slaves and as the inherent result of witnessing the evils of slavery. Scenes of sexual intimacy between master and slave prove more affectively complex, however, in *Incidents in the Life of a Slave Girl* (1861/2001), in which Harriet Jacobs grapples with how to represent her sexual relations with white men without losing the reader's sympathy. Toni Morrison's historical novel *Beloved* (1987) further challenges the tradition of the sympathetic slave mother by telling the story of a woman who tries to kill her three children in order to protect them from slavery, aiming for a more complex representation of the affective life of slavery than stark scenes of innocence and guilt. The powerful fusion of secular forms of religious feeling and maternal sentiment in abolitionist discourses provides a model for the representation of social suffering that has had a lasting impact on U.S. cultural politics in both popular entertainment and the news media. What Lauren Berlant (2008) has called the "unfinished business of sentimentality" persists not just in popular genres produced for women but also in realist and documentary forms of representation, including human rights discourses, in which spectacles of suffering are used to mobilize public action. Affectively charged representation is part of everyday life across the political spectrum, and images of political prisoners at Abu Ghraib, children of war, and unborn babies prompt ongoing debate about the politics of sensation, sentiment, and sympathy (Berlant 2004; Staiger, Cvetkovich, and Reynolds 2010).

Another important area of scholarship in which feeling and affect are central are discussions of trauma and cultural memory that have emerged in American studies as it reckons with the legacies of slavery, genocide, and colonialism. Although the urgencies of Holocaust memory have inspired the creation of public memorials and testimony as forums for emotional expression in Europe and elsewhere, slavery and genocide provide a specifically U.S. genealogy for trauma studies and cultural memory. In seeking to address traumatic histories, public cultures of memory raise questions about what emotional responses constitute a reparative

relation to the past and whether it is ever possible to complete the work of mourning, particularly while social suffering is ongoing. Drawing on psychoanalytic categories of mourning and melancholy, critical race theory and queer studies (especially work on AIDS) have produced new theories of melancholy or unfinished mourning as productive rather than pathological. These fields depart from psychoanalytic categories of affect and trauma in favor of vernacular vocabularies of affect in indigenous, diasporic, and queer cultures (Crimp 2002; Eng and Kazanjian 2002; Cvetkovich 2003). Queer studies has also made important contributions to embracing ostensibly negative emotions such as shame and melancholy, as well as theorizing queer temporalities that favor affectively meaningful representations of the past rather than accurate or realist documentation (Love 2007; E. Freeman 2010).

While these critical histories of affect as a cultural and social construct have been extremely generative in American studies, a second important line of research has returned to theories of embodiment and sensation to ask new questions about the material basis for affect, emotions, and feelings. The use of the term "affect" by Gilles Deleuze and Félix Guattari to describe the impersonal intensities, forces, and movements that cause bodies and objects to affect and be affected by one another has been especially influential in recent scholarship (Deleuze and Guattari 1987; Massumi 2002b; Stewart 2007; Puar 2007). Deleuze's work usefully displaces psychoanalysis and decenters the individuated subject of cognition, locating unconscious bodily processes and sensory life at the center of social life. Deleuze has also been a major catalyst for new materialist notions of affect that distinguish more sharply between "affect" and "emotion," preserving "affect" for noncognitive processes and using "emotion" to describe socially constructed behavior.

Clearly, the multidisciplinary question of what it means to be a sensory being cannot be confined to one theoretical school, and American studies and cultural studies have been invigorated by proliferating forms of affect studies. Phenomenology and cultural geography have provided resources for materialist histories of sensory experience as well as new accounts of the relations between bodies, objects, and environments and of terms such as "mood" and "atmosphere" (Ahmed 2006; Thrift 2008). Neurobiology and cognitive science have been embraced by scholars in the humanities interested in the interface between brain and body in constituting sensory experience, including reading and other forms of aesthetic and cultural reception (E. Wilson 2004; Zunshine 2006). Animal studies and ecocriticism contribute to a posthumanist concept of humans as integrated with animals, things, and nature and to understandings of affective experience as bodily sensation and vital force (Haraway 2008; Grosz 2011; J. Bennett 2010). With the project of overturning old hierarchies between mind and body, cognition and feeling, reason and emotion largely accomplished, affect studies is now promoting new interdisciplinary inquiry across science and humanities. In so doing, it offers answers to the long-standing problem in social theory of how to think the relation between the psychic and the social worlds and provides resources for building new cultures of public feeling.

2

African

Kevin K. Gaines

The keyword "African" has been and remains a touchstone for African-descended peoples' struggle for identity and inclusion, encompassing extremes of racial denigration and vindication in a nation founded on the enslavement of Africans. Both the African presence throughout the Americas and its significance for constructions of national culture in the United States have remained fraught with racialized and exclusionary power relations. In a nation that has traditionally imagined its culture and legislated its polity as "white," "African" has often provided for African Americans a default basis for identity in direct proportion to their exclusion from national citizenship.

As scholars ranging from Winthrop Jordan (1969) to Jennifer L. Morgan (2004) have noted, there was nothing natural or inevitable about the development of racial slavery in the Americas. Nor was the emergence of the racialized category of the African as permanent slave foreordained. European travelers who recorded their initial encounters with Africans did not perceive them as slaves. But their ethnocentric self-regard informed their descriptions of Africans as extremely different from themselves in appearance, religious beliefs, and behavior. European constructions of the bodily difference, heathenism, and beastliness of Africans mitigated occasional observations of their morality and humanity. As European nations experimented with systems of forced labor in the Americas, initially enlisting indigenous peoples and European indentured servants as well as Africans, ideologies of African inferiority facilitated the permanent enslavement of Africans as an expedient labor practice. With the legal codification of lifetime African slavery, European settlers completed the racial degradation of African men and women, a process anticipated in Enlightenment conceptions of difference and hierarchy. In keeping with the contingency of its origins, the idea of the African in America was subject to change and contestation. An awareness on the part of travelers and slave owners of ethnic and regional distinctions among peoples from Africa yielded to the homogenizing idea of *the* African. Throughout the eighteenth century, slave owners in the Caribbean and North America attributed rebellions to "wild and savage" Africans, leading, on occasion, to restrictions on the importation of African slaves.

During the nineteenth century, free African Americans held an ambivalent attitude toward all things African. It could hardly have been otherwise, given the existential burdens of chattel slavery and the exclusion of Africa and its peoples from Enlightenment ideas of historical agency, modernity, and civilization. Prominent African Americans such as the shipping merchant Paul Cuffee championed emigration to West Africa. Despite his personal success, Cuffee despaired at the prospects for African-descended people to achieve equality in the United States. Inspired by the global antislavery movement, as well as the establishment of the British colony of Sierra Leone as an asylum for Africans rescued from the slave trade, Cuffee believed that emigration would allow Africans and African Americans to realize their full potential. But Cuffee led only one voyage of settlers to West Africa, leaving his entrepreneurial and evangelical objectives unfulfilled. African American enthusiasm for emigration was further dampened by the rise in the early nineteenth century of an explicitly racist colonization movement. The impetus for this movement, which sought the removal of free blacks and emancipated slaves to Africa,

came from powerful whites, including slave owners and members of Congress.

Free blacks resented the proslavery motives of colonizationists and increasingly rejected an identification with Africa largely as a matter of self-defense. While the initial wave of schools, churches, mutual-aid societies, and other institutions established by northern free blacks in the late eighteenth century often bore the name "African," this nomenclature was largely abandoned by the mid-nineteenth century. The reasons for this shift were complex, including demands for U.S. citizenship, black abolitionists' opposition to the colonization movement, the dwindling population of African-born blacks, and an acknowledgment, at some level, of a multihued African American community resulting from the systemic rape of enslaved black women by white male slave owners. Above all, the term epitomized the stark conditions of exile faced by African Americans, excluded from U.S. citizenship and society and deprived of an affirming connection to an ancestral homeland. Even for leaders of the African Methodist Episcopal (AME) Church, founded in Philadelphia in 1816 when white Methodists refused to worship alongside blacks, wariness toward Africa and a deep suspicion toward its indigenous cultures informed their efforts to evangelize the continent (J. Campbell 1995).

While emigration and colonization movements resulted in the resettlement of relatively few African Americans, the violent exclusion of African Americans from southern politics after emancipation renewed the appeal of Africa as a foundation of African American identity. As Africa came under the sway of European missions and colonialism, the involvement of AME Church missions in Africa and the scholarship of Edward W. Blyden (1887/1967) helped promote among some African Americans a general interest in the welfare of Africans and a greater tolerance for indigenous African cultures. Blyden's work was part of a long-standing African American intellectual tradition seeking to vindicate Africa by documenting its contributions to Western civilization (Moses 1998). Such scholarship, combined with the worldwide impact of Marcus Garvey's post–World War I mass movement, helped sow the seeds of African nationalism and anticolonialism. The Garvey movement, which flourished amid a national wave of urban race riots and antiblack violence, built on popular emigrationism and inspired African-descended peoples all over the world with its secular gospel of economic cooperation toward African redemption, even as some African American intellectuals dismissed it as a quixotic "back to Africa" movement. Such controversy may well have informed subsequent debates among black studies scholars over whether it was valid to speak of African cultural retentions, or "survivals," among the descendants of enslaved Africans in the Americas. The sociologist E. Franklin Frazier and the social anthropologist Melville Herskovits represent the opposing positions in the debate (Raboteau 1978). Frazier believed that the traumas of enslavement and the rigors of urbanization had extinguished all cultural ties to Africa. Herskovits based his support for the idea of African cultural retentions on his research on Caribbean societies and cultural practices. If recent scholarship in history, anthropology, linguistics, religion, literary and cultural studies, historical archaeology, and population genetics is any indication, Herskovits's position that some African cultural practices persisted in the Americas appears to have prevailed.

As African national independence movements capitalized on the decline of European colonialism after World War II, the idea of the African underwent yet another profound revision in the minds of many African Americans, from intellectual and popular stereotypes of African savagery to images of black power and modernity. The emergence of newly independent African nations beginning in the late 1950s became a source of pride for many people of African descent. Even as blacks believed that the new African presence in world affairs signaled the continent's full participation in, if not redefinition of, the modern world, members of the U.S. and European political establishment opposed African demands for freedom and true self-determination, trafficking, more or less discreetly, in racist attitudes. In 1960, widely touted as "the year of Africa," more than thirty African states gained national independence; that year also witnessed the bloody repression of demands for freedom in apartheid South Africa and the Congo. For many northern urban African Americans a generation removed from the violence of the Jim Crow South and facing marginalization in such cities as New York, Chicago, and Detroit, new African states and their leaders, including Ghana's Kwame Nkrumah and the Congo's Patrice Lumumba, rivaled the southern civil rights movement in importance. When Lumumba was assassinated during the civil disorder in the Congo fomented by Belgium, African Americans in Harlem and Chicago angrily demonstrated against the complicity of Western governments and the United Nations in the murder. In doing so, they joined members of the black left and working-class black nationalists in a nascent political formation that envisioned their U.S. citizenship in solidarity with African peoples, uniting their own demands for freedom and democracy in the United States with those of peoples of African descent the world over (Singh 2004; Gaines 2006).

Within this context of decolonization, the term "African" became a battleground. To the architects of U.S. foreign policy, African American solidarity with African peoples and their struggles exceeded the ideological boundaries of U.S. citizenship. African American criticism of U.S. foreign policy and advocacy on behalf of African peoples transgressed the limits imposed by a liberalism whose expressed support for civil rights and decolonization was qualified by Cold War national security concerns (and opposed outright by segregationist elements). As some African governments joined U.S. blacks in denouncing violent white resistance to demands for equality, U.S. officials' assertions of the American Negro's fundamental Americanness became a staple of liberal discourse. Their view was echoed in press accounts asserting that Africans and American Negroes were fundamentally estranged from one another. No doubt many African Americans still looked on Africans with ambivalence. However, this normative, liberal, and assimilationist notion of African American identity and citizenship provided a context for subsequent debates among African Americans during the Black Power era of the late 1960s and beyond over the terms of an authentic black identity. Contested claims about authentic blackness, particularly when inflected with issues of gender and sexual orientation, can and have had a divisive and self-destructive impact among African Americans (E. Johnson 2003).

As a Janus-faced U.S. nationalism trumpeted its civil rights reforms—seemingly in exchange for consent to its political and military repression of African and, in the 1960s, Vietnamese nationalists—mainstream civil rights leaders endeavored, without success, to formalize an African American position on U.S. foreign policy. It was Malcolm X, among African American spokespersons, who most effectively articulated a growing frustration with the federal government's domestic and foreign policies toward black and African peoples (Gaines 2006). Along with such post–World War II figures as

Paul Robeson, St. Clair Drake, and Lorraine Hansberry, Malcolm X reanimated W. E. B. Du Bois's decades-old assertion that African Americans sought no less than full U.S citizenship without sacrificing their "Negro" identity and heritage, helping African Americans to embrace rather than shun the designation "African" (Plummer 1996; Von Eschen 1997; Meriwether 2002).

During the 1980s, African American leadership, including many elected officials, waged an effective civil disobedience campaign against the apartheid regime in South Africa and the Reagan administration's support for it. The rapid acceptance of the term "African American," championed by Jesse Jackson and others and used in the context of the antiapartheid struggle, represents a profound reversal of decades of shame and ambivalence. Yet it is unclear what relationship the general (though by no means universal) acceptance of "African" as a marker of U.S. black identity today bears to the black transnational consciousness that developed during the 1960s and that flourished during the Free South Africa movement. A major legacy of these social movements for black equality and African liberation has been the legitimation of scholarly investigations of the African foundations of African American history and culture, including studies of the African diaspora and what Paul Gilroy (1993) has termed the "Black Atlantic."

At the beginning of the twenty-first century, the term "African" remains highly contested in politics and popular culture. On the one hand, crises of poverty, famine, disease (including the AIDS epidemic), and armed conflict reinforce an Afro-pessimism in the Western imagination not far removed from the colonial idea of the "Dark Continent," a place untouched by civility and modernity. While the human toll of such crises is undeniable, the U.S. media generally devote far less attention to democratically elected civilian governments, some of which have supplanted brutal and corrupt military dictatorships supported by the West during the Cold War. These representations continue to view Africans and African Americans through alternately romanticizing and demeaning prisms of race.

On the other hand, the term "African" has come full circle within a society capable of sustaining wildly contradictory views of race. Apart from the usual Afro-pessimism, the African has been incorporated in some accounts into the quintessential U.S. immigrant success narrative, as the upward mobility of highly educated African immigrants is portrayed as an implicit reproach to underachieving native-born African American descendants of slaves. The idea of the otherness of African immigrants in relation to the native-born U.S. black community was widely debated during the 2008 presidential campaign of Barack Obama. Some African American pundits asserted that Obama's African parentage made him less authentically black than U.S.-born African Americans descended from slaves and, arguably, less entitled to the black vote than his rival in the Democratic primary in 2008, Hillary Rodham Clinton. This view was discredited as Obama's candidacy gained momentum and as African Americans equated Obama's run for the presidency with African Americans' historical struggles for equality. Obama's election was celebrated internationally, including throughout Africa and in the Kenyan village of his father's family. As the first African American president, Obama has faced an unusual level of attacks to his person and the dignity of his office, often of a blatantly racist nature. Right-wing pundits and politicians routinely portray Obama's African heritage as a threat to the republic; Newt Gingrich, during his 2012 run for the presidency, claimed that Obama's "Kenyan, anti-colonial" worldview was proof of his disloyalty and subversive influence (Costa 2010).

Whatever their origin or occasion, media and political narratives emphasizing tensions between African Americans and African immigrants are the present-day equivalent of Tarzan movies, whose effect is to erase the history and modernity of transnational black subjectivities. While recent scholarship in American studies has called for a rethinking of the black-white color line in U.S. race relations, the tensions expressed by the question of who is an "African" and who is an "African American" are symptomatic of the nation's continued struggle over the significance of the African presence, past and present, real and symbolic. Of course, the contested meaning and legacy of the African presence is not peculiar to the United States, as many Latino immigrants to the United States bring with them histories and identities shaped by the vexed legacy of racial slavery in their countries of origin. The foundations of Latin American societies, with their diverse populations of Africans, indigenous peoples, Europeans, and Asians, suggests that the expansion of the Hispanic population in the United States does not render the black-white color line obsolete but rather makes it all the more salient as a benchmark for social affiliation.

AFRICAN   KEVIN K. GAINES

3

America

Kirsten Silva Gruesz

"We hold these truths to be self-evident," begins the main body of the Declaration of Independence, and the definition of "America" may likewise seem utterly self-evident: the short form of the nation's official name. Yet the meaning of this well-worn term becomes more elusive the closer we scrutinize it. Since "America" names the entire hemisphere from the Yukon to Patagonia, its common use as a synonym for the United States of America is technically a misnomer, as Latin Americans and Canadians continually (if resignedly) point out. Given the nearly universal intelligibility of this usage, their objection may seem a small question of geographical semantics. But "America" carries multiple connotations that go far beyond the literal referent of the nation-state. In the statement "As Americans, we prize freedom," "American" may at first seem to refer simply to U.S. citizens, but the context of the sentence strongly implies a consensual understanding of shared values, not just shared passports; the literal and figurative meanings tend to collapse into each other. The self-evidence of "America" is thus troubled from the start by multiple ambiguities about the extent of the territory it delineates, as well as about its deeper connotations.

Seeking out the meaning of America might be said to be a national characteristic, if that proposition were not in itself tautological. The question prompts responses representing every conceivable point of view, from the documentary series packaged as *Ken Burns's America* (1996) to prize-winning essays by schoolchildren invited to tackle this hoary topic. Foodways, cultural

practices, and even consumer products are readily made to symbolize the nation's essence ("baseball, hot dogs, apple pie, and Chevrolet," as a highly effective advertising campaign put it in the 1970s). Such metonyms gesture, in turn, at more abstract notions: Freedom, Liberty, Democracy. Whether implicit or explicit, responses to the enigma of Americanness tend to obscure the conditions under which they were formulated. Who gets to define what "America" means? What institutions help enforce or undermine a particular definition? Under what historical conditions does one group's definition have more or less power than another's? Without looking critically at these questions of nomenclature, "American" studies cannot claim self-awareness about its premises or its practices.

Because the meaning of "America" and its corollaries—"American," "Americanization," "Americanism," and "Americanness"—seems so self-evident but is in fact so imprecise, using the term in conversation or debate tends to reinforce certain ways of thinking while repressing others. In the slyly comic *Devil's Dictionary* (1911), pundit Ambrose Bierce includes the term only in the form of its opposite: "un-American, adj. Wicked, intolerable, heathenish." If using the adjective "un-American" shuts down genuine argument by impugning your opponent's values, as Bierce implies, then the power to define what does count as "American" is a considerable one.

By the time Bierce penned this undefinition, the use of "America" as a synonym for "the United States" was a habit already deeply ingrained, thanks in part to nationalistic writers of the nineteenth century, such as Walt Whitman. Whitman's original preface to *Leaves of Grass* tries to get at the essence of the nation by using both terms in rapid-fire succession: "The genius of the United States is not best or most in its executives or legislatures, nor in its ambassadors or authors or colleges or churches or parlors, . . . but always most in the common people." "America is the race of races," he continues. "The Americans of all nations at any time upon the earth have probably the fullest poetical nature. The United States themselves are essentially the greatest poem" (1855/1999, 4–5). Whitman's vision of America / the United States celebrates "the common people," the heterogeneous mixing of immigrants into a "race of races," and everyday, vernacular speech as the stuff of poetry. Yet Whitman also includes scenes from Mexico, Canada, and the Caribbean in his panoramic vision of America, revealing not only the expansionist beliefs Whitman held at the time but the extraordinary persistence of this older sense of America as the name for the whole of the New World (another misnomer sanctified by the passage of time, since millions of indigenous inhabitants neither saw it as new nor imagined it on the abstract scale of the Europeans).

Against Columbus's insistence that the landmass he had "discovered" was Asia, the Italian explorer Amerigo Vespucci first dubbed it a "New World" in his treatise by that name. It was not Vespucci himself but a contemporary mapmaker, Martin Waldseemuller, who then christened the region "America," originally referring only to the southern continent. Later cartographers broadened the designation to include the lesser-known north—a further irony of history. To this day, alternative theories of the naming of the hemisphere flourish, finding new devotees on the Internet. Solid evidence links a British merchant named Richard Ameryk to John Cabot's voyages along the North Atlantic coast, leading to speculation that Cabot named "America" for his patron a decade or so before Waldseemuller's map. Others have argued that the name comes from Vikings who called their Newfoundland settlement "Mark" or "Maruk"—"Land of Darkness." Still others have claimed, more circumstantially, that

the root word derives from Phoenician, Hebrew, or Hindu terms, suggesting that one of these groups encountered America before Europeans did. Similar etymological evidence has been interpreted to show that the term ultimately stems from a word for Moors or Africans, so that "America" really means "land of the blacks." "America" is thus a product of the same misunderstanding that gave us the term "Indian." Given this similarity, one final theory about the term's origins is particularly provocative. An indigenous group in Nicaragua had referred to one gold-rich district in their territory as "Amerrique" since before the Conquest, and Mayan languages of tribes further north use a similar-sounding word (Jonathan Cohen 2004). These discoveries have led to the radical proposition that the name "America" comes from within the New World rather than being imposed on it. The continuing life of this debate suggests that what is really at stake is not some ultimate etymological truth but a narrative of shared origins; each claim grants primacy and symbolic (if not literal) ancestry of the Americas to a different group.

The fact that only one of these fables of the origin of the word "America" involves an indigenous name is revealing. Throughout the colonies, settlers tended not to refer to themselves as "Americans," since the term then conveyed an indigenous ancestry—or at least the associated taint of barbarism and backwardness—that they were (with certain romanticizing exceptions) eager to avoid. Instead, they nostalgically called their home spaces "New-England," "Nieuw-Amsterdam," and "Nueva España," reflecting the fact that, for most people, local identities took precedence over larger, abstract ones: a problem that the architects of nationhood eventually had to solve. There were some exceptions, however. The sixteenth-century Dominican priest Bartolomé de las Casas initiated an argument that raged across both Americas over whether Vespucci had usurped an honor rightly due Columbus; he proposed rechristening the region "Columba," and many place-names in Latin America pay homage accordingly. Las Casas gained a considerable following in the English-speaking world, and two of the most powerful writers of the later Puritan period, Samuel Sewall and Cotton Mather, recorded their wish to evangelize the whole of the New World so that it would "deserve the significant name of *Columbina*" (Sewall 1697/1997, 59). Mather even went so far as to describe himself as an "American" in the introduction to his historical chronicle *Magnalia Christi Americana* in 1702, well before the national sense of the term was even imaginable. Until the beginning of the nineteenth century, then, "America" and its analogs in Spanish, French, and other European languages designated the whole of the New World. Of the many figurative meanings that the American hemisphere has acquired over time, most involve notions of novelty, new beginnings, and utopian promise.

The Mexican historian Edmundo O'Gorman (1961) influentially wrote that America was "invented" before it was "discovered," demonstrating that Europeans had long imagined a mythical land of marvels and riches that they then projected onto the unfamiliar terrain. After Columbus, earlier Christian models of a three-continent globe were amended to include America as the fourth. To create two-dimensional representations of a world now known to be round, Renaissance mapmakers split the globe visually into distinct hemispheres—Europe, Africa, and Asia as the Eastern, and the Americas isolated into the Western. This geographical convenience has become so naturalized that it remains difficult for us to envision, for instance, the interlinked world of the Pacific Rim or the proximity of the points on the transatlantic triangle trade of slaves, sugar, and rum. Similarly, the idea of "Latin America"—comprising not just the continent of South America but a hefty portion of North America as well—is a product of cultural practices rather than any innate geophysical reality: in the nineteenth century, Spanish-speaking elites began using the term to defend and distinguish Franco-Iberian Catholic values from Anglo-Saxon Protestant ones. As Walter Mignolo writes, "Once America was named as such in the sixteenth century and Latin America named as such in the nineteenth, it appeared as if they had been there forever" (2005, 2).

The associations that Europeans projected onto this "new" hemisphere were not always positive, even though the wealth of the American colonies was absolutely vital to the historical shifts we associate with modernization. The common representation of a "virgin land" waiting to be explored, dominated, and domesticated relegates the natural world to the passive, inferior position then associated with the feminine. The French naturalist George Louis Leclerc de Buffon even argued in 1789 that since the region was geologically newer, its very flora and fauna were less developed than Europe's—a claim Thomas Jefferson (1787/1984) took pains to refute, using examples from South as well as North America. Nonetheless, the notion of the novelty of the Americas persisted, extending to the supposedly immature culture of its inhabitants as well.

Early debates over literature and fine arts in the English, Spanish, and French Americas all focused on the question of whether the residents of a land without history could cultivate a genuine or original aesthetic. Some Romantic writers tried on Indian themes, while others spun this "historylessness" in America's favor. The philosopher G. W. F. Hegel delivered an influential address in 1830 that claimed, "America is therefore the land of the future, where, in all the ages that lie before us, the burden of the World's History shall reveal itself—perhaps in a contest between North and

South America. It is a land of desire for all those who are weary of the historical lumber-room of old Europe" (1837/1956, 86). (Note that Hegel still uses "America" to indicate the whole region, not just the United States.) Claims about the New World's salvational role in global history, then, gestated from without as well as from within. Sewall and Mather's wish to elevate Columbus over Vespucci was revived after the Revolutionary War in the iconographic figure of the goddess Columbia. In the hands of artists and poets, this imaginary female figure lent a tinge of classical refinement to the nation-building project; the African American Phillis Wheatley (1775/2001) penned one of the very first poems to deploy this image. The figure of Columbia was quite popular during the century that followed, prompting patriotic musings on "the Columbian ideal" as well as events such as the 1893 World's Columbian Exposition in Chicago, calculated to draw international attention to a nation that increasingly celebrated modernity and progress. Voluptuous Columbia continued to appear on coins into the early twentieth century, but there is no contemporary visual icon that corresponds allegorically to the name "America."

It was perhaps inevitable that the hazy ideas projected so persistently onto the name of the hemisphere and, subsequently, the U.S. nation would spawn other coinages to describe dynamic social processes. "Americanism" and "Americanization" had entered common usage by the beginning of the nineteenth century, referring at first to evolving linguistic differences from the English spoken in Great Britain but expanding their connotations into the general realm of culture. "Americanization" became an everyday word at the turn of the twentieth century, a period of surging immigration, signifying the degree to which those immigrants altered their customs and values in accordance with the dominant view of Americanness at the time. It remains to be seen whether the "Americanization" of immigrants can absorb new meanings beyond this model of one-way assimilation.

Given the long-standing tendency to define America in mythic terms, we must be skeptical of the common boast that the United States is the only modern nation founded on an idea—democratic equality—rather than on a shared tribal or racial ancestry. Such a claim to exceptionalism has been particularly appealing to intellectuals, who traffic in ideas. In the early years of American studies as an academic discipline in the 1950s, the field's foundational texts located the essential meaning of "America" variously in the history of westward movement, in philosophical and economic individualism, or in the privileging of the future oriented and the new. As the discipline has evolved, it has increasingly attempted to show how such mythic definitions arise in response to historically specific needs and conditions. When we go in search of what is most profoundly American, scholars now insist, we blinker our sights to the ways in which the actual history of U.S. actions and policies may have diverged from those expectations. Moreover, any single response to the prompt to define "America" (meaning the nation-state, not the continent) tends to imply that this larger idea or ideal has remained essentially unchanged over time, transcending ethnic and racial differences. From the nineteenth century forward, "America" and its derivations have generally been used to consolidate, homogenize, and unify, rather than to invite recognition of difference, dissonance, and plurality.

Since the 1990s, interdisciplinary work in American studies has mainly focused on illustrating the ways in which "American national identity is . . . constructed in and through relations of difference," as one former president of the American Studies Association put it (Radway 2002, 54). She went so far as to suggest that the organization rename itself in response to challenges raised around the time of Columbus's quincentenary by proponents of an "Americas" or "New World" studies. Such a transnational approach would revive the hemispheric scale of America and consider U.S. cultural productions and social formations in relation to those of Latin America, the Caribbean, and Canada. Rather than Alexis de Tocqueville and Michel Crèvecoeur, its canon of commentators on the meaning of "America" highlights lesser-known figures such as the Cuban José Martí—who in an 1891 speech famously distinguished between "Nuestra" (Our) America, with its mestizo or mixed-race origins, and the racist, profit-driven culture he saw dominating the United States. Martí, like the later activist-writers of African origin W. E. B. Du Bois and C. L. R. James, was critical of the growing interventionist tendencies of the United States in the Western Hemisphere and sought to shift the connotations of the term in provocative ways. In addition to recovering such underappreciated thinkers, comparative Americanist work often locates its inquiry in spaces once relegated to the periphery of scholarly attention, such as the Spanish-speaking borderlands that were formerly part of Mexico. As contact zones between North and South, Anglo and Latino, such areas produce hybrid cultural formations that inflect mainstream U.S. culture with that of the "other" America.

Undoing what most Latin Americans see as an imperial arrogation of the name of the hemisphere by the most powerful nation in it has been central to the project of a pluralized, relational Americas studies. Bell Gale Chevigny and Gari Laguardia, in the preface to their landmark essay collection *Reinventing the Americas*, write that "by dismantling the U.S. appropriation of the name 'America,' we will better see what the United States is and what it is not" (1986, viii). The work of divorcing the names that Whitman (and others) wedded together so powerfully has stumbled a bit on the lack of a ready adjectival form in English. A few writers, such as the late Chicano scholar Juan Bruce-Novoa (2004), have recalled into service the neologism that Frank Lloyd Wright coined in the 1930s to describe his nonderivative, middle-class house designs: "Usonian." Others, including Chevigny and Laguardia, simply substitute "U.S." or "United Statesian" for "American," arguing that the very awkwardness of such terms has a certain heuristic value, recalling us to a historical moment before the pressure toward consensus and national unity became as pervasive as it is today.

Perhaps such consciousness raising about the power of "self-evident" terms could indeed begin the slow work of altering social relationships and structures of political power. Yet the plural form of "Americas" and the seemingly more inclusive geography of North America have found their way into some political formations that reinforce, rather than challenge, U.S. hegemony in the hemisphere—such as the North American Free Trade Agreement (NAFTA) and the U.S. Army School of the Americas, a military training center for Latin Americans whose graduates were implicated in multiple cases of human rights violations in the 1980s and 1990s (and which was subsequently renamed the Western Hemisphere Institute for Security Cooperation). In these examples, the seemingly more inclusive term works opportunistically rather than critically, suggesting that in the future, the usage of "Americas" may require the same kind of scrutiny that we have just brought to "America."

4

Asian

John Kuo Wei Tchen

"Orientals are carpets!" is a common Asian American retort today, one that rejects the linkage between objects of desire—whether hand-woven carpets made in central and western Asia or porcelains made in China—and the people who make them. During the late-1960s phase of the civil rights movement, second- and third-generation, college-age, mainly Chinese and Japanese Americans from the United States and Canada protested the term "Oriental," seeking to replace it with the seemingly less fraught term "Asian." But as in any debate about naming practices, the names rejected and defended reflect differing points of view, as groups trouble certain terms and adopt others in order to shape and reshape meanings for themselves. "Asia," "Asian," and "Asiatic" are still common, though the latter is far less preferred. Variations such as "Asianic," "Asiaticism," "Asiatise," "Asiatall," "Asiatican," and "Asiatically" are now archaic.

Each of these terms comes loaded with particular spatial orientations rooted in temporal relationships. "Asia" has Arabic, Aramaic, Ethiopian, and Greek origins signifying "was or became beautiful," "to rise" (said of the sun), "burst forth" or "went out," and "to go out." Demetrius J. Georgacas (1969, 33) speculates that "Asia" comes from the ancient Greeks, who adopted a cuneiform Hittite word *assuva* when traveling to the western shores of Anatolia (present-day Turkish Asia) around 1235 BCE. *Assuva*, in turn, may have originally been a pre-Persian name referring to a town in Crete with an ancient temple to Zeus or a "land or country with good soil" (73–75). Georgacas adds that Greek mariners first articulated a nautical boundary between the lands of the rising sun and those of the setting sun by traversing the saltwater straits of the Aegean through the Dardanelles, the Sea of Marmara, the Bosphorus, the Black Sea through the Straits of Kerch, and ending in the Sea of Azov, where the landmass to the north did not have such a divide (11–12). Hence "Asia" as "east" began as a local definition.

Asia in these contexts appeared as separated by water from the Greek world, leading to the inaccurate *idée fixe* of a separable landmass and people. The categorization of continents that emerged from this idea reproduced early notions of racial superiority and inferiority. By the fifth century CE, "Asiatic" was clearly associated with vulgarity, arbitrary authority, and luxurious splendor—qualities deemed antithetical to Greek values (Hay 1957, 3). An early eleventh-century "T-O" map reveals a clear religious cosmos of the world. A "T" within a circle divides three continents: Asia, marked "oriens," is over Europe and Africa (or Libya), which are both marked "occidens." The "T" itself represented both a Christian cross and the Nile River, believed by some people to be the divide between Africa, Asia, and the Mediterranean (ibid., plate 1b, 54). Noah's sons, Japheth, Shem, and Ham, were said to have dispersed to Europe, Asia, and Africa, respectively, thereby fixing their characters to geographic spaces. For Western Christians, the Ottoman Empire to the east was formidable. As their city-states became more secular and colonized non-Christian lands westward, northward, and southward, Renaissance intellectuals redefined "civilization" and "progress" as moving westward like the arc of the sun. A double shift took place: the West became synonymous with Christianity, and Western ideologues claimed direct continuity with Greek civilization.

In this centuries-long process, the appropriation of the word "Europe" for this Western Christian political culture also projected the imagined heathenism affixed to peoples onto the continents of "Asia" and "Africa." Intercultural influences that produced overlapping renaissances in the Mediterranean world were appropriated as *the* (one and only) Renaissance, at once Eurocentric and colonizing. Taxonomist Carolus Linnaeus (1735) formulated "four races of mankind," from primitive Africans to civilized Europeans, with Asians or "Mongoloids" said to be the "semi-civilized" peoples of once-great material civilizations now stifled by despotic rulers. The formulation by Karl Marx (1867/1976) of "the Asiatic mode of production" as despotic bore the assumptions of this worldview. The rising European and colonial middle classes desired Asian goods, with their cachet of luxury, opulence, and decadence—a practice emulating the European courts' consumption fashions. Yet this fascination was also laced by threat. Startled by Japan's swift defeat of China, Kaiser Wilhelm II first dreamed of an impending "yellow peril" in 1895. The *Fu Manchu* novels of Sax Rohmer (Arthur Sarsfield Ward) soon followed, selling millions of copies throughout the twentieth century and popularizing representations of the "Near East," as ascribed by self-named "Occidentists," as utterly opposite and alien to the European self (Said 1978). This alterity was both derisive and romantic, coding "Asian" difference as gendered and sexualized. French Orientalists, for example, were fascinated by the eroticism of Persian *odalisques*, such as those represented in Jean-León Gérôme's paintings. This alterity enabled the self-delusional Eurocentric myth of a singular Western modernity: "In adopting the name 'Europe' as a substitute for Western Christendom, the Modern Western World had replaced a misnomer that was merely an anachronism by a misnomer that was seriously misleading" (Georgacas 1969, 29).

This misnaming has a long history. In 1507, German mapmaker Martin Waldseemuller named "America" after the Italian explorer Amerigo Vespucci's charting of South America. At that moment, a fourth continent upset the tripartite "T-O" map, and the Americas became the place where populations—indigenous, Africans, Europeans, and Asians—intermingled. Spanish colonials established the Manila–Acapulco trade from 1565 to 1815, bringing Filipinos/as, Chinese, and other "Asians" to the "New World." By 1635, Chinese barbers were reportedly monopolizing the trade in Mexico City. Chinese silk shawls and other desired goods traveled the Camino Real north to Santa Fe. Filipino sailors resettled in the French colonial lands of Louisiane. As the northeastern ports of the newly established United States began direct trade with China in 1784, people, goods, and influences crisscrossed with ports of the Pacific and Indian Oceans. Yet with Euro-American colonization, transplanted Eurocentric ideas of "Asia," "the Orient," and "the East" were reproduced ever further westward. The more the people of the Americas shared this Eurocentrism, the more their national identities proved to be a variation of white *herrenvolk* nationalism.

Despite this long genealogy, "Asian" bodies in the Americas have been viewed as phenotypically foreign—a demarcation of otherness as foundational as the "T-O" map. "Far Eastern" bodies, ideas, and things were mapped onto existent binaries of "Near Eastern" Orientalism. Anglo-American phrases emerged, such as "the yellow peril," "Mongoloid idiot," and "Asiatic hordes," along with names for diseases such as "Asiatic cholera" and the omnipresent "Asian flu." "Asiatics" were portrayed as threatening and inferior to white Euro-American masculinity. The Asian American critique of stereotypes is useful here. Writer-critics Jeffrey Paul Chan and Frank Chin (1972) have delineated "racist hate" as what most U.S. Americans imagine anti-Asian racism to be and "racist love" as the affections formed by the dominant culture toward those Asians who conform to stereotype. The exotic-erotic lotus-blossom geisha, for example, is the object of Orientalist desire—an extension of the *odalisque*. And detective Charlie Chan always solved the white man's mystery with good humble humor. At the same time, white, straight, male control has been repulsed (and titillated) by the dominatrix Dragon Lady type or "the devil incarnate" Fu Manchu role.

Contemporary U.S. notions of "terrorism" are undergirded by such stereotypical structures of thought. When media mogul Henry R. Luce (1941) celebrated the "American Century" as a mid-twentieth-century enlightenment project for the world, the primary area of U.S. economic and political expansion was westward into the Pacific. For 170 years, U.S. military actions and wars in the Pacific Rim have been justified by national security and self-interest. The Asia Pacific War, usually understood as a response to Japan's expansionism and efforts to formulate an "Asian Co-Prosperity Sphere," might be better understood in this broader context of competition for Pacific and Asian resources and markets. Historian William Appleman Williams (1992) charted the linkages between U.S. western expansionism and U.S. "foreign" policy annexations into the Pacific. "Manifest Destiny" did not stop at the shores of California. A list of U.S. military, diplomatic, and trade initiatives clearly delineates deep, sustained U.S. involvements in the Asia Pacific region. Witness the U.S. involvement in the British-led opium trade and wars with China (1830s), Commodore Perry's "opening" of Japan (1853), the annexation of Hawai'i, Guam, and the Philippines (1898) and Samoa (1900), the countless military actions of the twentieth century establishing strategic military bases, and the early twenty-first-century battle with the "Axis of Evil."

Military actions, missionary work, and trade, along with labor recruitment and immigration policies, linked the fate of Asians and Pacific Islanders in the United States to national foreign policy in Asia and the Pacific. Liberation movements necessarily became critiques of U.S. expansionism and self-interest, while policies toward Asia and the Pacific were articulated to domestic civil rights. The Harvard historian and adviser to the U.S. war against Japan Edwin O. Reischauer is one example. He urged improved treatment of interned Japanese Americans to counter Imperial Japan's criticism of Western racism and imperialism—the primary argument for developing a pan-Asian and pan-Pacific Japanese-controlled "prosperity" confederation. While pan-Asianism has mainly been identified with the reactionary expansionism of the Japanese empire, it is important to note that there have been many moments when pan-Asian ideas and actions emerged from revolutionary nationalists—often adapting U.S. ideals of freedom and liberty. Tokyo in the 1900s brought together many left-leaning Chinese and Koreans with Japanese socialists; anarchists and various radicals gathered in Paris before World War I; and the Bandung Conference in 1955 articulated an Asian and African "Third World" unity. These movements have argued for multiple modernities, not one singular "Western" path. The ongoing post-civil-rights-era "culture wars" have cast Asian American and other identity-based rights movements as a de facto "Balkanizing" of Euro-America (Schlesinger 1998; Huntington 2004b). More progressive scholars argue for the ongoing struggle to expand the meaning of "we, the people" and "the American experiment" at home and democracy and human rights abroad.

Given this long and complex history, the challenges for American studies and cultural studies scholarship and practice are numerous. A thorough critique of Eurocentric knowledge needs to continue and to be extended into curricula. As Naoki Sakai (2000) insists, modernity needs to be pluralized to recognize multiple paths for a people's development. Those who have experienced disempowerment and marginalization help us understand and gain insight into the ways reality is constructed and policies are formulated. This insight, when cultivated with deeper historical, cultural, social, and political analysis, restructures what we understand and how we understand it. In addition, it enables the recognition and translation of diverse and dynamic economic, cultural, and political developments in various parts of "east," "southeast," "south," "central," and "western" Asia (all these directional terms are partial and misleading). This rethinking can begin with the available literature of those Asians, Pacific Islanders, and Asian Americans writing and being translated into English but must be extended to help U.S. Americans understand the local struggles of grain farmers in Kazakhstan or female Nike factory workers in Bangladesh in terms truthful to those people's own worldviews. This requires dialogue and the insistence that disempowered peoples gain the capacity to "name" their own world.

How the United States and various Asian governments respond to the political-economic rivalries of the "New World Order" will frame the spaces in which this scholarship and activism can take place. Calls for pan-Asianism, used in various ways in different places and at different times, can contribute to a process that opens up participation and grassroots mobilizations, or they can serve to close down understanding by offering simplistic solutions to complex political-economic questions. Uneven development and hierarchical knowledges challenge us to better imagine and work for a fair and equitable global vision. "Development" and "modernization" must be reformulated to produce sustainable local practices without romanticizing a prelapsarian past.

Here, feminists, labor activists, and students who have access to both local and particular knowledges and transnational networks, via the Internet, have led the way, while ambitious corporate power players from "developing nations" and peoples have become the new comprador managers of internationalizing North American, European, and Asian finance capital. The contestation of values and meanings is critical to our future collective well-being. Like other keywords of these globalized struggles, it is the fate of "Asian" to be contested locally and regionally—in contending, politicized practices of naming.

5

Black

E. Patrick Johnson

The word "black" has a long and vexed history both inside and outside the United States. Typically used as a neutral reference to the darkest color on the spectrum, the word has also taken on negative cultural and moral meanings. It describes both something that is "soiled," "stained," "evil," or "morally vapid" and people of a darker hue. The *American Heritage Dictionary* provides a typical example of this dual usage. One of the entries under "black" as an adjective is "gloomy, pessimistic, dismal," while another is "of or belonging to a racial group having brown to black skin, especially one of African origin: *the Black population of South Africa.*" The slippage in the latter definition from "brown to black" highlights the ways in which the term's negative cultural and moral connotations are racialized through reference to not-quite-white but also not-always-black bodies. This slippage maintains hierarchies among the races scaled from white to black. While the origin of this mixed usage of the term "black" is hard to pin down, negative associations of cultural and moral blackness with dark-skinned people appear regularly during the Renaissance, as in Shakespeare's play *Othello*, in which the dark-skinned protagonist of the same name is referred to as a "Barbary horse" and a "lascivious Moor." Over time and in opposition to the dominant discourses of their historical moments, people who belonged to these racialized groups have often followed Othello's lead by reappropriating the term "black" to signify something culturally and morally empowering and, in some instances, a quality superior to whiteness.

As this brief overview suggests, the adjective "black" is, in the words of the *Oxford English Dictionary*, "a word of difficult history." Part of that difficulty has to do with the various geographical and historical contexts of its usage. In relation to U.S. slavery, the term was not as prominent a descriptor for enslaved Africans as were the derogatory "nigger" or the seemingly more benign "Negro" and "colored." After emancipation, the term "black" gained increased prominence in the legal and political realms as the 1865 "black codes" were enacted to restrict the rights of the newly freed by reinforcing white supremacy during Reconstruction (Meier and Rudwick 1976). For the people directly affected by those codes, the term "black" still did not hold as much political weight as "Negro" and "colored" until later in the twentieth century. The result is that "black" was not used in the names of the political organizations that emerged in the late nineteenth and early twentieth centuries, such as the National Association of Colored Women (NACW), founded in 1895, and the National Association for the Advancement of Colored People (NAACP), founded in 1909.

The now common "African American" (or hyphenated "African-American") has a similarly complex history. It did not become a popular term until almost a century later, in the late 1980s. A black army veteran from Alabama by the name of Johnny Duncan claims that he was the first to use the term in his poem "I Can," which he wrote for a 1987 Black History Month calendar. In the last four lines of the poem, Duncan writes, "The last 4 letters of my heritage and my creed spell 'I can,' heritage being Afr-i-can and creed being Amer-i-can." According to Duncan, Coretta Scott King first introduced Jesse Jackson to the poem in 1989 when she showed him the calendar. In 1990, at a speech in New Orleans, Jackson read the poem and began using the term "African American" (Duncan 2010). Like the term "black," "African American" has a complex and highly politicized history: some people of African descent still prefer "black" because they do not associate themselves with Africa, while others embrace "African American" precisely because of its explicit acknowledgment of an African heritage. Still others deploy "black" as a way of marking global affiliations that exceed "America" (Gilroy 1993; Singh 2004).

In black intellectual circles at the turn of the twentieth century, the term "black" began to emerge as an antiracist response to ideologies of white supremacy disseminated through science. W. E. B Du Bois, for example, delivered a paper in 1887 at the founding conference of the American Negro Academy in which he critiqued the biological determinism prevalent in nineteenth-century scientific discourse. The form of racism that Du Bois attacked maintained that physical differences between the races account for social and psychological differences—that black (i.e., dark and not-yet- or not-quite-white) skin corresponds to a lower socially developed human form. Du Bois critiqued this racist science by calling attention to the role that history, law, and religion—humanistic rather than scientific theories—have played in the differences among the races. This critique was important because it called attention to the effects of history and sociocultural factors to explain racial differences as opposed to biophysical ones. His argument was the foundation for his most oft-quoted line from *The Souls of Black Folk*— "The problem of the twentieth century is the problem of the color-line"—and for his notion of "double consciousness" (1903/1997, 45).

Du Bois's critique of racial essentialism is foundational to approaches in American studies and cultural studies that have become known as racial constructivism. These approaches focus on historical processes of racialization, suggesting that essentialist racial identity categories are stable only due to their repeated references in the context of specific racial projects (J. Butler 1990; Omi and Winant 1986/1994). Theorists today stress the need to read race as a result of dialogic processes between material bodies and sociocultural influences. An important forerunner of these theories and theorists, Du Bois's critique was aimed at racist scientific discourses promulgated not just by whites but also by leaders in the black community, such as Marcus Garvey and his Universal Negro Improvement Association (UNIA), which promoted the return to Africa as well as racial uplift and a radical black consciousness. Du Bois's critique of race discourse and Garvey's mobilization of that discourse to promote political consciousness around blackness prefigured debates in the 1960s during the emergence of the civil rights movement, as black leaders and artists began to struggle to expand notions of blackness (Du Bois), while also solidifying a common definition around which divergent factions could organize as a community against racism (Garvey) (Blight and Gooding-Williams 1997; Dawson 2001; Ongiri 2010).

These forms of political and cultural activism drew on a rich and often ignored history of cultural production during the Harlem Renaissance. In the 1920s, a consolidation of black pride formed in the African diaspora, especially in the French Caribbean and in Paris through what became known as the Négritude movement. The Martinique poet Aimé Césaire coined the term "negritude" as a way to recuperate the French *nègre*, often translated as "nigger," to signify something closer to the more prideful "black" that was circulating in North America (Nesbitt 1999). Négritude was further developed and revised by a number of thinkers and writers, ranging from poet, philosopher, and Senegalese president Léopold Sedar Senghor to the influential Martinique psychoanalyst Frantz Fanon (Senghor 1964; Fanon 1963/2004, 1967a).

Emerging within this global frame and in the context of the civil rights movement, the word "black" became highly politicized. It replaced terms such as "colored" and "Negro" that had become associated with Jim Crow laws and outdated views of people of African descent as benignly subordinate to whites. It also indexed a conscious effort to reappropriate the negative connotations of the term in order to instill race pride among blacks. The term became a part of the name of almost every political organization or movement, including the Black Panther Party and the Black Arts Movement. The heightening of what became known as "black consciousness" and "black nationalism" in the 1960s was critical for the deployment of the term "black" as a cultural mode of being, an analytic, and a site of organized resistance to the global history of white supremacy. Political figures such as Malcolm X and Bobby Seale and organizations such as the Student Nonviolent Coordinating Committee (SNCC) and the Black Panther Party encouraged blacks to disavow white values, beliefs, and ways of knowing and to replace them with black or African worldviews. Signifying oppositionally on the notion that black was somehow inferior to white, Americans of African descent deployed the term "black" to demonstrate their rich cultural heritage through diverse aspects of both expressive and consumer culture—clothing (dashikis), music (rhythm-and-blues and soul music), hair (the afro and braids), language ("black English"), theater (Black Arts Repertory Theater), foodways (soul food), and literature (the Black Arts Movement). Vernacular expressions that reinforced this race pride also circulated during this time: "Black is beautiful. Brown is it. Yellow is something. White ain't shit."

James Brown's 1968 hit "Say It Loud (I'm Black and I'm Proud)" became a signature anthem.

As during the Harlem Renaissance, art and politics were intimately intertwined during this period as the Black Arts Movement emerged as the cultural front of the Black Power Movement. The poetic and theatrical expressions of Amiri Baraka (LeRoi Jones), Haki Madhubuti (Don L. Lee), Sonia Sanchez, Nikki Giovanni, and others reflected the imbrication of aesthetics and politics. These artists and performers spoke of their art both as weapons against oppression and as the vanguard of black creative expression. Kimberly Benston argues that for these black artists of the 1960s, "writing, properly reconceived and directed as utterance and as act, was advanced as a signal instrument of cultural liberation" (2000, 2). Cultural liberation meant an adherence to what was coined "the black aesthetic," a set of principles and standards by which all expressive arts by people of African descent should conform and to which they should aspire. Addison Gayle codified the aesthetic dimensions of this struggle in *The Black Aesthetic* (1971), a collection of essays that elaborated the goals and characteristics of Black Arts. Stephen Henderson's *Understanding the New Black Poetry* (1973) was similar to Gayle's book but with a focus on the tenets of black poetry and its distinguishing features. The artists and intellectuals who were a part of the movement held a range of political views and beliefs about how best to empower the community, but the one through line was a common belief in an authentic or essential blackness.

The effects of this strategic deployment of black essentialism were twofold. On the one hand, the movement enabled a proliferation of artistic expression. The publishing houses, theaters, and intellectual activity it produced made possible the emergence of area and ethnic studies departments devoted to the study of race in academic institutions. Black student riots and takeovers at institutions of higher education across the country demanded that administrators take seriously the intellectual and artistic contributions of people of African descent, which undoubtedly grew out of the fomenting Black Power and Black Arts Movements (Baker, Diawara, and Lindeborg 1996). On the other hand, the movement's reliance on essentialist understandings of blackness created a complex matrix of politics about who could be included under "black" as an umbrella term. While the male leadership of the Black Power Movement believed that black women were a part of the category "black," their views about the role that women should play in the movement mitigated their inclusion. Other identity markers such as sexuality and class status also determined the degree of one's blackness, with homosexuality being viewed as a white disease that had infected the black community and middle-class status viewed as a site of total political capitulation to the white status quo (Cleaver 1968; V. Smith 1998; E. Johnson 2003). This tendency toward selective exclusion and inclusion entered into and structured academic debate as scholars and activists focused on the question of what and who constitutes blackness (Asante 1987; Baker 1987a; Gates 1987; Joyce 1987a, 1987b; Johnson and Henderson 2005). One result of this struggle is that most departments and programs battled over nomenclature, with suggestions for naming ranging from "Black Studies" and "Afro-American Studies" in the 1960s and early 1970s to "African American Studies," "Africana Studies," and "African and African Diasporic Studies" from the late 1970s to the present.

These struggles over naming and the meaning of blackness coincided with the emergence of structuralism and poststructuralism in the academy. These approaches to the study of culture threw into question notions of authenticity and stable meanings of texts. Some black theorists, especially literary critics, drew heavily on poststructuralism to expand what might count as a "black" text and who might count as a "black" author. These critics often focused on black women writers (M. Henderson 1989), gays and lesbians (B. Smith 1982), or a general engagement with the ways black texts signify beyond a specific referent (Gates 1978; Baker 1986). They gained a platform in a white academy friendly to both poststructuralism and racial antiessentialism but not without pushback from traditional black scholars who saw the adoption of mostly Western theories to analyze black literature as leading to the devaluation of its political and cultural intent (Christian 1987; Joyce 1987a).

Outside the United States, usages of the term "black" followed a similar pattern as they entered into and catalyzed debates about identity and identity politics. In several contexts, the term does not necessarily have as a referent Africa or people of African descent. Aboriginals in Australia are referred to as "black" (Broome 2010), and the subcaste of people in India known as "dalit" or the "untouchables" are referenced as "black," as were many Indians during British colonialism (L. James 2000; Rajshekar 2009). With the advent of mass immigration from the British colonies to the metropole during the 1970s and '80s, the term "black" began to be used to reference any former colonial subject: West Indian, African, South Asian. One result was the intellectual formation known in Britain as black cultural studies (Gilroy 1991, 1993; Mercer 1994; S. Hall 1973, 1992b). These writings were influential on black critical thought in the United States and encouraged scholars to conceive of blackness as a much more capacious signifier, provoking them to rethink racialized knowledge production, identity formation and history, and the circulation of blackness within a global context (Gilroy 1991; Favor 1999; Walcott 2000; E. Johnson 2003; Michelle Wright 2004; Elam and Jackson, 2005; Hine, Keaton, and Small 2009). In each of these contexts, the designation of blackness had as much to do with politics as phenotype. Even in the United States, groups we now think of as "white" were earlier described as "black." The Irish, for example, were considered the "blacks of Europe" due to their status as British colonials. They became white only once they had emigrated to the United States and ascended the socioeconomic scale (Ignatiev 1995).

Over the past decade, an interest in postidentity studies has fueled a new revision of blackness and its meanings. Mixed-raced scholars writing about their own life experiences (Senna 1999, 2010; R. Walker 2002) and mixed-raced artists who claim multiple identities (e.g., Mariah Carey, Alicia Keys, Halle Berry) have engaged the rhetoric of the U.S. "postracial" moment since the election of Barack Obama (Elam 2011). While this interest in postraciality might, on the surface, suggest that the importance of "black" as a racial signifier is waning, we need only look to the most prominent of the self-identified mixed-raced figures such as Tiger Woods and Barack Obama to understand how the historical weight of blackness haunts the present. If the history of the term "black" has taught us anything, it is that racialized symbols—those that are disparaging and those that are affirming—never quite fade from sight or consciousness but constantly evolve alongside the people who create them.

6

Border
Mary Pat Brady

Were we to imagine an earlier iteration of this keywords project—one published around, say, 1989—"border" would most likely have been left off the list entirely, though "margin" or maybe "minor" might well have been included. In the intervening years, as violent border conflicts erupted across the world and as the U.S. government heavily militarized its border with Mexico, the term has become prominent in academic work. Accounting for this shift—understanding the concept's fortunes, as it were—entails movement among academic concerns, theoretical conversations, and sociopolitical and economic developments over the last quarter of the twentieth century and the first decade of the twenty-first. To be sure, a loosely defined field of "border studies" has been around in some form or another since Frederick Jackson Turner (1893/1920) argued for the significance of the frontier and Herbert Eugene Bolton (1921) published *The Spanish Borderlands: A Chronicle of Old Florida and the Southwest* and certainly since the end of Word War II, when regional area studies began to receive sustained governmental support. During this period, the most prominent borders were located between East and West Germany, North and South Vietnam, and the officially segregated U.S. South and the unofficially segregated U.S. North. By the mid-1980s, however, the United States had failed in its effort to maintain the border between North and South Vietnam, segregation had been rendered illegal if not eliminated in practice, and efforts to dismantle the border between East and West Germany were gaining momentum. At the same time, philosophers, artists, novelists, and scholars who had been meditating on the less prominent international border between Mexico and the United States began to gain broad attention and to publish significant new work.

That new work emerged along with the effort to create a North American Free Trade Zone, the subsequent Zapatista revolutionary response, the acceleration of other globalizing forces, and the attendant anxieties these forces generated among citizenry of various nations. These tendencies led to political and grassroots efforts to further militarize national borders, to narrow access to citizenship, and to withdraw humane support for workers without papers. Borders were very much in the news because of the ongoing violence of national borders around the world, particularly in regions immediately affected by the breakup of the Soviet Union, the Palestinian-Israeli conflict, the continuing impact of anticolonial struggles, and regional economic recessions. Furthermore, during this period, capital accelerated its transition from its base in the nation-state to a new global scale that entailed more flexible modes of accumulation and citizenship. Under a series of new trade agreements, national borders no longer contained national economies as they had in prior decades. This economic shift accelerated a broad new series of global flows of capital, resources, jobs, and people across national and regional borders. Alongside these developments, researchers in African American and postcolonial studies, feminist theory, poststructuralism, and the cultural studies of the Birmingham school, attuned to the experiences of exile and diaspora, drew attention to the manner in which various kinds of borders are made and unmade (C. Fox 1999; Derrida 1993). Thus, scholars became particularly interested in the theoretical analyses of Chicano and Chicana intellectuals who connected the study of ethnicity, racialization, and immigration to empire building, imperialism, and international relations (Paredes 1958; Gutiérrez-Jones 1995; Saldívar 1997).

Perhaps most significant among these new border theorists was the late philosopher Gloria Anzaldúa. Already well-known among feminists of color as coeditor of the groundbreaking anthology *This Bridge Called My Back* (Moraga and Anzaldúa 1981), Anzaldúa, in *Borderlands/La Frontera: The New Mestiza* (1987), mapped the violence of U.S. colonialism, patriarchy, and capitalism by exploring some historical aspects of the Texas-Mexico border. In doing so, Anzaldúa drew attention to the violent history of anti-Mexican racism, noting the borderland rapes, murders, land grabs, and police detentions largely ignored in standard U.S. histories. At the same time, she roundly critiqued what she saw as misogynist and homophobic practices prevalent in both Anglo and Mexican cultures (Saldívar-Hull 2000). In a brilliant act of reappropriation, she mined the term "border," unveiling its metaphoricity in an effort to envision the impact of the material border in less degrading and more sustainable ways. In keeping with the critical theoretical work of other feminists of color, Anzaldúa questioned the production and maintenance of binaries, their exclusionary force, and the maxims that suggest that living with contradiction necessarily entails psychosis. Instead, she mobilized a second spatial metaphor—that of the *frontera* or borderlands—to insist that one can embrace multiple contradictions and refuse the impossible effort to synthesize them fully, thus turning apparent oppositions into sources of insight and personal strength.

Rapidly disseminated in the United States and elsewhere, this concept of the *frontera* or borderlands enabled other writers to consider culture not through a dominant narrative of synthesis but from a more subaltern perspective of heterogeneity and messiness.

"The borderlands are physically present," Anzaldúa (1987, 19) writes, "wherever two or more cultures edge each other, where people of different races occupy the same territory, where under, lower, middle and upper classes touch, where the space between two individuals shrinks with intimacy." This deliberately universalizing turn provided a language for discussing difference while invoking an imaginary geography. It allowed other scholars and performance artists to build on Anzaldúa's insights, focusing particularly on the conceptual possibilities contained in metaphors of borders, border crossings, and borderlands. Some, such as Guillermo Gómez-Peña (1990), Néstor García Canclini (1995), and Homi K. Bhabha (1994), found much to celebrate in the hybridizing effects of borders. They too argued for the latent power and innovative possibilities of conflictive regions and binaries and suggested that working with contradictions, drawing humor and insight from them rather than repressing or resolving them, would challenge an epistemological structure that enabled economic oppression, racism, misogyny, and homophobia.

"Border" subsequently became a common analytical tool and reference point for scholars working across the fields of American studies, romanticism, medieval history, and cultural studies more generally (Aparicio 2003). Prominent journals of critical theory and philosophy organized special issues around the theme of "borders." At the same time, global corporate elites celebrated the arrival of a world in which national borders appeared no longer to prohibit the movement of people and material. Since these celebrations of a borderless world often occurred at the very moment when nations enacted economic blockades and restricted the informal movements of poor people across national borders, the contradictory function of borders could not be ignored. These contradictions highlighted the extent to which militarized borders have become crucial to capital management—they serve as revenue producers for states, as wage depressers for corporations, and as mechanisms for tying bodies to state power. In short, geopolitical borders have become both abjection machines and state-sponsored aesthetic projects in which states authorize and decorate their own sovereignty (M. Brady 2000, 2002; P. Villa 2003; De Genova, 2002; Salter 2006).

Within academic research in particular, the term "border" began to do some very peculiar work. Because of its simultaneous material and metaphoric resonances, "border" could be used to locate an argument by apparently materializing it, while often dislocating it from any historically specific geopolitical referents. Such a function might not have been so available had borders not been so regularly the subject of news reports. Because of the unending violence of many geopolitical borders, including the thousands of people who have died attempting to cross the Mexico-U.S. border, scholars could use the term and implicitly invoke its violence without documenting or narrating that violence with any real precision (Berestein 2005). Beginning with a geopolitical term, border theorists have developed an epistemological approach equally cognizant of "real" borders and of their fantastic, fantastically violent effects.

And yet it must be noted that the sociopolitical transformations of the first decade of the twenty-first century have added still further nuance to the keyword. Technological and regulatory changes have shifted state power such that the border that Anzaldúa so famously characterized as an "open wound" no longer exists (Schmidt Camacho 2008). It is mobile; it follows us around. Or, as Gilberto Rosas (2006) argues, the border has "thickened." In order to accommodate the deterritorialization of capital and wealth, the border's traditional work as an instantiation of sovereignty over a territory and citizenry has been irrevocably dislocated, unmoored from its Cartesian coordinates through practices that combine policing and emergency services, schooling, and banking with immigration law enforcement. The border is now a process far more than a place. This rescaling of "border" challenges its *tocaya*, or twin term—"citizen"—at the very moment when activists and scholars have begun to question the viability of the pact between state and subject that "citizen" articulates and that borders instantiate (Schmidt Camacho 2010; Boyce Davies and M'Bow 2007; Otiono 2011; Sassen 2009; Waligora-Davis 2011). Should such efforts succeed in dismantling the structures of national citizenship and establishing a global citizenry with universal rights, the border in many of its manifestations will be drained of its power.

7

Capitalism
David F. Ruccio

While the capitalist system is generally celebrated by mainstream economists, American studies and cultural studies scholars will search in vain through their writings for actual discussions of the term "capitalism." Instead, neoclassical and Keynesian economists refer to the "market economy" (in which individuals and private firms make decisions in decentralized markets) or just "the economy" (defined by scarce means and unlimited desires, the correct balancing of which is said to characterize all societies) (Stiglitz and Walsh 2002; Bhagwati 2003; Krugman and Wells 2004; Samuelson and Nordhaus 2004).

In contrast, discussions of the term "capitalism" have long occupied a central position in the vocabulary of Marxian economic theory. References to capitalism in American studies and cultural studies draw, implicitly or explicitly, on the Marxian critique of political economy: a critique of capitalism as an economic and social system and a critique of mainstream economic theory. Karl Marx and latter-day Marxists criticize capitalism because it is based on exploitation, in the sense that capitalists appropriate and decide how to distribute the surplus labor performed by the direct producers, and because it periodically enters into crisis, imposing tremendous costs on the majority of people. They also criticize the work of mainstream economists for celebrating the existence of capitalism and for treating capitalist institutions and behaviors as corresponding to human nature (Mandel 1976; Resnick and Wolff 1987; Harvey 1989).

Much of this scholarship draws on Marx and Friedrich Engels's critique of political economy in the

Manifesto of the Communist Party (1848) and the three volumes of *Capital* (1867, 1884, 1894). In the *Manifesto*, Marx and Engels compare capitalism to other forms of economic and social organization such as feudalism and slavery. What they have in common is that all are based on class exploitation, defined as one group (feudal lords, slave owners, and capitalists) appropriating the surplus labor of another (serfs, slaves, and wage laborers). At the same time, capitalism exhibits a distinct dynamic. For the first time in history, it "established the world market," making it possible for the capitalist class to "nestle everywhere, settle everywhere, establish connexions everywhere" and giving "a cosmopolitan character to production and consumption in every country" (1848/1976, 486, 487). It leads to radical and continuous changes throughout the economy and society, since, as Marx and Engels famously put it, "all that is solid melts into air" (1848/1976, 487).

If the goal of the *Manifesto* was to challenge the prevailing belief that capitalism had eliminated classes and class struggles, the point of *Capital* was to analyze the specific conditions and consequences of the class dimensions of a society in which the capitalist mode of production prevails. Capitalism presumes that the products of labor have become commodities, in the sense that the goods and services that human beings produce have both a use value (they satisfy some social need) and an exchange value (they can be exchanged for other commodities or money). The existence of commodity exchange, in turn, presupposes a culture congruent with the "fetishism of commodities": a culture whereby individuals come to believe and act such that they have the freedom to buy and sell commodities, that the commodities they exchange are equal in value, that the commodity owners meet one another as equals in the marketplace, that individuals have well-defined property rights in the commodities

they sell and purchase, and that they are able to calculate the ability of external objects to satisfy their needs and desires. The existence of commodity exchange is not based on the essential and universal human rationality assumed within mainstream economics from Adam Smith to the present. Nor can the cultures and identities of commodity-exchanging individuals be derived solely from economic activities and institutions. Rather, commodity exchange both presumes and constitutes particular subjectivities—forms of rationality and calculation—on the part of economic agents (Amariglio and Callari 1993).

In both the *Manifesto* and *Capital*, capitalism refers to a system in which capitalists are able to produce commodities that will, at least in principle, yield them a profit. The source of the profit is the value created by the laborers who have been forced (historically, through a process Marx referred to as "primitive accumulation," and, socially, through capitalist institutions and cultures [1867/1976, 1:871–940]) to exercise the specifically capitalist "freedom" to sell their ability to labor as a commodity. Under the assumption that all commodities (including labor power) are exchanged at their values, a surplus value arises based on the ability of capitalists to appropriate the surplus labor performed by the wage laborers and to realize that extra labor by selling the commodities that are produced. Struggles consequently arise over the "rate of exploitation" (the ratio of surplus value to the value of labor power) and over the subsequent distributions of surplus value (to managers, state officials, and other capitalists, who receive portions of the surplus). The keyword "capitalism" thus designates not just an economic structure but also the conflicts, contradictions, and subjectivities inherent in that structure. Both the initial emergence and the subsequent reproduction of capitalism, if and when they occur, often lead to social dislocations and acute crises; they are also conditioned by the most varied cultures and social identities.

In the case of the United States, the past two centuries have witnessed the widening and deepening of capitalism, both domestically and internationally. Initially a market for foreign (especially British) capitalist commodities, the original thirteen colonies oversaw the establishment and growth of domestic capitalist enterprises, which sought both raw materials and markets for final goods within expanding geographical boundaries and across a heterogeneous class landscape. One result was that noncapitalist (communal, independent, slave, and feudal) producers were eventually undermined or displaced, thereby causing waves of rural peoples (men, women, and children of diverse racial and ethnic origins) to migrate to existing and newly established cities and to sell their labor power to industrial capitalists. The opening up of new domestic markets (through the determined efforts of retail merchants, advertisers, and banks), capitalist competition (which drove down the unit costs of production), and government programs (to establish a national currency and to regulate trusts and working conditions) spurred further capitalist growth. The continued development of capitalist manufacturing provoked vast international migrations of laborers: initially, from Africa and western Europe; later, and continuing to this day, from Latin America, Asia, eastern Europe, and Africa (Dowd 1977; Duboff 1989; Amott and Matthaei 1996).

The movement of capital that accompanied the expansion of markets and the search for cheaper raw materials transformed regions outside the industrialized Northeast, including the relocation of textile mills to the South, the creation of foundries and automobile factories in the Midwest, the development of the oil industry in the Southwest, and the flourishing of capitalist agriculture and the movie industry on the West Coast. Capital was also exported to other countries to take advantage of lower wage levels and other cost advantages, thereby introducing economic and social dislocations similar to those that had occurred inside the United States. In both cases, governments, business groups, and social movements (such as trade unions, civil rights organizations, and political parties) struggled over the economic and social conditions and consequences of the new industrial capitalist investments—the boom and bust cycles of domestic economic growth, large-scale movements of populations, the formation of new social identities, and imperial interventions. The uneven development of capitalism at home and abroad has left its mark on the culture of the United States (Kaplan and Pease 1993; Jacobson 2000).

In the first decade of the twenty-first century, as during the Great Depression of the 1930s and many other times throughout U.S. history, capitalism entered into an economic and cultural crisis. The conditions leading up to the current crisis have put new issues on the agenda of American studies and cultural studies—the exponential growth of inequality (Collins, di Leonardo, and Williams 2008), the role of economists in creating the crisis (Grossberg 2010b), the increasing importance of the financial sector (R. Martin 2010), the continued racialization of the housing market through subprime lending practices (Lipsitz 2011), and the heightened role of communication technologies and culture in processes of capital accumulation (Fuchs et al. 2010). The severity of the crisis has cast doubt on the legitimacy of neoliberalism and of capitalism itself (J. Clarke 2010).

In the analysis of this nexus of capitalism and U.S. culture, we face three major challenges that in turn open up new paths of investigation for American studies and cultural studies. The first concerns globalization. It is often assumed that the internationalization of the U.S. economy and society is a radically new phenomenon, something that burst on the scene in the 1980s. However, when measured in terms of movements of people (migration), goods and services (imports and exports), and money (capital inflows and outflows), the globalization of capitalism achieved in that decade levels that are quite similar to those experienced almost a century earlier (Ruccio 2003). Because of these similarities and others (particularly the rise in the rate of exploitation and, with it, the increasingly unequal distribution of income and wealth), it is a mistake to describe contemporary developments as unprecedented (Phillips 2002). This is not to say that the forms of capitalist development during the two periods are the same. One of the challenges for students of U.S. culture is to register these differences—such as the outsourcing of jobs, the growth of Wal-Mart, the spread of financial markets, the conduct of wars to protect petroleum supplies, and the emergence of new media and communication technologies—without losing sight of the past.

The second challenge is to avoid treating capitalism as a purely economic system, separate from culture. The influence of capitalism on the culture industry, including the rise of a capitalist film industry and the export of U.S. culture (Miller et al. 2001; Wayne 2003), has been widely studied and debated. What is less clear is that the capitalist economy is saturated by cultural meanings and identities. From this perspective, each moment of capitalism, from the existence of commodity exchange to the export of capital, is simultaneously economic and cultural. The point is not to substitute cultural studies for political economy but to recognize and analyze, concretely and historically, the cultural conditions of capitalism. Money, commodities, labor power, surplus value, profits: all of these economic forms require the performance of historically and socially constructed meanings and identities. It is also important to understand the role of economic thought in influencing the development of U.S. capitalism and U.S. culture generally. These topics remain open, though a fruitful place to begin is by understanding the role that "languages of class" play in creating new class identities (Gibson-Graham, Resnick, and Wolff 2001), the complex interplay of capitalist and noncapitalist economic imaginaries (Watkins 1998), and the need to rethink the economy and economic knowledge (Grossberg 2010a).

The third potential stumbling block is the treatment of capitalism as an all-encompassing, unitary system that has colonized every social arena and region of the globe. While capitalism certainly represents a powerful project for making and remaking the world, deploying the concept of capitalism as a complete mapping of the economic and social landscape has the effect of obscuring noncapitalist forms of economic organization and cultural sense making. "Capitalocentrism" (akin to the role played by "phallocentrism" and "logocentrism" with respect to gender and language, respectively) hides from view the diverse ways in which people in the United States and elsewhere participate in individual and collective noncapitalist economies— including barter, communal production, gift giving, and solidarity—that fall outside the practices and presumed logic of capitalism (Gibson-Graham 1996; Ruccio and Gibson-Graham 2001). On this view, U.S. culture is heterogeneous and contradictory with respect to different class structures. It contains elements that foster and reproduce capitalism and, at the same time, its noncapitalist others.

8

Citizenship

Lauren Berlant

Although we tend to think of citizenship as something national, originally the citizen was simply a certain kind of someone who lived in a Greek city: a member of an elite class who was said to be capable of self-governance and therefore of the legal and military governance of the city. But the ancient history of the term tells us little about the constellation of rights, laws, obligations, interests, fantasies, and expectations that shape the modern scene of citizenship, which is generally said to have been initiated by the democratic revolutions of the eighteenth century (B. Anderson 1991; B. Turner 1993; Mouffe 1995). Most simply, citizenship refers to a standing within the law (this is often called *formal* citizenship); *jus soli* citizenship allots citizenship to people born within the geographical territory, and *jus sanguinis* awards citizenship by way of a parental inheritance.

At the same time, citizenship is a relation among strangers who learn to feel it as a common identity based on shared historical, legal, or familial connection to a geopolitical space. Many institutional and social practices are aimed at inducing a visceral linkage of personal identity with nationality. In the United States, this process has often involved the orchestration of fantasies about the promise of the state and the nation to cultivate and protect a consensually recognized ideal of the "good life"; in return for cultural, legal, and military security, people are asked to love their country and to recognize certain stories, events, experiences, practices, and ways of life as related to the core of who

they are, their public status, and their resemblance to other people. This training in politicized intimacy has served as a way of turning political boundaries into visceral, emotional, and seemingly hardwired responses of "insiders" to "outsiders." Thus, we can say that citizenship's legal architecture manifests itself and is continually reshaped in the space of transactions between intimates and strangers. The term "civil society" is often applied to these scenes of *substantive* citizenship, though discussions of civil society tend to focus only on the rational aspects of communication and interaction that contribute to the state's reproduction of mainstream society, and not to the ordinary affective or interactive aspects of social exchange (Habermas 1999).

The concept of sovereignty is a crucial bridge between the legal and the substantive domains of U.S. citizenship. This term presupposes a relation between the nation's legal control over what happens in its territory and the presumption that citizens should have control over their lives and bodies, a condition of limited personal autonomy that the state has a responsibility to protect. But the promise of U.S. citizenship to deliver sovereignty to all of its citizens has always been practiced unevenly, in contradiction with most understandings of democratic ideals (Rancière 1998). The historical conditions of legal and social belonging have been manipulated to serve the concentration of economic, racial, and sexual power in the society's ruling blocs.

This shaping of the political experience of citizens and noncitizens has been a focus of much recent scholarship and political struggle. These discussions contest the term "citizenship" in various ways: "cultural citizenship" describes the histories of subordinated groups within the nation-state that might not be covered by official legal or political narratives (T. Miller 1993, 2001; Ong 1996; R. Rosaldo 1999); "consumer citizenship" designates contemporary practices of social belonging and political pacification in the United States (Shanley 1997; Cronin 2000; L. Cohen 2003); "sexual citizenship" references the ongoing struggle to gain full legal rights for gendered and sexual minorities (Berlant and Warner 2000; Cott 2000; M. Kaplan 1997); and "global citizenship" describes a project of deriving a concept of justice from linkages among people on a transnational or global scale (Falk 1994; Bosniak 1998; Hardt and Negri 2000). This list could be vastly expanded. Patriotic citizenship, economic citizenship, and legal citizenship have all been shaped not just within a political public sphere, not just within the logic of mass culture and consumer capitalism, but also within a discussion among various collective interest groups struggling over the core norms, practices, and mentalities of a putatively general U.S. population.

The histories of racial and sexual standing in the United States provide the clearest examples of the uneven access to the full benefits of citizenship. But historically citizenship has also shaped less recognized kinds of distinction. Central among these is that U.S. citizenship has always involved tensions between federal and state systems. Indeed, for most of U.S. history, state citizenship had priority, and the history of civil and suffrage rights centrally involved arguments over the relative priority of state versus federal law. For example, the 1967 Supreme Court case *Loving v. Virginia* (388 U.S. 1), which deemed it unconstitutional to forbid marriage among heterosexuals identified as being of different races, nullified "antimiscegenation" laws not only in Virginia but in thirty-seven other states as well. In so doing, the Supreme Court argued that it is a general rule of U.S. citizenship that marriage cannot be governed by racial restrictions. Prior to that, states were more

important than the nation in determining the racial component of legal marriage among heterosexuals, as well as in many other sexual, familial, and commercial matters, including the legal standing of Mormon, lesbian, gay, and women's marital practices, age of consent, marital rape, reproduction (e.g., abortion, surrogacy, and adoption), and child protection.

Given these complex legal and social histories, U.S. citizenship may be best thought of as an intricate scene where competing forces, definitions, and geographies of freedom and liberty are lived concretely. Citizenship is the practical site of a theoretical existence, in that it allows for the reproduction of a variety of kinds of law in everyday life. It is an abstract idea on behalf of which people engage in personal and political acts, from cheating on taxes to pledging allegiance to fomenting revolutions. It is also, importantly, an ordinary space of activity that many people occupy without thinking much about it, as the administration of citizenship is usually delegated to the political sphere and only periodically worried over during exceptional crises or the election season.

Recent scholarship has pursued this insight into the everyday life of citizenship by exploring some of the most contested scenes in which citizenship has been battled over in U.S. history: immigration, voting rights, sexuality, and labor. Immigration and suffrage have been closely linked at least since the U.S. Naturalization Act of 1790 allowed only "free white persons" to be naturalized as full U.S. citizens. Implicitly this act began the shift from a definition of citizenship as the *ownership of property* to citizenship as the *ownership of labor*, since the word "free" in this act defined freedom as not being economically enslaved—that is, free to sell one's labor in a market for wages (Glenn 2004). The history of U.S. immigrant rights (and exclusions) is thus tied up with desires to control the conditions under which certain populations would be "free" to perform labor in the United States without access to many of the privileges of "free white persons," such as the vote and the legal standing to enforce contracts (Haney-López 1996; Lipsitz 2006; Roediger 1999).

So, for example, between 1882 and 1952, virtually all Asian immigrants except for a small number of Filipino laborers were excluded from full U.S. citizenship. During this period, the United States was also opening and closing the gates to Latin American peoples, especially Mexicans, hundreds of thousands of whom were forcibly repatriated to Mexico a number of times, following fluctuations in capitalists' needs and white racial anxieties about disease and moral degeneracy, along with the usual and always false fear that "alien" poor people take more from the economy than they contribute to it. The courts adjudicating these shifts veered between using racial science and "common knowledge," especially in the visual register, as justification for discrimination (Honig 1998; Jacobson 1998, 2000; Roberts 1998). Similarly, arguments for *and* against suffrage for women appealed to common sense, racist science, and biblical authority to protect patriarchal privilege. Suffrage was achieved only when President Woodrow Wilson found it politically expedient to use an image of emancipated femininity to establish U.S. modernity and moral superiority on a global scale (Berlant 2002). Federal and state manipulation of voting rights continues to threaten the representation of many citizens, especially the poor and the incarcerated.

The same pseudoscientific rationales that maintained white supremacy in the performance of U.S. citizenship were also crucial in shaping reproductive law. It may not seem a question of citizenship when a court determines, as it did in the early twentieth century, that it is proper to sterilize women deemed mentally ill, intellectually limited, or epileptic. But the presumption was that these women would be incompetent as mothers and would pass their incompetence on to their children and that the nation would be burdened by the social and economic costs of reproduction by the poor. Poor women and women of color, especially African American and Native American women, were isolated by this juridical-medical ideology: in California, until the late nineteenth century, Native American children could be taken from their families without due process; until 1972, the state of Virginia routinely sterilized poor women without their consent if their offspring were deemed vulnerable to taking on a "degenerate" form (Ginsburg 1998; Stern 1999b). These examples demonstrate that certain perquisites of citizenship, such as the material experience of sovereignty and sexual "privacy" (a modern development within sovereignty), have often been unavailable to the poor, thereby privileging the wealthier classes and the sexually "normal."

What connects these cases to the keyword "citizenship" is not that they are denials of state-protected *rights* (there has never been a "right" to medical care in the United States). Rather, the contradiction between the sovereignty of abstract citizens and the everyday lives of embodied subjects has been structured by the administration of class hierarchies alongside formal democracy. So it is no surprise that citizenship norms and laws have been highly contested in the workplace as well. Should places of business be allowed to function by different standards than the public domain? Should the protections of citizenship punch out when the worker punches in? Should there be different rules for free speech and political speech on private property and public property? These and other legal questions of citizen sovereignty are put to the test in labor relations. It was not until the last decades of the nineteenth century that workers won the right to an eight-hour day; and during the post–World War II era, many employers made "concessions" to their workers, such as the family wage, health insurance, pensions, and protecting workers from undue physical harm on the job. None of these concessions would have happened without the organizing energy of the labor movement, as we can see when, in tight economic times, corporations renege on contracts with workers, and states cut back on oversight of corporations' economic, environmental, and worker-health practices. Most histories of U.S. citizenship would not place worker rights at the center of a consideration of the practice of equality in the law and social spaces. But insofar as citizens and workers live citizenship as an experience of sovereignty in their everyday lives, the conditions of labor and the formal and informal rules about organizing worker demands for employer accountability have to be at the center of the story.

Many other vectors of normative and legal adjudication that have structured citizenship could be isolated and enumerated, such as human rights, family law, public education, military conscription, real estate zoning, tax structure, religion, and various state entitlement programs. Such seemingly separate domains are actually mutually defining. What, for example, has Christianity had to do with U.S. citizenship, given the constitutionally mandated prohibition of an official state religion? While some theorists have correlated the development of modern public spheres with the secularization of the shared social world, this evolutionary liberal model has recently been shattered by a cluster of different arguments: that the founding fathers were installing political modernity within the strictures of a Protestant morality of conscience; that the history of legislation around marriage, the family, and children has inevitably been influenced by religious movements advocating for and against traditional patriarchal control; that religious organizations have shaped powerfully the historical relation of the public and the private in terms of rights and proprieties; that the development of the welfare state and the civil rights understanding of the economic basis of rights was crucially shaped by religious thinkers (Harding 2001; Morone 2003; Bruce and Voas 2004). At the same time, local communities often engender notions of proper citizenship through churches, schools, and other institutions that involve face-to-face social participation (Ong 1996). The religious question has also been central to the story of the citizenship of Mormons, Native Americans, and many immigrant groups, involving taxation, reproductive rights, free speech, public education, and diverse discussions of the material relation of morality to political and economic concerns.

Many of the progressive developments in U.S. citizenship would not have been achieved without the internationally based struggles of socialism, feminism, and the labor movement. Today, the United States feels pressure from other international movements dedicated to transforming its practices of citizenship: religious movements (Christian fundamentalism and evangelicalism, Islam, Catholicism); antineoliberalism (antiglobalization movements dedicated to a sustaining rather than exploitative and depleting version of global integration); international legal and policy institutions (the United Nations and the International Court of Justice; Doctors without Borders). While international institutions tend to be oriented toward a one-world model of justice, resource distribution, and peace, there is no singular direction or vision of the good life projected by these movements. Antineoliberalism is a *motive* rather than a program, coordinating liberal reformist models of ameliorative activity (environmentalism, welfare statism) with more radical anarchist, queer, antiracist models of refusal and demand. Global religious movements link anticapitalist (antipoverty) messages with a variety of assertions of local sovereignty against the abstract imperialism and general liberality of the modernist state.

Innovations in communication and transportation technology, most notably the Internet, have revitalized and even enabled new inter- and transnational movements and have often produced new understandings of citizenship (Dahlberg 2001; Graeber 2002; Poster 1999). Local determination is not a major stress point among Internet utopians: personal attachments across the globe are made possible by the speed of information transmission. The seemingly infinitely expanding possibilities of niche political developments and micromovements have reanimated citizenship as an aspirational concept in discussions of diverse communities, real and imagined. Thus, the nation-state as such has become only one player in struggles over political and social justice, so much so that many states feel threatened by the transnational flow of information and have responded with censorship. Still, the delocalization of citizenship has not made the world simply postnational. Corporations are like empires; both work transnationally to reshape national standards of conduct. So too the activity of ordinary people to force accountability and to imagine new possibilities for democratic collective life and the sovereignty of people—whether or not they are citizens—continues to revitalize the political sphere everywhere.

9

Class
Eric Lott

As an analytical tool and historiographical category, "class" has an important place in American studies and cultural studies, if only because so many people have thought it irrelevant to the study of the United States. Unlike Europe's old countries, with their feudal pasts and monarchical legacies, the United States, it has often been said, is a land of unlimited economic and geographical mobility. Abraham Lincoln was only one of the most notable believers in "American exceptionalism," the idea that the United States, uniquely among the globe's nations, assigned its citizens no fixed class definition and afforded boundless opportunity to those who would only work hard and look beyond the next horizon. The reality is much more complicated, as scholars and critics have to some extent always known and over the past forty years have demonstrated in studies of U.S. class formation, cultural allegiance, and artistic expression.

Some form of class consciousness has existed in North America at least since white settlers arrived; John Winthrop's (1630/1838) well-known sermon aboard the *Arbella*, "A Modell of Christian Charity," in part justifies the existence of class differences by making them crucial to God's plan of binding through charity the socially stratified community of Puritan believers. The descendants of those believers became an ever-rising post-Puritan middle class, as German sociologist Max Weber (1905/1958) famously suggested when he linked the "Protestant ethic" with capitalist economic energies. Simultaneously, the development of a specifically working-class or "plebeian" consciousness came out of the early U.S. situation of class stratification, and the scholarly dilemma ever since has been how to account for such stratification historically, socially, and culturally.

Closely related to such categories as "station," "status," "group," "caste," and "kind," "class" resonates with implications of value, quality, respectability, and religious virtue. Goodness is gilded in much U.S. cultural thought, and it has been difficult to pry capital loose from rectitude. A related difficulty is that class can seem a natural and fixed category; certainly one strain of social and historical analysis in American studies has been marked by a static account of class and class belonging, with discrete strata exhibiting characteristic habits and allegiances and existing in hierarchical formation. In one of the best theoretical accounts, Erik Olin Wright (1985) makes useful distinctions among class *structure*, class *formation*, and class *consciousness*. Class structure is that ensemble of social relations into which individuals enter and which shapes their class consciousness; class formations are those organized collectivities that come about as a result of the interests shaped by the class structure or system. As Wright sums it up, classes "have a structural existence which is irreducible to the kinds of collective organizations which develop historically (class formations), the class ideologies held by individuals and organizations (class consciousness) or the forms of conflict engaged in by individuals as class members or by class organizations (class struggle), and . . . such class structures impose basic constraints on these other elements in the concept of class" (28).

These distinctions help keep in view the fact that class and classification are dynamic processes, more the result than the cause of historical events. Class, as British historian and cultural studies scholar E. P. Thompson (1963) insisted, is a *relational* category,

always defined against and in tension with its dialectical others. In response to British cultural theorist Raymond Williams's (1958, xvi) claim that culture should be defined as a "whole way of life," Thompson (1961a, 33; 1961b) redefined culture as a "whole way of conflict," structured in dominance and constantly contested by its various social actors. Work on class in American studies has done much to substantiate Thompson's thesis, and the connections between Thompson's historical reconstruction of British working-class formation, Williams's influential model of cultural studies, and American studies scholarship focused on class have been often intimate.

This emphasis has battered time-honored and influential ideas about U.S. culture and society, such as Frederick Jackson Turner's "frontier thesis" (1893/1920), in which westward-roving U.S. Americans continually reestablish the conditions for social mobility and rising wages, or Louis Hartz's lament that a hegemonic "liberal tradition" rendered U.S. Americans incapable of thinking outside the contours of social consensus (1955). American studies scholars have shown, for example, how self-conscious, articulate, and combative early working-class or "artisan republican" ideologies were in waging rhetorical—and sometimes actual—war on what they termed the "nonproducing classes" or "the upper ten." Sean Wilentz's *Chants Democratic: New York City and the Rise of the American Working Class, 1788–1850* (1984b) is one of the finest studies of the former, while Stuart Blumin's *The Emergence of the Middle Class: Social Experience in the American City, 1760–1900* (1989) is one of the best on the latter. Both capture how extensively the cultural and affective life of social class shaped democracy in the United States.

Each of these studies exemplifies a body of historiography that first emerged in the 1960s to explain the shape and nature of various class formations. Wilentz is the beneficiary of the "new social history," of which Herbert Gutman (1976) was perhaps the chief U.S. representative. Subsequent studies of the labor process, shop-floor cultures, workers' leisure activities, and other matters have decisively demonstrated the tenacious, conflictual character of working-class belonging—even, or most particularly, when that belonging is overdetermined by being African American or female (Peiss 1986; Kelley 1994). Meanwhile, extensive studies of bourgeois or middle-class cultural formations in major books by Warren Susman (1984), Jackson Lears (1981), and many others have shown how ruling-class desires and cultural investments have influenced everything from modern art to modern therapy, as well as the degree to which such canonical ideas as the "American character," "American progress," and the "American Dream" are inflected by class. Perhaps most illuminating have been studies by such scholars as Christine Stansell (1986), Richard Slotkin (1985), Hazel Carby (1987), Alan Trachtenberg (1982), and Lizabeth Cohen (2003) that examine the complex interrelations among various class fractions and formations.

One of the common findings of the latter sort of study is how often cross-class interaction works not to dissolve class boundaries but to buttress them. Examples include middle-class philanthropic enterprises that wind up solidifying bourgeois formations and alienating their would-be working-class wards, and African American strategies of racial uplift that too often demonize the black working class. For this reason and others, the category of class has been immensely useful in American studies as an analytical tool capable of unpacking the sometimes surprising dynamics of cultural and textual processes and products, from social clubs and theatrical performances to dime novels and Disney films. The

class segregation of mid-nineteenth-century U.S. theaters, for example, has earned a whole tradition of scholarship, with its attention to class-bound characters, plots, settings, and themes; much the same has been done for the history of U.S. fiction, which has, scholars argue, differing trajectories based not only on plot, character, and outcome but also on mode of production and distribution. Cultural forms hardly recognized at all under erstwhile rubrics of U.S. cultural expression—balladry, mob action, table manners, amusement parks—have found a place in scholarly debates precisely as classed forms of cultural life. The saloon is now recognized no less than the literary salon as a space of cultural and social self-organization.

Just as importantly, quintessential public artifacts of U.S. culture such as New York City's Central Park need to be understood as complex mediations of conflicting class, party, and historical factors. Witness too studies of U.S. newspapers, in which various class accents have been seen to vie for control of a given editorial tendency, newsworthy event, or style of audience address. The key, and often exhilarating, emphasis in such studies is that U.S. cultural forms do not so much belong to a given class or class fraction as they become sites in which class struggles are fought out. In recent years, studies of American "hemispheric" and global class struggles have moved to the fore, whether focused on the emergence of internationalist social movements (Reed 2005), the character and function of manufacturing sweatshops (Ross 1997), or the place of U.S. cultural formations in the world system (Denning 2004).

At their best, class-sensitive versions of American studies and cultural studies are animated by the attempt to grasp the complex dialectic of work and leisure—the structuring of U.S. society by the unequal and uneven social relations of labor and the ways in which those relations give rise to a vast array of cultural forms. The social location of the artist, the assembly-line production of films and cheap fiction: whatever the case, class analysis has immeasurably benefited our understanding of the cultural scene. The United States may be an exceptional place—what country is not?—but it has seen its fair share of class conflict in the sphere of culture, conflict that is intense, productive, and ongoing.

10

Colonial

David Kazanjian

"Colonial" has very old roots. The Latin word *colonia* was used during the Roman Empire to mean a settlement of Roman citizens in a newly conquered territory. Often these citizens were retired soldiers who received land as a reward for their service and as a display of Roman authority to the conquered inhabitants. For Roman writers, *colonia* translated the Greek word *apoikia*, which meant a settlement away from one's home state, as opposed to the *polis*, meaning one's own city or country as well as a community of citizens, or the *metropolis*, literally one's mother city or mother country.

Despite these etymological ties to the violence and power of conquest, the English word "colony" was until the eighteenth century as likely to mean simply a farm or a country estate as a settlement in conquered land subject to a parent state. The cognate "colonial" was not coined until the late eighteenth century (it is not in Samuel Johnson's 1755 dictionary), when it was used as an adjective to mean "of a colony" and as a noun to mean "a person from a colony," most often referring to Europeans who conquered and settled in North America and the West Indies.

This eighteenth-century usage acquired an important and odd wrinkle in the United States, one that is particularly relevant to U.S. variants of cultural studies: "colonial" and "colonist" have often been used as if they were simple descriptors for early Americans and unrelated to conquest. For instance, while the recent popular dictionary *Colonial American English* does not include a definition for the word "colonial," it does define "colony" as "a government in which the governor is elected by the inhabitants under a charter of incorporation by the king, in contrast to one in which the governor is appointed" (Lederer 1985, 54). Here, we can see how far this usage strays from the word's roots in conquest by suggesting that "colonial" signifies a kind of democracy. Indeed, "colonials," "American colonists," "the colonial period," and "colonial literature" in the U.S. context have often invoked images of plucky settlers fleeing persecution in Europe, overthrowing their oppressive European rulers, establishing rich new states and cultures against all odds through hard work, and founding a free, democratic, and unified nation. The word "colonial" thus oddly comes to connote resistance *to* the violence and power of conquest.

In 1847, the influential political economist Henry Charles Carey (1967, 345) extended this usage in a way that links it to a history of American exceptionalism: "The colonization of the United States differs from that of the two countries we have considered [Britain and France], in the great fact that they [the United States] desire no subjects. The colonists are equal with the people of the States from which they sprang, and hence the quiet and beautiful action of the system." While Britain and France send their citizens to the far corners of the world to conquer territory and subjugate native inhabitants, Carey tautologically claims, the United States was founded by colonists who colonized themselves. As he goes on to argue, the resulting nation is both exceptional, or unique in the history of the world, and exemplary, or destined to be emulated by the rest of the world.

This U.S. understanding of colonization expresses a deeply nationalist mythology that continues to thrive today: the United States was founded exclusively on the just and noble principles of freedom, equality, and democracy, and it continues to spread those principles around the world. This mythology has been challenged from a number of directions. Scholars and activists in African American and Native American studies have shown how the "quiet and beautiful action" that Carey describes actually involved some of the most brutal systems of dispossession that the modern world has known: the conquest of Native American lands, the enslavement and genocide of native peoples and Africans, and the establishment of a vast transatlantic and transcontinental system of race-based chattel slavery. Much of this scholarship has argued that these practices were not simply aberrations from or exceptions to the history and culture of the United States but rather constitutive of all that it was to become.

Forms of dispossession in which colonists take up permanent residence in the territories they appropriate are called "settler colonialism." As Karl Marx (1867/1976) explained in the first volume of *Capital*, such dispossession—along with the enclosure of the agricultural commons throughout Europe, the expropriation of peasants from those expropriated lands, and the transformation of those peasants into wage laborers, global migrants, and settler colonials—was a central means by which capitalists, starting in the sixteenth century, accumulated the wealth they needed to increase the productive efficiency of agricultural and industrial production and to extract ever-increasing rates of surplus value from peasants, the poor, and indigenous and enslaved populations. Mythologized as "primitive accumulation" by classical political economists, accumulation by dispossession was in fact the brutal condition of possibility for modern global capitalism and its attendant political form, the nation-state (Emmanuel 1972). The white settler foundations of the United States—in which European settler colonials violently expropriated lands from Native Americans—can thus be linked with other histories of settler colonialism across the Caribbean, Latin America, and

Canada, as well as in South Africa, Australia, and New Zealand (Wolfe 2006; Black Hawk 1833/2008; Goldstein and Lubin 2008; Andrea Smith 2010; Byrd 2011; Morgensen 2011; Goldstein 2012). The concept of settler colonization has also been used to link more recent examples of dispossession, such as the black settler colonization of Liberia and the Zionist project in Israel, to this long history of capitalism's rise to hegemony (Massad 2006; Afzal-Khan and Seshadri 2000; Pedersen and Elkins 2005; Kazanjian 2011, 2012). Indeed, accumulation by dispossession has been extended to contemporary neoliberal policies throughout the globe, policies that have managed waves of economic crisis from the 1970s forward, including the privatization of public assets, seizures of indigenous lands, and the rise of so-called financialization (Harvey 2003).

Attention to histories of settler colonialism unsettles the myth of the North American colonial as a "quiet and beautiful," even heroic actor. Take as an instance of this myth the text that can be said to have founded it: the Declaration of Independence. The Declaration represents North American colonials as innocent victims of British tyranny ("Such has been the patient sufferance of these Colonies"), as well as harmless witnesses to violence against Native Americans, by blaming both the Crown and Native Americans themselves for Indian resistance to colonization ("the present king of Great Britain . . . has endeavored to bring on the inhabitants of our frontiers the merciless Indian savages"; Jefferson 1776/1984, 19, 21). Even as white settlers were doing battle with Indians, they paradoxically drew on their fantasies about Indians to fashion their own identities as American colonials distinct from their British brethren. Sometimes they "played Indian," as Philip J. Deloria (1998) has carefully recounted, in private societies and at protests such as the Boston Tea Party. At other times, they combed through Indian graves to show that America had its own ancient history to rival that of Europe (Jefferson 1787/1984). And increasingly after the Revolution, white U.S. American writers depicted Indians in order to distinguish "American" from "English" literature. Performed alongside violence against Native Americans, this fashioning of a U.S. American identity helped to generate the mythology of the innocent North American colonial who became a heroic rebel and eventually an exceptional U.S. citizen.

While the Declaration of Independence does not mention slavery directly, in an early draft it did include a passage that both criticized slavery and perpetuated the mythology of North American colonials as innocent victims of conquest. The passage personified the entire transatlantic slave trade in the king ("He has waged cruel war against human nature itself") and equated enslaved Africans with free white settlers as fellow victims ("he is now exciting those very people [slaves] to rise in arms among us, and to purchase the liberty of which he has deprived them, by murdering the people on whom he also obtruded them" [Jefferson 1776/1984, 22]). By suppressing the alliance between Europeans and North American colonials in the system of chattel slavery, this passage transforms the latter from conquerors to conquered. Unabashedly proslavery colonials found even this argument too threatening to their interests and fought successfully for its deletion.

By recovering and reinterpreting early colonial and national texts that were crucial in their day but had long been excluded from disciplinary canons, twentieth-century scholars have traced histories and practices of dissent that challenged the mythological conception of the American colonial. New social historians have reminded us that the list of men who signed the Declaration of Independence is not simply a list of heroic rebels; it is a list of elites. Their Declaration would have had no force behind it had poor people throughout the colonies not been struggling for decades against exploitation at the hands of wealthy and powerful colonials as well as British authorities. The North American colonial looks neither innocent nor uniform from the perspective of an early dissident such as Stephen Hopkins, who helped to organize a rebellion and then a furtive utopian community after a Virginia Company vessel shipwrecked on Bermuda in 1609 (Strachey 1610/1964); or Richard Frethhorn, an indentured servant who was transported to Virginia in 1623 and wrote back to his parents of the brutal conditions he faced (Jehlen and Warner 1997, 123); or Anne Bonny and Mary Read, two cross-dressing women pirates who worked with the predominantly male pirate population of the early eighteenth century to disrupt the social and cultural norms, and the emerging imperial state, of the British Empire (Hogeland and Klages et al. 2004, 98-106); or rural colonial rebels who challenged the British colonial elite for control over land and political decision-making before the American Revolution and then took on the early social and political elite in the Shays Rebellion of 1786 (Alfred Young 1976, 1993; Zinn 1980; G. Nash 1986; New Social History Project 1989-92; Raphael 2001).

In the eighteenth and nineteenth centuries, African Americans and Native Americans took the lead in challenging the mythology of the North American colonial. In 1829, a free black tailor and activist from Boston named David Walker published a pamphlet that excoriated whites for their systematic racism and called on blacks to claim the land that slavery had forcibly made their own, effectively recalling the etymological roots of "colonial" in the violence and power of conquest as well as disrupting analogies between white settler colonials and slaves (1829/1995, 74-76). William Apess, a Pequot born in 1798, published an 1833 essay in which he charged that U.S. Christians failed to live up to the Revolutionary ideals of freedom and equality as well as the spirit of Christianity: "By what you read, you may learn how deep your principles are. I should say they were skin-deep" (1833/1992, 160). Even in the title of his essay ("An Indian's Looking-Glass for the White Man"), Apess reverses the dynamic of "playing Indian"; he claims a European technology, the looking-glass, and turns it on white men so that they may see themselves not as innocent colonials but as violent colonizers.

This minority tradition of challenging the mythology of the U.S. American colonial was renewed after the U.S.-Mexico War of 1846-48 by Mexicanos, Tejanos, and, in the twentieth century, Chicanos who insisted that it was U.S. imperialism—not innocent, plucky settlers—that made them as well as the entire geography of the Southwest and California part of the United States. Chicanos in the second half of the twentieth century collaborated with African Americans, Asian Americans, and Native Americans to appropriate the word "colonial" by situating their own histories in the context of Third World liberation movements ("Alcatraz Reclaimed" 1970/1971; "El Plan" 1969/1972; Ho 2000). Black activists Stokely Carmichael and Charles Hamilton (1967, 5-6) exemplify this mode of analysis in their book *Black Power: The Politics of Liberation in America*: "Black people are legal citizens of the United States with, for the most part, the same *legal* rights as other citizens. Yet they stand as colonial subjects in relation to the white society. Thus institutional racism has another name: colonialism. Obviously, the analogy is not perfect." By acknowledging the imperfections of this "internal colonization" argument at the very moment of formulating it, Carmichael and Hamilton foreground both the difficulty and the importance of thinking about the keyword "colonial" in an international context.

Such international thinking took place in the early United States as well: Walker's *Appeal*, for instance, is addressed to "the coloured citizens of the world." And it continues today: in an echo of the Declaration of Independence's claim that white North American colonials are victims of imperialism along with slaves and Indians, some contemporary scholars have suggested that the United States should be considered a postcolonial nation (Ashcroft, Griffiths, and Tiffin 1989; Buell 1995). In contrast, others have picked up on the implications of the internal colonization thesis and insisted on the differential relations among variously racialized minorities and whites (Spivak 1993; Sharpe 1995; Saldaña-Portillo 2001). The latter scholarship relies on rich historical understandings of the differences among modes of imperialism, particularly white settler colonialism, comprador capitalism, and neocolonialism.

Contemporary scholars have also shown how a historical understanding of these differences requires a close attention to gender and sexuality. Indeed, we can hear an echo of gender and sexuality in the very word "colonial." As noted earlier, the Latin *colonia* was a translation of the Greek word *apoikia* (literally, "away from the domestic sphere"), which itself was opposed in Greek to the *polis* and the *metropolis*, "the city" and "the mother country." This distinction survives in English in the opposition between "metropole" and "colony." If the home or domestic sphere is figured as maternal, then the colonial sphere is readily figured as public, political, and masculine, which makes the word "colonial" subject to the vast feminist scholarship on the separation—or inseparability—of public and private spheres (Kerber 1980; Isenberg 1998; Davidson and Hatcher 2002). One aspect of this scholarship is exemplified by studies of North American colonial women such as Anne Hutchinson, who challenged the male dominance of mainstream Puritanism in seventeenth-century New England (Kerber and De Hart 2004, 25–120). Other studies suggest that the very concept of the domestic invokes the process of domestication, the incorporation and subjection of that which is not yet fully domesticated (A. Kaplan 2002).

It is thus not surprising to see early champions of women's work in the domestic sphere, such as Catharine Beecher (1841), imagine in imperial terms the ordering and unifying of the home as an ever-expanding process destined to encompass the entire world. In addition, black women who were enslaved in the Americas, as well as contemporary black feminist critics, have shown how the gendering of the colonial had deep racial implications (A. Davis 1983; H. Wilson 1859/1983; Hartman 1997; Prince 1831/2000; Spillers 2003). Eighteenth-century laws that based a black person's status as free or enslaved on that of the mother encouraged the sexual exploitation of black women by white men. Consequently, the black domestic sphere became, to white men, a breeding ground for slavery. To further complicate matters, feminist postcolonial scholars have shown how the colony as such is often figured as feminine in order to make it subject to the power and authority of the metropole, while others have complicated this general model by tracking the uneven deployments of gender across the postcolonial world (Mohanty, Russo, and Torres 1991; McClintock 1995; Yuval-Davis 1997; Spivak 1999). Queer studies has also opened up the study of sexuality in the colonial context, examining closely the ways heterosexuality was made culturally and legally normative among early North American colonists, and in turn revealed the challenges that sexually dissident cultures presented to this normativity (J. Goldberg 1992; Burgett 1998).

The complex history of the word "colonial" indexes the equally complex politics that have characterized U.S. imperialism. In the first decades of the twenty-first century, debates about colonialism, and settler colonialism in particular, remain at the forefront of research in American studies and cultural studies. As struggles over the future of the U.S. empire proliferate, it is all the more urgent for cultural studies to take stock of the history of such a contested keyword.

11

Community
Miranda Joseph

In the late twentieth- and early twenty-first-century United States, the term "community" is used so pervasively that it would appear to be nearly meaningless. The term is often deployed more for its performative effect of being "warmly persuasive" than for any descriptive work it accomplishes (Raymond Williams 1976/1983, 76). Carrying only positive connotations—a sense of belonging, understanding, caring, cooperation, equality—"community" is deployed to mobilize support not only for a huge variety of causes but also for the speaker using the term. It functions this way for companies such as Starbucks and Target, which have programs and pamphlets in their stores proclaiming their commitment to community, as well as for the feminist scholar who seeks to legitimize her research by saying she works "in the community." It is deployed across the political spectrum to promote everything from identity-based movements (on behalf of women, gays and lesbians, African Americans, and others) to liberal and neoliberal visions of "civil society," to movements seeking to restore or reaffirm so-called traditional social values and hierarchies.

The relentless invocation of "community" is all the more remarkable given the persistent critique to which it has been subjected. In the late twentieth century, scholars examined its use in the contexts of identity politics, liberalism, and nationalism, in each case pointing to its disciplining, exclusionary, racist, sexist, and often violent implications (Joseph 2002). Feminist activists and scholars have argued that the desire for communion, unity, and identity among women tended in practice to make the women's movement white, bourgeois, and U.S.-centric (Martin and Mohanty 1986). Feminist critics of liberalism have pointed out that the supposedly abstract political community constituted through the liberal state actually universalized exclusionary gendered and racial norms (Wendy Brown 1995). Critics of European and postcolonial nationalisms have historicized the communal origin stories used to legitimate those nationalisms and emphasized the hierarchies and exclusions likewise legitimated by those narratives. Poststructuralist theories have underwritten many of these critiques, enabling scholars to argue that the presence, identity, purity, and communion connoted by "community" are impossible and even dystopic fantasies (I. Young 1990). In light of these critiques, many scholars have tried to reinvent "community," to reconceptualize it as a space of difference and exposure to alterity (Mouffe 1992; Agamben 1993). Such stubborn efforts to build a better theory and practice of community only emphasize that the crucial question to pose about "community" as a keyword is this: Why is it so persistent and pervasive?

One answer to this question lies in the realization that many deployments of the term can be understood as instances of a larger discourse that positions "community" as the defining other of capitalist "modernity." As Raymond Williams (1976/1983) notes, "community" has been used since the nineteenth century to contrast immediate, direct, local relationships among individuals with something in common to the more abstract relations connoted by capitalist or modern "society." While community is often presumed to involve face-to-face relations, capital is taken to be global and faceless. Community concerns boundaries between us and them that are naturalized through reference to place or race or culture or identity; capital, on the other hand, would

seem to denature, crossing all borders and making everything and everyone equivalent. The discourse of community includes a Romantic narrative that places it prior to "society," locating community in a long-lost past for which we yearn nostalgically from our current fallen state of alienation, bureaucratization, and rationalization. This discourse also contrasts community with modern capitalist society structurally; the foundation of community is supposed to be social values, while capitalist society is based only on economic value. At the same time, community is often understood to be a problematic remnant of the past, standing in the way of modernization and progress.

This narrative of community as destroyed by capitalism and modernity, as supplanted by society, can be found across a wide range of popular and academic texts; one might say that it is one of the structuring narratives of the field of sociology (Bender 1978). And it took on a fresh life in the works of communitarians such as Robert Bellah (Bellah et al. 1985), Robert Putnam (1993), Amitai Etzioni (1993), E. J. Dionne (1998), and others, all of which are aimed at least in part at nonacademic audiences. These works inevitably misread Alexis de Tocqueville's *Democracy in America* (1835/2004) as describing a now-lost form of local community that they believe would, if revived, promote democracy and economic prosperity and solve many contemporary problems, including drug use, crime, and poverty.

The discursive opposition of community and society provides a crucial clue to the former's pervasiveness in contemporary discourse; community is a creature of modernity and capitalism. Williams optimistically suggests that modernity positively constitutes communities of collective action. In *The Country and the City* (1973, 102, 104), he argues against the nostalgic idealization of preenclosure communities that he finds in late eighteenth- and early nineteenth-century British literature, pointing out that preenclosure villages supported "inequalities of condition" and that "community only became a reality when economic and political rights were fought for and partially gained." More pessimistically, Nikolas Rose (1999, 172, 174) reads the invocation of community as a central technology of state power, arguing that "community" is used to invoke "emotional relationships" that can then be instrumentalized. He suggests that the communities so invoked are required to take on responsibilities for "order, security, health and productivity" that were formerly carried by the state. And certainly there is substantial evidence for his argument in the proliferation of public-private partnerships, neighborhood watch programs, restorative justice initiatives, and the like, all of which mobilize familial and communal relations to promote subjection to law and order rather than to fight for economic or political rights (Lacey and Zedner 1995; N. Lacey 1996; Joseph 2006).

Community thus can be understood as a necessary supplement to the circulation of state power and capital; as such, it not only enables capital and power to flow, but it also has the potential to displace those flows. Because the circulation of abstract capital depends on the embodiment of capital in particular subjects, the expansion and accumulation of capital requires that capitalists engage in an ongoing process of disrupting, transforming, galvanizing, and constituting new social formations, including communities. Community is performatively constituted in capitalism, in the processes of production and consumption, through discourses of pluralism, multiculturalism, and diversity, through niche marketing, niche production, and divisions of labor by race, gender, and nation.

This complex relation of community to capitalism is particularly evident in the promotion of nonprofit and nongovernmental organizations (NPOs and NGOs)—"civil society"—in the context of "development" in the United States and internationally. In the United States, nonprofit organizations are said to express community and often stand in for community metonymically. They are the institutional sites where people contribute labor or money to "the community." And they are posited as the form through which community might be reinvigorated as a complement to capitalism, providing those goods and services that capitalism does not. In the context of "development," NGOs have been explicitly promoted as a means for developing human and social capital and involving the poor in development projects—as, in other words, sites for constituting liberal capitalist subjects and subjectivities. At the same time, the necessity for such organizations suggests that subjects are not always already capitalist subjects. And in fact, the promotion of NPOs and NGOs has often been explicitly intended to stave off socialism or communism; for example, in the post-Soviet era, "community," in the guise of NGOs, featured prominently in the promotion of "civil society" in both former communist countries and "developing" countries of the "Third World" (Joseph 2002). The incorporation of subjects as community members at the site of the NGO can be understood as hegemonizing, wedding potentially resistant subjects (potentially or actually communist subjects) to capitalism.

The centrality of community to capitalism becomes more explicit in the context of globalization. Politically diverse iterations of globalization discourse, both popular and academic, argue that capitalism depends on communities, localities, cultures, and kinship to provide the social norms and trust that enable businesses to function and that globalized capitalism is and should be more attuned to particular communities, localities, and cultures (Piore and Sabel 1984; Fukuyama

1995). While a number of scholars have portrayed the localization and culturalization of capitalism as a positive development, creating opportunities for local or communal resistance (Lipietz 1994; Mayer 1994), others have emphasized the weakness, dependence, and vulnerability of the local (Peck and Tickell 1994). The claim that capitalism only recently discovered community is, however, problematic. It suggests that communities, and the economic inequalities among them, have not themselves been constituted by capitalism. To the contrary, the explicit deployment of community within globalization discourse tends to legitimate economic inequalities and exploitation as the expression of authentic cultural difference even as it articulates all communities and cultures as analogous sites for production and consumption (Melissa Wright 1999).

The project of examining "the seductions of community" remains a crucial one (Creed 2006). Exploring the ways in which community is constituted by or complicit with capital and power can reshape our understandings of the dimensions of our communities and the connections among them. Such exploration might enable us to recuperate and rearticulate the needs and desires for social change that are so often co-opted by the uncritical deployment of the term.

12

Contract

Amy Dru Stanley

"Contract" is at least as old as the Old Testament and as new as the market transactions of the moment—local, national, and global. It encompasses the provinces of religion and commodities, state and civil society, public and private exchange, the rights of persons and the rights to property. Puritan theology speaks of covenants, Enlightenment liberalism of social contracts, political economy of commercial contracts, the law of liberty of contract. Informed by those traditions, U.S. culture has long been infused by contract. Just after the Civil War, a primer handed out by Yankee liberators to former slaves testified to contract's vast province: "You have all heard a great deal about contracts, have you not since you have been free? . . . Contracts are very numerous; numerous as the leaves on the trees almost; and, in fact, the world could not get on at all without them" (Fisk 1866, 47). The lesson of freedom was not simply that contract was essential but that it was virtually a fact of nature. In other words, "contract" stood as a keyword of U.S. culture. Never was this more so than in the nineteenth century, when contract prevailed as a metaphor for social relations in free society.

Implicit in the vocabulary of contract is a set of fundamental terms denoting human subjectivity, agency, and social intercourse. As opposed to prescriptive duties or formally coercive bonds of personal dominion and dependence, a contract is, in principle, a purely voluntary obligation undertaken in the expectation of gaining a reciprocal benefit—an equivalent of some sort, a quid pro quo, or, in the language of the law, "consideration." Thus, contract implies both individual volition and mutual exchange, reconciling freedom and obligation, creating rights and duties, and imposing social order through myriad transactions among ostensibly free persons. Above all, contract implies conditions of self-ownership. In order to cede a portion of liberty by choosing to incur duties, contract makers must, in theory, be sovereigns of themselves—possessive individuals, entitled to their own persons, labor, and faculties. A lasting axiom of Enlightenment thought is that contract derives from and governs individual will and that free will is tethered to rights of proprietorship. Early in the nineteenth century, G. W. F. Hegel (1821/1979, 58) philosophized that under a contract a person "ceases to be an owner and yet is and remains one. It is the mediation of the will to give up a property . . . and the will to take up another, i.e. another belonging to someone else." Or as a U.S. American professor of political science explained half a century later, "I cannot make that the property of another *by contract* which is not *mine* already" (Woolsey 1878, 74). Equally enduring in this intellectual tradition is the notion that contract's fundamental properties—self-ownership, consent, and exchange— belonged fundamentally to men. That notion, like the very meaning of "consent," "exchange," and "self-ownership," has provoked a long-standing dispute over the cultural significance of contract.

Notably, contract is not simply a language, a metaphor, a set of principles, or a worldview. A contract is also a palpable transaction. It is a social relation—an exchange relation—involving what the eighteenth-century British legal theorist Sir William Blackstone (1765–69/1979, 118) called the "rights of things" and the "rights of persons." Abstract principles of entitlement and volition find concrete embodiment in contracts of state, of church, of sale, of debt, of labor, and of marriage. In the realm of U.S. law, the nineteenth

century has long been considered the age of contract— with contract figuring as the legal apparatus of classical political economy and laissez-faire liberalism. Yet the authority of contract reached well beyond the law, and contract law itself was heir to older religious and political traditions. In the Middle Ages, contracts of rulership reflected Christian doctrine as well as Roman codes, and ancient, informal customs of covenant shaped the advent of early contract law (Gordley 1991). In the modern era, the roots of contract extend back to understandings of the origins of the state, the Puritan church, and market society in the seventeenth and eighteenth centuries and, following the paths of the common law, became embedded in debates over the meaning of slavery and emancipation (Hopfyl and Thompson 1979).

Since the British settlement of North America, the tenets of self-ownership, consent, and exchange remained central to contract theory and practice; yet the meaning of those tenets subtly altered as they were understood to validate changing institutions and social relations. The doctrine of covenant, or contract, lay at the heart of dissenting Protestantism, reconciling divine supremacy and human agency, explaining the relationship between God and humanity as a bargain, and establishing consent as the basis for human obedience to biblical edicts. The Enlightenment theory of the social contract gave secular political formulation to this notion of voluntary submission to the rule of law, thereby legitimating the obedience of citizens to the authority of the state in return for protection of their lives and property. Here, contract entailed volition and reciprocity, while also justifying a degree of subordination. But, as a paradigm of commercial society, contract came to embody exchange between individuals who were formally equal as well as formally free. It defined the relations of the free market rather than the rules of sovereignty. For Adam Smith (1776/1937, 31) and his disciples, contract presupposed "rough equality" among persons involved in commodity exchange. And the antislavery claim of the nineteenth century was that contract represented the absolute antithesis of chattel bondage, with the abstract rights of freedom concretely lodged in the contracts of wage labor and marriage, which entitled ex-slaves to own and sell their labor and to marry and maintain a home.

Most famously, contract has been associated in U.S. culture with the career of classical liberalism, an association that past and present critics have deemed the source of contract's most infamous illusions and contradictions. The criticisms have become canonical and are virtually synonymous with those directed at other core liberal institutions and intellectual traditions: laissez-faire political economy, the negative state, the market calculus of supply and demand, commodity relations, possessive individualism, the abstractions of rights theory. In contract, so the argument goes, the core liberal tenets of formal equality and freedom cloak actual differences of power, thereby obscuring the underlying social inequalities, dependencies, and informal compulsions that nullify the vaunted rights of individual contract freedom. Since the early nineteenth century, this argument has been advanced by wage workers seeking to form unions and fashion collective work contracts; by ex-slaves resisting free labor's coercions; by churchmen, reformers, and intellectuals critical of the moral callousness and inequities of the free market; and by statesmen and jurists, such as Justice Oliver Wendell Holmes, who, in his landmark dissent in the 1905 *Lochner v. New York* case (198 U.S. 45 (1905)), insisted that the Fourteenth Amendment had been wrongly construed to enshrine liberty of contract as an absolute constitutional right. As one freedman vividly decried the falsity of the contract regime, "I would not

sign anything. I said, 'I might sign to be killed. I believe the white people is trying to fool us'" (Henry Adams, quoted in Sterling 1976, 6).

Another strain of critique has brought to light the contradictions of contract in affirming individual rights while also validating sexual inequality on the basis of putatively immutable physical difference. Thus, the "sexual contract" stands alongside the "social contract," anointing men with property in women, who accordingly are dispossessed of rights to their own persons, labor, sexuality, and property (Pateman 1988). That was the outcry of generations of feminists against the marriage contract, which gave the husband dominion over his wife, binding her to serve and obey him in return for his protection and support. "If the contract be equal, whence come the terms 'marital power,' 'marital rights,' 'obedience and restraint,' 'dominion and control?'" Elizabeth Cady Stanton protested in 1868. "According to man's idea, as set forth in his creeds and codes, marriage is a condition of slavery" (Stanton 1868a, 1868b). Subject to the will of a master, the wife had no rights of contract, a fact that led Stanton and others to bitter comparisons between marriage and chattel slavery. Prostitution also figured as an analogy for marriage; reformers argued that both were contracts centered on the sale of sex as a commodity and in which women were not fully free or equal to men. The point was that only in the context of an ideal marriage, contracted freely between husband and wife who were utter equals, could sex be a legitimate token of exchange; otherwise, sex counted as a uniquely inalienable aspect of self (Stanley 1998).

Yet to highlight only the critical tradition is to lose sight of the emancipatory prospects of contract. Absent such insight, the cultural power of contract ideals becomes inexplicable, even mysterious. For the generation who witnessed the transition from slavery to freedom and argued over the meaning of that transformation, contract offered a way of making sense of the changes in their world and of distinguishing between the relations of freedom and slavery. Contract opened up ways of thinking about the perplexities of a culture that condemned the traffic in slaves while otherwise celebrating the boundlessness of the free market. It did not offer a common vantage point to differently situated persons but instead provided some common principles for expressing differing visions of the genuine meaning of self-ownership, consent, and reciprocal exchange. It was a language of aspiration as well as of criticism.

Objections to existing contract relations often translated into demands for universalizing and authenticating the ideals of contract—for more perfectly realizing contract's promise, as opposed to rejecting it outright. However much ex-slaves disavowed the equation of freedom and the wage contract, they tended to choose willingly to marry, and many expressly invoked their "rights under . . . contract" in challenging the control of ex-masters (Loyd 1865/1990, 614–15). Notably, however much freedwomen joined with freedmen in affirming the collective dimensions of emancipation, they simultaneously asserted individual rights of property and person and protested the inequalities of marriage. At least some black women, both those born as slaves and those born free, explicitly strove to be self-owning. That was also the vision of generations of white feminists who proclaimed equal rights of contract as a central goal. And however much some critics condemned the entire wage system, many more, through methods ranging from unions and labor legislation to partnerships, cooperatives, and Christian brotherhood, sought to bring greater equality to the wage contract.

Precisely because contract held such emancipatory meaning, its ideals also could mask existing inequalities.

That ideological paradox endures along with more palpable contract practices. Today, however, public debate dwells less on the legitimacy of contract than it did a century ago, when the age of contract waned with the advent of the welfare state and the new creeds of liberalism advanced by reformers in the Progressive Era. Then, intellectuals and reformers disputed whether industrial capitalism subverted or sustained individual liberty of contract; indeed, many concluded that contract freedom had become illusory. And that conclusion still finds credence among some scholars today, who agree with the famous interpretation put forth by law professor Grant Gilmore in *The Death of Contract* (1974, 95–96): "The decline and fall of the general theory of contract and, in most quarters, of laissez-faire economics, may be taken as remote reflections of the transition from nineteenth-century individualism to the welfare state and beyond." But, again, the association of contract simply with the ideal world of Adam Smith is too narrow. "Contract" remains a keyword of both U.S. culture and the study of that culture, signifying not only free-market capitalism, consensual government, and the rule of law but also the sovereignty of self that underlies the right of free individuals to choose what to do with their bodies and property. It is not hard to imagine emissaries of the global dispersion of U.S. culture distributing primers just like those put in the hands of freed people after the Civil War.

13

Copyright

Kembrew McLeod

Embedded within the word "copyright" is a simple and succinct self-definition. It means, quite literally, the right to copy. Unlike "intellectual property," a term that did not come into common usage until the mid-twentieth century, "copyright" has been used for centuries, dating from 1735. The term accurately describes what this legal doctrine is and how it functions. Often understood as a synonym for "copyright," "intellectual property" is actually a deceptive neologism. That is because copyrighted, patented, and trademarked works are not in fact *property*—they are instead protected by government-granted rights that are limited in how they can be enforced. The term "intellectual property" functions ideologically because it naturalizes an association with physical property that does not exist in law. This encourages many false analogies, such as the common claim that the unauthorized download of a song or a film is like breaking into someone's car and driving it away. The comparison is misleading because stolen physical property is no longer accessible to the owner, something that is not true when a copyrighted work is appropriated. Put in economic terms, physical property is a rivalrous good, and copyrighted works are nonrivalrous because their use by one consumer does not preclude their simultaneous consumption by another (Boyle 2010; Lessig 2002).

Copyright applies to all types of original expression, including art, choreography, literature, music, songs, maps, software, film, and graphic design. A work only needs to rise to the most minimal level of originality to be copyrightable, though it is important to note that one cannot copyright an idea—only the *expression* of an idea. This distinction is known among legal theorists as the "idea-expression dichotomy." It may seem obvious that a copyrighted work cannot be produced without an author—whether corporate or human—but upon closer inspection, "the author" reveals itself to be an unstable and slippery category. During the first half of the eighteenth century, before copyright law as we know it existed, two competing conceptions of authorship prevailed. On the one hand, the author was thought to be much like a "craftsman" who created poems by mining linguistic raw materials and following literary conventions, not unlike a carpenter. On the other hand, the author was viewed as one who transcends workmanlike procedures and channels something higher, such as a muse or God. These two understandings of authorship shared the assumption that authors had no right to own their creations. After all, how could one claim exclusive ownership over a product constructed with commonly shared words or, for that matter, something that originated from a divine source (Vaidhyanathan 2001; Woodmansee and Jaszi 1994)?

Over the course of the eighteenth century, a more individualist notion of authorship emerged as the result of several important economic and cultural changes. The patronage system that had supported artistic production was breaking down during the transition from feudalism to early capitalism, and there was nothing that prevented one's creative labor from being appropriated in a literary marketplace where reproduction had been mechanized. Authors were struggling to make a living from the written word. Without any consensus about what authorship was, literary works could not be legitimated as property in commonsense notions of ownership. Responding to this vacuum, many writers and thinkers very consciously attempted to redefine texts as commodities. The resulting legal battles that codified copyright as a legal doctrine were informed by emerging Enlightenment notions of what constitutes originality, authorship, and ownership. In eighteenth-century England and nineteenth-century Germany, authorship increasingly became associated with economic discourses about property and Romantic notions about "original genius." Within this context, it became possible for authors (or, more commonly, publishers) to secure the exclusive "right to copy." Put simply, copyright law emerged out of contradictions produced by the rise of capitalism, the invention of the printing press, and the commodification of culture (M. Rose 1995; Woodmansee and Jaszi 1994).

In 1710, Britain passed the Statute of Anne, which is widely recognized as a predecessor to modern copyright. Then, in 1790, the U.S. Congress enacted the world's first copyright law. The U.S. Constitution states that copyright is intended to "promote the progress of science and useful arts, by securing for limited times to authors and inventors the exclusive right to their respective writings and discoveries" (art. I, § 8, cl. 8). As many legal scholars have noted, the primary constitutional objective of copyright is to promote the creation and dissemination of knowledge, inventions, and creative expression. Because the United States was a very young country, it had no established culture or literary tradition to call its own. As a project of nation formation, the Constitution treated copyright law as a tool that could solve this problem. It was conceived as a kind of bribe that gave authors a limited right to commercially exploit their work—after a maximum term of twenty-eight years, previously copyrighted works entered the public domain so anyone could make use of them. This is one example of how the U.S. Constitution treated the author as the secondary

beneficiary of copyright law; the public interest always came first (Boyle 2010; Coombe 1998; Wirtén 2008).

The framers of the Constitution articulated a theory of copyright that rewarded creativity, but they did not want to give creators complete control over their work in ways that would inhibit the "progress of science and useful arts." As a result, the concept of fair use developed into a robust legal doctrine that was eventually codified into U.S. federal law in 1976. The fair use statute allows people to quote from or repurpose elements of copyrighted works without asking permission, as long as it is for educational, critical, journalistic, or other transformative purposes. Like the word "copyright," fair use is intuitively named: it applies to any usage that a reasonable jurist would consider *fair*. One of the most influential U.S. Supreme Court cases involving fair use was the *Sony Corp. of America v. Universal City Studios, Inc.* (464 U.S. 417, *reh'g denied*, 465 U.S. 1112 (1984))—better known as the 1984 Betamax case—which legalized the videocassette recorder. In this 5–4 decision, Supreme Court Justice John Paul Stevens makes clear copyright law's constitutional mandate. Its purpose, Justice Stevens argued in the majority opinion, is *not* to provide a special private benefit to an individual or corporation: "The limited grant is a means by which an important public purpose may be achieved. It is intended to motivate the creative activity of authors and inventors by the provision of a special reward, and to allow the public access to the products of their genius after the limited period of exclusive control has expired. The copyright law, like the patent statutes, makes reward to the owner a secondary consideration" (*Sony*, 464 U.S. at 429). This assertion is grounded in the "limited" rights language found in the U.S. Constitution, as well as subsequent case law that developed over the course of two centuries (Aufderheidi and Jaszi 2011; Hilderbrand 2009; Litman 2001; McLeod 2007).

Today, fair use functions as a free-speech safety valve within copyright law, one that has become even more important since the U.S. Congress extended the term of copyright in 1998. The Sonny Bono Copyright Term Extension Act lengthened these protections by twenty years: copyright protection now lasts ninety-five years for corporate authors; for individuals, it lasts their entire lifetime, plus seventy years. In contrast, between 1790 and 1978, the average work passed into the public domain after just thirty-two years. This precedent honored the constitutional mandate that stipulated copyright protections should last for "limited times." Some people sarcastically refer to the Bono Act as the Mickey Mouse Protection Act, and with good reason. Without it, *Steamboat Willie*—the first appearance of the transmedia rodent—would have fallen into the public domain in 2003, and several other valuable classics would have followed. The constitutionality of this extension was challenged, but in 2003, the Supreme Court upheld the right of Congress to determine how long was meant by "limited." As a result of this law, nothing would enter the public domain for another twenty years, not until 2019. This means that the right to copy and transform many decades-old works remained in the hands of individual and corporate copyright owners, who had veto power. This environment makes it difficult, legally, to reshape and react to the popular culture that surrounds us because so much of it is locked up, out of reach (Aufderheidi and Jaszi 2011; Boyle 2010; Coombe 1998; Lessig 2002).

Beyond the controversies that greeted the advent of the photocopier, the videocassette recorder, and other disruptive duplication technologies, we can trace the origins of the contemporary copyright wars to the practice of digital sampling that emerged in the mid-1980s. "Sampling" refers to the act of digitally rerecording pieces of preexisting music and placing those bits in a new song. Artists have always borrowed from each other, but hip-hop musicians took these appropriation practices to their furthest logical conclusions. Sampling can be viewed as an extension of earlier African American musical traditions such as the blues, jazz, and gospel. During the 1970s, hip-hop DJs in the South Bronx reimagined the turntable as a device that could *create* music, rather than just *replay* songs. In the 1980s, hip-hop artists reinvented newly emerging digital sampling technologies by making them do things their inventors never imagined. As with the sharing of MP3 music files today, many artists and record companies believed that digital sampling was the equivalent of stealing. By 1991, the music industry began rigorously enforcing copyright law, and the industry developed a cumbersome and expensive "sample clearance" system. All samples, even the shortest and most unrecognizable, now had to be approved and paid for. Since this period, the cost of licensing samples has continued to increase, as have the costs associated with negotiating those licenses. This made it impossible for certain kinds of music to be legally made, especially those collage-heavy records that typified hip-hop's "golden age"—a period that lasted roughly from the mid-1980s to the early 1990s (Demers 2006; McLeod 2007; McLeod and DiCola 2011).

Many artists and critics have argued that the contemporary sample licensing system had a negative impact on the creative potential of hip-hop before it had a chance to flower. These critics argue that the growth of twentieth-century jazz would have been similarly stunted if jazz musicians—who regularly "riffed" on others' songs—had been burdened by the requirement of getting permission from music publishers for even the smallest melodic quotations. It is important to note that the licensing log jam produced by the modern-day "clearance culture" has implications that stretch far beyond the concerns of the hip-hop world. Music, including sample-based music, is regularly integrated into television shows, movies, videogames, and user-generated online content. When one is dealing with songs that sample songs that contain other samples, the stack of licenses one must acquire can grow quite tall. The same is increasingly true of remixed video content. As a cultural practice and a legal lightning rod, sampling has implications that stretch far beyond the domain of musical remixing. The crisis it provoked within copyright regimes was the canary in the intellectual property coal mine. Sampling kick-started a conversation about copyright years before the latter became front-page news after the file-sharing service Napster debuted in 1999. Hip-hop artists in the mid-1980s raised many of the same ethical and economic questions that people are still wrestling with now but on a broader scale. Today, new technologies give most people the *ability* to copy, whether or not they legally have the *right* to copy. Given the complexity of this situation, it is unlikely that these contradictions will be resolved anytime soon (Boon 2010; McLeod and DiCola 2011).

14

Corporation

Christopher Newfield

In current usage, the keyword "corporation" is synonymous with "business corporation," generally referring to a for-profit organization that can operate at the discretion of its owners and managers free of social and legislative control. The term is derived from the Latin *corporatus*, the present participle of *corporare*, which means "form into a body," and appeared in English by 1530. A business corporation can own property; buy, sell, and control assets, including other corporations; pay or avoid taxes; write or break contracts; make and market products; and engage in every kind of economic activity. At the same time, the persons involved in a corporation have under most circumstances no liability for its debts. Since 1900, the corporation has been the dominant form for organizing capital, production, and financial transactions. By 2000, the corporation had become a dominant force in the global economy, the only alternative to the state as an organizer of large-scale production, a rival to national governments, and a powerful presence in the world's cultures. Of the world's hundred largest economies in 2000, forty-seven were nation-states and fifty-three were corporations.

American studies and cultural studies generally have focused not on the corporation or the corporate form but rather on features of culture and society that the corporation has affected (Trachtenberg 1982; Horwitz 1987; Michaels 1987). This research has produced major reconsiderations of civil rights, community formation, consumerism, culture industries, discrimination, environmental justice, imperialism and colonialism, labor, political agency, and underdevelopment, domains where business has played a major and sometimes controlling role. But the corporate world as such has only rarely been an object of study in itself. The prominent critic Fredric Jameson (1993, 50) noted the reluctance of cultural studies to "look out upon the true Other, the bureaucrat or corporate figure." The situation has changed little since that time; for instance, the word "corporation" does not make a single appearance in a comprehensive bibliographical essay on the 2005 American Studies Association website (Reed 1999).

Before the mid-nineteenth century, the corporation was a public franchise—a ferry or turnpike company, for example—that received a profit in exchange for reliable service to the common or public good. After the Civil War, corporations increasingly came to reflect private economic interests. Though the Supreme Court, in the early case *Trustees of Dartmouth College v. Woodward* (17 U.S. 518 (1819)), had held that a public charter possessed the legal status of a private contract, most of the legal foundations for this change were laid in the 1870s and 1880s. In the *Slaughter-House Cases* (83 U.S. 36 (1873)), the Supreme Court denied that labor had a property interest in a job that required compensation upon dismissal, which left the firm itself as the sole legitimate property interest. In *Santa Clara County v. Southern Pacific Railroad Company* (118 U.S. 394 (1886)), the Court asserted, without supporting argumentation, that the corporation was a legal person and could not have its property regulated in a way not in conformity with the due process provisions of the Fourteenth Amendment. Through a series of small but unswerving steps, the courts freed the corporation from both public purpose and direct legislative will.

This movement toward corporate independence consolidated several important features of the corporate form. One was limited liability, in which the shareholder was personally insulated from claims for damages or the repayment of debts. Limited liability made it easier to attract a large amount of capital from many investors while retaining concentrated control, since the investor was less likely to insist on control in the absence of liability. Through two further changes, corporations gained the right to own stock in other companies, a right that had been denied to ordinary proprietorships, and stabilized the managerial authority of boards of directors (Roy 1997). A firm could grow through cross-ownership or, even without ownership, could control other firms through interlocking board memberships. This legal framework gave the firm's executives significant independence from the firm's owners, a framework that was influentially defined as the separation of ownership and control (Berle and Means 1932). This phenomenon allowed the corporation even greater distance from the surrounding society, for it was relatively sheltered not only from immediate legislative influence and community pressure but also from the collective will of its own investors. The simultaneous development of concentration of control and immunity from interference transformed the corporation from a public trust into a potential monopoly power with most of the capacities of a parallel government.

Twentieth-century corporate law took the existence of the corporation for granted and sought not to regulate the form so much as to regulate particular industry sectors and management practices. The landmark Sherman Anti-Trust Act (1890) was so vague that its powers were in effect created through enforcement or through later legislation such as the Hepburn Act (1906) and the Mann-Elkins Act (1910), which focused on the power to regulate monopoly pricing or constrain concentrated ownership, and the act was extended through later New Deal legislation such as the Glass-Steagall Act (1933) and, still later, the

CORPORATION CHRISTOPHER NEWFIELD

Bank Holding Company Act (1956). The courts generally rejected the idea that big is bad; rather, plaintiffs had to show that big had a materially bad effect. To the contrary, by the late twentieth century, enormous size was seen by regulators as a competitive necessity; in the 1980s, "ten thousand merger notifications were filed with the antitrust division. . . . The antitrust division challenged exactly twenty-eight" (L. Friedman 2002, 392). One legal historian summarized the situation by saying that "corporation law had evolved into a flexible, open system of nonrules" that "allowed corporations to do whatever they wished" (ibid., 389).

Support for the corporation came more frequently from courts and legislators than from public opinion. The labor movement consistently challenged three of the corporation's most important impacts on working conditions: the accelerated absorption of skilled, relatively independent workers into the factory system; Taylorization, in which mass production was transformed into a routinized assembly-line process strictly regulated for maximum time efficiency; and managerialism, whose meaning for labor was unilateral control of pay and working conditions by layers of management separated from and generally set against labor. More than a century of major strikes—such as those at Carnegie's steel works at Homestead, Pennsylvania (1892), the Loray Mill in Gastonia, North Carolina (1929), and the Flint Sit-down Strike (1936), down through the United Parcel Service strike (1997), the Los Angeles janitors strike (2000), and the Chicago teachers strike (2012)—were among the most visible expressions of popular opposition to the corporation's independence of, or sovereignty over, the wider society in which it operated.

Corporate power prompted a decades-long movement for "industrial democracy" that sought to put corporate governance on a constitutionalist and democratic footing. Some observers saw collective bargaining, finally legalized by the Wagner Act (1935), as an industrial civil rights movement that transformed management into a government of laws (Lichtenstein 2002, 32–38). But labor never did achieve meaningful joint sovereignty with management in the context of the large corporation. The Taft-Hartley Act (1947) required all trade-union officials to sign an affidavit that they were not Communists, impugning the collective loyalty of labor leaders (managers were not required to sign), and also forbade cross-firm and cross-industry labor coordination (ibid., 114–18). Union membership and influence declined precipitously from the 1970s onward, and the idea of industrial democracy had by the end of the century virtually disappeared from public view. Even as the corporation continued to rely on the state for favorable environmental legislation, tax law, educated workers, and the like, it consolidated its relative autonomy from employees and the public.

Over this period, the corporation became part of the culture of the United States and other countries, and the resulting corporate culture had four dominant features. First, consumption became central. When the corporation collectivized labor and coordinated the production process on a large scale, it enabled the mass production of consumer goods for the first time. This led to increases in the general standard of living and to the rise of a consumer society in which consumption came to be a virtually universal activity and a primary means of expressing personal identity and desire. Second, democracy was equated with capitalism. Mass production and consumption, freedom, self-expression, and personal satisfaction came to be seen as interchangeable and as enabled by corporate capitalism; consumption came to eclipse, if not exactly replace, political sovereignty. Conversely, democracy's best outcome seemed to be affluence rather than public control of the economy and other social forces. Third, efficient organization became synonymous with hierarchical bureaucracy. As the twentieth century wore on, it became increasingly difficult to imagine truth, power, or innovation arising from personal effort, insight, and inspiration unharnessed by economic roles, or effective cooperation without command from above. Fourth, philosophical, spiritual, cultural, and social definitions of progress were eclipsed by technological ones. The rapid commercialization of technical inventions—radio, radiology, transistors—became the measure of the health of a society, and thus society came to require healthy corporations. Building on a long tradition of corporations presenting themselves as public benefactors (Marchand 1998), by the 1980s and 1990s, they were regarded by most political leaders and opinion makers as the leading progressive force in society.

Across these changes, the economy began to appear as a natural system, accessible only to highly trained experts in production, management, and finance and resisting all attempts to soften its effects through public services and social programs. In this new common sense, society had to adapt to the economy, and the corporation was the privileged agent of that adaptation. By 2000, the majority of U.S. leaders appeared to accept the priority of economic laws to social needs, and the corporate system as the authentic voice of those laws. Concurrently, U.S. society lost its feel for the traditional labor theory of value. Real value now seemed to be created by a combination of technological invention and corporate activity. At the end of the twentieth century, cheap manual labor and advanced mental labor had become more important than ever to steadily increasing corporate revenues, and yet the individual's labor contribution was less valued and more difficult to picture.

The tremendous cultural power of the corporate form has not spared it turbulence and even decline. Annual economic growth in the United States and Europe slowed markedly in the 1970s, as did rates of increase in profitability and productivity. Business efforts to maintain profit margins led to continuous price increases that in turn increased wage demands and overall inflation. The United States lost its unchallenged economic preeminence as countries such as France, Germany, Italy, and Japan fully recovered from the devastation of World War II and as the newly industrializing countries of Asia became important competitors. Oil-price shocks and the end of the Bretton Woods currency system were only the most visible sign of this changing economic order (Rosenberg 2003). Internal pressures added to external ones. Job satisfaction was low enough to prompt an important study from the Nixon administration's Department of Labor, and "human relations" management theory increased its attacks on Taylorist regimentation (Newfield 1998). These trends contributed to a sense among some observers that the large corporation was part of the problem, that it had become too inflexible, hierarchical, and expensive to lead the way in a new era of "post-Fordist" globalization (Harvey 1989).

In response to these threats, corporations began a rehabilitation campaign, recasting themselves as the world's only true modernizers, capable of moving the economy and society relentlessly forward, often against their will (T. Friedman 2000, 2005). Though presented as news, nearly all of these claims were tried-and-true standards of the economic liberalism of previous periods: that the markets are inherently efficient and self-regulating in the absence of government interference; that attempts to stabilize employment and incomes place unnatural burdens on these efficient markets, as do consumer protections, banking restrictions, environmental legislation, regional planning, and the like; that the tireless search for ever-cheaper labor, now fully internationalized, is legitimate because it benefits consumers; that corporate giants can "learn to dance" by "reengineering" their companies to simplify their cumbersome bureaucratic layers and routines (Kanter 1990; Hammer and Champy 1993); and that corporations have rejected monopoly in favor of entrepreneurship. By the turn of the twenty-first century, no single corporation or corporate group could be called an empire, but as a group, corporations had unchallenged sovereignty over the economy.

Or almost unchallenged. Economic problems persisted: overall growth remained historically weak while economic inequality mounted steadily, work became less secure, and the public was treated to a long series of trials for corporate fraud. Opposition to corporate influence grew at the end of the twentieth century, though the strongest movements appeared outside the United States. Examples included Argentina, which had modified the regime imposed on it in the 1990s by the U.S.-dominated International Monetary Fund; India, where protests against development projects and intellectual property regimes sponsored by multinational corporations became routine; Malaysia, whose conservative regime rejected U.S. recipes for recovery from the economic crisis of 1997–98; Mexico, where nongovernmental organizations began to build social infrastructure; Venezuela, where strong popular support for social development proved capable of prevailing in elections; and Bolivia, where native peoples toppled two presidents in their attempt to nationalize natural gas reserves. In the United States, protests against the World Trade Organization and the "Washington Consensus" broke out in Seattle in 1999, though they did not become as widespread or sustained as they have been elsewhere.

In the first decades of the twenty-first century, the corporation has been at the center of several major developments. Following the September 11, 2001, attacks on New York and Washington, D.C., some corporations became directly involved in military operations as private contractors (Singer 2003; Dickinson 2011). In various sectors, the privatization of public functions and their revenue streams became an important business strategy. Information and communications technology reached in new ways into private life, ranging from customized marketing and Internet-based data collection via Amazon, Facebook, Google, and similar firms (Andrews 2012) to the collection and delivery to the government of unprecedented and still-unknown quantities of personal data for security and surveillance purposes (Greenwald 2013). Legislation and legal decisions allowed corporations to exert new levels of political management. The most famous case, *Citizens United v. Federal Election Commission* (558 U.S. 310 (2010)), sanctioned new corporate bodies, often organized as nonprofits, to channel unlimited private funds into elections (Briffault 2012). One basis for the majority's opinion was the Court's recognition in *Santa Clara* and other cases that "First Amendment protection extends to corporations" (*Citizens*, 558 U.S. at 25). The Court affirmed the precedent that "the Government cannot restrict political speech based on the speaker's corporate identity" (*Citizens*, 558 U.S. at 30).

The decisive trend may turn out to be the diverging economic fates of corporations and the middle class, whose prosperity had been the core political justification for tax, trade, employment, and innovation policies that favored business interests. Economically, the 2000s was a "lost decade," and the mainstream media routinely disseminated evidence that whatever else corporations had been doing for the previous decades, they had not given the majority of the

U.S. workforce an inflation-adjusted raise (Mishel et al. 2012; Parlapiano 2011; Schwartz 2013). The sense of economic failure was confirmed by the financial crisis of 2007–8 and the diverging fates of Wall Street, which recovered, and Main Street, which did not. The growing sense that corporations produced inequality rather than prosperity triggered another form of resistance, the Occupy call in 2011 for a society run by and for the 99 percent. Evidence continues to grow that the hierarchical, multidivisional corporation of the twentieth century—with its enormous managerial and executive costs, its monopoly market goals, its mixtures of empowerment and authoritarianism, its definitions of value that exclude social benefits—is less functional and affordable than most leaders had assumed (D. Gordon 1996; Ross 1997; Bamberger and Davidson 1999). And yet any process of inventing postcorporate economic forms would require deeper public knowledge of corporate operations than prevails in the wealthy countries of the early twenty-first century, as well as clearer, more imaginative definitions of democratic economics.

15

Culture

George Yúdice

The concept of culture has had widespread use since the late eighteenth century, when it was synonymous with civilization and still indicated a sense of cultivation and growth derived from its Latin root, *colere*, which also included in its original meanings "inhabit" (as in "colonize"), "protect," and "honor with worship" (as in "cult"). According to Raymond Williams (1976/1983, 87–93), the noun form took, by extension, three inflections that encompass most of its modern uses: intellectual, spiritual, and aesthetic development; the way of life of a people, group, or humanity in general; and the works and practices of intellectual and artistic activity (music, literature, painting, theater, and film, among many others). Although Williams considers the last to be the most prevalent usage, the extension of anthropology to urban life and the rise of identity politics in the 1980s (two changes that have left a mark on both cultural studies and American studies) have given greater force to the communal definition, particularly since this notion of culture serves as a warrant for legitimizing identity-based group claims and for differentiating among groups, societies, and nations. More recently, the centrality of culture as the spawning ground of creativity, which in turn is the major resource in the so-called new economy, has opened up a relatively unprecedented understanding of culture in which all three usages are harnessed to utility.

The meaning of "culture" varies within and across disciplines, thus making it difficult to narrate a neat linear history. Nevertheless, one can discern a major dichotomy between a universalist notion of development and progress and a pluralistic or relativistic understanding of diverse and incommensurate cultures that resist change from outside and cannot be ranked according to one set of criteria. Beginning in the late eighteenth century, universalist formulations understood culture as a disinterested end in itself (Kant 1790/1952) and aesthetic judgment as the foundation for all freedom (Schiller 1794/1982). Anglo-American versions of this universalism later linked it to specific cultural canons: Matthew Arnold (1869/1994, 6) referred to culture as "the best which has been thought and said in the world" and posed it as an antidote to "anarchy"; T. S. Eliot (1949, 106) legitimated Europe's claim to be "the highest culture that the world has ever known." Such assertions, which justified U.S. and European imperialism, are newly disputed in postcolonial studies (Said 1993), but they were already rejected early on by defenders of cultural pluralism and relativism, such as Johann Gottfried von Herder (1766/2002), who argued that each particular culture has its own value that cannot be measured according to criteria derived from another culture. This critique of the culture-civilization equation had its ideological correlate, first formulated by Karl Marx and Frederick Engels (1845–46/1972), in the premise that culture is the superstructure that emanates from the social relations involved in economic production; hence, it is simply a translation of the ruling class's domination into the realm of ideas.

The view of culture—and the civilizing process—as a form of control is consistent with the turn in cultural studies and cultural policy toward a focus on the ways in which institutions discipline populations. In the post-Enlightenment, when sovereignty is posited in the people, the institutions of civil society deploy culture as a means of internalizing control, not in an obviously coercive manner but by constituting citizens as well-tempered, manageable subjects who collaborate in the collective exercise of power (T. Miller 1993; Bennett 1995). The universal address of cultural institutions, ranging from museums to literary canons, tends either to obliterate difference or to stereotype it through racist and imperialist appropriation and scientism, sexist exclusion and mystification, and class-based narratives of progress. Populations that "fail" to meet standards of taste or conduct, or that "reject culture" because it is defined against their own values, are subject to constitutive exclusion within these canons and institutions (Bourdieu 1987). Challenges to these exclusions generate a politics of representational proportionality such that culture becomes the space of incremental incorporation whereby diverse social groups struggle to establish their intellectual, cultural, and moral influence over each other. Rather than privilege the role of the economic in determining social relations, this process of hegemony, first described by Antonio Gramsci (1971, 247), pays attention to the "multiplicity of fronts" on which struggle must take place. The Gramscian turn in cultural studies (American and otherwise) is evident in Raymond Williams's (1977/1997, 108–9) incorporation of hegemony into his focus on the "whole way of life": "[Hegemony] is in the strongest sense a 'culture,' but a culture which has also to be seen as the lived dominance and subordination of particular classes."

But hegemony is not synonymous with domination. It also names the realm in which subcultures and subaltern groups wield their politics in the registers of style and culture (Hebdige 1979). Indeed, in societies such as the United States, where needs are often interpreted in relation to identity factors and cultural difference, culture becomes a significant ground for extending a right to groups that have otherwise been excluded on those terms. The very notion of cultural citizenship implies recognition of cultural difference as a basis for making claims. This view has even been incorporated in epistemology to capture the premise that groups with different cultural horizons have different and hence legitimate bases for construing knowledge; they develop different "standpoint epistemologies" (Haraway 1991; Delgado Bernal 1998). The problem is that bureaucracies often establish the terms by which cultural difference is recognized and rewarded. In response, some subcultures (and their spokespersons) reject bureaucratic forms of recognition and identification, not permitting their identities and practices to become functional in the process of "governmentality," the term Michel Foucault (1982, 221) uses to capture "the way in which the conduct of individuals or groups might be directed." On this view, strategies and policies for inclusion are an exercise of power through which, in the U.S. post-civil-rights era, institutional administrators recognize women, "people of color," and gays and lesbians as "others" according to a multiculturalist paradigm, a form of recognition that often empowers those administrators to act as "brokers" of otherness (Cruikshank 1994).

These contemporary struggles over cultural citizenship and recognition can be traced to earlier battles over the attributes according to which anthropologists and sociologists in the 1950s and '60s catalogued certain non-European and minority populations as "cultures of poverty." This diagnostic label, first formulated by Oscar Lewis in 1959, references the presumed characterological traits—passivity, apathy, and impulsivity—that in underdeveloped societies impede social and economic mobility. We see at work here the narrative of progress and civilization that had been the frame within which anthropology emerged more than a hundred years earlier. Most anthropologists' method had been comparative in a nonrelativistic sense, as they assumed that all societies passed through a single evolutionary process from the most primitive to the most advanced. Culture, which has been variously defined as the structured set or pattern of behaviors, beliefs, traditions, symbols, and practices (Tylor 1871; Boas 1911; Benedict 1934; Mead 1937; Kroeber and Kluckhohn 1952) by means of which humans "communicate, perpetuate and develop their knowledge about and attitudes toward life" (Geertz 1966/1983, 89), was the ground on which anthropologists, even into the 1920s, sought to track the origins of all societies as well as their progress toward (European and/or Anglo-American) modernity.

In partial contrast, the relativist or pluralist cultural anthropology that arose in the 1920s and is often associated with Franz Boas (1928) began to critique the scientific racism that underwrote many of these accounts, to question the premise that any such accounting could be objective, and to argue that there were neither superior nor inferior cultures. Nevertheless, Boas and his U.S. and Latin American followers (Kroeber 1917; Freyre 1933/1956; Benedict 1934; Mead 1937; F. Ortiz 1946) believed that culture could be studied objectively, as a science, so long as description and analysis were not hamstrung by the anthropologist's cultural horizon. Many of the U.S. studies were explicitly designed, in Margaret Mead's words, to "giv[e] Americans a sense of their particular strengths as a people and of the part they may play in the world" (1942/1965, xlii).

By the end of the 1950s (coincident with the rise of cultural studies in Britain and American studies in the United States), the Boasian legacy as well as other salient anthropological tendencies such as British structural-functionalism and U.S. evolutionism waned and other trends rose in influence: symbolic anthropology (culture as social communication and action by means of symbols; Geertz 1966/1983), cultural ecology (culture as a means of adaptation to environment and maintenance of social systems; M. Harris 1977), and structuralism (culture as a universal grammar arranged in binary oppositions that rendered intelligible the form of a society; Lévi-Strauss 1963). These largely systemic analyses then gave way in the 1980s to a focus on practice, action, and agency as the main categories of anthropological explanation and also to a self-reflexivity that put the very enterprise of cultural analysis in question. Self-reflexive or postmodern anthropology criticized the writing practices of ethnographers for obscuring the power relations that subtend the ethnographic encounter, the status of the knowledge that is derived from that encounter, the relationship of ethnography to other genres (Marcus and Fischer 1986; Clifford and Marcus 1986), and even the analytical and political usefulness of the concept of culture itself (Abu-Lughod 1991; Gupta and Ferguson 1992; R. Fox 1995). Related developments in postcolonial studies focused on transnational hybridity in contradistinction to national cultural homogeneity. With the introduction of television and other electronic media, mass migrations from former colonies to metropolitan centers, and modern transportation and communications technologies, cultures could no longer be imagined as circumscribed by national boundaries. Metaphors such as montage and pastiche replaced the melting pot in accounts of Brazilian culture (Schwarz 1970/1992; Santiago 1971/1973), echoing "Néstor García Canclini's description of popular culture as the product of 'complex hybrid processes using as signs of identification elements originating from diverse classes and nations'" (Dunn 2001, 97, quoting García Canclini 1995; see also Appadurai 1996). More recently, García Canclini (2004) has added *access* to new information and communication technologies as another dimension to consider when weighing the effects that globalization has on culture-based understandings of difference and equality.

For many U.S. scholars, this troubling of culture as a category of analysis opened up a critique of the ways in which culture expanded in the late twentieth century to serve as an almost knee-jerk descriptor of nearly any identity group. While this expansion responds to the political desire to incorporate "cultures of difference" within (or against) the mainstream, it often ends up weakening culture's critical value. Especially frustrating for critics working in these fields is the co-optation of local culture and difference by a relativism that becomes indifferent to difference and by a cultural capitalism that feeds off and makes a profit from difference (Eagleton 2000). If a key premise of modernity is that tradition is eroded by the constant changes introduced by industrialization, new divisions of labor, and concomitant effects such as migration and consumer capitalism, then recent theories of disorganized capitalism entertain the possibility that the "system" itself gains by the erosion of such traditions, for it can capitalize on it through commodity consumption, cultural tourism, and increasing attention to heritage. In this case, both the changes and the attempts to recuperate tradition feed the political-economic and cultural system; nonnormative behavior, rather than threatening the system in a counter- or subcultural mode, actually enhances it. Such a flexible system can make action and agency oriented toward political opposition seem beside the point.

These critical responses to corporate and bureaucratic modes of multicultural recognition are useful, but they often lack a grounded account of how the expedient use of culture as resource emerged. Today, culture is increasingly wielded as a resource for enhancing participation in this era of waning political involvement, conflicts over citizenship (I. Young 2000), and the rise of what Jeremy Rifkin (2000, 251) has called "cultural capitalism." The immaterialization that is characteristic of many new sources of economic growth (intellectual property rights as defined by the General Agreement on Tariffs and Trade and the World Trade Organization) and the increasing share of world trade captured by symbolic goods (movies, television programs, music, tourism) have given the cultural sphere greater importance than at any other moment in the history of modernity. Culture may have simply become a pretext for sociopolitical amelioration and economic growth. But even if that were the case, the proliferation of such arguments, in forums provided by local culture-and-development projects as well as by the United Nations Educational Scientific and Cultural Organization (UNESCO), the World Bank, and the so-called globalized civil society of international foundations and nongovernmental organizations (NGOs), has produced a transformation in what we understand by the notion of culture and what we do in its name (Yúdice 2003). Applying the logic that a creative environment begets innovation, urban culture has been touted as the foundation for the so-called new economy based on "content provision," which is supposed to be the engine of accumulation (Castells 2000). This premise is quite widespread, with the U.S. and British hype about the "creative economy" echoing in similar initiatives throughout the world (Caves 2000; Landry 2000; Venturelli 2001; Florida 2002).

As should be clear, current understandings and practices of culture are complex, located at the intersection of economic and social justice agendas. Considered as a keyword, "culture" is undergoing a transformation that "already is challenging many of our most basic assumptions about what constitutes human society" (Rifkin 2000, 10–11). In the first half of the twentieth century, Theodor Adorno (1970/1984, 25) could define art as the process through which the individual gains freedom by externalizing himself, in contrast to the philistine, "who craves art for what he can get out of it." Today, it is nearly impossible to find public statements that do not recruit art and culture either to better social conditions through the creation of multicultural tolerance and civic participation or to spur economic growth through urban cultural development projects and the concomitant proliferation of museums for cultural tourism, epitomized by the increasing number of Guggenheim franchises. At the same time, this blurring of distinctions between cultural, economic, and social programs has created a conservative backlash. Political scientists such as Samuel Huntington have argued (once again) that cultural factors account for the prosperity or backwardness, transparency or corruption, entrepreneurship or bureaucratic inertia of "world cultures" such as Asia, Latin America, and Africa (Huntington 1996; Harrison and Huntington 2000), while the Rand Corporation's policy paper *Gifts of the Muse: Reframing the Debate about the Benefits of the Arts* has resurrected the understanding of culture as referring to the "intrinsic benefits" of pleasure and captivation, which are "central in . . . generating all benefits deriving from the arts" (McCarthy et al. 2005, 12). The challenge today for both cultural studies and American studies is to think through this double bind. Beyond either the economic and social expediency of culture or its depoliticized "intrinsic" benefits lies its critical potential. This potential is not realizable on its own but must be fought for in and across educational and cultural institutions.

16

Democracy

Fred Moten

Democracy is the name that has been assigned to a dream as well as to certain already existing realities that are lived, by many people, as a nightmare. The dream is of government by the people, government in which the common people hold sway, in which the dispensation of the commons—"the universality of individual needs, capacities, pleasures, productive forces, etc., created through universal exchange" that Karl Marx called wealth—is collectively determined, in which the trace of any enclosure of the commons whatever is an object of the severest vigilance since such dispensation will have been understood as ending not in tragedy but in romance (Marx 1858/1993, 488; Hardin 1968). This is the fantasy of democracy as fantasy, as the contrapuntal arrangement of the many voices of the whole. The materialization of this dream will have been real democracy.

Authority in democracy can be exercised directly, in the immediate participation of each member of a given polity, or it can be ceded to representatives of the people, mediated not only by an individual person but also by whatever persons, codes, forms, and structures constitute the mode in which a representative is chosen. Every element that intervenes between the commons and authority carries with it a danger for the democracy to come; every idea and procedure that limits or circumscribes common participation is, similarly, a danger. And of the myriad ways in which the democratic dream is deferred and direct participation eclipsed, the most important are those in which the consent of the governed is manufactured by governors

and boards of governors in the name of saving already existing democracy. When considering "democracy" as a keyword in culture and cultural studies in the United States, one must come to grips with the severity of the difference between what exists and what is yet to come under the name of democracy while inhabiting a state that constantly announces itself to be democracy's very incarnation.

It is partly by way of the shrill ubiquity of such celebratory announcements that we become aware that democracy in the United States has always been in crisis. This fact is indexed by constant contradictory assertions that the United States is democracy's unique and solitary home and that the nation has the right and duty violently to export what it calls democracy. What it has meant to be a part of the intellectual cohort of the U.S. ruling class, at least in part, is to have participated in the ongoing identification and amelioration of that crisis. The constant crisis of democracy in the United States— something recognized with clarity in the normative national intellectual formation from James Madison to Samuel Huntington, something whose proper management is celebrated every four years, with every presidential inauguration, in what is often reverently and uncritically described as a ritual of continuity, a series of spectacles in which the abortive nature of repetitive beginning is everywhere present, though almost nowhere remarked, *as exclusion*—is precisely that democracy constantly threatens to overflow its limits, to emerge from the shadows in the outlaw form of an excluded, denigrated middle. It is not that which is given but that which invades, as it were, from an alienated inside, from the interior that it has been the business of already existing democracy, throughout the long history of its devolution, to expunge and criminalize (whether in the form of a duplicitous speaking for that middle by the ones who call themselves conservatives or in the forms of abandonment and dismissal, of condescension and mischaracterization, of that middle by the ones who call themselves progressives). Thus, U.S. democracy is, on the one hand, what exists now as crisis management and, on the other hand, the set of acts, dispositions, improvisations, collectivities, and gestures that constitute and will have constituted the crisis.

Noam Chomsky, who has had much to say about what Huntington calls "the crisis of democracy," is fond of invoking John Dewey as a kind of conceptual antidote to Huntington (Crozier, Huntington, and Watanuki 1975). Early in the last century, Dewey already recognized that "politics is the shadow cast by big business over society" (Chomsky 2005). We could expand on this now by saying that U.S. democratic politics is a mode of crisis management whose most conspicuous and extravagant rituals—elections and the inaugural celebrations and protests that each in its way confirms them—operate at the level of the demonstration. Elections in the United States are meant, finally and above all, to demonstrate that an election took place—a central consideration for structures of authority that depend on the eclipse of democratic content by the ritual reanimation of supposedly democratic forms. We might examine, along with Chomsky and Edward Herman, the history of the U.S.-mandated demonstration election that is a central element of U.S. foreign policy in the American Century, while emphasizing the fact that such demonstrations were first enacted domestically (Chomsky and Herman 1979). We operate within a long history of the self-nomination of the elect and their restriction of elections and, more importantly because more generally, a long history of antinomian political voicing that, as poet and critic Susan Howe (1993) points out, goes at least as far back as Anne Hutchinson. Straining against pseudodemocratic formality is a question whose utterance defines alternative membership. Where will democracy, which is to say the democracy that is coming, have been found? The answer remains on the outskirts of the U.S. American *polis*.

It remains possible and necessary, then, for anyone who aspires to do cultural studies in the United States to consider and to participate in what Chomsky (2005, 35) calls the "public attitudes that are kept in the shadows." When one dreams, along with C. L. R. James (1956), of the government of cooks, of government that cooks or swings in ways that belie facile identifications of the music that cooks and swings with what is called, or what already exists under the name of, American democracy, when one imagines the common and fantastic counterpoint and countertime that moves in perpetual disturbance of the American exception and the imperial acquisitiveness and domestic predation, the ongoing endangering of internal and external aliens, that exception is supposed to justify, then one could be said to move in as well as toward the outskirts and shadows—which are, in fact, the social essence—of the *polis*. Intimations of this city, which is not on a hill but underground, are given in those occult forms where participation and mediation, participation and representation, interact by way of linkage and articulation rather than eclipse: for instance, in the paramusical, intervallic space where Ray Charles's voicing and phrasing submits itself to the force of an exteriority that comes, paradoxically, from his own, alien interiority; or in speculative-fiction writer Samuel R. Delany's paraliterary excursions into the diffuse origins of the city and of writing, where he extends his continuing invocation of what one of Delany's critics, fellow novelist Joanna Russ, calls "the subjunctivity of science fiction" in order both to illuminate and to inhabit that excess of the mundane that characterizes (the politics of) everyday life in the shadows (Russ 1995; Laura Harris 2005).

Such illumination, such *theoria*, such fantasy, links Delany and Charles because in both it is enabled by their placement in the tradition of black radicalism, a tradition of alternative vision predicated on the enabling inability to see (which is to say the capacity and curse of seeing through) the glaring light of already existing democracy and its demonstrations. Something Al Sharpton once said of Charles—that his blindness is the condition of possibility of a rendition of "America the Beautiful" that is at every moment infused with phonographic insight and foresight— helps us to understand how Delany's documentary writing on Times Square is given only through the lens of submerged cities and fragmentary texts of lands that have never, or have not yet, been (Charles 1972; Delany 1994, 2001). Charles and Delany see shades of red and blue that are wholly outside the spectrum of intellectual and pseudointellectual democratic management. Moreover, Sharpton, against the grain of his own obscurantist tendencies, makes clear what must be understood, at least in part, as the Afro-diasporic constitution—and invasion (the incursion of what Cedric Robinson [1983/2000] conceptualizes as the eternal internal alien, the *metoikos*)—of a problematic Greek revival, the violently suppressed and nevertheless ongoing work that W. E. B. Du Bois (1935/1998) called the "black reconstruction of democracy in America."

Reading and rereading work such as that of Du Bois sharpens our awareness that the United States is the land of formal democratic enclosure and, moreover, the land in which critical analysis of such oxymoronic forms is relegated to the shadows. Such analysis occurs in nonstandard languages and styles; at the same time, whatever democratic energy that remains in the practically empty interior of our democratic forms makes itself manifest as dissatisfaction with those forms. Of course, the irregularity of common cries and common dreams is manifest as both mourning and optimism at the very outset and from the very outskirts of the *polis*. Recent analyses of the constitutive irruption of the outside (and the outsider) in Athenian democracy bear this out while providing transcendental clues regarding the constant irruptions into the democracy that now exists of the democracy that comes (Loraux 1998; Butler 2000). At the same time, democrats of the outside, the partyless democrats who like to party, who rock the party, recognize that the presence of that future prompts a constant and total mobilization against, moves as if in regulation of, such irruption (Hanchard 2006). Democracy is the rupture of any exclusion, however common that exclusion might appear to be, the recalibration of the *polis*, of the city, by and according to the most irregular measures. In the United States and in every place subject to U.S. authority, there are multitudes who work to discover it.

17

Diaspora

Brent Hayes Edwards

Until only a few decades ago, "diaspora" was a relatively esoteric word restricted in meaning to the historical dispersion of particular communities around the Mediterranean basin. Since then, it has become a privileged term of reference in scholarship, journalism, and popular discourse, used broadly and at times indiscriminately to denote a number of different kinds of movement and situations of mobility among human populations. *Diaspora* is a Greek word, a combination of the prefix *dia-* (meaning "through") and the verb *sperein* (meaning "to sow" or "to scatter"). It was used in the Septuagint, the translation of the Hebrew Torah prepared for the ruler of Alexandria in Egypt around 250 BCE by a specially appointed group of Jewish scholars. Subsequently, the word came to be employed as a self-designation among the Jewish populations that spread throughout the Mediterranean during the Hellenic period.

In recent deployments of the term, it is sometimes assumed that *diaspora* was used to translate a relatively wide number of Hebrew words in the Septuagint, including words relating both to scattering and to exile. However, as scholars of the Hellenic period have long pointed out, the Greek word never translates the important Hebrew words for exile (such as *galut* and *golah*) (Davies 1982). Instead, *diaspora* is limited to the translation of terms describing literal or figurative processes of scattering, separation, branching off, departure, banishment, and winnowing. Most of these terms, such as *tephutzot* (or "dispersal"), are derived from the Hebrew root *pvtz* ("scatter"). In the Septuagint,

many such terms are found in passages dealing with the divine expulsion of the Jewish people, particularly in the books of Leviticus and Deuteronomy, as in Leviticus 26:33, which reads, "And I will scatter you among the heathen, and will draw out a sword after you: and your land shall be desolate, and your cities waste."

In fact, there is a deeply significant distinction in the Jewish intellectual tradition between "diaspora" and "exile." Often "diaspora" is used to indicate a state of dispersal resulting from voluntary migration, as with the far-flung Jewish communities of the Hellenic period. In this context, the term is not necessarily laced with a sense of violence, suffering, and punishment, in part because Jewish populations maintained a rich sense of an original "homeland," physically symbolized by the Temple in Jerusalem. (Strikingly, Jewish settlements around the Mediterranean were commonly called *apoikiai*, or "colonies.") Very differently, the term "exile" (*galut*) connotes "anguish, forced homelessness, and the sense of things being not as they should be" (Wettstein 2002, 2) and is often considered to be the result of the loss of that "homeland" with the destruction of the Second Temple in 70 CE. As Haim Hillel Ben-Sasson (1971, 275) explains, "The residence of a great number of members of a nation, even the majority, outside their homeland is not definable as *galut* so long as the homeland remains in that nation's possession. . . . Only the loss of a political-ethnic center and the feeling of uprootedness turns Diaspora (Dispersion) into *galut* (Exile)."

This nuanced history is almost always overlooked in the current appropriations of the term "diaspora" that render it as a loose equivalent for a range of other words, conflating it with "exile," "migration," "immigration," "expatriation," "transnationalism," "minority or refugee status," and "racial or ethnic difference." Scholars have also debated the "primacy" of the Jewish model in any definition of "diaspora" (Tölölyan 1996; Boyarin and Boyarin 2002). Yet the genealogy of the term in the Jewish intellectual tradition itself might be taken as an indication that the Jewish diaspora should not be considered to be an "ideal type," as some scholars of comparative diasporas would have it (Safran 1991). "Diaspora" is first of all a translation, a foreign word adopted in the Jewish intellectual discourse of community. As such, it should serve as a reminder that there is never a "first," single dispersion of a single people but instead a complex historical overlay of a variety of kinds of population movement, narrated and imbued with value in different ways and to different ends. As the historian Erich Gruen (2002, 19) has explained with regard to Jewish populations in the Hellenic period, "a Greek diaspora, in short, brought the Jewish one in its wake." With regard to the study of the movement of peoples under globalization in the contemporary period, this history of usage should make us skeptical of an overarching concern with the movement of groups considered as discrete or self-contained and compel us to focus on the ways in which those movements always intersect, leading to exchange, assimilation, expropriation, coalition, or dissension. This is to say that any study of diaspora is also a study of "overlapping diasporas" (E. Lewis 1995, 786–87; Brent Edwards 2003b).

In the United States, the term "diaspora" has been invoked in interdisciplinary academic initiatives, first and foremost in attempts to institutionalize Africana and black studies programs, as well as in popular culture at least as early as the late 1960s. Yet it became especially prevalent in scholarly discourse as a result of the international influence in the late 1980s and early 1990s of a group of intellectuals associated with the Centre for Contemporary Cultural Studies at the University of Birmingham (Brent Edwards 2001). In the writings of Stuart Hall and Paul Gilroy, "diaspora" is invoked expressly in a critique of previous scholarship in cultural studies and labor history by Raymond Williams, Richard Hoggart, and E. P. Thompson, among others, which was limited above all by its implicit assumptions about the racial character of Englishness. It is reductive to discuss such forms of national belonging, Hall (1993) and Gilroy (1993) argued, without taking into account the ways in which English identity itself has been defined through the exclusion of a range of "others," particularly populations of the former British colonies who have been forcibly denied the rights and privileges of citizenship. This critique opened an entire arena of study, as the younger generation of Birmingham scholars began to consider culture "within the framework of a diaspora as an alternative to the different varieties of absolutism which would confine culture in 'racial,' ethnic or national essences" (Gilroy 1987, 155).

Despite the antiessentialism of the Birmingham model, diaspora has been theorized most often in relation to the scattering of populations from sub-Saharan Africa in particular, as a result of the slave trade and European colonialism. As some scholars have cautioned, given the historical peculiarities of the African diaspora, this model should not be taken as a template for any inquiry into the dynamics of diasporic forms of community (Tölölyan 1996; Brent Edwards 2001). Moreover, diaspora structured in terms of race may be qualitatively different from diaspora structured in terms of religion (as evident, for instance, in recent scholarship on the "Sikh diaspora"), nation (as in the "Indian diaspora," the "Cuban diaspora," or the "Palestinian diaspora"), ethnicity (as in the "Berber diaspora" or some definitions of the "Chinese diaspora"), region (as in the "Caribbean diaspora"), or sexuality (as in the "queer diaspora").

Especially in historical and sociological work on diaspora, much scholarship continues to take what Kim Butler (2001, 193) has termed the "checklist" approach, testing a given history of dispersal against a set of typological characteristics: to be "authentic," a diaspora must involve, for instance, the forced migration of a people to two or more locations; a collective memory or narrative of the homeland; the maintenance of autonomous group identity against the backdrop of the host environment; and, in some versions, a persistent network of ties to the homeland or ongoing agitation for its redemption. In contrast, "diaspora" tends to be used in American studies and cultural studies scholarship as a term that runs against the grain of any fixed notion of belonging; cultural identity is thereby understood as necessarily "unstable points of identification or suture," as Stuart Hall (1990, 226) puts it: "not an essence but a *positioning*." This emphasis on diaspora as a politics of process or practice, especially in anthropology and literary studies, has resulted in scholarship investigating the uneven and dialogic interplay of material, ideological, and discursive phenomena in transnational cultural circuits (Nandy 1990; Warren 1993; E. Gordon 1998; Matory 1999; Yelvington 2001). Some of this scholarship insists on language difference as a key structural feature of transnational culture and thus theorizes diaspora through the intricacies of translation (Rafael 1988; Gruesz 2002; Brent Edwards 2003a; Hofmeyr 2004).

Given that "diaspora offers an alternative 'ground' to that of the territorial state for the intricate and always contentious linkage between cultural identity and political organization," the term represents a challenge to any mode of knowledge production framed around the nation-state as an organizing principle (Boyarin and Boyarin 2002, 10). In this sense, the term reframes and transforms the discussion of a wide variety of issues in an area-based field such as American studies. Seen through the lens of diaspora, some of the traditional, even paradigmatic concerns of American studies, such as immigration and assimilation, are thrown into question or rendered peripheral (Mishra 1996). With regard to community affiliation and self-description in the contemporary conjuncture, it is crucial to consider the reasons that groups that not long ago might have called themselves "minorities" are increasingly calling themselves "diasporas" (Clifford 1997). An emphasis on diaspora also necessitates a new approach to the study of foreign policy, as evinced in the growing scholarship that has begun to consider the impact of "mobilized" diasporic pressure groups on U.S. foreign affairs (Mathias 1981; Edmondson 1986; Shain 1994–95; Von Eschen 2004). The term likewise opens up new avenues of inquiry into the history of U.S. imperialism, not just in relation to its attendant dispersal of military, labor, diplomatic, and administrative populations but also because of the ways in which transnational population movements in the Americas, especially those involving groups of people considered "others" in the U.S. nation-state, necessarily take shape in the shadow of U.S. globe-straddling ambitions.

18

Digital

Tara McPherson

In the twenty-first century, we tend to associate the word "digital" with computation, but its origins hark back to ancient times. The term derives from *digitus* in classical Latin, meaning "finger," and, later, from *digit*, which refers both to whole numbers less than ten and to fingers or toes. Digital procedures long predate the development of electronic computers, and we might understand a number of earlier devices or systems to operate by digital principles. For instance, the abacus is a simple digital calculator dating from 300 BC, while Morse code and Braille represent more recent digital practices. What each of these examples has in common—from fingers to digital computers—is a particular use of the digital to refer to discrete elements or to separate numbers. This focus on the discrete and the separate is central to the functioning of today's digital electronics, which, at a basic level, operate by distinguishing between two values, zero and one. While the digital predates computation, today the two terms are closely linked, and the adjective "digital" is typically a shorthand for the binary systems that underpin computation. Thus, we are living through a "digital revolution," are at risk of an increasing "digital divide," and are plugged into "digital devices" that play "digital audio" and store our "digital photographs." Some of us practice the "digital humanities." The slippage between the digital and computation seems so complete that it is easy to assume that the two terms are synonymous.

Computers have not always been digital. In the early decades of modern computation from the 1940s through the 1960s (and as we moved from mechanical to electrical machines), scientists were developing both analog and digital computers. Analog computers derived from earlier devices such as the slide rule. While the abacus used discrete beads to represent individual digits, the slide rule displayed a continuous scale. On an analog clock, time sweeps smoothly around a circular face; a digital clock represents time via discrete numbers, not as a continuous flow. Electronic analog computers functioned by analogy; that is to say, they built models of the problem to be solved and usually worked with continuous values rather than with the discrete binary states of digital computation. They converted the relationships between a problem's variables into analogous relationships between electrical qualities (such as current and voltage). They were often used (and still are) to simulate dynamic processes such as air flight and to model the physical world. Digital computers work differently. They process digital data as discrete units called bits, the zeroes and ones of binary code. A transistor in a digital computer has two states, on or off; a capacitor in an analog computer represents a continuous variable. The digital privileges the discrete and the modular; the analog represents continuity. As humans, we perceive the world analogically, as a series of continuous gradations of color, sound, and tastes.

Historians of computation typically narrate the transition from analog to digital computing as a story of efficiency and progress. Such evolutionary accounts suggest that digital machines win out because they are more precise, have greater storage capacities, and are better general-purpose machines. These teleological schemes can make it hard to understand the many cultural, economic, and historical forces that are in play during any period of technological change. Much recent scholarship has attended to the specificity of the digital, defining its key features and forms (Wardrip-Fruin and Montfort 2003). Lev Manovich observes in his important *The Language of New Media* (2001) that digital media can be described mathematically, are modular, and are programmable, that is, are subject to algorithmic manipulation. He proposes that media and cultural studies should turn to computer science to understand the digital. General histories of computers and much of new media theory tend toward evolutionary or formalist explanations for the emergence of the digital as the dominant computational paradigm, but we might also understand the shift as cultural and historical along a number of registers.

Instead of asking "what is the digital?" American studies and cultural studies might shift focus and ask, "how did the digital emerge as a dominant paradigm within contemporary culture?" Why, if we experience the world analogically, did we privilege machines that represent the world through very different methods? Scholars have begun to answer this question by highlighting the ways in which the move from analog to digital computing promoted notions of "universal" disembodied information while also concealing the computer's own operations from view (Fuller 2008; Galloway 2004; Hayles 2012; Lanier 2010). The ascendancy of digital computation exists in tight feedback loops with the rise of new forms of political organization post–World War II—including neoliberalism, a mode of economic organization that encourages strong private property rights, expansive free markets, and corporate deregulation—as well as with the rise of modern genetics (Chun 2011).

During this period, early developments in digital computing were also intertwined with shifting racial codes. The introduction of digital computer operating systems at midcentury installed an extreme logic of modularity and seriality that "black-boxed" knowledge in a manner quite similar to emerging logics of racial visibility and racism, the covert modes of racial formation described by sociologists Michael Omi and Howard Winant (1986/1994). An operating system such as UNIX (an OS crucial to the development of digital computers) works by removing context and decreasing complexity; it privileges the modular and the discrete. Early computers from 1940 to 1960 had complex, interdependent designs that were premodular. But the development of digital computers and software depended on the modularity of UNIX and languages such as C and C++. We can see at work here the basic contours of an approach to the world that separates object from subject, cause from effect, context from code. We move from measuring to counting and from infinite variation to discrete digit. We move from the slide rule, which allowed the user to see problem, process, and answer all at once, to the digital calculator, which separated input from output, problem from answer. There is something particular *to the very forms* of the digital that encourages just such a separation (McPherson 2012a).

We may live in a digital age, and the privileged among us might feel closely connected to our digital devices, but the sensations we feel as we touch our keyboards and screens are analog feelings, rich in continuous input and gradations of the sensory. We must remember that the digital is embedded in an analog world even as it increasingly shapes what is possible within that world. "Digital" emerges from and references particular histories, and these histories have consequences. By examining how these histories came to be, we will better understand and, perhaps, shape our present.

19

Disability

Kanta Kochhar-Lindgren

As a keyword in American studies and cultural studies, the site of a political movement, and the name of an interdisciplinary field, "disability" articulates vital connections across the many communities of people with disabilities, their public histories, and a range of cultural theories and practices. People with disabilities have too often been rendered invisible and powerless because of a mainstream tendency to valorize the normal body. As a result of disability activist work emerging from the civil rights movement, legal reforms, and grassroots activist work, the framing of disability has shifted from an emphasis on "disability" as a medical term to one of disability as a social construction. In the 1980s, disability activists began to move into the academy and to formulate a wide range of scholarship around the keyword. In the first phase, their work centered largely on the analysis and reform of public policy. By the early 1990s, a second phase in the humanities began to analyze the implications of representation on how people think about disability. In more recent years, disability scholarship has shifted to a focus on theories of intersectionality (the ways in which disability interacts with other modes of power and privilege) and transnationality (the ways in which nation-based frames of analysis misrecognize networks of affiliation that cross national borders).

Among the factors that contributed to the development of the term and its specific genealogies in relation to the rise of disability studies, the most prominent are the civil rights movement of the 1960s, disability activism in the 1960s and '70s, and the implementation of the Americans with Disabilities Act (ADA) in the 1990s. Spearheaded by Ed Roberts's advocacy for independent living, disability activism in the United States began in the 1960s at two university campuses, the University of Illinois and the University of California–Berkeley, where demands for alternatives to the previously dominant rehabilitation model led to the creation of the Center for Independent Living. This activism led to a number of important shifts in U.S. law, such as Section 504 of the Rehabilitation Act of 1973, intended to grant the right of equal access to federal programs to people with disabilities, and the Education of All Handicapped Children Act (renamed IDEA in 1990). The latter act led to the mainstreaming of children with disabilities by mandating equal access to public education and one free meal a day for all children with physical or mental disabilities. Equal access to public transportation also became more common as a result of grassroots activism and subsequent legal interventions. The 1990 ADA accords people with disabilities the right to protection against employment discrimination.

While these legal and policy reforms were promising, law and practice were and often are not in accord, as evinced by the fact that a large percentage of the cases brought before the Supreme Court under the ADA have not been decided in favor of the disabled person (R. O'Brien 2001). Partly as a result of this gap, recent work on disability has turned to questions of cultural representation and the impact of those representations on social practice. This shift in the ways in which scholars and activists approach the question of disability highlights how the disabled body—whether diseased, deaf, blind, physically handicapped, or cognitively different—marks the other of the able body, an unmarked norm that gained its force as an implicit corollary to Enlightenment notions of citizenship and work. From the 1860s to the 1970s, so-called ugly laws institutionalized this pattern of normalization in a number of U.S. cities by keeping individuals with "unsightly" or "disgusting" disabilities out of public spaces and off the streets (Schweik 2009). In Chicago, for example, the 1881 law read, "No person who is diseased, maimed, mutilated or in any way deformed so as to be an unsightly or disgusting object or improper person to be allowed in or on the public ways or other public places in this city, or shall therein or thereon expose himself to public view, under a penalty of not less than one dollar nor more than fifty dollars for each offense" (Chicago Municipal Code, § 36034). At the turn of the twentieth century, eugenics programs, fostered in part at the Carnegie Institution's Cold Spring Harbor complex in Long Island, New York, furthered this approach by implementing state-sanctioned sterilization as a means of limiting the proliferation of the disabled and other populations deemed undesirable (Carlson 2001; Black 2003). Recent disability scholarship has traced the transnational impact of these policies, including the implementation of killing centers in Nazi Germany (Snyder and Mitchell 2006). The common pattern of removing the disabled from everyday life reinforced and continues to reinforce the valorization of the able-bodied paradigm, the authority of the medical model of treatment to classify and to control the disabled, and the common understanding of the disabled body as a site of abjection, all based on an "out-of-sight, out-of-mind" logic.

These various attempts to codify, isolate, and fix the disabled were congruent with nationalism's tendency to classify and regulate diverse populations. The institutionalization of the deaf provides one example of this tendency. Beginning in the early nineteenth century in Europe and spreading quickly to the United States, the regulation of deaf people is illustrative of the drive to remove people with disabilities from the cultural mainstream, thus creating institutional sites where they could begin to form unique subcultures. The first school for the deaf, the American Asylum for the Education and Instruction of Deaf and Dumb Persons, was founded in 1817 by Thomas Hopkins Gallaudet in Hartford, Connecticut; by 1863, there were thirty-two such schools in the United States. This form of institutionalization led to the education of a large deaf community as well as the development of a community identity enabled by a shared language, American Sign Language (ASL). In response to these developments, proponents of nationalism in the period advocated for monolingual societies, resulting in the suppression of the use of sign language and the promotion of oralism. Educators influenced by social Darwinism argued that the use of sign language indicated intellectual inferiority and lack of social and cultural progress. Even in deaf schools, new technologies and elocution methods were developed to train the deaf to behave as if hearing. It was not until disability activism began to gain force in the 1960s that the Gallaudet University professor and linguist William Stokoe validated ASL as a full language in its own right through his extensive research into its linguistic structures (Stokoe, Casterline, and Croneberg, 1965). This research enabled deaf schools such as Gallaudet University to incorporate ASL in their instructional methods and the deaf community to be identified as a linguistic minority analogous to ethnic minorities. It led the deaf students at Gallaudet to protest successfully for the hiring of the first deaf university president in 1988 (Christiansen and Barnartt 2002; Burch 2004).

This history of a single disability demonstrates how social practices maintain and reinforce disability as a category of the marginalized other, what the consequences of that othering are, and how these techniques of othering are exacted on the body. These practices have serious implications not only for how we treat the disabled but also for how we understand the limits of the human body, since disability is the only minoritized identity group that can be joined by what activists call TABs, the "temporarily able-bodied." Scholars, along with activists and people with disabilities, have frequently remarked on the characteristic first response of the able-bodied to the disabled as being one of unease (L. Davis 1995). Subjected to strong cultural mores about the normal body as a site of orderliness, even progressive and radical able-bodied responses tend to repress anxiety about dealing with sensory, physical, or cognitive differences (E. Samuels 2002). Yet there is much to be gained from a critique of knowledge produced about and through theories of the body, difference, and disability. Donna Haraway's (1991) work on cyborgs, for instance, is helpful for its articulation of a disability identity and its theorization of the use of prosthetics as a mixture of human and machine. Similarly, Rosemarie Garland-Thomson has applied Eve Kosofsky Sedgwick's (1990) distinction between "minoritizing" and "universalizing" theories of sexual difference to disability. While the former links the politics of disability to a specific population, the latter opens onto a broader understanding of disability as "structuring a wide range of thought, language, and perception" (Garland-Thomson 1997, 22; see also Porter 1997).

As this brief survey indicates, disability studies, alongside related work in American studies and cultural studies, seeks to revise the place that disability holds in various cultural imaginaries, challenging the tendency to consider disability a personal problem, a source of pity or charity, or something that can be overcome with the help of medical intervention. The consolidation of a discrete interdisciplinary field of disability studies

emerged through the pioneering work of Paul Longmore (Longmore 2003; Longmore and Umansky 2001), Simi Linton (1998), Rosemarie Garland-Thomson (1997), David Mitchell and Sharon Snyder (2001), and Lennard Davis (1995). At the same time, a number of scholars are working at and across the edges of that field to create new connections regarding the significance of disability, including linkages to genetic engineering (Asch and Fine 1988; Asch and Parens 2000), immigration and labor studies (Longmore 2003; Baynton 1998), literary studies (Mitchell and Snyder 1997, 2001), everyday life (Garland-Thomson 1997; R. Adams 2001; Schweik 2009), performance studies (Kuppers 2003, 2011; V. Lewis 2005; Sandahl and Auslander 2005; Kochhar-Lindgren 2006; Henderson and Ostrander 2010), philosophy (Silvers 1998), medical humanities (S. Gilman 1995), deaf and race histories (Krentz 2007), deaf history (Brueggeman 2009), and queer and disability identity (McRuer 2006; McRuer and Mollow 2012). Across all of this work, the framing of disability as a cultural problematic rather than a fixed category extends important work already being done on the body, eugenics, biopolitics, immigration, nation building, and the practice of everyday life.

While this innovative scholarship has advanced a more nuanced understanding of the underlying assumptions that make disability the other of normalcy, one of the problems in using disability as an organizing trope is that it often artificially consolidates a wide array of physical and mental differences under a single term. Like other keywords that organize identity-based legal and cultural fields, the term helps to politicize our understanding of disability but also tends to create an abstract concept in which the particularities of divergent histories are erased. In order to recuperate a more embodied reference point for disability and to claim a more visible social space in the public sphere, a number of disability scholars have begun to address the importance of reclaiming individual bodily experience through art, performance, and literature (Corker 2001; Mitchell and Snyder 2001; Snyder and Mitchell 2001; Siebers 2004; Kochhar-Lindgren 2006). With regard to the fields of American studies and cultural studies, the ongoing challenge will be to identify disability as a discrete category, while also pluralizing our understanding of its manifestations. Considered as a keyword that indexes this challenge, "disability" has newly problematized and invigorated work on the body by naming an identity category that enables us to understand the lived experiences of bodies and their many sensorial differences.

20

Diversity

Jodi Melamed

What is the best way to manage unlike human capacities in the name of human progress and improvement? This deceptively simple question has preoccupied Western political modernity, especially in the United States. The positive connotations often adhering to the keyword "diversity"—a term commonly used to reference human differences broadly considered—arise from its importance in high-status discourses that have sought to discern the best management of human differences, including eighteenth-century liberal political philosophy, nineteenth- and twentieth-century natural science (especially the so-called race sciences), and twentieth- and twenty-first-century law and education policy. In contrast, research in American studies and cultural studies has come to look on the endeavor of managing human differences in a suspicious light (Ferguson 2012). It recognizes that ideologies of progress and development from Manifest Destiny to multiculturalism have consistently, and sometimes in surprising ways, divided people into good (desirable) and bad (undesirable) forms of human diversity, creating hierarchies that evaluate groups as more or less civilized, capable, advanced, or valuable according to a shifting catalogue of criteria (Horsman 1981; Cacho 2012; Melamed 2011). This research suggests that these attempts to divide humanity are symptomatic of a fundamental contradiction between political democracy, which defines citizens as equal and working cooperatively for collective well-being, and capitalism, in which individuals of unequal material means and social advantages compete with one another for profit (Lowe 1996).

Viewed in this light, discourses of diversity are a form of crisis management; they portray the inequality that capitalism requires as the result of differing human capacities, inaccurately representing groups dispossessed by and for capital accumulation as being in need of the improvements of civilization, education, or freedom. The result is that "diversity" has come to be seen as an ambiguous term that endows its referent—human differences—with only an indistinct and opaque legibility, making it easier to displace the causes of capitalism's structural unevenness onto naturalized fictions of human differences. Karl Marx's example of the nursery tale told by bourgeois political economists to explain the origin of capitalist wealth speaks to this cultural process (1867/1976). The tale involves two kinds of people who lived long ago: diligent, frugal elites who conserved the fruits of their labor so their progeny could become capitalists; and lazy, spendthrift masses who burned through their substance in riotous living so their heirs (wage laborers) have nothing to sell but themselves. This fable about the origins of human diversity (versions of which are still told every day) substitutes for the real acts of force that have expanded capital flows, including conquest, enslavement, land grabbing, and accumulation through dispossession (Harvey 2003). Diversity operates here as a ruse that naturalizes social inequality by inverting cause and effect.

The intertwined usage histories of the keywords "diversity" and "race" are central to this ruse. They appear together first across two disparate yet interrelated domains that influenced the organization of U.S. modernity in the eighteenth and nineteenth centuries: liberal political philosophy and the race sciences. Both of these discourses were concerned with discerning and cultivating human differences, though to very different ends. Liberal political philosophers ranging from Jean-Jacques Rousseau (1762/1968) to John Stuart Mill (1859/1869) advocated the free play of the "good" diversity of European talents, interests, and beliefs as the means and end of a free society. In contrast, the race sciences of the period were concerned with controlling "bad" diversity, conceived as the biological inferiority of nonwhite races, through sterilization, termination, incarceration, and exclusion. Harry Laughlin, for example, the United States' leading eugenicist in the first half of the twentieth century, argued in the context of debates over the passage of the Johnson-Reed Act in 1924 that "progress cannot be built on mongrel melting-pots, but it is based on organized diversity of relatively pure racial types" (Laughlin and Trevor 1939, 18). The naturalization of race in relation to the category of diversity is what made credible these otherwise contradictory frameworks for understanding human difference. Concepts of diversity and race worked together to define "the white race" as so superior to others that freedom and self-cultivation were only beneficial and available to them, thus assuaging conflicts between philosophical commitments to individual liberty and the realities of economic systems dependent on the coercions of slavery, poverty, and industrialization.

During and after World War II, white supremacy and biological concepts of race were discredited by an accumulation of sociopolitical forces including worldwide rejection of German National Socialist (Nazi) racism and antisemitism, anticolonial and antiracist struggles, and global labor migrations from the rural South to the metropolitan North (Winant 2001). As a result, the usage of the terms "diversity" and "race" became even more complexly related. The geopolitical context shaping their new meanings and relationship was the rise of the United States to the position of Cold War superpower and leading force for the expansion of transnational capitalism. In order to accomplish these postwar leadership goals, the United States began to sanction and promote a specific kind of liberal antiracism. The intent of this form of antiracism was to modernize and extend freedoms once reserved for white/European Americans to all U.S. inhabitants regardless of race. These liberal freedoms became the meaning and goal of antiracism: possessive individualism, the right to self-cultivation, abstract legal equality, and access to the field of economic competition. Yet strengthening political democracy by ending white monopolies on liberal freedoms could not serve as an antidote for the structurally uneven relationships developed within global capitalism. The problem was and is that the conceptual framework for liberal antiracism overlapped with the knowledge architecture of global capitalism through the promotion of individualism and economic competition as foundational for racial equality and capitalist development.

As conflicts between democratic ideology and capitalist economy continued to emerge under new conditions, questions of how to best manage unlike human capacities in the name of progress, reform, and improvement continued to provide cover for the next phases of global capitalism. The ruse of racialization lives on: forms of humanity are valued and devalued in ways that fit the needs of reigning political-economic orders. Conventional understandings of race as skin color or phenotype no longer dominate the process. Instead, criteria of class, culture, religion, and citizenship status assume the role that race has played historically, positioning individuals who benefit from differential power arrangements as "fit" for success (good diversity) and those who are structurally exploited or excluded by power arrangements as "unfit" (bad diversity). As "racial difference" gets redefined as "cultural," the language of diversity takes on the burden

previously borne by race. Though race never vanished as a means of managing difference, the emphasis on culture creates a situation that is both flexible and productive, allowing new categories of difference and diversity to evolve in relation to the crises perpetrated by global capital.

Beginning in the 1970s, law and educational policy became the dominant domains for these discussions of how to manage human differences in the name of progress and reform, with affirmative action law being most prominent. Beginning with Supreme Court Justice William Powell's watershed decision, *Regents of the University of California v. Bakke* (438 U.S. 265 (1978)), affirmative action discourse has conditioned the meaning of diversity and, in the process, redefined how the state can recognize and act on racial inequality. In his decision, Justice Powell deployed the keyword "diversity" no less than thirty times. His point was to invalidate all but one of the reasons offered by the University of California–Davis School of Medicine for reserving a few admission slots for students identified as "economically and/or educationally disadvantaged" or members of "minority groups" (*Regents*, 438 U.S. at 274). He found it unconstitutional to use race in admissions to counter discrimination, to break up white monopolies on medical training, or to increase the well-being of communities of color (by training more physicians of color). The only admissible ground for taking race into consideration was "obtaining the educational benefits that flow from a diverse student body" (*Regents*, 438 U.S. at 306). By ruling that "educational diversity" is protected under the free speech clause of the First Amendment, Powell negated material social change as a racial justice goal, replacing it with consideration for higher education's mission to provide all students with opportunities for self-cultivation through exposure to diversity. The decision rests on the capacity of diversity to abstract and generalize human differences in a way that forestalls more precise and relational analysis. It positions "racial justice" as anathema to "genuine diversity," defined only vaguely as "a far broader array of qualifications and characteristics" (*Regents*, 438 U.S. at 315).

Twenty-five years later, the next wave of Supreme Court affirmative action cases (*Grutter v. Bollinger*, 539 U.S. 306 (2003), and *Gratz v. Bollinger*, 539 U.S. 244 (2003)) were decided in a context where universities, corporations, and government agencies had all adapted to this definition of diversity by hiring an array of diversity managers, diversity consultants, and diversity directors, many of whom were assigned the task of finding the most efficient and profitable way to manage human differences of race, ethnicity, gender, culture, and national origin. Sandra Day O'Connor makes this logic apparent in her findings for *Grutter v. Bollinger*: "Diversity [in education] promotes learning outcomes and better prepares students for an increasingly diverse workforce" since "major American businesses have made clear that the skills needed in today's increasingly global marketplace can only be developed through exposure to widely diverse peoples, cultures, ideas, and viewpoints" (*Grutter*, 539 U.S. at 330). O'Connor's reasoning reflects a new common sense developed within multinational corporate capitalism. Bestsellers such as *The Diversity Toolkit: How You Can Build and Benefit from a Diverse Workforce* (Sonnenschein 1999) and *Managing Diversity: People Skills for a Multicultural Workplace* (Carr-Ruffino 1996) promised to teach corporate managers, in the words of the World Bank's Human Resources website, "to value [human] differences and use them as strategic business assets" (Office of Diversity and Inclusion 2013). One might argue that more is at stake than hiring multiracial, female, and lesbian/gay/bisexual/transgender (LGBT) employees to rainbow-wash corporate agendas. Corporate diversity's deeper violence is to claim all differences—material, cultural, communal, and epistemological—for capital management, that is, to recognize no difference that makes a difference, no knowledges, values, social forms, or associations that defer or displace capitalist globalization.

In the first decades of the twenty-first century, diversity's referent tends to slip back and forth, indexing with equal frequency both human differences in general *and* idealized attributes of the global economy. This slippage corresponds to the rise of neoliberal ideology and its mantra that competitive markets are the best way to manage unlike human capacities and other resources in the name of growth and improvement. Within the vocabulary of neoliberalism, diversity affirms the goodness of values such as "freedom" and "openness" and helps these values penetrate previously anti- or noncapitalist domains of social life, including education, religion, family, nonprofit organizations, and social services. As early as 1962, Milton Friedman argued in *Capitalism and Freedom* that truly free and prosperous societies arise only beside an unregulated market, which has "the great advantage" that it "permits wide diversity" (1962/2002, 15). This argument has become mainstream, in part as a result of the work done by the term "diversity" in portraying access to all the world's goods and services as the key to entry into a postracist world of freedom and opportunity.

Are there alternatives to this yoking of discussions of human difference to the goal of capital accumulation? One countervocabulary that emerges alongside the rise of diversity as a form of corporate management involves an alternative keyword: "difference." In contrast to "diversity," the roots of the term "difference" are found in the Afro-Asian solidarity movements of the 1950s and 1960s and the social movement activism of the 1970s.

These movements sought to evade the contradictions of the Cold War by arguing that the different experiences of postcolonial societies—differences grounded in the history of having undergone and defeated white supremacist colonization, in cultural epistemologies unlike those of the West, and in indigenous and non-Christian religious practices—meant that they should not have to fit into either capitalist or communist frameworks, with their shared values of productivity and geopolitical dominance (R. Wright 1956/1995; Von Eschen 1997). The term thus valorized nonnormative and marginalized social subjects as agents of change, insisting that cultures and communities forged by people calling themselves Black, Brown, American Indian, Asian, Militant, Radical, Lesbian, Feminist, and Queer were too valuable to be lost to assimilationist versions of "global diversity." "Difference" pointed toward economic justice, based on an understanding of the racialized, gendered, and sexualized nature of political economy, such as that developed in women of color feminism (Moraga and Anzaldúa 1981; Hong 2006; I. Young 1990).

Since the 1970s, American studies and cultural studies scholarship has been caught up in the conflict encapsulated by this struggle between discourses of diversity and difference. The stakes of the struggle are large. Whereas discourses of diversity suggest that group-differentiated vulnerability to premature death is a problem *for* democratic capitalist society and resolvable within its political economic structures, discourses of difference insist that the globalization of capitalism and its compatibility with only weak forms of political democracy *is* the problem. "Diversity" consequently appears in American studies and cultural studies scholarship with both positive and negative connotations. Sometimes, as in the groundbreaking *Heath Anthology of American Literature*, the term "diversity" appears in a positive light, signifying the belief that a politics of multicultural recognition can dramatically increase racial democracy in the United States (Lauter 1994). At other times, the category of diversity is itself the problem. Often, this skepticism about the term is accompanied by commitments to support social movement knowledges, ranging from women of color feminism to diasporic queer activism, whose critical interventions demand a reckoning with material relations of enduring structural inequality propped up by liberal-democratic and multicultural norms. The result is that much scholarly effort has gone into preventing critical knowledge interventions, such as intersectional analysis, subaltern studies, Indigenous studies, and queer of color analysis, from being subsumed within the generalizing rhetoric of diversity.

As market rationality saturates the usage of diversity within universities today, this scholarship draws on the genealogy of difference to point to the limits of diversity discourse as a means of advancing democratizing projects. In sharp contrast to the vague manner in which diversity discourse presents human differences, it cultivates new ways of thinking about the structural, historical, and material relations that determine who can relate to whom and under what conditions (Hong 2006; Manalansan 2003; Nguyen 2012; Reddy 2011). Innovating new comparative analytics, such scholarship replaces "diversity" with terms such as "partition," "transit," "affinities," "assemblage," and "intimacies" to expose and imagine otherwise the connections and relations that sustain capital accumulation at the cost of generalized well-being (R. Gilmore 2012; Byrd 2011; Puar 2007; Lowe 2006; Hong and Ferguson 2011; Chuh 2003).

21

Domestic

Rosemary Marangoly George

The keyword "domestic" conjures up several different yet linked meanings. It evokes the private home and all its accouterments and, in a secondary fashion, hired household help. It also refers to the "national" as opposed to the "foreign" and to the "tame" as opposed to the "natural" or "wild." American studies and cultural studies scholarship has only recently begun to think through the connections among these usages of the term and to make visible the racial and class bias of much of the scholarship on domesticity in relation to the United States.

Theorizing the domestic has been integral to many academic disciplines: architecture and design, anthropology, sociology, history, economics, philosophy, psychoanalysis, and literary and cultural criticism. Expressed in binary terms such as male/female, public/private, and production/reproduction, a relatively stable home/work dichotomy has formed the basis of scholarly writing on domesticity across these disciplines. Newer studies of domesticity are more attentive to its complex political entrenchment in the so-called public and private: to the entanglement of the domestic with nationalist discourses and, in feminist economic analyses, to the home as a workplace where industrial "homework" is done. Researchers such as Jeanne Boydston (1990) and Alice Kessler-Harris (1990) see the impact of domesticity on the determination of wages and on labor issues that were hitherto understood to be purely market driven. In studies of women's labor history in the West and the reliance on domestic ideologies to buttress capitalist expansion,

Eileen Boris (1993) notes that while a home/work split was an essential component for industrialization, the two arenas were also fundamentally constitutive of each other. Thus, domesticity, in these discussions, has ideological functions that do not stop at constructions of the private life of individual persons, of homes and families.

Much work on domesticity has focused on the white middle classes. This work tends to trace what is essentially an Anglo history of the "American" home from its utilitarian use in the seventeenth century as an unadorned place for storage and shelter to the emergence of the cult of domesticity or true womanhood in the mid-nineteenth century, to the mid-twentieth-century articulation of the home as a prison where countless white, middle-class women suffered unnamable sorrows (Matthews 1987). The prevalence and familiarity of this story indexes both the success and the limitations of liberal feminism as a social movement. Even as it sought to reformulate domesticity in relatively gender-equitable ways, liberal feminism failed to address other factors that shape the domestic arena, most notably the economic and racial connections that hold different domestic sites adjacent and yet unequal within a national or global framework.

A very different genealogy of domesticity in the United States can be traced through the history of the domestic (as household servant) over the same three centuries. This history moves from the seventeenth-century use of indentured servants and "hired help" who worked alongside family members in the household to the use of servants and slaves in the eighteenth and nineteenth centuries, to the centrality of domestic laborers in establishing U.S. notions of ideal domesticity in the mid-twentieth century. It is worth speculating that what Betty Friedan referred to in the first chapter of *The Feminine Mystique* (1963) as the "problem that has no name," the anxieties that beset countless white women in the late 1950s, arose in part because the era of ample, cheap domestic labor came to an end as women of color found other employment avenues open to them. In recent years, career women in the United States may be reversing this trend, as they increasingly turn to nonfamilial domestic labor, provided mainly by a service economy made up of documented and undocumented immigrants and other women of color, in order to juggle the tasks of maintaining both a career and high standards of child care and home maintenance. A complex network of economic, racial, and gendered arrangements needs to be in place on a national and international footing before respectable middle- and upper-middle-class homemaking is successfully achieved in the United States (M. Romero 1992; Parreñas 2001).

Scholarship on European and U.S. imperialism has also begun to examine the "spatial and political interdependence of home and empire," what Amy Kaplan (1998, 25) has called "Manifest Domesticity." Such scholarship demonstrates that the domestic sentimentalization of the white, middle-class home from the nineteenth century onward was intimately intertwined with the ongoing and violent expansion of U.S. interests across the North American continent and beyond. One example of this work is Laura Wexler's (2000, 8) notable study of late nineteenth- and early twentieth-century women photographers and the multiple ways in which "nineteenth-century domestic photographs shaped the look and power of white supremacy at the century's end." Wexler argues that Frances Johnston's photographs of Admiral George Dewey and his crew, taken in 1899 aboard the battleship *Olympia* after they had routed the Spanish forces in the Philippines, celebrate and consolidate the "American" heroism that Dewey and his band of sailors embodied

even as these photos bear witness to the "American" domestic world that was re-created on the ship. Such "domestic images" function both to deny and to showcase the violence with which the differences between home and alien spaces or alien peoples are constructed, managed, and policed (ibid., 21).

Research of this type demonstrates that the domestic is a dynamic and changing concept, one that serves as a regulative norm that continually refigures families, homes, and belonging. In its early forms, the domestic was a primary site where modernity was made manifest; the concept of family changed from a largely temporal organization of kinship into a spatially organized sphere of activity. In narratives and practices of domesticity, the trauma of such transformation is absorbed (imperfectly at times), and the domestic is reissued as usable or, in rare cases, abandoned altogether. The wholesomeness associated with the domestic, as in Witold Rybczynski's (1988, 217) assessment of "domestic well-being [as] a fundamental human need that is deeply rooted in us, and that must be satisfied," is rarely discarded even when specific domestic arrangements are. Even liberal-radical accounts that seek to contest the mainstream-conservative reduction of domesticity to the nuclear family often remain firmly committed to family values. These values may be alternative, but they nonetheless retain the pleasures of the normative: private comfort, safety, exclusivity. And at the national level, the demand for the comfort and safety of the enfranchised citizenry has put into place a rigorous screening process that excludes from the "homeland" those who threaten "the American way of life," even as it lets slip in an underclass whose labor is necessary for maintaining the domestic comforts of everyday life.

Much of the literary and cultural studies scholarship on the rise of these normative forms of domesticity focuses on the mid-nineteenth century, when a new ideology of the home and of women's role in its maintenance took hold of the U.S. imagination. Catharine E. Beecher's *A Treatise on Domestic Economy for the Use of Young Ladies at Home and at School* (1841) was a significant inaugurator of this ideology, since it newly venerated the white, middle-class home and placed central responsibility for it in the hands of the housewife. This widespread rhetoric sentimentalized both the home and the housewife as the sources and locations of national virtue and was manifest in a variety of cultural texts, including women's magazines such as *Godey's Lady's Book* (published 1830–98), religious tracts, newspapers, home-design innovations, home-management guides, and the "domestic fiction" written in this period. In the late twentieth century, a whole generation of U.S. feminists investigated the cultural impact of the latter phenomenon, produced by what Nathaniel Hawthorne famously called the "d——d mob of scribbling women" (1855/1987, 304). Influential studies such as Ann Douglas's *Feminization of American Culture* (1977) and Jane Tompkins's *Sensational Designs* (1985) revised the U.S. literary canon by insisting on the importance of mass culture in the nineteenth century and of women as powerful consumers and producers in this arena. David Reynolds (1989), Lora Romero (1997), and others have argued that "the reign of women [should be understood as] a cultural artifact produced by the antebellum period" (Romero 1997, 14) rather than as an accurate assessment of the power of middle-class white women in the antebellum years.

Regardless of the degree to which the nineteenth-century cult of domesticity authorized white women in the context of U.S. cultural production, the "domestic fiction" formula reigned supreme. When African American women writers in the late nineteenth century utilized this genre, it was indicative of the different political charge of domesticity for a people struggling with the burden of slavery that had placed heavy prohibitions on both the means and contents of such pleasures. Denied access to reading, writing, state-recognized marriage, and homeownership, denied the luxury or right to play the pure lady of the house or even to be a child learning at her mother's knee, these writers produced domestic fiction that revealed very little dissonance between attending to the claims and duties of domestic life (especially motherhood) and attending to those of activism on behalf of the race. The establishment and celebration of happy marriages within domestic havens in these black women's writings did powerful political and cultural work in a period when the attainment of a private sphere, whether through homeownership or by other means, was something fought for daily even as it was recorded and celebrated in cultural texts (Tate 1992; DuCille 1993). More than a century later, welfare reform programs and policies, the recruitment of disproportionate numbers of people of color into the armed forces and police, and racially biased criminal sentencing and incarceration patterns all indicate that, in Aída Hurtado's (1989, 849) words, "there is no such thing as a private sphere for people of Color except that which they manage to create and protect in an otherwise hostile environment." Whether we look at housing-loan records, zoning laws, civic amenities in specific neighborhoods, the location of toxic industries, the differential funding to schools, or levels of prenatal care, we see that state intervention into domestic life continues to be systematically beneficial to white, middle- and upper-class citizens and detrimental to the everyday lives of lower-class whites and people of color.

Partly due to this complex history, "domestication" has often been deployed for metaphorical purposes in academic discourse, including feminist discourse, to signify the opposite of radical thought, a usage that draws on the opposition of the domestic to the wild. The literary and cultural critic Rachel Bowlby (1995, 73), for instance, notes that domestication "refers generally to processes of simplification, assimilation and distortion—any or all of these—to which the theory in question falls victim or which it is powerless to resist." Yet if we consider the name chosen by the founders of Kitchen Table / Women of Color Press, we encounter a radical feminism that harnesses the wisdom and labor of this homely location to a far-reaching feminist politics. As in the nineteenth century, "marriage," "family," and "homemaking" continue to be differently inflected terms and spaces for different groups of people and are fabricated with local variations across national borders and social classes. What is truly remarkable are the ways in which dominant domestic ideologies and practices have become globally hegemonic as a result of colonial and capitalist expansion and modernization, even as they have entered into contestation with other local forms of domesticity. Class, race, and geographic location place heavy inflections on domesticity, and yet, like love, childhood, and death, the domestic is most often portrayed as transcending all specifics or, rather, as blurring all distinctions in the warm glow of its splendor. Ultimately, the enormous attention that domesticity has received, and the enshrinement of heterosexuality therein, has severely stymied the representation and even recognition of other forms of establishing intimacy and affiliation.

22

Economy
Timothy Mitchell

The term "economy" in its contemporary sense came into use only quite recently. It is often assumed that the idea of the economy, defined as the relations of material production and exchange in a given territory and understood as an object of expert knowledge and government administration, was introduced by political economists such as William Petty, François Quesnay, and Adam Smith in the seventeenth and eighteenth centuries, or even by Aristotle. In fact, however, this use of the term developed only in the 1930s and 1940s and was well established only by the 1950s (T. Mitchell 2005).

In earlier periods, "economy" (usually with no definite article) referred to a way of acting and to the forms of knowledge required for effective action. It was the term for the proper husbanding of material resources or the proper management of a lord's estate or a sovereign's realm. "Political economy" came to mean the knowledge and practice required for governing the state and managing its population and resources (Tribe 1978; Poovey 1998). Michel Foucault (1991) connects the development of this expertise to the wider range of practices known as "government," in an older sense of that term referring not to the official institutions of rule but to a variety of forms of knowledge and technique concerned with governing personal conduct, managing the health and livelihoods of a population, and controlling the circulation of material and political resources.

What is the difference between the older meaning of "economy," understood as a way of exercising power and accumulating knowledge, and the contemporary idea of "the economy," understood as an object of power and knowledge? Foucault (1991, 92) does not address this question but simply relates the two meanings by suggesting that "the very essence of government—that is the art of exercising power in the form of economy—is to have as its main object that which we are today accustomed to call 'the economy.'" This conflation has led several scholars to argue that the economy emerged as a distinct object in the late eighteenth or early nineteenth century. Others read Karl Polanyi's (1944/2001) argument that in the same period market relations were "disembedded" from society as another version of this idea. Polanyi, however, is describing the emergence not of the economy but of society, formed as an object of political discourse in response to the increasingly unrestrained relations of what he calls "market economy."

The emergence of the economy in the mid-twentieth century differs from the era of nineteenth-century governmentality in at least three important senses. First, economists and government agencies defined the economy in a way that enabled them to claim new powers to measure it, manage it, and make it grow. They defined it not in terms of human labor, the management of resources, or the accumulation of national wealth but as the circulation of money. The economy is the sum of all those transactions in which money changes hands, and its size and growth are calculated by estimating this sum. Second, the idea of the economy belongs to the postimperial era of nation-states, in which human sociality is understood as a series of equivalent national units. Each of these units claims the right to its own national state, replacing the earlier system of European colonial empires, and each is thought to be composed of a series of distinct sociotechnical spaces: a society, an economy, and a culture (T. Mitchell 2002). Third, the

emergence of the idea that state, society, economy, and culture exist as separate spheres, which collectively fill the space of the nation-state, coincided with the twentieth-century development of the social and cultural sciences as distinct professional and academic fields. Political science, sociology, economics, and anthropology (and the study of national literatures and histories in the case of Western societies) each contributed to the making of its respective object, providing it with concepts, calculations, agents, and methods of evaluation. Portrayed as merely an object of knowledge, the economy, along with these other spheres, was in fact enmeshed in the new forms of academic expertise and professional knowledge.

Acknowledging the role of economics and other professional expertise in making the economy does not mean that the economy is just a "representation" or merely a "social construction." Making the economy involved a wide range of sociotechnical projects that embedded people and things in new machineries of calculation, new techniques of accounting, and new impulsions of discipline and desire. The development of marketing and brand identity, the management of the flow of money by corporate and national banks, New Deal programs such as electrification and the building of dams, colonial development schemes and the postwar projects of development agencies and the World Bank: all contributed to the organization of worlds that could now be described and measured as the economy.

Firmly established by the 1950s, the modern idea of the economy was soon subject to criticism. Researchers pointed out that its measurement does not take proper account of unpaid labor, especially the work of maintaining and reproducing households, which is performed largely by women. It cannot measure illegal, unreported, or unregistered economic activity, such as the global arms trade or the informal, small-scale farming, manufacturing, and commerce that play a large role in many countries. It treats the natural world only as resources to be consumed and cannot express the cost of the exhaustion of nonrenewable resources, the destruction of species, or irreversible changes in the global climate.

These criticisms were made by writers and researchers mostly operating outside the academic discipline of economics. But even economists began to acknowledge the increasing difficulty of accurately measuring or describing the economy. The growth in the production of film and music, tourism and information, telecommunications and the Internet, legal and consulting services, health care, and other forms of expertise and culture created economies whose products seem increasingly ethereal. Even in the case of consumer goods such as food, clothing, cars, and electronics, the creation of value through brand identity and through the shaping of fashion and taste has made the economic world seem less material and more difficult to measure or predict.

These changes in the economy have sometimes been described in American studies, as in cultural studies more broadly, as marking the transition to a postmodern stage of capitalism (Jameson 1991; Lowe and Lloyd 1997). Such accounts homogenize the changes and attribute them to the force of an underlying logic of the development of capital. They also invoke an earlier era, modernity, in which representations were more firmly anchored to material realities. The genealogy of the concept of the economy cautions against this view. There was never an era in which a simple, material reality could be captured and represented as the economy. The possibility of representing the economy as the object of economic knowledge rested on the proliferation of sociotechnical processes of representation. It was the spread of new forms of representational practice that made it possible to attempt the social-scientific representation of that world. The economy, the new object of economics, was constructed out of not only numerical quantifications but an entire process of branding, product development, information production, and image making that formed both the possibility of the modern economy and the increasing impossibility of its representation.

The contemporary idea of the economy has also been affected by the rise of neoliberal economics, which has turned attention away from the economy and back toward the seemingly simpler idea of "the market." The trouble is that markets, like economies, must be made. They are produced not by the natural working of self-interest but by the complex organization of desire, agency, price, ownership, and dispossession. Economics (especially in a wider sense of the term, encompassing fields such as accounting and management) helps to produce these arrangements, by providing instruments of calculation and other necessary equipment (Callon 1998), just as it helped to produce the economy. However, while the idea of the economy refers to a specific territory, usually the nation-state, the market has no particular spatial connotation. It can refer to the trading floor of a futures exchange or a transnational network. Unlike the economy, therefore, it does not invoke the role of the state, as the power that governs economic space and defines its task as the management and growth of the economy and the nurturing and regulation of economic actors. The regulation of markets and the forming and governing of market agencies is dispersed at numerous levels.

The idea of the economy survives today as much as a political concept as an object of economic theory. A sign taped to the wall in the Democratic Party campaign headquarters for the 1992 U.S. presidential election proclaimed, "It's the economy, stupid!" Placed there, it is said, as a reminder of where the campaign should keep its focus, it reminds us today of the work that is done to make the existence of the economy appear obvious and its truths uncontestable. It also should remind us that the goal of fixing what the economy refers to has remained surprisingly resilient. While the field of cultural studies, American and otherwise, has paid much attention to other organizing concepts, such as nation, class, gender, society, and of course culture itself, it has often left the idea of the economy untouched. There have been a number of interesting studies of different "representations" of the economy. These usually assume, however, that the economy itself remains as a kind of underlying material reality, somehow independent of the intellectual equipment and machinery of representation with which it is set up and managed. In the same way, academic economics is often criticized for misrepresenting the "true nature" of the economy. The task now is to account for the great success of economics and related forms of expertise in helping to make the economy in the first place.

23

Empire
Shelley Streeby

For most of the twentieth century, the intellectual and political leaders of the United States denied that the nation was an empire. Then around 1994, things began to change, with the neoconservatives aligned with the Project for a New American Century (PNAC) openly embracing the idea of an American empire capable of ruling the post–Cold War world. This shift is a good example of the process Raymond Williams describes in *Keywords* (1976/1983, 11–26), whereby changes in the significance of words occur rapidly at times of crisis. For Williams, World War II decisively shaped the remarkable transformations in the meanings of certain keywords that inspired his book. In the twenty-first-century United States, the response of the Bush administration to 9/11, which sociologist Giovanni Arrighi calls "a case of great-power suicide" (2009, 82), precipitated a similar crisis.

While PNAC's embrace of empire was a departure from the Cold War framing of the Soviet Union as an evil empire and the United States as the free world's defender, such an embrace was not a new phenomenon. In 2003, Vice President Dick Cheney's Christmas card contained the following quotation, attributed to Benjamin Franklin: "And if a sparrow cannot fall to the ground without His notice, is it probable that an empire can rise without His aid?" (Bumiller 2003). As this citation demonstrates, ideas about empire as a tyrannical, Old World vice competed from the moment of the founding of the nation with arguments about the divine exceptionality of American empire. Many founders feared the proximity of other empires—British, French, and Spanish—in other parts of the Americas. In competition with these powerful states, U.S. leaders often asserted, in spite of the prior claims of indigenous peoples, a natural right to the continent on the basis of both geography and the ongoing practices of settlement and colonization by U.S. migrants. Empire, in this context, named both a risk and an opportunity. As Montesquieu (1748) warned, empires threatened republics with corruption and decline by engendering luxury, intermixing alien peoples, and requiring standing armies. The question was whether imperialism and republicanism could be reconciled.

Thomas Jefferson's Louisiana Purchase of 1803 pushed this question to a crisis by massively increasing the size of the United States and clarifying the nation's imperial ambitions. Since then, many advocates of empire have repeated Jefferson's statement that U.S. expansion increases freedom's space and thereby contributes to an "empire for liberty," while others have echoed the logic that vast territories endanger republics. Such warnings often rest on comparisons to the rise and fall of other empires, including Rome, Spain, and England, and worries over annexing new lands. William Prescott's 1843 *History of the Conquest of Mexico* encouraged many people to imagine that U.S. soldiers retraced the steps of Spanish conquistadors as they marched on Mexico City during the U.S.-Mexico War (1846–48). Crises in India and Ireland also made the British Empire an unsettling point of comparison, as in 1847, when Theodore Parker compared the U.S. invasion of Mexico to England's "butchering" of Sikhs in India and seizure of lands in Ireland (1863/1973, 26). The annexation of new territories reanimated debates over the extension of slavery as well as the incorporation of Catholics and nonwhites into the nation (Streeby 2002). Empire and slavery thereby became fatally conjoined, and the lands acquired after 1848 further divided the nation, pushing it toward Civil War.

While midcentury historians such as Parker made bleak comparisons to other empires, many advocates of the war used words other than "empire" to describe U.S. expansion. In 1845, *Democratic Review* editor John O'Sullivan (1845, 5) famously suggested it was the nation's "manifest destiny to overspread the continent allotted by Providence for the free development of our yearly multiplying millions." The concept of Manifest Destiny situated the New England Puritans as God's chosen people in the Promised Land and built on John Locke's influential argument that land ownership was justified by use, as well as Jeffersonian theories that agrarian democracy extended freedom's space. The concept gave divine sanction to U.S. expansion and made it feel natural and right to white settlers and their descendants, thereby shaping the common sense of scholars who distinguished "continental" expansion across North America from empire, understood as the possession of colonies and settlements overseas. This distinction allowed scholars to claim that the United States did not act as an empire throughout the nineteenth century, a claim that is clearly counterfactual.

As a result, the U.S. expansion into the Philippines in the 1890s became widely regarded within conventional histories as an aberrant period in which the United States uncharacteristically acted as an empire. The "new" overseas empire required the extension and protection of networks of U.S. commercial interests, investments, and military bases in addition to or instead of the annexation of lands (LaFeber 1963). The truth is that little of this activity was new. From early on, the United States tried to influence, control, or even take over "overseas" places such as Cuba, and the notion of a commercial empire was strongly articulated as early as the 1860s by Abraham Lincoln's secretary of state, William Seward. While U.S. leaders retreated

EMPIRE SHELLEY STREEBY

from the previous pattern of annexing territories and making them into states after the 1890s, this shift was more of an innovation in empire's administration than a break. Indeed, by calling the 1890s empire "new" and distinguishing continental expansionism from overseas imperialism, scholars naturalized the violent displacement of indigenous people, even as they implied that empire was an exception in U.S. history rather than the norm.

The idea that the 1890s was an aberrant period of empire belies the extent of U.S. military and commercial intervention around the world in the decades that followed. Theodore Roosevelt stated in his 1904 corollary to the Monroe Doctrine that "chronic wrongdoing, or an impotence which results in a general loosening of the ties of civilized society, may in America, as elsewhere, ultimately require intervention by some civilized nation, and in the Western Hemisphere . . . may force the United States, however reluctantly, . . . to the exercise of an international police power" (Roosevelt 1904, 831). The idea that the United States is an international police power defending civilization has often justified interventions in Latin America, and although Roosevelt's frank endorsement of empire differs from other, seemingly benevolent attempts to build international institutions, such as Woodrow Wilson's founding of the League of Nations in 1919, both shared a vision of the United States as a "world cop" (Hardt and Negri 2000, 177). Wilson spoke of preserving peace while Roosevelt claimed war kept men strong and defended civilization against savagery, yet Wilson sent U.S. troops to intervene in Russia, Mexico, Haiti, Central America, and the Dominican Republic during his presidency. The seeming benevolence of Wilson's hierarchical internationalism derived from his rearticulation of U.S. intervention around the globe in idealistic Jeffersonian language as the extension of universal values: his 1917 declaration that the United States was devoted to making the world "safe for democracy" has often been echoed by U.S. war hawks, most recently by George W. Bush during the early-twenty-first century "war on terror."

But if U.S. leaders have used the word "empire" as a way to justify U.S. imperialism from the beginning, it is important to recognize that the deployment of the term to speak back to U.S. power is equally enduring. In the brilliant "Eulogy on King Philip" (1836/1992), for instance, the itinerant preacher, orator, and organizer of the Mashpee Revolt William Apess compared the leader of the Pequot Rebellion in Massachusetts favorably to George Washington and other "emperors" of the past as he exposed the "inhumanity" of the English colonization of Massachusetts. And over the course of U.S. history, many other American Indian writers have found it necessary to take on this enduring task of disturbing the historical and ongoing disavowal of the colonization of indigenous people. Since the "creation of the United States as a political entity," as Jodi Byrd puts it, "American Indians have existed in a space of liminality, where what was external was repeatedly and violently reimagined and remade as internal in order to disavow the ongoing colonization of indigenous people that is necessary for the United States to exist" (2011, 136). In other words, the colonizers of North America, who came from "external" faraway places, reimagined themselves as "internal" to the nation even as they violently displaced the indigenous people who were already living there.

It is not surprising, then, that despite the complicated hierarchies involved in the production of mediated narratives by indigenous people, such as *Life of Black Hawk* (Black Hawk 1833/2008) and *Geronimo: His Own Story* (Geronimo 1905/1996), these texts, along with John Rollin Ridge's *The Life and Adventures of Joaquin Murieta* (1854/1977), foreground the violent reimagining of the external as internal and the traumatic spaces of liminality that empire engenders in ways that disturb its disavowal. Later, decolonization and civil rights struggles in the 1960s and 1970s made the word "empire" important again as a metaphor for the struggles of other aggrieved groups, though as Byrd cautions, when imperialism becomes an "empty referent that can be claimed by any marginalized group, to use it to describe the historical and spatial positionality of indigenous nations is a colonial violence that undermines sovereignty and self-determination" (2011, 137). That is, when "empire" becomes a metaphor, the specificity of the violent displacement of indigenous people as the origin story for the nation may disappear from view in ways that diminish and disregard indigenous nations' prior claims to sovereignty and self-determination.

Like these Native American thinkers, intellectuals aligned with transnational social movements have recognized the risks of using empire as a metaphor. Writers and scholars such as Cyril Briggs, Alexander Berkman, Hubert H. Harrison, Emma Goldman, C. L. R. James, Ricardo and Enrique Flores Magón, and Lucy Parsons worked in the early decades of the twentieth century to link histories shaped by empire without leveling differences among marginalized groups, though many of them were punished, imprisoned, and deported for doing so (Streeby 2013). From this perspective, the widely influential 1993 anthology *Cultures of United States Imperialism*, edited by Amy Kaplan and Donald Pease, is best understood as a contribution to ongoing debates within American studies, not as an origin point. The book grew out of a 1991 conference that was organized "in the shadow of three macropolitical events—the end of the cold war, the Persian Gulf War, and the Columbus quincentennial" (Pease 1993, 22). Kaplan focused in her introduction on imperial amnesia, arguing that "imperialism has

been simultaneously formative and disavowed in the foundational discourses of American Studies" (1993, 5). And several contributors engaged British cultural studies, including José David Saldívar, who located himself within the University of California–Santa Cruz's Center for Cultural Studies as he used Raymond Williams's theory of the "country-city opposition" to analyze "the experimental anthropological and anti-imperialist literary work of Américo Paredes" (1993, 292–93). Such transnational connections helped put empire on the agenda of American studies, following the lead of Stuart Hall (1992a), Paul Gilroy (Centre for Contemporary Cultural Studies 1982; Gilroy 1991), and others who had worked hard in the previous decades to persuade their colleagues to confront the way imperialism had shaped and constrained imaginings of the English people-nation and culture.

This return of empire as an object of inquiry also coincided with reformulations of American studies away from a primary focus on history and literature. Despite the dominance of these disciplines in the affiliations of contributors to *Cultures of United States Imperialism*, the social sciences are represented, and the impact of interdisciplinary formations such as women's studies and ethnic studies is evident. This broadening of the disciplines and interdisciplines contributing to American studies and the conversation about empire continued apace in the flagship journal of the American Studies Association (ASA), *American Quarterly*, during the 2000s. It has also been evident at the ASA's annual meetings, which have focused in recent years on topics ranging from "American Studies and the Question of Empire: Histories, Cultures and Practices" in 1998 to "Dimensions of Empire and Resistance: Past, Present, and Future" in 2012.

Within these diverse discussions of empire, new tensions have emerged, even among scholars critical of "empire studies." One influential example of these tensions is Caroline Levander and Robert Levine's *Hemispheric American Studies* (2008a), which was also a special issue of the journal *American Literary History*, garnered many grants, and inspired panels at an array of professional conferences. Although the scholarship of the book's contributors was wide ranging, their disciplinary affiliations were more homogeneous: twelve of eighteen worked in English departments, two in literature, two in Spanish, and two in American studies. The editors began their introduction by focusing on "Americanist literary criticism" but ultimately aspired to address the question of how to "reframe disciplinary boundaries within the broad area of what is generally called American Studies" (2008b, 3). "Empire studies" emerges as the bad other for the editors, who worry that "recent tendencies to conceive of the U.S. in the American hemisphere solely in terms of empire and imperialism tend to overlook the complex series of encounters that collectively comprise national communities in the Americas," such as the "hemispheric cultural flows" that move in multiple directions (7). Their counterstrategy therefore proposes to approach "literary and cultural history from the vantage point of a polycentric American hemisphere with no dominant center" (7).

There are several kinds of hemispheric projects at play in this collection, but Levander and Levine's conceptualization of a hemisphere with no dominant center risks disregarding enduring asymmetries of power. The keyword "hemisphere" can serve neither as a panacea for the ills of empire nor as a replacement for the keyword "empire," since U.S. corporations and imperialists have also promoted their own versions of a hemispheric America. As Amy Kaplan explained in her 2003 ASA presidential address, both words have vexed histories, and neither will satisfactorily resolve complicated problems of institutional and geopolitical power.

Kaplan's insights present scholars with three specific challenges as they approach the question of empire. First, debates about empire should be recast in transnational, historical, and comparative contexts in ways that complicate simplistic characterizations of empire studies. A focus on empire need not obscure connections made below, above, and beyond the level of the nation, as well as multidirectional exchanges among diverse parts of the world and voices from other places. Second, scholars of empire should recognize difference, contradiction, and disruption, rather than turning the story of U.S. empire into a seamless narrative (McAlister 2005). Third, work on U.S. empire should be comparative and multilingual, not exceptionalist or conducted only in English. Chicana/o, Latina/o, and Latin American studies scholars, many of whom use the word "empire" themselves, have been making this point for a very long time. Indeed, the work of some of the contributors to *Hemispheric American Studies*, including Jesse Alemán and Kirsten Silva Gruesz, contradicts the editors' ambitions to distinguish strongly between the "hemispheric" from empire studies.

The turn—or return—to empire in American studies, particularly within the subfields of American literary studies and American cultural studies, was relatively late in coming. At the inception of cultural studies in the U.S. academy, it was neither as interdisciplinary as its British counterpart nor as invested in responding to contemporary social problems. The English department was often its home in the United States, while the Centre for Contemporary Cultural Studies at Birmingham and its collective projects, including important books such as *The Empire Writes Back* (Ashcroft, Griffiths, and Tiffin 1989), were part of an interdisciplinary formation responding to contemporary struggles. In the United

States, interdisciplinary and problem-based fields such as ethnic studies often confronted the category of empire earlier because of their closer connections to social movements struggling over imperialism and colonialism, such as the Chicana/o movement and the antiwar movement. When we define American studies in terms of programs and institutions, we must recognize the way it emerged as a post–World War II form of area studies that had ties on some campuses to the CIA, the Cold War security state, and U.S. empire. But we should also attend to what George Lipsitz has called that "other American studies, the organic grassroots theorizing about culture and power that has informed cultural practice, social movements, and academic work for many years" (2001, 27).

The pressing question today is whether American studies will be shaped in the future by disciplinary retrenching, impossible attempts to depoliticize the production of knowledge, and the cutting of interdisciplinary programs and departments in the neoliberal university, or whether it will remain open to that other, grassroots American studies of which Lipsitz writes, as well as the interdisciplinary crossings that are crucial for connecting the university to social movements. It would be strange to have "empire" recede from the American studies lexicon while debates over U.S. global military involvement and the decline and fall of the "American empire" continue to make it meaningful to broader publics and audiences. Even as we reflect on the limits of empire as a paradigm and consider the perils and possibilities of hemispheric and other frameworks, American studies scholars need the keyword "empire" to respond to what is happening in the world around us.

24

Ethnicity
Henry Yu

The term "ethnicity" gained widespread currency in the mid- to late twentieth century, naming a process by which individuals or groups came to be understood, or to understand themselves, as separate or different from others. This meaning of "ethnicity" commonly referred to the consciousness of exclusion or subordination, though it also indexed social practices—language, religion, rituals, and other patterns of behavior—that define the content of a group's culture. The spread of this theory of ethnic culture created two mutually exclusive, analytically separate categories: "ethnicity," defined as cultural traits, was utterly divorced from the workings of the physical body, defined as "race." When anthropologists such as Franz Boas (1940) of Columbia University and sociologists and anthropologists from the University of Chicago began to teach students in the early twentieth century that cultural characteristics were the most interesting social phenomena for study, they spread at the same time the idea that any attention to physical characteristics was intellectually inappropriate. Attacking justifications for racial hierarchy grounded in biology, social scientists used the concept of ethnicity as a weapon against racial thinking.

"Ethnicity" thus became the term that named an alternative to the earlier biological emphases of racial hierarchy. In *Man's Most Dangerous Myth: The Fallacy of Race* (1942), one of the most significant antiracist books published in the twentieth century, the anthropologist Ashley Montagu argued that race as a category of analysis should be dropped as a dangerous invention and that "ethnic group" was a more neutral term. "Ethnicity" became synonymous with cultural difference, and any theory dependent on physical characteristics was dismissed as racist. Similarly, the attempt by anthropologists such as Ruth Benedict (1934) to array societies in a spectrum of cultures aided this flattening of all human distinction into a matter of cultural or ethnic difference. Possibilities for the elimination of racial prejudice (defined specifically as the expression of conscious attitudes about a group of people considered racially different) depended on a very specific definition of race as a form of consciousness. Race was a myth because it had no basis in biology, yet race as a consciousness about the importance of a set of physical attributes could still exist. Because consciousness of race was claimed to be merely one form of ethnic consciousness, race and ethnicity were concepts simultaneously distinct and indistinct from each other.

The subsuming of race under the broader category of ethnicity was both a significant attempt at offering a solution to racial conflict and a sign of the persistent difficulties with distinguishing between the two. As a matter of consciousness, the racial culture of "Negro Americans" was no different in kind than the ethnic culture of "Polish Americans," and purely cultural processes of assimilation could eliminate all differences between them. However, there were chronic difficulties with the distinction between race and ethnicity. W. Lloyd Warner and Leo Srole's widely read *Social Systems of American Ethnic Groups* (1945) exemplified the paradox inherent in this distinction. According to them, the host society accepted some groups more easily than others. Class differences tended to fragment ethnic groups, and the class mobility of some members of ethnic groups was the major determinant of acceptance within the host society. Most difficult to accept, however, were those groups seen to be racially different. Although Warner and Srole argued that group conflict was a matter of ethnic identification (in the sense that the host society viewed a group as different, and the group viewed themselves as different), they also assumed that there was some characteristic that set apart ethnic groups that were racially defined. The "future of American ethnic groups seems to be limited," Warner and Srole concluded; "it is likely that they will be quickly absorbed. When this happens one of the great epochs of American history will have ended and another, that of race, will begin" (295).

This sense that a great epoch of ethnicity was about to end at midcentury was a product of a crucial social transformation in the decades following the explicitly racialized immigration exclusion policies of the late nineteenth and early twentieth centuries. By the 1920s, U.S. social scientists (some of whom were themselves either migrants or children of migrants) had created a body of theories of race and culture that had grown out of studying mass migration (Yu 2001). The most significant of these studies were associated with sociologists such as William I. Thomas (Thomas and Znanieki 1918–20) and Robert E. Park (1950) at the University of Chicago. Park and Thomas were at the forefront of an attempt to advance a new theory about social interaction based on the concept of culture. In opposition to earlier theories about the importance of inherited characteristics and physical bodies in determining human behavior, cultural theories emphasized the centrality of consciousness, of the mental attitudes and forms of self-understanding that people communicated through writing, speech, and other media. One of the most important of these theories concerned what Park and Thomas labeled "cultural assimilation," the process by which two groups communicated with each other and came to share common experiences, memories, and histories.

Applied specifically to U.S. immigrants, the theory of assimilation promised that any migrant, no matter how different in language, religion, or other social practices at the moment of arrival, could learn to assimilate national cultural norms. This historically progressive vision of the United States became the foundation for later arguments about ethnic consciousness, self-identity, and group identity.

At the same time, the twentieth-century "alchemy of race" (Jacobson 1998) had its origins in the mechanisms by which European immigrants who were defined at the beginning of the century as racially different came to be seen as "white" ethnics by the end of the century (Brodkin 1998). Along with the intellectual transformation wrought by cultural theory, popular writers such as Louis Adamic, who was himself of recent immigrant ancestry, pushed for an overcoming of the nativist divide between old and new U.S. Americans. In books such as *From Many Lands* (1940) and *Nation of Nations* (1944), Adamic reconceived the United States as a land of immigrants, subsuming what had earlier been major dividing lines such as religion and language into mere differences of ethnic culture. At the same time (and with Adamic's assistance), organizations such as the National Council of Christians and Jews, founded in 1928, were striving to unify Protestants, Catholics, Orthodox Christians, and Jews into a so-called Judeo-Christian tradition. This period also saw widespread mass-cultural arguments for the end of religious discrimination, perhaps most visibly in 1950s Hollywood motion pictures such as *The Ten Commandments* (1956) and *Ben-Hur* (1959). The focus on the assimilation of religious differences, powerfully propelled by wartime propaganda against the genocidal science of Nazism, helped label anti-Semitism and anti-Catholicism as un-American. By the end of the 1950s, class mobility fueled by the postwar Montgomery GI Bill and federal subsidies of suburban housing had made Adamic's dream of an amalgamation of new and old seem viable.

The truth is that such programs of social engineering were predominantly focused on men able to pass as white. Immigrants who had been treated in the period between 1890 and 1920 as racially different (Slavs, Jews, southern Europeans such as Italians, Greeks, and Armenians) were now transformed into white ethnics, mere varieties of white people. Just as dividing lines over religion, which had seemed intractable a generation before, were now reduced to mere denominational differences, all such culturally defined elements of difference had disappeared into a generic whiteness marked only superficially by vestiges of ethnic culture. Ironically, the civil rights movement of the 1950s helped reinforce this process of ethnic transformation. Jewish American intellectuals of the 1930s and 1940s had been at the forefront of political coalitions with African Americans seeking civil rights. Similarities in discrimination and exclusion at work and in the legal segregation of housing and public facilities had drawn Jewish and African Americans together to fight for civil rights. However, paralleling the larger transformation of white ethnics, Jewish Americans by the end of the civil rights era had become solidly white, even if anti-Semitism remained in vestigial and virulent forms. The civil rights movement for blacks ended up helping immigrant groups that previously had been the targets of racial nativism to amalgamate into a new ethnic "whiteness."

Despite these formidable intellectual and political problems, "ethnicity" has continued to be used widely as a description of and prescription for social life. Indeed, the acceptance and eventual celebration of ethnic difference was one of the most significant transitions of the twentieth century. Coincident with the increasing awareness of migration at the beginning of the century, a cosmopolitan appreciation of exotic difference arose. Writing in the days before World War I, a number of New York intellectuals embraced the rich diversity of the city, forecasting that the eclectic mix of global migrants was the future of U.S. society. Randolph Bourne's vision of a "transnational America" (1916) and Horace Kallen's description of "cultural pluralism" (1915) argued against the xenophobia that fueled the immigration exclusion acts of the same period, replacing it with an embrace of the exotic. The consumption by elite whites of the music and art of the Harlem Renaissance in the 1920s, along with periodic fads for Oriental art and so-called primitive tribal objects, reflected an embrace of the different as valuable. The celebration of exoticism in theories about the cosmopolitan self laid the groundwork for two major developments concerning ethnicity. The first was the theoretical foundation for the commercialization of ethnic difference; the second was the creation of a new definition of elite, enlightened whiteness.

Beginning with the fascination with exotic art forms in modernism, but also embodied in the hunger for ethnic food and objects, a tasteful appreciation of the exotic became part of an educational program to combat racism and ignorance in the 1960s. At the same time that education was touted as the answer to race relations, ethnic music and other forms of exotic art and entertainment were offered at first as alternatives to the mass productions of popular culture and by the 1990s as important commodities distributed and consumed in the marketplace. Interestingly, the rise and spread of a cosmopolitan embrace of exotic difference helped expand the boundaries of whiteness. One of the ways in which those individuals formerly excluded as racially or ethnically suspect could "whiten" themselves was by embracing cosmopolitan ideas. Those who continued

to express racist opinions were subsumed under the newly enlarged rubric of white racists (a category that "whitened" former ethnics at the same time that it tarred them as ignorant bigots of the lower classes). The embrace of cosmopolitan ideals offered a way of becoming an elite, enlightened white. Whether it was black music or Chinese food, an appreciation of exotic difference signaled one's aspiration to a higher class status. These ideas were spread through advertising and by an education system that began in the 1940s to promote this outlook on ethnicity and class.

By the end of the twentieth century, objects associated with ethnicity enjoyed a popular boom as commercial goods. Ethnic objects that had assumed the status of collectible art (such as African tribal masks and Native American totem poles), items of everyday use (such as Chinese woks and chopsticks or Scottish tartan kilts), performances of identity that could be consumed (ethnic music and dance): all were packaged as desirable objects of consumption. Ethnicity was something to be collected by a tasteful consumer able to appreciate an array of objects. This commercialization of ethnicity also allowed those who were identified as different to turn that identification into an object with value. Musical styles such as rhythm and blues, rock and roll, soul, rap, and hip-hop were marketed through an association with their black origins. By the 1970s, the commercialization of ethnicity extended to those ethnics who had been targets of xenophobia but were now comfortably white. White ethnics could continue to express cosmopolitan appreciation for the exoticism of nonwhites, but they could also embrace signs of their own ethnicity without fear of exclusion from the privileges of whiteness. White ethnicity was thus securely different from nonwhite racial ethnicity, and white ethnics drew on a history as victims of discrimination in ways that attenuated their own enjoyment of the privileges of being white, even as it evoked parallels to the historical suffering of nonwhites.

There are many long-term legacies of this history of ethnicity, including the rise of "whiteness studies" and the current use of the term "ethnicity" in the U.S. media to describe a wide array of subnational and transnational conflicts. The ethnic cultural theory that underwrites these legacies derived its popular appeal from the combination of two elements. One was the description of how European immigrants were transformed into white ethnics during the mid-twentieth century; the other was the hope that this social process would also work for U.S. Americans subordinated as nonwhite. However, the extension of what Nathan Glazer (1983, 92) called the "ethnic analogy" to the problems of racial hierarchy has often foundered because of a widespread belief that ethnicity is a matter of choice. This mistake is a direct result of the way the concept was modeled on the extension of the privileges of white supremacy to those who could voluntarily erase signs of their foreign origins and the withholding of those privileges from those who could not. The process of forgetting the historical origins of ethnicity in white supremacy continues today in arguments about its definition.

25

Fashion
Thuy Linh Tu

What is "fashion"? In contrast to "clothing" and "garments" (words that name the materials that are the basis of fashion) or sewing and tailoring (the processes that produce those materials), "fashion" names a relatively new cultural form. The term originated in the fourteenth century, derived from the French *facon* (meaning "manner, mode, or appearance") and the Latin *factionem* ("making or doing"). In its etymological origin, "fashion" referred to the acts of making and of displaying—to both object and labor—but this relationship has become increasingly obscured in the term's contemporary usage. A word that once implied both the object produced and the mode of its production is now commonly used to reference only the former, as fashionistas and fashion scholars alike become less concerned with who makes clothing (and under what conditions) than who wears it (and what this might say about their class positions, gender roles, ethnic affiliations, sexual proclivities, cultural zeitgeist, and so on).

Several historical developments contributed to the emergence of this new concept of fashion. Historians cite the introduction in the seventeenth century of the French couturier's guild, which allowed tailors to create clothing for nonaristocrats, as a key moment (E. Wilson 1985/2003). Once the couturiers set up shop, it became possible for anyone who could afford their services to be à la mode—to buy clothing, made by hands other than their own, which emphasized style rather than simply function. The rise of the industrial revolution in the nineteenth century, which allowed clothing to be made quickly and cheaply; the maturation in the mid-twentieth century of fashion design as a professional field separate from tailoring and sewing; the consequent growth of designer brands in the late twentieth century: all worked to imbue clothing with value beyond usefulness or even quality (N. Green 1997; McRobbie 1998; Entwistle 2000). These developments contributed to the transformation of clothing into fashion by turning clothing into a cultural object, one whose meaning is understood to be produced and circulated primarily through consumption and display.

Driven by rapidly changing style rather than need or utility, fashion came to be understood not just as clothing but also as a symbolic process. Foundational theorists of this understanding of fashion, ranging from Roland Barthes and Georg Simmel to Pierre Bourdieu and Dick Hebdige, have stressed the symbolic functions of fashion. For Simmel (1957), one of the earliest theorists, fashion serves in large part to maintain social distinctions, particularly class distinctions. Echoing Thorstein Veblen's earlier comments about the consumption habits of the leisure class (1899/1994), Simmel argued that members of lower classes wear certain styles of clothing to imitate those of the upper classes; the latter, in turn, dress to distinguish themselves from the former, often changing styles as they become more widely adopted. Indeed, knowing what is in and out of fashion becomes an important form of cultural capital and social power, in Bourdieu's formulation (1973).

Subsequent writings have disputed the kind of top-down model espoused by these early theorists, pointing out that fashion can circulate from street to runway, from subcultures to showrooms (Hebdige 1979), and that it can be a democratizing force, as Gilles Lipovetsky has provocatively argued (1994). Despite the different emphases of these theorists, they generally conclude that fashion is primarily about display and is one important way in which we visibly distinguish ourselves as groups and individuals. Fashion, they tell us, links our physical body to a social body and, like other cultural forms, allows us to construct meaning through acts of consumption and presentation. Popular discussions of fashion emphasize as well the importance of display, whether in "make-over" shows such as *What Not to Wear*, where a change in clothing provides visual proof of a change in person, or in "behind-the-scenes" programs such as *Project Runway*, where the making of fashion pales in comparison to its parade down the runway.

Yet not all consumers (or producers) of clothing can be fashionable. Almost all accounts of fashion locate its emergence within Western industrialized societies—societies capable, technologically and epistemologically, of change, growth, and modernization. As a result, fashion has become a global form—European couture can now be found from Accra to Abu Dhabi—that is primarily understood as being a product of the West. What the non-West has, instead, is garment, dress, costume, and attire, none of which is, strictly speaking, fashion or fashionable. What the non-West makes are either low-end garments for transnational firms or native costumes, neither of which is represented as demanding the input of local designers. In the former instance, the designer resides elsewhere; in the latter, the designer does not exist at all (those garments emerging, presumably, out of a collective tradition). In this sense, fashion is not just a product of Western modernity; it is also an index of the capacity to be modern. Clothing, as opposed to fashion, becomes one of the most visible ways in which a culture gets constructed as unchanging, backward even.

Such ideological distinctions have had the effect of cordoning off certain places and peoples as fashionable, with some important social and economic implications.

Consider as an example the early twenty-first-century convulsions around Arab dress. In the first decade of the century, designer labels from Givenchy and Versace to Galliano and Dior all dabbled in so-called Arab styles, sending them down the Parisian runway at the same moment that then French president Nicolas Sarkozy declared full-body coverings "not welcome" in France. Or think about the ways that Western cities—Paris, London, Milan, New York (and, much more recently, Tokyo)—are commonly accepted as sites of fashion production and taste construction, while cities in the non-West are embraced only as places for the less profitable or more labor-intensive garment production. As a result, countries such as China get courted as consumers of fashion, even as their own designers find it incredibly difficult to gain a foothold in the fashion marketplace—to be seen as producers of fashion.

When we make claims about fashion, then, about who and what is fashionable or unfashionable, we allow the term to embody a set of social, cultural, and economic positions. Far more than what we put on our bodies, fashion is one of the ways we mark, name, produce, and consume the various forms of difference that animate our social world. As such, fashion indexes much more than how we consume goods or display our identities. A critical approach to fashion requires that we take into account the term's full meaning, that we consider both make and mode, consumption and production, the material and the symbolic. Indeed, as recent scholars have shown, fashion can reveal how these are all in fact connected (Tu 2011; Paulicelli and Clark 2009; Root 2010).

26

Finance
Randy Martin

Finance today signals a whole range of ways in which culture, economy, and polity—the very fabric of material and symbolic life—have become interwoven. It maps a terrain where expert knowledge jostles uneasily with tacit understandings of the world, where enormous wealth becomes entangled with everyday poverty, where the future mingles with the present and the faraway with the very near. "Finance," as a noun or verb, along with "financialization" as a name for the process by which financial habits of thought have become prevalent across a wide array of fields and activities, has meanings and applications that shift depending on usage. This variation renders the term all the more challenging to grasp, even as the calamitous specter of households, businesses, nations, and global markets in default has made private matters of credit and debt objects of public consideration.

One reason for this confusion is that "finance," considered as a keyword, presents meanings that are both logically and practically conflicted. It appears in popular and academic discussions as a realm of imaginary speculation unmoored from the material labors of production and circulation, even as it points in those same discussions to the collapse of the distinction between the imaginary and the real. It is said to be both the source of our economic woes and the key to our future prosperity. Its complex mathematical formulae are held up as perfect information processors, self-regulating and best run without public oversight or government interference; yet the prominence of finance has spawned reams of rules and regulations.

When financial markets froze in 2008 and trillions in U.S. taxpayer dollars were put up as collateral to restore their health, the conventional meanings of public and private interests reversed. Once offered as proof of the reasonableness of private markets to organize and satisfy collective needs and wants, finance suddenly occasioned scenes of popular rage, confusion, and anxiety.

"Finance" once signified more narrowly. The *Oxford English Dictionary* traces the term to fifteenth-century French provenance, where it referred to settling a dispute or debt, paying a ransom, or supplying a contracted provision—the "fin" or final point of a transaction or exchange. It was not until the turn of the nineteenth century that the term's usage began to point toward the science of managing fiscal affairs in governments and corporations, along with what became the modern language of credit and economy (Poovey 2008). "Finance," in this context, refers to a means of amassing capital by underwriting the risks associated with the promise of future wealth through the issuance of bonds and other instruments of credit. Throughout the nineteenth century, finance capital fueled industrial and imperial expansion as investment houses developed increasingly sophisticated technologies for managing and profiting from economic risk and speculation. Out of these origins in the nineteenth and early twentieth centuries, financial logics and terms of art entered everyday speech only in the last quarter of the twentieth century. With the turn toward market-based thinking in public policy debates, finance began to provide a generalized vocabulary for modeling the management of risk across a wide array of arenas, ranging from the consequences of weather patterns to the assessment of schoolchildren's learning to disease and terrorism as threats to security (R. Martin 2002).

The colleges and universities in which this essay is most often read provide one instance of this financial turn in policy discourse. From the granting of land to create public universities through the nineteenth-century Morrill Act to subsidies for student tuition and campus operations in the twentieth century, major initiatives in higher-education policy have focused on inclusion and access. The assumption guiding these initiatives is that education is a public good essential to upward economic mobility and informed democratic citizenship. Beginning in the 1980s (partly as a result of the rise of the so-called knowledge economy and its ability to make intellectual pursuit profitable), financialization began to recast education as a private investment. For individual students, this shift has made college planning something to manage from cradle to grave, with families putting money into financial instruments such as stock-market-based 529 savings plans at birth. At the same time, public and private tuition continues to rise, as does average student-loan debt (the current number is over $20,000 per pupil). Taken as an aggregate, student-loan debt is approaching a trillion dollars and, as of 2011, exceeds consumer credit-card debt. For institutional investors in the global financial markets, this level of borrowing makes student loans a source of revenue or liquidity, particularly when the debt is bundled or securitized in ways that transform it into a long-term stream of income. The expectation that tuition (and debt) will continue to rise is now being used as collateral by some public-university administrations to secure favorable terms on bonds for construction projects. These strategic investments rationalize inequalities and cross-subsidies from lower-cost, instruction-intensive fields in the humanities and social sciences to the higher-cost fields of science, technology, engineering, and medicine that might promise returns on investment if enough money is risked. Contemporary metrics of educational excellence—national and international rankings, endowment size, grant making, intellectual property—eclipse other student-centered considerations of what education might be for and which values it should uphold (Meister 2011; R. Martin 2011; Newfield 2008).

As both a term and a technology, finance plays its greatest role when these types of substantial changes in the way business is conducted are afoot. Historians have detected patterns across periods of rapid monetary expansion: the rise of finance as a means of wealth making corresponds to the social decline of locations where finance is centered. Examples are Florence during the Renaissance (the early 1500s), Spain at the end of its century of conquest (the late 1500s), the Dutch at the end of their period of expansion (the late 1700s), and the British Edwardians at the sunset of their empire (the late 1900s). In each of these eras, the concentration of financial wealth and the leveraging of resources through finance capital were accompanied by dramatic polarizations between haves and have-nots, both between the imperial center and its colonial peripheries and within the center itself. In each instance, the middle class that helped to usher in the new wealth fell on hard times. The historical pattern distinct to financialization can be traced through the rapid accumulation of wealth that anoints a new global center of economic activity, the relative shift from industry to finance as the preferred mode of capital accumulation, the resulting rise of income polarization and decline of the middle class, and the resort to state coercion as the only means of governing an increasingly polarized population (Braudel 1981–84/1992; Arrighi 1994).

The United States entered this historical pattern when it began to take over dominance in global financial affairs from Britain at the end of the nineteenth century. In the early decades of the twentieth century, the United States expanded overseas, and its workers were converted through a process known as Fordism into middle-class consumers with access to credit for the cars and houses of their (American) dreams. After a decade of depression and doubt whose nadir corresponded to relinquishing the gold standard as the means of undergirding currency value, the nation emerged victorious from World War II as the guardian of a system of international exchange that pegged the worth of all currencies to the dollar. The United States enjoyed the economic and political privileges of monetary sovereignty since it controlled the rules of the game as a result of the Bretton Woods agreements of 1944 (agreements that installed the International Monetary Fund and the World Bank as global financial institutions). But it also took on the responsibilities of being the standard currency. In the 1970s, economic growth among European and petroleum-exporting countries outstripped the U.S. government's ability to hold adequate dollar reserves. As the financial architecture installed at Bretton Woods unraveled, exchanges of money, credit, and debt became the province of a massive multinational financial-services complex.

The significance of this shift cannot be overstated. As a result of the slow transition from industry to finance as the cardinal mode of wealth making in the United States, the government's role as guardian of the economy shifted from stimulating growth and developing the nation's human capital to guaranteeing the security of transnational monetary flows and shifting financial risk onto its citizenry (Hacker 2006). From the 1970s to the present day, organized labor has come under assault due to its commitment to viable working-class lives, and wages have flatlined or declined. Expanding consumer credit and access to appreciating equity (stock-based pensions or mortgage-based homeownership) has taken up the slack of wealth production for the middle class. The credit wings of venerable manufacturers such as General Motors and General Electric have become their most profitable divisions. As finance has become more pervasive, the concept of risk has also risen in significance. Understood as the calculable measure of potential future gain, the capacity to act now by living in anticipation of what may come to pass, risk makes of finance both a calculation and a feeling. When queried as to the ideal mix of investments, financial planners invite their clients to answer for themselves, "Can you sleep at night?" This question shows that financial decision-making may be more emotional than rational or, in the words of Raymond Williams (1977/1997, 128–35), that it may provide a "structure of feeling"—an inchoate and emergent sensibility underlying many aspects of contemporary life. As financial thinking has spread from the rarified precincts of capital to the sinews and microfibers of middle-class planning and self-fashioning, both assets and populations have begun to be sorted according to who can bear or manage risk (the virtuous self-managers of risk) and who cannot (the "at-risk" populations in need of management).

When the decades of heightened financial risk taking incentivized by neoliberal policy reforms boiled over in the crisis of 2007–8, the understanding of finance as a parasite on something else called the real economy took hold. The effects of this conventional way of thinking about finance were diverse: anti-Semitic images of greedy bankers running Ponzi schemes were recycled from the Crusades and the Christian prohibitions on usury; racialized representations of "at-risk" populations reawakened ideological associations of poverty with the failures of individual self-control. Odd political bedfellows were created as Tea Party populists chafed at taxpayer money propping up failed banks and liberal Democrats blamed insufficient regulation for the creation of financial firms that were too big to fail, thus giving the scoundrels a pass. Leftists declared with a mix

of hope and longing that the burst bubble portended a capitalist collapse (R. Brenner 2003; Foster and Magdoff 2009). At the same time, these political effects distracted attention from the structural significance of the contemporary interweaving of economics, politics, and culture. Finance devoured or outpaced regulation, relied heavily on state intervention, and exacerbated the coercive aspects of the market. It relied on a double vision of moral hazard and moral panic. The first worried about rewarding the bad behavior of the bailed out, both rich and poor; the second referred to those blemished subprime-mortgage borrowers who, as carriers of bad debt, required preemptive action through foreclosure (R. Martin 2010).

For both cultural studies and American studies, this interweaving of the material and the symbolic—what Marxists refer to as the economic base and political superstructure—should provide an opportunity to recognize the ways in which productive activities are now closely integrated with financial circuits of social reproduction. This recognition provides a suppler grasp of the current situation. Whereas Karl Marx invited us to treat the culture of capitalism from the vantage of its apparent singularity, the commodity, the cognate analytic move today requires that we approach the culture of finance from its most salient manifestation, the derivative (Bryan and Rafferty 2006; LiPuma and Lee 2004). Derivatives are financial contracts that work like insurance policies; a premium is paid by an investor to hedge against the unanticipated outcomes of speculation on future events. As such, derivatives have a face or notional value many times what they are bought and sold for. On the eve of the subprime-mortgage crash in 2007, derivative contracts had a face value of over a quadrillion dollars, nearly fifteen times the global gross domestic product—the standard measure of the value of goods and services. These instruments for speculating on and managing risks by bundling together attributes of commodities-in-exchange (interest, mortgage, currency exchange, and other variable rates) were the principle medium of profit making among the investment banks and hedge-fund managers who purportedly drag raced the economy off the cliff in 2008.

The challenge we face today demands that we neither moralize about derivatives as financial instruments nor await the next cyclical downturn to be able to say "I told you so." Rather, we need to trace the generalized social logic of risk that the derivative epitomizes so as to locate new horizons of possibility for human association. Derivatives provide financial leverage; they take local attributes and render them of interest to global circuits of exchange. Mortgage rates, once governed by neighborhood savings and loans, are now spliced together according to their credit rating and traded internationally. These far-flung, highly diversified portfolios quickly came back to bite investors and homeowners, restructuring entire neighborhoods along the way. This is the spatial dimension of the derivative. Its temporal aspect works similarly since it makes the future actionable in the present. This ability to act on opportunities before all their conditions have been realized is one feature of the culture of neoliberal and market-based thought and policy with which we live today. But it may also underwrite the confidence in speculation that characterizes the do-it-yourself counterculture of hacking, mash-ups, and self-production. The temporality of finance insinuates the future in the present; the possible becomes actionable now.

If finance were not imagined as an end in itself, it could become a means of making common claims on the enormous aggregations of wealth in our midst. The result could be a rethinking of our mutual indebtedness, away from the intonations of moral turpitude that blame the individual victims of financial miscalculation and toward more expansive and appreciative claims that we are able to make on one another (Dienst 2011). For cultural studies and American studies, finance should force us to consider the means we use to value how we perform, what we produce, where we are accountable and mutually interdependent. In the early twenty-first century, finance has brought an end to a certain U.S.-centered dreamscape, but it should also allow us to mine its ruins to see what else we might make of the surpluses it has created. It names the politics we have made but have not yet found the means to value.

27

Freedom
Stephanie Smallwood

"Freedom" is a keyword with a genealogy and range of meanings that extend far beyond the history and geographical boundaries of the United States, even as it names values that are at the core of U.S. national history and identity. From the Declaration of Independence to Operation Enduring Freedom (the name given to the post-9/11 U.S. military intervention in Afghanistan), the term is at the root of U.S. claims to being not only exceptional among the world's nations but a model that others should follow. The *Oxford English Dictionary* defines "freedom" in abstract terms as "the state or fact of being free from servitude, constraint, [or] inhibition." But dictionary definitions cannot reveal the materiality of the specific contests through which freedom has attained its central place in modern Western understandings of self and society. While the term's etymological roots and core attributes date to the classical societies of ancient Greece and Rome, "freedom" gained its contemporary significance in the context of western Europe's transition from an ancien régime (comprising passive subjects over whom monarchs claimed divinely sanctioned absolute rule) to the era of the secular state (comprising citizen-subjects who consent to be governed through social contract).

Against the divinely ordained absolute rule of a singular sovereign in the seventeenth and eighteenth centuries, the discourse of freedom posited the popular sovereignty of the civic collective—a plurality composed of autonomous individuals possessed of purportedly natural, and therefore primordial, rights. This rights-bearing individual was the newly ascendant

being around whom the core tenets of political freedom took shape—liberalism's claim that government exists to protect and guarantee the rights of the individual, the republican celebration of representative rule, and the leveling discourse of equality. Two related features that powerfully shaped this individualist understanding of freedom in the early modern West were its possessive quality and its universalist rhetoric. "Every man has a property in his own person," John Locke wrote in his highly influential *Second Treatise of Government* (1690/1988). Reflecting the penetration of market relations across northwest Europe in the seventeenth century, Locke's framing meant that freedom was conceptualized as something that resulted from an individual's ability to possess things and as something one experienced as though it was a possession itself (Macpherson 1962).

This understanding of freedom is paradoxical. The individual celebrated by the modern Western theory of freedom was male, and his purportedly self-produced economic independence derived at least in part from the labor of wives, children, servants, and other dependents whose political subjectivity was subsumed under his patriarchal authority. Shifting discourses of gender, race, and class, among others, rendered these relations of appropriation natural and self-evident elements of freedom's core conditions of possibility (K. Brown 1996; G. Brown 2001; J. Morgan 2004). By the end of the eighteenth century, the ideal of an expanding horizon of self-possessed (male) individuals was nowhere more fully realized than in British North America, where white men enjoyed lives remarkably independent of traditional institutions such as the family, church, or state, making them "the freest individuals the Western world had ever known" (Appleby 1992, 155). At the same time, the independent state that emerged out of the American Revolution gave the doctrine of possessive individualist freedom its ultimate expression with its institutionalization of racial slavery (D. Davis 1975; Blackburn 1988; Berlin 1998). Although the triumvirate of "life, liberty, and property" (or generalized "pursuit of happiness") was a commonly deployed phrase across the eighteenth-century Anglo-Atlantic world, these abstractions took materialized form for Thomas Jefferson, Patrick Henry, and other slaveholding architects of the radical American experiment in political freedom through the transmutation of property in one's "own person" into property in the full personhood of others.

Numerous writers of the period recognized that holding property in the personhood of others while waging a war for freedom defined as universal individual autonomy charted a path of logical inconsistency. "Would any one believe," Patrick Henry wrote in private correspondence, "that I am Master of Slaves of my own purchase! I am drawn along by ye general inconvenience of living without them, I will not, I cannot justify it" (1773/1957, 300). That a "people who have been struggling so earnestly to save *themselves* from slavery" were nonetheless "very ready to enslave *others*" was a problem put before Jefferson by his friend Richard Price (1785/1953, 259). Henry's admission that slavery produced "conveniences" that he would not relinquish offered an answer to Price's concern.

Among the most trenchant interpretive interventions regarding the relationship of freedom to slavery has been the suggestion that the former was produced by the latter. It was no accident that the leading authors of a North American revolutionary theory of freedom were men whose experience of individual autonomy derived from slavery. Put simply, the North American theory of freedom used racial exclusion to solve the problem posed by its egalitarian rhetoric. The elite planter, middling proprietor, and poor tenant were "equal in not being slaves"—equal, that is, in being white. The new republic's universal freedom was marked by color from its inception (E. Morgan 1975, 381; Fields 1990; C. Harris 1993; Dain 2002; Waldstreicher 2010). Jefferson gave voice to this racialized and racializing freedom in his *Notes on the State of Virginia* when he concluded a lengthy exegesis on slavery and race with the opinion that black inferiority troubled the prospect of slave emancipation. For Jefferson, granting freedom to enslaved African Americans introduced the "second" and "necessary" step of forced exile: once freed, the emancipated African American would have to be "removed beyond the reach of mixture" (1787/2002, 181). Half a century later, Abraham Lincoln likewise gave voice to the mainstream white sentiment that black freedom within the space of the U.S. nation-state was unthinkable (1854/1953).

The understanding of freedom produced by the founding and early maturation of the U.S. nation-state thus turned on an understanding of possessive individualist freedom whose purported expansiveness was from the start circumscribed by gendered and racialized structures of exclusion and domination (Saxton 1990; Roediger 1991, 1999; Bederman 1995; Zagarri 2007). Because it relied on the theory that some humans were categorically superior to others, its universalist rhetoric worked not to realize individual autonomy for all humans but to secure the particular interests of propertied white men by naturalizing those interests and the relations of subordination required to produce and sustain them (Trouillot 1995; Lowe 2006; Welke 2010). But these dominant understandings of freedom did not emerge without contestation. From the antislavery movement of the antebellum period through subsequent "rights" movements on behalf of women, African Americans, workers, Chicanos, Native Americans, homosexuals, and Asian, Latino, and other immigrant communities, the boundaries of freedom have been redrawn and stretched beyond anything that its propertied white male architects would recognize or condone (V. Deloria 1969/1988; Okihiro 1994; Foner 1998; Mariscal 2005; MacLean 2006).

Explaining these contestations of the meaning and practice of freedom has been one of the most important interpretive challenges for scholars. At stake in this question are two problems: how to tell the story of the expansion of freedom and how to assign responsibility for the positive transformations of freedom in U.S. society. The mainstream response to these questions, generally associated with liberalism, understands the universalist rhetoric of the founding discourse of North American freedom as predestining freedom's expansion across time and space. It positions events such as the Emancipation Proclamation, the ratification of the Nineteenth Amendment to the U.S. Constitution, the 1964 Civil Rights Act, and the *Roe v. Wade* Supreme Court decision as signposts along the march toward an ever-more-true expression of the nation's ideals. This narrative tends to locate the nation's founding patriarchs at its center, making their genius the catalyst that sets freedom's expansion in motion. The underlying logic produces the claim that to fault the nation's founders for what they did not do (their failure to extend freedom to nonwhites and women) is to miss the larger and more important point: namely, that it was their revolution that "made possible the eventual strivings of others—black slaves and women—for their own freedom, independence, and prosperity" (Wood 1992, 368).

Countering this narrative, a diverse body of scholarship has argued that the problem with this liberal approach to the paradox of freedom is that it represents the movement from past to present teleologically—as an already known eventuality. By figuring historical outcomes as evidence to support characterizations of the past as we wish it to have been, it disavows the lives and stories of those whose subjugation produced the very conditions for modern freedom's emergence and whose own freedom was a dream made real only by their revolutionary initiative. At stake here is not just recognition of agency for its own sake but an accounting for the material politics of insurgent agency in pursuit of more radical understandings of freedom. One of the key achievements of this scholarship has been to illuminate the politics of freedom's expansions and transformations across U.S. history (Du Bois 1935/1998; Hartman 1997; Linebaugh and Rediker 2000; Smallwood, 2004; Bruyneel 2007). This work, which is varied in its subjects, methods, and conceptual approaches, shares an understanding of the expansion of freedom not as inevitable but as produced by the radical organizing and activism of those for whom freedom was never intended. Their struggles have generated understandings that run counter to the liberal progressive narrative of freedom's inevitable expansion, reflecting what one scholar has called the "historical politics of time-making" (W. Johnson 2002, 152).

The theory and practice of the black freedom struggles of the twentieth century provide one illustrative instance of a sense of temporality at odds with the liberal progressive narrative. Half a century after legal emancipation, the Great Migration carried millions of black southerners to cities such as New York, Chicago, and Los Angeles "looking for a free state to live in" and was characterized as a "second emancipation" (Foner 1998, 174; Grossman 1989; F. Griffin 1995; Hunter 1997; Sernett 1997; P. Ortiz 2005). Civil rights activists in the South likewise understood their struggle to make real the freedoms promised a century earlier by such Reconstruction measures as the Fourteenth and Fifteenth Amendments to the U.S. Constitution as a "second reconstruction" (Woodward 1955; Kennedy

1963). This lexicon of serial repetition suggests that the passage of time marks not the steady, linear progression from slavery to freedom but rather the crisis and (dis)orientation of being stuck in the time and place of slavery. Unable to move into a reliably free present, one cannot confidently assign slavery to the past. This circular temporality is captured in the metaphor used by Rev. Willie David Whiting, a black Floridian who was initially rejected at the polls in the 2000 U.S. presidential election on the false charge that he was a convicted felon, when he described his experience in testimony before a U.S. Civil Rights Commission: "I felt like I was sling-shotted back into slavery" (Adam C. Smith 2003). The same insight is expressed by the protagonist of Ralph Ellison's *Invisible Man*, who warns of history's "boomerang" effect (R. Ellison 1952/1995, 6; Singh 2004, 55).

Meaningful analysis of such a lexicon of freedom and archive of struggle requires a willingness to take seriously its alternate understanding of the social conditions from which its temporality derives. Following the murder of James Chaney, the black civil rights activist killed along with white co-workers Andrew Goodman and Michael Schwerner during the "Freedom Summer" campaign to register black voters in Mississippi in 1964, Ella Baker decried the fact that Chaney's was not the only black body desecrated in the region's muddy waters. "Until the killing of black mothers' sons is as important as the killing of white mothers' sons, we who believe in freedom cannot rest," she famously proclaimed (quoted in Ransby 2003, 335). The refrain "we who believe in freedom cannot rest" was revived by protesters in 2013 when a Florida court found that George Zimmerman was not criminally responsible for the death of Trayvon Martin, the unarmed black teenager he pursued and shot in "self-defense" (McGrory 2013; M. Edelman 2013). The mass incarceration of black men, the Supreme Court's gutting of the 1965 Voting Rights Act, and the Zimmerman verdict can all be taken to indicate that time need not march forward in lockstep with freedom's steady expansion. Rather, the temporality of black freedom always threatens to carry the unfreedoms of the past forward into the present (A. Davis 2003, 2012; R. Gilmore 2007; Blackmon 2008; Michelle Alexander 2010). Replete with phrases and terms such as "turn back the clock," "rollback," and "reversal," discussion of current legal challenges to women's health and reproductive rights suggests another domain in which freedom's temporality does not conform to the steady forward progression posited by the liberal narrative (Roberts 1998; Stolberg 2009; Sanders 2012).

We must also recognize that as the dominant liberal understanding of freedom produces its subject through bourgeois, heteronormative, and patriarchal regimes of social control, it renders all who do not fit within those norms as deviant and subject to disciplinary regulation (Foucault 1975/1995; Wendy Brown 1995). To the extent that historical projects to expand the boundaries of freedom have reified and benefited from such regulatory regimes rather than questioning and troubling them, they have served to (re)produce barriers to emancipation for women of color, homosexuals, transgendered persons, differently abled persons, and other nonnormative subjects. Bringing otherwise-unaccounted-for experiences and practices of these groups into view reveals the intersectional politics of freedom's meanings and illuminates some of the most radical (and also most easily silenced) understandings of freedom. Whether rejecting the "freedom" to marry, refusing reformist agendas of rescue and uplift, or critiquing the "free labor" regimes of global capitalism, these alternative understandings foreground the disciplinary structures of hierarchy and control on which the normative liberal discourse of freedom turns and question whether winning membership in the circle of possessive individualist freedom is a viable strategy for effective emancipation (L. Davis 1995; Stanley 1998; Byrd 2011; Lowe 2009; Ferguson 2004; Hong 2006).

International and transnational frameworks offer equally important critiques of liberal understandings of freedom. From the seventeenth century to our present moment, the concept of freedom has been instrumental in authorizing colonial violence and has underwritten U.S. imperial agendas (Kaplan and Pease 1993; Von Eschen 1997; Renda 2001; Jung 2006; Smith-Rosenberg 2010). On the receiving end of U.S. foreign-policy initiatives, the concept of freedom has also served to render peoples "liberated" by U.S. interventions as indebted beneficiaries of the purported "gift" of freedom (Rodríguez-Silva 2005; Yoneyama 2005; Nguyen 2012). The disturbing imbrications of this "gift" have come to be especially evident in the post-9/11 era of the U.S. security state. In 2010, the Matthew Shepard and James Byrd, Jr. Hate Crimes Prevention Act was signed into law by being tethered to the National Defense Authorization Act. Pairing civil rights with national security, this legislation extends federal protection against hate crime to actual or perceived members of the gay/lesbian/bisexual/transgender/queer (GLBTQ) community through the mechanism of the largest-ever appropriation of funds to the nation's military. That such a coupling has not drawn critique suggests a contemporary political culture in which freedom is produced with and through violence. What does it mean, we must ask, to pursue "homosexual emancipation" through the "sustenance and growth of the military," particularly when victims of unmanned drone strikes are increasingly the target of U.S. military action undertaken under the banner of "freedom" (Reddy 2011, 5; Melamed 2011; Randall Williams 2010)?

A growing body of American studies and cultural studies scholarship suggests that the duality of freedom and various unfreedoms is best understood not as a paradox awaiting resolution by the teleological unfolding of the United States' ever-more-perfect and self-correcting expression of its destiny. Rather, it should be seen as evidence that the possessive individualist freedom enshrined in U.S. modernity depends on and requires the unfreedom of some category of fellow humans. Given this long and complex history, it may be that the pressing question today is whether a fully universal human liberation is thinkable through normative logics of freedom in the United States.

28

Gender

Jack Halberstam

In American studies and cultural studies, as in the humanities more broadly, scholars use the term "gender" when they wish to expose a seemingly neutral analysis as male oriented and when they wish to turn critical attention from men to women. In this way, a gender analysis exposes the false universalization of male subjectivity and remarks on the differences produced by the social marking we call "sex" or "sexual difference." Poststructuralist feminist theory queries this common usage by suggesting that the critique of male bias or gender neutrality comes with its own set of problems: namely, a premature and problematic stabilization of the meaning of "woman" and "female." In 1990, Judith Butler famously named and theorized the "trouble" that "gender" both performs and covers up. In doing so, she consolidated a new form of gender theory focused on what is now widely (and variably) referred to as "performativity." In recent years, this focus on gender as something that is performed has enabled new modes of thinking about how the transgendered body is (and can be) inhabited, about the emergence of queer subcultures, and about practices that promise to radically destabilize the meaning of all social genders.

As a term, "gender" comes to cultural studies from sexology, most explicitly from the work of psychologist John Money (Money and Ehrhardt 1972). Money is credited with (and readily claimed) the invention of the term in 1955 to describe the social enactment of sex roles; he used the term to formalize the distinction between bodily sex (male and female) and social roles (masculinity and femininity) and to note the frequent discontinuities between sex and role. Since sex neither predicts nor guarantees gender role, there is some flexibility built into the sex-gender system. This reasoning led Money to recommend sex reassignment in a now infamous case in which a young boy lost his penis during circumcision. Given the boy's young age, Money proposed to the parents that they raise him as a girl and predicted that there would be no ill effects. Money's prediction proved disastrously wrong, as the young girl grew up troubled and eventually committed suicide after being told about the decisions that had been made on his/her behalf as a baby.

This case has reanimated claims that gender is a biological fact rather than a cultural invention and has led some medical practitioners to reinvest in the essential relationship between sex and gender. It has also been used by some gender theorists to argue that the gendering of the sexed body begins immediately, as soon as the child is born, and that this sociobiological process is every bit as rigid and immutable as a genetic code. The latter claim (concerning the immutability of socialization) has been critiqued by poststructuralist thinkers who suggest that our understanding of the relation between sex and gender ought to be reversed: gender ideology produces the epistemological framework within which sex takes on meaning rather than the other way around (Laqueur 1990; Fausto-Sterling 1993).

All of these arguments about how we ought to talk and think about sex and gender assume a related question about how the modern sex-gender system came into being in the first place. Different disciplines answer this question differently. In anthropology, Gayle Rubin's work on "the traffic in women" (1975) builds on Claude Lévi-Strauss's structuralist analysis of kinship (1971) to locate the roots of the hierarchical organization of a binary gender system in precapitalist societies in which kinship relied on incest taboos and the exchange of women between men. Esther Newton's (1972) ethnographic research on drag queens in Chicago in the 1960s and 1970s finds gender to be an interlocking system of performances and forms of self-knowing that only become visible as such when we see them theatricalized in the drag queen's cabaret act. In sociology, Suzanne Kessler and Wendy McKenna (1990) have produced a brilliant handbook on the production of gendered bodies, providing readers with a vocabulary and a set of definitions for the study of gender as a system of norms.

Working across these disciplinary formations, American studies and cultural studies scholarship on gender continues under numerous headings and rubrics. Researchers studying the effects of globalization have paid particular attention to transformations in the labor of women under new phases of capitalism (Enloe 1989; Kempadoo and Doezema 1998). Scholars working on race have traced very specific histories of gender formation in relation to racial projects that attribute gender and sexual pathology to oppressed groups. In African American contexts, for example, black femininity has often been represented as vexed by the idealization of white femininity on the one hand and the cultural stereotyping of black women as strong, physical, and tough on the other (Hammonds 1997). Other scholars seeking to denaturalize cultural conceptions of manhood have examined masculinity in terms of new forms of work, new roles for men in the home, the function of racialized masculinities, new styles of classed masculinity, the impact of immigrant masculinities on national manhood, and the influence of minority and nonmale masculinities on gender norms (Bederman 1995; Sinha 1995; Harper 1996). Queer theorists have detached gender from the sexed body, often documenting the productive nature of gender variance and its impact on the way gender is understood and lived.

In all of these research contexts, gender is understood as a marker of social difference, a bodily performance of normativity and the challenges made to it. It names a social relation that subjects often experience as organic, ingrained, "real," invisible, and immutable; it also names a primary mode of oppression that sorts human bodies into binary categories in order to assign labor, responsibilities, moral attributes, and emotional styles. In recent years, cultural work dedicated to shifting and rearticulating the signifying field of gender has been ongoing in queer and transgender subcultures. Drag-king shows, for example, have developed along very different lines than their drag-queen counterparts (including those documented by Newton). While drag queens tend to embody and enact an explicitly ironic relation to gender that has come to be called "camp," drag kings often apply pressure to the notion of natural genders by imitating, inhabiting, and performing masculinity in intensely sincere modes. Whereas camp formulations of gender by gay men have relied heavily on the idea that the viewer knows and can see the intense disidentifications between the drag queen and femininity, drag-king acts more often depend on the sedimented and earnest investments made by the dyke and trans performers in their masculinities. Drag-king acts disorient spectators and make them unsure of the proper markings of sex, gender, desire, and attraction. In the process, such performances produce potent new constellations of sex and theater (Halberstam 1998).

Understood as queer interventions into gender deconstruction, drag-king performances emerge quite specifically from feminist critiques of dominant masculinities. In this sense, they can be viewed as growing out of earlier practices of feminist theory and activism. Consider Valerie Solanas's infamous and outrageous 1968 *SCUM Manifesto* (SCUM stood for "Society for Cutting Up Men"), in which she argued that we should do away with men and attach all the positive attributes that are currently assigned to males to females. As long as we have sperm banks and the means for artificial reproduction, she argued, men have become irrelevant. While Solanas's manifesto is hard to read as anything more than a Swiftian modest proposal, her hilarious conclusions about the redundancy of the male sex ("he is a half-dead, unresponsive lump, incapable of giving or receiving pleasure or happiness; consequently he is an utter bore, an inoffensive blob," etc. [1968/2004, 36]) take a refreshingly extreme approach to the gender question. The performative work of the manifesto (its theatricalization of refusal, failure, and female anger and resentment; its combination of seriousness and humor) links it to contemporary queer and transgender theaters of gender. Like Solanas's manifesto, drag-king cultures offer a vision of the ways in which subcultural groups and theorists busily reinvent the meaning of gender even as the culture at large confirms its stability.

It is revealing, then, that Solanas is at once the most utopian and dystopian of gender theorists. While Butler, in her commitment to deconstructive undecidability, cannot possibly foretell any of gender's possible futures (even as she describes how gender is "done" and "undone"), Solanas is quite happy to make grand predictions about endings. Many academic and nonacademic gender theorists after Solanas have also called for the end of gender, noted the redundancy of the category, and argued for new and alternative systems of making sense of bodily difference (Bornstein 1994; Kessler 1998). But socially sedimented categories are hard to erase, and efforts to do so often have more toxic effects than the decision to inhabit them. Other theorists, therefore, have responded by calling for more categories, a wider range of possible identifications, and a more eclectic and open-ended understanding of the meanings of those categories (Fausto-Sterling 2000). It

seems, then, that we are probably not quite ready do away with gender, or with one gender in particular, but we can at least begin to imagine other genders.

Whether by manifesto or reasoned argumentation, scholars in the fields of American studies and cultural studies have made gender into a primary lens of intellectual inquiry, and the evolution of gender studies marks one of the more successful versions of interdisciplinarity in the academy. Indeed, as U.S. universities continue to experience the dissolution of disciplinarity, a critical gender studies paradigm could well surge to the forefront of new arrangements of knowledge production. At a time when both students and administrators are questioning the usefulness and relevance of fields such as English and comparative literature, gender studies may provide a better way of framing, asking, and even answering hard questions about ideology, social formations, political movements, and shifts in perceptions of embodiment and community. Gender studies programs and departments, many of which emerged out of women's studies initiatives in the 1970s, are poised to make the transition into the next era of knowledge production in ways that less interdisciplinary areas are not. The quarrels and struggles that have made gender studies such a difficult place to be are also the building blocks of change. While the traditional disciplines often lack the institutional and intellectual flexibility to transform quickly, gender studies is and has always been an evolving project, one that can provide a particularly generative site for new work that, at its best, responds creatively and dynamically to emerging research questions and cultural forms, while also entering into dialogue with other (more or less established) interdisciplinary projects, including cultural studies, American studies, film studies, science studies, ethnic studies, postcolonial studies, and queer studies.

GENDER JACK HALBERSTAM

29

Globalization

Lisa Lowe

"Globalization" is a contemporary term used in academic and nonacademic contexts to describe a late twentieth- and early twenty-first-century condition of economic, social, and political interdependence across cultures, societies, nations, and regions that has been precipitated by an unprecedented expansion of capitalism on a global scale. One problem with this usage is that it obscures a much longer history of global contacts and connections. In the ancient world, there were empires, conquests, slavery, and diasporas; in medieval and early modern times, Asian, Arab, and European civilizations mingled through trade, travel, and settlement. Only with European colonial expansion, beginning in the sixteenth century and reaching its height in the nineteenth, did global contacts involve western European and North American dominance; the rise of Western industrialized modernity, made possible by labor and resources in the "new world" of the Americas, was, in this sense, a relatively recent global interconnection. Yet today, the term "globalization" is used to name a specific set of transformations that occurred in the late twentieth century: changes in world political structure after World War II that included the ascendancy of the United States and the decolonization of the formerly colonized world; a shift from the concept of the modern nation-state as bounded and independent toward a range of economic, social, and political links that articulate interdependencies across nations; and an acceleration in the scale, mode, and volume of exchange and interdependency in nearly all spheres of human activity.

Even with this caveat, globalization is not a self-evident phenomenon, and the debates to which it gives rise in American studies, cultural studies, and elsewhere mark it as a problem of knowledge. For economists, political scientists, sociologists, historians, and cultural critics, globalization is a phenomenon that exceeds existing means of explanation and representation. It involves processes and transformations that bring pressure on the paradigms formerly used to study their privileged objects—whether society, the sovereign nation-state, national economy, history, or culture—the meanings of which have shifted and changed. Globalization is both celebrated by free-market advocates as fulfilling the promises of neoliberalism and free trade and criticized by scholars, policymakers, and activists as a world economic program aggressively commanded by the United States and enacted directly through U.S. foreign policies and indirectly through institutions such as the World Bank, the International Monetary Fund, and the World Trade Organization, exacerbating economic divides, with devastating effects for the poor in "developing" countries and in systematically "underdeveloped" ones (Amin 1997; Stiglitz 2002; Pollin 2003).

Political scientists argued in the 1980s that the global expansion of the economy had created asymmetries among nations and regions that provided sources of "complex interdependence" (Keohane and Nye 1989). Adherents of the "neoliberal" school of political science, dominant for nearly two decades, agreed that international laws and institutions, global commerce, and diplomatic networks of cooperation had lessened the need for war and militarism. Yet since 2001 and the unilateral U.S. invasions of Afghanistan and Iraq, the U.S. government has embraced "neoconservative" political thinking, reviving "neorealist" arguments from the Cold War period to contend that despite economic or social links between nations, "national security" has never ceased to be the most important issue and that war constitutes a viable, "rational," and effective instrument of policy and of wielding power (Kagan and Kagan 2000). Such lethal contentions about the nature of global conditions have demonstrated that the epistemological problem of what can be known about globalization is never distant from ethical or political issues of life and death.

Sociologists adopted Max Weber's (1968) early twentieth-century observations about the contradictions of rationalizing modernity within a single society to study globalization as an acceleration and expansion of capitalist bureaucracy through transnational corporations (Sklair 1991). In this view, globalization both deepens the interconnection *and* widens the dissymmetries represented as "core" and "periphery" in an earlier "world-system" (Wallerstein 1976). At the same time, cultural critics observed that flexible capital accumulation and mixed production fragmented subjectivities and collectivities according to a "cultural logic of postmodernism" (Jameson 1991), an apparent shrinking or elimination of distances and a general compression of time (Harvey 1989). The rise of a new "global" culture composed of cross-border communities, multilingual immigrants, and syncretic religions revised earlier presumptions that place, culture, language, and identity could be mapped neatly onto one another (Gupta and Ferguson 1992; Sassen 1998; Fregoso 2003). The coexistence of migrant diasporas and indigenous peoples creates material imaginaries dictated less by citizenship and traditional national sovereignty than by new social identities and overlapping affinities (Appadurai 1996; Clifford 1997). At the same time, some social identities are policed, and criminalized, by the refortified articulations of "national security" states.

One position in debates about the globalization of culture argues that globalization is a form of cultural imperialism that has eroded nation-states and flattened national cultural differences through the vast spread of consumerism (Miyoshi 1993). Another emphasizes that global encounter, migration, and contact have produced more hybrid forms of "cultural complexity" (Hannerz 1992). The best critical cultural studies of globalization move beyond the polarized theses of cultural imperialism or hybridization, or the simplified idea that culture flows from center to margin, overcoming or corrupting the periphery. To study "culture" within globalization is to understand it neither as merely commodified nor as simply the inert effects or ideological correlative of transnational capitalism. Rather, contemporary culture, as the "structure of feeling" of globalization (Raymond Williams 1977/1997, 128–35), mediates the uneven spaces linked through geohistorical, political, economic, and social logics (P. Taylor 1999). Whether it is the medium through which groups are persuaded to live and die as patriotic subjects or the inspiration for their transgression or protest, "culture" expresses dynamic contradictions precisely at those intersections, borders, and zones where normative regimes contact, enlist, restrict, or coerce. Critical studies of the place of the United States within global processes may demonstrate, through the study of culture, that normative modes differentiate as they regulate, and discipline as they include and assimilate.

American studies follows this line of inquiry by situating U.S. culture (its traditional object) in an international context, from its origins up through contemporary globalization. It identifies in cultural products (literature, music, art, mass and popular cultures) and in cultural practices (the organization of cities and public spaces, schooling, religion) both the longer world history within which the United States

GLOBALIZATION LISA LOWE

emerged and the contemporary U.S. understanding of itself within a global entirety, increasingly yet unevenly mediated through electronic information technologies. Manuel Castells (2000) has suggested that state, military, and economic processes are now entirely coordinated, in real time across distances, through the vast reach of global information networks. As "information" becomes a pervasive new medium of global production, "cultures" of globalization will include information technologies, such as the Internet, as sites of both production and critique.

The restructuring of the U.S. economy by globalization has entailed a shift from vertically integrated national industries to transnational finance capitalism, a conversion of traditionally male jobs in manufacturing to more feminized forms of service operations, and an unsettling of historical neighborhoods by the influx of new transnational migrants. Communities of color in deindustrializing U.S. cities of the 1980s were hit hard by loss of jobs as manufacturing moved to export-processing zones in Asia and Latin America, even as the urban poor suffered from the simultaneous reduction of social welfare and buildup of the U.S. prison system (R. Gilmore 1998). Transnational immigration that appeared to bring more racial and ethnic diversity often rendered these worsening inequalities more complex and certainly more difficult to decipher. New comparative work on race considers U.S. cities as locations for understanding the history of racial inequalities and its rearticulation within neoliberal political and economic policies from the 1980s onward (James Lee 2004). Urban geographers have noted the colossal increase of impoverished, dispossessed populations in cities around the world, disconnected from industrialization or economic growth (M. Davis 2007b), while political theorists have observed the consolidation of U.S. capitalism through explicit war and covert military operations in East and Central Asia, the Pacific, Central America, and the Middle East (Mamdani 2004/2005; Shigematsu and Camacho 2010).

For some scholars in American studies and cultural studies, globalization signifies the "end" of modern U.S. myths of purity: of "man" as the white race, redeemed by the authenticity of rural life, as leader of the "free world" and "the American century." For others, it is a "crisis," a "chaos of governance," and the "end" of the Enlightenment, liberal humanism, or civil society. Noting the weakening of states and the waning social power of subordinated groups, some suggest that globalization changes the balance of power between "civilizations." Projected apocalyptically, it appears as a "clash of civilizations" between Western modernity and the Confucian-Islamic East (Huntington 1996). Others interpret Chinese modernization as a probable sign of emerging Asian economic supremacy (Krugman 1997). Still others herald the impact of antiglobalization movements, transnational feminism, global environmentalism, and international human rights activism and evaluate the possibilities for countering poverty and creating sustainable growth (Lowe and Lloyd 1997; Alexander and Mohanty 1997; Sen 1999). Some observe that transnational capitalism not only effects a "denationalization" of corporate power but also draws new workforces that express themselves in movements articulated in terms other than the "national," for example, in transnational feminist work by U.S. and UK women of color and immigrant women from the formerly colonized world (Sudbury 1998; Mohanty 2003; Hong 2006). Globalization not only "unbundles" the territorial organization of sovereignty, defying earlier maps of "core" and "periphery"; it also changes the means, agents, and strategies employed in contesting the "new world order." Global cities such as

New York, London, Tokyo, and São Paulo gather both the infrastructure to coordinate global finance and the transnational migrant workers who perform the service labors for these operations (Sassen 1991; Eade 1997). Women, immigrants, political prisoners, refugees, "squatters," and other nonstate subjects are among the important new social actors who are transforming how we ought to conceive of ethics, justice, and change in globalization.

30

Government
Leerom Medovoi

In common usage, the word "government" often refers to the individuals or parties that operate the state (as in "I support this government"). But it can equally refer to the institutional features of the state (as in a "constitutional" or "aristocratic" form of government). One result of this dual usage is that the practices of governance and the institution of the state are often treated as the same thing, even though their implications are quite different. The modern state, as a form of governance, is typically bound to the idea of the nation and its popular sovereignty. By contrast, government understood as an act of governing originally referred to such diverse activities as moral self-control, household management, or even the sailing of a ship (*Oxford English Dictionary*). One can today still talk about "governing" one's behavior, a budget, or an organization. "Government" thus refers first and foremost to the regulation of activity. The fact that the term has become so closely tied to the state, despite these broader meanings, reveals much about the path taken by modern strategies of power.

One influential approach to this paradox begins in a series of famous lectures by the French historian and philosopher Michel Foucault (2009). Foucault argues that government first emerged as a political idea during the sixteenth century, as an explicit alternative to the rule of the Machiavellian prince, whose goal was simply to stay in power. Foucault then points out that the prince's sovereign power was essentially circular, a force that sought only to maintain itself. In contrast, early advocates of government emphasized how a state might best mobilize people and things toward such concrete ends as wealth, health, or trade. With this new conception of government, the modern state for the first time began to regulate ordinary people's everyday lives. This shift from sovereign authority to governmental power initially meant greater efficiency in achieving various ends as defined by the state, but it gradually came to delineate a newly specified domain of human action (the economy) that the state would be specially tasked with governing, particularly through its management of populations. Both Foucault and Mitchell Dean have described this process as the "governmentalization" of the state or as the rise of "governmentality" (Foucault 2009; Dean 2009).

Some scholars have suggested that governmentality actually finds its practical origins in the histories of early modern slavery and colonization, both of which sought early on to regulate the labor, health, sexuality, and docility of subjected populations with the aim of increasing their productivity (Stoler 1995; D. Scott 1995; Lowe 2006). During the eighteenth century, these goals of colonial governmentality began to infiltrate the political projects of popular sovereignty in Britain, France, and the early United States, where the ideal of a democratic state presupposed a citizenry whose conduct made it capable of regulating itself. Governmentality thus helped to produce a modern distinction between the normal citizen, who is capable of self-governance, and abnormal subjects, against whom the ends of self-government must be secured and defended, often violently: blacks, queers, rebellious workers, criminals, or otherwise "unhealthy" populations. The resulting policing practices reveal important continuities between colonial governmentality and the modern state's deployments of race, sexuality, and other markers of population (Reddy 2011).

Viewing government as a new kind of political logic or rationality helps us to think about the rise of the modern state. It also allows us to consider the governmental dimension of social and cultural life. The policing of a population's conduct, after all, is hardly limited to state action. It has historically come to involve such disparate phenomena as fashion, education, public opinion, sexuality, and media arts. The range of venues where governmentality is enacted suggests that the political science approach to government—one that focuses on the state as a separate sphere of power and influence—could be fruitfully linked to humanistic and historical studies of the various cultural techniques through which the conduct of modern populations is regulated. The Australian cultural theorist Tony Bennett (1992) argues that we can best combine studies of government and culture by focusing on questions of cultural policy. Since culture is not simply a system of signifying practices or a way of life but also a "domain of morals, manners, codes of conduct" (26), it can be approached as both the object of government (what it seeks to change) and its instrument (how government seeks to intervene).

This proposition has begun to receive serious reflection in American studies (Bratich, Packer, and McCarthy 2003) and has been put to work by individual scholars. In recent years, it has resulted in a wide range of promising studies, including ones that explore the rise of demography in the nineteenth century in the United States as a spatial strategy of power (Hannah 2000), the uses of race making in administering post-9/11 "homeland security" (Grewal 2003), and the capacity of consumer niche marketing to regulate the social life of populations (Binkey 2007). Perhaps the most sustained investigations into U.S. cultural governmentality, however, are to be found in the historiography on U.S. sexuality, which has long studied the strategies of power served by the regulation of sexual conduct. John D'Emilio and Estelle Freedman (1988/1997), for instance, have explored how the ethos of sexual freedom motored twentieth-century consumption imperatives, while Julian Carter (2007) has shown how protocols of sexual heteronormativity worked to justify and maintain white supremacy after emancipation.

The origins of a non-state-based governmentality date back to the rise of classical liberalism in the eighteenth century. Classical liberalism differs greatly from what we mean by liberalism today (a welfare-state approach to the population's well-being, associated with John Maynard Keynes). As enshrined in such texts as the Declaration of Independence, classical liberalism is an ancestor of both modern liberalism and modern conservatism, advocating a political vision of personal liberty and human rights. Yet classical liberalism was no mere ideology. It was also a practical strategy of using indirect means to govern "at a distance," as Nikolas Rose and Peter Miller have put it (2008, 173–85). Liberalism rejects sovereign power—the direct state intervention into the life of the population—as an effective strategy of government. The colonial rebels thereby rejected the rule of the British monarch not on the grounds of sovereign right (he should not be ruling over this people) but on the grounds of poor government: he failed to secure the ends of "Life, Liberty, and the Pursuit of Happiness," which the Declaration presents as the sole reason that "governments are instituted among men." Likewise for Thomas Paine (1776/2005), while a state simply *was*, a government could be better or worse at achieving its proper ends: security and freedom.

Liberal governmentality gained special impetus in the United States, where the word "state" came to refer to the thirteen (and now fifty) states, each of which retained its status as a quasi-sovereign entity. "Government," meanwhile, became the only available word to describe the federal system by which these states would be constitutionally bound together for the sake of improved commerce, self-defense, and other economic ends. Liberalism advocates a minimal state as a means of achieving increased human freedom from government. The trouble is that not everyone is found suited to freedom, and against those populations, sovereign power has often been exercised by way of incarceration in prisons, asylums, or military camps. But for the "normative" population that can regulate itself, it turns out that freedom is actually the means to achieving a minimal state. By "freeing" us from state-run health care, we are made individually responsible for monitoring and arranging our own medical needs. By "freeing" us from state media "propaganda," we make consumer choices that actually pay a culture industry to regulate our opinions, tastes, and behavior. And by having us perform such governmental work ourselves, the cost of operating the state can be reduced and government made more "efficient." This is why, to paraphrase Nikolas Rose, freedom is not the antithesis of government but in fact one of its key inventions (1999).

For this project of a self-governing population, it turns out that culture and older definitions of "government" (moral conduct, household management) still matter. When conservative antitax activist Grover Norquist (2001) says that he wants to reduce government to the size that he can "drown it in the bathtub," he is expressing in particularly blunt terms the liberal dream of good government: the population takes on its own shoulders (through notions of personal responsibility, community service, proper sexual conduct, work habits, consumer activity) all of the regulatory objectives of the state. This idea is also reflected in more radical traditions, as in Henry David Thoreau's opening creed in "On Civil Disobedience," where he asserts that not only does he accept the slogan that the government is best that governs least but even that "that government is best which governs not at all" (1849/1966, 277). Is this not, in effect, the fantasy of an exercise of power so efficient that it requires no exertion of force whatsoever?

The more recent orthodoxy about politics and economics that is referred to as "neoliberalism" represents the latest permutation in liberal governmentality. Under neoliberalism, as political theorist Wendy Brown (2003) explains, social life is reorganized in ways that subject it to game theory rationality. The exercise of freedom is framed as the maximization of personal strategic investment in our own human capital, thereby encouraging choices that might serve governmental ends. The U.S. right wing claims to hate big government, but seen in this way, the freedom they espouse is simply a displacement of the technologies of government from the state to the scene of civil society. They prefer their government in homes, supermarkets, and neighborhood associations, understood as sites of competition, rather than through the agency of the state bureau.

The theory of governmentality, in all its forms, expands our notion of what government is or has been. Above all, it calls our attention to the self-serving and indeed misleading account of power that classic liberal governmentality propagates when it draws distinctions between the state (allegedly the unique seat of government) and civil society (the domain of personal freedom). Liberalism conveniently indicts the state as a force of repressive political power, even while it quietly insinuates the regulation of the populace ever deeper into civil society. This process only continues under neoliberal governmentality, which actively reshapes society as well as the state in the image of the market. In so doing, neoliberalism simply extends a longer tradition of governmentality here described. Whether acting as social individuals, cultural consumers, sexual agents, or citizens of the state, we have come to build the political order that governs us by exercising our freedoms.

31

Immigration
Eithne Luibhéid

Immigration is one of the most frequently discussed and multivalent concepts in scholarship on the U.S. experience. A subcategory within studies of "migration," "immigration" refers in the *American Heritage Dictionary* to the activity of "enter[ing] and settl[ing] in a region or country to which one is not native." The usage note at "migrate" adds, "*Migrate*, which is used of people or animals, sometimes implies a lack of permanent settlement, especially as a result of seasonal or periodic movement. *Emigrate* and *immigrate* are used only of people and imply a permanent move, generally across a political boundary." As this definition indicates, many kinds of relocation may be described in everyday vernacular as "immigration." In partial contrast, academic studies of immigration generally focus on geographic relocations across political boundaries, usually of nation-states. These relocations are often imagined as permanent, thus differentiating immigrants from groups such as temporary migrant laborers, tourists, business visitors, and international students. The note at "migrate" confirms this usage: "*Emigrate* describes the move relative to the point of departure. . . . By contrast, *immigrate* describes the move relative to the destination: *The promise of prosperity in the United States encouraged many people to immigrate.*"

Definitions such as this one tend to make nation-states seem natural, to overstate the extent to which both emigration and immigration involve individual choice, and to make mobile people visible primarily as problems for the state to manage. In contrast, the treatment of immigration in much recent work in

American studies and cultural studies focuses on historicizing the construction of nation-states and the peoples who populate them. It was only in the late nineteenth century that nation-states began to monopolize control over migration across international borders and to justify such controls as a matter of national sovereignty. During the second half of the nineteenth century, as waves of immigrants arrived from Europe, Asia, and the Americas, the United States nationalized its immigration policies and implemented them in increasingly exclusionary ways. Claims that immigration control involved national sovereignty were reinforced in the 1880s and 1890s through efforts to exclude Chinese immigrants on racial grounds. A national sovereignty framework meant that Congress's powers over immigration were not constrained by the Constitution and legitimized reduced due process protections and explicitly discriminatory practices including race-based exclusion (Erika Lee 2007). In the 1890s, the United States also acquired significant overseas territories, including the Philippines, Puerto Rico, Hawai'i, and Guam. In this expanding imperial context, immigration control gained significance as an expression of and tool for constituting an explicitly racialized national sovereignty.

The link between immigration control and national sovereignty both reinforced and was aided by the rise of a centralized state bureaucracy. Given the filtering demands of immigration policy, officials needed ways to establish clearly who belonged to the nation-state. This need, in turn, required the development of identity documents and systems of verification such as the passport, which became widely used after World War I (Torpey 2000). These documentation practices tied individuals to bureaucratic identities in ways that allowed for their monitoring and surveillance. Such practices did not map identities that people already had; rather, they were tools to divide up and classify populations in relation to state-making projects at local, national, and imperial levels. They depended on, deployed, and refined forms of racial, colonial, and sexual knowledge about bodies, and they relied on technologies such as photography and fingerprinting that developed in the context of empire, the transformation of policing, and the rise of human sciences (Wiegman 1997). Contemporary uses of biometric technologies have extended this history in new ways (Noiriel 1991).

Through these processes, "the immigrant" became defined as a person who crosses a nation-state boundary and takes on the legal status of "alien," with associated regimes of identification, surveillance, rights, and constraints. The figure of the "illegal immigrant" is produced through similar processes. Popularly treated as a sociological category, the "illegal" or undocumented immigrant actually refers not to any particular type of person but to the shifting ways in which the nation-state produces registers of legitimate and illegitimate entrants. While undocumented immigrants are denied many fundamental rights, their labor is often welcomed, even demanded. Furthermore, the construction of certain migrants as undocumented connects to histories of inequality between the United States and other nation-states within an imperial global order. For example, many scholars suggest that Mexicans have become the paradigmatic undocumented immigrants through historical, legal, political, and economic processes that derive from enduring neocolonial relationships between the United States and Mexico (Nevins 2002; M. Ngai 2004). Efforts to police undocumented immigrants are thoroughly implicated in the production of the nation-state in a manner that emphasizes its territorial borders. Since undocumented immigrants live inside the national territory, however, borders within the nation-state have also proliferated in a manner that often racializes Latin Americans, Asian Americans, and Middle Easterners as "foreigners" (while equating citizenship with whiteness).

Understanding that immigration control "illegalizes" particular migrants in an act of state power requires revising the common conception of immigration as a simple matter of individuals deciding to relocate permanently to another nation-state. This conception has been elaborated through theories of immigration as a consequence of push/pull forces or cost/benefit economic decision-making. These theories suggest, in line with the *American Heritage Dictionary*, that immigration is primarily driven by people making rational decisions to migrate due to poor conditions at home (poverty, repression, violence) and the promise of a better life elsewhere (wealth, freedom, peace). Other theories, in contrast, offer richer and more accurate understandings of the dynamics of immigration by exploring how histories of imperialism, invasion, investment, trade, and political influence create what Saskia Sassen (1992) theorizes as bridges linking regions within nation-states. While individuals certainly make choices, their choices are constrained and enabled by the global, national, and local histories that Sassen describes. And they are also influenced by social networks including family, friends, and community members and by intermediaries such as labor recruiters, attorneys, and smugglers.

Bridges for migration may also be created through more symbolic means, including narratives and images of immigration and immigrants (Chavez 2008). Common representations characterize the United States as a "nation of immigrants," a "melting pot," or a "multicultural mosaic." Such images naturalize histories of genocide, slavery, racialized patriarchy, and economic exploitation as necessary moments of national consolidation, thus contributing to a culture that normalizes and privileges white, male, middle-class, and heterosexual statuses. Images produce these normalizing effects in part by drawing on forms of expertise created and inhabited by sociologists, demographers, economists, policymakers, and health professionals. Such expertise never involves simply collecting and analyzing facts that already exist; rather, there is an ongoing and reciprocal relationship between governance and knowledge production. These types of expertise function in a complex relationship to more critical modes of scholarship. For instance, in the early twentieth century, Robert Park (1950) and the "Chicago school" social scientists effectively established the sociological study of immigration. Many of Park's concepts—such as the four-stage assimilation cycle of competition, conflict, accommodation, and assimilation—remain with us today. Park's scholarship contested the racist orthodoxy of his day but ultimately preserved whiteness and masculinity as unmarked national norms into which migrants were expected to assimilate and through which they were governed (Yu 2001).

Nonetheless, the meanings of images, representations, and forms of knowledge are always open to revision—as shown by immigrants and allies who have organized to counter negative imagery, to resist state practices of criminalization and marginalization, and to propose new forms of living, working, and belonging (Buff 2008; Das Gupta 2006; Louie 2001). Contemporary activism focuses on new political and laboring subjects who often live transnational lives, may be undocumented, and negotiate multiple forms of exploitation. Immigrant activism builds on and transforms historic struggles for civil, labor, feminist, queer, and anticolonial rights, offering new organizing strategies through social media and cross-border linkages and revitalizing challenges to exclusionary models of citizenship and the nation-state. At the same time, since immigrant activism has historically served to inculcate newcomers into normative forms of belonging, contemporary organizing must continually negotiate the tension between normalization and resistance.

With the contemporary turn in American studies, cultural studies, and immigrant activisms toward models of transnationalism, globalization, diaspora, and borderlands that map more varied trajectories of migration, scholars have begun to rethink many of the foundational concepts of immigration scholarship, including static or place-bound ideas of culture, community, nation, race, gender, identity, and settlement (Gutiérrez and Hondagneu-Sotelo 2008). Much of this rethinking challenges concepts that are framed by trajectories of evolutionary development within the boundaries of the nation-state. Instead, newer work attends to contradiction, relationality, and back-and-forth dynamics. It strives to undo conceptual binaries, to challenge evolutionary narratives, to theorize liminal positions, and to resituate borders as contact zones. These studies rethink immigrant agency and resistance by connecting material conditions to subject-formation processes, while emphasizing multiple, interlocking inequalities at different scales (Segura and Zavella 2007; Zavella 2011).

Scholarship focused on sexuality can usefully illustrate these multidisciplinary efforts to reconceptualize the study of immigration. Though often overlooked or naturalized in immigration scholarship, sexuality is directly implicated in racial, gender, class, cultural, and imperial inequalities. It thoroughly structures and is restructured by immigration, not merely at the level of metaphor and symbol but also materially. For example, when the United States established military bases and sent troops to Asia for "rest and recreation" in the latter half of the twentieth century, it also generated bridges for immigration to the United States shaped by interlocking sexual, racial, gender, and economic inequalities within a (neo)colonial framework. More generally, links between capitalism and sexual identities, ideologies, imaginaries, and practices continue to influence immigration movements (Brennan 2004). Contemporary neoliberalism, which relies on and naturalizes racialized, patriarchal heterosexuality as a tool of governance (particularly through "family values" discourses and political projects), simultaneously extends this complex history and contributes to the erasure of sexuality within mainstream thinking about immigration.

While histories of (neo)colonialism, economic inequality, racism, and (hetero)sexism on a global scale materially shape immigration, U.S. laws and policies remain largely unresponsive to these complexities. Instead, they respond within a nationalist framework that privileges normative heterosexuality channeled into marriage and family. The heterosexual family has long served as a model for nation making that inscribes and naturalizes important hierarchies, including a patriarchal order that constructs women's sexualities as the property of males and a racial and cultural order that valorizes whiteness (McClintock 1993). The heterosexual family and its associated hierarchies provide the abstract model, concrete mechanism, and means for assessing and generating discourses about various social processes affecting immigrants (Berlant 1997). Take the example of racial and ethnic "mixing," which has been a central concern in the governance and study of immigration. "Mixing" has generated two of the major discourses that have structured popular and academic thinking about immigration—the color line and the melting pot—and the heterosexual family has been central to each.

In regard to the color line, antimiscegenation laws, which were grounded in the history of slavery, were in many cases revived or extended to prevent single immigrant men from Asia, Africa, and Latin America from becoming sexually involved with native-born white women. Single immigrant women were also figured as potentially threatening—most vividly in nineteenth-century claims that Chinese women who engaged in sex work were corrupting white men and boys, stripping them of their money, and infecting them with deadly diseases. Patriarchal marriage within the boundaries of one's "race" and "ethnic group" was deemed a good solution to all manner of potential social disorders associated with immigrant sexuality—including challenges to the color line. Yet when sexuality was channeled into marriage within racialized immigrant groups, the resulting childbearing often became constructed as a threat to the color line in a different way. Immigrants have regularly been accused of deliberately attempting to "(re)colonize" parts of the United States through birthing children who were legal citizens but were considered racially and culturally "unassimilable." The accusations have prompted cycles of exclusionary and eugenic measures in areas including health care, education, social welfare, immigration and citizenship law, and border management.

At the same time, the heterosexual family has been viewed as a mechanism to assimilate immigrants into "American" culture and citizenship; in this respect, it has also been the focus of "melting pot" discourses, desires, strategies, systems of governance, and modes of representation, including versions of assimilation, pluralism, Americanization, and multiculturalism. For example, interracial and interethnic marriage has regularly been characterized as the most effective mechanism to erase the color line and has been studied accordingly (Yu 2001). Similarly, the promotion of companionate marriage in both popular discourse and social science research has provided a technology for immigrant assimilation and driven more than a century of public policies and programs.

This history of "mixing" points to a larger issue. Normative heterosexuality has served as the unexamined ground for elaborating many foundational concepts in the study and governance of immigration. The core concept of "assimilation," for example, came to serve as a model for immigrant life that draws on and recapitulates the norm of heterosexuality as the desired outcome of a developmental process on which racial and national hierarchies depended (Somerville 2000). Generational conflict within heterosexual immigrant families became the model for conceiving and narrating cultural change. "Settlement"—another key concept in mainstream immigration scholarship—similarly hinged on whether immigrants entered into patriarchal marriages. Models of family, culture, community, economic advancement, race, and nation presumed heterosexuality as their actual mechanism and as the normative standard for evaluation. Recent scholarship that centers on sexuality in a manner that recognizes its direct imbrication in racial, gendered, colonial, and class regimes has contributed to rethinking these and other foundational concepts—not only in nation-centered accounts of immigration but also in global, diasporic, and transnational models of migration that implicitly rely on heterosexual logics (Manalansan 2006). This reworking of key concepts is useful for all scholars of immigration, whatever their discipline or approach, since it provides a basis for rethinking the epistemologies, methodologies, and representational forms that govern our collective understanding of the histories and futures of migration within and across national borders.

32

Indian

Robert Warrior

"Indian" is a word that has deep and conflicting roots in the history of the Western Hemisphere and in the contemporary imaginations and attitudes of those who live in the Americas. The issue of the proper usage of this term and those related to it ("Native American," "American Indian," "Amerindian," "Native," "Indigenous," and "First Nations," among others) can be frustrating since the question is so basic; that is, it does little to open up the depths of historical or contemporary indigenous experiences. But it is also a way of beginning a discussion of what students and practitioners of American studies and cultural studies ought to be learning and researching about the aboriginal history of the Americas.

Broad agreement exists that the term "Indian," referring to people in the Americas, originated in Christopher Columbus's mistaken idea that he had discovered a new route to India when he arrived in the Caribbean. Since Columbus's errors of navigation and nomenclature, variations on this term have often been used derisively, as in its bastardized form "Injun" or in its contemporary use in Mexico and other places south of the United States to describe people thought of as poor, backward, and racially disadvantaged. In light of this, most scholars in Native American studies and many Native people themselves advise against the use of the word "Indian" alone as a noun (singular or plural) in favor of "American Indian," though the adjectival form (as in "Indian culture") is widely acceptable in the United States. This preference seems to derive from the fact that "American Indian" is a unique term but is also roughly equivalent in form to other terms that delineate ethnic and racial difference and identity in the United States, such as "Italian American," "Asian American," and "African American."

"Native American" has gained currency more recently in the United States and Europe, though some American Indian people bristle at its use, in part because "Native American" would seem to refer to anyone who is born on the continent and perhaps also because the term gained momentum among sympathetic non-Indian people in the 1970s—as if these sympathizers assumed that American Indian people, like African Americans, must surely have wanted to be referred to differently and so came up with what they imagined Indians wanted to be called. Still, one clear advantage of the term "Native American" is that it includes all indigenous people of the countries in the Americas. In the United States, that means it references Alaskan Eskimos, Inuits, Aleuts, and Native Hawai'ians, none of whom consider themselves American Indians. "Native," a shortened form, has become a preferred term among many academics, students, and others.

The issue of proper nomenclature is nowhere near settled, and specific usages usually reflect regional and national histories and realities. In Mexico and other South and Meso-American countries in which "Indian" (or "Indio") is highly insulting, "indigenous" (or *indigena*) has come into usage. Many people within these same indigenous communities also reject the term "Latin America" to describe those countries, since, as indigenous people (many of whom do not speak Spanish), they do not consider themselves Latin. In Canada, the main political term for indigenous groups is "First Nations," and the people who belong to those nations are "Aboriginal," "Native," or "First Nations" people.

Although nothing close to a consensus exists among Native people as to a preferred term for themselves in general, wide agreement has developed over the past several decades that it is most appropriate to use the names that specific tribal groups have for themselves (Diné, Dakota, Yupik, Ojibwe, or Yakama) or at least the names by which they have come to be known since the European colonization of the Americas (Navajo, Sioux, Eskimo, Chippewa, or Yakima, respectively). This specificity generally affords respect for the vast differences among the indigenous peoples of the Americas, standing in marked contrast to references to *the* Indian, *the* Native American, or *the* original American, which are monolithic and help bolster the misimpression that all indigenous people are the same. This preference has grown up alongside social and political movements focused on the needs and prospects of individual tribal nations and local communities, rather than the more broadly defined politics of the 1970s. While that earlier era of activism and protest witnessed calls for wholesale changes in Indian affairs, the period since has seen a concern for economic development, cultural preservation, governmental reform, and community control at the local level.

In spite of these areas of wide agreement, many individual Native people in the United States feel completely comfortable calling themselves and other people "Indians." A shortened form, usually represented in writing as "Ind'n" (or now, in the sort of shorthand people use in the digital world, "ndn"), speaks to the persistence and acceptability of the term in urban, rural, and reservation settings. Thus, while the movement toward understanding oneself as a member of a specific tribal group is one contemporary dynamic, a significant sense of generational cohesiveness is also common among indigenous youth.

The fact that most college students do not even have this basic knowledge about how to refer to indigenous people of the Americas speaks to how little the average student who grows up in the United States learns about Natives in elementary and secondary school. Much of this ignorance results from the persistence of poor school curriculums in regard to the history and contemporary realities of Native life, but it also reflects the fact that the vast majority of U.S. schoolchildren have had little or no exposure to living, breathing Indian people, except perhaps on a family vacation through the Southwest or someplace else where large concentrations of Natives live. Nor do they encounter Native recording artists, television or film actors, authors, or politicians, though there are some exceptions, both historical (including Will Rogers, Jim Thorpe, the ballerina Maria Tallchief, and Vice President Charles Curtis) and contemporary (including activist/actor Russell Means, singer Rita Coolidge, and professional golfer Tiger Woods, who is Native along with being Thai, white, and African American). Even in the major cities with the highest concentrations of Natives (Minneapolis and Oakland, for instance), no single neighborhood has much more than 10 percent Natives living in it.

Indian people, then, for the most part live either in enclaves in which they are a major focus of social life (reservations or towns bordering them) or in places where they are mostly invisible to the people with whom they share the world. Outside of occasional news stories on exceptionally severe social problems (poverty, substance abuse, unemployment, poor health) or feature stories on cultural events (powwows, art exhibits), neither local nor national media pay much attention to Native issues. While this might be said for any number of other groups in the Americas, none share the history or contemporary situation of Native Americans. To use just the most obvious example, no other group in the United States or Canada has an entire federal bureaucracy dedicated to it as Natives do with, respectively, the Bureau of Indian Affairs (BIA) and the Department of Indian Affairs (DIA). Taxpayers in these countries support their governments' day-to-day managing of the lives of Native people in spite of the fact that few of those taxpayers can say much about what their money funds.

Being inclusive of Native American experiences in American studies thus requires something more than creating a new branch of the field that accounts for yet another group clamoring for the attention of scholars and students. Craig Womack makes this point forcefully in his work on Native American literature. "Tribal literatures," he writes, "are not some branch waiting to be grafted onto the main trunk. Tribal literatures are the *tree*, the oldest literatures in the Americas, the most American of American literatures. We *are* the canon. Without Native American literature, *there is no American canon*. . . . Let Americanists struggle for *their* place in the canon" (1999, 6–7). Native American studies is an invitation for American studies to rethink its understanding of the continent and the people who have made it their home. It requires attention to the ways in which historians have often skewed their work at the expense of an accurate portrait of how Native people have developed their own sophisticated ways of life, including responses to the circumstances that the European colonization of the Americas brought to them. But confronting ignorance also entails recognition of the contemporary realities that Native people inhabit.

Though American studies, when it has paid attention to Native Americans at all, has mostly focused on historical topics, other recent approaches in the field could create deeper scholarly understandings of features of contemporary Native life. Native American literature and visual art, for example, are now established as serious areas of artistic achievement and scholarly study; but numerous forms of contemporary Native expression have yet to capture much of the attention of the scholarly world, and interdisciplinary work could reveal important levels of meaning. Sporadic attempts have been made over the past two decades to establish Native versions of speculative fiction, graphic novels, and comic books (Justice 2005; Mindt 2005). These attempts, many of them interesting in and of themselves, could lead to rich discussions about what it means for indigenous youth to grow up without representations of themselves in most of the popular culture they experience. Similar work could be done in contemporary Native music, including jazz, rock, and hip-hop, or in the blending of traditional and contemporary crafts. Studies have barely begun of the development of professionalism or entrepreneurialism among Natives or of women's involvement in traditionally male roles. Along with striking a balance between the historical and the contemporary, American studies students and scholars would do well to balance topics that are trendy (Native American "Barbie" or cruise packages marketed to Native professionals) with those that are not (the structure of the BIA and the history of federal Indian policymaking).

Impressive gains have been made in American studies, cultural studies, and other academic fields over the past three decades in developing stronger scholarship regarding Native people, their histories, and their contemporary lives. Given that virtually every square foot of the Americas has an aboriginal past and much of the hemisphere has an aboriginal present, a fair question would seem to be why there has not been more. Students and scholars alike would do well to ask themselves whether American studies can consider itself "American" without American Indians being much more central to how the field defines itself.

33

Indigenous

J. Kēhaulani Kauanui

The keyword "indigenous" has varied genealogies in the fields of American studies and cultural studies. American studies scholarship has tended to use the terms "Indian" and "Native" to refer to indigenous peoples of North America, whereas the field of cultural studies has typically used the terms "Native," "Indigenous," and, in some contexts, "Aboriginal" interchangeably. "Indigenous" peoples in what is regarded by most people as the United States (although the very boundaries of the nation-state are contested by enduring indigenous presence and assertions of sovereignty) include American Indians and Alaska Natives (including Inuits and Aleutians) who constitute 566 federally recognized tribal nations and villages (Bureau of Indian Affairs 2012). From the island Pacific and Caribbean, there are also Native Hawaiians, American Samoans, Chamorros (Guam and the Northern Mariana Islands), and Taino/ Jibara-identified people (Puerto Rico). While all of these peoples can make cases for distinct political statuses based on their indigeneity, four historical and political realities set American Indians apart: they were the original inhabitants of what is now considered the United States; their existence necessitated the negotiation of political compacts, treaties, and alliances with European nations and the United States; they are recognized sovereigns and subject to the U.S. trust doctrine, a unique legal relationship with the U.S. federal government that entails protection; the United States asserts plenary power over tribal nations that is exclusive and preemptive (Wilkins and Stark 2011, 33–37).

In both scholarly and political discussions today, usages of the terms "indigenous" and "indigeneity" emerge from this colonial history and as critical responses to it. One result is that the question of who and what counts as "Indigenous" seems to cause anxiety for just about everyone. The *Oxford English Dictionary* traces the etymology of the adjective "indigenous" to late Latin: *indigen-us*, meaning "born in a country, native" (< *indigen-a*, "a native"), and defines the term as "born or produced naturally in a land or region; native or belonging naturally *to* (the soil, region, etc.)," as well as "inborn, innate, native" and "of, relating to, or intended for the native inhabitants." This emphasis on nativity or birth often leads to assertions such as "everyone is indigenous to *some* place," a universalizing commonplace that makes the term meaningless by erasing the political history of specific indigenous struggles over land claims. Well into the twentieth century, white, Anglo-Saxon "nativists" used this logic to claim land within and beyond the borders of the United States. They dismissed the presence of a wide range of indigenous peoples (along with newly arrived migrants) by claiming, themselves, to be "native-born."

For these reasons, the general definition of "indigeneity" as "born or produced naturally in a land or region" is far too simple. It cannot account for the wide range of relations to region and nation of the more than 370 million indigenous people who are spread across seventy countries worldwide (United Nations 2005). Some indigenous peoples define themselves by their historical continuity with precolonial and presettler societies; others by ties to territories and surrounding natural resources; others in relation to distinct social, economic, or political systems; and still others by their distinct languages, cultures, and beliefs. A 1986–87 definition proposed by United Nations (UN) Special Rapporteur José Martínez Cobo remains most influential today: indigenous peoples are "those which, having a historical continuity with pre-invasion and pre-colonial societies that have developed on their territories, consider themselves distinct from other sectors of the societies now prevailing in those territories, or parts of them" (United Nations 2009, 5). The UN Permanent Forum on Indigenous Issues suggests that "the most fruitful approach is to identify, rather than define indigenous peoples" on the basis of the fundamental criterion of self-identification, rather than by a single set of shared characteristics (United Nations 2005).

The principle of self-identification functions to rebut counterfactual claims that indigenous peoples are either entirely extinct due to genocide or diluted due to racial and cultural mixing. Histories of genocide within the legacy of conquest are pervasive, as settler colonial societies—those built through permanent settlement of a foreign population to another land, where land is the central resource targeted for seizure—have typically expanded their territory by waging wars against indigenous peoples (Stannard 1992; Wolfe 2006). Jean M. O'Brien (2010) traces the genealogy of the myth of indigenous extinction to white settler ideologies that required that there be no "natives" who could trump their own nativist claims to land or country. In order to assert that the Indians had vanished, nineteenth-century U.S. historians and their readers embraced notions of racial purity rooted in the period's scientific racism—the belief that races were organized in an evolutionary hierarchy that began with savagery, moved through barbarism, and ended with Christian civilization. One result was that most living Indians were cast as "mixed" and thus no longer truly Indian. The erasure and subsequent memorialization of indigenous peoples served the colonial goal of refuting Indian claims to land and rights and became a primary means by which European Americans asserted their own "modernity" while denying it to putatively "primitive" Indian peoples. One effect of this history is that indigenous peoples have been subject to standards of authenticity based on a colonial logic of biological and cultural purity—notions undergirded by succeeding schools of physical and cultural anthropology.

Within the field of American studies, "indigenous"—as opposed to "native" or "Indian"—has only recently become an important keyword, largely because of interventions by Native American studies scholars (Deloria 2003; Warrior 2003; J. O'Brien 2003). "Indigenous" has increased its prominence for several reasons: it links U.S. movements to the global political struggle to press for the right of self-determination for indigenous peoples; it offers a more inclusive category with less derogatory baggage than "Indian"—which, as indigenous peoples in the Americas have pointed out, is itself a misnomer; it usefully opposes the tendency in the United States to group indigenous Pacific Islanders within the panethnic rubric "Asian Pacific Islander," which problematically conflates indigenous Pacific Islanders with Asian Americans (Kauanui 2004).

The relatively wider circulation of the term "indigenous" within cultural studies may result from that field's more extensive engagement with postcolonial studies, especially in the British Commonwealth states of Canada, Australia, and Aotearoa / New Zealand, all of which acknowledge that they are settler colonial societies. In contrast, cultural studies in the United Kingdom has tended to focus on how postcolonial migrant subjects from South Asia, the Middle East, Africa, and the Caribbean have reshaped British society and the United States. As a result, the concept of diaspora has been valorized over and above indigeneity within UK cultural studies (Diaz and Kauanui 2001). There have been some provocative exceptions to this generalization in research that has troubled the false binary between diaspora and indigeneity by teasing out differences between these two approaches to postcolonial politics and theory (Diaz 1987, 1989, 1994, 1995; Clifford 1997, 2001; Teaiwa 1998, 2005; Kauanui 2007).

The emphasis in both American studies and cultural studies on the constructed as well as the contested nature of identities—the insistence that culture and identity are neither innocent nor pure—has too often and too quickly led scholars in those fields to dismiss assertions of indigenous identity as essentialist (Diaz and Kauanui 2001). They have assumed that claims to "indigeneity" are necessarily grounded in a belief in an underlying and unchanging "essence." While scholarship in cultural studies has offered nuanced critiques of power from the political and historical experiences of failed (or ongoing) revolutions in the First World (critiques of race, ethnicity, class, gender, sexuality, and science), indigeneity has rarely been taken up as a category of analysis. While there has been some productive work in this area on the way indigenous peoples have been racialized (Sturm 2002; Garroutte 2003), the concept of race does not map so neatly onto American Indians or any other indigenous peoples since the question of indigeneity is rooted in a distinct relationship to land and territory that has consequences for sovereignty (Wilkins and Stark 2011). And while postcolonial studies (a field that responds to and analyzes the cultural legacy of colonialism and imperialism) has offered sustained criticism on the unfinished nationalist liberation movements in the Third World, it rarely addresses the still-colonized "Fourth World"—a term coined in 1974 by George Manuel and Michael Posluns to name the "indigenous peoples descended from a country's aboriginal population and who today are completely or partly deprived of the right to their own territories and its riches" (Manuel and Posluns 1974, 40; see also Shohat 1992).

The strategies used by dominant groups to undercut indigenous claims to sovereignty vary and are deeply rooted. Consider as an example the contemporary contestation over the Discovery doctrine, a concept that originated in a 1493 papal bull written to legitimate Columbus's second voyage to the Americas and subsequently used to justify colonial powers' claims to lands belonging to sovereign indigenous nations. The doctrine established Christian dominion and subjugated non-Christian peoples by invalidating or ignoring aboriginal possession of land in favor of the government whose subjects explored and occupied a territory whose inhabitants were not subjects of a European Christian monarch. Today, there is a widespread movement among indigenous peoples to demand that the Vatican revoke the 1493 edict, especially since European and Euro-settler nations continue to use the doctrine to rationalize the conquest of indigenous lands in order to perpetuate the legal fiction of land possession.

Contestations over issues such as the Discovery doctrine are further complicated by the fact that conceptions of indigenous sovereignty tend to be framed by indigenous peoples themselves as a responsibility rather than as a right. This philosophy is reflected in a common saying heard throughout Native America—"the land does not belong to us; we belong to the land"—and serves to counter hegemonic claims made by settler colonial regimes. For instance, U.S. federal Indian law and policy have long been premised on Old Testament narratives of the "chosen people" and the "promised land," as exemplified in the 1823 Supreme Court ruling *Johnson v. M'Intosh* (21 U.S. (8 Wheat.) 543 (1823)), a landmark decision that held that private citizens could not purchase lands from Indian tribes. The foundations of the Court's opinion lay in the Discovery doctrine (Robert Williams 2005). Since this ruling has never been struck down, the U.S. government considers tribal nations as mere occupants with use rights. Those who are indigenous are not even allowed collective property rights of ownership over land—as is the case for domestic dependent nations (federally recognized tribes) with regard to their reservations. This legal imposition can also be traced to the eighteenth-century view that indigenous peoples' life ways were incommensurate with civic life—that they were living in a "state of nature," the supposedly "natural condition" of humankind before the rule of man-made law and a state of society with established government.

Today, states continue to impose this notion of the "premodern" savage as a mechanism of control in their negotiations with indigenous peoples' legal status and land rights. One result is that there is no global consensus that indigenous peoples have the right to full self-determination under international law—which would allow for the development of Fourth World nation-states independent from their former colonizers, like the states of the postcolonial Third World. Because the basic criteria defining colonies under international law include foreign domination and geographical separation from the colonizer, indigenous peoples have been at a disadvantage in the application of decolonization protocols to indigenous nations. This limitation reflects the long-term battle over whether indigenous peoples should be considered "peoples" in the context of Chapter XI of the UN Charter of 1945, which includes the Declaration Regarding Non-Self-Governing Peoples in Article 73, and within UN General Assembly resolution 1514, which reads, "all peoples have the right to self-determination; by virtue of that right they freely determine their political status and freely pursue their economic, social and cultural development."

Even after the UN General Assembly's passage of the Declaration on the Rights of Indigenous Peoples in 2007, there is still no consensus. The Declaration—a nonbinding, aspirational document—came after decades of global indigenous activism that led to the 1982 establishment of the Working Group on Indigenous Populations (WGIP), under the UN Economic and Social Council. The Declaration was stalled for many years due to concerns by states with regard to some of its core statements—namely, the right to self-determination of indigenous peoples and the control over natural resources existing on indigenous peoples' traditional lands. Numerous African and Asian states also took exception to the term "indigenous," suggesting that their entire populations counted as such (even though many of those same states have indigenous minorities within their borders), while Anglo settler states opposed the use of the plural noun "peoples," which signifies collective legal rights under international law.

This difference in legal interpretation over the concepts of "self-determination" and "peoples" was reflected in the 2007 proposal presented to the General Assembly, in which the four votes against the Declaration came from white settler states, all with a strong indigenous presence: Australia, Canada, New Zealand, and the United States. Article 46 continues to limit claims of secession and independence by indigenous peoples: "Nothing in this Declaration may be interpreted as implying for any State, people, group or person any right to engage in any activity or to perform any act contrary to the Charter of the United Nations or construed as authorizing or encouraging any action which would dismember or impair totally or in part, the territorial integrity or political unity of sovereign and independent States." Despite this limitation, the Declaration is the most comprehensive international instrument addressing the rights of indigenous peoples. It calls for the maintenance and strengthening of indigenous cultural identities and emphasizes the right to pursue development in keeping with indigenous peoples' respective needs and aspirations. It states that indigenous peoples have the right "to the recognition, observance and enforcement of treaties" concluded with states or their successors. It also contains a number of provisions that stipulate "free, prior and informed consent"—the right of indigenous peoples to approve or reject proposed actions or projects that may affect them or their lands, territories, or resources (United Nations 2007).

Looking toward the future, the fields of American studies and cultural studies will need to engage the keyword "indigenous" in ways that acknowledge and interact with this global political history. This necessity is particularly pressing after the turn in both fields away from nation-based approaches and toward transnational modes of understanding politics, power, and culture. The problem and paradox is that the transnational approach of American studies and, to a lesser degree, cultural studies rarely includes indigenous peoples *as nations* in the first place because they are not nation-states. And yet it is states that are legally (as well as morally) accountable to indigenous peoples *as peoples*. The growing field of Native studies (as exemplified by the Native American and Indigenous Studies Association, established in 2008) can be instructive for American studies and cultural studies in providing models of scholarly work that takes up this problematic relation between "nation," "state," and "people."

34

Islam

Brian T. Edwards

The arrival of Islam as a religion in the United States is far from new, yet neither the religion nor its adherents received much attention in American studies or cultural studies until Islam became a media and popular fixation, especially after September 11, 2001. In this sense, scholarly interest in Islam has responded to the obsessions of the U.S. public sphere, where the religion is poorly understood and often defined in imprecise or fallacious ways, resulting in inaccurate references to and representations of both Islam and the "Muslim" or "Arab" worlds. Locating "Islam" as a keyword for American studies and cultural studies thus requires an exploration of related terms such as "Muslim" and "Arab." While not all Arabs are Muslim, and only about one-quarter of all Muslims are Arab, U.S. public discourse has often collapsed the religion and the ethnicity through the logics of Orientalism, wherein the inscription of a unified Other located in the "Orient" buttresses the equally fictitious sense that there is a unified West or "Occident" (Said 1978; Prashad 2007).

Anyone studying U.S. culture therefore needs to consider how "Islam" has at least three different referents. First, it designates a poorly understood and massively misrepresented global religion. Second, it is a catchall term that U.S. Americans have used to describe a variety of intertwined religious, ethnic, or racial others, some of them Muslim but not all. Third, it names a complex sociological reality that includes waves of migration and large-scale religious conversions that have brought millions of Muslims to the United

States. In the keyword "Islam," these three referents become intertwined.

The monotheistic religion now called Islam first emerged in the Arabian Peninsula when, in 610 CE, during the month called Ramadan, an Arab businessman named Muhammad received the first of a series of revelations from God. Two years later, Muhammad began to preach to others. Muhammad did not at first think of himself as founding a new religion but as bringing an older faith in the One God to the Arabs, who had not had their own prophet before (K. Armstrong 2002). The God of the Arabs (*al-Lah*, which in Arabic means, simply, "the God") before Muhammad was a single deity whom many Arabs considered the same as the one worshipped by Jews and Christians in the neighboring Byzantine and Persian Empires. When Muhammad began to recognize himself as a prophet for the Arabs, he saw his message as extending that of a line of prophets from Abraham, Moses, David, and Solomon to Jesus, all of whom are mentioned in the Qur'an and considered prophets by Muslims. The Qur'an calls Jews and Christians *ahl al-kitab*, or People of the Book, and commands Muslims to say to them, "our God and your God is one, and to Him we have submitted" (Qur'an 29:46, trans. Muhsin Khan).

Muhammad's preaching focused on the creation of a just society and the sharing and distribution of wealth, a message that resonated in the city of Mecca, where he lived. For the following two decades, Muhammad continued to receive revelations in the form of verses of Arabic. Though Muhammad was illiterate, the Qur'an (which means "recitation" in Arabic) as received or revealed to him was considered a masterpiece of the use of language and poetry. Indeed, its sophistication and beauty was so immediate and overwhelming that it convinced even some of the most skeptical and resistant in Muhammad's day to convert to the new religion. To the present, versions of the Qur'an translated into other languages are considered secondary and not to be the Qur'an at all. The title of the English translation, for instance, is often rendered as "The Meaning of the Holy Qur'an," to indicate the secondary status of the translation. While Islam has become the second-largest religion in the world, with an estimated 1.5 billion adherents (about one-fifth of the population of the world), the vast majority of whom do not speak Arabic, the Qur'an in Arabic is its centerpiece.

The word *Islam* appears eight times in the Qur'an, while the word *Muslimun*, the Arabic plural form of *Muslim*, is much more common (Gardet 1978). Both words derive from the trilateral Arabic root *s–l–m*, meaning "to surrender" and also "to prostrate oneself." A "Muslim," understood etymologically, is thus someone who surrenders to God. This trilateral root also gives us the Arabic word *salaam*, meaning "peace." Of course, etymology only goes so far in explaining the history of the word and its uses. Gardet, in the widely respected *Encyclopedia of Islam*, notes that though the word "Islam" is relatively rare in the Qur'an, it was increasingly used to designate the faith in the titles of Arabic-language works during the classical period (i.e., the Middle Ages in Europe), far surpassing the word *iman* (or "faith"), a word that earlier scholars had often erroneously equated with it. Scholars of Islam note the centrality of the idea of a community (*umma*) of believers whose submission and surrender to God, beyond merely following God's commandments, grants them admission to the *umma* of Muslims.

Muhammad was an influential figure, both while he was alive and after his death. While alive, he was a charismatic individual, a great preacher, and an extremely talented political and military leader. In 622, Muhammad, along with roughly seventy Muslim families living alongside him in Mecca, departed for the city of Medina. This migration (or *hijra*) represented Muhammad's breaking with the tribe and the creation of a new community, a just society in which politics and religion intermingle (K. Armstrong 2002). After the death of Muhammad in 632, three *khalifa* (or caliphs, meaning "representatives") were chosen to lead the Muslims, each succeeding another, all of them close associates of Muhammad. However, when the third caliph, Uthman, was assassinated, a contest over succession emerged, leading to a period called a *fitna* (or "confusion"), as different communities of Muslims rallied around two possible successors. These two different lines became the basis for the major division between the Shi'a and Sunni denominations or branches of Islam. Both Shi'a and Sunni denominations, and variants on them such as the Isma'ili branch of Shi'a Islam and the Nation of Islam, which affiliates with the Sunni branch, are prevalent in the United States today (Curtis 2009).

Those who eventually called themselves the Shi'a (from *Shi'at Ali*, meaning "followers or partisans of Ali") support Muhammad's son-in-law and cousin Ali ibn Abi Talib. Ali became the fourth caliph in 656 but was assassinated five years later. His followers consider him the First Imam of the Islamic Community. His murder and the eventual slaughter of his second son, Husain, the grandson of Muhammad, by the troops of the rival Umayyad caliph as Husain marched to Iraq to take up leadership, are considered by Shi'a as symbols of the perpetual injustice pervading human life. The response to the killings of Ali and Husain established patterns that carried forward in time: "[They] seemed to show the impossibility of integrating the religious imperative in the harsh world of politics, which seemed murderously antagonistic to it" (K. Armstrong 2002, 43). For a long time, Shi'a tended not to be invested in practical affairs of state (postrevolutionary Iran, a Shi'a

majority state, is a recent exception). In contrast, the Sunni (whose name refers to the *sunna*, or "customs," namely, the religious practice of Muhammad himself) have in most Arab countries been more numerous and more concerned with politics and are in the majority (roughly 85–90 percent of Muslims globally, though in the Middle East the divide is roughly 60–40 Sunni-Shi'a). Still, the differences between Shi'a and Sunni—which many observers argue are primarily political, not spiritual—have in many cases been overstated in Western discourse, and there are numerous examples of peaceful cohabitation between adherents of the two branches (Mamdani 2005).

Today, with 1.5 billion Muslims, six different schools of *fiqh* (jurisprudence) between the Sunni and Shi'a branches, and variations among nationally or locally inflected traditions and customs, "Islam" could hardly be considered the monolith that mainstream commentators in Western media have sometimes claimed it is. What many scholars consider fundamental to contemporary Islam is the practice of its five central tenets or pillars (though Shi'a do not call them pillars of Islam). Namely, the *shahada* (profession of faith), prayers five times per day, fasting during the month of Ramadan, the giving of charity or alms (*zakat*), and taking a *hajj* or pilgrimage to Mecca at least once in a lifetime. But given the diversity of the religion as practiced globally, Islam's tolerance of the interruption of day-to-day affairs, and a much greater secular impulse in many of the Muslim-majority countries than is generally appreciated in the West (so-called cultural Muslims), these are often ideals rather than practices.

While the origins of Islam were far from the United States in place and time, Islam has long fascinated people in the United States. In recent years, scholars in American studies have investigated the history of this interest and key moments when U.S culture engaged the global religion from a distance or when U.S. international projects led individuals from the United States to a closer encounter with lands where Islam was the majority religion. A point of debate in such scholarship is whether there is a prevailing continuity in U.S. representations of Islam—thus a continuation of what Edward Said called the "fabric" of Orientalism (1978, 24) and transposition of French and British traditions into U.S. discourse—or whether discontinuities and persistent historical amnesia have led different generations to redefine and recharacterize Islam and Muslim lands and peoples without cognizance of previous generations' patterns of so doing (see McAlister 2001; Brian Edwards 2005; Marr 2006; Makdisi 2007; Nance 2009; Berman 2012).

Scholars trace the U.S preoccupation with Islam as far back as the seventeenth-century European settlement in North America. Timothy Marr has called this persistent obsession "American Islamicism," which he describes as motivated by the "need to acknowledge Islam as an important world phenomenon" and the "desire to incorporate its exotic power within national genealogies" (2006, 1–2). In early and antebellum North America, there was a surprising diversity of images of Islam that exhibit an ambivalent response to the religion and to Muslims: both revulsion and attraction. The former is represented by Captain John Smith, who had violently fought Turks in the Ottoman Europe prior to his arrival at Jamestown, Virginia; the latter can be seen in the missionary impulse of Mary Fisher, an important Quaker who left New England in 1658 to preach the Christian gospel in Turkey (Marr 2006). In either case, early concerns with Islam were more international (or "planetary") than we have traditionally understood.

In the early eighteenth century, West African Muslims arrived on North American shores as slaves. Their prompt and forced conversion to Christianity did not free them from bondage but was a condition of it. In the late eighteenth century, during the popular fascination with white slavery and the Barbary pirates of North Africa, this point was highlighted by novelist Royall Tyler (1797) and satirized by Benjamin Franklin (1790), both of whom made readers aware of the paradox that U.S. citizens held captive in North Africa who converted to Islam were immediately freed by their captors, while African slaves who were forced to convert to Christianity in the United States were not. This intriguing connection in what can be seen as eighteenth-century comparative accounts of captivity was, along with the more general obsession with white captivity in Muslim lands, a moment when Islam seemed to matter immediately to the United States (Sayre 2010).

Through the nineteenth century into the early twentieth, there were other occasions when individuals living in the United States were fascinated with Islam and Muslims. Islam figured in antebellum antislavery and temperance movements, played a large role in Herman Melville's and Washington Irving's cosmopolitan literary engagements, and ran through Ralph Waldo Emerson's deep interest in classical Persian poetry (Marr 2006; Dimock 2006). In popular culture, the rise of the Shriners, belly dancers, and mystics domesticated Muslim iconography and forms; and the Nation of Islam emerged from the African American community in Detroit in 1930, innovating a starkly different understanding of the religion practiced in the Arab world (Nance 2009). Recent scholars in American studies have plumbed these overlooked archives, but some have disputed whether to attribute an increasingly visible fascination with Islam and Muslim practices to a longer history of U.S. imperial designs and have been critical of adopting Edward Said's model of "Orientalism" for the case of the United States (Said

1978; McAlister 2001; Nance 2009). To be sure, present concerns have deeply inflected popular and scholarly understandings of the history of U.S. engagement with the Arab Muslim world, requiring further research and careful historicization (Brian Edwards 2005, 2010).

Across this complex history, there is a tension between Islam as signifier of the *foreign* and Islam as *domestic* practice and sociological phenomenon. As a domestic practice and phenomenon, Islam existed in North America earlier than commonly recognized and is more prevalent in the United States than generally known. Despite its arrival with West African slaves in the eighteenth century, Islam did not survive with substantial numbers (the forced conversion of Muslim slaves to Christianity had a major effect). With the decline and dissolution of the Ottoman Empire in the late nineteenth and early twentieth centuries, a second wave of Muslims arrived in the United States, many of them from Syria, Lebanon, and Turkey. A third major wave of Muslim migration to the United States followed the easing of restrictions on immigration after the passage of the Immigration Act of 1965. While numbers are always contested and difficult to know because the U.S. Census does not collect data on religion, credible estimates of the current Muslim population in the United States range from 1.8 to 7 million, with a generally accepted number hovering around 6 million (Cainkar 2010). The major communities of Muslims are South Asian, Arab, and African American. Among African American Muslims, conversion to Islam has been a major factor, and the Nation of Islam continues to play a major role and to demonstrate that there is a significant disparity among practices of Islam in the United States and abroad (Abdo 2006; Curtis 2009).

Since 2001, the experience of Muslims in the United States has become especially fraught and difficult because of the popular obsession with Islam as a source of global terrorism and the misapprehension and misrepresentation of the global religion as scapegoat for the actions of individuals. If nothing else, the history of the Western fascination with Islam teaches us that American Orientalism or American Islamicism has for centuries generalized and collapsed a multiplicity of Muslim sects, schools, and practices (including secular nonpractice) into a monolithic or misrepresented symbol of foreignness. In the twenty-first century, anxieties about the waning of U.S. cultural and economic hegemony—the advent of what has been called the "post-American world" (Zakaria 2008)— have often been channeled into simplistic and single-minded accounts of the second-largest religion in the world, using as evidence details from tiny minorities. Books such as Dave Eggers's nonfiction work *Zeitoun* (2009), set in New Orleans during Hurricane Katrina; Moustafa Bayoumi's academic reportage *How Does It Feel to Be a Problem?* (2008), based on interviews in Brooklyn in the wake of 9/11; and Amaney Jamal and Nadine Naber's collection *Race and Arab Americans before and after 9/11* (2008) have shown how such anti-Muslim and anti-Arab stereotyping threaten to repeat the worst aspects of U.S. racism and to extend the Orientalism of past centuries into the present. More recently, the venomous expressions of hatred unleashed during the 2010 debates over the building of an Islamic community center in downtown Manhattan (the so-called 9/11 Mosque) and the media feeding frenzy that surrounded a small-town Florida pastor named Terry Jones, who captured global attention with the bait of burning copies of the Qur'an, demonstrate the resilience of Islamicism in the United States and the interplay of global and domestic in present discussions of Islam.

35

Labor

Marc Bousquet

In April 1968, Martin Luther King, Jr., was assassinated while organizing mass protests in support of an illegal strike by Memphis sanitation workers. Like many activists of his day, he saw a series of connections among discrimination by race, sex, and workplace exploitation. He asked, "What does it profit a man to be able to eat at an integrated lunch counter if he doesn't earn enough money to buy a hamburger and a cup of coffee?" (1968). In response to intersecting modes of oppression, King and others believed that liberatory social movements needed to pursue shared goals. The long tradition of such intersectional labor analysis includes the oratory of Frederick Douglass (2000) and the sociology of W. E. B. Du Bois (1995a, 1995b); the feminist anarchism of Lucy Parsons (2004) and Emma Goldman (1969); the revolutionary communist poetry of Langston Hughes (1973) and Amiri Baraka (1999); as well as the socialist feminism of Roxanne Dunbar-Ortiz (2006), Donna Haraway (1985), Angela Davis (1983), Barbara Ehrenreich (2001), and Leslie Feinberg (1993), among countless others.

The intersectional view of power exists in significant tension with common uses of the term "labor" to name a distinct or "special" interest group. In mainstream journalism and school curricula, the word most commonly refers to organized labor, especially politically influential trade-union membership. For many people, this mainstream usage calls up images of sweat and industrial grime, especially the meatpackers, miners, and autoworkers in films such as Paul Schrader's *Blue Collar* (1978) or Barbara Kopple's Oscar-winning

documentaries *Harlan County, U.S.A.* (1976) and *American Dream* (1990). The problem with this usage is that it obscures a far more diverse reality. At present, the most unionized U.S. occupations are education and civil service (about 40 percent), as compared to 10 percent of miners and factory workers (U.S. Bureau of Labor Statistics 2011). If image reflected reality, our notion of a typical union member might be fiftyish and female, an Inuit teacher, a Puerto Rican corrections officer, or a Korean American clerk at the Department of Motor Vehicles. The gulf between simplistic media imagery and diverse reality raises critical questions regarding the tendency to stereotype labor as a chiefly white and male, well-organized, "blue collar" special interest group characterized by a culture of rough, manly, almost effortless solidarity.

Associated with agricultural or mechanical toil and modest social standing in earlier usages dating from the Middle Ages, "labor" emerged as a keyword in the nineteenth century for critical theorists and social reformers addressing questions of political and economic modernity. Along with the democratic revolutions and emergence of a capitalist economy, the rising self-organization and social consciousness of individuals who worked in order to live produced a new social category: "laborers." This category—and the lived experience that enabled it—led to the recognition by social theorists that organized workers constituted a powerful, socially transformative class of persons. A wide array of theorists, both radical and conservative, recognized that this class embodied interests that were clearly distinguished from those of people whose incomes derived from ownership rather than their own efforts (the possessors of capital, or the capitalist class) (Blanc 1839; Marx and Engels 1848/1976).

Critical to understanding any deployment of the term "labor" during this period is the revolutionary *labor theory of value.* Plainly put, this theory is based in the idea that the value of goods derives from the labor necessary to their production (Adam Smith 1776/1937; Ricardo 1817; Marx 1844, 1867/1976; Mandel 1974). Karl Marx praised capitalism for its "constant revolutionizing of production" and agreed that it was generally an improvement for many ordinary workers over previous forms of economic organization. But he also observed, drawing on the sensationalist working-class literature of the period, that the system operated vampirically; it diverted a large fraction of labor-generated value to persons who owned the industrial means of production (that is, the investing class that purchases machinery and factories, hires the brain power of inventors and engineers, pays workers in advance of sales, and so on). In this sense, capital is nothing more than dead labor, as Marx put it, thriving and accumulating "by sucking living labor, and lives the more, the more labor it sucks" (1848).

This usage by Marx and other early social theorists emerged in connection with labor's militant self-organization in the nineteenth century. The labor movement's understanding of itself as a socially transformative class or group is broadly evident in the newspapers, essays, dialogues, and plays produced by workers in labor fraternities and working women's associations. Women in New England mills built some of the earliest and most militant working-class organizations in the country and, like their male counterparts, produced a countercultural literature of dissent, provocation, and solidarity ("Women Working, 1800–1930"). This literature-from-below described a profound antagonism between labor and capital, describing laborers' working conditions as the return of slavery, the end of democracy, and the return by stealth of aristocracy to North American soil. Between the middle of the nineteenth and the middle

of the twentieth century, countless workers drew on this literature as they developed that "one big union" model of *industrial unionism,* as practiced by the Industrial Workers of the World (IWW, or Wobblies), the Congress of Industrial Organizations (CIO), and the pioneering Knights of Labor.

Influenced by E. P. Thompson and the Birmingham school of cultural studies, U.S. scholars such as Stanley Aronowitz (1974), Sean Wilentz (1984b), David Montgomery (1987), and Paul Buhle (1987) aligned themselves with these activists and reformers as they produced a *new labor history.* What was new about this history was its understanding of working people as cultural producers, not merely the consumers of cultural artifacts produced for them by others. Extending this legacy, the cultural historian Michael Denning (1997) chronicles how the rich and complex culture produced by and for union members—often dissident or radical union members seeking to change the culture of their unions for the better—shaped the broader culture and its politics, most notably in the left-wing popular art of the 1930s and '40s. Until the campaign of repression launched by McCarthyism, most unions, mainstream and radical, had significant membership crossover with socialist, communist, or anarchist movements aimed at revolutionary working-class liberation, typically adopting an intersectional view toward oppression by race and sex (Maxwell 1999; Rabinowitz 1991; Coiner 1995; Kelley 1994).

Largely as a result of feminist activism and research, the activities that we understand as labor have expanded enormously since the early 1970s. Pointing out that the creation, training, and care of (traditionally) male wage workers depends, all over the globe, on the often unwaged, traditionally *female labor of reproduction,* Selma James and Mariarosa Dalla Costa (1972) led an innovative "wages for housework" campaign and radicalized our understanding of the labor process. James and Dalla Costa objected to the common understanding of *reproductive labor* as referring to the generally unwaged activities of child rearing by parents and other caregivers in the family and community. Instead, they usefully expanded the insight that capitalism's visibly waged activities depend on an elaborate supporting network of unwaged effort. This insight altered a long-standing agreement between radical and conservative nineteenth-century theorists that the political economic analysis of capitalism should focus only on wage labor, particularly labor that led directly to the employer's profit, such as factory work.

As a result of this feminist intervention into labor history and politics, new areas of analysis came into focus: unwaged labor, as in child rearing and housework; donated labor, as in volunteerism or internship; waged labor in the nonprofit sector, such as teaching, policing, and civil service; free creative or intellectual work; subsistence labor in small agriculture; forms of forced labor such as slavery, indenture, and prison labor; labor in illegal or unregulated circumstances, as in sweatshops or sex work; working "off the books" in otherwise legal activities such as babysitting and food service. Underscoring all of the teaching, feeding, nursing, transportation, clothing, and training involved in "producing" an industrial worker, feminists and analysts in the Italian autonomist tradition, such as Paolo Virno and Tiziana Terranova, argued that the value represented by consumer goods is produced in a *social factory*, a vast web of effort that intersects at the point of assembly but is not limited to it (Virno 2010).

This is not just a critical or theoretical observation. As any college student or recent graduate can attest, nearly all forms of contemporary enterprise are restructuring the labor process to maximize the contributions of unwaged, underwaged, or donated labor: from volunteers, students, apprentices, and interns; from regular wage workers who communicate by email and take phone calls at home or in transit; from local government, which pays for worker training and security services; from permanently "temporary" workers who are not entitled to benefits; or from outsourced workers who are superexploited by contractors, often in another country. The persons who contribute much of this unaccounted-for labor include women, students and teachers, migrants, guest workers, the undocumented, workers in the service economy, clergy, and civil servants. Many of them are seduced into donating or discounting their labor by canny management that portrays the discount as a fair exchange for workplaces that are perceived as fun, creative, or satisfying (Ross 2004, 2009). Persons in all of these intensely racialized laboring groups played a leading role in the worldwide revolutionary ferment of the 1960s. While they often intersected with each other in both planned and spontaneous ways, the new social movements they participated in were largely independent (or *autonomous*) of traditional sources of power to shape the course of the state, such as political parties and the dominant trade unions. The school of thought that came to be known as autonomism emphasizes their power independent of organized political parties and trade unions, and the intersection of workers' interests across economic sectors and national borders.

Grasping labor as social productivity includes the crucial understanding that contemporary capitalism captures profit from many activities not generally understood as labor. Consider social media as an example. Many kinds of businesses directly monetize recreational or self-expressive social activity, as in the *social sourcing* of revenue-producing content on YouTube, the *Huffington Post*, and other media-sharing sites. Users also make a second, less obvious gift of countless related activities—the labor of rating content, publicizing it (by passing links along), and surrounding the content with entertaining commentary. This phenomenon was notably described by Maurizio Lazzarato (1996) as *immaterial labor*, a kind of labor previously reserved to privileged or professional taste makers such as professors, critics, public-relations and advertising workers, and journalists. The breadth of this social productivity includes students' low-wage, underwaged, and donated labor in work-study or internship arrangements. But that is only the tip of the iceberg. Students create value for campuses in myriad ways, from athletics and performance to donated journalism, service learning, running extracurriculars for other students, and so on. Facebooking one's social life or working out in the fitness center can be understood as making a donation to the campus brand (Bousquet 2008, 2009).

Where capital cannot seduce labor, it seeks to rule by other means. The capitalist reaction to labor insurrection worldwide has been state adoption of economic *neoliberalism* and the steady *globalization* of the production process (Harvey 1989). This means that much of the work involved in producing goods consumed in the United States—even putatively "American" brands such as Apple, Levi's, and Harley-Davidson—is the labor of Chinese, Mexican, Indonesian, African, and Indian workers. Organizations such as China Labor Watch and films such as *China Blue* (2005) document, across industries, persistent patterns in Chinese manufacture: typically hiring primarily young, single, female workers between the ages of sixteen and twenty-five, who will burn out or be fired because of worker abuse ranging from violence and toxic chemical exposure to eighty- and ninety-hour workweeks, often with net salaries (after deductions for employer-provided dormitory housing, food, and other necessities) of less than thirty cents an hour. In response to the domination that many workers experience in capital's globalization-from-above, it seems inevitable that laborers will have to build a worldwide solidarity in self-defense—a visionary workers' globalization-from-below.

36

Latino, Latina, Latin@

Juana María Rodríguez

The oldest and most conventional of this keyword's variants, "Latino," is commonly used as an ethnic designation that distinguishes Latin Americans living in the United States from those living in their countries of origin. Even this seemingly straightforward variant sustains a hefty set of internal contradictions and has a decidedly blurry genealogy. While commonly used as an adjective modifying everything from voting blocs to musical categories, neighborhoods, and foodways, the exact referent of the term remains indeterminate even as it seems to imply specific populations, geographies, histories, colonialisms, languages, and cultural practices. The problem is that each of these potential referents carries significant contradictions and erasures. The gendered nature of the Spanish language presents its own stylistic challenges. In Spanish, *latino* (masculine) or *latina* (feminine) as a noun or adjective is gendered in relation to specific objects. In English, the masculine form is usually applied universally, or else a slash is used to register two possible gendered possibilities: Latino/a. More recently, a linguistic convention emerging from queer online communities has taken up the *arroba* to create terms such as Latin@ or amig@s, marking instead where someone is "at" in terms of gender (J. Rodríguez 2003).

The most widespread use of the term "Latin@" is as a geographic reference to peoples in the United States who originate from Latin America. This definition immediately invokes cartographic debates about the precise borders of Latin America, where Latin America as a specific cultural and historical construct is understood as distinct from both South America and North America. Mexico is, of course, in North America, and prior to the 1848 Treaty of Guadalupe Hidalgo, it included 525,000 square miles of what is now U.S. territory, including California, Utah, and Nevada, along with parts of Colorado, Wyoming, New Mexico, and Arizona. This history of annexation disrupts the commonplace association of "Latin@" with immigration or "foreign" origin. The terms "Chicano" and "Chicana" (often spelled "Xicano" and "Xicana") emerged in the 1960s as politically inflected alternatives to "Mexican American" to mark the distinct cultural and political characteristics of people of Mexican ancestry living in the United States, to differentiate these populations from more recent immigrants, and to reclaim an imagined historical past rooted in *Aztlán*, a constructed designation used to name the lands annexed by the United States (Rosales 1997; Noriega and Sandoval 2011). These occupied territories contained sizable indigenous communities that have remained culturally and legally distinct from their Mexican, Chican@, and U.S. neighbors, which should serve as a caution against collapsing distinctions between Latin@s and Native Americans in the region. Broad attempts to imagine Latin America as beginning at the Rio Grande and ending at the southernmost tip of Chile elide the various nation states that do not share a Spanish or even Iberian colonial history. As the numbers of Brazilians in the United States have grown, they are increasingly being included in the designation "Latin@," but populations that immigrate to the United States from countries historically associated as French, Dutch, or English colonies in South and Central America, such as Belize, Suriname, Guyana, French Guiana, and the Falkland Islands, are less likely to be imagined as forming part of what is understood as Latin@.

The various countries, cultures, and colonies of the Caribbean also press on attempts to categorize "Latin@"

through recourse to geography. Puerto Ricans are certainly a visible and recognizable portion of what is termed "U.S. Latin@s," yet the island's current colonial status as an unincorporated territory of the United States adds an additional consideration. The tendency to understand "Latin@" as implying a migratory relationship to the United States differentiates it from the term "Latin American," with the effect that Puerto Ricans both on and off the island are implicated in its usage. Despite their U.S. passports, many Puerto Ricans living on the mainland (often termed "Nuyoricans" to signal their significant presence in New York or "Diasporicans" to mark broader migratory trajectories) are ethnically stigmatized as foreign or ethnic others in relation to an imagined Anglo-Saxon populace. In contrast, Puerto Ricans on the island experience their relationship to the mainland through the legal, economic, militaristic, linguistic, and cultural force of U.S. colonial power. The lived consequences of their colonial status include being U.S. citizens who cannot vote in U.S. presidential elections and have no vote in Congress. Other islands such as Hispaniola, which is shared by both the Dominican Republic and Haiti, create additional problems of categorization. While Dominicans, as Spanish speakers, might more easily self-identify as Latin@s, French- and Creole-speaking Haitians are more likely to use the geographic referent "Caribbean" if they wish to stake a claim to a pannational, regionally situated, ethnic identity. The numerous nations and islands of the Caribbean, with their messy tangle of serial colonialism, multilingualism, and interregional migration, create particular challenges for a geographic understanding of the term "Latin@." Nor does recourse to shared Iberian conquest bring clarity to the term. After all, Spain and Portugal have had colonial investments in the Philippines, Cape Verde, Macao, Mozambique, Morocco, Guinea Bissau, Angola, and elsewhere. Upon migration to the United States, these populations have rarely been viewed as Latin@.

Questions of race—as a categorical designation separate from ethnicity, geography, or nationality—further complicate attempts to define "Latin@." Colonialism, slavery, migration, and interracial reproduction through marriage, concubinage, and rape have produced phenotypically diverse and racially stratified Latin American and Latin@ populations. Centuries of racialized slavery throughout the hemisphere have resulted in numerically larger populations of African Americans in South American than in North America. In the United States, the "one-drop" rule historically designated anyone with African heritage as black. In Latin America, understandings of race generally allow any mixture that includes European to be defined as something other than black or indigenous, thus producing a much wider range of terms designating specific racial mixtures, including terms such as *mulato*, *mestiza*, *pardo*, and *trigeño*. Some Latin American countries have linked their identities to concepts such as *mestizo* (which has also been taken up widely in U.S. Latin@ discourse), attempting to indicate a racially mixed and nationally unified population. The risk of these universalizing gestures is that they can erase or marginalize specific racial, ethnic, and religious minorities, particularly indigenous, African, and immigrant populations. Despite the discourse of racial multiplicity and coexistence that is often associated with Latin@s, racial hierarchies that privilege whiteness within mixed-race spectrums remain the norm throughout the hemisphere. These regionally and nationally disparate ways of understanding racial categories are rearticulated and transformed through their association with a U.S. racial order (Román and Flores 2010).

Reflecting these categorical ambiguities and in response to shifting political pressures, the U.S. Census has used a range of criteria in its efforts to enumerate these populations (C. Rodríguez 2000). In 1940, the census collected data on "persons of Spanish mother tongue"; in 1950 and 1960, the criteria shifted to "persons of Spanish surname"; in 1970, the census asked if "this person's origin or descent was Mexican, Puerto Rican, Cuban, Central or South American or Other Spanish"; in 1980, it used the phrase "Spanish/Hispanic origin or descent," identifying individuals as racially white unless they specifically indicated otherwise. These early uses of "Hispanic" included immigrants from Spain, emphasized the "Spanish" roots of Latin America, and promoted an identification with whiteness. Politically and culturally, the term "Latino," which was first adopted in the 2000 census, shifted the focus to origins in Latin America. The 2000 census also marked the first time that individuals who identified themselves as "Latino or Hispanic" were also asked to indicate their race and the first time an individual could check multiple boxes for race. This effort to refute an assumed whiteness on behalf of Latin@s is significant as a means to enumerate the presence of Afro-Latin@s, Asian-Latin@s, and those with mixed racial identifications, even as these hyphenated terms can likewise perpetuate a definition of "Latin@" that exists separate from these racial currents.

Throughout the second half of the twentieth century, U.S. studies of these diverse populations participated in the politics of these naming practices. The field was divided between Chicano studies on the West Coast and Puerto Rican studies on the East Coast. These scholarly explorations emerged from the civil rights movements of the late sixties and early seventies and were generally centered on questions of identity, language, history, community, and lived experiences of discrimination. In early Chican@ cultural production and activism, the labor conditions of farmworkers

figured centrally, as did protests against police violence and political demands for expanding educational access and diversifying existing curricula (Rosales 1997). Puerto Rican cultural and political projects tackled more broadly the daily realities of urban poverty, street violence, racial discrimination in the United States, and the cultural complexities brought about by the *guagua aérea*, or air bus, of circular migration between San Juan and New York City (Flores 2000; Laó-Montes and Dávila 2001). On both coasts, much of the political writing of the civil rights era was formed through heterosexist and masculinist concepts of nationalism that stressed patriarchal dominance in familial and activist hierarchies, often using cultural narratives of "tradition" to buttress binary gender distinctions and social roles (Blackwell 2011; R. Rodríguez 2009). These gendered critiques of nationalist politics were not unique to Latin@s, but they were forcefully given voice in the breakthrough cultural phenomenon that was *This Bridge Called My Back*, edited by Chicana lesbians Cherríe Moraga and Gloria Anzaldúa (1981). Moraga (1983) and Anzaldúa (1987) became leading figures in feminist of color movements and pushed forward efforts to address heterosexism in Latin@ communities and white ethnocentrism in U.S. feminist and gay and lesbian communities of the era. Since then, significant critical work produced at the intersection of Latin@ studies and queer theory has intervened into both streams of inquiry, complicating the political and performative function of identity (Muñoz 1999, 2009; Quiroga 2000, J. Rodríguez 2003; Soto 2010).

In the early twenty-first century, issues surrounding immigration have dominated public discourse on Latin@s and have resulted in crucial investigations into education, public health, law, and public policy (García Bedolla, 2009). As migration patterns have shifted, regionalism and site-specific investigations within urban centers such as Los Angeles, Miami, New York, Hartford, and Chicago and within different areas of the Southwest, particularly border towns, have gained prominence as a means of interrogating the implications of the localized diversity of Latin@ populations, often in relation to other racialized communities (Fernandez 2012; Laó-Montes and Dávila 2001; Schmidt Camacho 2008). Scholarly investigations of Latin@ art, literature, and more recently, music have dominated humanistic investigations within Latin@ studies. This work has highlighted themes related to gender roles and family; home, cultural belonging, and displacement; colonial histories and processes of racialization; and the complexities involved in translating languages and cultures across borders, regions, and bodies (Aparicio 1998; Flores 2000; Lima 2007; Parédez 2009; Pérez 2007; Vargas 2012). Increasingly, the multinational and generationally differentiated nature of Latin@ communities has shifted scholarly attention to investigate how *latinidad*, a term used to highlight the constructed nature and political possibilities of pan-Latin@ expression, gets deployed. This turn has also prompted some scholars to critique the term "Latino," suggesting that it functions most effectively as a marketing strategy, a way to designate diverse but aggregated populations in order to better serve the economic needs of specific local, regional, national, and transnational markets (Dávila 2001). Future directions in the field of Latin@ studies are poised to make productive use of the complexity of the term by fully interrogating its historical and regional specificity alongside transnational currents, drawing on the interdisciplinary history of the field to interrogate how bodies, gestures, ideas, language, popular culture, and forms of social connection circulate across disciplinary, regional, and imaginary borders.

37

Law
Dean Spade

The word "law" is most commonly used with reference to what the *Oxford English Dictionary* calls "the body of rules . . . which a particular state or community recognizes as binding on its members." It also refers to statements of fact or truth that are based on observable patterns of physical behavior, as in the "law of gravity" and other "scientific laws." These two uses of the term—a body of rules and an established scientific truth—are related. Liberal legal systems, including U.S. law, claim to be grounded in universal truths, even as they create bodies of rules specific to a particular society or community. The dominant story about the U.S. legal system, as told from the perspective of its founders and those who govern, is that it exists to establish and preserve freedom, equality, and certain individual rights. Law, in this account, is the neutral arbiter of fairness and justice. The background assumption is that law codifies a set of agreed-upon reasonable limits on human violence or disorderly behavior and that citizens freely submit to the legal system in order to be protected from the violence that would occur without enforcement of rules.

The concept of "the rule of law" supports this commonsense understanding of the law by asserting the legitimacy of legal rules that apply to all, are created through clear and consistent procedures, and are enforced by an independent judiciary (Hart 1961; Raz 1977/1999). In this framework, the rule of law refers to the technical application of neutral principles, and courts are cast as autonomous from the political pressures that influence the elected branches of government; they are the accessible place for parties experiencing unfairness, inequality, or impediments to freedom to assert their rights (Sarat 1982). For example, the case *Brown v. Board of Education* (347 U.S. 483 (1954)), in which the U.S. Supreme Court declared that race segregation in public schooling was unconstitutional, is often said to demonstrate the promise of U.S. law to resolve injustice and promote universal fairness and equal rights. This case is a critical part of a widely disseminated national narrative about how the white supremacist and patriarchal norms codified in the founding documents of the country were eventually eradicated through proper interpretation and enforcement of neutral constitutional principles. From this vantage point, white supremacy was a problem of law resolved through law; the rule of law thus appears to be a seamless and self-correcting system.

Scholars and activists have critiqued this image of U.S. law (and liberal legalism more generally), questioning the assumption that law is a neutral set of universal principles analogous to scientific laws. The alternative account points out that the founding of the United States and the establishment of a system of participatory democracy raised great anxieties among the wealthy colonial elites authoring its legal structure. They identified a need to prevent the potential redistribution of wealth that might be demanded by less wealthy white men who were newly entitled to political representation. For this reason, the key rights protected by the new legal system were property rights (Mensch 1982). Important critiques of this system emerged in the 1920s when a group of theorists known as the legal realists suggested that an awareness of social conditions should inform purportedly neutral legal reasoning. Supreme Court Justice Oliver Wendell Holmes argued that the legal system used the pretense of neutral principles to promote laissez-faire economic theory for the benefit of those groups with the most economic and social power. He noted that judicial decisions striking down laws passed to protect workers in the name of enforcing the liberty of contract in *theory*, as in the famous case *Lochner v. New York* (198 U.S. 45 (1905)), ignored the *reality* of the contexts in which workers contract with employers and cast as neutral conditions that actually benefited wealthy people and perpetuated the exploitation of everyone else (G. White 1986).

The realists were neither the first nor the last to argue that U.S. law was founded to protect and preserve the concentration of wealth and property. The critical legal studies movement that emerged in the 1970s, the critical race theory movement of the 1980s, and the various social movements that engage with the law (including indigenous mobilizations, antiracist movements, and various strains of feminism) all have contributed to an analysis of the U.S. system of property law as securing racialized and gendered property statuses from the start. The legal rules governing indigenous and enslaved people articulated their subjection through the imposition of violent gender norms, such as the enforcement of natal alienation among slaves and European binary gender categories and gendered legal statuses among indigenous people (C. Harris 1993; Andrea Smith 2005; Roberts 1993). The statuses and norms established by these systems were (and are) racializing and gendering at the same time. They do not create rules for all women or all men or all white people or all native people or all black people; instead, they reproduce intersectional social hierarchies by inscribing within the law specific subject positions that are simultaneously racialized and gendered.

Contemporary writers influenced by these overlapping critical traditions and social movements continue to argue that the purported universality of the freedom, equality, and rights established in

U.S. law operates in ways that perpetuate the theft of land and labor by a very small group at the expense of the majority. Feminists have deconstructed the legal distinction between private and public spheres, observing that this division has relegated the violence and harm that women experience routinely (often in unregulated, unpaid or underpaid domestic labor) to the private sphere in a way that precludes relief under the law (Taub and Schneider 1982). Critical race theorists have pointed out how the idea that certain choices are private, such as the decision by white parents to move away from jurisdictions where public schools have been integrated, has been used by courts to declare that law cannot be used to remedy de facto racial segregation in education (*Miliken v. Bradley*, 418 U.S. 717 (1974); A. Freeman 1995). From this perspective, U.S. law has established processes of racialization and gendering from the outset, since the purportedly universal categories of citizenship that it deploys were operationalized in ways that secured colonial, racial, wealth, and gender hierarchies (Burns 1982; Gómez 2007; Ngai 2004;Valverde 2007).

These types of analyses cast doubt on the idea that the legal system is a place where those who are left out can and should assert their rights. Representations of the law as a vehicle for delivering freedom and equality are commonplace in the United States. Yet venues of potential rights enforcement such as voting, litigation, and legislation are not accessible to all people because of wealth concentration, campaign finance rules, gerrymandering, voter suppression practices, media consolidation, and the reality that the legal profession and judiciary are dominated by white, wealthy people. Formal legal equality has been established on some fronts, but material inequality is still in place and, for many populations, expanding. During the "post-civil-rights" period when we have all supposedly become

equal under the law, we have witnessed a growing wealth gap and the drastic expansion of racially targeted criminalization and immigration enforcement systems. This contradiction is particularly striking in relation to a legal system that declares itself "color-blind" and claims to have overcome white supremacy. The trouble with these assertions is that legal reform comprehends discrimination very narrowly, primarily forbidding intentional discrimination against individuals on the basis of race (and other categories such as sex and disability) in areas such as employment, public accommodations, and housing. The ongoing conditions facing marginalized groups—widespread disparity in access to education, health care, and employment; overexposure to poisonous pollution and police violence and imprisonment—cannot be traced to the intentional actions of individual discriminators (A. Freeman 1995). Due to the logic of "color blindness" advanced by discrimination law, programs aimed at remedying these widespread conditions of maldistribution, such as affirmative action initiatives that use race as a factor in distributing life chances in university admissions or job applications, can be declared unlawfully discriminatory and prohibited (*Parents Involved in Community Schools v. Seattle School District No. 1*, 551 U.S. 701 (2007); Gotanda 1991; *Fisher v. University of Texas at Austin*, 132 S. Ct. 1536 (2012)).

A focus on legal reform as the site of social and political transformation also misrecognizes and misrepresents demands of populations facing marginalization and maldistribution. It fails to comprehend how the violences of white supremacy, patriarchy, ableism, and other systems of meaning and control work together to produce particular vulnerabilities. Critical race theorist Kimberlé Crenshaw famously describes this phenomenon as "intersectionality" (1995). Crenshaw asserts that political resistance mobilized to fight racism *or* sexism frequently disregards intragroup difference. She demonstrates that single-axis strategies tend to address only the harms facing the privileged subject of that specific axis, leaving those who are facing intersecting forces of oppression outside the scope of the remedies. For instance, when white feminist activists advocate increased criminal punishment as a solution to sexual and domestic violence, women of color who live in communities terrorized by policing and immigrant women who fear that police contact might lead to deportation for themselves, their loved ones, or neighbors are marginalized. In response, women of color activists have critiqued white feminists for focusing their analysis exclusively on gender and failing to understand that expanding punishment systems will not make women of color and immigrant women safer. They have also exposed how anticriminalization campaigns, when they focus only on the concerns of men of color, can ignore problems of sexual and gender violence that women of color face. (Critical Resistance and INCITE! Women of Color Against Violence 2006).

These critical inquiries into the politics of legal reform and the U.S. legal system have raised significant questions for scholars and activists operating across a wide range of social movement contexts. The debate about hate crime legislation in queer and trans politics is an example. Some advocates of lesbian/gay/bisexual/transgender (LGBT) rights have worked to pass legislation designed to increase the penalties for people convicted of crimes motivated by bias and to require criminal punishment agencies to collect data about such crimes. They argue that hate crimes perpetrated against queer and transgender people are common and often underprosecuted and that these laws will help establish that this kind of violence will not be tolerated. In response, queer and trans scholars and activists who oppose hate crime laws as a method of

addressing the problem of violence point out that these laws do nothing to prevent homophobic or transphobic violence. Rather, they provide increased resources to a criminal punishment system that targets queer and trans people, people of color, and poor people (Spade 2011). They point out that the United States currently imprisons 25 percent of the world's prisoners while having only 5 percent of the world's population and that over 60 percent of people in U.S. prisons are people of color, with one in three black men experiencing imprisonment during their lifetimes (Bonzcar 2003; Sabol and Couture 2008). Viewed within this context, hate crime laws use violence against queer and trans people to rationalize further expansion of a system that is actually one of the leading perpetrators of violence against them (Whitlock 2001; Mogul, Ritchie, and Whitlock 2011; Sylvia Rivera Law Project 2009; Sylvia Rivera Law Project et al. 2009). Debates about whether to seek access to institutions long understood by feminist, antiracist, and anticapitalist critics as fundamentally violent and harmful, such as legal marriage and military service, have similarly divided queer and trans social movements (Farrow 2005; Kandaswamy, Richardson, and Bailey 2006; Bassichis, Lee, and Spade 2011; Queers for Economic Justice 2010).

Embedded in the keyword "law," then, is a series of questions about the location and efficacy of legal reform within social movement activism. Do legal reform projects necessarily legitimize and expand violent and coercive systems, or can they be used to dismantle such systems? Can U.S. law or particular legal and administrative systems in the United States (criminal punishment systems, immigration systems, tax systems) be redeemed and reformed in ways that reduce violence and create a fairer distribution of wealth and life chances, or do such efforts merely co-opt and neutralize resistance formations? Are the key categories and concepts of legal liberalism (individual freedom, equality, citizenship) ultimately about exclusion and the maintenance of racialized and gendered systems of maldistribution, or can they be mobilized to transform those systems? There can be no doubt that the language of "rights" and "equality" has come to have deep emotional meaning for people in struggle. The trouble is that this language shifts the transformative demands of social movements into legal reform strategies that do not deliver sufficient change. Given this contradiction, what relationship should change seekers have to law-based rights and equality rhetoric? These questions are important entry points for exploring what law means, inquiring into structural matters of governance and power, and crafting new cultural and political narratives about difference, progress, and redemption.

38

Liberalism

Nikhil Pal Singh

"Liberalism" is one of the most important terms in Anglo-American and, more broadly, Euro-American political and philosophical discourse. It derives from the English term "liberal," which initially referred to a class of "free men" as opposed to the unfree—that is, people embedded within or bound by one or another form of socially restrictive hierarchy (Raymond Williams 1976/1983, 179–81). "Liberalism" has never shed the class meanings and elitist connotations at its root and origin, in large part because it indexes tensions and ambiguities at the heart of what are now referred to as liberal-democratic nation-states. At the same time, the term "liberal" has also retained long-standing associations with universality, open-mindedness, and tolerance linked to an advocacy of individual freedom and an antipathy to socially determined, collectively defined forms of ascription. As such, it has had special purchase for scholars of U.S. politics and culture, from Louis Hartz's seminal critique in the 1950s to the contemporary affirmations of Michael Ignatieff, as intellectual assertions about a consistent and thoroughgoing liberalism generally underpin a discourse of American exceptionalism (Singh 2004).

Colloquial uses of the term "liberal" complicate efforts to understand liberalism as one of the foundational intellectual discourses of political modernity. The conventional discussion in the United States illustrates this clearly, as "liberals" have been under sustained attack by "conservatives" for the past thirty years for what is alleged to be a reckless disregard for traditional values and moral virtue and for a sentimental adherence to overly inclusive notions of human rights, political participation, economic distribution, and international norms. While these arguments reflect broad antinomies internal to the political history of liberalism, they also manifest a particular historical conjuncture in a much longer struggle over the prior meanings and future directions of a liberalism that is broadly shared across a spectrum of particular political positions.

Liberalism, in this larger sense, has been characterized by deep continuities as well as periodic revisions to the political, economic, and normative dimensions underlying its defining orientations. The latter can be summed up rather easily with reference to the *Oxford English Dictionary*, which defines liberalism as "respectful of individual rights and freedoms, favoring free trade and gradual political and social reform that tends toward individual freedom and democracy." This definition, replete with its characteristic repetition ("freedoms," "free," "freedom") and allusion to vague temporalities of progress ("gradual," "tends toward"), encapsulates some of the key attributes and ambiguities of liberalism. Central to every version of liberalism is an insistent, quasi-naturalistic link between human and market "freedom." What remains ambiguous is the specific historical character of liberalism's supposedly inherent "tendency" toward "democracy" and social "reform."

The modern conflation "liberal democracy" quietly resolves this central and enduring problematic for liberalism and its adherents: how to combine an expansive, even utopian, defense of individual freedom with a stable and cohesive structure of social organization. Theorists of liberalism have looked toward two institutional mechanisms to manage this fundamental task: the self-regulating market and one or another form of political democracy or representative government, incarnated in the nation-state. At least provisionally, therefore, we might distinguish between two strains within liberalism: *market liberalism* as exemplified by the work of Adam Smith, in which the individual is imagined as *homo œconomicus*, a person whose conduct is naturally coordinated and regulated through competition and trade with others with minimal state interference; and *political liberalism*, exemplified by the work of John Stuart Mill, in which individuals are posited as *citizen-subjects*, formally equal within a civic order whose political institutions are designed to balance and preserve individual liberty and equality (Adam Smith 1776/1937; Mill 1859/1999; Wendy Brown 2003).

One of the strongest critics of both variants of liberalism, Karl Marx (1867/1976) argued that capitalist market relations could only emerge in societies where human equality had attained the status of a popular prejudice. Despite the fact that the two variants—freedom as the freedom of unregulated market activity and freedom as a "tendency" toward political equality—share a conception of the abstract and interchangeable human individual as the basis of all social organization, the coordination between them has been highly uneven and has required a range of innovative thought experiments and institutional arrangements to give a "commonsense" cast to what is in fact a contradictory and unstable cohabitation. A work that illuminates this tension (and an important touchstone for liberalism as an intellectual project) is John Locke's *Second Treatise of Government* (1690/1988), which envisions individuals in the state of "natural liberty," defined by an unlimited impulse to accumulate status and possessions, who consensually enter into a "social contract" with one another, arrogating their theoretically unlimited natural rights within civil society and in turn establishing a government whose legitimacy rests on its ability to secure the life, liberty, and property of its members.

Locke's theory implants property rights and class inequality at the heart of the liberal order by restricting political participation and decision-making to men of property and status, namely, those whose preexistent social credentials and private accumulation (that is, what they have supposedly "earned" in the "state of nature," *before* they voluntarily entered into civil society) is most in need of protection and legitimation (Macpherson 1962). Amplifying this critique, several thinkers suggest that Locke's theory of natural rights rests on a broad range of social norms and conventions that the "individual, equipped with universal capacities, must negotiate before these capacities assume the form necessary for political inclusion" (Mehta 1999, 63). Those who do not have an adequate stake in the social order, including the propertyless, those who are temporarily or permanently unable to exercise reason (i.e., children and the insane), and those whose presumed conjugal or domestic status supersedes their claim to public individuality (i.e., women) can in this view be governed without their consent (Pateman 1988).

The problems of political domination, exclusion, and inequality within liberalism are deepened dramatically when we consider the historical record of liberal-democratic nation-states founded in racial slavery and colonial expansion. Lockean liberalism in this context encodes a split view of the "state of nature," one that is idealized and viewed retrospectively from the standpoint of established civil society and another that is historical, composed of people who purportedly lack reason and who thus exist (in Locke's words) like "wild Savage Beasts, with whom Men can have no Society or Security" (Locke 1690/1988, 96). This liberalism contrasts an already "moralized" state of nature, defined by private property, with a wild, uncultivated nature. Indeed, this is the basis for Locke's famous advancement of historically extant justifications for the dispossession of Native lands in British settler colonies—North America in particular: Indians did not possess any property rights due to their failure to create value through commercial cultivation or the steady, patient admixture of their labor with the land. Although Locke opposed hereditary slavery, he himself was heavily invested in the transatlantic slave trade, revealing what was at best an inconsistency and at worst the divided normative vision that gradually codified "racial" difference as a principle technology naturalizing exclusion within liberal-democratic societies.

How an unlimited—indeed a universal and universalizing—concept of human freedom could be so consistently combined with and underpinned by differentialist logics of exclusion and exploitation—of the propertyless, of women, of slaves and aboriginal peoples—became the most vexing theoretical and political problem of twentieth-century liberalism. One of the crucial, unresolved debates among critics and defenders of liberalism is whether political exclusion is inherent within liberalism or whether it is an artifact of historically contingent divergences between the theoretical universalism of liberalism and exclusionary social practices of liberal societies founded on race, class, and gender inequality. The latter view opens up the possibility of a politically productive dynamic in which demands for political and civic equality among excluded groups and categories of persons (women, racial and sexual minorities, colonized subjects, disabled people) have steadily advanced the convergence of the theoretical universalism of liberalism and the social and political boundaries of liberal-democratic nation-states across the world-system (Myrdal 1944).

Even if one resists the strong teleological presumption behind this last claim, it is possible to suggest that the idealized schematics of liberal universalism yielded distinctive patterns of political struggle and transformation. As Karl Polanyi (1944/2001, 155) argued, nineteenth-century liberal doctrines of laissez-faire capitalism actually promoted "an enormous increase in the administrative functions of the state"—to enclose common lands, to create pools of wage labor, to police vagrants, to provide relief for the poor, to open colonial markets, to manipulate money and credit, and so on. At the same time, these powerfully destabilizing processes and events engendered countermovements for the reasonable "self-protection of society," in the form of trade unions, voluntary associations, public health initiatives, and rural and environmental conservation, as well as anticolonial movements for national sovereignty. What Polanyi called the "double movement" developed over time into a strong critique of the ideology of the self-regulating market, culminating in the social institutions and economic redistributions of the modern welfare state.

Against the backdrop of the crisis of the Great Depression, the U.S. philosopher John Dewey (1935, 56) denominated "renascent liberalism" as those efforts of "organized society" to develop and use political administration to produce the actual and not merely the theoretical liberty of the national citizenry. This meant first and foremost the emergence of state-directed policies toward equalizing the distribution of the national income. The key innovations here were in the economic domain and are generally ascribed to the British economist John Maynard Keynes, who argued for a more extensive regime of market regulation, economic planning, and public spending against the old "orthodoxies" of laissez-faire capitalism. Although Keynes was undoubtedly concerned to stave off revolutionary challenges from below, it is reasonable to ask whether the kind of social liberalism developed under the auspices of Keynesian economic policy is a fundamental deviation from what we still want to call liberalism. Polanyi (1944/2001, 242), for example, described "socialism" as "the tendency inherent in an industrial civilization to transcend the self-regulating market by consciously subordinating it to a democratic society," and he viewed the U.S. New Deal as a decisive step in that direction.

Other writers have been less sanguine about the inner tendencies of liberalism, particularly against the backdrop of mass democracy. In the face of the political crisis of post–World War I Germany, for example, political philosopher (and later Nazi jurist) Carl Schmitt (1923/1985, 15) presciently warned that "states of emergency" would force liberal-democracy to "decide between its elements." Schmitt identified democratic unanimity with sovereign capacity to decide on exceptions to the law, and he argued that this conjunction revealed the political anemia of liberal proceduralism (that is, parliamentary deliberation, separation of powers, and protection of individual rights). Advancing a sharp critique of the universalizing claims of liberalism, Schmitt defined democracy as "the equality of equals" and the production of a homogeneous form of life (16). In doing so, he once again envisioned a doubled space where the rule of law and right enjoyed by "civilized" peoples was predicated on the violent suppression and control of contiguous or adjacent "wild" spaces, as exemplified by European (and U.S.) colonial history.

Writing at the height of the McCarthy period in the United States (but with a different political agenda and sympathies), Louis Hartz (1955, 9) decried what he called the "dogmatic liberalism of a liberal American way of life." According to Hartz, this "liberal tradition," despite its expansive individualism, was inherently conservative and "conformitarian," possessing a "deep and unwritten tyrannical compulsion" at its core that led to periodic outbursts of nationalist hysteria, moral panics, "deportation deliriums," and "red scares" (12). Hartz's critique marks a seminal moment in the development of a critical American studies discourse as it emerged from wider streams of reflection on the meaning and import of culture in the moment of U.S. global ascendancy. For despite his generally cynical and ironic standpoint, Hartz proposed an "unconscious" or "mass Lockeanism" as the key to the national character and as an answer to the old American exceptionalist saw "Why is there no socialism in the United States?" The puzzle for Hartz was that "Americanism" so consistently "combined McCarthy with [Woodrow] Wilson" (13). Thus, U.S. liberalism was marked both by a cosmopolitan, expansionist drive to "transform things alien" and by insular, parochial withdrawals into home and nation (286).

Hartz's critique lent itself to a certain political quiescence; it also underplayed the ongoing racial and imperial crisis of modern liberalism. In this sense, thinkers from the political left and those associated with new social movements of the 1960s and 1970s developed more powerful critiques of post–World War II liberalism (particularly as it had been leavened with anticommunism) as a regime of political compromise and coordination within the North Atlantic world that forestalled more radical potentials for working-class self-organization at home and decolonization abroad. Thus, anticolonial theorist Frantz Fanon (1963/2004, 80, 103) denounced the "universal violence" of a Pax Americana that preserved what he called "luxury socialism" for Europe, while subjecting the rest of the world to a violent and capricious decolonization, under the shadow of global nuclear annihilation. From within modern welfare states, feminist and antiracist activists excoriated the racial and gender hierarchies and differential inclusions that continued to skew material distribution and symbolic recognition for those who had long been subordinated within the liberal order. A further line of criticism, associated with Michel Foucault (1975/1999), cast the long historical development of the administrative or governmental state as a deepening of disciplinary techniques and normalizing logics that enmeshed individual subjects in an extensive network of power relations and intensive systems of social control.

Even as liberalism was attacked from the left, however, it was, to paraphrase British cultural studies scholar Stuart Hall (1978), moving to the right. As Irving Kristol famously quipped in the late 1960s, a neoconservative was merely a liberal who had been "mugged by reality." The image of a mugging invoked the specter of black street crime, the alleged soft tolerance of "liberal" inclusion, and rage at the perception that the United States had lost its moral claim to be the world's exemplary liberal democracy in the wake of the Vietnam War. It is clear that since the 1970s another renovation of liberalism—often arrayed under the moniker "neoliberalism"—has been under way and gaining momentum. A hybrid (like all forms of liberalism), neoliberalism resurrects "pre-Keynesian" assumptions that free markets automatically generate civic order and economic prosperity, even while it gradually eviscerates democratic norms of political participation by an informed citizenry, reimagining both individuals and groups as primarily "entrepreneurial actors" (Wendy Brown 2003, 5).

A significant challenge for critical intellectual work in the coming years will be to track the political contours and consequences of neoliberalism in a moment of resurgent U.S. imperialism. As Locke (1690/1980, 29) famously wrote, "In the beginning, all the world was America." Today it appears at times that we have come full circle, with the United States attempting to turn the world into itself. "A deep continuity connects U.S.

global ambition from the eighteenth to the twenty-first century," something that may have a lot to do with Hartz's Lockean political unconscious (N. Smith 2004, 11). A danger is that the U.S. face of neoliberal globalization, with its consumptive excesses, blunt force, casual racism, and crude market calculus, augurs the exhaustion of the politically productive, incipiently democratic "double movement" of liberal universalism and liberal exclusion and a turn to something far more ominous. As long as liberalism continues to dominate the political horizon, however, the ongoing and wholly consequential struggle to determine the character of its distinctive precipitates of economic liberty and political equality, individual freedom and normative exclusion, reformist perfectionism and counterrevolutionary animus, cosmopolitan vision and provincial blindness, are likely to continue.

39

Literature

Sandra M. Gustafson

Derived from the Latin *littera*, or "letter," "literature" for many centuries referred to a personal quality ("having literature") that meant possessing polite learning through reading. To call someone "illiterate" in the seventeenth century did not mean that the person could not read; it meant that the individual was not possessed of learning, notably knowledge of the classics. Any formal written work—for instance, a scientific treatise, a sermon text, a work of philosophy, or an ethnographic narrative—counted as "literature." Then around 1750, the historical associations of literature with literacy and polite learning began to change. Literacy rates rose, printing presses became more common, and the products of the presses became increasingly varied. Reading styles slowly shifted from intensive reading of a few works to wide reading of many works, authorship emerged as a distinct profession, and printed works were increasingly treated as intellectual property. All these factors undermined the association of literacy with polite learning and affected the definition of literature, until eventually it was restricted primarily to works of imaginative literature, notably poetry, drama, and fiction (Kernan 1990; Amory and Hall 2000; McGill 2003).

This account of the emerging conception of literature summarizes developments in Europe and in creole communities in the Americas. Some distinctions are worth stressing. The colonies of British North America were among the most literate societies of their day. The Protestant tradition, which stresses the authority of scripture and the priesthood of all believers, justified the extension of literacy as a tool of spiritual enlightenment and of redemption from bondage to sin. Literacy contributed as well to religious community, uniting like-minded people around the reading of the Bible (Amory and Hall 2000). A parallel but secular narrative that links literacy, enlightenment, political freedom, and the body politic emerged somewhat later, gaining prominence in the age of revolution (D. Hall 1996). Often entwined, these two liberationist narratives explained and promoted the high rates of literacy, particularly in New England, where the Common School movement joined other efforts to expand access to education during the antebellum period.

Even as literacy came to be understood as the basis for an informed citizenry and an essential component of democratic civic responsibility, the expanding array of reading materials available to the literate was a matter of concern to guardians of social order. From the beginning of the nineteenth century, when ministers and cultural elites fretted over the potential of the novel to distract women and the lower classes from their prescribed tasks and roles, to Anthony Comstock's campaign against "dangerous books" at the end of the century, to current debates about "banned books" and the Internet, the increasing availability of cheap and often sensational or politically charged texts produced a backlash from those who believed that literature should function as a tool of social discipline (Davidson 1986/2004).

Works of literature could be used to nurture critique as well as conformity. Among those who identified critique as a central function of literature were the writers now associated with the project of creating a U.S. national literature, notably Ralph Waldo Emerson, Henry David Thoreau, Margaret Fuller, Walt Whitman, and Herman Melville. Writing at the moment when European national identities coalesced around distinct literatures constituted by a shared language and allegedly bearing the marks of the genius of the "race" that produced them, writers associated with the Transcendentalist and Young America movements began in the 1830s to create what they considered to be a distinctively "American literature" (Matthiessen 1941; Widmer 1999). Literature came to be defined less in relation to categories of fiction and nonfiction than by its efforts to manifest a uniquely "American spirit" through its subject matter and form. Some writers and reformers argued that the uniqueness of "American literature" could be found in its use of critique to nurture social progress (M. Gilmore 1985).

Such overtly nationalistic literary efforts were more the exception than the rule on the literary scene of the United States, however. Until 1891, when an international copyright law was passed giving foreign authors intellectual property in their works, the U.S. book and periodical markets were dominated by reprints, many of them works by English writers. Moreover, in contrast to the more centralized publishing institutions of Europe, the U.S. book market was regional and heterogeneous until after the Civil War. In many instances, the market was multilingual, with regional presses publishing works in a wide range of languages, particularly German, Spanish, and French. The multilingual nature of the U.S. market grew with the acquisition of formerly French and Mexican territories and with the enormous influx of immigrants after the Civil War (Sollors 1998; Shell 2002; McGill 2003; Loughran 2007).

The consolidation of a mass book market in the twentieth century tempered but did not eliminate the heterogeneity of the literary marketplace in the United States. For many decades, literature was defined by its representative and inclusive nature. The consolidation of a more exclusive, more narrowly "literary" canon during the Cold War was soon challenged, first by the democratization of universities that began in the 1950s and later through the canon-busting movements of the 1960s through the 1980s. The rise of ethnic literatures and the emergence of performance art contributed to these broadening trends as well. Other factors influencing the expanded notion of the "literary" include the development of interdisciplinary methodologies and programs; the rise of theory within English departments; and the impact of British cultural studies, with its emphasis on social forms, media, and "communication." Debates about "cultural literacy" led to the conceptualization of multiple literacies (Graff 1987; Kernan 1990).

The challenges that these social, cultural, and intellectual movements pose to a narrow conception of literature are not novel features of a debased modern mass culture, as is sometimes argued. Manuscript, performance, and electronic forms of verbal expression have always complicated and resisted the consolidation of a restrictive, print-based sense of the literary. For instance, the circulation of poetry in manuscript form had an important vogue in the middle of the nineteenth century, at the height of what is often called "print culture," a trend most famously instantiated in the fascicles of Emily Dickinson (Cameron 1992; Howe 1993; Martha Nell Smith 1998; Gustafson and Sloat 2010). Beginning in the late nineteenth century, and with growing vigor during the following century, artists' books reflected a vital interest in visual elements and nonprint modes of literary production (Drucker 1995).

For much of the nineteenth century, political and religious forms of oratory were central to the world of letters. Even as U.S. writers suffered the contempt of the English reviewers and the competition of foreign reprints, the nation's orators were celebrated (not always without irony) as peers of Demosthenes and Cicero. Oratory was perceived as the ideal verbal art, a consummate republican form. Compilations of "great American speeches" were produced in substantial numbers. Critics wrote books analyzing the qualities and strengths of various orators. Elocution was a popular subject of study, and students rehearsed Patrick Henry's famous words in schools. In 1851, Daniel Webster's collected speeches were published, perhaps the first such collection to appear during an orator's lifetime. Thirty years later, his speeches were still being analyzed for their contributions to U.S. American letters. The influence of oratory runs through the essays, fiction, and poetry of the antebellum period and constitutes an important element in the era's literary culture. Performance art, poetry readings, stand-up comedy, and other verbal arts are all heirs of the spoken word from this earlier era (Gustafson 2000, 2011).

The continued influence of oral genres has been particularly important for U.S. ethnic writers. Alphabetic literacy not only was in some instances prohibited to African Americans and Native Americans, as in the slave codes outlawing literacy training. It also came with the added burden of being identified as a skill derived from and properly belonging to whites and often used to advance their interests through false treaties and unjust laws. For some ethnic-minority verbal artists, literacy was a tool of oppression and, at times, of self-division, separating an individual from a community distinguished by oral forms of verbal art. In the twentieth century, writers and other artists associated with the Black Arts Movement, as well as many Native American writers, reflected on the paradoxes of oppression and liberation intrinsic to the alphabetic literacy central to their artistic projects. U.S. literary history cannot be fully understood without reference to the oral forms that it excludes in its very name, the forms that modern critics call "orature," a term invented by the Ugandan linguist Pio Zirimu and developed by Ngũgĩ wa Thiong'o (Lauter 1990; Ngũgĩ 1998; Gustafson 2000).

Today the rise of electronic media poses important challenges to print culture. Beginning in 1990, a series of books and studies has tracked the impending "death of literature," linking its demise to social trends such as the democratization of the university and, increasingly, to technological developments, notably the rise of the World Wide Web. These critics characteristically employ the most restrictive definition of "literature," limiting it to poetry, drama (in a book, not on the stage), and, above all, the novel. The novel has special status for these writers, who often take it to be the paradigmatic literary form because of its length, the "linear" reading that it encourages, and the solitude and consequent richness of subjectivity that novel reading is supposed to produce. They trace certain forms of social order and cultural organization to widespread engagement with "the literary," in this narrow definition (Birkerts 1994; Edmundson 2004).

These claims for and about literature have not gone unchallenged. One of the most striking recent developments in American studies and cultural studies is the emergence of a critical discourse focused on recognizing and understanding the range of textual media and their varied modalities of creative verbal and visual expression. Studies of electronic media, some of which travel under the flag of the digital humanities, demand that scholars rethink the heterogeneous nature of textuality and the varied forms of reading that these textualities produce (McGann 2001; Hayles 2008). This approach opens new avenues for interpreting older textual forms, such as "Aboriginal oral, glyphic, artefactual modes, and conceptualizations of communication" (Battiste 2004, 121; see also M. Cohen 2009). It foregrounds the specific historical and contemporary institutions and practices that are organized by alphabetic literacy. It also engages a broader archive in its effort to document the interactions between the products of such literacy and those who produce and consume them.

40

Marriage

Elizabeth Freeman

Marriage seems to be an ordinary fact of life, not a contested concept. In U.S. culture, however, the term "marriage" has pointed to two simultaneous but incompatible functions. As a component of U.S. kinship law, marriage sanctions particular sexual alliances, from which property relations are determined. It thereby defines a sphere of protected sexual and economic interests, whose exterior is marked by sexual "deviants." Yet as an aspect of modern emotional life in the United States, marriage is also the ideological linchpin of intimacy—the most elevated form of chosen interpersonal relationship. At the core of political debate and much critical debate in American studies and cultural studies is whether marriage is a matter of love or law, a means of securing social stability or of realizing individual freedom and emotional satisfaction. These have become national questions; marriage seems so tied to collective national identity and democratic practices that many U.S. Americans view it as an expression of patriotism. This linkage is more than rhetorical. As well as structuring sexuality and gender, marriage law undergirds U.S. citizenship, because it is implicated in the property relations, racial hierarchy, immigration policy, and colonialist projects that have determined national membership.

Historically, the institution of marriage has been regulated by both church and state, a merging partly responsible for its contradictory meanings. Christian scriptures stipulate that marriage makes a man and a woman into "one flesh." But Christian marriage also takes place within a larger, communal body of Christ whose members are united by spiritual bonds rather than the property relations of aristocratic families. Protestants, in giving governments control over marriage in the mid-sixteenth century, elevated the couple as the primary social and economic unit. The burden of caretaking shifted from Christian communities, aristocratic paterfamilias, and the government to spouses and parents. Here, legal issues (the loss of institutionalized provisions for the economically distressed) were reconfigured into emotional ones (family feelings). Western European popular culture eventually solidified this ideological triumph of love over law and property. The literary genre of the sentimental novel, emerging in the eighteenth century, secularized the Christian image of a couple embedded in and figuring a community bound by love, rather than terrorized by hierarchical class relations or, later, legal interference.

In England and its American colonies, the conflicting functions of marriage became implicated in questions of nationhood beginning with a clash in Enlightenment political theory. Following Sir Robert Filmer (1680), the male-headed, hierarchical Puritan household was considered an arm of the government. Later colonial and Revolutionary-era thinkers, however, adhered more closely to Locke's doctrine that the private "voluntary compact" between a man and a woman historically preceded and provided the basis for democratic relations in the public sphere, while remaining separate from it (Locke 1690/1988, 43; Norton 1996). This ideal of consensual, private marriage suffused Revolutionary rhetoric in the eighteenth century (Fliegelman 1982). Thus, the founders of the United States saw marriage as a template for the ideal society, in which a people freely consented to leadership rather than submitting to a hierarchy (Cott 2000). Intimacy, as they imagined it, would mirror kinship; love would meet law and even prefigure it. Correspondingly, marriages in the new republic were seen as rehearsals for or reenactments of a proper citizenship grounded in family feelings (Kerber 1980).

One problem with this use of marriage as a figure for liberal democracy was that marriage has long structured the asymmetrical power relations that constitute gender. The unwritten spousal contract, most visible in nuptial vows and suits for divorce or separation, assigned economic support and physical protection to men. In exchange, women's duties included sexual intercourse, childbirth, housework, and child rearing. Thus, the term "marriage" also implied patriarchy, for men controlled the economic and physical well-being of their wives and children. It implied domesticity for women, who exercised their power in the home only. But this contract was not actually drawn between two legal individuals. Following the common laws of England even after the Revolution, U.S. women who married were *femes coverts*, with no legal existence independent from that of their husbands. Women could not own separate property, keep their earnings, sign contracts, or vote to change this system. In these and other practices, men and women were considered as one, and the one was the husband. Debates in American studies about marriage were prefigured by early republican writers who analogized coverture and political tyranny. "Remember the Ladies," wrote Abigail Adams (1776/1988, 10) to her husband. "Do not put such unlimited power in the hands of the Husbands. Remember all men would be tyrants if they could."

Analogies between marriage and other forms of political inequality continued in the abolitionist era and beyond, as white feminists equated wifehood with slavery (Sánchez-Eppler 1993). Until the 1970s, the cultural expectation of husbandly economic support in exchange for wifely domestic support removed middle-class women from the workforce and provided uncompensated labor for working men and the institutions that employed them. As feminists eventually argued, marriage creates domestic labor, the unpaid work of women who process raw materials for workers' consumption and socialize children for the workforce (Delphy 1977). Socialists argued that marriage further bolsters the system of capitalism by keeping profits in the private family (Engels 1884/1972). It turns wealth into a matter of inheritance rather than lifetime accumulation, preventing redistribution to a larger public and thereby enforcing work for pay among the propertyless class. Yet the Protestant legacy has meant that marriage is also viewed as an individual solution to poverty, far preferable, for conservatives, to a welfare state. In 2003, for instance, the U.S. Congress passed a bill (H.R. 4) mandating that every state receiving welfare funds establish objectives for promoting marriage.

Still, to speak of marriage as a form of slavery, or even as an essential feature of market capitalism, fails to address its racial politics. Marriage law served as a means of securing white dominance. Slaves could not marry; free black people were legally forbidden to marry whites in many states from the 1660s to 1967; and rights to inheritance were denied to the black partners of whites and their children (Saks 1988). One effect of this history was that many African Americans saw the right to marry as fundamental to achieving full citizenship. After the failure of Reconstruction, black fiction writers often used the sentimental marriage plot to allegorize the civil justice they had been denied (Tate 1992). But not all African Americans have taken marriage to be a sign of or path to freedom. When in 1865 the Freedman's Bureau insisted that all former slave unions be legitimated by license or ceremony, some freedpeople, especially women, declined to register their unions (K. Franke 1999). A century later, when the infamous report on the black family by Daniel Patrick Moynihan (1965) appeared, it blamed the social woes of African Americans in part on "matriarchal" households in which unmarried women were the primary or only breadwinners. This interpretation of African Americans' kinship structures racialized, gendered, and sexualized poverty, setting the stage for the welfare reforms of the 1980s and beyond.

The racial politics of marriage have also inflected its role in colonial projects within the United States, as well as in the nation's immigration law. By legitimizing, promoting, and protecting the monogamous heterosexual relationships of citizens and automatically extending citizenship to those born within them, nation-states make national belonging seem a matter of nature and not law. Marriage legitimates birthright, which trumps mere residence as a means of access to citizenship (Stevens 1999). Thus, European settlers in the colonies persecuted Native Americans in part because their kinship systems and sexual practices sometimes included polygamy, easy divorce, and premarital sex. During the period of American Indian removal, the government allocated plots of land using Anglo, not Indian, kinship as a grid. Once the federal government took full control over immigration in 1891, marriage became a means of excluding racialized groups from entry or permanent resident status in the United States. Asians and Muslims, for instance, were often excluded under laws barring polygamists and prostitutes from entry. Since the lifting of racial quotas, immigrants have had an easier time entering the United States as family members than as laborers. The laws currently linking marriage explicitly to citizenship, known as family reunification laws, have their precedent in a 1907 statute mandating that the nationality of an American woman follow the nationality of her husband (Cott 2000). Although this law was repealed in the 1930s, it provided a blueprint for the preferential treatment of foreign spouses over other immigrants. Lesbian and gay international couples, however, have been denied this benefit.

While for the federal government marriage provides the very architecture of citizenship, the individual states actually have jurisdiction over marriage. Thus, federal law has only rarely intervened positively to define marriage or to prohibit particular kinds of marriage between free people. The first of these interventions occurred in 1862, when Abraham Lincoln signed the Morrill Act prohibiting polygamy in the territories. In 1890, the Mormons were forced to give up polygamy as a condition of statehood for Utah. The next federal intervention was the Defense of Marriage Act, signed by Bill Clinton in 1996. George W. Bush followed suit with a campaign for a constitutional amendment prohibiting same-sex marriage. An arguably theocratic state reemerged with these official enforcements of Christian, monogamous, heterosexual marriage. Even as a national lesbian and gay movement has promoted gay marriage, voters and government officials have moved furiously to prevent it, at least until very recently.

The power of marriage as a guarantor of gender identity and sexual hierarchy, a paradigm of democratic consent, an island of economic security, a mechanism for racial solidarity, and the scaffolding of citizenship itself explains the passion of these debates (Duggan 2004). Despite the constitutional separation of church and state, the Protestant model of marriage has historically been a prerequisite for belonging to "America." Merely allowing same-sex couples this privilege will not change that. The critical tasks ahead include continuing to ask what other hierarchical institutions marriage serves or is implicated in. At the same time, we must look beyond marriage and couplehood by working to democratize support for the diverse household structures and emotional bonds that organize people's lives.

41

Media

Lisa Nakamura

"Media" is a word with unusual weight in the United States. It appears in the name of a discipline—media studies—as well as numerous subfields, such as media industry studies, feminist media studies, comparative and transnational media studies, and most recently, digital media studies. "Participatory media," "interactive media," and "social media" are all relatively new terms that describe the production and consumption of digital texts, images, and sounds through the World Wide Web and mobile applications that use social networks such as YouTube, Pandora, Facebook, and Twitter. The quick uptake and incorporation of these new media into everyday life in the United States and globally have resulted in a proliferation of usages of the keyword "media."

Though "media" is the grammatical plural of the singular "medium," the word is most often used in the singular. It is easy to portray "the media" in negative terms as "addictive" and socially isolating, as a purveyor of harmful stereotypes and violent images, yet media scholars working in the cultural studies tradition have tended to focus less on this preoccupation and more on the ways that the media creates a sense of identity and practices of social belonging for its users. Some of the earliest thinkers to take the media as an object of critical analysis were Continental philosophers such as Theodor Adorno (2001) and Walter Benjamin (1968), who worked in a mostly German tradition known as "critical theory" or the Frankfurt school. Like the later French writer Jean Baudrillard (1994), they were deeply interested in

the increasing ubiquity, cheapness, and profusion of printed images, recorded sounds, and moving image sequences. They saw these new media technologies as signaling a profound social shift. Technological advances starting with the printing press and moving on to photography, film, and digital devices and networks enabled copies to circulate more widely than ever before, bathing individuals in a constant flow of images that had meant something very different when they were singular and traveled less freely. In the foundational 1936 essay "The Work of Art in the Age of Mechanical Reproduction" (1936/1968), Benjamin both mourns the loss of the unique "aura" that original artworks possessed and ushers in the study of the media as an academic discipline. Benjamin's focus on the automation of media production has inflected media studies in the United States and elsewhere with an abiding concern with the technology, politics, and economics of media as well as its content.

Members of the Frankfurt school shared Benjamin's interest in mechanically reproduced or "mass" media, and their stance toward it was fundamentally suspicious. At the same time, this group, particularly Adorno, was among the first to take the power of the "mass media" seriously and to recognize it as a cultural apparatus deserving of its own set of theories. In his 1963 essay "The Culture Industry Reconsidered" (1963/2001), Adorno argued eloquently for a critical and pessimistic view of "monopolistic mass culture," or the sale of culture for profit, a phenomenon that he considered fundamentally at odds with aesthetic quality and the public good. Adorno reserved special scorn for news magazines and television, particularly genres such as Westerns and musicals, which were not only full of empty spectacle and numbing repetition but earned enormous sums for companies that exploited both workers *and* audiences. He is careful to note that his objection to "mass media" and "mass culture" has nothing to do with his moral judgments of its audience and its taste preferences. Indeed, his critique of mass media is that it is not popular *enough*, meaning it does not "arise spontaneously from the masses themselves" but is rather a commodity, a product "tailored for consumption by masses" (98).

In sharp contrast to Adorno, Marshall McLuhan had a sunnier, even utopian attitude toward the role of media in society. In *Understanding Media: The Extensions of Man* (1964/2003), he was eager to consider electronic media forms such as television, radio, and film as specific forms of technological practice. While we no longer envision television as "hot" or radio as "cool," as McLuhan advocated, digital media scholars have taken up his work after a period of neglect during the eighties. What they find useful is McLuhan's envisioning of electronic media forms such as television and radio not just as ways to get information and entertainment but also as having distinctive affective qualities and as extensions of the human body and brain. Benedict Anderson's influential 1983 *Imagined Communities*, for instance, found a new and receptive audience in the 2000s and beyond because it explained national identity and nationalism as artifacts of a particular medium—print—and the sociocultural formation he called "print capitalism." Drawing on historical materials from diverse anticolonial movements (beginning with the American Revolution), Anderson found that newspapers did far more than report happenings in a particular regional locale. They also brought the nation into being by creating a readership that came to view or imagined itself as sharing a common identity. Media, in this account, do more than convey information or even ideology. They create communities. Anderson claimed that national identity was less a function of birthplace or legal standing within a citizenry than it

was an "imagined" or virtual state—called into being by the process of mediation itself. A form of media such as print, in this account, functions as a space or medium of cultural interpellation.

One trouble with this account is that not everyone uses or is positioned by the media in the same way. The postcolonial response to this line of argument emphasizes the ways that unequal access to media power and the tools of media production results in exclusion of specific populations from the nation on both a symbolic and a very real level. People of color, women, sexual minorities, and other subaltern individuals possess less power within the media system, which has often represented them in stereotyped, limited ways. In other words, mass media do not hail all bodies equally (Loomba 2005). When the Internet and the World Wide Web were adopted more widely in the midnineties, the so-called Web 1.0 period, it seemed that McLuhan's dream of intimate democratic community through media—what he called "the global village"—had come true. However, it quickly became clear that the Internet was far from radically democratic. Not every body had an equal or voluntary relation to it in terms of access or authorship. The feminist philosopher Donna Haraway argued eloquently that the computer age has made it impossible to separate the body from technology (1991). Biotechnologies enabled by computing devices entangle us in webs and assemblages of human and machine, since the human body *is* literally a form of media—informational technologies are interwoven with and inform our bodily existence. Haraway's critique of these technologies, particularly the military and commercial technologies that gave rise to our current media system, has proven very influential to science and technology studies scholars as well as to feminist media scholars. Her work also draws attention to the systemic role that gendered and raced labor plays in building the integrated circuits needed in electronic and, later, digital media devices.

Consider as an example of this system the deep and often unacknowledged connections between internal colonization, settler colonialism, and computing hardware. From 1965 to 1975, the Fairchild Corporation's Semiconductor Division operated a large integrated-circuit manufacturing plant in Shiprock, New Mexico, on a Navajo reservation. During this period, the corporation was the largest private employer of Indian workers in the United States. The circuits that the almost entirely female Navajo workforce produced were used in devices such as calculators, missile guidance systems, and other early computing devices. To address this type of history, media criticism and analysis will have to turn away from a narrow focus on representations of stereotypes as the most central form of media influence and toward an attention to the intersections of the design, implementation, and production of media technologies themselves. This materialist or archaeological approach to media, digital or otherwise, urges us to examine not just how media represent or interpellate different cultures, genders, and identities but also how media devices are produced and marketed. Mobile media such as cellphones, for instance, require rare metals such as coltan, which is extracted from the Congo and finds its way to the rest of the world in a system that echoes earlier forms of resource extraction under colonialism. These practices, along with technological constraints and affordances and less known histories behind the screen, are inseparable from the way that digital media mean (Ernst 2013). Recent scholarship focused on materialist media archaeologies in the digital realm has contributed greatly to the fields of American studies and cultural studies by mapping the links between media infrastructures' origins, design cultures, and informing principles, as well as the hidden or neglected histories of marginalized groups in computing (Chun 2011; McPherson 2012b; Sandvig 2012).

Earlier digital media scholarship tended to represent new forms of media production and distribution as tools for liberation. Recent scholarship adopts a more critical stance, stressing the ways in which mass media are often fundamentally at odds with the aesthetic and economic needs of the people they claim to liberate. This critical stance has become increasingly important with the rise of digital "participatory media." For the past twenty years, digital media have been posited as a way for individuals to exert more control over their own identities through media making and distribution. The advent of social media such as Facebook, Twitter, blogging, and other forms of user-generated content management and distribution have ushered us into the age of Web 2.0, the "participatory web." It is true that more and more of us are "participating" by contributing our content, images, location information, and "likes" and "dislikes" in exchange for these services. And the production of mash-ups, amateur video, and sampled sound recordings can indeed enable users to create countercultural and critical new messages (Jenkins 2006). Yet the observation that users make, create, and distribute certain types of digital media content such as memes, mash-ups, and video does not mean that mass media's problems, including rampant racial, gender, and sexual misrepresentation and exclusion, are no longer present. Women and people of color have not been well served by the mass media, which has thrived on the circulation of racist and sexist ideologies as a means of marketing commodities (Banta 1987; McClintock 1995; Ewen and Ewen 2006). Digital media have given users new opportunities to exploit images of race and gender as part of memetic culture (Nakamura 2008; Nakamura and Chow-White 2012). Whether scholars of media choose to focus on neglected histories of media forms; the way that media represents bodies, identities, sexualities, or genders; or other aspects of media altogether, the everydayness of digital media will require us to pay more attention to the media platforms and communities, digital and otherwise, where so many of us live our lives.

42

Migration

Alyshia Gálvez

"Migration" was initially used in early sixteenth-century French to refer to human movement across space. These early usages date to the initial period of European conquest and colonization of the Americas, arguably the first phase of what is today referred to as globalization (Wolf 1982). The contexts of these usages were largely historical and literary, referring to the expulsion of Adam from Eden or the travel of a person from one town to another. A century later, "migration" was deployed by natural scientists in reference to the migration of birds, salmon, and butterflies. This naturalistic use of the term predominated into the twentieth century, as the natural and social sciences came to view animal and human actions, relations, and movements in an empiricist light, as objective and apolitical (Foucault 1976/1990, 1975/1995). Human migration was thus dehumanized, reduced to a mechanistic response to availability of resources. Whether nomadic groups crossing the ice bridge in the Bering Sea twenty thousand years ago or Canada geese flying south for the winter, humans and animals can be expected to move to where they find the necessities of life. Pioneering studies of human migration in the fields of geography and demography were influenced by this orientation, charting "laws of migration" and the "push" and "pull" factors that expelled migrants from their homes and attracted them to new lands (Ravenstein 1885; Everett Lee 1966).

As this usage history indicates, "migration" is a general term, encompassing many different kinds of movement, including immigration (migration *to* a nation) and emigration (migration *from* a nation), as well as flows *within* a nation such as rural-to-urban migration (urbanization) and urban-to-suburban migration (suburbanization). Globally, the magnitude of movement is greater now than at any other point in human history: as many as a billion people are migrants, a quarter of them transnational and three-quarters internal or domestic migrants (Suárez Orozco, Suárez-Orozco, and Sattin-Bajaj 2010). At present, there are two main ways that the term "migration" is deployed in relation to these movements. First, "migration" refers to the movement of populations in space. While this use is less common in the United States, it continues to be dominant in some international and supranational contexts. The Migration Policy Institute (2012), for instance, dedicates itself to "the study of the movement of people worldwide," while Migrant Rights International (2012) describes itself as a "global alliance of migrant associations and migrant rights, human rights, labor, religious, and other organizations that operate at the local, national, regional or international level."

The second use of the term occurs when the topic of interest is a specific subset of the phenomena encompassed by migration: when migrants cross national borders. This selective emphasis has been dominant in the field of American studies and, to a lesser extent, cultural studies. It typically excludes other meanings, including forms of involuntary migration that are categorized under headings such as human trafficking and refugee policy. While refugee and asylum issues are addressed in many industrialized nations as part of foreign aid and humanitarian assistance, they are typically distinguished from the desire of people to relocate to such nations for economic or social reasons. In short, nation-states and institutions make distinctions between different kinds of migration—between "immigrants" and "refugees"—that are in many ways arbitrary but can have

life-and-death consequences for those who receive these designations. In the United States, unauthorized flows of newcomers, who are classified generally as "economic migrants" and referred to as "illegal immigrants," fall into the bureaucratic jurisdiction of law enforcement agencies including Immigration and Customs Enforcement, or ICE.

Since the mid-twentieth century, "migration" has been used most often in U.S. contexts only with modifiers or prefixes: "transnational migration," "emigration," and "immigration." "Migration" is thus made specific in everyday usage. In American studies and cultural studies, these usages shape both fields of inquiry. In the mid-twentieth century, it was still common to use "migration" as a general term referring both to "foreign" immigration and "internal" migration, as in Sidney Goldstein's "Migration: Dynamic of the American City" (1954). It is almost unthinkable to imagine a study such as Goldstein's today: comprehensive of both immigration and internal migration trends in the United States. The same is true in less scholarly contexts. Discussions of the contemporary movement of African Americans to the South, a reversal of earlier flows usually referred to as the "Great Migration," are described in a 2011 *New York Times* article as a movement, an exodus, a return, and only once as a "migration" (Bilefsky 2011). "Migration" in popular usage signifies more narrowly than it once did; it has become almost synonymous with "immigration."

This selective use and semantic narrowing of terminology reflects the preoccupation in the United States with national security, borders, and their regulation. Only the circulation of people across U.S. borders is cast as relevant to public policy and debate about migration. This limited use of the term is prevalent not only in the United States but also in other countries classifiable as "immigrant receiving" such as the United Kingdom, France, and Chile. In these national contexts, the use of the term to refer primarily to the specific phenomenon of cross-border migration has the effect of making migrants and their movements seem a thing of the past. In a time of unprecedented militarization of U.S. borders, migration becomes, at best, a quaint remnant of more innocent times and, at worst, an aggressive act of defiance against the rule of law. From the normative viewpoint of receiving nations, *immigration* is a problem to be regulated through the orderly flow of those who respect the sovereignty of nations, while migration remains an unregulated, unplanned movement of populations ignorant or defiant of the borders they cross and the states that seek to regulate those borders.

Applied to the history of migration in the United States, these assumptions mean that Europeans passing through Ellis Island in the early twentieth century were *immigrants*, subject to the nation's interest in regulating admission, while Mexican workers traveling to pick crops were *migrants*, their movement pegged to a natural cycle of the cultivation, ripening, and harvest of fruits and vegetables, their entry not always controlled by bureaucracy, and their return assumed. Even when the work was industrial, not agricultural, and regulated, the term "migrant worker" was used, with time limits and return implied. In the early to mid-twentieth century, regular migrant flows across the border, even without authorization, were not viewed as terribly controversial because workers were thought likely to return from where they came at the conclusion of the season. Policies such as the Bracero program (a guest-worker program in existence from 1942 to 1964) were premised on the notion of cyclical flows. Like migratory birds, migrant workers were thought to respond to instinctual rhythms of labor supply and scarcity. Cyclical movement, not settlement, continues

to be implied in the use of the term "migration" in the United States today.

This distinction between immigration as a regulated, bureaucratic, and legal process and the more naturalistic usages of the term "migration" legitimizes the flows of some people and delegitimizes others. Contemporary social life is thought to be governed by "the rule of law," borders, and state sovereignty. Migration becomes a political issue to be regulated and managed by nation-states. No longer are there large-scale guest-worker programs with temporary visas for seasonal work in the United States. Even the relationship between agriculture and seasonality has been obscured as supermarkets are filled with fruits and vegetables imported as often from another hemisphere as from local agricultural regions. In the context of globalization, the notion of the seasonality of labor supply and demand and the right of human beings to move across borders to seek a living (upheld in the United Nations' Universal Declaration of Human Rights) are increasingly viewed as threats to national sovereignty, while migrants themselves are less tolerated than ever and viewed as anachronistic and even insufficiently civilized. The most frequently cited argument for withholding legalization from undocumented immigrants is the notion that they must "show respect for the law" at the same time that the law has shifted, becoming ever more stringent and restrictive over time. In this way, the term "migration" does the semantic work of dehumanizing people who travel across borders of various kinds, depicting them as out of step with current modes and juridical structures of citizenship and belonging.

The category of immigrants is reserved for those who do not need to migrate but are highly skilled and highly mobile individuals who stand patiently at the door, awaiting the clearance of legal and bureaucratic obstacles to entry. By the same logic, "illegal immigrants"

MIGRATION ALYSHIA GÁLVEZ

are the inverse, imagined as those who are not skilled or educated, and certainly not patient, viewed as "cutting the line" or "jumping the fence." Even when viewed charitably, as "economic" migrants, they are denied the status of *im*migrants due to unauthorized entry or impermanent visa status, their complex array of motivations for movement reduced to simple self-interest. Rather than a unidirectional, authorized, and regulated flow, migrants are assumed to be sojourners, a fleeting presence, soon to return or, if not, subject to forcible return or deportation (G. Chang 2000; Chavez 1988; De Genova 2005; Hondagneu-Sotelo 1995). Given the vast diversity of migration experiences, both internal and transnational (see Maria García 2006; Swinth 2005), greater awareness of how the term is used to dehumanize and delegitimize migrants and their motivations is more critical than ever.

43

Modern
Chandan Reddy

"Modern" is among the most difficult words in our critical vocabulary either to define or to abandon. Within different disciplinary contexts, both the origins and the features of the modern are differently inscribed. Philosophy locates the onset of the modern in the eighteenth-century secularization of knowledge about the human and material world, while history and political science periodize it alongside the generalization of the sovereign nation-state after the Treaty of Westphalia in 1648 and the emergence of the citizen-subject after the French Revolution of 1789. For economics, the modern began with the emergence of capitalist market economies following the British Industrial Revolution, whereas literary studies traces it to the invention of the printing press and the gradual universalization of schooling and literacy. The hallmarks of modernity as defined by these intellectual traditions include the development of free labor, universalist notions of culture, and abstract notions of equality. As 85 percent of the globe's land mass was forcibly submitted to colonial rule, Western intellectuals and their publics, enthralled by the birth of "modernity," promoted "progress" by fixating on these features as the endpoint of colonial "development." It was, as one British poet wrote on the eve of the U.S. colonization of the Philippines in 1899, "the white man's burden" to shine the light of modernity globally (Kipling 1899).

Derived from the Latin terms *modernus* and *modo* (meaning, respectively, "of today" and "recently"), "modern" first entered the English language around the twelfth century as a term to denote a newness that required legitimation in contrast to classical antiquity. Yet it was only with the rise of the European Enlightenment in the mid-eighteenth century that "modern" took on "the sense of a qualitative claim about the newness of the times, in the sense of their being 'completely other, even better than what has gone before'" (Osborne 1995, 10, quoting Koselleck 1985/2004, 228). By the nineteenth century, the modern possessed an epochal character, promising a *qualitative* transformation from the past, now itself understood as composed of discrete epochs with distinct features. Shaped by its relation to other terms such as "progress," "development," "freedom," "revolution," "society," and "civilization," "modern" was no longer a mere temporal descriptor. Instead, it signified a "newness" previously unavailable in human consciousness and societies, a distinctive orientation of thought toward the future rather than tradition, and a uniquely "scientific" worldview that located Europe as a coherent geography and temporal center of global history (T. Mitchell 2000). Largely through the force of British and European colonialism, the term was no longer contrasted with "antiquity" but instead with "backwardness," a category that encompassed both "older civilizations" in decline and "primitive societies" frozen in an earlier moment of human history. Whole societies, peoples, and art forms were now classifiable as primitive, degenerate, or modern, with the latter positioned at the leading edge of historical time and serving as the measure of human perfectibility.

By the mid-nineteenth century, the keyword "modern" thus began to function much as it does today, connoting something both temporal ("that which is most recent" within the context of developmental linear time) and spatial (the grouping of otherwise diverse phenomena into a single category or class).

Modern peoples, practices, and objects are said to share a qualitative uniqueness that merits the reflexive practices by which modern societies interpret their particular historicity as representative of universal human progress. By this logic, to designate a thing, practice, place, or person as "modern" is to point to the signs by which reflexive acts of interpretation identify the modern condition (Habermas 1987). Virginia Woolf's (1924/1989, 421) famous modernist declaration, "On or about December 1910, human character changed," exemplifies how these meanings overlap: the use of a date to mark both a unique, irreversible event in chronological calendar time and a specific temporalized event, qualitatively new, bearing on universal "human experience." As a representative statement of a broad aesthetic movement, it also conveys the sense of artistic modernism as centrally preoccupied with new *practices of representation*, a critical aspect of the reflexive scrutiny necessary for the modern age.

Emerging out of the same historical conjuncture as artistic modernism, the discipline of sociology describes the modern as coincident with the development of Western industrial capitalist societies. For mainstream sociologists, the defining features of modernity are mass citizenship, official bureaucracy, a national division of labor, long-term capital accumulation, the separation of social spheres, organized leisure, rational individualism, secularization, and a state monopoly on violence across a geographically bounded society. Identifying these features has enabled sociologists since the mid-twentieth century to study societies comparatively, recommending "modernization" to those areas of the globe that, lacking these features at the social and institutional levels, were characterized as socioeconomically "backward." Modernity thus became a regulative ideal with multiple empirical coordinates, the presence or absence of which could be verified by specialists in particular "area studies." In the 1950s, the economist and political scientist W. W. Rostow distinguished between "traditional" and "modern societies," describing the latter as possessing economies that could "take off" or, in other words, could experience continuous long-term growth through processes "internal" to their separate national economies (N. Gilman 2003). As U.S. Cold War anticommunism extended to the newly decolonized world through various modernization strategies, Rostow's takeoff model legitimated overt and covert interventionist wars and development policies in Asia and Latin America, coding them as acts that protected economies and societies from the perverting drives of communism (Escobar 1995; Saldaña-Portillo 2003). The irony that the task of "modernizing" non-Western economies sanctioned U.S. neocolonial interventions did little to undermine the theory's popularity or effectiveness in mapping a world of closed national economies in different stages of universal economic development, each "protected" by the benevolence of U.S. policies of modernization.

For some researchers and scholars today, the category of the "postmodern" names a break with the modern occasioned by the emergence of finance capital; a global division of labor across transnational communities; a decline of liberal freedom; the expansion of the prison-military-industrial complex; a loss of "nature"; an explosion of digital technologies and other simulacra; and an increasingly racialized, gendered, and sexualized cultural politics (Harvey 1989; Soja 1989; Baudrillard 1994). These theorists of postmodernism historicize ruptures in modernity as an effect of an advanced or late capitalism, naming postmodernity as the condition of late capitalism and postmodernism as its dominant cultural logic (Jameson 1991). In doing so, they repeat a modernist impulse, namely, the desire for a knowable

social totality graspable by a unitary epistemological subject. In response, postcolonial scholars have stressed that the postmodern critique of linear development ought to offer the opportunity for a radical displacement of "Western modernity" and the knowledge regimes that create and sanction our ignorance of the complex local histories that mediate modern processes (Spivak 1988). They see in the postmodernist stress on crisis, particularly of form and meaning, the recognition of the breakdown of unified Western histories and epistemological categories for regulating discrepant postcolonial modernities, as well as the disavowal of that recognition (Chakrabarty 2000).

To understand the origins and significance of this more thoroughgoing critique of modernity, we need to situate it as an engagement with the political economy of global Euro-American colonialism. Haunted by the racialized social practices that enabled metropolitan prosperity, the category of the modern has abetted the mischaracterization of that prosperity as universal progress, thus displacing the contemporaneity of colonial social formations and temporalizing the peripheries of the world system as nonmodern (Amin 1976). In this context, earlier conceptions of the modern should be seen as the effect of practices of intellectual abstraction that seek to extricate the West from the actual strategies and relations of accumulation that organized its domination of the world economy, including the violence, destruction, and privation that accompany its prosperity (Benjamin 1950/1968). The social formations that have emerged out of practices of continental genocide (A. Franke 1998), slavery (E. Williams 1944/1994), territorial colonialism (Chandra 1980), and imperialism (Du Bois 1995a) have rarely been understood as modern. Instead, the term has named the practices and concepts through which Euro-American societies narrate their originality as the universal development and futurity of all human societies, occluding the global social relations, divisions of labor, and market economies through which they were built. Epistemologies of race and gender have mediated knowledge of these social forces, inventing the "West" not as a set of differentiating practices within a world economy or global modernity but rather as a closed European historical space moving through linear time (Said 1978).

A different view of the modern can be found in the work of contemporary interdisciplinary scholars, particularly in the fields of historical sociology, postcolonial anthropology, and cultural studies. Here, the term indexes an attempt to understand the *multiple* modernities that have been produced through worldwide capitalism and that cannot be reduced to or understood through a universal norm, such as the nation-state. In American studies scholarship influenced by this research, explorations of racial, gender, and sexual formations that exceed the nation form have produced important critiques of the epistemologies that organize dominant and normative conceptions of U.S. modernity (C. Robinson 1983/2000; Ferguson 2004; Singh 2004). Some of this scholarship has found in the "female African slave," the "Asian coolie," and the "undocumented diasporic worker" the standpoint through which alternative, nonnational modernities might be explored (Anzaldúa 1987; Camp 2003; Jung 2006). Some of it has stressed the ways in which U.S. modernity (and postmodernity) represses the intra- and international "regional" modernities of racialized working peoples, appraising these alternative *late* modern geographies as disjunctive social spaces that undo the nation's capacity to unify historical difference (Bonus 2000; Agarwal and Sivaramakrisnan 2003). And some scholarship has located *late* modernity in the standpoint of the perverse, privileging nonnormative forms of sexual and gender embodiment that normative modern subjects persistently repudiate as pathology and atavism (Eng 2001; Shah 2001; Manalansan 2003; Gopinath 2005). In each instance, these critical studies of late modernities have interrogated the epistemologies through which we have come to know ourselves as modern; the racial, gendered, and sexual genealogies constitutive of these epistemologies; and the ethical and political implications of acknowledging the social relations and histories that these epistemologies have generated as our "nonmodern" shadow.

To situate these various interventions within the context of late modernity is to suggest that our task today may be to ruminate collectively on the erasures, gaps, and incompletions that are a necessary part of any endeavor to tell the story of our modernity. But it is also to note that the conditions for these endeavors are not locatable, as they are for many postmodernists, exclusively in transformations to the structure of capital or in the breakup of the nation-state. They are equally to be found in the demographic transformation of the university through antiracist struggle, in postcolonial migrations, and in the internationalization of the disciplines that have enabled a "return of the repressed" within modern epistemologies (Hong 2006, xiii; see also Gulbenkian Commission 1996). For scholars attentive to these shifts, modernity poses a question that one cannot fully answer, since no single perspective or location can survey the social totality, and each paradigm of thought must be critically scrutinized for what it encourages us to let go, forget, or disperse as historical detritus. The resulting research cannot seek merely to create a more inclusive "American modernity" by applying modern disciplinary knowledge to otherwise neglected social identities and histories. Rather, it needs to situate the formations of modern knowledge within global histories of contact, collaboration, conflict, and dislocation, examining in each instance how the category of the modern has distorted those global histories, producing unity out of hybridity and development out of displacement. These modernist misrepresentations are reproduced in the contemporary norms by which we feel and know ourselves to be modern subjects. But they also appear in the inability of modern knowledge to attend to "nonmodern" social practices and formations. In the contradictions of our late modernity, these emerging practices and formations offer the opening for a different politics of knowledge, what one scholar has called the "politics of our lack of knowledge" about modern societies, their colonial histories, institutional forms, and possible futures (Lowe 2006, 206).

44

Nation

Alys Eve Weinbaum

"Nation" has been in use in the English language since the fourteenth century, when it was first deployed to designate groups and populations. Although the concept of "race" was not well defined in this period, the *Oxford English Dictionary* (*OED*) retrospectively refers to such groups and populations as "racial" in character. In the modern period, the *OED* continues, the meaning of "nation" came to refer to large aggregates of people closely associated through a combination of additional factors, including common language, politics, culture, history, and occupation of the same territory. Though it appears that an initial racial connection among nationals was later supplanted by a widened range of associating factors, the early understanding of "nation" as based in race and "common descent" remains central to discussions of the term to this day, either as a retrospective imposition of the sort orchestrated by the *OED* or as a "natural" grounding. An important contribution of American studies and cultural studies has been to interrogate race as a description and sometimes a synecdoche for nation and to insist that an uncritical conflation of race and nation constitutes a pressing political and theoretical problem. Indeed, as numerous scholars argue, ideas of race and racist ideologies continue to subtend the expression of nationalism in the United States, which is unsurprising given that the founding and consolidation of the nation was pursued as a project of racial nationalism that arrogated full belonging (if not citizenship) to whites or, in nineteenth-century parlance, to people of Anglo-Saxon descent.

Beginning in the late eighteenth century, when "nation" first accrued consistent political usage and "national" became a routine noun used to designate individual subjects, the constitution of political units (nation-states) composed of so-called nationals began to center around identification of the factors that would ideally cohere large aggregates and bestow belonging on individual members of such groups. During the nineteenth century, generally referred to as the century of modern nationalism, principles of inclusion and exclusion were hotly debated by political pundits favoring immigration restriction or curtailment and various population-control measures that, over time, profoundly shaped the racial, ethnic, and class composition of nations by designating those who could rightfully belong and by circumscribing that belonging through restriction on the reproductive pool and designation of the progeny of "mixed" unions as "illegitimate" or "foreign." Such nineteenth-century debates exposed nation formation as deeply ideological—as involving processes of self-definition and self-consolidation as often dependent on the embrace as on the persecution of differences, especially those construed as racial in character.

Even as nationalization centers on the construction of a people, it also raises questions of land and territory. In the case of settler colonial nations such as the United States, South Africa, and Israel, nationalization has depended on the transformation of a territory into a "homeland"; on the defeat, enslavement, and genocidal destruction of "natives"; and on the subsequent expropriation of land from people already inhabiting it. In this sense, nation building and imperialism ought to be seen as closely and historically allied. As Seamus Deane (1990, 360) eloquently explains, "Nationalism's opposition to imperialism is . . . nothing more than a continuation of imperialism by other means." Imperialism arises contemporaneously with modern nationalism because the two forms of power have needed each other. The ideology of racial, cultural, and often moral superiority that is used to justify imperialism is also always at least in part national, and vice versa. Like imperialism, nation building is an ideological and material project that involves continuing reorganization of space, bodies, and identities. It is at once individual and collective, internally and externally oriented, destructive and productive, and all too often brutally violent.

Although philosophers and political scientists writing in the transatlantic context tend to agree on the range of factors that may be used to identify nations and the nationals belonging to them, they continue to argue over the nature of the elusive glue that binds individuals into nations. Ernest Renan (1882/1990) suggests in his famous lecture "What Is a Nation?," first delivered at the Sorbonne and often regarded as the gambit that inaugurated contemporary debate, that language, culture, and territory are not in and of themselves enough to constitute a nation. Rather, to all these must be added a common substance capable of binding disparate individuals into a people. And yet, paradoxically, this substance is far too ephemeral to be readily or decisively distilled. Approximating religious faith or spirituality but not reducible to either, nationalism, Renan suggests, is nothing more or less than an inchoate feeling, albeit an extremely consequential one. By contrast with citizenship, a set of political and civil rights guaranteed to nationals on the basis of their legal belonging within the nation, "nationness" and feelings of national belonging are far harder to pin down.

This vexing question of what binds nationals to one another has led contemporary theorists to argue that nations are fictions given solidity through political and juridical processes that transform them into material practices, including population control and eugenic containment, immigration restriction and curtailment, and full-scale genocide. As a materialized fiction, national belonging may thus be understood as what Raymond Williams (1977/1997, 128–35) has labeled, in a different context, a "structure of feeling": an emergent sentiment not easily articulated but so deeply and fully inhabited by individuals and collectivities that it appears to them as primordial, inevitable, and enduring. Thus, on the one side (commonly denoted as uncritically nationalist, often jingoistic), we find the nation discussed as a "natural" formation. On the other side (which holds itself above nationalism or opposes it in the form, for instance, of socialist internationalism or Enlightenment cosmopolitanism), we find the nation posited as a harmful construction. In this latter view, nationalism is seen as fomenting dangerously partisan solidarities, and the nation is seen as a fiction that is made to cohere through ideological pressures that masquerade as "natural" but are in fact self-interested, self-consolidating, and ultimately driven by capitalist and imperialist imperatives. As world-systems theorists such as Immanuel Wallerstein (2004) argue, nations can be regarded as racialized economic and political units that compete within a world marketplace composed of other similar units. As the globe divided into core and periphery, into regions made up of those who labor and those who exploit such labor, nations located in the core often rationalized their economic exploitation of those of the periphery by racializing it.

Although individuals may move from one nation to another, thus losing or being forced by law to forgo one form of citizenship for another, feelings of national belonging cannot be forcibly stripped away. Indeed, such feelings are often willfully carried with individuals and groups as they migrate. In the United States, the bipartite, sometimes hyphenated, identities of some nationals—Italian Americans, Irish Americans, Polish Americans—express such national retention or carryover. In these instances, which must be contextualized within a framework of voluntary migration, the designations "Italian," "Irish," and "Polish" indicate a desire to retain a previous national identity now regarded as cultural or ethnic. In other instances, self-constituting invocations of national identity have been transformed into a critique of dominant nationalism or into an alternative imagination of nation, as with the forms of insurgent Third World nationalism examined by the theorist of decolonization Frantz Fanon (1963). In such instances, the new or invented nationalism competes either to exist alongside or to displace the dominant national identity, which is viewed as a violent imposition. In the Americas, this is perhaps most evident in movements for Native sovereignty that work to build tribal nations or in the form of Chicano nationalism that claims Aztlán as both a mythical homeland and a name for the portion of Mexico taken by the United States after the U.S.-Mexico War of 1846–48.

In the case of modern diasporas, we witness yet another form of oppositional nationalism, one occasioned by forced displacement and shared oppression. In those instances in which a homeland no longer exists or has never existed, or in which a diasporic people seek to constitute a new nation unconstrained by the dictates of geography, ideas of nation and national belonging come into sharp focus. Consider the black nationalism that had its heyday in the United States and the decolonizing world in the 1970s, or Queer Nation, an activist organization that gained prominence in the United States during the 1980s and early 1990s. Although very different in political orientation, both movements appropriated the idea of the nation to contest dominant forms of nationalism and to reveal the constitutive exclusions that enable national hegemony. Somewhat paradoxically, the imaginative creation of these collectivities revealed, even as it mimicked, the constructed nature of hegemonic nations formally recognized as political states.

This idea of hegemonic nations as ideologically constructed or "imagined communities" is most famously elaborated by Benedict Anderson, who, in the early 1980s, theorized the emergence of the modern nation out of the nationalist revolutions that took place throughout the Americas in the late eighteenth and early nineteenth centuries. As Anderson (1983, 19) argues, nations are brought into being by peoples whose access to print culture enables collective imagination of involvement in a political and cultural project that extends back into an "immemorial past" and "glides into a limitless future." Anderson built his theory on modern European historiography (especially Eric Hobsbawm's work [1983]) that argued that nations produced themselves by inventing traditions that enabled them to constitute populations as historical and cultural entities meaningfully joined over time and in space. Anderson is also indebted to critical theorist Walter Benjamin (1950/1968, 262), who theorized the "homogeneous, empty time" characteristic of modernity—a temporality that Anderson regards as necessary to national imagining and that he calibrates to a set of technological developments, principally the invention of the printing press and the tabloid newspaper. Together, print culture and the thinking of "nation time" that it enabled allowed people living in a given territory and speaking and reading a similar language to materialize connections to one another in a synchronic and cohesive manner that was previously unthinkable.

Numerous scholars of Third World nationalisms have taken issue with Anderson's Eurocentric and teleological view of national development and have called attention to his overemphasis on print culture, thus exposing his theory's dependence on the application of European-style nationalism throughout the world and on the presupposition of universal literacy as a requirement of national development. Yet others have used the idea of the nation as an "imagined community" to argue for the special relationship between nationalism and print culture and between nation and narration more generally. As postcolonial theorist Homi Bhabha (1990b, 1) avers in a formulation self-consciously indebted to both Renan and Anderson, "Nations, like narratives, lose their origins in the myths of time and only fully realize their horizons in the mind's eye. Such an image of the nation—or narration—might seem impossibly romantic and excessively metaphorical, but it is from . . . political thought and literary language that the nation emerges . . . in the west."

The idea that nations need narratives to exist—that they need to be narrated into being—has resonated for an entire generation of American studies scholars. Their research suggests that elite and popular cultural texts, including public spectacle and performance, are and have been used to consolidate and contest various nationalist projects. Some of these scholars focus on texts manifestly intent on nation building (e.g., the *Federalist Papers*) or on offering alternatives to hegemonic nationalism (e.g., W. E. B. Du Bois's *The Souls of Black Folk* [1903/1997]), while others dwell on those that are less transparent in their ideological commitments but that may be read against the grain to expose the processes through which nationalist sensibilities are generated and torn apart (e.g., Gertrude Stein's *The Making of Americans* [1925/1995] and Américo Paredes's *George Washington Gómez* [1990]). Literary scholars working on U.S. culture from the Revolutionary War through the present have been at the forefront of such inquiry, focusing on canonized traditions and on texts authored by those who have been historically minoritized within the nation. Such writings frequently expose the ideologies of racism, sexism, and heterosexism that lie at the heart of U.S. nationalism (Berlant 1991, 1997; D. Nelson 1992, 1998; Wald 1995; Lowe 1996).

Central to this scholarship is an understanding that, in the United States and elsewhere, the relationship between nationalism and racism can be characterized as one of historical reciprocity in that modern nationalism expresses itself as racial (Balibar 1994). With the centrality of this relationship in mind, researchers have focused on histories of Native American genocide, African American enslavement, and immigration to the United States over the past three centuries. As such work attests, westward expansion of the frontier in the eighteenth and nineteenth centuries was facilitated by racist ideologies that viewed Indians as "lesser breeds" whose removal or extermination was necessary to the establishment of Anglo-Saxon civilization (Horsman 1981; Hietala 1985; Rogin 1996). Four hundred years of enslavement and disenfranchisement of Africans was the steep price paid for the creation of whiteness as a form of "status property" (C. Harris 1993, 1714) that functioned as a guarantor of national belonging and citizenship rights. After the Civil War and well into the twentieth century, the nativist and restrictionist policies toward immigrants from southern and eastern Europe and Asia allowed for further consolidation of the United States as a white nation whose population could be imagined as principally Anglo-Saxon and thus as free of the taint of "foreign blood." As detailed case studies have demonstrated, ethnicized immigrant groups have shed the taint of their otherness through expressions of various forms of racism. Indeed, entrance into the national fold has invariably depended on a

group's ability to differentiate and distinguish itself as white and free (Roediger 1991; Theodore Allen 1994; Jacobson 1998). Central here are both internally directed racism, responsible for keeping the national body "pure" by separating "true" nationals (free whites) from nonnationals (slaves and natives), and externally directed racism, or xenophobia, which clearly defines the nation's borders and keeps "undesirable" immigrant populations (those deemed "unassimilable") out.

Feminist and queer scholarship has further complicated our understanding of the dialectic between race and nation by demonstrating that men and women participate differently in nation building and that reproductive heterosexuality plays a decisive role in the creation of nationalist ideologies, which are, in turn, deeply gendered and heteronormative. As such scholarship makes plain, it is misguided to study nations and nationalism without bringing to bear a theory of gender power and an understanding of the historically sedimented relationship of nation building to reproductive politics (Parker et al. 1992; McClintock 1995; Kaplan, Alarcón, and Moallem 1999). Women commit themselves to and are either implicitly or explicitly implicated by others in the production of nations, nationals, and nationalism in a number of ways: as active participants in nationalist struggles for liberation; as mothers, the biological reproducers of subjects and national populations; as upholders of the boundaries of nations through restrictions on reproductive sexuality and the circumscription of marriage within ethnic and racial groups; as teachers and transmitters of national culture; and as symbolic signifiers of nations (Yuval-Davis and Anthias 1989).

Though often overlooked, the reproductive dimensions of the idea of nation are embedded within the term (derived as it is from the Latin root *natio*, "to be born"). Likewise, the idea that nationals are literally reproduced has been naturalized and rendered invisible within many national cultures. In the United States, birth to a national is one of the principal bases on which both national belonging and citizenship are granted (Stevens 1999). In practice, the idea that national populations are reproduced by racially "fit" or "superior" mothers has been used to justify a range of eugenic policies that allow some women to reproduce while restricting others. Nazi Germany is the most glaring example of such eugenic celebration of national motherhood and of the control of reproductive sexuality. However, it is too seldom acknowledged, particularly when the Nazi example is invoked, that the mainstream eugenics movement of the early part of the twentieth century emerged not in Europe but in the United States, where it was widely celebrated as a means to "strengthen" the national populace by "breeding out" so-called degenerate members of society, including immigrants, people of color, homosexuals, and the "feeble-minded" (Ordover 2003).

The idea that nationals and nations are reproduced is not only or simply a material reality but also an elaborate ideology positing that the essence of nationality is itself reproducible. Within this ideology, protection of the "naturalness" of heterosexual reproduction becomes central, as does the construction of women's wombs as repositories of racial identity (Weinbaum 2004). Buried within the ideology of national reproduction is a concept of the female body as the source from which nationals spring and the related idea that national populations are racially homogeneous and can be maintained as such only if sexual unions that cross racial and ethnic lines are carefully monitored and even more carefully represented. Significantly, in the United States, it was not during the antebellum period that interracial sex was most forcefully legislated against and a mixed nation (a so-called miscege*nation*)

vociferously denounced but, rather, after the Civil War, emancipation, and incorporation of African Americans as citizens. In other words, although master-and-slave sex was routine, it was only after black people began to be regarded as nationals and were granted at least some of the rights held by other (white) citizens that sexuality across racial lines was deemed threatening to the national body.

The continuous policing of reproductive sexuality that is characteristic of most forms of modern nationalism ought to lead us to the realization that just as nationalism is an ideology inextricably intertwined with racism, so too are racism and nationalism bound together with sexist and heterosexist reproductive imperatives. From this perspective, it becomes clear that in order to fully limn the idea of nation, it is necessary to refocus the study of the keyword on discussions of the ideological and material processes that exploit existing racial, gender, and sexual hierarchies in the production of nations, nationals, and feelings of national belonging. Such a reorientation ideally should begin with the idea that the nation is differently produced in each instantiation and historical conjuncture and within the context of each raced, gendered, and sexualized social and political formation.

45

Neoliberalism

Lisa Duggan

The word "neoliberalism," first used during the 1930s, came into widespread circulation in the 1990s to name a utopian ideology of "free markets" and minimal state interference, a set of policies slashing state social services and supporting global corporate interests, a process (neoliberalization) proceeding in company with procorporate globalization and financialization, and a cultural project of building consent for the upward redistributions of wealth and power that have occurred since the 1970s. But neoliberalism might best be understood as a global social movement encompassing all of these political goals. In American studies and cultural studies, the concept has gathered force as a description of current tendencies in global politics and a critique of those tendencies, even as its meanings have dispersed.

Though the term tends to be used differently across the social sciences and the humanities, there is wide agreement that neoliberalism is a radicalized form of capitalist imperialism, centered in the United States and Anglo-Europe, that has developed unevenly across the globe since the 1970s. Most scholars trace its intellectual genealogy to the Mont Pelerin Society and the ideas of Friedrich Hayek (1944), Ludwig von Mises (1949) and economists of the Austrian school, and to the writing and activities of Milton Friedman (1962/2002) and the Chicago school, developed and circulated since the 1940s. These economists defended classical liberalism and market-based economies grounded in individualism and published scathing critiques of the centralized government regulation and redistributive social benefits provided by capitalist welfare states as well as socialist societies.

These minority views moved toward centers of power during the 1970s, beginning with the overthrow of the democratically elected socialist government of Salvador Allende in Chile by the Chilean military and internal elites, with the assistance of the CIA and the advice of the University of Chicago–based economists surrounding Milton Friedman, often called the "Chicago Boys." Neoliberal reforms—privatization of state enterprises, opening up to foreign business ownership and expatriation of profits, cuts to social services—were accomplished along with violent suppression of dissent. When these policies were later modified to meet the challenges of economic stagnation in the mid-1970s, neoliberalism as state policy (rather than a utopian theory opposed to the state) began to appear as a practical set of strategies for maintaining capitalism in the face of global social movement challenges and for reinforcing or installing elites with access to an increasing share of economic and political power. As David Harvey (2005) and Naomi Klein (2007) describe the genealogy of neoliberalism since the Chilean coup, successive experiments developed means of extracting resources on the U.S. imperial model (as had occurred in earlier interventions in Nicaragua and Iran, among many others), the installation of unaccountable governing structures, the transfer of profits out of social services supported by progressive taxation, and the maintenance of widening inequalities.

These events and tactics function as experiments by creating or exploiting crisis conditions to test key economic hypotheses central to the theory of neoliberalism, as political institutions and modes of decision-making are simultaneously reshaped to entrench neoliberal power brokers. Such experiments include the 1975 New York City fiscal crisis that slashed social services and gave bankers and bond holders unprecedented control over the city's finances; the 1980s "structural adjustment" programs forced on Latin American economies through the practices of the International Monetary Fund (IMF) that created and exploited sovereign debt to enforce investor domination of the political process; and the 2003 U.S. invasion of Iraq, where the administrator of the U.S.-controlled Coalition Provisional Authority of Iraq, Paul Bremer, presided over massive privatization of state enterprises opened to foreign control. These experiments developed policies in localities at the periphery of U.S. imperial power that might then be generalized for use in the center, both nationally, as in the rebuilding of New Orleans after Hurricane Katrina, and transnationally, as in the imposition of austerity policies in the European Union after the 2008 economic crisis and recession. By the 1990s, such policies had been fittingly labeled the Washington Consensus.

Within the imperial purview of the United States and the policies of U.S.-dominated global institutions including the IMF, the World Bank, and the World Trade Organization, these neoliberal policies express ongoing tensions and contradictions. As an ideological revival of classical liberalism in radicalized form, neoliberalism constitutes an attack on the twentieth-century capitalist welfare state, with its modest redistributions and state regulation of corporate power. Critiques of the theories of John Maynard Keynes (1936), the welfare-state liberal capitalism that he championed during the Great Depression of the 1930s, and the Keynesian economic policies dominant in the United States and Anglo-Europe from the 1940s to the 1980s have been a crucial focus of neoliberal intellectual and policy elites. As a set of strategies, set in place over time through trial and error, via both force and consent, neoliberalism-in-practice has often deviated from the theories of the intellectuals. Overlapping at times with neoconservative security-state policies that deploy centralized military power for imperial violence and war, neoliberalism has functioned historically less as a clearly defined set of ideas and theories and more as an internally contradictory mode of upward redistribution of wealth and power and an extension of the practices of imperial extraction of resources from economies of the global South.

But U.S. imperial power has not been the sole source of global neoliberal reform. From the "opening" of China to world capitalist markets in the 1980s, through the new business and trade policies of post-Soviet Russia and postapartheid South Africa in the 1990s, to the policies enacted via the 1992 Maastricht Treaty on European Union, many global, local, and national forces have produced the uneven spatial and temporal landscape of neoliberalism. Some scholars acknowledge this unevenness but emphasize the hegemonic force of global neoliberalism since 1980. These writers focus on the power of the dominant economic system in reshaping global societies and politics (Harvey 2010). Others acknowledge global neoliberalism's historical power but emphasize the highly variable landscape of exceptions to neoliberalism and of neoliberalism as exception under other economic regimes around the globe. This group includes many researchers who are as interested in tracking the limitations of neoliberalism's influence as in documenting its power (Ong 2006).

Despite these differences, there is wide agreement among scholars on the foundational causes and enduring effects of global neoliberalism. As a response to the economic and political challenges to capitalist dominance in the mid-twentieth century, neoliberalism organized the uneven, contradictory efforts of global corporate and political elites to maintain and concentrate power. The effect of widening global inequalities is indisputable (Galbraith 2012; Stiglitz 2013). But within this consensus, approaches to the study of neoliberalism within American studies and cultural studies are broadly various. Sociologists, geographers, and urbanists tend to take a structural approach, emphasizing the overall logic and force of neoliberal policies as they spread over time and space (N. Smith 1983; N. Brenner 2004). Anthropologists are more likely to point to the contingencies of those policies and to the power of resistance to them, especially in the global South (Sawyer 2004; Tsing 2011). Scholars located in the literary humanities tend to analyze the cultural project of neoliberalism, its modes of subject formation, along with its affective traces (G. Harkins 2009; Berlant 2011). Layered alongside these divisions are other theoretical differences. Marxist scholars offer narratives of political economic conflict and change, focused on the class conflicts that shape the shifting forms of capitalism and the state (Harvey 2005; N. Smith 1983; N. Brenner 2004). Writers influenced by Michel Foucault examine the broad dispersion of power among institutions that regulate populations, including schools, prisons, the health care industries, popular culture, and media, and the ways that self-disciplining subjects who comply with neoliberal expectations are produced (N. Rose 1999; Povinelli 2011).

Across all of these fields, postcolonial and transnational studies scholars have offered the most pointed set of challenges to the standard narratives of spreading neoliberal hegemonies since the 1970s. Rather than focus primarily on the structural impact of late capitalism, procorporate globalization, and financialization on states, economies, cultures, and everyday lives, these scholars have noted the myriad ways in which challenges to Western colonial modernity have shaped, rather than simply resisted, the ideas and practices of neoliberalism. These scholars expand on postcolonial and decolonial studies of the cultural work of racial taxonomies, gendered narratives, and sexual discourses in producing dominant forms of Western modernity and empire since the sixteenth century (McClintock 1995; Stoler 2010; M. Jacqui Alexander 2005). They have noted the role of decolonization and of feminist, queer, and ecological social movements, as well as of class and labor politics, in producing constantly morphing responses to and from ruling institutions (Grewal 2005; Reddy 2011).

This group of scholars enables expansive ways of thinking about social change. If we follow their lead in going beyond notions of neoliberal hegemony, uneven developments, or dominance and resistance, we can begin to trace the interactions among complexly intertwined axes of power. The global landscape of social movements contesting the impact of neoliberalism today—all of which treat the boundaries between state, economy, and culture, public and private, as dynamic and fluid—might be best understood as an ongoing set of dispersed yet interconnected efforts at achieving more just forms of globalization (Duggan 2003).

46

Normal

Robert McRuer

"Normal," because of its easy associations with typical, ordinary, or unremarkable, appears to many people as a benign word, nothing more than a neutral descriptor of certain groups, bodies, or behaviors that are more common than others. Yet more than almost any other keyword in American studies and cultural studies, "normal" carries with it a history of discursive and literal violence against those who could never hope to be described by the term. Sexual minorities, disabled people, racialized populations, immigrants, and many others have at times found themselves among the motley group that the Chicana lesbian feminist Gloria Anzaldúa terms *los atravesados*: "those who cross over, pass over, or go through the confines of the 'normal'" (1987, 3). For Anzaldúa and innumerable other critics of the normal, this border crossing has consequences. Lives lived beyond the confines of the normal have been marked as illegitimate and targeted for surveillance, control, correction, confinement, and even elimination.

The history of the keyword "normal" is relatively short compared to that of most words in the English language, despite the fact that the term structures contemporary cultures in powerful and nearly ubiquitous ways. The *Oxford English Dictionary* (*OED*) notes that the idea of "normal" as "constituting or conforming to a type or standard; regular, usual, typical; ordinary, conventional" was not in common usage until 1840. This usage roughly coincides with the French statistician Adolphe Quetelet's (1835) widely influential notion of *l'homme moyen*, or average man, an abstract human being with particular qualities that could be measured and graphed. Characteristics that were "abnormal," according to the new understandings of statistics developed by Quetelet and others, were those located outside a "normal" bell-shaped curve (L. Davis 1995). Over the course of the nineteenth century, statistical measurement became an imperative: not only *could* human characteristics be observed and plotted on graphs and charts, but they *should* be, in order to identify (and potentially correct) that which was abnormal (L. Davis 1995).

By the end of the century, this imperative produced a second usage traced in the *OED* of "normal" as descriptive of a person "physically and mentally sound; free from any disorder; healthy." Here, the word's appearance of carrying mere statistical meaning (as average or mean) masks its ability to bear moral judgment and to privilege certain groups (as normal) while subordinating others (as deviant). Only at the beginning of the twentieth century did the term begin to name a person who might be understood as "heterosexual" (a term that itself was coined only in 1868) (J. Katz 1995). In less than a century, then, a word with a Latin etymology that meant "conforming to or organized by a rule" began to carry, in most European languages, dominant meanings that Anzaldúa and other scholars of American studies and cultural studies now critique.

Across this history, the normal was not simply being identified and described; rather, as the philosopher Michel Foucault makes clear, an entire culture and machinery of "normalization" were emerging. Normalization entailed the widespread production of knowledge and discourse about those who were "abnormal." Technologies of normalization developed over the nineteenth century. These technologies, ranging from medical or psychiatric charts to judicial records, targeted "dangerous individuals" who deviated from a standard, or "norm," and on whom corrective power thus needed to be exercised (Foucault 1999/2003). Normalizing power, in these contexts, is not simply repressive; it works by producing ways of knowing, recognizing, and categorizing individuals. Power is therefore best understood as a relation, as something always in motion, rather than an inert substance or property. Put differently, power is not simply *held* by one privileged group and *exercised* on another, weaker or "disempowered," group. Instead, power is at work everywhere, constructing—literally materializing— normal and abnormal subjects.

Discourses of normalcy and abnormalcy were generated in, and traveled through, institutions such as schools, prisons, asylums, and hospitals and were codified by the "expert opinion" of people authorized by such institutions. Enforcing normalcy and identifying and containing abnormalcy were particularly important for an emerging industrial capitalist order, which needed the majority of people to function as able-bodied laborers in a "work-based" rather than a "need-based" system. Tests, measurements, questionnaires, and other "validating devices" shaped by a range of authorities (doctors, psychiatrists, government officials, insurance agents) were developed both to keep the majority of normal people in the work-based system and to stigmatize those sorted, through a newly invented "clinical concept of disability," into the need-based system (D. Stone 1984). These processes did more than make the association of "normal" and "able-bodied" appear to be completely natural. Over the nineteenth and twentieth centuries, they required that disabled people—those forced to appeal to the very institutions that had deemed them abnormal and dependent—had to pass through "ceremonies of social degradation" to demonstrate their eligibility for the work-based system (L. Davis 1995; Longmore 2003).

Flourishing throughout the nineteenth century and into the twentieth, freak shows, which put on display people with congenital disabilities and racialized groups, made abnormalcy spectacular in a somewhat different way. Freaks were constructed through a discursive transformation of individual (and otherwise unremarkable) characteristics: William Henry Johnson, an African American man with a cognitive disability, became the "What Is It?" exhibit; Charles Tripp, performing everyday tasks with his toes, became the "Armless Wonder" (Bogdan 1988). Attendees at freak shows could reassure themselves of their own normalcy as they observed the display of freakish others (Garland-Thomson 1997; Clare 1999). The complex web of power relations staged by freak shows generated that which was abnormal, delineated that which was normal, and depended on embodied "evidence." Here and elsewhere, the project of enforcing normalcy had particularly profound ramifications for disabled people, who were increasingly positioned by experts and laypeople alike as having abnormal bodies (L. Davis 1995).

The emergence of "unsightly beggar laws" in urban areas in the late nineteenth and early twentieth centuries (laws that prohibited "diseased, maimed, or unsightly" bodies from being in public spaces) likewise functioned to spatialize a distinction between normal citizens and those whose bodies or behavior marked them as deviant and in need of correction. Disability activists later termed these ordinances "ugly laws," recognizing the extent to which they could be, or had been, deployed to control or contain people with disabilities (Schweik 2009). Such containment was often quite literal, as the rate of institutionalization of disabled people skyrocketed as the nineteenth century ended (Trent 1994). The move to displace individuals and populations deemed abnormal reached its most lethal conclusion in eugenic policies that flourished at the turn of the twentieth century. In both Europe and the United States, these policies encouraged the sterilization of disabled people, with the explicit goal and justification of extending normalcy for future generations (Snyder and Mitchell 2006). In Nazi Germany, the phrase "life unworthy of life" was eventually used to describe disabled people, and thousands were killed alongside millions of Jewish people and others (homosexuals, gypsies, religious minorities, political dissidents) who went beyond the confines of the new eugenic normal (Garland-Thomson 2007).

By the mid-twentieth century, scholars had begun to map and critique the contours of normal and abnormal and the mechanisms used to divide one from the other. Foucault's former teacher Georges Canguilhem, a philosopher and historian of science, traced the ways that the biological, scientific, and statistical division of the world into "normal" and "pathological" was always saturated with political and ideological concerns and never entailed simple or neutral measurement (1966/1989). Erving Goffman studied the workings of stigma and argued that people with "spoiled identities," outside the realm of the normal, had to manage, fastidiously, their encounters with others (1963). This management might be what Goffman called "stigmaphobic" (if one essentially insisted on one's normalcy and distanced oneself from more deviant others) or "stigmaphilic" (if one embraced, or even reveled in, one's outsider status), but it was constant.

Anzaldúa and other feminists, particularly feminists of color in the in the 1970s and 1980s, extended these early efforts toward a critical understanding of normalization, focusing on how regimes of normalcy were constructed through overlapping and mutually reinforcing systems of age, race, class, gender, and embodiment (Moraga and Anzaldúa 1981; B. Smith 1982; Ferguson 2004). "Somewhere on the edge of consciousness," Audre Lorde wrote, "there is what I call a *mythical norm*, which each one of us within our hearts knows 'that is not me.' In america, this norm is usually defined as white, thin, male, young, heterosexual, christian, and financially secure" (1984a, 116). Disability studies scholars surveyed the uneven and unequal ways that bodies had been cast as normal and abnormal, and perhaps most famously, the interdisciplinary field of queer studies began to excavate the ways that normal was both naturalized as "heterosexual" and made compulsory (Rich 1980/1983; de Lauretis 1991; M. Warner 1999). By the end of the century, queer disability studies began to posit that "compulsory heterosexuality" was thoroughly interwoven with "compulsory able-bodiedness" (McRuer 2006; McRuer and Wilkerson 2003).

In the same period, feminist and queer theory more generally began to rename "compulsory heterosexuality" as "heteronormativity" in order to convey the ways in which technologies of normalization operate not simply through logics of repression or compulsion but through forms of power that privilege, naturalize, and institutionalize heterosexuality (Berlant and Warner 1998). Eventually, queer theory moved from a textured delineation of the workings of "heteronormativity" to accounts of the ways in which gay men and lesbians themselves participate in what was dubbed "homonormativity," especially as the organizations running the mainstream movement began to seem more and more like corporations and to emphasize disproportionately integrationist issues such as the right to marry or serve in the military (Duggan 2002). Transgender theorists, in turn, insisted that homonormativity consisted not only in contemporary gay and lesbian desires for normalcy and assimilation but also in a privileging of normative masculine and feminine experiences and embodiments (Stryker 2008; Spade 2011).

Normal ways of being and living have generally been accorded a privacy denied to abnormal lives; that privacy has been secured through social forms such as the heterosexual (and reproductive) couple. Resistant alternatives to regimes of the normal thus argue for forms of being-in-common that are public, accessible, and collective. This expansive sense of public culture, which might be comprehended as both queer and disabled (or "crip," as some scholars have begun to theorize it), are particularly vital now, because conceptualizations of "normal" have shifted during an era of neoliberal capitalism. Brian Massumi (2002a), Slavoj Žižek (2010), and other critical theorists have argued that contemporary capitalism no longer deploys a logic of "totalizing normality"; instead, neoliberal capitalism focuses on and markets constant change, flexibility, "difference," and, indeed, freakiness. Put differently, neoliberal capitalism arguably embraces the freaky or abnormal, domesticating or taming it as it sells it back to us. The more expansive and accessible public cultures offered by feminist, queer, and disability theorists seek to recognize and resist this embrace as just one more form of normalization (and indeed privatization), blocking a more democratic materialization of queer, freaky, and crip public cultures.

47

Orientalism

Vijay Prashad

In 1849, Henry David Thoreau wrote, "Behold the difference between the Oriental and the Occidental. The former has nothing to do in this world; the latter is full of activity. The one looks in the sun till his eyes are put out; the other follows him prone in his westward course" (1849/1985, 120). Thoreau's "Orientals" included the people of India and China, although his contemporaries often added the people of the Arab world. At the same time, Thoreau and other Boston Brahmins used the even more vaguely defined term "Occidental" to refer to Anglo-Protestant civilization (and only rarely included Catholics and non-Anglos). The point they made was simple: the world had to be sundered between East and West. The former once had a great history, but it had since descended into timelessness and stasis; the latter remained dynamic and cultivated wisdom. Thoreau, being a pacifist, forswore the values of conquest, but his confreres did not. They shared his revulsion toward the contemporary Orient and yet wanted to dominate it. He only wanted its knowledge.

A critical analysis of this Orientalist discourse is made easier because of the valuable work of such scholars as Anwar Abdel Malek (1963) and Edward Said (1978), as well as the field that is now known as postcolonial studies. This tradition lifted the commonplace category of Orientalism and filled it with analytical meaning. Before Abdel Malek and Said, the term referred to the academic study of all that lives in the lands outside Europe, the Americas, sub-Saharan Africa, and Russia. Orientalists toiled away on the languages and cultures of regions of the world not often considered to be central to the activity of the U.S. and European academy. Said, in contrast, wrenched the term out of its disciplinary context and demonstrated how European and U.S. government bureaucrats, academics, cultural workers, and common sense defined and circumscribed knowledge about the "Orient." The first step of Orientalist discourse is to sunder the world into a West and an East. Here the lonely academic and the public imperialist share a remarkable feat. Both collect vastly different areas of the world into a zone called the "East," albeit the former for purposes of study, the latter for conquest and rule. The premise for both the academic and the imperialist is that these diverse regions can be assembled into a singular "Orient" and, in consequence, that their own lands can be seen as an equally singular "Occident." The second step is to impute values to these zones, with the West being productive, dynamic, adult, and masculine, while the East is slothful, static, childlike, and feminine. Once these two steps have been accomplished, it is easy to say that the West must have dominance over the East. Frequently, Orientalist discourse provided a useful justification for colonialism, as colonial rulers attempted with varying degrees of success to fashion real, living cultures into their image of the "Orient," while older historical traditions and the resistance of colonized peoples made such a divine act impossible.

As with any good theory, this early critique of Orientalism has its flaws. Some of these are conceptual, as pointed out by the literary critic Aijaz Ahmad. Said is unclear whether Orientalism is the ideology of colonialism or is rooted in the very psyche of European thought. If it is the latter, then Said's use of the term is an "Orientalism-in-reverse," in which the "West" has an inherently flawed understanding of the rest of the world (Ahmad 1992, 183). Additionally, Said underestimates the strong tradition within Arabic writing that draws

ontological distinctions between East and West. The concept of Orientalism also suffers from an overly general application. It may aptly describe the English and French, though not the German, view of what they called the "Near" or "Middle East." Without alteration, however, it would not be of much use for understanding U.S. intellectual and political policy toward either Asia or the Middle East. Literary critics and historians have demonstrated that U.S. Orientalism was both heterogeneous and "far more mobile, flexible, and rich than the Orientalism binary would allow" (McAlister 2001, 270). While Thoreau shared a great deal with his English colleagues, he did not condone colonialism: "They may keep their rupees," he wrote of "Orientals"— he sought only their wisdom (1855/1958, 398). This was already a difference.

To fully understand U.S. Orientalism, we thus need to locate it within the context of the emergence of the U.S. empire as a truly global behemoth. U.S. imperialism was rooted in the wars against Amerindians, in the push westward after the Revolutionary War, in the Monroe Doctrine's implications for South and Central America, and in the war to supplant Spain in the Caribbean and the Philippines. Still, the United States remained a junior partner to the dynamic northwestern European empires (Dutch, English, French) until the close of World War II. Only during the Cold War did the United States become the political leader of the advanced capitalist states. At the same time, nationalist movements around the world and the horror of the Holocaust finally delegitimized formal racism on a global scale, producing the Universal Declaration of Human Rights in 1948, the many United Nations conventions against racial discrimination, and the intellectual work of the United Nations Educational, Scientific and Cultural Organization (UNESCO). Whereas earlier forms of Orientalism could quite openly truck in racist stereotypes, the U.S. Orientalism of the era had to adjust to this assault on racism and direct colonial dominion.

U.S. domestic law eventually submitted to the dictates of international opinion and of the civil rights movement, overturning the Jim Crow laws of the South. Alongside the Civil Rights and Voting Rights Acts came a 1965 revision of U.S. immigration law that finally allowed legal entry and naturalization to Asians (another complex category), who had either been barred or subjected to quotas for much of the twentieth century. The state claimed that its new immigration policy was designed to counter "Communist propaganda" about U.S. racism against Asians (Prashad 2000). U.S. pundits and policymakers welcomed highly skilled Asians, whose demographic advantages then became a foil for the indisputably wretched condition of most people of color. In 1966, *U.S. News & World Report* noted that the experience of Chinese Americans confirms "the old idea that people should depend on their own efforts—not a welfare check—in order to reach America's 'promised land'" (158). Asians worked hard to make it "at a time when it is being proposed that hundreds of billions of dollars be spent to uplift Negroes and other minorities" (158). The sorting logic of this new U.S. immigration policy began to blur older categories of racist discourse. The post-civil-rights epoch inaugurated a discourse of color-blind racism, in which the rhetorics of economic efficiency and cultural difference masked claims about racial inferiority. This shift is crucial to an understanding of U.S. Orientalism.

But just because the media began to praise Asians, in part by substituting the newer keyword "Asian" for the older keyword "Oriental," does not mean that Asians were sheltered from rebuke. The state allowed the racism nurtured by the long history of Orientalism to flourish in civil society, despite having disavowed it as public policy. The language and emotive charge of racism often drew its power from the ongoing U.S. wars in Asia. Beginning with the wars in the Philippines in the nineteenth century, the U.S. media and military pummeled the public and the troops with racist imagery of the Japanese (during World War II), the Koreans (during the Korean War), the Vietnamese (during the Vietnam War), and the Chinese (during the seemingly endless animosity toward Communist China). The examples are legion, from virulent comments from a U.S. military officer in Korea who threatened to "give these yellow bastards what is coming to them" (quoted in Cumings 2005, 287) to the experience of Japanese American troops in Vietnam ("This is what the Viet Cong looks like, with slanted eyes," said a drill instructor as he pointed to a Japanese American recruit; quoted in Whelchel 1999, 104).

Today, U.S. Orientalism remains inherently ambiguous and heterogeneous—deeply committed to U.S. primacy and to multiculturalism. It posits that Asians are both required and repellent, both necessary to the economy (and as a weapon against other people of color) and a danger to society. Asia is also laid out on an international plane: the fears of outsourcing are linked directly to the rise of India and China as an alternative to U.S. supremacy. Asians in the United States cannot distance themselves from these global dynamics, as racist events substitute planetary-scale anxiety for the bodies of actual people (the 1982 beating of Vincent Chin, a Chinese American man, for the deindustrialization of Detroit in relation to the rise of the Japanese auto industry is an early example). Thoreau's views still resonate because it is commonplace to appreciate the culture of the ancient "East" and goods from the modern "East" and, at the same time, to be uneasy about the actual people who inhabit that entire region. Bindis and temporary tattoos are easier to accept than are those who wear bindis on a regular basis.

If, however, those who would wear bindis choose not to, and simply work hard, they then become acceptable. That is the contradiction of U.S. Orientalism.

The analytical category Orientalism thus enables an analysis of the ambiguity of U.S. imperialism, which is driven by the twin goals of supremacy and liberation. The Iraqis and Afghans could not liberate themselves, the logic goes, because they are supine, so the GIs must liberate them, especially Iraqi and Afghan women (Armstrong and Prashad 2005). So the U.S. army arrives as a force of liberation. At the same time, the army secures raw materials and creates markets for global corporations and for the dynamic of advanced capitalist states. The urge to liberate is as fundamental as the requirement to subordinate. What is forbidden in the Orientalism of our period is for the "native" to speak in its vital variety—and, because that voice is muted, the native might choose means that are unspeakable. That too is the price of Orientalism.

48

Performance
Susan Manning

In many studies of the arts, "performance" is defined as the set of artistic choices an actor, dancer, or musician makes in realizing a preexistent text—whether that text is a dramatic script, a choreographic design, or a musical score. Over the past few decades, however, some scholars in American studies and cultural studies have redefined "performance" as a mode of cultural production composed of events bound in time and framed in space. Whereas the traditional usage of the noun "performance" implies an opposition to "text," the new usage understands it as a framed event that may well deploy textual elements but cannot be reduced to the realization of preexistent scripts or scores. Like other modes of cultural production, performance takes the form of diverse genres that emerge, alter, and disappear over time. Indian ceremonial, jubilee and Jonkonnu, melodrama, minstrelsy, vaudeville, world's fairs, modern dance, the Broadway musical: all are distinct genres of performance that have circulated within and without U.S. culture.

American studies and cultural studies have adopted a new usage for the verb "perform" as well as for the noun "performance." To perform generally means to carry out, to complete, or to accomplish as well as to act in a play, to execute a dance step, or to play a musical instrument. In its new usage, the connotation of the verb shifts from the achievement of an action to the embodiment of an identity. This usage derives from theories in the social sciences and humanities. Kenneth Burke's *The Philosophy of Literary Form* (1957), Erving Goffman's *The Presentation of Self in Everyday Life* (1959), Victor Turner's

The Ritual Process (1969), and Edward Hall's The Hidden Dimension (1969) all conceptualize social structure and communication in terms of theatrical imagery. Individuals take on roles in scenarios and, verbally and nonverbally, perform their identities for others in the scene. Adapting this language of theatricality, scholars today talk about how social actors perform race, ethnicity, gender, sexuality, class, profession, region, and nationality. This usage of "perform"—and its synonyms such as "stage," "rehearse," "dramatize," "enact"—implies a process whereby physical bodies accrue social identities. It also underscores how some bodies become legible as "masculine" or "black" or "mainstream," while other bodies become legible as "feminine" or "white" or "marginal."

Taken together, the new usages for the noun and verb constitute the field of performance studies and propose two interrelated critical projects for the fields of American studies and cultural studies. Consider the example of performance at the turn of the twentieth century in U.S. culture. As Lawrence Levine (1988) has demonstrated, the hierarchy of high and low culture emerged during this period. Levine's paradigmatic example is Shakespeare. Through most of the nineteenth century, Shakespeare's plays appeared regularly on U.S. stages, both as full-blown productions, often starring visiting British actors, and as subject matter for farcical afterpieces, burlesque, and even blackface minstrelsy. Theaters during the antebellum period drew spectators from the immigrant working class as well as from established elites, and in these public spaces, workers and business owners shared their pleasure and familiarity with Shakespeare. Toward the end of the century, however, Shakespeare migrated from cross-class venues to a newly created realm of high culture, as elites created distinctive venues (the art museum, the symphony hall, the independent theater) separate from the changing spaces for popular culture (the dance hall, the amusement park, the sports stadium). Attending one venue rather than another became a way for people to assert—to perform—their class identities in an era of mass urbanization, industrialization, and immigration.

Strikingly, the cross-class theater of the antebellum era was for men only. Although actresses appeared onstage, only a few women ventured into the theater as spectators, and these women carried the social stigma of "public women," or prostitutes, whatever their actual livelihood. Only after the Civil War, as theaters split along class lines, did women begin to attend in significant numbers. In fact, one hallmark of the newly respectable theater was its accessibility to white, middle-class female patrons, made possible in part by changing codes for audience behavior. Earlier, male spectators had engaged in rowdy behavior, becoming as much a part of the show as the stage action. But after the Civil War, innovations in stage design and lighting accompanied new protocols for quietly attentive spectatorship. Thus, middle-class female theatergoers extended the domestic ideology of the first half of the nineteenth century into the public space of the theater, even as they challenged the strictures of that ideology by venturing out into the city. White, middle-class women's attendance at theaters performed changing conceptions of gender during an era when women first entered universities and the professions and began to organize for the vote.

The division between high and low culture carried racialized connotations as well. In fact, the terms "highbrow" and "lowbrow" derived from late nineteenth-century phrenology, which differentiated "civilized" from "primitive" races according to the shape and size of the human cranium. Thus, the new arena of high culture highlighted its connection with European culture and dismissed performance genres influenced by non-European cultures, most especially jazz music and jazz dance. Originating within African American subcultures during the early decades of the twentieth century, jazz soon attained a broad popularity among the urban working class and white middle class. Although high culture routinely borrowed the inflections of jazz, it disavowed the influence, even while the new technologies of recorded sound commodified jazz as a national sound. These dynamics continued to shape U.S. performance—and racial identities—for decades to come.

This brief case study demonstrates a type of inquiry made possible by new definitions of "performance" as a noun and "perform" as a verb. However, such cross-genre inquiry is not yet widespread in American studies and cultural studies, most probably because it requires scholars to look across the disciplinary histories of dance, music, theater, popular entertainment, and exhibition. Doing so enriches our explorations because we then can trace the complex relations between expressive forms, individual identities, and social formations. The potential for cross-genre inquiry in performance studies is not limited to U.S. cultures or even to the cultures of the Americas but holds across diverse national and regional boundaries.

Far more widespread is scholarship that redefines the verb "perform." It has become commonplace for scholars to discuss the performance of race, gender, class, and so on. These scholars are indebted to the theory of performativity that the feminist philosopher Judith Butler derived from the philosopher of language J. L. Austin (Butler 1990; Austin 1962). Attempting to understand gender as a socially constructed rather than a biologically inherent quality, Butler described it as a "stylized repetition of acts," a set of "bodily gestures, movements, and styles" that signal masculinity or femininity, corporeal signs endlessly repeated and subtly modified over time (1990, 139–40). Following Butler's lead, scholars proposed that other axes of social identity and difference operate in similar ways.

The widespread acceptance of theories of performativity has come under critique from several angles. From one perspective, these theories do not give sufficient weight to material determinants of social identity. This holds especially true for subordinate racial and class positions. To describe middle-class status as the performance of consumer choice makes more sense than to describe the status of the impoverished as a performance. A performance of what? one might ask. Using the term "performance" in this context implies an unimpeded agency that belies the realities of economic inequality and systematic discrimination.

From another perspective, theories of performativity do not sufficiently account for the varying dynamics of everyday life and framed events. This holds especially true for cases of impersonation across race and gender, both onstage and offstage. Scholars have used such cases to illustrate their theories of performativity, but in so doing, they typically blur and confuse the distinction between theater and life. Butler, for example, has advanced a controversial interpretation of drag balls staged in Harlem by African American and Latino men, as documented in Jennie Livingston's film *Paris Is Burning*, arguing that the performers' citation of social norms of femininity ultimately reinforce those norms (Butler 1993). More sustained ethnographic research reveals a radically different set of meanings for the participants in the drag balls, whose offstage lives of homelessness, sex work, and subsistence wages counter their glamorous onstage personae (Jackson 2002). Butler's misreading in part results from her overemphasis on gender and her underestimation of race and class as categories for analysis.

That Butler relied on a film documentary to draw conclusions about a performance event is also telling.

PERFORMANCE SUSAN MANNING

To borrow Raymond Williams's (1982) terminology, performance has become a residual cultural form over the past hundred years, displaced first by film and radio, then by sound recording and television, and now by digital technologies. In retrospect, the emergence of the hierarchy of high and low anticipated the eclipse of performance and the rise of media as dominant cultural forms. This shift cannot be disentangled from contemporary usage of the noun "performance" and the verb "perform." The language of theatricality deployed by Burke, Goffman, Turner, and Hall in the 1950s and 1960s reflects the increasing mediatizing of culture evident during those decades, and the momentum has only intensified since then—hence the seeming irony of our preoccupation with performance at precisely the cultural moment when encounters with live bodies bound in time and framed in space have become increasingly rare occurrences. Our fascination with physicality and embodiment reveals the underside of our mediatized age. The interdisciplinary terrain of performance studies, through its multiple intersections with American studies and cultural studies, reflects an intellectual and institutional response to a larger shift toward media culture over the past century.

49

Politics

Kandice Chuh

"Politics," in its most common usage, refers to the activities of governance, including efforts to attain or retain the power to control those activities. In this sense, the term refers to an interest in how the state (the regulating structures and governing practices of the nation) works and under what or whose authority. This understanding of "politics" is clearly present in both American studies and cultural studies, most markedly in the work of political scientists and legal scholars. However, both fields have long had a broader interest in how and with what consequences the power to govern operates. How and why are resources distributed as they are, and to the benefit or disadvantage of which populations? Who gets to be represented in and who is excluded from participation in governance? What ideas and institutions legitimize the exercise of authority, and how can existing practices and structures be transformed? In what ways do cultural products and practices shape the relationship of individuals and groups to power and authority? How is life itself regulated as a matter of power and authority? Answers to these questions draw on a different meaning of the term "politics," one that stresses contestation over the power to define legitimate authority and recognizes that politics shape everything from the organization and activities of educational and legal institutions to the valuing of some aesthetic practices over others. It is for this reason that phrases such as the "politics of knowledge," "the politics of culture," "the politics of gender," and so on commonly frame the work undertaken in American studies and cultural studies.

The term is most often used in the phrase "the politics *of*" or as the nominalized adjective "the political," and its significance in American studies and cultural studies may be seen in two ways: first, as marking an awareness of the historical conditions of the emergence of these fields and, second, as pointing toward an inquiry into the kind of work that critics in these fields undertake. Common narratives explain the establishment of American studies within U.S. universities as closely related to the global politics of the Cold War era—what may be understood as Cold War *geo*politics. These narratives suggest that, alongside other area studies (e.g., Asian studies), American studies was institutionally legitimated because of the interests of the U.S. nation-state in having detailed knowledge about other nations and regions as it entered into empire-building activities globally (Kaplan and Pease 1993). These stories of the field's establishment closely align it with the politics of U.S. national interests. American studies today, however, tends to be defined by its difference from such nationalist inclinations. What had been a heavy reliance on empirical studies designed to provide information about the United States and its populations has given way to a much richer and more diverse critical sensibility. This transformation echoes the changes to the historical contexts and corollary politics of the movement from the Cold War to the post–Cold War era and reflects the impact of the globally dispersed social movements of the post-civil-rights era.

The shift to a more diversified field of study also reflects the influence of academic discourses and theoretical insights of the late part of the twentieth century, including cultural studies. The field of cultural studies is generally understood to have been established in the 1970s and '80s, with roots in the British class struggles of that era. Key figures such as Simon During (1993/2007), Stuart Hall (1980), and Lawrence Grossberg (Grossberg, Nelson, and Treichler 1992), in accord with the demands of the social movements of the late twentieth century, argued for attention to the ways in which universities play a significant role in the organization of society into different classes. Universities and their dominant ways of producing and disseminating knowledge—their dominant epistemologies and pedagogies—have historically contributed to the uneven distribution of power and resources. Debates over what gets studied and taught, by whom, and how were framed in these founding texts of cultural studies as a politics of knowledge. These debates changed the landscape of what could be taken up and taught as legitimate objects of knowledge. For example, the legitimation of the study of popular culture is an effect of the struggles over the politics of knowledge of this time. Politics, then, are one way of understanding the history of the fields themselves.

Feminist, queer, postcolonial, and ethnic studies politics, theories, and traditions have been driving forces in the kinds of questions that animate these fields. Not all of the work undertaken in American studies or cultural studies attends to matters of power and difference, which is a central concern of these discourses and the social movements with which they are intimately connected. But it is arguable that the most compelling work draws on the energies that issue from thinking through race, sex, gender, sexuality, empire, and bodily norms, along with class, as intersecting axes of analysis. In these ways, American studies and cultural studies are largely organized by questions that are at once political (they address matters of authority and power) and epistemological (they ask how knowledge is produced and what value it is given).

The politics of the field formations of American studies and cultural studies thus draw attention to the boundary between the realms of politics and culture, knowledge and society. What is American studies? What is cultural studies? What are their stakes and objectives? Persistently and deeply concerned with these foundational questions, both fields have made it possible to recognize the role of politics in the ways that culture is shaped and expressed, the role of culture in giving meaning to political processes, and the role of academic discourses and institutions in making it possible to attend to questions of power and authority. Engagement with these kinds of issues often draws on political theorists and philosophers associated closely with Marxist thinking and related theories of ideology and hegemony, which have had enormous impact on the ways that power and its relationships to the people is conceptualized (Althusser 1971/2001; Gramsci 1971) and on the material aspects of art and culture (Benjamin 1936/1968; Raymond Williams 1976/1983). The theorization of power in terms of *biopolitics* has enabled a crucial understanding of politics as a mechanism by which life is given or taken (Foucault 1975/1995). Other critics have generated key insights into the affective dimensions of life, culture, and politics (Berlant 1991, 2011); the rise of neoliberalism as an ideology of governance (Duggan 2003; Wendy Brown 2005); the ways in which sex and race shape knowledge production (Ferguson 2012); the history of popular culture and social movements (Lipsitz 1990b, 1998/2006); the interrelation of race and gender, capitalism and national identity formation (Lowe 1996); and the performative dimensions of racial and sexual embodiment and identification (J. Butler 1993; Muñoz 1999, 2009).

At the same time, contemporary scholarship in American studies and cultural studies also focuses critical attention on the boundaries of "the political" itself. Partly in response to the dominance of the kinds of critiques associated with the politics of identity

and representation, recent work has encouraged an expansion of the topics, sites, and methods of cultural studies analyses in American studies. Identity and representation in this context refer to sociopolitical identities—those of race, gender, age, and so on— and how they are constructed and with what effects. Enormously powerful in showing how such identities matter to the lives, cultures, and histories of the United States—powerful, that is, in showing that there *is* a politics of identity—these approaches have been criticized for defining the objectives of politically engaged work in terms of dominant representational politics. For instance, analyses of the history of racism in the United States that focus primarily on the objective of attaining citizenship and the rights that accompany it operate within the nation's normative framework by promoting identity understood in nationalist terms as the achievement of social justice. A critique of that type of analysis encourages questioning the adequacy of national identity as the solution to social and economic problems, rather than encouraging identification with it (Moten 2003; Reddy 2011).

This emphasis on the boundaries of the political has made it clear that politics are too narrowly defined when attached to the frameworks of identity and representation that are sanctioned by the nation-state. These critiques have led to efforts to expand and theorize "the political" itself. Partly, these efforts can be observed in the variety of "turns" that cultural studies and American studies have taken—toward the transnational, the hemispheric, the global, the aesthetic, the ethical, the affective, and so on—with each named "turn" attempting to generate paradigms for critical inquiry that are better able to apprehend the complexity of power structures and dynamics and their effects. Likewise, the currency and traction of terms such as "indigeneity," "sovereignty," "disability," "the commons," and "ecocriticism" reflect the changing critical and political landscape of both American studies and cultural studies. Some of these moves attempt to alter the spatial protocols by which "Americanness" is conceptualized and studied, to illuminate the politics of the nation and of citizenship. Others may be better understood as more explicitly rewriting "the political" itself. One example is the increased interest in the cultural and material significance of affect. Driven largely by feminist and queer theorists, this attention to "the politics of affect" inverts the usual association of politics with reason and the public sphere and of feeling with sentiment and domesticity (Berlant 1991, 2011; Clough and Halley 2007; Cvetkovich 1992, 2003; S. Ngai 2005).

In these ways, the space of American cultural studies—the overlap between American studies and cultural studies—is a site through which the complexity and breadth of both "politics" and "the political" can be apprehended as an aspect of world-making ideologies (such as imperialism and nationalism) and ordinary lives, of ways of knowing and of sorting knowledge, and of the distribution of life and death. By insisting on asking what constitutes "the political," this vein of scholarship importantly necessitates awareness of how its definition delimits what can be studied, known, and potentially transformed.

50

Prison

Caleb Smith

The United States now incarcerates more people than any other country in the world, both as a percentage of its own population and in absolute numbers. The federal government operates a far-reaching network of immigrant detention centers and war prisons, including the notorious camp at Guantánamo Bay. Like the domestic warehouses of mass incarceration, these are spaces where the boundaries of legal personhood and cultural identity are contested. While prisons have been expanding, many other public institutions have disappeared or withered; those that remain, such as schools and housing projects, seem increasingly prison-like. Critics have described the United States as a "prison nation," arguing that imprisonment, which serves various functions elsewhere, has become a core mission of the U.S. state, an end in itself (Herivel and Wright 2003). To claim that the United States, as a nation, is distinguished by its prisons is to pose a problem, not to resolve one, since prison stands for so many enduring contradictions—between assimilation and exclusion, deracination and racialization, subject formation and abjection.

"Prison" is an ancient word. The *Oxford English Dictionary* suggests an etymological link between "prisoner" and "prize," perhaps because captives taken (*pris*) in war, according to some customs and codes, could be sold into servitude or otherwise exploited by their captors. In the modern era, following the Atlantic revolutions, "prison" came to name an institution designed for the long-term incarceration of convicted criminals. Thus, prisons were distinguished from jails, which are places of detention where inmates await trial or punishment. Led by reformers from the northeastern United States, many European and North American criminal justice systems gradually abandoned public punishments—hanging, whipping, branding, and other forms of disfigurement and shame—and established imprisonment as the new standard. The first wave of reform promised to rationalize and humanize the penal system, to re-create the prison as a scene of reflection and rehabilitation. To emphasize these new ideals, the reformers called their institutions "houses of correction" or "penitentiaries." Since the 1960s, scholars in American studies, cultural studies, and the interdisciplinary field of critical prison studies have excavated the causes and consequences of these transformations. Their research suggests that, even as the prison came to signify a revolution in punishment, it never fully severed its ties to the forms of captivity associated with empire, war, and slavery. Today, imprisonment's genealogical bonds to those kinds of large-scale violence seem more durable than its frayed connection to such concepts as justice and the rule of law.

Interdisciplinary and activist scholarship uses prison as a critical concept, analyzing the penal system in terms other than the official ones which are used to justify that system or to improve it from within. Scholars have submitted the discourses of legitimation and reform to a dual critique, analyzing them from alternative theoretical perspectives and, at the same time, attending to inmates' own accounts of their experience. Some of this work promotes specific policy changes, such as an end to solitary confinement or life sentencing. Increasingly, though, critical prison studies has allied itself with the radical project of ending imprisonment altogether—a "new abolitionism" (J. James 2005). From the start, this critique confronted an institution so normalized that it was difficult to imagine any alternative. To make the prison visible as an object of controversy, Michel Foucault's influential *Discipline and Punish: The Birth of the Prison* took a genealogical approach, writing a "history of the present" (1975/1995, 31). With the rise of the penitentiary, according to the received wisdom, punishment ceased to wound the body and dedicated itself to rehabilitating the soul. Foucault rejected this narrative, arguing that the modern prison was a scene of unending struggle. It was "born" when techniques of disciplinary training, surveillance, and control that had first been developed elsewhere—in the military, the workshop, and the school—were used to reorganize the penal system. These disciplines produced prisoners as objects of specialized knowledge and as subjects responsible for the regulation of their own actions. Rather than releasing the state's hold on the body, the shift from spectacular torture to prison discipline actually tightened its grip.

Foucault's research focused on western Europe, but the movements that produced the first penitentiaries were transatlantic in scope; and the boundary between torture and its civilized alternatives was drawn most vividly at the edges of empires (Asad 2003). In the United States, prison reform was aligned with other enlightened causes—temperance, antislavery, even democracy itself. By the 1830s, prison reformers had the support of powerful evangelical organizations, and two world-famous penitentiary systems were competing for prestige. Pennsylvania's "solitary system" placed every inmate in solitary confinement. New York's "congregate system" enforced group labor in factory-like workshops. The rivalry was the topic of a fierce pamphlet war, but it also obscured some deeper continuities; soon it was taken for granted, at least in the free states, that imprisonment would be the standard punishment for most serious crimes. Already, the penitentiary had become a key component in the international reputation of the United States. Charles Dickens (1842) and Harriet Martineau (1837) joined the debate, and Alexis de Tocqueville compiled his notes for *Democracy in America* (1835/2004) while he was studying U.S. penitentiaries for the French government. These visitors suspected that the penitentiary systems would disclose something essential about the character of the new republic, where punishment had been reconceived as an implement of humanization and enlightened justice. In the solitary confinement cell, the United States fashioned its ideal citizens; in the prison workshop, it built its model of a well-regulated society.

Critical histories of the penitentiary have explored how the new institution, promising rationality and humanity, reinforced hierarchies of race and class and tightened social control (W. Lewis 1965; Rothman 1971; Dumm 1987; Meranze 1996). Seeing prison reform less as a humanitarian movement than as a tactical shift in the exercise of power, this approach connects the penitentiary to other institutions designed for surveillance and training: the industrial factory, the asylum, the technical college, and the Indian school. Today, however, the penal system rarely promises rehabilitation, and historians have come to doubt that the genealogy of the prison can be traced exclusively to the nineteenth-century penitentiary. Studies of U.S. war prisons, for instance, have situated contemporary torture and indefinite detention within far-reaching histories of imperialism (M. Brown 2005; A. Kaplan 2005; Dayan 2007). And new work on the highly racialized regime of mass incarceration has discovered precedents in the antebellum plantation and its successors, convict leasing, the prison farm, and Jim Crow segregation (Wacquant 2002; Oshinsky 2008; Michelle Alexander 2010). These new genealogies have tended to set aside the term "penitentiary," with its reformist and religious connotations, in favor of

"prison," emphasizing that the object of critique is not a machine for remaking subjects but a scene of abjection, dehumanization, and death (C. Smith 2009).

Despite the rhetoric of reform, the true "uses of incarceration in the United States," Colin Dayan argues, have always been "to criminalize, exclude, and do such violence to persons that they are returned to their communities—when they are—diminished and harmed sometimes beyond repair, or redress" (2011, xiv). This sense of prison as a zone of exclusion and mortification undergirds an increasing scholarly interest in prison literature and in fieldwork that documents inmates' accounts of their own lives. Several studies and collections have emphasized imprisonment as a defining aspect of African American experience and expression, linking the project of prison abolition to the nineteenth-century abolitionists' antislavery campaigns (Philip 1973; H. Franklin 1978; T. Green 2008). Others have asked what modes of consciousness and resistance remain available within the conditions of disciplinary isolation and social death (Rhodes 2004; D. Rodríguez 2006; Guenther 2013). When the prison is understood as an implement of vengeance whose true aim is to annihilate, not to rehabilitate, the self, inmates' own documentary accounts and creative testimonials are of special value to a critical practice that identifies itself with the activist struggle to end imprisonment.

What does it mean to speak of the prison today? In recent decades, new developments have made the penal system an object of critical and popular controversy. The privatization of some facilities introduces a profit motive and allows corporations to screen their practices from public oversight by invoking the legal protections that guard trade secrets. The large-scale incarceration of undocumented immigrants is explained in terms of sovereignty and citizenship, rather than correction. The same is true of indefinite detention (or internment) and torture in "the new war prison" at Guantánamo (J. Butler 2004a, 53). And solitary confinement, now euphemized as "administrative segregation" or "special housing," has been redefined as a strategy for system-internal securitization, imposed at the discretionary authority of bureaucratic officials. Hunger strikes, riots, and other acts of resistance by inmates have called attention to a human rights crisis. In the academy and in the public sphere, critics have pointed to the widening and scandalous gap between the actual functions of prisons and their traditional role as public institutions of criminal justice. Some of these scandals may seem to partake of the logic of the "exception," instances of sovereign power operating outside the ordinary rule of law (Agamben 2005). But they can also be connected to the normal functioning of a new kind of prison system, unlike any other in the world.

Between 1975 and 2000, the total number of inmates in U.S. facilities jumped from just under 380,000 to almost two million, an increase of more than 500 percent, driven largely by harsh, racially targeted sentencing laws for drug offenses (Wacquant 2009). The result was "mass incarceration," imprisonment on a scale that is unprecedented in U.S. history and unequaled anywhere else in the world. In an effort to understand and resist this dramatic turn, scholars have advanced several critiques. Most agree that the rise of mass incarceration was not primarily a response to a rise in crime, but each has its own account of what the prison has become. One argument points to the decline of the ideal of rehabilitation and the resurgence of a vengeful popular attitude, accompanied by spectacular, sensationalized images of crime and punishment in mass culture (F. Allen 1981; J. Whitman 2003; M. Brown 2009). Another points to a thriving "prison industrial complex," a coalition of state and private interests which exerts such a strong influence on policy that the main business of criminal justice in the United States is simply to continue expanding the nation's prisons (Parenti 1999; A. Davis 2001).

A third argument, associated with critical legal studies, suggests a shift in the very nature of government. With deindustrialization, the welfare state gave way to the "penal" or "carceral" state. As neoliberal reforms dismantled the midcentury's institutions of welfare and public health, governments began using jails and prisons to manage forms of social insecurity—mental illness, drug addiction, and poverty—that had previously been addressed by other means (Simon 2007; Wacquant 2009; Dolovich 2011). Critical prison studies has begun to advance the radical proposition that the penal system no longer maintains *any* meaningful connection to popular conceptions of justice, whether reformist or retributive, but operates instead to identify disorderly groups and to redistribute bodies in geographic space, warehousing them in a state of *incapacitation* (Feeley and Simon 1992; R. Gilmore 2007). The prison, in these analyses, is the centerpiece of a penal system that has shifted its focus away from the offender, toward target populations; away from justice, toward security; away from rehabilitation, toward the smooth functioning of its own institutional machinery. Prison today names both the principal implement of domestic state violence and the object of an intensifying critical resistance.

51

Public

Bruce Robbins

According to the *Oxford English Dictionary*, "public" originated from the Latin *populus*, or "people," apparently under the influence of the word *pubes*, or "adult men." The term's considerable authority, based on its claim to represent the social whole, has continued to bump up against evidence that large classes of people have been omitted from it, as women and children are omitted from *pubes*. In American studies, relevant debates have focused on the continuing applicability of this ancient notion within a specialized modern division of labor in which no one has knowledge of the whole (Dewey 1927; Lippman 1927); on whether the apparent decline of public life (as in Robert Putnam's "bowling alone" thesis [2000]) might reflect the larger percentage of U.S. women now doing paid rather than voluntary work; on whether "public spaces" in the past were ever really democratically accessible to all; and on how open or universal the goals, values, and membership of so-called identity politics movements ought to be. Recent critics, skeptical that such a thing as a social whole exists except at the level of ideology, have sometimes implied the desirability of removing the word from circulation. If there has been no moratorium, this is in part because current usage also acknowledges a need for the term's appeal against state despotism, a key motive for its rise in the eighteenth century, and against the free market economy, in which many observers see a newer, decentralized despotism.

Recoiling from the singular, putatively comprehensive usage (*the* public), cultural studies has undertaken to recognize the existence of multiple publics, especially among excluded or marginalized groups. Examples include Oskar Negt and Alexander Kluge's (1993) hypothesis of a proletarian public sphere, as well as the publics formed by political organizing, sexual role playing, and diasporic affiliation on the Internet. These objects of ethnographic and sociological attention are often described as "counterpublics." The coinage is perhaps premature, for oppositionality remains to be demonstrated; to be smaller than or separate from X is not necessarily to oppose X. Nor can it be assumed that what is countered is the normative force of publicness itself. To speak of an excluded group as a "public" is again to claim representation of a social whole (though a smaller one) and thus to invoke an authority that can be disputed on similar grounds. The multiplication of publics (the plural still causes distress to my computer's spell checker) offers no escape from the term's onerous but alluring authority.

Empirical questions of who is and is not included in a given public—a necessary component of cultural studies projects and one that always threatens to unsettle the term's authority—thus cannot overthrow it completely. Normativity seems to be hardwired into usage. As Michael Warner (2002) suggests, speech is public only when it is addressed, beyond any already-existing group of members, to an indefinite number of strangers. As a result, the public is always open to the charge of being merely a wishful fiction, but by the same token, it is immune to merely empirical verification, perpetually in excess of any delimited membership. This excessiveness, which is honored far beyond scholars responding to the works of Jürgen Habermas (1999), helps explain the term's tolerance for near redundancy. "Public" can be added as an adjective to a noun that would already seem to be public. The events of September 11, 2001, Judith Butler (2004a, xi) writes, "led public intellectuals to waver in their public commitment to principles of justice." There is no such thing as a *private* intellectual; "intellectual" already implies a concern for more than the (presumed) privacy of academic, field-specific knowledge. Similarly, a commitment that was kept secret would hardly deserve to be called a (true) commitment. Yet usage supports the supplement, which exhorts intellectuals and commitments to become, by strenuous effort, more fully and passionately that which they already are.

In addition to the distracting discrepancy between empirical reference and normative exhortation, "public" lends itself to other sorts of confusion. As a singular noun, it hesitates between social wholes of different scale and nature: between a collective organized as a body and an unorganized, unselfconscious aggregate; between the opinions of the empirically existing members and their conjectural long-term interest or welfare; between the inhabitants of a nation, and—in a sense that has recently returned from obsolescence—the world at large, all of humankind. If the public is what *pertains* to the social whole, other important ambiguities result from the distinct relations to that whole that are hidden away in "pertain": that which is *potentially accessible* to the community, that which is *already visible to* and *viewed by* the community, that which *belongs to* or *is controlled by* the community, that which *affects* or is *of significance to* the community, that which is *authorized by* the community, and that which is done *in the service* or *on behalf of* the community.

In this context, "community," which seems indispensable to the definition of "public," also provides an important contrast to it. Like "culture," another contiguous and overlapping term, "community" seems less tolerant of universal ethical principles, warmer to its members, and more hostile to strangers and self-estrangement. The referential indefiniteness of "public" leaves it more open, if also cooler and more abstract. But both "community" and "culture" also have senses that are closer to "public."

Related ambiguities result from a sliding set of oppositions between "public" and the diverse meanings of "private," a term that derives from the Latin *privatus*, or "withdrawn from public life." Shades of difference in "private" correspond to comparable differences in "public"; for example, the demand for citizen participation (which is asserted against private apathy) differs from the demand for scrutiny and debate (which is asserted against governmental restriction of access). Along with capitalist globalization and the revolution in digital technology, another major factor influencing usage of both terms has been the drive for gender equality. Here the clear movement has been toward an expansion of sites and occasions deemed public. For men, both the family and the workplace had seemed to belong to the domain of privacy, hence deserving protection from state interference. The women's movement refused this public/private distinction, redescribing the family as a domain of patriarchal injustice that must be opened up to public scrutiny and rectified by means of state action. With women adding salaried work outside the home to their unpaid work within it, the workplace too has been added to the public. Yet feminists have also questioned the seeming limitlessness of this enlargement. To what extent should sex be subject to scrutiny and regulation? As Jean Cohen (2002) notes, issues such as reproductive rights, gays in the military, and sexual harassment in the workplace seem to demand a reworking, rather than an abolition, of the public/private distinction.

"Private" has come to signify both the domain of capitalist economics and the domain of personal freedom and domestic intimacy. To allow the deeply cherished emotions associated with intimacy to extend to the world market is to bestow a handsome gift of friendly propaganda on defenders of large corporations and international finance. Any demand for public regulation of the economy thus becomes an unwanted and unwarranted intrusion into one's most personal space. Relevant cultural studies projects include the critical analysis of intellectual property, copyright law, file sharing, and digital sampling, all of which investigate the fate of public access to cultural products and scientific knowledge, incursions into the public domain by private ownership, and movements to restore public rights (open access) to research results produced with the help of public funding.

But capitalism's effects on usage of "public" and "private" have been paradoxical. On the one hand, capitalism is associated with privatization and the shrinkage of the public. On the other, market-fueled digitalization is celebrated for democratically multiplying the shapes, rhythms, and vectors of publicness and for allowing people to socialize with minimal interference from their spatially tethered and symbolically coded bodies or from the usual gatekeepers controlling for social status and professional expertise. (The same divide structures debates in architecture and urban studies over the fate of public space.) Yet digital technologies are also blamed for overextending the domain of the public. The degree of invisible nonstop surveillance made possible by new techniques of data retrieval, ranging from information on buying habits collected by retailers and marketers to governmental assaults on privacy and civil liberties, has intensified the term's further connotation of shaming exposure.

Like "private," "public" derives ideological force from the confusing of distinct senses and situations. The term switches between what is owned, decided on, and managed by the community and what is merely observed by and relevant to the community—that is, between the public as active participant (modeled on the organized political group) and the public as passive spectator (modeled on the theatrical audience and reading public). "Public" thus can imply that the active, participatory aspects of politics are present within the more passive, aestheticized context of spectatorship. This switch encourages a tendency to inflate the degree and significance of agency available in the act of cultural consumption—the suggestion, say, that shopping and striking are comparable practices. Yet this ambiguity also raises such productive questions as how distinct the two sorts of publicness are and what role theatricality and symbolism can play within politics. The same ambiguity drives media research into how, when, and whether what is public in the minimal sense of *visibility* (celebrity, publicity) translates into what is public in a weightier sense such as *sociability* or *organized political will* (activism, collaboration).

A closely related distinction helps clarify the even more interesting issue of the public's *scale*. The word has been used most frequently about various collectivities up to the scale of the nation, but not about international or multinational entities. This fits its association with zones of actual conversation and self-consciously shared destiny, which have historically been limited. Yet there is increasing consensus among students of both American studies and cultural studies that this limitation is intellectually and politically unacceptable. The concept of the public as a zone of causal connectedness—those actions relevant to or significant for the welfare of a given group, whether or not the group is in conversation with itself or with the begetters of the actions—is much vaster. In the era of the world market, not to speak of official and unofficial violence across borders, this zone has become increasingly international. Thus, the restrictively national scale of "public" (in the sense of conversation and control) is seen to be stretching and at the same time to need *further* stretching. Enlarging the scale of international attention, conversation, and opinion so as to match the scale of international causal connectedness—that is, bringing these two senses of "public" into congruence with each other—means resetting the boundaries of the relevant moral community so that those who are likely to be affected by a course of action, wherever they live, are among those invited to debate it. The United Nations, so-called nongovernmental organizations, transnational television stations such as CNN and Al-Jazeera, and the Internet are among the sociotechnical institutions whose impact on the possible constituting of a global public now ought to be under hopeful and suspicious examination.

52

Queer
Siobhan B. Somerville

"Queer" causes confusion, perhaps because two of its current meanings seem to be at odds. In both popular and academic usage in the United States, "queer" is sometimes used interchangeably with the terms "gay" and "lesbian" and occasionally "transgender" and "bisexual." In this sense of the word, "queer" is understood as an umbrella term that refers to a range of sexual identities that are "not straight." In other political and academic contexts, "queer" is used in a very different way: as a term that calls into question the stability of any such categories of identity based on sexual orientation. In this second sense, "queer" is a *critique* of the tendency to organize political or theoretical questions around sexual orientation per se. To "queer" becomes a way to denaturalize categories such as "lesbian" and "gay" (not to mention "straight" and "heterosexual"), revealing them as socially and historically constructed identities that have often worked to establish and police the line between the "normal" and the "abnormal."

Fittingly, the word "queer" itself has refused to leave a clear trace of its own origins; its etymology is unknown. It may have been derived from the German word *quer* or the Middle High German *twer*, which meant "cross," "oblique," "squint," "perverse," or "wrongheaded," but these origins have been contested. The *Oxford English Dictionary* notes that while "queer" seems to have entered English in the sixteenth century, there are few examples of the word before 1700. From that time until the mid-twentieth century, "queer" tended to refer to anything "strange," "odd," or "peculiar," with additional negative connotations that suggested something "bad," "worthless," or even "counterfeit." In the late eighteenth and early nineteenth centuries, the word "queer" began to be used also as a verb, meaning "to quiz or ridicule," "to puzzle," "to cheat," or "to spoil." During this time, the adjectival form also began to refer to a condition that was "not normal," "out of sorts," "giddy, faint, or ill."

By the first two decades of the twentieth century, "queer" became linked to sexual practice and identity in the United States, particularly in urban sexual cultures. During the 1910s and 1920s in New York City, for example, men who called themselves "queer" used the term to refer to their sexual interest in other men (Chauncey 1994). Contemporaneous literary works by African American writers such as Nella Larsen (1929) and Jean Toomer (1923/1969) suggest that the term could also carry racialized meanings, particularly in the context of mixed-race identities that exposed the instability of divisions between "black" and "white." But it was not until the 1940s that "queer" began to be used in mainstream U.S. culture primarily to refer to "sexual perverts" or "homosexuals," most often in a pejorative, stigmatizing way, a usage that reached its height during the Cold War era and that continues to some extent today. In the early twenty-first century, "queer" remains a volatile term; the *American Heritage Dictionary* even appends a warning label advising that the use of "queer" by "heterosexuals is often considered offensive," and therefore "extreme caution must be taken concerning [its] use when one is not a member of the group." The term has also carried specific class connotations in some periods and contexts. On the one hand, as one participant in a 2004 online forum put it, "'Queer' is a rebellion against those posh middle-class business owners who want to define gaydom as being their right to enjoy all the privileges denied them

just cos they like cock" (Isambard 2004). On the other hand, these class connotations are unstable. "If I have to pick an identity label in the English language," wrote poet and critic Gloria Anzaldúa, "I pick 'dyke' or 'queer,' though these working-class words . . . have been taken over by white middle-class lesbian theorists in the academy" (1998, 263–64).

The use of "queer" in academic and political contexts beginning in the late 1980s represented an attempt to reclaim this stigmatizing word and to defy those who have wielded it as a weapon. This usage is often traced to the context of AIDS activism that responded to the epidemic's devastating toll on gay men in U.S. urban areas during the 1980s and 1990s. Queer Nation, an activist organization that grew out of ACT UP (AIDS Coalition To Unleash Power), became one of the most visible sites of a new politics that was "meant to be confrontational—opposed to gay assimilationists and straight oppressors while inclusive of people who have been marginalized by anyone in power" (Escoffier and Bérubé 1991, 14). In subsequent decades, queer political groups have not always achieved this goal of inclusiveness in practice, but they have sought to transform the homophobic ideologies of dominant U.S. culture, as well as strategies used by existing mainstream lesbian and gay rights movements, many of which have tended to construct lesbian and gay people as a viable "minority" group and to appeal to liberal models of inclusion (Duggan 1992).

The movement to gain legal rights to same-sex marriage demonstrates some of the key differences between a lesbian/gay rights approach and a queer activist strategy. While advocates for same-sex marriage argue that lesbians and gay men should not be excluded from the privileges of marriage accorded to straight couples, many queer activists and theorists question why marriage and the nuclear family should be the sites of legal and social privilege in the first place. Because same-sex marriage would leave intact a structure that disadvantages those who either cannot or choose not to marry (regardless of their sexual orientation), a more ethical project, queer activists argue, would seek to detach material and social privileges from the institution of marriage altogether (Ettelbrick 1989; Duggan 2004).

Sometimes in conversation with activist efforts and sometimes not, queer theory emerged as an academic field during the late 1980s and early 1990s. Drawing on the work of Michel Foucault, scholars who are now referred to as queer theorists argued that sexuality, especially the binary system of "homosexual" and "heterosexual" orientations, is a relatively modern production. As Foucault (1976/1990) argued, although certain acts between two people of the same sex had long been punishable through legal and religious sanctions, these practices did not necessarily define individuals as "homosexual" until the late nineteenth century. While historians have disagreed about the precise periods and historical contexts in which the notion of sexual identity emerged, Foucault's insistence that sexuality "must not be thought of as a kind of natural given" has been transformative, yielding an understanding of sexuality not as a "natural" psychic or physical drive but as a "set of effects produced in bodies, behaviors, and social relations by a certain deployment" of power (105, 127). Moving away from the underlying assumptions of identity politics and its tendency to locate stable sexual subjects, queer theory has focused on the very process of sexual subject formation. If much of the early work in lesbian and gay studies tended to be organized around an opposition between homosexuality and heterosexuality, the primary axis of queer studies shifted toward the distinction between normative and nonnormative sexualities as they have been produced in a range of historical and cultural contexts.

For this reason, a key concept in queer theory is the notion of "heteronormativity," a term that refers to "the institutions, structures of understanding, and practical orientations that make heterosexuality seem not only coherent—that is, organized as a sexuality— but also privileged" (Berlant and Warner 1998, 548n2). Heteronormativity, it is important to stress, is not the same thing as heterosexuality (though the two are not entirely separable); indeed, various forms of heterosexuality (adultery, polygamy, and interracial marriage, among others) and heterosexual practices (e.g., fornication, sodomy) have historically been proscribed in certain contexts rather than privileged (Rubin 1984; C. Cohen 1997; Burgett 2005). Rather, heteronormativity is a form of power that exerts its effects on both gay and straight individuals, often through unspoken practices and institutional structures.

Because queer critique has the potential to destabilize the ground on which any particular claim to identity can be made (though, importantly, not destroying or abandoning identity categories altogether), a significant body of queer scholarship has warned against anchoring the field primarily or exclusively to questions of sexuality. Instead, these scholars have argued, we should dislodge "the status of sexual orientation itself as the authentic and centrally governing category of queer practice, thus freeing up queer theory as a way of reconceiving not just the sexual, but the social in general" (Harper et al. 1997, 1). In local, national, and transnational contexts, such a formulation allows us to contest constructions of certain issues as "sexual" and others as "nonsexual," a distinction that has often been deployed by U.S. neoconservatives and neoliberals alike to separate "lesbian and gay" movements from a whole range of interconnected struggles for social justice.

The field of queer studies has challenged this tendency by using intersectional approaches that begin from the assumption that sexuality cannot be separated from other categories of identity and social status. Whereas some early queer theorists found it necessary to insist on understanding sexuality as a distinct category of analysis, one that could not be fully accounted for by feminist theories of gender, it is now clear that sexuality and gender can never be completely isolated from each other (Rubin 1984; Sedgwick 1990). Indeed, Judith Butler (1990, 5) has shown that our very notions of sexual difference (male/female) are an effect of a "heterosexual matrix." A significant body of scholarship, largely generated out of questions raised by transgender identity and politics, has insisted on the pressing need to revisit and scrutinize the relationships among sex, gender, and sexuality, with an emphasis on recalibrating theories of performativity in light of materialist accounts of gender (S. Stone 1991; Prosser 1998; Valentine 2007; Spade 2011).

If queer theory's project is understood, in part, as an attempt to challenge identity categories that are presented as stable, transhistorical, or authentic, then critiques of naturalized racial categories are also crucial to its antinormative project. As a number of critics have shown, heteronormativity derives much of its power from the ways in which it (often silently) shores up as well as depends on naturalized categories of racial difference in contexts ranging from sexology and psychoanalysis to fiction and cinema (Somerville 2000; Eng 2001). Heteronormativity itself must be understood, then, as a racialized concept, since "[racially] marginal group members, lacking power and privilege although engaged in heterosexual behavior, have often found themselves defined as outside the norms and values of dominant society" (C. Cohen 1997, 454). This insistence on putting questions of race at the center of queer

approaches has been vigorously argued most recently in a body of scholarship identified as "queer of color critique" (Muñoz 1999; Ferguson 2004).

At the same time that intersectional approaches have become more central to queer studies, the field has also increasingly turned to the specificities of nation-based models and the dynamics of globalization and imperialism. Scholars have begun to interrogate both the possibilities and the limitations of queer theory for understanding the movement of desires and identities within a transnational frame, as well as the necessity of attending to the relationship between the methods of queer theory and colonial structures of knowledge and power (Povinelli and Chauncey 1999; Manalansan 2003; Gopinath 2005). The resulting interest in the "nation" and its constitutive role in processes of racialization and sexualization has raised new questions about the ways that queer theory might usefully interrogate the nation's less charismatic companion—the state (Reddy 2011). Jacqueline Stevens (2004, 225), for instance, has envisioned queer theory and activism as a site for articulating "a revolution against all forms of state boundaries, . . . the unhindered movement and full-fledged development of capacities regardless of one's birthplace or parentage."

If the origins of the term "queer" are elusive, its future horizons might be even more so. While the term itself has a contested and perhaps confusing history, one of the points of consensus among queer theorists has been that its parameters should not be prematurely (or ever) delimited (Sedgwick 1993; Berlant and Warner 1995). The field of queer studies is relatively young, but as it has made inroads in a number of different academic disciplines and debates, some critics have asserted that the term has lost its ability to create productive friction. Pointing to its seeming ubiquity in popular-cultural venues, others criticize the ways that the greater circulation of "queer" and its appropriation by the mainstream entertainment industries have emptied out its oppositional political potential. Whether we should be optimistic or pessimistic about the increasing visibility of "queer" culture remains an open question. Meanwhile, scholars continue to carefully interrogate the shortcomings and the untapped possibilities of "queer" approaches to a range of diverse issues, such as migration (Luibhéid and Cantú 2005), temporality (Edelman 2004; Halberstam 2005; E. Freeman 2010; Rohy 2009), region (Herring 2010; Gopinath 2007; Tongson 2011), indigeneity (Justice, Rifkin, and Schneider 2010; Morgenson 2011), and disability (McRuer 2006). Whatever the future uses and contradictions of "queer," it seems likely that the word will productively refuse to settle down, demanding critical reflection in order to be understood in its varied and specific cultural, political, and historical contexts.

53

Race

Roderick A. Ferguson

The study of race incorporates a set of wide-ranging analyses of freedom and power. The scope of those analyses has much to do with the broad application of racial difference to academic and popular notions of epistemology, community, identity, and the body. With regard to economic and political formations, race has shaped the meaning and profile of citizenship and labor. In relation to corporeality, race has rendered the body into a text on which histories of racial differentiation, exclusion, and violence are inscribed. Analyzed in terms of subjectivity, race helps to locate the ways in which identities are constituted.

Many of these insights are the intellectual effects of antiracist political struggles, particularly ones organized around national liberation and civil rights. In the United States, the minority movements of the 1950s and 1960s fundamentally changed the ways in which racial minorities thought about their identities and cultures and the ways that race worked within U.S. society (Omi and Winant 1986/1994). In doing so, these movements intersected with sociological arguments that displaced notions of race as a strict biological inheritance and forced scholars to confront it as a category with broad political and economic implications. For the first time, there was mass mobilization around the deployment of the linguistic, historical, and artistic elements of minority cultures as a means of challenging racial oppression within the United States. Black, Chicano, and Asian American political and cultural groups emerged out of this context. In addition to cultural recovery, these groups argued for land redistribution, the end of police brutality, and community control over economic development. Race emerged out of these movements as an expression of cultural and political agency by marginalized groups. This was the notion of race that underwrote the ethnic studies movements of the 1960s and 1970s, including the student protests of 1968–69 that inaugurated the Division of Ethnic Studies at San Francisco State University. There and elsewhere, departments of Asian, Chicano, Native, and black studies worked to challenge race as a mode of exploitation within U.S. society in particular and Western nations more generally (Marable 2000).

At the same time, insights about the various meanings of "race" have also arisen out of movements that countered these largely nation-based forms of racial politics. As postcolonial and poststructuralist theorists have illustrated, race is more than a way of identifying and organizing political coalitions against forms of state repression and capitalist exploitation; it is also a category that sets the terms of belonging and exclusion within modern institutions. David Theo Goldberg (1993, 87) captures this tension nicely: "[Race] has established who can be imported and who exported, who are immigrants and who are indigenous, who may be property and who are citizens; and among the latter who get to vote and who do not, who are protected by the law and who are its objects, who are employable and who are not, who have access and privilege and who are (to be) marginalized." In other words, race both accounts for the logics by which institutions differentiate and classify, include and exclude, and names the processes by which people internalize those logics. Critical theorists of race such as Goldberg have pointed out that ideals of political agency that rely on notions of race, including those derived from ethnic studies, have often bought into the same unspoken norms of racial regulation that they elsewhere critiqued

(Crenshaw 1995; Lowe 1996; Chuh 2003). Feminist and queer critiques of racial ideologies and discourses have complicated the matter further. As women of color and Third World feminists have argued since the mid- to late 1970s, civil rights and national liberation struggles shared important and largely unappreciated affiliations with the very racist regimes to which they were responding, affiliations concerning mutual investments in heterosexual and patriarchal forms of power (C. Clarke 1983; Combahee River Collective 1983; A. Davis 1997; Ferguson 2004).

One way of extending the interpretations by women of color and Third World feminists of the gendered and sexualized infrastructure of racial discourse is to attend to the ways in which that infrastructure was produced within a genealogy of morality. Morality, in this context, has a much broader definition and application than its more restricted modern understanding, which sees it largely in terms of gender and sexual restrictions. In classical social theory, morality refers to the social powers and privileges that come with political and civil enfranchisement, thus referencing a horizon of possibility rather than an ambit of restrictions and limitations. It was precisely this quality of morality—its promise of enlargement and endowment—that made conservative and liberatory demands for freedom into vehicles for all types of regulations. Morality was both the promise of freedom and the qualification of that promise through regulation. When women of color and Third World feminists troubled the gender and sexual footings of antiracist social movements, they were actually struggling against the moral inheritance of those movements—not simply the gender and sexual norms of those movements but also the imperative to stipulate freedom through regulation. Thinking about race within that genealogy allows us to see how a critical interrogation of race must address the gender and sexual itineraries of both conservative and liberatory politics. It permits us to further tease out the unexpected affiliations that revolutionary and nationalist definitions of race share with liberal-democratic and colonial deployments of race.

Several theorists have followed these leads by locating the procedures of racialization within the moral discourse of Western modernity. By doing so, they have interpreted modernity as an epistemological procedure that produces racial knowledge, a material formation that engenders the racial foundations of political economy, and a discursive formation that fosters racial subjects. Goldberg (1993, 14), for instance, situates our understanding of racial modernity within moral notions that constitute "personal and social identity." Take as an example Jean-Jacques Rousseau's linkage of race and morality in *The Social Contract*. According to Rousseau, man's transition from the state of nature to civil society effects a moral change in "him," one that delivers man to the morally constituted domain of civil society. In the state of nature, man is "governed by appetite alone"; in civil society, he is ruled by justice rather than instinct and through this subjection ascends to freedom and rationality. Man thus becomes a moral being who is part of a civil order that gives his "actions the moral quality they previously lacked" (1762/1968, 64–65). Rousseau's formulation of morality as an entrance into freedoms that are both social and personal can help us to see the ways in which morality expresses a racialized genealogy that links emancipation and subjection.

Through the history of racial formations, we can outline these connections between emancipation and subjection. Indeed, that history reveals how a commitment to political ideals of freedom and liberty was often understood in explicitly racial terms and how it required forms of gender and sexual governance.

In the Caribbean plantation economy, for instance, slaveholders and colonizers stood as symbols not only of whiteness and freedom but also of gender and sexual morality. The bodies of nonwhite Caribbean subjects—blacks, "coloureds," and indentured Indians—were unevenly constructed as outside the parameters of gender and sexual propriety (M. Jacqui Alexander 1994). In the nineteenth-century United States, black women's bodies were similarly constructed as the antithesis of true womanhood, a womanhood presumably embodied by white femininity. Responding to this construction became a simultaneously moral and political agenda for black feminists during and beyond this period. As historian Darlene Clark Hine (1989) has argued, African American clubwomen subscribed in the late nineteenth century to Victorian ideologies of gender and sexual propriety as a means of subverting negative stereotypes about black women's sexuality. In doing so, these clubwomen entered civil society by invoking forms of mastery and discipline, underlining and extending the connection between their relative freedom and the subjection of others.

In the early twentieth century, this racialized genealogy shaped the emergence of sociology as a discipline that tried to assimilate U.S. residents and citizens to the presumably rational ideals of liberal democracy. That discipline worked to reconcile communities of color, particularly African Americans, to the gender and sexual regimes of morality in part by pressuring them into normative U.S. citizenship. For instance, W. E. B. Du Bois (1900/1978) argued for a partnership between the census (to track the social problems afflicting African American communities) and an emerging sociological profession (to lift African Americans from the moral residues of those problems). U.S. sociology in the early to mid-twentieth century matured into a discipline that responded to the social changes of industrialization and migration by extending these moral prescriptions, including Gunnar Myrdal's famous recommendation that African Americans adhere to the gender and sexual ideals of heterosexual patriarchy as a means of achieving citizenship—a recommendation that used the "instability of the Negro family" to argue that Negro culture is a "distorted development, or a pathological condition, of the general American culture" (1944, 928; see also Ferguson 2005). By advocating the rational ideals of liberal democracy, sociology linked the political to the social morality of citizenship. In other words, a commitment to the political ideals of citizenship entailed a fidelity to the nuclear family, conjugal marriage, and heterosexual monogamy. Given this genealogy, a critical interrogation of race needs to locate the links between citizenship and gender and sexual regulation. By studying race through its emergence within this genealogy, we obtain an understanding of political agency as the extension of power and discover how political freedom is tied to gender and sexual subjection.

Apprehending political agency through its connections to gender and sexual subjection is also a way of understanding the antiracist movements that decried regimes of race. Anticolonial and antiracist movements represented powerful challenges to racial regimes of colonial and liberal capitalist states. But they often did so without theorizing how those practices were constituted out of heterosexual and patriarchal relations. Antiracist social movements within Africa, Asia, the Caribbean, and North America not infrequently became sites where women, especially, were subject to gender and sexual oppression and regulation. As Cynthia Enloe (1989, 44) notes, "nationalism typically has sprung from masculinized memory, masculinized humiliation and masculinized hope. Anger at being 'emasculated'—or turned into

a 'nation of busboys'—has been presumed to be the natural fuel for igniting a nationalist movement." In the U.S. context, Angela Davis (1997) observes that the liberatory ideals of the civil rights and Black Power movements were constituted on unexamined heterosexual and patriarchal norms. As anticolonial and antiracist movements figured liberation and freedom either as the acquisition of rights that would eventually empower racially marginalized men or as the decolonization of colonized spaces for those men, these movements produced freedom and liberation as the extension of regimes of heterosexuality and patriarchy. As such, the antiracist critiques developed in these settings could only apprehend part of race's genealogy as a social formation. Such analyses often failed to see how national liberation and rights-based action fostered new forms of power. Antiracist and anticolonial movements evinced a moral commitment to liberation and rights that did not necessarily entail a commitment to dismantling gender and sexual hierarchies.

In contrast, women of color and Third World feminist formations directly addressed freedom's connection to gender and sexual regulation. In doing so, these formations provided what is referred to today as an intersectional model for a more complete consideration of the moral genealogy of racial projects. The Combahee River Collective (1983, 277), for instance, argued in its organizational statement, "We need to articulate the real class situation of persons who are not merely raceless, sexless workers, but for whom racial and sexual oppression are significant determinants in their working/economic lives." Emerging from the failures and contradictions of national liberation and civil rights, this statement calls for a theory and practice of freedom that link differences of gender, sexuality, and class within specific epistemological and material formations. Subsequent work on the history of women of color and Third World feminisms illustrates how the regulatory architecture of emancipatory projects resulted in postcolonial state formations that rearticulated the moral agendas of colonial regimes (M. Jacqui Alexander 1994). Hence, postcolonial states represented the dawn of dubious forms of neocolonial freedom that depended on economic subordination to advanced capitalist states whose claims to universal freedoms were undermined by internal processes of exclusion at the level of gender and sexuality. Those processes, as M. Jacqui Alexander (1991) points out, eventuated in much regulatory activity, including the criminalization of lesbianism in the Caribbean.

In the United States, the gendered and sexual legacies of civil rights have powerfully illustrated the ways in which rights-based projects extended (and continue to extend) regimes of gender and sexual normativity. We might understand the critical cultural and political practices of queers of color as inheriting women of color feminism's critical assessment of liberation and emancipation. Groups such as Other Countries, Gay Men of African Descent, and the Audre Lorde Project have pointed to the historical and material limits of universal gay identity and the limited assumptions about freedom that such an identity presumes. The contemporary gay and lesbian movement has been organized along the axes of participation in the military, access to marriage and adoption, and protection from hate crimes, an agenda that has also been a means of fostering a universal gay identity (Spade and Willse 2000). In doing so, this mainstream movement has revealed itself as excluding the interests of queers marginalized by some intersectional combination of gender, race, and class. This analysis points to the ways in which hegemonic queer cultures presume the rationality of gay visibility, a visibility ritualized through the coming-out process and institutionalized through gay rights agendas. The study of race as it is applied to queer formations demonstrates how the mainstream gay rights movement fosters forms of white privilege and displaces queers of color, particularly those marginalized by class and nationality. We might therefore say that today's racialized gay rights agendas emanate from the dialectic of freedom and unfreedom that arises out of an equally racialized genealogy of modern morality. Work by queer scholars who engage questions of racialized modernity intervenes into the study of race by observing how the array of nationalist and normative formations has expanded within the contexts of diaspora and contemporary globalization. Today, as it has for at least three centuries, the study of race names the different permutations of morality that continue to shape social formations according to freedom's relationship to unfreedom.

54

Racialization

Daniel Martinez HoSang and Oneka LaBennett

In contrast to keywords such as "race" and "racist," "racialization" is relatively new to American studies and cultural studies. The term has a diverse lineage but is most often associated with the work of Michael Omi and Howard Winant (1986/1994), who helped make the concept of racialization a central analytic within both fields. Omi and Winant utilize the term to "signify the extension of racial meaning to a previously racially unclassified relationship, social practice or group. Racialization is an ideological process, an historically specific one" (64). In contrast to static understandings of race as a universal category of analysis, racialization names a process that produces race within particular social and political conjunctures. That process constructs or represents race by fixing the significance of a "relationship, practice or group" within a broader interpretive framework. Working within this paradigm, scholars have investigated processes and practices of racialization across a wide range of fields, including electoral politics, music, literature, sports, aesthetics, religion, public policy, and social identity.

Any use of the term "racialization" requires some account of the theoretical status of race within popular culture and mainstream social science. Inherent in Omi and Winant's definition are three assumptions common to much of the critical scholarship on race in the United States since the 1970s: race functions as a signifier of social identity, power, and meaning, rather than as a biological or hereditary characteristic; racial meaning is a dynamic, fluid, and historically situated *process* of social and political ascription (James Lee 2009); race can be generative of diverse ideological frameworks that justify many forms of social hierarchy and power. Response to this definition has been varied. On the one hand, some sociologists and historians have questioned race as a theoretical concept and a category that can explain social outcomes, suggesting that any use of the term "race"—or "racialization"—as an explanatory category ultimately serves to reify or legitimate it as a fixed and stable category of human existence (Das Gupta et al. 2007; Fields 1990; Gilroy 2000; Loveman 1999; Miles and Torres 2007). On the other hand, scholars such as Cornel West (1994) and Kimberlé Crenshaw (1990) reason that race cannot be abandoned as an analytical concept since, as Winant notes, "U.S. society is so thoroughly racialized that to be without racial identity is to be in danger of having no identity" (1994, 16).

All of these deployments of the term "racialization" draw on and diverge from earlier usages that carried different theoretical and normative assumptions regarding the basis of racial hierarchies. As early as 1899, one can find references to the term "deracialization," a process described as the removing or eradicating of racial characteristics from a person or population. A coinage that emerged from social Darwinism, this usage of the term locates parochial or retrogressive traits as expressions of racial difference that could be eliminated through education, acculturation, or the mixing of populations, thus rendering a "deracialized" group or subject. By the early 1930s, this notion of deracialization as a process of homogenization and incorporation gave way to uses of "racialization" that referenced a process of bodily differentiation capable of explaining the development of distinct "racial stocks" to which different groups of Europeans allegedly belonged. For example, Sir Arthur Keith, a prominent physical anthropologist, conceptualized "race-feeling" as "part of the evolutionary machinery which safeguards the purity of race" (1928, 316). Keith and his colleagues theorized that nature embedded race within human populations as a means toward the betterment of humankind through differentiation. Racialization thus described a positive and necessary process by which Anglo and Nordic racial supremacy and biological purity could be sustained and reproduced (Barot and Bird 2001, 602–6).

As the scientific imprimatur to claims of white supremacy withered in the aftermath of World War II and the state racism of Nazi Germany, references to "racialization" receded from academic and popular discourse. The term then reemerged in Frantz Fanon's influential *The Wretched of the Earth* (1963/2004). Writing in the context of anticolonial struggles in North Africa, Fanon contrasted social conditions that were "racializing" against those that were "humanizing," demonstrating how racial oppression organizes and constrains a universal recognition of human capabilities (Essed and Goldberg 2000; Barot and Bird 2001; Fanon 1963/2004). In Fanon's usage, racialization, or the hierarchical production of human difference through race, is posed as a necessary precondition for colonial domination and a hindrance to the process of internal self-making among Black subjects. The influence of Fanon's equation of racialization and dehumanization is apparent in a wide range of scholarly work that interrogates the social construction of race, especially in postcolonial scholarship (Said 1978; Bhabha 1994; Rabaka 2010). This work has exposed the legacies of racialized colonial discourses, noting the ways that racial meaning structures the construction of "the Orient" in western European artistic, literary and political discourse and interrogating how the emergence of the United States as an empire has depended on an array of racial formations: the historical racialization of Asians as dangerous threats to the nation; the contemporary racialization of the same population as "model minorities"; and the post-9/11 racialization of the "uncivilized" Muslim/Arab as an object of racial terror and as a population requiring U.S. intervention, supervision, and domination (Prashad 2007; Lee and Lutz 2005; Razack 2012).

In a parallel use of the term, scholars of social policy have examined the ways in which debates over issues such as welfare, immigration, crime, reproductive rights, and taxes in the United States have become thoroughly racialized since the 1960s. As the civil rights movement effectively challenged formal policies of race-based segregation and discrimination, the concept of racial "color blindness" became the dominant principle within official legal and political discourse (Gotanda 1991). Within this framework, discriminatory practices and ideals are supposedly inadmissible in policy debates and legal deliberations. But public controversies about whether the government should provide cash assistance to low-income families (Fujiwara 2008; Quadagno 1994) or militarize national borders or cover abortions in publicly financed health-insurance programs (E. Gutiérrez 2008; K. Baird 2009; Richie, Davis, and Traylor 2012) or raise property taxes to improve schools (Edsall and Edsall 1992) or prosecute a "War on Drugs" (Michelle Alexander 2010) all draw on and produce a dense set of racial meanings. The simultaneous withdrawal of public funding for social welfare programs, along with the systematic reduction of property and income taxes perceived to support those programs, is often tied to assumptions about the racial identities of the beneficiaries of those policies. In this sense, these debates are racialized.

Contemporary scholarship has also complicated our understanding of processes of racialization by attending to the intersections of gender, class, age, and sexuality and by venturing beyond the national boundaries and Black/white dichotomy that has long dominated the literature on race (Crenshaw 1995). Along these lines of inquiry, the meanings attached to the racialized body have led to wide-ranging questions. How can the concept of racialization challenge the double or triple vulnerability of Muslim immigrant women with disabilities (Dossa 2009)? What do the debates surrounding U.S. immigration policies reveal about the racialization of the "illegal immigrant" as a displaced nonperson who embodies criminality (T. Sandoval 2008)? How has the racialization of Black women in the United States depended on notions of the pregnant Black woman's body as representative of the "undeserving poor" (Bridges 2011)? How does religion structure and articulate processes of racialization for followers of Islam and Judaism and for Hindus (Joshi 2006)? Comparative and intersectional analyses of the colonization of indigenous peoples in a number of regions and the colonization of nations in Africa and the Caribbean similarly link processes of racialization and globalization (Das Gupta et al. 2007). Work in this vein has focused on topics including the globalized production of knowledge about race, the cultural dimensions of globalization, transnational migration, feminism and the politics of decolonialization, consumption, and global economies (M. Jacqui Alexander 2005; Appadurai 1996; De Genova 2005; Ferreira da Silva 2007; C. Freeman 2000; Gilroy 1993; Thomas and Clarke 2006).

A promising trajectory within the current scholarship on racialization explores the ways in which the hierarchies of humanity that the concept of race has historically signified increasingly become articulated through the logics of neoliberalism, militarism, and security. In a discussion of the post–World War II global shift toward official antiracisms, Jodi Melamed

has argued that the "trick of racialization" is that it displaces differential valuations of humans into global ordering systems which yield new, more covert expressions for privileged racializations such as "liberal," "multicultural," and "global citizen," alongside stigmatized racializations such as "unpatriotic," "monocultural," and "illegal" (2011, 2). The state's formal antiracism becomes pressed into service to defend or justify unbridled U.S. military occupation, widening economic inequalities, muscular immigration enforcement, and the expansion of prisons and police authority within the United States (Cacho 2012; De Genova 2012; Singh 2012). These diverse usages of the term "racialization" across a range of fields and disciplines—including sociology, ethnic studies, anthropology, cultural studies, and American studies—will continue to be foundational to conveying relations of power and authority within and beyond U.S. political culture, even as its referents continue to change and evolve.

55

Religion

Janet R. Jakobsen

The keyword "religion" names one side of a pair of terms—"religion" and "secularism"—each of which is defined by its opposition to the other. In this relational definition, religion is that which is not secular, is associated with the sacred rather than the profane, and is aligned with dogma rather than reason. As delineated through this series of oppositions, the concept of religion draws together a wide range of practices across cultures that may not have much in common with one another. The conflation of various practices under the sign of religion has its origins in the thought of Enlightenment writers such as David Hume (1757/1993), for whom religion named the universal experience that marked the unity of human beings, even as it served to distinguish among humans on the basis of their different religions (R. Baird 2000). In the process, even practices that had no reference to a god, such as Buddhism, were assimilated to a category of religion organized around the Protestant concept of "faith." The use of this Protestant heuristic can be seen today in U.S. public discourse, in which the most common way of speaking of multiple religious groups is to refer to "faiths" (as in the Jewish "faith," despite the fact that most forms of Judaism prioritize practice over faith).

Working from Protestantism as the model of religion implied that other practices must either conform to its norms or suffer by the comparison. As David Chidester (1996) has shown, for example, the peoples of southern Africa were treated at different stages in the colonial history of the region as if they had no religion, a religion like the ancient roots of Christianity, or a fundamentally different species of the genus religion. At each stage, the European understanding of southern African religion enabled particular forms of colonial interaction. In the final stage, when colonial rule was consolidated, southern Africans were seen as essentially like European Christians in that they "had" a religion but also as essentially different in their particular religion. This difference provided crucial conceptual support for the institutionalization of unequal treatment.

The Enlightenment idea of religion has remained powerful from the colonial past through the postcolonial present, as the keyword "religion" continues to mobilize a broad range of politics along the lines of race, nation, gender, and sexuality. U.S. racial categories grew out of what was originally a distinction between Christians and "strangers," a categorization that differentiated between Christian indentured servants and African slaves (Sweet 2003). But as Africans converted to Christianity, this distinction shifted toward a racial category that was understood to be unchangeable and, thus, not subject to conversion. At the same time, a truly *un*reasonable refusal to convert, as was the case with some Native Americans, was also increasingly taken as a marker of an inherent difference (Murphree 2004). In this view, only those who were *un*reasonable would refuse to see the light of Christianity, and racial difference was invoked to buttress the idea of such a profound difference. This intertwining of religious and racial identities continues to be evident in U.S. public life, as exemplified by the frequent presumption that Arabs must be Muslim and Muslims must be Arab.

The linkage of race and religion is also implicated in a politics of gender and nation. As Minoo Moallem (2005) has argued, gendered ideas about Islam contribute to the idea of "fundamentalism" as that which distinguishes "the West" from Islam. Particularly since the Iranian revolution in 1979, "a turning point in . . . the representation of Islamic fundamentalism outside of Iran" (6), Muslim "fundamentalists" have been repeatedly portrayed through a masculinity that is "irrational, morally inferior, and barbaric" and a femininity that is "passive, victimized, and submissive" (8). In contrast to Muslim "fundamentalism," the West is presumed to be "free" (secular or religious in a nonfundamentalist sense), and Western gender relations serve as the marker of that freedom.

The idea of religious fanaticism or "fundamentalism" is crucial to this set of associations. Like the category of religion, "fundamentalism" is a term that originally developed in the context of Protestantism, specifically in a 1920s conflict within U.S. Protestantism over the literal interpretation of the Bible. In dueling pamphlets ("The Fundamentals" and "Will the Fundamentalists Win?"), fundamentalists were positioned as those who threatened liberal Protestants (Marsden 1980). Though the term has been extended to refer to other forms of conservative religion (most frequently Islam) for which biblical literalism is not an issue in the same way that it is for Protestantism, the sense of threat imputed to fundamentalism in the original conflict is maintained (and even magnified) when the term "fundamentalism" is applied to other religions. Like Hume's category of religion, the term "fundamentalism" does the work of positing some "religions" as reasonable and others as threatening.

The intertwining of religion and secularism is part and parcel of prevalent mythologies of "Americanness." The apparently contradictory positioning of the United States as a simultaneously secular *and* Christian country is based in a familiar narrative of national origin, in which religion—here again a mostly Protestant Christianity—plays a leading role. This dominant narrative, taught in virtually every U.S. public school, includes the settlement of the continent by the New England Pilgrims in search of religious freedom, the institution of religious freedom in the First Amendment to the Constitution, the separation of church and state that was the basis of a putatively free and secular public sphere, and the rise of religious pluralism with successive waves of immigration. It is also possible, though certainly less common, to relate this narrative in a way that acknowledges the implication of religion in the violent underside of the establishment of the nation-state. This counternarrative includes the destruction of indigenous cultures and societies, the use of the Bible to legitimate slavery, and the role of Christian missionary activity in U.S. imperialism throughout the world.

There can be no doubt that religion has been used to legitimate violence, both in the history of establishing the United States and in various contemporary religious movements—whether those of religious extremism in the United States or worldwide. When the category of religion is deployed to legitimate violence either domestically or abroad, it is appealing to turn to secularism as an answer. Yet a turn to the secular will not provide a simple escape. This is because the Enlightenment terms with which we still live render religion and secularism as intertwined. The entangled opposition between the two terms is as likely to fuel conflict and violence as is taking up one side or the other. To be able to accuse an enemy of either failing to be religious or being unreasonably religious provides fuel for conflict and legitimation for violent action.

To see how religion and secularism are historically and conceptually intertwined is to understand why those who are "secular" are not necessarily less violent or more progressive than those who are "religious." Many major social justice and peace movements throughout the world—from Catholic base communities fighting poverty in Latin America to the peaceful resistance of

Tibetan Buddhism to the civil rights movements of the United States—have religious roots. The question for anyone who would use "religion" as a term of analysis in American studies and cultural studies is neither to distinguish the religious from the secular nor to ask "What is religion?" but to consider how the use of the term affects social relations and practices. This shift in perspective leads to a focus on the effects of claiming that something—a work of art or other cultural object, a person, a social movement—is, or is not, religious. Wars—both international and cultural—can be fueled by such claims; asking questions about how such claims are made can provide alternatives to violence, whether among religions or between religious and secular actors.

56

Rural

Scott Herring

The simple life often evoked by the keyword "rural" belies its extraordinary complexity. Across the centuries, many hands have wielded this term for contradictory purposes: to exalt and exhaust the nation's natural resources, to malign and glorify nonurban citizens, and to incite and squelch revolutions. As a word that invites and resists reduction, "rural" can signal a pastoral landscape on one hand and neglect the labor that cultivates it on the other. It can conjure a bucolic retreat at odds with dynamic histories of political, socioeconomic, and racial conflict. It can appear outdated in our postindustrial era of globalization and expansive megacities, yet it persists in the conservative rhetoric of small-town values as well as the radical manifestoes of eco-activism.

Some of these tensions originate from overlapping—and historically entrenched—uses of "rural" as a noun and as an adjective. As a noun, "rural" can refer to any geographic place (the countryside, the outskirts, the woods) distinct from a city. According to the *Oxford English Dictionary*, "rural" is "opposed to urban" and defined by its presumed contrast to the metropolis. This geography can, however, be material (clay soil, prairie wheatgrass), or it can be metaphoric (a poetic arcadia, a Delta blues folk song). As an adjective, "rural" applies to those who occupy these nonurban spaces as well as their everyday life practices. It has been used as a pejorative social category (a hayseed) as well as a positive one (a hardworking husbandman). These distinctions collide and evolve across genres and historical periods.

It comes as no surprise, then, that the interlocking disciplines of American studies and cultural studies attend to the definitional intricacies of "rural." While a tendency to privilege urban-based phenomena persists in cultural studies, foundational works such as Raymond Williams's *The Country and the City* examine how meanings of "rural" contribute to understandings of capitalism, aesthetics, urbanization, and nationhood. In that centuries-spanning literature review, Williams assesses how "rural" accrues cultural and economic significance as he simultaneously reproaches those who cast nonurban inhabitants as "broken and ignorant" (1973, 190). Exploring links between "rural" and synonyms such as "country," Williams finds that a cultural hierarchy "between country and city, as fundamental ways of life, reaches back into classical times" (1). Yet while country/rural has often been subordinate to city/urban, the keyword remains an important resource for patriotic nationalism. "In its general use, for native land," Williams stresses in *Keywords*, "country has more positive associations than either nation or state" (1976/1983, 81).

Scholars in American studies have likewise explored how the term informs social belonging and nation building from the colonial era to the present. In the inaugural 1949 volume of *American Quarterly*, University of Minnesota sociologist Lowry Nelson published an essay titled "The American Rural Heritage" that discussed some of the keyword's overlapping applications. Nelson outlined the "material" and "nonmaterial" aspects of rural life in the United States, whereby "material culture" such as farmland and agricultural instruments could be found alongside "nonmaterial aspects, including especially the agrarian ideals" (1949, 225). Both characteristics, he felt, contributed to "laying the foundation of our society and its institutions," and Nelson's attempt to showcase

the positive role played by agrarianism points to the centrality of the rural in scholarly accounts of national origins and the countryside (225).

This idealized vision of rural citizenry and native land had been prevalent for some time. Romantic depictions of rural life reach back to Thomas Jefferson's *Notes on the State of Virginia* (1787/1984), a commendation of yeomanry that paints agrarianism as a cornerstone of the new republic: "Those who labor in the earth are the chosen people of God, if ever he had a chosen people" (197). Confirming Williams's observation regarding the metaphoric meaning of native land, this claim fuses the idea of rural with the ideal of the country. It finds echo in writings by French immigrant J. Hector St. John de Crèvecoeur, whose influential *Letters from an American Farmer* (1782/1981) praised rural living across the eastern-seaboard states even as the text lamented what Jefferson's condoned—the enslavement of Africans who toiled the earth. Scholars of U.S. culture have shown that these idealizing portraits of country people— both evoking a pastoral tradition begun by Greek poet Theocritus—were accompanied by frequent dismissals of rural populations on behalf of urban elites across the late eighteenth and early nineteenth centuries (Bushman 1992). We may also recall that the slur "poor white trash" surfaced by the mid-nineteenth century to denigrate nonmetropolitan spaces and nonurban working-class whites alike (Wray 2006).

As this last link suggests, fraught connections among class, race, and other identity categories inform changing ideas of rural existence. The rise of sharecropping across the rural South after the U.S. Civil War set the stage for the largest relocation in the nation's history—the Great Migration of largely rural African Americans to industrializing cities beyond the Mason-Dixon line starting in the early twentieth century (F. Griffin 1995). Many impoverished white farmers threw

RURAL   SCOTT HERRING

their weight behind the People's Party (Populist Party) in 1891 to protest the overreach of corporate interests, and the coalition both invited and abused relationships with African American agrarians throughout its various permutations (Goodwyn 1978). Occurring at a moment of escalating urbanization, these watershed events were matched by rural betterment programs such as Theodore Roosevelt's Country Life Commission (1908–9) that addressed the rural as a backward and unhygienic locale in desperate need of modernization (Roosevelt 1909). Such biases were aided by a newfound interest in racially degenerate "hill folk," an interest supported by proponents of eugenics (Danielson and Davenport 1912).

By the mid-twentieth century, many rural inhabitants in the United States did not consider themselves God's chosen people, yet some managed to improvise creative encounters with nonurban spaces. In 1942, the U.S. government launched the Bracero Program, an exploitative agricultural guest-worker program for transnational Mexican migrants that lasted officially until 1964 (D. Cohen 2011). The shift to industrialized farming and the gradual dominance of monoculture crops made agriculture more efficient (Fitzgerald 2003), but it weakened the single-family farm unit. A round of rural white migration to industrialized cities such as Chicago stoked moral panics over metropolitan "hillbilly ghettoes" and cast a harsh light on these migratory laborers (A. Harkins 2005). In 1964, Lyndon B. Johnson pronounced a War on Poverty, his response to depressed living conditions in Appalachia and one that investigated the plights of impoverished rural Native and Hispanic populations across the Great Plains, the West Coast, and the Southwest.

Soon thereafter, countercultural back-to-the-land movements followed these ongoing geographic calamities. Extending long-standing traditions of U.S. utopianism, hippies embraced the keyword to launch rural art colonies and small-scale farms across the nation. Sexual minorities also organized around the rural in hopes of finding spaces and mind-sets conducive to social and sexual experiments. Several of these communes—lesbian separatist collectives and radical faerie gatherings—flourish to this day and offer respite to a variety of queers across class, race, and generation (Povinelli 2006). As with earlier representational battles, country life remained a material and cultural space stocked with possibility and constriction. In pliable imaginaries that featured clashing themes of technological progress, geographic displacement, population decline, and agrarian idealism, the rural was at once a utopia to till and a place to leave behind.

In the twenty-first century, scholars continue to track how "rural" has been put to novel cross-purposes as the term surfaces across competing systems of knowledge and emergent forms of material culture. Food co-ops that support local agriculture struggle to vend alongside multinational agribusiness ventures that use countrified corporate logos. Once-pejorative identity markers such as "redneck" have become a questionable basis for regional race pride as theme parks such as Dollywood and culture industries such as Nashville's Music Row cater to white working-class nostalgia. Privileged exurbanites turn abandoned farmland outside the metropolis into rural retreats, and a conservative populism with little resemblance to its late nineteenth-century predecessor maintains prominent sway over voters with the fantasy of small-town America. Sexual minorities continue to occupy rural spaces that are both welcoming and inhospitable (John Howard 2001; E. Johnson 2008; Herring 2010); and transborder migrants create social networks that connect nonurban U.S. spaces to larger communities within and beyond the hemisphere (Stephen 2007). Millions who will never own a shovel tend to their virtual farms with online games. Frozen only in stereotype, the rural exists in a state of perpetual development and decline.

These recent innovations counter the idea of nonurban environments as uncomplicated geographies, and scholarship continues to trace the cultural richness inherent in the unfolding idea of rural life. Across anthropology, religious studies, gender studies, and critical race/ethnic studies (to name but four), scholars have investigated impoverished West Virginia hollers (Stewart 1996), African American return migration to the rural South (Stack 1996), sexual liberation and small-town campus life in Kansas (B. Bailey 1999), and the global rise of the Ozarks as the crown jewel of Christian-based capitalist endeavors (Moreton 2009). The intellectual vistas of these wide-ranging inquiries suggest that the rural offers a productive means of grappling with—and working through—contemporary issues of social welfare, leisure, labor, consumption, mobility, and sexual citizenship that are both particular to rural populations and shared by other geographic locales. This is especially true for those who have historically experienced a tortuous relationship to land—the minority populations who continue to feel the material and nonmaterial unevenness of agrarian ideals cited by Nelson in his *American Quarterly* essay.

Hence, even as the metropolis may appear ascendant since the start of the twentieth century, thinking with "rural" offers a rich vocabulary for articulating the aspirations and the injustices faced by many people in what counts for present-day modernity. As a symbolic space that is all too real, the rural remains an enduring theme in the wake of the global city and in conversation with it. Both reactionary and radical, the countryside continues to provide rich soil for mobilization and quietism. Its heritage is to remain a problem area for American studies and cultural studies.

57

Secularism
Michael Warner

"Secularism" is a late coinage in English, dating from the 1850s, when it was adopted by reformers who regarded the church and capital as the joint enemies of the worker (Holyoake 1854). But because the word is used by cultural critics in many antithetical senses, it occasions great confusion. The United States is sometimes held to be the model of secular democracy and sometimes the most religious of all major modern democracies. Can both be true?

The root "secular" derives from the Latin for "the age"; in the Christian tradition, the secular is the temporal or the worldly. The spiritual/secular opposition is fundamental, but Christian attitudes toward the secular have ranged from hostility to fervent immersion and have seldom been simple. It was at one time possible, for example, to speak of "secular clergy," by which was meant ordinary parish priests, as opposed to the religious of the monastic orders.

Protestantism heightened the contrast, and Puritans especially differentiated spiritual and secular functions as part of their critique of the established church. Thus, they relegated marriage to secular authorities and avoided the ecclesiastical courts. But they did not imagine the secular to be outside of Christianity, let alone outside of the abstract category "religion." "Religion," as Wilfred Cantwell Smith pointed out in his classic *The Meaning and End of Religion* (1964), had until recently the sense of piety rather than of any category of belief systems and institutions. Only in the late eighteenth century could Christianity and Islam be seen as tokens of the same type. So although the new secularism of the Puritans may have fed the growth of the autonomous state, the aim was to purify rather than relativize religion.

"Secularism" refers sometimes to social conditions that can be embraced by the religious and nonreligious alike. Disestablishment is the most obvious of these; it was an idea developed largely by Baptists and other dissenters, at a time when virtually no one in North America expressed open antagonism to religion (Hamburger 2002). Somewhat more broadly, "secularism" refers to the idea that the complex set of social transformations called "secularization" can be embraced as a good thing. This idea, too, can be held for religious or nonreligious reasons; there are many Christian theologians who regard the conditions of secularization as restoring to Christianity a purity that it had lost through the corruption of institutional power and temporal preoccupations. For them, the litmus issues that are widely thought to indicate religious conviction—opposition to abortion, gay marriage, or evolution—are temporal concerns corrupting religion.

"Secularism" can also refer to atheism or freethought, though the term was coined largely to give the sense of a substantive ethical vision rather than the merely negative sense of infidelity or nonbelief. "Freethought" is a continuous tradition in Anglo-American culture, dating from the second half of the seventeenth century, though it was more vilified than evinced in North America. Some versions of freethought are religious in many senses of the term. Most emphasize reason as the guide to religious truth. The earliest proponents of freethought in North America include Ethan Allen, Thomas Paine, and Elihu Palmer; all were deists, and Paine vigorously denounced atheism (Morais 1934). Their innovation was to make freethought a popular rather than elite cause. Nineteenth-century freethought had even more radical aspirations and was frequently elaborated as part of other movements, especially labor, feminism, antislavery, and pacifism. Among its greatest exponents were Frances Wright, Robert Ingersoll, and Ernestine Rose.

More radically still, "secularism" sometimes refers to an active quest for the elimination of religion, a quest that can be tied to projects as different as positivism, structuralism, and the post-Nietzschean move to expunge Christian moralism and redemptive theology from the culture. Despite the prominence of these antihumanist versions of secular thought, "secular humanism" emerged in the twentieth century as the target of fundamentalists, who often identify it with science, mass culture, liberal jurisprudence, and many other phenomena that may or may not be tied to humanist or other views of the secular.

More rarely, "secularism" can be embraced as a kind of spiritual worldliness in a way that is distinguished from Christianity, or the theological, but not necessarily from religion per se. William Connolly's *Why I Am Not a Secularist* (2000), despite the irony of its title, advocates a nontheist worldliness that—in contrast to what he regards as liberal statist secularism—would not be sharply distinguished from religious subjectivities or practices. It can be argued that some of the Transcendentalists—Ralph Waldo Emerson and, even more so, Henry David Thoreau and Walt Whitman—represent this kind of secularism as well.

Connolly joins several other recent scholars—Charles Taylor (2002, 2004), Talal Asad (1993, 2003), and Leigh Schmidt (2000)—in seeing secularism not as the absence of religion or as an antagonist to religion but as a specific cultural formation in its own right, with its own sensibilities, rituals, constructions of knowledge, and ethical projects. Schmidt, for example, has documented a reeducation of the senses connected with the eighteenth-century critique of revelation.

Secular culture in this sense remains comparatively understudied, possibly because—as Asad argues—one of its features is the consolidation of "religion" as an object of social-scientific knowledge in a way that takes for granted the secular character of explanation itself.

Secularism is often associated with the Enlightenment and with rationalism, but neither of these intellectual movements took hold in British America in the way that is often assumed by critics whose view of the Enlightenment is based on the French version. The deist movement that was so notable in England after the 1690s made only an indirect impact in the colonies before the Revolution. (Benjamin Franklin is one exception, and even he supported evangelical movements and clergy, largely on pragmatic grounds.) The anticlericism that marked the French Enlightenment was also conspicuously absent from the colonies. The American Enlightenment, indeed, was often led by clergy (H. May 1976).

In classic studies by Carl Schmitt (1986), Carl Becker (1932), M. H. Abrams (1971), and others, the Enlightenment is seen historically as transposing religious values into nontheological equivalents, the significance of which often depends on the religious background that has been suppressed. Thus, progress is secularized providence, utopia is secularized heaven, and sovereignty is secularized omnipotence. Hans Blumenberg (1983), however, has countered that these stories mistakenly assume a theological origin and neglect the new context, function, and impulse of secular themes.

By the end of the eighteenth century, it had become possible to speak of religion in a comparative sense, defined principally by belief. This understanding still reigns as common sense in the United States, but it does not go without saying; many kinds of religious practice have little to do with belief or sincerity of conviction.

The Protestant quest for saving faith no doubt lies behind this assumption, but so does the development of the denominational system, in which churches are no longer taken to be national or territorially comprehensive, as they had been in the long history of the Catholic, Anglican, and even Congregationalist systems. Instead, they began competing for voluntary adherents in overlapping territories. Being outside a particular church no longer meant being alienated from a fundamental institution of belonging and public culture, thus opening more space for the secular. Yet this same system marked the rise of evangelicalism and the aggressive promotion of religious faith to a public of strangers. This association is so strong that it makes sense to speak of an evangelical public sphere, developing first with the so-called Great Awakening and exploding after the 1790s. The way this combination of disestablishment and denominationalism created fertile conditions for religiosity is what struck Alexis de Tocqueville (1835/2004) so forcibly.

For many scholars of the sociology of religion (P. Berger 1963, 1969; Stark and Finke 1992, 2000; Swatos and Olson 2000), this pattern is seen as a "marketplace of religion." The metaphor is highly questionable, since the key features that define a market—including abstract value, price as a mechanism for coordinating supply and demand, territorial integration of regulation—are absent. This model also leads people to think of religion as a constant and thus to overlook its transformation and construction.

Rodney Stark and Roger Finke have argued strongly that the marked and enduring religiosity of U.S. culture refutes what they call "the secularization thesis." In their view, the secularization thesis is the idea that modernity necessarily entails a decline of religious belief. They point out that religious adherence—at least as measured by church attendance—was much lower in the premodern Middle Ages than in the United States of the past two centuries. "To classify a nation as highly secularized when the large majority of its inhabitants believe in God is absurd," they write (2000, 62).

But this view depends on an extremely reductive view of secularization. The more robust understanding of secularization is that a variety of social changes—bureaucratization, the rationalization and professionalization of authority, the rise of the state, the separation of the economy, urbanization, and empirical science—change the position of religious institutions in the social landscape (D. Martin 1969, 1978; Weber 1983; B. Wilson 1998). Clergy compete with other public intellectuals; other grounds of legitimacy and authority are available; and the society itself is understood to be distinct from a confessional body. This understanding of secularization does not necessarily predict a decline in belief. In fact, the understanding of religion as defined primarily in terms of subjective belief could be seen as *evidence* of this larger transformation. Thus, it would not at all be absurd to say that U.S. society, marked by high levels of belief in God, is highly secularized precisely because mental and voluntary adherence is the principal way that religion is salient.

Charles Taylor (2004) has elaborated this point. Modern social imaginaries, in his view, are secular in several senses, though they also allow for new kinds of religiosity. They take the social to be an order of mutual benefit in which governments answer to essentially prepolitical ends (natural rights, happiness, flourishing), directly comprehending all constituents. Political and social life is increasingly understood in a secular temporality of simultaneous and directional activity, rather than in a higher time of origins or ritually realized eternity. Religion can exist, even thrive, under the conditions of modern social imaginaries, but it is newly enframed. One major change, in Taylor's view, is the widespread assumption that religious convictions, to be truly authentic, should be the result of an individual path toward spirituality. Thus, what is often called the "privatization of religion" is not just a reduction or restriction but involves new ethical imperatives and a backgrounded understanding of the social.

Working against this trend, however, are several new kinds of public religion, from the prophetic character of the African American church (Chappell 2004) to what Robert Bellah (1970, 1975) calls "civil religion," by which he means not just a veneration of the nation's founding, documents, and rituals of citizenship but a faith in a deity that providentially superintends the nation. In many contexts, U.S. Americans speak of God in a way that is nominally ecumenical. Eisenhower is supposed to have remarked, "Our government makes no sense unless it is founded in a deeply felt religious faith—and I don't care what it is" (Henry 1981, 35). George W. Bush similarly speaks of a nation "guided by faith" without specifying what that faith is in (Bumiller 2002). This vagueness bespeaks secularism, in that it is thought to be multiconfessional and disestablished. But the divine is assumed to be personal and historical: a being that actively addresses individuals and nations and has specially appointed a world-historical mission for the United States. This political religion is secular in an important sense: its proof lies not in spiritual truth or a higher time but in the politics of the present. The Gettysburg Address is a classic example of this crypto-Protestant secular providentialism (Tuveson 1968). This strain of redemptive nationalism explains why those who speak of America's God believe themselves to be in a mainstream of U.S. history against advocates of church-state separation—who nevertheless also see themselves as in the mainline of Constitutionalism.

Among the greatest challenges in thinking about secularism is that although the term acquired its significance from the development of Christian culture, it was globalized in the period of the European empires to apply to cultures where local religions did not have the same tradition of distinguishing themselves from the secular. Thus, in many parts of the world, including the Islamic world, secularism and Christianity are often presented not as opposites but as twin faces of Western dominance. Some of the strongest critiques of secularism have come from postcolonial India (Bhargava 1998). Secularism might thus be seen as a mode of political organization closely connected with global capitalism, and it is ironic but not simply inconsistent that secular governance in other countries is promoted with missionary and even violent fervor by the most evangelical Christian wing of U.S. politicians.

The dialectic unfolding of these ironies is lost on common sense, which continues to hold as self-evident that secularism means governmental neutrality, that religion is a universal category of subjective belief, and that the two are locked in combat. These convictions distort any attempt in American studies, cultural studies, or elsewhere to confront such ultimate questions as finitude, mortality, nature, fate, and commonality.

58

Slavery

Walter Johnson

"Slavery has never been represented, slavery never can be represented," said the novelist, antislavery lecturer, and former slave William Wells Brown in 1847 (1847/1969, 82). Brown referred, in the first instance, to the world-making violence of the system of kidnapping, dispossession, and labor extraction that emerged in the fifteenth century and persisted almost to the dawn of the twentieth. But he referred in the second instance to a sort of epistemological violence, a murderous, forcible forgetting of the history of slavery. Only slavery's victims—if it is possible to use the word "only" in the context of so many millions of stolen lives—might have truly told the story he wanted to tell. Brown reminds us that we approach the history of slavery by way of whispers and shadows, where truth has often been hidden in half truth in order to be saved away for the future. We approach it, that is to say, across a field of argument in which the history of slavery has often been conscripted to the economic, political, and imperial purposes that have hidden inside the word "freedom."

Over the four centuries of Atlantic slavery, millions of Africans and their descendants were turned into profits, fancies, sensations, and possessions of New World whites. The vast majority of the enslaved were agricultural workers whose lives were devoted to the production of staple crops (sugar, tobacco, indigo, coffee, and cotton). Their labor provided the agricultural base of European mercantile capitalism and much of the surplus capital that, by the late eighteenth century, was being invested in the development of European industry. North America was alone among New World slave societies in having a self-reproducing slave population. Elsewhere, particularly in the Caribbean and Brazil, the murderous character of the slaveholding regime (the life expectancy of Africans put to work cultivating sugar in the Americas was seven years from the time they stepped ashore) meant that slaveholders depended on the Atlantic slave trade as a replacement for biological reproduction.

The history of New World slavery was characterized by daily resistance on the part of the enslaved, terrific brutality on the part of the enslaving, and frequent military conflict between the two. Daily forms of resistance took the form of everything from mouthing off and shamming sickness to flight, arson, and assault. The slaveholders' violent responses, which seem at first to emblematize the license of unchecked power, upon closer inspection reveal the brittleness of their control; mastery had constantly to be—could only be—shored up through brutality. Everyday forms of resistance helped slaves come to trust one another enough to plan a hemisphere-wide series of insurgencies—some on a very small scale, some mobilizing thousands at a time—which varied widely in their ideology and aspiration but which continually presented the possibility that the "Atlantic World" might be remade as a "Black Atlantic" (C. James 1938/1989; Genovese 1979; Stuckey 1987; Gwendolyn Hall 1992; Gilroy 1993; da Costa 1994; Sidbury 1997; Berlin 1998; W. Johnson 2002; Dubois 2004; Jennifer Morgan 2004). Indeed, the military and diplomatic history of the New World was distilled in the alembic of black revolt. From the Maroon Wars in Jamaica to the Haitian Revolution to the American Revolution, the Civil War, and the Cuban Revolution, armed and insurgent blacks (and the almost unspeakable threat they represented to white leaders) decisively shaped the course of European and American history.

The foundational role of African and African American labor and resistance in the history of European imperialism and the economic growth of the Atlantic economy was reflected in the institution's role in shaping Atlantic culture. Institutions of law and governance, structures and styles of authority, religious faith and medical knowledge, cultural forms ranging from popular amusements to sentimental novels and autobiographies: all of these emergent forms of European modernity bore the stamp (often forcibly obscured) of slavery. So, too, did the ongoing identification of blackness with the condition of dispossession, and the disposition to insurgency.

The long nineteenth century, beginning with the Haitian Revolution in 1792 and culminating with the legislative emancipation in Brazil in 1888, marked the passing of slavery from the governing institutional solution to problems of labor, empire, and difference, to a residual social form (persisting to this day, it should be said) with tremendous discursive power. The end began with the idea that the opposite of slavery was neither redemption (as the Christian emphasis on sin as a form of slavery would have it) nor mastery (as the idea of history as a sort of race war would have it) but "freedom." The emergent antislavery version of enslavement was one that tried to demonstrate the ways in which slavery deformed the course of right and history by specifying its evils: its epochal barbarities and quotidian tortures, its corruptive tyranny and degrading license, its economic and moral backwardness, its unfreedom. And over the course of the nineteenth century, this new view increasingly contested a proslavery argument that slavery itself represented the unfolding course of "freedom": the alignment of social institutions with natural (racial) history, the propagation of the earth for the benefit of its masters, the temporal manifestation of an institution that was both ancient in provenance and providential in design. Beginning with the Haitian Revolution, it was the antislavery argument about slavery that won: African American slavery came to be seen as the antithesis of "freedom."

Though the term "slavery" referred over the course of that century-long argument to a condition that was historically specific to black people, it came to serve as a sort of switchboard through which arguments over the character of "freedom" could be routed and defined: the archaic pendant to the emergent future. By using the word "slavery" to describe institutions ranging from wage labor and marriage to prostitution and peonage, nineteenth-century reformers sought to extend the moral force of the argument against African American slavery to other sorts of social relations. Their efforts were generally met with an insistence that slavery was a condition that was (or had been) unique to African Americans, who were, with emancipation, presumed to be experiencing "freedom."

The framing of slavery as archaic and freedom as emergent has a complex history in Western political economy. In both Smithian and Marxian thought, slavery remained an almost wholly unthought backdrop to the unfolding history of capitalism in Europe. For Adam Smith, slavery was destined to fall away before the superior capacity of wage labor to motivate workers through their own self-interest; the inferior motivation of bonded labor was in the Smithian tradition taken as a given rather than recognized (and theorized) as the result of the resistance of enslaved people (Oakes 2003). For Karl Marx, slavery was a moment in the history of primitive accumulation—the initial process of dispossession out of which capitalist social relations were subsequently built. It was the past to the present of "capitalism" (understood here as that system of social relations characterized by "free" labor and the factory mode of production) with which he

was primarily concerned (Marx 1867/1976, 1:667–712; W. Johnson 2004). To this day, much of the scholarship on slavery done in each of these traditions—so radically opposed in so many other ways—shares the common metanarrative shape of outlining a "transition" from slavery to capitalism.

The marking of slavery as an archaism, destined to be superseded by the emergent history of freedom, even as it provided the term with enormous critical potential, made it (and the history of the millions of martyrs it contains) useful to those who defined freedom in terms of national belonging or economic license. In this usage, as found in nineteenth-century reform and political economy, the relationship between slavery and freedom is figured as one of temporal supersession. The United States is no longer figured as a place where the contest between the two is to be fought out but as a place where it has been uniformly and once and for all completed. As George W. Bush put it in his 2001 inaugural address, the history of the United States is "the story of a slave-holding society that became a servant of freedom." He went on to elaborate this claim, asserting that "the very people traded into slavery helped to set America free" through their struggle against injustice (2003). In the historical vision expressed by (but certainly not limited to) Bush's addresses, the history of slavery has been turned into a cliché, a set of images that have been emptied of any authentic historical meaning through their sheer repetition in connection with their supposed extinction at the hands of "freedom." The history of slavery in this usage exists in a state of civil servitude to the idea of "American freedom."

A countercurrent within mostly Marxist and black radical thought—notably W. E. B. Du Bois (1935/1998), C. L. R. James (1938/1989), Eric Williams (1944/1994), Stuart Hall (2002), Sidney Mintz (1985), David Brion Davis (1975), and Cedric Robinson (1983/2000)—has insistently contested the temporal framing of the relationship of slavery to freedom as one of linear progress. By insisting on the place of slavery in the history of European and American capitalism—on the way that the palpable experiences of freedom in Europe and the Americas and the narrowness of an idea of freedom defined as the ability to work for a wage both depended on slavery—they have framed the relationship between the two terms as being one of dynamic simultaneity. They have, that is to say, insistently pointed out practices of servitude at the heart of the history of freedom, a set of insights that gives new and subversive meaning to Bush's phrase "servant of freedom."

The idea of the simultaneous coproduction of slavery and freedom lies at the heart of the case for reparations for slavery. This ongoing case has a history in the United States that dates to Reconstruction, and it represents a powerful (if also powerfully stigmatized by the intellectual and cultural mainstream) refiguration of the relationship of capitalism, slavery, freedom, past, and present. By reworking the history of the exploitation of Africans in the Americas—by whatever means, under whatever mode of production, mystified by whatever Western category of analysis—as a single extended and ongoing moment of time, the heterodox historiography of reparations calls on us to recognize slavery as an element not of the national (or hemispheric) past but of the global present.

59

Space

George Lipsitz

In order for history to take place, it takes places. American studies and cultural studies scholars have drawn on the ideas and insights of critical geographers Henri Lefebvre (1991), David Harvey (2000), Yi-fu Tuan (1977), Cindy Katz (2004), Ruth Wilson Gilmore (2007), Laura Pulido (1996), and many others to explore the creative possibilities and the moral meanings attributed to particular spaces and places. The politics and poetics of space permeate the culture of the United States as a nation through moral values that get attached to the open ranges of the western frontier and the far reaches of empire overseas; that contrast the barrio, the ghetto, and the reservation with the propertied and properly gendered suburban home; that juxtapose the finite limits of social space with the infinite possibilities of cyberspace and outer space. In both scholarly research and everyday life, the moral meanings attributed to these spaces and places have often been resolutely and creatively contested.

For European political philosophers during the Renaissance, corruption came from time—from the particularity of historical events—while the universality of space was presumed to promote virtue and morality. After the discovery and conquest of the Americas, these ideas helped fuel the hope that the virtues of the ideal space they associated with what they called "America" could provide escape from the corruptions of European time. As historian David W. Noble argues, idealized fantasies about pure and virtuous space have permeated the political and expressive cultures of the United States from the era of colonization and conquest up to the present day. The idea of a free "America" especially excited European thinkers because they had come to believe that free nations needed to be composed of homogeneous populations with strong ties to the national landscape, to "timeless spaces" where citizens could dwell in harmony with one another. European Americans who imagined that the purity of "American" space might offer them a refuge from the corruptions of European time developed what Noble calls "the metaphor of two worlds"—the idea that the territory of the United States would be an island of virtue in a global sea of corruption (2002, xxxiv). Later institutionalized inside U.S. national culture, this metaphor depends on binary oppositions between the pure spaces of New World freedom and their contamination by despised and demonized groups overseas or at home marked as "other." In order to have pure and homogeneous spaces, "impure" populations have to be removed or marginalized, destroyed or dominated. Noble argues that belief in a redemptive national landscape performed important cultural work in constituting the United States as an imagined community grounded in white masculine property and power.

Imagined utopian spaces have long served as idealized escapes from the problems of real places. Images of the pastoral rural landscape and the rugged western frontier permeate works of expressive culture by writers, painters, and composers (H. Smith 1950; Kolodny 1984; L. Marx 1964/2000). In the nineteenth century, literary and philosophical works by Transcendentalists and paintings of the Hudson River school imbued the national landscape with democratic possibility. In the twentieth century, musical compositions by Virgil Thompson and Aaron Copland echoed writings by historians Frederick Jackson Turner (1893/1920) and William Prescott Webb (1931/1981) that identified the open spaces of the western frontier as unique sources of democratic regeneration. These imagined free spaces were constructed discursively in opposition to the constraints that settled society seemed to impose on freedom-seeking U.S. Americans. Herman Melville's Ishmael in *Moby-Dick* in 1851 and Mark Twain's Huck Finn in 1885 may be the best known of many fictional heroes who have been eager to take to sea or to "light out for the territory" to avoid facing the contradictions of settled society (Melville 1851/1971; Twain 1885/1985).

Of course, neither Ishmael nor Huck fled "civilized" space alone. Both were accompanied by people of color on whom they depended for moral instruction and guidance. People from communities of color could not access the metaphor of two worlds because it required their subordination, humiliation, exclusion, sometimes even their annihilation. The putatively empty and timeless North American discursive space that settler colonists expected to serve as a space of refuge from the corruptions of European time was actually a physical place inhabited by indigenous people with long histories and distinct customs. The heroism of conquest, settlement, and westward expansion depended on genocidal wars against Native Americans, slavery imposed on Africans, lands seized from Mexicans, and the exploitation of laborers in and from Asia and Latin America. Rather than imagining the national landscape as common ground to be shared, the moral geography of settler colonialism required conquest, slavery, and empire. As white civilization and its corruptions penetrated the West, it became increasingly difficult for people in the United States to believe that they inhabited the democratic landscape of their dreams. The end of slavery, the rise of the interracial egalitarian coalition formed around what W. E. B. Du Bois (1935/1998, 184) called "abolition-democracy," mass immigration from Europe, and working-class mobilizations for justice all challenged the homogeneity and harmony central to the dominant national spatial and social imaginary.

Rather than reckon honestly and openly with the internal contradictions and conflicts that rendered domestic society unable to produce the freedom and democracy that had been promised, many white U.S. Americans looked outward, seeking in the global marketplace the perfect harmony and happiness they had failed to produce in the national landscape. If the United States of America could not be an island of virtue in a global sea of corruption, the sea had to be transformed to be like it (D. W. Noble 2002). But the United States itself also had to be made more homogeneous. In the face of the increasing public presence and growing power of communities of color, the imagined free spaces of the frontier had to be fabricated in the segregated suburb, in the normative, properly gendered, and prosperous household (E. May 1988; Massey 1994; Marsh 1990) A distinct spatial imaginary propelled the creation of subdivisions designed to secure comparative advantages from what political economist Robert Reich (1991) calls "the secession of the successful" into gated exclusive communities governed by ever smaller subunits of government set up to hoard amenities and advantages for their residents (McKenzie 1994). Just as pastoral North American space was once viewed as the ideal escape from the corruptions of European time, the rewards and privileges of whiteness have configured U.S. suburbs as the means of escape from the responsibilities and obligations of national citizenship. In segregated white communities, the intersection of race and space produced a radically restricted spatial imaginary, one that reinforced the rewards, privileges, and structured advantages of whiteness through commitments to hostile privatism and defensive localism (Lipsitz 2011).

Because aggrieved communities of color could not access for themselves the amenities and advantages of places shaped by the white spatial imaginary, they have often manifested a different approach to discursive space and physical place that has had enormous cultural and political appeal for people of all races. As the philosopher Charles Mills notes, the white spatial imaginary tells people of color that they belong "somewhere else," that "you are what you are in part because you originate from a certain kind of space, and that space has those properties in part because it is inhabited by creatures like yourself" (1997, 42). Yet populations living in ghettos, barrios, and reservations have turned segregation into congregation through social movements that depict space as valuable and finite, as a public resource for which all must take responsibility. The competing spatial imaginaries of the national political culture have influenced a variety of works of expressive culture. The art of John Biggers and Betye Saar, the fiction of Paule Marshall, plays and essays by Lorraine Hansberry, and the creation of collectives of musicians by Horace Tapscott and Sun Ra all exemplify this alternative to the dominant spatial imaginary (Lipsitz 2011). The American studies and ethnic studies scholars Robert Alvarez (2005), Arlene Dávila (2004), Raul Villa (2000), and Mary Pat Brady (2002) have delineated the complex cultural consequences of racialized space for Latinos, while Linda Trinh Vo (2004), Leland Saito (2009), and Chiou-ling Yeh (2008) have produced similar studies of Asian American communities.

The Black spatial imaginary has been a particularly generative force for new spatial and racial ideas exemplified in the work of the jazz pianist, composer, band leader, and political visionary Sun Ra. The dual meaning of "space" as both a continuous empty expanse of territory and the physical universe beyond the Earth's atmosphere enabled Sun Ra to expose how relations among races in the United States are also relations among spaces. In the early 1970s, he picked the phrase "space is the place" as the title for a song, an album, and a feature film. As part of a long-standing effort on his part to use flamboyant self-dramatization and performance to make a serious point, Sun Ra presented himself as a visitor from outer space appalled by the racism he discovered on the planet Earth. The jazz musician's mischievous play with the words "space" and "place" contained obvious implications about race. In these works, Sun Ra imagined utopian travels in space as a direct contrast to and a direct rebuke of "Earthy" spatial imaginaries: housing segregation based on a long history of restrictive covenants, racial zoning, mortgage redlining, steering, block busting, and mob violence that relegated people of different races to different spaces. Sun Ra's target audience had firsthand experience with the more than sixteen hundred urban renewal projects starting in the 1930s that destroyed the economic and emotional ecosystems of minority communities (Fullilove 2004, 20). The spatial imaginary that guided Sun Ra's eccentric art and public persona had more to do with the problems of segregated spaces on the planet Earth than with the utopian possibilities of travel through the universe. His artistry emerged from and spoke to a Black spatial imaginary based on mutuality and solidarity that developed over decades in Black communities where residents turned divisive segregation into celebratory congregation.

Like other artists, activists, and intellectuals from aggrieved communities, Sun Ra attempted to make the familiar realities of racialized space appear unnatural and therefore unnecessary. His adopted public persona as a purported interplanetary traveler from Saturn blended long-standing strains of Afro-diasporic tricksterism with emerging currents of Afro-futurism. He invoked the cosmos to contrast an imagined freedom in outer space with the confinements confronting Black people on the planet Earth (Szwed 1998; Kilgore 2003). Similarly important spatial imaginaries have been developed through political mobilizations to forge new spaces of inclusion and opportunity. The Chicano movement of the 1960s and 1970s united citizens and noncitizens through brilliant deployments of the mythic and poetic "land of Aztlán" as a discursive space uniquely suited to positioning group struggle within and across borders. This spatial imaginary recruited people of Mexican origin in both Mexico and the United States without condoning the conquest and suppression of indigenous peoples by both nations. It positioned Chicano activists to battle for both national civil rights and global human rights (Bebout 2011). The intercommunalism of the Black Panther Party leader Huey P. Newton created a cognitive mapping that connected Black struggles for self-determination in Oakland, California, to peasant resistance to imperialism in Vietnam. In Newton's view, the United States was not a nation into which Blacks should assimilate but rather an empire that they should oppose (Singh 2004). Queer Latina activists mobilizing in San Francisco's Mission District in the 1990s in response to official indifference to the AIDS epidemic converted a storefront on a busy street into a welcoming space for progressive and culturally sensitive political education and organizing among people from different national-origin groups (J. Rodríguez 2003).

Insurgent struggles have often made history take place by seizing space and deploying it for unexpected purposes. On Thanksgiving Day in 1969, activists identifying themselves as Indians of All Nations seized and occupied the abandoned prison on Alcatraz Island. The name Indians of All Nations turned aggregate anti-Indian racism into a new form of solidarity by asserting a unified panethnic identity. The activists cited a provision of a treaty between the Lakota nation and the federal government as a guarantee that members of all tribes had the right to seize unused government land (Smith and Warrior 1996). They used the sentimental appropriation of Indian history in this national holiday to call attention to the original seizure and occupation of North America by white settler colonialists that preceded the first Thanksgiving. They dramatized the desperate situation facing indigenous people by becoming the first people in history to break *into* jail. The action underscored the culpability of the federal government by seizing national park property as reparations for lands confiscated from Indians elsewhere. Similarly, the American Indian Movement desacralized the physical places of westward expansion through the Trail of Broken Treaties caravan from Alcatraz to Washington, D.C., in 1972. Signifying on the forced removal of the Cherokee and Choctaw people to Oklahoma on the brutal Trail of Tears in 1831, the caravan traveled in the opposite direction of westward expansion, foregrounding white duplicity in the title of the march. It stopped along the way in the racialized spaces of reservations and urban ghettos, turning them from forgotten and abandoned places into spaces supplying new recruits for the campaign.

There are lessons to be learned from these activist mobilizations. By organizing in actual locations over the discursive meanings of space and place, they have drawn attention to the ways in which new relations among races require renegotiation of relations among places. They signal that space is not merely a barren expanse, the universe around the Earth, or an empty temporal interval. It is a dynamic place where important discursive and political work can be done when people recognize that space is the place in which to do it.

60

Subject
Tavia Nyong'o

Hey you! Yes . . . you! Now that I have your attention, let me ask you a question. How did you know it was you I was addressing? I didn't call you by your name, after all. In fact, I don't know your name or any other distinguishing characteristic. Nonetheless, I called out, and you turned your attention to me. There is a lot of power in what just happened, more than you might initially suspect. Or maybe you *do* already suspect. Perhaps you are already conscious of the coercion in my addressing you in this abrupt and unceremonious manner. Maybe you rankle a little at my interruption of what you intended to be doing, my disruption of what you were expecting to find here in this essay. Who am I, you may be asking, to presume to command your attention as I have just done?

"Subject" first emerged as a keyword in the fields of cultural studies and American studies as an effort to understand situations just like this one: situations in which a subjective response emerges out of a seemingly impersonal call or hail. What "subject"—or the closely related term "subjective"—means in such situations is anything but clear. A subject (from the Latin verb for "to throw under") is something that comes under the influence of an external authority or force. Some examples may suggest the breadth and subtlety of the concept.

In the colonial era, North American settlers were "loyal subjects" of the British Crown. When, in the course of human events, revolutionary white men felt obliged to throw off their imperial yoke, they felt "a decent respect to the opinions of mankind" required them to justify this act through an open declaration of independence. Even in revolutionizing themselves, they continued to guide their conduct and speech in relation to an abstract, external authority (Fliegelman 1993).

During the notorious Tuskegee syphilis experiment, conducted by the U.S. government from the 1930s to the 1970s, hundreds of impoverished black men were "experimental subjects" of an inhumane medical study in which they were denied treatment in order to track the "natural" progress of their disease. And recently, a historian discovered prior tests conducted by the U.S. Public Health Service in Guatemala, in which humans were *deliberately* infected with syphilis (Reverby 2009). These medical crimes resulted in the creation of institutional review boards (IRBs) that now govern research on what are called "human subjects."

The standardized test you probably took to qualify you for the college-level course in which you may be reading this essay made you a "psychological subject." Your aptitude or capacity for reasoning was assessed, and the results affected which educational opportunities would be open or closed to you. The legitimacy of such assessments in organizing economic and educational opportunity in a democratic society has been intensely researched and debated since the test was first invented (Lemann 2000). Many people argue that they are illegitimate in a democratic society and lie on the discredited foundations of eugenic science.

In each of these examples, the *political* character of subjectification—the process of becoming a subject—should be clear. In each case, the *historical* character of the subjectifying power that precedes and makes the subject may not be obvious. Subjectification bears a history, but it is a history that is often masked. One is seemingly "born" owing allegiance to the British monarch or to the opinions of humankind. One "happens" to be a black sharecropper in the Jim Crow South or a Guatemalan prostitute and therefore available for use in a government experiment on the efficacy of penicillin. One is simply "gifted" with the ability to achieve in school, as "revealed" by the SAT or other tests, and thus merits more or better education than someone who is less highly ranked. The hidden history of these processes of subjectification allows their results to appear impersonal and objective. This *naturalizes* the structural effects that subjectification has on how we are formed as subjects—how we live or die, what rights we possess or lack, what we know or are kept ignorant of. Subject positions are not merely a set of "boxes" or "labels" with no real substance to them; they are not something we can elect to freely "identify with" or not. They inform who we feel ourselves to be in our "innermost selves" and how we are entangled in our most objective and immediate environment. They form the ground on which we stand, when and if we take a stand. Even when we refuse or rebel against our subjectification, we do so *as* subjects.

Scholars who use the term "subject" to explore processes of subjectification draw on a variety of theoretical traditions, ranging from Marxism and psychoanalysis to Foucauldianism and feminism. A common theme in many of these traditions is the observation that subjectification works most powerfully when it is felt most consensually. Of course, brute force, or the realistic fear of it, can also be subjectifying. But so can the protection from violence, the provision of medical care, the granting of legal rights, the enlightenment of the mind with education or knowledge (Hartman 1997). American studies has long been interested in the terrain of "soft power" and "tender violence": it has tracked the winning of "hearts and minds" and the "rites of assent" through which the formerly excluded are incorporated into the fabric of society (Abel 1997; Bercovitch 1993; Wexler 2000).

Such processes are stories of subjectification. If violence tends to render humans as objects, power turns them into subjects (Scarry 1985). But the power that subjects us does not emanate from a single mythical source, like the sovereign body of the king (Kantorowicz 1957). It is continuously reproduced in moments of hailing such as the one with which this essay began, the hail that made you, however temporarily, into a "learning subject," a subject to my expertise and scholarly authority.

To be sure, my authority in this scene of instruction is tenuous. For one, it is mediated by my own ongoing subjectification. In order to teach you about the keyword "subject," I rely on your ongoing cooperation and comprehension, however partial or skeptical. The pedagogic power that renders you a learning subject is a negotiation in which I attempt to anticipate and provide for your instruction, while you "follow along" in hopes of "mastering" the subject. At least this is what happens in one ideal scenario, which may not resemble yours or mine. Perhaps we decide to read against the grain, to wrest this essay away from its seeming intent, to employ it for different purposes.

As a democratic educator, I should welcome such creativity as a sign of the consensual nature of our negotiation, as proof that you are a *free* subject in this learning scenario and not any kind of conscript. But who am "I" in this case? I am not the "grammatical subject" of this sentence, psychoanalysis has argued, but the *split* between that grammatical "I" and the body that speaks though the "I" (Fink 1995). That speaking body is forever finding, losing, and dispersing itself in the grammatical subject "I" that ostensibly secures and stabilizes its authority. According to the psychoanalytic view of the subject, I am not the master of the discourse I would pass along to you—especially not when I claim to speak in the first person. Rather than imagine a power-free context for the subject, situations in which we are somehow free to be who we really are independent of others, we might do better to seek fuller accounts of *intersubjectivity*, that is, to better understand the *relations of power* at work—whether behind the scenes or quite openly on the surface—in our various scenes of subjectification.

Cultural studies, including the traditions of critical theory on which it draws, has trained scholars to be suspicious of situations that present themselves as free of coercion or constraint (Horkheimer and Adorno 1944/2002). This suspicion raises the important question of whether knowledge about the subject implies power over the subject. To answer that question, let us return to the scene with which I began, one that I have borrowed from the Marxist philosopher Louis Althusser (1971/2001). In Althusser's example, it is not an author but a police officer yelling, "Hey you!" Althusser wanted to know why we turn when we hear this hail (he called it an "interpellation") and what happens when we do. Althusser was searching for a critical account of how and why working people "consent" to their domination and exploitation in capitalist societies. Integrating the insights of Marxism and psychoanalysis, Althusser developed an account of a subject who was given a *forced choice* to belong to the capitalist order (as enforced by schools, police, and other "apparatuses" of the state). Since "you" could refer to anyone, in deciding that it nonetheless is "me" whom the police officer is addressing, "I" become a subject *for* the police. The resulting analysis emphasizes both the relations of production in society and the institutions that hold those relations in place despite our possible wishes otherwise.

If I am "stopped and frisked" by the New York Police Department because I am a young black or Latino male or have to show my papers in Arizona because I fit another racial profile, I may understand that this interpellation by the state is in violation of rights conveyed by the U.S. Constitution. But knowing this does not in itself give me choice. "You" *could* mean me, and so I turn. I am structurally—"always already"—hailed by the police officer. In Althusser's account, my subjectivity is in a crucial sense an *effect* of the policeman's power. Other critical theorists contest this point: Slavoj Žižek (1999) argues that there is always an inextricable core of irrationality to subjectivity that interpellation cannot reach (although neither can the individual subject). And the philosopher and historian Michel Foucault famously argued that "where there is power, there is resistance": the hail that produces the subject is also the swerve of the subject against its power or authority (1976/1990, 95). There is a minimum of momentum always available for escape.

You may have already noticed an ambiguity running throughout these usages of the term "subject" to denote the process of being hailed by an external power. You may suppose that it is better, all other things being equal, to be a "subject" than to be an "object." But this common usage of the term smuggles into language the confusing assumption that subjects always possess agency and objects always lack it. When feminists critique the objectification of women or antiracists critique the stereotyping of people of color, they do not always rely on the liberal humanism that privileges subjects over objects. Scholars have begun to question the underlying assumptions regarding subjective agency and even to argue that it is distributed more broadly and unpredictably across "subjects" and "objects" than we may expect (J. Bennett 2010). They have asked how and in what ways objects also resist (Moten 2003). And they have shown how the norms that the subject cites can be subverted through the very act of citation, which can expose their natural self-evidence as a fiction (Butler 1990).

If objectification is a problem, subjectification is no straightforward solution. It may be better understood as a beneficial harm or poisonous cure since the results of subjectification are indeterminate and ambiguous with regard to the goals of greater agency and more capacious identity (Derrida 1981). Foucault illustrates this point through the powerful example of modern sexuality. Most modern subjects feel themselves to possess an innate sexuality and sexual orientation. The struggle for women's rights and lesbian/gay/bisexual/transgender (LGBT) rights in the United States has been waged, in large part, over this idea of sexuality as central to who we are as subjects, especially as it pertains to the freedom to dispose of one's body as one wills, to enter and exit sexual relationships, to choose to reproduce or not, and to create families and communities of our choosing. Foucault, himself a gay man, certainly supported feminism and LGBT rights as political tactics with efficacy in the contemporary historical moment. But he also pointed out that sexuality, seen as an innate or personal "thing" that we discover, accept, and express, is itself a relatively recent invention, not a human invariant. Prior to the nineteenth century, when categories such as "heterosexual" and "homosexual" came into being, both reproductive and nonreproductive sex could be organized quite differently than they are today and could have quite different ramifications for subjectivity (Foucault 1976/1990). This history should make us particularly suspicious of our conviction that our sexuality is a secret we somehow repress or an orientation we need to speak openly in order to be liberated. Even as the concept of sexual orientation has been a vehicle for the liberation of queer and transgender people, it has also produced new knowledges about subjects that can be dangerous for them (Epstein 1996; Massad 2007). This risk may not lead us to abandon either the use of the term "sexual orientation" or the feeling that we possess one, but it may keep us wary about the ambiguous nature of the concepts we use regarding the subject.

As the example of sexuality indicates, an awareness of these relations of power at work in processes of subjectification can make it tricky to approach history as a narrative in which we progress from coercion to freedom. The trouble is that any narrative about the making of subjects will lack an external point of view from which we speak, since there is no objective standpoint from which we might talk about subjectivity. Put differently, objectivity is one of many ruses through which the relations of power that produce subjectification are sustained (Novick 1988). Rather than narrate history as a process of the gradual liberation of humans from various forms of prejudice and domination, we might want instead to tell a story of the emergence, layering, and gradual erosion of different practices of subject formation. These practices, in turn, reflect different regimes of knowledge-power, that is, different ways of knowing about and managing subjectivity. The resulting tale may not be one of liberation; rather, it may be a *genealogy of the subject* (Foucault 1994). The resulting politics may involve a drive not to "be who we are" but to "refuse who we are." The critical commitment to a genealogical approach to the study of subject formation is important because it immerses us in a critical understanding of how power hails, solicits, empowers, debilitates, chooses, and abandons subjects. Genealogy also calls for our ethical commitment to those who, while historically subjugated, have not vanished but still crowd our consciousness, hungry ghosts if only we would hear (A. Gordon 2008).

Thank you for your attention. This lesson is concluded. You're free to go.

61

Technology
Jentery Sayers

When used in everyday speech today, the keyword "technology" refers primarily to physical devices. Yet this usage was not common until the second half of the twentieth century. During the seventeenth century, "technology" was either a systematic study of the arts or the specific terminology of an art (Casaubon 1612; Bentham 1827; Carlyle 1858). An encyclopedia, dictionary, or publication like *Keywords for American Cultural Studies* would have been called a technology. Related terms such as "tool," "instrument," and "machine" described physical devices (Sutherland 1717; Hanway 1753). In the nineteenth century, "technology" became the practical application of science, a system of methods to execute knowledge (Horne 1825; Raymond Williams 1976/1983), or a discipline of the "Industrial Arts" focused on the use of hand and power tools to fabricate objects (G. Wilson 1855; Burton 1864). During the twentieth century, the meaning of "technology" gradually expanded to include both the processes of a system and the physical devices required of that system (D. F. Noble 1977). By midcentury, it was used as a modifier to characterize socioeconomic developments, as in the use of "high-technology" or "high-tech" to describe complex applications of specialized machines in industrialized economies.

Scholars of American studies and cultural studies working on the history of technology have emphasized its social, cultural, and economic dimensions. They have tended to resist complicity in technological determinism (technology as the sole cause of cultural change), technological instrumentalism (technology as value neutral), technological positivism (technological progress as social progress), and technological essentialism (technology as having some intrinsic nature or essence). In fact, American studies and cultural studies approaches to technology are best described as "nonessentialist." The central premise of nonessentialism is that neither technologies nor histories of technology can be divorced from the social and cultural contexts of their production, circulation, or consumption (Ross 1990). American studies and cultural studies approaches begin with the claim that technologies can be made, interpreted, and used in multiple and often contradictory ways (Ihde 1990; Feenberg 1999; Haraway 1985). They share with "constructivist" approaches common to both fields a focus on the ways in which social conditions and meanings shape how people create, perceive, and understand technologies. But they also underscore why the technical particulars of technologies—how technologies turn this into that (Fuller 2005)—really matter (Galloway 2006; Gitelman 2006; Bogost 2007; Kirschenbaum 2008). They frequently note that a technology can articulate complex relations between actors in a given network, rendering decisions for them beyond their own knowledge or awareness (Latour 1987; Kittler 1999; Galloway 2004; Chun 2011). From a nonessentialist perspective, technologies are never simply "extensions" of human beings or human rationality (McLuhan 1964/2003). Instead, technologies exist in recursive and embodied relationships with their operators, and they must be understood through their social, cultural, economic, and technical processes, all of which are material.

In order to better understand this approach, consider a key moment in the history of technology: the Luddite rebellions that started in Nottingham, England, in 1811. Composed largely of experienced artisans in the hosiery and lace trades, the Luddites broke wide-frame looms—a new technology of the moment—because looms threatened their livelihood by automating their craft and reducing the costs of hosiery and lace production. The rebellions spread beyond Nottingham (to Derby, Yorkshire, and elsewhere) and to other industries (cotton, cropping, and wool). They ultimately failed to stop the proliferation of wide-frame looms, and their legitimacy was undermined by the Luddites' violent attacks on magistrates, merchants, and other townspeople. Yet the rebellions are historically important because the Luddites anticipated the gradual shift from technology as "the theory and accurate description of useful arts and manufactures" (Zimmerman 1787, iii) to technology as the material application of science in industries such as textile manufacturing. To adapt a metaphor from Karl Marx (1867/1976), the Luddites understood how technology was becoming "frozen labor" or, put differently, "work and its values embedded and inscribed in transportable form" (Bowker and Star 1999, 135).

A nonessentialist approach to technologies such as wide-frame looms suggests that machines were an important factor in the shift toward "frozen labor" during the nineteenth century, but they were not its sole cause. Instead, machines represented and even enabled the social, cultural, and economic forces of industrial capitalism: the rise of factories (L. Klein 2008); the alienation, systemization, and automation of handicraft; the widespread investment in efficiency; and the decrease of human error through scientific management and standardized workflows (F. Taylor 1911/2010). Nonessentialist approaches also recognize how the implications of technology are interpreted differently across different settings and populations. For working-class Luddites, the wide-frame loom implied the deskilling of certain crafts and the eventual obsolescence of existing occupations; for engineers such as Charles Babbage (1832), it pointed toward innovation, heightened productivity, decreased costs, and increased accuracy in manufacturing. Such differing perspectives reproduced asymmetrical relations of class and power.

These class and power differences are important to remember when observing how industrialization corresponded with the formation of technology as an academic discipline during the mid-nineteenth century. At that time, the word began to appear in university names, such as the Massachusetts Institute of Technology, which opened in 1865. As a discipline, technology was associated with the humble and economically useful "Industrial Arts," rather than the noble and aesthetically useful "Fine Arts" (G. Wilson 1855). It was also a set of technical skills possessed by an individual: "His technology consists of weaving, cutting canoes, [and] making rude weapons" (Burton 1864, 437). In many universities, such skills were deemed inferior to the mental labor of science and literature. During debates with biologist T. H. Huxley, the nineteenth-century poet and critic Matthew Arnold defined technology as mere "instrument-knowledge" (1882/1885, 107), peripheral to culture and the civilizing pursuits of spiritual and intellectual life (Mactavish and Rockwell 2006). Although Huxley and Arnold disagreed about the role that science should play in education, neither considered technology a discipline worthy of the ideal university. Weaving, cutting canoes, and making rude weapons were routines delegated to the working class, not the late nineteenth century's educated elite.

The nineteenth-century definition of "technology" as a practical application of science persisted well into the twentieth century, especially through the proliferation of phonography, photography, cinema, radio, and other utilitarian modes of mechanical reproduction (T. Armstrong 1998). The effects of this proliferation were perceived variously across contexts, but a common question during the first half of the twentieth century was how—through technology— politics were aestheticized and aesthetics were politicized (Benjamin 1936/1968). The totalitarian regimes of fascism and Nazism aestheticized their politics through references to technological innovation. They rendered automobiles, airplanes, cameras, radios, and typewriters beautiful objects: symbols of progress, modernity, efficiency, and mastery over nature (Marinetti 1909/2006; *Triumph of the Will* 1935). Once aestheticized, technologies such as cinema helped mask totalitarian violence through commodity culture and mass distribution, prompting the Frankfurt school philosopher Herbert Marcuse to write, "the established technology has become an instrument of destructive politics" (1964/2002, 232).

Like the Luddites, Marcuse and other neo-Marxists were critical of the tendency to reify politics and labor through technologies and aesthetics (Horkheimer and Adorno 1944/2002; Dyer-Witheford 1999). Their response required the politicization of aesthetics through the same modes of mechanical reproduction. For instance, early cinema was used for purposes other than formalizing and disseminating totalitarian ideology. It also fostered opportunities for shared experience (in the theater), collective witnessing (of narratives, images, and audio), and better understanding of how consciousness, perception, and social relations are produced in the first place (Benjamin 1936/1968; Kracauer 1960/1997; Hansen 2011). This response prevented technology from being reduced to an instrument or agent of positivism. Rather, it positioned technology as one element in a complex system of material processes and conditions. The more practical this system appears, the more instrumental, determinist, or positivist it becomes (Postman 1993). In this sense, "practical" is nearly synonymous with a "natural," "intuitive," or "invisible" technology (Heidegger 1977/1993; Weiser 1991; Norman 1998).

This common affiliation of technology with practicality explains why nonessentialist approaches are central to American studies and cultural studies: they resist the tendency either to give technologies too much authority in everyday life or to relegate people to unconscious consumers, who are incapable of intervening in systems, applications, or devices of any sort (Braverman 1974/1998; D. F. Noble 1995). They also highlight the fact that technology becomes gendered, sexualized, and racialized through its naturalization or routinization. Historically, technology has been culturally coded as masculine (Wajcman 1991; Balsamo 1996; Rodgers 2010), and it has consistently served the interests of "able" bodies, prototypical whiteness, and heteropatriarchy (Haraway 1985; A. Stone 1996; Nakamura 2002, 2008; Sterne 2003; T. Foster 2005; E. Chang 2008; Browne 2010). Yet it is important to recognize that bias or supremacy is not somehow inherent to technologies or their technical particulars. It emerges from the social, cultural, and economic conditions through which technologies are articulated with interpretive processes and embodied behaviors.

In response to this recognition, some American studies and cultural studies practitioners encourage a "technoliteracy" influenced by computer hacking, technical competencies, new media production, and critical making (Wark 2004; Hertz 2009; Ratto 2011; Losh 2012; McPherson 2012a). Andrew Ross (1990) defines "technoliteracy" as "a hacker's knowledge, capable of reskilling, and therefore of rewriting the cultural programs and reprogramming the social values that make room for new technologies" (para. 43). Technoliteracy thus complicates Matthew Arnold's

reduction of technology to mere instrument-knowledge since it refuses to draw a neat division between physical devices and social values. More important, it involves actively intervening in technologies—at the level of systems, applications, and devices—as key ingredients in the everyday production of knowledge and culture. Thus, the question for nonessentialist investments in technoliteracy is. Technology, but for whom, by whom, under what assumptions, and to what effects?

In our so-called digital age, many people would assume that interventions in technological processes are accessible to more people than ever before. After all, the Internet has been depicted as a decentralized, democratizing, and even immaterial "cyberspace" of radical freedom—a hacker's paradise of do-it-yourself coding, performance, and publication (Gibson 1982; Barlow 1996/2001; Hayles 1999). The trouble is that proliferation should not be conflated with access or intervention. As the very word "technology" is subsumed by industry terms such as "iPad," "Twitter," "Droid," and "Facebook," not to mention the ubiquity of verbs such as "Bing," "Skype," and "Google" (Vaidhyanathan 2011), the values, procedures, and biases of high-technology systems, applications, and devices grow increasingly opaque or invisible to most people, who are simply deemed "users." On the one hand, strategies for social control and regulation persist and expand through code, algorithms, metrics, protocols, and networks, which—when compiled— exceed the knowledge base of any given individual or group (Galloway 2004; Beller 2006; Chun 2006, 2011). On the other hand, scholars and users of technology are reimagining the implications of technology and technoliteracy, especially through collaboration, experimental media, and social justice initiatives (Daniel and Loyer 2007; Juhasz 2011; Anthropy 2012; Cárdenas 2012; Goldberg and Marciano 2012; Women

Who Rock 2012; Cong-Huyen 2013; Lothian and Phillips 2013).

Collaborative work around technologies allows practitioners to build alternative infrastructures, tools, and projects that are difficult (if not impossible) to construct alone (Davidson 2008; Sayers 2011). Meanwhile, experimental media afford multimodal approaches to scholarly, cultural, and creative expression, anchored not only in text but also in video, audio, images, programming, and dynamic visualizations (McPherson 2009). Such expression is central to many social justice initiatives that rely on witnessing, interviews, process documentation, real-time data, intercultural dialogue, and community-based participatory action research (Ang and Pothen 2009). When blended together, collaboration, experimental media, and social justice research suggest an exciting new trajectory for American studies and cultural studies, one that invites practitioners to engage the history and future of technologies at the intersection of thinking and doing, critiquing and making, immersion and self-reflexivity.

62

Terror

Junaid Rana

"Terror" is a complex word that refers both to physical violence and to the emotional response produced by that violence. While this dual meaning has persisted for centuries, the term's connotations have shifted in the modern era in relation to the perceived source of such force. In contrast to earlier usages that reference punitive measures of the state, such as political violence and persecution, terror is now used to name threats posed by nonstate actors. Though amplified in the United States after 9/11, this shift began in the context of conflict with militant left and liberation struggles throughout the nineteenth and twentieth centuries, the rearticulation of radicalism with anti-Americanism and terrorism during the 1970s, and the advent of wars on drugs, crime, and terror in recent decades. The result is a notion of terror that is shorthand for an abstract, state-sanctioned war against a multivalent idea (terrorism) and an ambiguous actor (the terrorist). This meaning obscures the history of state violence administered in the United States, and increasingly across the globe, to control and dominate particular populations. As such, the rhetoric of terror narrows the discourse of dissent and debate toward state-sanctioned ideologies and otherwise permissible views, beliefs, and actions.

The origin of this concept of terror is often attributed to revolutionary France in the 1790s. The Jacobin state led by Maximilien Robespierre conceived of terror as a means of enforcing state justice and patriotic duty. Targeting internal and foreign enemies for mass executions by guillotine, the Reign of Terror, as this period of state repression came to be known, created a populist notion of state virtue and public service that imposed a swift and severe form of justice (Robespierre 1794/2007). Of particular importance was the idea that citizen-led policing through surveillance and open persecution expressed one's patriotic duty to the sovereign nation. This development in modern citizenship, along with an emphasis on abstract rights, led Edmund Burke, in his classic of modern conservatism, *Reflections on the Revolution in France* (1790/2009), to conclude that revolutionary France would devolve into tyrannical rule and state-imposed violence on its citizens. Replies to this position came from Thomas Paine in his *Rights of Man* (1791/1999) and Mary Wollstonecraft's *A Vindication of the Rights of Man* (1790/2009) and *A Vindication of the Rights of Women* (1792/2009). Both argued against Burke's promotion of hereditary rights and for individual liberties based in an equal society. The importance of these dueling positions to the debate on relations among terror, liberalism, and modern statecraft continue in the present era.

In the nineteenth and early twentieth centuries, the term "terror" continued to evolve. In Europe, governments associated terror with the strand of revolutionaries identified with anarchism, a varied antiauthoritarian political philosophy that sought to end fascism and, in some cases, to overthrow the state through political violence, including bombings and targeted assassinations. These ideas quickly traveled to North American shores and contributed to a range of radical politics. Key moments in the history of violence involving anarchist struggles in the United States include the 1886 Haymarket affair at a labor demonstration in Chicago, in which a bomb exploded, meant for the police, who then opened fire and wounded over sixty protestors (Avrich 1984; J. Green 2006); the 1901 assassination of President William McKinley; and the 1920 Wall Street bombing by a horse-drawn wagon,

considered the precursor to modern car bombing (M. Davis 2007a). In the twentieth century, the convergence of violent militancy with the labor movement led to two periods often referred to as Red Scares in which the U.S. government imposed far-reaching and severe measures of control to prevent the spread of terror. The first, beginning in the 1900s and lasting through the 1920s, targeted alleged anarchist and communist activity, most notably in the infamous raids of Attorney General A. Mitchell Palmer. The second, in the late 1940s and 1950s, was led by Senator Joseph McCarthy, as he attempted to expand and exploit popular fears of communism as a means of discrediting a variety of leftist and progressive political ideologies.

In the second half of the twentieth century, the meaning of "terror" in the United States continued to shift in ways that served to control domestic populations and to shape foreign policy. Richard Nixon's "law and order" platform of the late 1960s took the institutional form in 1972 of the Committee to Combat Terrorism, which sought to purge and eliminate domestic political and ideological opponents (Collins 2002). In the 1970s, terrorist studies took off as an intellectual field, as a special brand of political science and public policy, creating a form of expertise based in public service and political experience (Herman and O'Sullivan 1989). The study of terrorism became a cottage industry, as the same experts who researched and reported on terrorism were largely responsible for crafting U.S. domestic and foreign policy as elected or appointed officials or political lobbyists. Later, in the 1980s, Ronald Reagan expanded this policy approach as part of a battle against foreign and domestic communism and the alleged support of international terrorism, using the term "evil empire" to describe the Soviet Union for the first time in a speech to the National Association of Evangelicals in 1983. Under Reagan, counterterrorism, widespread surveillance, and covert operations increased, as did the power of intelligence experts groomed in the academy and independently funded think tanks.

Over the same period, the sociological and geographical referent of terror began to shift to Islam and the Arab and Muslim world. As many scholars have demonstrated, the discourse of terror is part of an image and information war that is waged through representational meanings and popular consent (Alsultany 2012; W. Mitchell 2011). The association of terrorism with the strategy of targeted hijackings and the Palestinian struggle for self-determination were linked in U.S. mass media and popular culture throughout the 1970s (Said 1981; Shaheen 2001). Associated with a wide array of stereotypes concerning oil and terrorism, these representations positioned the origins of terror as foreign, ignoring domestic and right-wing militant groups in the United States. The gap in policy analysis blindsided government officials and the news media in the 1995 bombing of the federal building in Oklahoma City by Timothy McVeigh, an attack first attributed to Islamic militants rather than domestic groups associated with the white supremacy movement (Linenthal 2001). Since 9/11, terrorism has become inseparable from the idea of Islamic radicalism—a phrasing that combines Islamic militancy with antileft sentiments. This rhetorical strategy resurrects and repurposes the Red Scares of the early and mid-twentieth century, linking radicalism, Islam, and terror. Reminiscent of the McCarthy hearings, the congressional hearings in 2011 launched by Representative Peter King to examine the supposed radicalization of Muslims in the United States epitomizes the establishment and widespread reach of Islamophobia (Kumar 2012; Lean 2012; Sheehi 2011).

For all of these reasons, popular understandings of terror and terrorism conceal a longer history of state terror in the United States and beyond its borders. The U.S. government has sought to control a wide array of militant organizations on the right and left, including the Communist Party USA, the Ku Klux Klan, the American Nazi Party, and the Nation of Islam, by labeling them terrorists. In relation to these and other organizations, terror is associated with militancy and branded as anti-American and unpatriotic activity. This association neutralizes arguments about inequality and ongoing forms of social and economic violence while making racists equivalent with antiracists. Such governmental scrutiny has overwhelmingly focused on progressive social movements, including antinuclear and environmental groups, the labor movement, queer activists, radical intellectuals, feminist groups, and other liberation struggles and solidarity groups. During the 1960s and 1970s, for example, the Black Panther Party and the American Indian Movement were subjected to forms of surveillance, infiltration, and systematic repression that included alleged murders and assassinations by the FBI's counterintelligence program known as COINTELPRO (Churchill and Vander Wall 1990/2001). Domestically, the tactics and strategies of covert intelligence gathering have expanded since 9/11 to spy on Muslims, in addition to numerous political groups such as the Occupy Movement, throughout the United States by local, state, and federal authorities (Aaronson 2013; Apuzzo and Goldman 2013).

After 9/11, the War on Terror established under the presidency of George W. Bush extended counterintelligence tactics by mobilizing military operations in global wars across the Middle East, Central Asia, and South Asia in places such as Iraq, Afghanistan, and Pakistan, while also reinforcing a domestic security apparatus built on an expanded system of policing, surveillance, detention, and deportation (De Genova and Peutz 2010; Shiekh 2011; Rana 2011). The War on Terror draws on previous campaigns of the U.S.

government, including the War on Crime and the War on Drugs, that marked the inner city of the United States and international locations largely in the global South as racialized sites in need of regulation and control. Despite the popular understanding of terror as a form of destruction by nonstate actors in the contemporary era, modern state violence through overt and covert means overwhelmingly surpasses that of so-called terrorists (Asad 2007). The impact of such violence is apparent in the media representations and emergent social structures associated with the U.S. government and military. Iconic representations such as those of the 2004 Abu Ghraib torture scandal reveal the complex social relations of U.S. imperial discourses (Danner 2004; Eisenman 2007; Puar 2005; Sontag 2003). The image of tortured Iraqis not only represents the horror of dehumanization in the site of carceral subjugation but, when defined broadly as political violence, implicitly defines enemies of the state in the terms of racialized bodies and the language of social hierarchy of the U.S. nation-state. In the administration of President Barack Obama, the War on Terror intensified through the proliferation of covert intelligence and the use of drone strikes to eliminate so-called terror targets, including U.S. citizens, on foreign soil.

These tactics of the U.S. government follow a history of state control and regulation that employs the terms "terror," "terrorist," and "terrorism" to curb dissent, to manufacture state enemies as terrorists, to obtain popular consent, and to hide state violence while further shifting the meaning of citizenship, fundamental rights, autonomy, and self-determination. Given this complex history, the challenge of critically engaging the concept of terror is to understand how it is deployed and for what purposes, particularly as the right to protest state uses of power become increasingly limited and curtailed.

63

Time

Valerie Rohy

A child can learn to "tell time," but telling time in American studies and cultural studies is anything but simple—not least because time is crucial to the act of telling, the work of narration. The *Oxford English Dictionary* defines "time" tautologically, as "a space or extent of time" and "a system of measuring or reckoning the passage of time." It eventually suggests that "time" can signify a "period or duration," but after a lengthy entry including "time out" and "time after time," the *concept* of time remains unspecified. As these circular definitions indicate, time often seems self-evident—it either needs no explanation or has no explanation, perhaps because its meanings are so prolific and so various.

Scholars in American studies and cultural studies have sought to unpack some of these meanings, starting with the distinction between time understood as a natural phenomenon and time recognized as a social construction. If you have a clock, you can determine how long it takes you to read this page, understanding time as a quantifiable physical reality. But when you reset your clock for Daylight Savings Time, you join a collective, state-sanctioned agreement that what was three o'clock yesterday is four o'clock today. Here time is not an empirical fact but a social fiction, an idea, or a system of ideas. In a very real sense, "all time is social time" (Adam 1990, 45).

The term "temporality" recognizes time as a product of social negotiation that may seem natural or self-evident to those who have internalized its logic and assumptions. This concept has enabled scholars to denaturalize time and to expose the heterogeneous temporalities operating in U.S. culture and beyond: psychic time, historical time, narrative time, reproductive time, queer time, hour and day, duration, time as commodity, modernism, memory and nostalgia, anachronism, musical tempos such as syncopation, time and hegemony, sequence, futurity, synchronization, timekeeping technologies, progress and teleology, anticipation, grammatical tenses such as the future anterior, childhood and aging, continuity and discontinuity, belatedness, and retroaction, each with its own ideological burden.

As these diverse temporalities indicate, time itself is subject to time—that is, to alterations brought by changing cultural, economic, and political circumstances. For example, the capitalist commodification of time ("time is money") is a relatively recent development. In a groundbreaking article, the British historian E. P. Thompson traced the eighteenth- and nineteenth-century shift from agrarian, task-oriented time to industrial clock time. Once employers purchased the time of laborers, particularly in factory settings, "time is now currency: it is not passed but spent"; and the lesson of how properly to spend this commodity is taught to children at school (E. P. Thompson 1967, 61, 84). Benjamin Franklin's late eighteenth-century autobiography stressed the monetary value of time well spent, offering a daily schedule meant to ensure that "every part" of one's business has "its allotted time" through all "twenty-four hours of the natural day" (1895, 155). That this "natural day" is wholly unnatural—that is, invented and contingent—hardly impedes the commodification of time throughout the United States, from North to South and city to farm.

This temporality was critical to the rise of modern capitalism, in which "time enters into the calculative application of administrative authority" (Giddens 1984, 135). Even the slaveholding, agrarian U.S. South, which might seem exempt from industrial clock time, adopted northern concepts of temporality, not merely in urban wage labor but also in rural slave labor (Mark Smith 1997, 8). Spending time in this way required a standardization of timekeeping, which in turn supported common notions of time as neutral and homogeneous. From the seventeenth century on, new technologies allowed more affordable and more accurate clocks and watches, even as other mechanical innovations changed time on a larger scale. In Great Britain, Greenwich Mean Time was adopted in 1847 to facilitate railroad schedules, and in the United States, what we now call Standard Time was instituted, again by the railroads, in 1883 (Bartky 2000).

This regularization of time not only promoted new kinds of social discipline but also produced new forms of national identity, as historian Benedict Anderson argues. Modern nationalism was enabled by the nineteenth-century rise of print culture and organized by what Anderson calls, borrowing from Walter Benjamin, "homogeneous, empty time": a shared sense of standardized, linear temporality and with it a national identity founded on continuous history (1991, 24). In contrast to Anderson, the postcolonial theorist Homi Bhabha suggests that national time is anything but homogeneous; rather, tensions between dominant and minority cultures create a disjunctive "double-time," which sets the "continuist, accumulative temporality" of progress against the nonlinear, recursive temporality that disrupts nationalist histories (1990a, 294). Other responses to Anderson have emphasized the heterogeneity of national time in the nineteenth-century United States, where the plurality of temporalities or ideas about time, including the particular temporality of the feminine domestic sphere, resists national consolidation (Pratt 2010; Thomas Allen 2008).

As this research suggests, time is always political, and its politics extend beyond the nation-state; indeed, matters of time inevitably engage with questions of space. Wai Chi Dimock, for example, argues that accounts of U.S. literature and culture can be limited by the short historical reach attendant on their national scope and proposes instead a larger temporal scale, an awareness of the *longue durée*, or "deep time," that would also expand the boundaries of American studies beyond the borders of the nation (2006, 3–4). While Dimock takes issue with Anderson's monolithic sense of national modernity, the notion that different cultures occupy different temporalities is itself problematic. The rhetoric of racism and colonialism often places the Other outside the time of the observer or outside of time as such. It renders "difference as *distance*," temporal as well as geographical, rather than acknowledging different cultures as coeval—that is, contemporaneous and linked by that temporal commonality (Fabian 2002, 16).

There is danger, then, both in universalizing time and in overparticularizing it. While we cannot assume that different cultures occupy different temporalities, we must also acknowledge that time is not identical for all; at every juncture, diachronic aspects of temporality—changes in time over time—are complicated by synchronic differences among different subjects in a particular moment. As Rita Felski explains, "The peaks and valleys of historical time may appear in very different places, depending on who is looking and whose fortunes are being tracked across centuries" (2000, 2). Like other feminist scholars, she notes the ways in which women's time differs from men's time not naturally but culturally, from the masculine bias of conventional historical periodization to the distinct rhythms of women's work in the home. Where sexuality is concerned, there is again no universal time. The heteronormative time line of psychic development equates maturity with genital, reproductive sexuality, consigning homosexuals to infantilism and arrested development. Concurrently, in what Lee Edelman (2004) calls reproductive futurism, homosexuality comes to represent all that threatens to foreclose futurity by replacing temporal progress with an unproductive force of monstrous repetition.

If time itself changes over time, so too do its representations, not least in accounts of the past. The rise of historicist methodologies in American studies and cultural studies over the past quarter century has been challenged by poststructuralist and postmodern views of history. The latter approaches not only recognize time as heterogeneous; they also resist totalizing metanarratives, claims of "objective" mastery, and the very possibility of a stable, positivist historical knowledge. Instead, we find accounts of U.S. culture that acknowledge the contingency of "history" and underscore the plurality of past and present. One such account is Jonathan Goldberg's (1995) reading of the temporality invoked by Thomas Harriot's chronicle of Virginia and other colonial discourses in the Americas, which strangely combine recounting the past and predicting the future, the history that is yet to come.

There is a certain irony, therefore, in any effort to historicize time, for history is always a construction of yesterday in today's terms; its chronology can only be anachronistic because it is relational, the past of a particular present. In a well-known argument, Fredric Jameson describes this postmodern insight as a "crisis in historicity": if modernity means linear, continuous time, postmodernity is the loss of that temporality (1991, 71). Yet he does so in classically historical terms, accepting the Marxist model of linear, teleological time and presuming the knowable facticity of the past (Hutcheon 2002, 61). The paradox is hardly unique to Jameson. While the project of historicizing time seeks to address the contingency of any chronology, old ideas of time inevitably return within it, reasserting conventional periodization and familiar narratives of sequential change. Indeed, any effort to theorize temporality is marked by its particular era. When Walt Whitman declared in *Leaves of Grass* that "these are really the thoughts of all men in all ages and lands," his claim echoed nineteenth-century notions of universal, homogeneous time despite his effort to transcend his historical moment (1855/1965, 45). There is no place outside time from which we can observe time.

64

Youth

Sunaina Maira

The keyword "youth" bears a potent and overdetermined symbolism that has made it both central to cultural studies and significant, if relatively marginal, in American studies. Critical conversations about youth span anthropology, sociology, psychology, education, history, and geography and cross over into interdisciplinary areas such as cultural studies, American studies, feminist studies, queer studies, and ethnic studies. Across these fields, the word "youth" is used in myriad ways, generally as a signifier of a developmental stage, a transition to adulthood, or a moment of socialization into or rejection of social norms. A universalizing notion of youth as a period of development that everyone experiences coexists with a particularized understanding of youth as subjects-in-the-making who are always embedded in specific historical and social contexts. This tension underlies the significance of the keyword and its appearance and disappearance in scholarly and political debates.

The most common definition of "youth" in the United States is a transitional period or stage of development between childhood and adulthood. It is associated with a condition of liminality—an uneasy location between one social space or political status and another. Youth are not yet adults and not quite citizens, so they must be shepherded into proper adulthood and, as they acquire that status, the social order. As such, "youth" is a signifier that is fraught with meaning. Discussions of youth in the United States tend to be preoccupied with "youth in crisis" (or "youth at risk" of crisis), concerns that young people are particularly susceptible to behaviors and lifestyles deemed criminal, subversive, or radical (Giroux 1996). Media-induced panics about youth—the gang banger, the mass killer, or the "homegrown" terrorist—are generally linked to deeper anxieties about social, political, or economic transformation that are displaced onto young people. Immigrant and second-generation youth are viewed as being caught in a "clash of cultures," neither authentically ethnic nor sufficiently "American" (Maira 2002). A perceived crisis in culture or civilization thus gets projected onto a generational category viewed as being inherently unstable. Youth are perceived by adults as being in need of protection, even when those adults question the social control and surveillance of youth by technologies of classification, policing, and imprisonment. Across the political spectrum, "youth" names an appealing site for narrating particular cultural anxieties and for evading or erasing other social problems.

The cultural construction of youth as in crisis or at risk is embedded in the evolving debate about how, where, and when to study youth. Until the 1960s or 1970s, the word "adolescence" was used much more commonly than "youth" to describe the idea of a transition into adulthood when social identities and political allegiances are formed. In 1904, G. Stanley Hall, a U.S. psychologist and the founding president of the American Psychological Association, published the first study to propose adolescence as a unique period in individual development, laying the groundwork for the now familiar association of youth with a universal developmental trajectory leading to autonomy and individuality. This notion of adolescence as a passage into adulthood was tied to economic and social shifts in the United States that produced the "teenager" and, later, "youth" after World War II. In the 1950s, the emerging leisure industries began to target a marketing niche—"teenagers"—who had new levels of disposable income and were located between compulsory childhood education (ages five to sixteen) and the adult labor force (generally ages twenty and above), helping to consolidate this generational category. New social and material conditions, including extended educational demands, diminishing economic opportunities, and shifts in child bearing and rearing practices, led to a prolongation of adolescence and a deferral of adulthood.

Even as the understanding of adolescence as a universal developmental stage gained traction in mainstream social science and popular culture, more critical approaches stressed the cultural and historical specificity of the concept. The anthropologist Margaret Mead argued persuasively in her pioneering, if controversial, ethnography *Coming of Age in Samoa* (1928/1961) that the notion of adolescence as a period of "storm and stress" was a peculiarly Western and U.S. view. At a time when the nature/nurture debate was raging and cultural relativists were challenging racist theories of individual and group development, Mead suggested that adolescence was shaped by culturally distinct views of the relationship of the individual to community, gender, sexuality, and labor. Psychosocial theories, particularly those influenced by the work of Erik Erikson (1944/1968), similarly defined adolescence as a period of identity development and the crystallization of ethical and political beliefs, shaped by a culturally specific set of rituals.

This debate about adolescence as a cultural or ideological framework is ongoing in various disciplines. A significant critique of developmental theories of youth was offered by feminist psychologists, such as Carol Gilligan (1982), who focused on the crisis facing white, middle-class girls and argued for a gendered rethinking of U.S. adolescence. More recently, Nancy Lesko (2001) argues that adolescence was shaped by a dominant belief in a "civilizing" process for young individuals. She observes that the notion of adolescence emerged from an assumption that the teenage years were the proper age during which to instill in (white) boys a desire for "a particular national and international order," which was their responsibility to uphold (Lesko 2001, 41). The codification of adolescence and, later, youth in the United States has always been intertwined with fears about loss of racial privilege, male dominance, and national unity—the various cultural "crises" that "youth" embody. The compulsion to classify young people's behaviors highlights the ways in which the trope of "youth as transition"—like youth in crisis or at risk—serves as a justification for the surveillance, incarceration, and management of young bodies in modern state systems, through educational, social welfare, labor, military, and prison regimes (Mizen 2002).

The preoccupation with youthful transgression resonates with early twentieth-century research on "deviant" adolescents and young adults by sociologists at the University of Chicago. From the 1920s through the 1950s, ethnographers focused on issues of social status, collective problem solving, and urban subcultures. The "delinquent" behaviors of young people were understood as responses to problems of social (class or racial) status in urban environments (J. Young 1971). The Chicago school paved the way for cultural studies work on youth cultures at the University of Birmingham. These scholars focused on youth at a time of social transition in postwar Britain, drawing on Marxist analyses of culture and resistance by the Frankfurt school and theorists such as Antonio Gramsci to develop youth subculture theory. The Birmingham school's research diverged from earlier studies of adolescence by focusing on the resources that mass culture could provide youth in responding to shifts in labor and leisure patterns (McRobbie and Garber 1976; Willis 1977; Hebdige 1979). This work helped crystallize what could be described as a shift from social science research on "adolescence" to cultural studies scholarship on "youth," youth subcultures, and youth cultures.

Seminal texts, such as Stuart Hall and Tony Jefferson's *Resistance through Rituals: Youth Subcultures in Post-war Britain* (1976), signaled the ambivalent assessment of the politics of youth culture typical of the Birmingham school scholars and their interest in the concept of "resistance," particularly in relation to class. Their analyses suggested that the youth subcultures of the 1960s and '70s, such as mod or punk culture, provided symbolic resolutions to the dilemmas facing the urban working class but also that they were not structural solutions to the crisis of class. Youth had to be situated within the larger economic and social contradictions that these subcultural rituals were invented to address but that they were unable, ultimately, to transform. This subculture theory focused on the production of youth itself, through ethnographic research that interrogated the articulation of class with generation, nation, and gender. The Birmingham school's work has been very influential even as it has been critiqued for overinterpreting subcultural possibilities of "resistance" and focusing primarily on the spectacular cultural practices of white, working-class young men (Gelder and Thornton 1997).

British subcultural theory has informed subsequent work on youth in cultural studies and American studies, much of which has inherited the preoccupation with and ambivalence about youth and resistance. While some of this scholarship in the United States has focused on the representational aspects of youth culture, generally relying on textual rather than ethnographic analysis, there is a growing body of work that has grappled with the politics of gender, sexuality, class, and race in young people's everyday lives. Influential studies such as those by Penelope Eckert (1989) and Douglas Foley (1994) have interrogated the reproduction of social inequalities through schooling, while other research has investigated the contradictory political meanings and spatial dimensions of youth subcultures and of oppositionality (Kelley 1997; LaBennett 2011; T. Rose 1994; Austin and Willard 1998; Skelton and Valentine 1998). Work in cultural studies and American studies has built on the Birmingham school's legacy to explore the work of "youth" as an expression of political crises or cultural anxieties. Catherine Driscoll, for instance, suggests that girlhood and the notion of adolescence in general "defines the ideal coherence of the modern subject—individuality, agency, and adult (genital) sexuality" (2002, 53). Driscoll argues that "the role of adolescence . . . as psychosocial crucible for becoming a Subject" is embedded in late modernity and in the narrative of maturing nationalism (50).

The lingering association of youth with liminality and with subjects that are not quite formed means that there are key questions about nationalism, the state, and citizenship that remain unaddressed in relation to youth in American studies. At the same time, there seems to be an easy reaching for the notion of youth in studies of cultural production and consumption. Cultural studies has claimed youth as a key analytic category due to the association of young people with popular culture's—and now digital media's—possibilities and pitfalls, in the wake of theories developed by scholars of the Frankfurt, Chicago, and Birmingham schools. Youth signifies both the romance of resistance and the tragedy of consumerist conformity. As such, it names the ambiguity lying between these primary tropes in cultural studies. Recent work on "youthscapes" (Maira and Soep 2005) responds to this ambiguity by integrating an analysis of the material realities and social practices of young people with that of cultural representations of youth. This analysis moves beyond the romantic/tragic binary of resistance/conformity that is so often pinned onto youth. The framework of youthscapes situates youth in relation to debates about transnationalism, the nation-state, and empire. In doing so, it provides an epistemological and methodological intervention in interdisciplinary studies of youth, a category that is not bound to the nation-state and that travels across disciplinary borders.

The simultaneous invisibility and dramatic visibility of young people in both public debates and scholarly work is the key to the puzzle of the appearance and disappearance of the keyword "youth." The developmental narrative of youth as not-yet-adults underlies the assumption that young people are incomplete citizens or social actors. This assumption intensifies the deeper fantasies about and fears of social change or stasis embodied by the specter of youth. The traditional investment of cultural studies in the heuristic of resistance means that youth continue to appear as a site where battles over status quo forms of national culture are fought. Across American studies and cultural studies, the category of youth continues to be central to debates about the making of national subjects, but it should also be considered when discussing crucial questions of rights, belonging, and the remaking of the social order in a globalized world and at a late moment of U.S. empire.

Works Cited

Aaronson, Trevor. *The Terror Factory: Inside the FBI's Manufactured War on Terrorism*. Brooklyn, NY: Ig, 2013.

Abdel Malek, Anwar. "Orientalism en crise." *Diogenes* 44 (Winter 1963): 107–8.

Abdo, Genieve. *Mecca and Main Street: Muslim Life in America after 9/11*. New York: Oxford University Press, 2006.

Abel, Elizabeth, ed. *Female Subjects in Black and White: Race, Psychoanalysis, Feminism*. Berkeley: University of California Press, 1997.

Abrams, M. H. *Natural Supernaturalism: Tradition and Revolution in Romantic Literature*. New York: Norton, 1971.

Abu-Lughod, Lila. "Writing against Culture." *Recapturing Anthropology: Working in the Present*. Ed. Richard G. Fox. Santa Fe, NM: School of American Research Press, 1991. 137–62.

Adam, Barbara. *Time and Social Theory*. Philadelphia: Temple University Press, 1990.

Adamic, Louis. *From Many Lands*. New York: Harper, 1940.

———. *Nation of Nations*. New York: Harper, 1944.

Adams, Abigail. Letter to John Adams, March 31, 1776. *The Feminist Papers: From Adams to de Beauvoir*. Ed. Alice Rossi. Boston: Northeastern University Press, 1988. 10–11.

Adams, Rachel. *Sideshow U.S.A.: Freaks and the American Cultural Imagination*. Chicago: University of Chicago Press, 2001.

Adams, Rachel, Benjamin Reiss, and David Serlin. *Keywords for Disability Studies*. New York: NYU Press, forthcoming.

Adamson, Joni, William Gleason, and David N. Pellow. *Keywords for Environmental Studies*. New York: NYU Press, forthcoming.

Adorno, Theodor. *Aesthetic Theory*. 1970. Trans. C. Lenhardt. Ed. Gretel Adorno and Rolf Tiedemann. London: Routledge and Kegan Paul, 1984.

———. *The Culture Industry: Selected Essays on Mass Culture*. Ed. J. M. Bernstein. London and New York: Routledge, 2001.

———. "The Culture Industry Reconsidered." 1963. *The Culture Industry: Selected Essays on Mass Culture*. Ed. J. M. Bernstein. London and New York: Routledge, 2001. 98–106.

Afzal-Khan, Fawzia, and Kalpana Rahita Seshadri, eds. *The Preoccupation of Postcolonial Studies*. Durham: Duke University Press, 2000.

Agamben, Giorgio. *The Coming Community*. Trans. Michael Hardt. Minneapolis: University of Minnesota Press, 1993.

———. *State of Exception*. Trans. Kevin Attell. Chicago: University of Chicago Press, 2005.

Agarwal, Arun, and K. Sivaramakrisnan. *Regional Modernities: The Cultural Politics of Development in India*. Stanford: Stanford University Press, 2003.

Agnew, Jean-Christophe. *Worlds Apart: The Market and the Theater in Anglo-American Thought, 1550–1750*. New York: Cambridge University Press, 1986.

Ahmad, Aijaz. *In Theory: Classes, Nations, Literature*. London: Verso, 1992.

Ahmed, Sara. *Queer Phenomenology: Orientations, Objects, Others*. Durham: Duke University Press, 2006.

Alarcón, Norma. "Anzaldúa's *Frontera*: Inscribing Gynetics." *Displacement, Diaspora, and Geographies of Identity*. Ed. Smadar Lavie and Ted Sweedenburg. Durham: Duke University Press, 1996. 41–54.

"Alcatraz Reclaimed." *Newsletter of the Indian Tribes of All Nations*, January 1970. Reprinted in *Chronicles of American Indian Protest*. Ed. Council on Interracial Books for Children. Greenwich, CT: Fawcett, 1971.

Alcoff, Linda Martín. "Who's Afraid of Identity Politics?" *Reclaiming Identity: Realist Theory and the Predicament of Postmodernism*. Ed. Paula M. L. Moya and Michael Hames-García. Berkeley: University of California Press, 2000. 312–44.

Alemán, Jesse "The Other Country: Mexico, the United States, and the Gothic History of Conquest." *American Literary History* 18.3 (Fall 2006): 406–26.

Alexander, J. Robert. *The Right Opposition: The Lovestoneites and the International Communist Opposition of the 1930s*. Westport, CT: Greenwood, 1981.

Alexander, M. Jacqui. "Not Just Any Body Can Be a Citizen." *Feminist Review* 48 (1994): 5–23.

———. *Pedagogies of Crossings: Meditations on Feminism, Sexual Politics, Memory, and the Sacred*. Durham: Duke University Press, 2005.

———. "Redrafting Morality: The Postcolonial State and the Sexual Offences Bill of Trinidad and Tobago." *Third World Women and the Politics of Feminism*. Ed. Chandra Talpade Mohanty, Ann Russo, and Lourdes Torres. Bloomington: Indiana University Press, 1991. 133–52.

Alexander, M. Jacqui, and Chandra Talpade Mohanty, eds. *Feminist Genealogies, Colonial Legacies, Democratic Futures*. New York: Routledge, 1997.

Alexander, Michelle. *The New Jim Crow: Mass Incarceration in the Age of Colorblindness*. New York: New Press, 2010.

Allen, Chadwick. *Blood Narrative: Indigenous Identity in American Indian and Maori Literary and Activist Texts*. Durham: Duke University Press, 2002.

Allen, Francis. *The Decline of the Rehabilitative Ideal: Penal Policy and Social Purpose*. New Haven: Yale University Press, 1981.

Allen, Theodore. *The Invention of the White Race*. Vol. 1: *Racial Oppression and Social Control*. London: Verso, 1994.

Allen, Thomas M. *A Republic in Time: Temporality and Social Imagination in Nineteenth-Century America*. Chapel Hill: University of North Carolina Press, 2008.

Alsultany, Evelyn. *Arabs and Muslims in the Media: Race and Representation after 9/11*. New York: NYU Press, 2012.

Althusser, Louis. "Ideology and Ideological State Apparatuses." *Lenin and Philosophy and Other Essays*. 1971. New York: Monthly Review Press, 2001.

Alvarez, Robert R., Jr. *Mangos, Chiles, and Truckers: The Business of Transnationalism*. Minneapolis: University of Minnesota Press, 2005.

Amariglio, Jack, and Antonio Callari. "Marxian Value Theory and the Problem of the Subject: The Role of Commodity Fetishism." *Fetishism as Cultural Discourse*. Ed. Emily Apter and William Pietz. Ithaca: Cornell University Press, 1993. 186–216.

Ambrose, Stephen E. *Eisenhower, the President*. Vol. 2. New York: Simon and Schuster, 1984.

American Dream. Dir. Barbara Kopple. Prestige Films/HBO, 1990.

Amin, Samir. *Capitalism in the Age of Globalization: The Management of Contemporary Society*. London: Zed Books, 1997.

———. *Unequal Development: An Essay on the Social Formations of Peripheral Capitalism*. Trans. Brian Pearce. New York: Monthly Review Press, 1976.

Amory, Hugh, and David D. Hall. *The Colonial Book in the Atlantic World*. Cambridge: Cambridge University Press, 2000.

Amott, Teresa, and Julie Matthaei. *Race, Gender, and Work: A Multicultural Economic History of Women in the United States*. Rev. ed. Boston: South End, 1996.

Andersen, Margaret. "Whitewashing Race: A Critical Perspective on Whiteness." *White Out: The Continuing Significance of Racism*. Ed. Ashley Doane and Eduardo Bonilla-Silva. New York: Routledge, 2003. 21–34.

Anderson, Benedict. *Imagined Communities: Reflections on the Origin and Spread of Nationalism*. London: Verso, 1983.

———. *Imagined Communities: Reflections on the Origin and Spread of Nationalism*. Rev. ed. London: Verso, 1991.

Andrews, Lori B. *I Know Who You Are and I Saw What You Did: Social Networks and the Death of Privacy*. New York: Free Press, 2012.

Ang, Ien, and Nayantara Pothen. "Between Promise and Practice: Web 2.0, Intercultural Dialogue and Digital Scholarship." *Fibreculture Journal* 14 (2009). http://fourteen.fibreculturejournal.org/fcj-094-between-promise-and-practice-web-2-o-intercultural-dialogue-and-digital-scholarship/.

Anonymous. *Of Cyvile and Uncyvile Life: A Discourse Where Is Disputed What Order of Lyfe Best Beseemeth a Gentleman*. London, 1579, S.T.C. 15589.

Anthropy, Anna. *Rise of the Videogame Zinesters: How Freaks, Normals, Amateurs, Artists, Dreamers, Drop-Outs, Queers, Housewives, and People Like You Are Taking Back an Art Form*. New York: Seven Stories, 2012.

Anzaldúa, Gloria. *Borderlands / La Frontera: The New Mestiza*. San Francisco: Spinsters / Aunt Lute Books, 1987.

———. *Borderlands / La Frontera: The New Mestiza*. Rev. ed. New York: Aunt Lute Books, 1999.

———. "To(o) Queer the Writer—Loca, escritora y chicana." *Living Chicana Theory*. Ed. Carla Trujillo. Berkeley: University of California Press, 1998. 263–76.

Aparicio, Frances R. "Latino Cultural Studies." *Critical Latin American and Latino Studies*. Ed. Juan Poblete. Minneapolis: University of Minnesota Press, 2003. 3–31.

———. *Listening to Salsa: Gender, Latin Popular Music, and Puerto Rican Cultures*. Hanover, NH: University Press of New England, 1998.

Apess, William. "Eulogy on King Philip, as Pronounced at the Odeon, in Federal Street, Boston." 1836. *On Our Own Ground: The Complete Writings of William Apess, a Pequot*. Ed. Barry O'Connell. Amherst: University of Massachusetts Press, 1992. 275–310.

———. "The Experiences of Five Christian Indians" ["An Indian's Looking-Glass for the White Man"]. 1833. *On Our Own Ground: The Complete Writings of William Apess, a Pequot*. Ed. Barry O'Connell. Amherst: University of Massachusetts Press, 1992. 117–162.

Appadurai, Arjun. *Modernity at Large: Cultural Dimensions of Globalization*. Minneapolis: University of Minnesota Press, 1996.

Appleby, Joyce. *Liberalism and Republicanism in the Historical Imagination*. Cambridge: Harvard University Press, 1992.

Apuzzo, Matt, and Adam Goldman. *Enemies Within: Inside the NYPD's Secret Spying Unit and Bin Laden's Final Plot against America*. New York: Touchstone, 2013.

Armstrong, Elisabeth, and Vijay Prashad. "Solidarity: War Rites and Women's Rights." *CR: The Centennial Review* 5.1 (2005): 213–53.

Armstrong, Karen. *Islam: A Short History*. Rev. ed. New York: Modern Library, 2002.

Armstrong, Tim. *Modernism, Technology, and the Body: A Cultural Study*. Cambridge: Cambridge University Press, 1998.

Arnold, Matthew. *Culture and Anarchy*. 1869. Ed. Samuel Lipman. New Haven: Yale University Press, 1994.

———. "Literature and Science." 1882. *Discourses in America*. London: Macmillan, 1885. 72–137.

Aronowitz, Stanley. *False Promises: The Shaping of American Working Class Consciousness*. New York: McGraw-Hill, 1974.

Arrighi, Giovanni. *The Long Twentieth Century: Money, Power and the Origins of Our Times*. London: Verso, 1994.

———. "The Winding Paths of Capital: Interview by David Harvey." *New Left Review* 56 (March–April 2009): 61–94.

Asad, Talal. *Formations of the Secular: Christianity, Islam, Modernity*. Stanford: Stanford University Press, 2003.

———. *Genealogies of Religion: Discipline and Reasons of Power in Christianity and Islam*. Baltimore: Johns Hopkins University Press, 1993.

———. *On Suicide Bombing*. New York: Columbia University Press, 2007.

Asante, Molefi. *The Afrocentric Idea*. Philadelphia: Temple University Press, 1987.

Asch, Adrienne, and Michelle Fine, eds. *Women with Disabilities: Essays in Psychology, Culture, and Politics*. Philadelphia: Temple University Press, 1988.

Asch, Adrienne, and Erik Parens, eds. *Prenatal Testing and Disability Rights*. Washington, DC: Georgetown University Press, 2000.

Ashcroft, Bill, Gareth Griffiths, and Helen Tiffin. *The Empire Writes Back: Theory and Practice in Post-colonial Literatures*. London: Routledge, 1989.

Asher, R. E., and J. M. Y. Simpson, eds. *The Encyclopedia of Language and Linguistics*. 10 vols. New York: Pergamon, 1994.

Attali, Jacques. *Noise: The Political Economy of Music*. Minneapolis: University of Minnesota Press, 1985.

Aufderheidi, Patricia, and Peter Jaszi. *Reclaiming Fair Use: How to Put Balance Back in Copyright*. Chicago: University of Chicago Press, 2011.

Austin, J. L. *How to Do Things with Words*. Cambridge: Harvard University Press, 1962.

Austin, Joe, and Michael Willard, eds. *Generations of Youth: Youth Cultures and History in Twentieth-Century America*. New York: NYU Press, 1998.

Avrich, Paul. *The Haymarket Tragedy*. Princeton: Princeton University Press, 1984.

Babbage, Charles. *On the Economy of Machinery and Manufactures*. Philadelphia: Carey and Lea, 1832.

Bacevich, Andrew. *The New American Militarism: How Americans Are Seduced by War*. New York: Oxford University Press, 2006.

Bailey, Beth. *Sex in the Heartland*. Cambridge: Harvard University Press, 1999.

Bailey, Peter. "Breaking the Sound Barrier." *Hearing History: A Reader*. Ed. Mark M. Smith. Athens: University of Georgia Press, 2004. 23–35.

Baird, Karen L., ed. *Beyond Reproduction: Women's Health, Activism, and Public Policy*. Madison, NJ: Fairleigh Dickinson University Press, 2009.

Baird, Robert. "Late Secularism." *Social Text* 64 (2000): 123–36.

Baker, Houston, Jr. "Belief, Theory, and Blues: Notes for a Post-structuralist Criticism of Afro-American Literature." *Belief vs. Theory in Black American Literary Criticism*. Ed. Joe Weixlmann and Chester J. Fontenot. Greenwood, FL: Penkeville, 1986. 5–30.

———. "In Dubious Battle." *New Literary History* 18 (Winter 1987a): 363–69.

———. *Modernism and the Harlem Renaissance*. Chicago: University of Chicago Press, 1987b.

Baker, Houston, Jr., Manthia Diawara, and Ruth Lindeborg. *Black British Cultural Studies: A Reader*. Chicago: University of Chicago Press, 1996.

Baldwin, James. *The Price of the Ticket: Collected Nonfiction, 1948–85*. New York: St. Martins / Marek, 1985.

Balibar, Etienne. *Masses, Classes, Ideas: Studies on Politics and Philosophy before and after Marx*. New York: Routledge, 1994.

Balsamo, Anne. *Technologies of the Gendered Body: Reading Cyborg Women*. Durham: Duke University Press, 1996.

Bamberger, Bill, and Cathy N. Davidson. *Closing: The Life and Death of an American Factory*. New York: Norton, 1999.

Banta, Martha. *Imaging American Women: Idea and Ideals in Cultural History*. New York: Columbia University Press, 1987.

Baptist, Edward E. *Creating an Old South: Middle Florida's Plantation Frontier before the Civil War*. Chapel Hill: University of North Carolina Press, 2002.

Baraka, Amiri. *The LeRoi Jones / Amiri Baraka Reader*. New York: Basic Books, 1999.

Barlow, John Perry. "A Declaration of the Independence of Cyberspace." 1996. *Crypto Anarchy, Cyberstates, and Pirate Utopias*. Ed. Peter Ludlow. Cambridge: MIT Press, 2001. 27–30.

Barnes, Elizabeth. *States of Sympathy: Seduction and Democracy in the American Novel*. New York: Columbia University Press, 1997.

Barot, Rohit, and John Bird. "Racialization: The Genealogy and Critique of a Concept." *Ethnic and Racial Studies* 24.4 (July 2001): 601–18.

Barrett, Michèle, and Mary McIntosh. *The Anti-social Family*. London: Verso, 1982.

Bartelson, Jens. *The Critique of the State*. Cambridge: Cambridge University Press, 2001.

Barthes, Roland. "Rhetoric of the Image." *Image, Music, Text*. Ed. and trans. Stephen Heath. New York: Hill and Wang, 1977. 32–51.

Bartky, Ian R. *Selling the True Time: Nineteenth-Century Timekeeping in America*. Stanford: Stanford University Press, 2000.

Bassichis, Morgan, Alexander Lee, and Dean Spade. "Building an Abolitionist Trans and Queer Movement with Everything We've Got." *Captive Genders: Trans Embodiment and the Prison Industrial Complex*. Ed. Nat Smith and Eric Stanley. Oakland, CA: AK, 2011. 15–40.

Battiste, Marie. "Print Culture and Decolonizing the University: Indigenizing the Page: Part 1." *The Future of the Page*. Ed. Peter Stoicheff and Andrew Taylor. Toronto: University of Toronto Press, 2004. 111–23.

Baudrillard, Jean. *Simulacra and Simulation*. Trans. Sheila Faria Glaser. Ann Arbor: University of Michigan Press, 1994.

Baym, Nina. "Melodramas of Beset Manhood." *The New Feminist Criticism: Essays on Women, Literature, and Theory*. Ed. Elaine Showalter. New York: Pantheon, 1985. 63–80.

Baynton, Douglas. *Forbidden Signs: American Culture and the Campaign against Sign Language*. Chicago: University of Chicago Press, 1998.

Bayoumi, Moustafa. *How Does It Feel to Be a Problem? Being Young and Arab in America*. New York: Penguin, 2008.

Bebout, Lee. *Mythohistorical Interventions: The Chicano Movement and Its Legacies*. Minneapolis: University of Minnesota Press, 2011.

Beck, Scott H., and Kenneth, J. Mijeski. "Indigena Self-Identity in Ecuador and the Rejection of Mestizaje." *Latin American Research Review* 35.1 (2000): 119–37.

Becker, Carl. *The Heavenly City of the Eighteenth-Century Philosophers*. New Haven: Yale University Press, 1932.

Bederman, Gail. *Manliness and Civilization: A Cultural History of Gender and Race in the United States, 1880–1917*. Chicago: University of Chicago Press, 1995.

Beecher, Catherine. *A Treatise on Domestic Economy for the Use of Young Ladies at Home and at School*. Boston: Marsh, Capen, Lyon, and Webb, 1841.

Beecher, Catherine, and Harriet Beecher Stowe. *The American Woman's Home; or, Principles of Domestic Science*. New York: J. B. Ford, 1869.

Bell, Daniel. *The End of Ideology: On the Exhaustion of Political Ideas in the Fifties*. Glencoe, IL: Free Press, 1960.

Bellah, Robert. *Beyond Belief: Essays on Religion in a Post-traditional World*. Berkeley: University of California Press, 1970.

———. *The Broken Covenant: American Civil Religion in Time of Trial*. New York: Seabury, 1975.

Bellah, Robert, Richard Madsen, William M. Sullivan, Ann Swidler, and Steven M. Tipton. *Habits of the Heart: Individualism and Commitment in American Life.* New York: Harper and Row, 1985.

Beller, Jonathan. *The Cinematic Mode of Production: Attention Economy and the Society of the Spectacle.* Lebanon, NH: Dartmouth University Press, 2006.

Bellion, Wendy. *Citizen Spectator: Art, Illusion, and Visual Perception in Early National America.* Chapel Hill: University of North Carolina Press, 2011.

Bender, Thomas, ed. *The Antislavery Debate: Capitalism and Abolition as a Problem in Historical Interpretation.* Berkeley: University of California Press, 1992.

———. *Community and Social Change in America.* Baltimore: Johns Hopkins University Press, 1978.

Benedict, Ruth. *Patterns of Culture.* Boston: Houghton, 1934.

Ben-Hur. Dir. William Wyler. Metro-Goldwyn-Mayer, 1959.

Benjamin, Walter. *Illuminations: Essays and Reflections.* Ed. Hannah Arendt. Trans. Harry Zohn. New York: Schocken Books, 1968.

———. "Theses on the Philosophy of History." 1950. *Illuminations: Essays and Reflections.* Ed. Hannah Arendt. Trans. Harry Zohn. New York: Schocken Books, 1968. 253–66.

———. "The Work of Art in the Age of Mechanical Reproduction." 1936. *Illuminations: Essays and Reflections.* Ed. Hannah Arendt. Trans. Harry Zohn. New York: Schocken Books, 1968. 217–51.

Bennett, Jane. *Vibrant Matter: A Political Ecology of Things.* Durham: Duke University Press, 2010.

Bennett, Tony. *The Birth of the Museum: History, Theory, and Politics.* London: Routledge, 1995.

———. "Putting Policy into Cultural Studies." *Cultural Studies.* Ed. Cary Nelson, Paula Treichler, and Lawrence Grossberg. New York: Routledge, 1992. 23–37.

Bennett, Tony, Lawrence Grossberg, and Meaghan Morris, eds. *New Keywords: A Revised Vocabulary of Culture and Society.* Oxford, UK: Blackwell, 2005.

Ben-Sasson, Haim Hillel. "Galut." *Encyclopaedia Judaica.* Vol. 7. Ed. Cecil Roth and Geoffrey Wigoder. Jerusalem: Encyclopaedia Judaica, 1971. 275–94.

Bensel, Richard Franklin. *The Political Economy of American Industrialization, 1877–1900.* New York: Cambridge University Press, 2000.

Benston, Kimberly. *Performing Blackness: Enactments of African-American Modernism.* New York: Routledge, 2000.

Bentham, Jeremy. *Rationale of Judicial Evidence: Specially Applied to English Practice.* London: Hunt and Clarke, 1827.

Bercovitch, Sacvan. *The Rites of Assent: Transformations in the Symbolic Construction of America.* New York: Routledge, 1993.

Bercovitch, Sacvan, and Myra Jehlen, eds. *Ideology and Classic American Literature.* Cambridge: Cambridge University Press, 1986.

Berestein, Leslie. "Border Desert Nearing Grim Record." *San Diego Union-Tribune,* August 10, 2005: A3.

Berger, John. *Ways of Seeing.* London: British Broadcasting Corporation / Penguin, 1972.

Berger, Peter. "A Market Model for the Analysis of Ecumenicity." *Social Research* 30.1 (Spring 1963): 77–93.

———. *The Sacred Canopy.* Garden City, NY: Doubleday, 1969.

Berger, Peter, and Thomas Luckmann. *The Social Construction of Reality.* New York: Doubleday, 1966.

Bergman, Jill, and Debra Bernardi, eds. *Our Sisters' Keepers: Nineteenth-Century Benevolence Literature by American Women.* Tuscaloosa: University of Alabama Press, 2005.

Berlant, Lauren. *The Anatomy of National Fantasy: Hawthorne, Utopia, and Everyday Life.* Chicago: University of Chicago Press, 1991.

———, ed. *Compassion: The Culture and Politics of an Emotion.* New York: Routledge, 2004.

———. *Cruel Optimism.* Durham: Duke University Press, 2011.

———. *The Female Complaint: The Unfinished Business of Sentimentality in American Culture.* Durham: Duke University Press, 2008.

———. *The Queen of America Goes to Washington City: Essays on Sex and Citizenship.* Durham: Duke University Press, 1997.

———. "Uncle Sam Needs a Wife: Citizenship and Denegation." *Materializing Democracy: Toward a Revitalized Cultural Politics.* Ed. Dana D. Nelson and Russ Castronovo. Durham: Duke University Press, 2002. 144–74.

Berlant, Lauren, and Michael Warner. *Intimacy.* Chicago: University of Chicago Press, 2000.

———. "Sex in Public." *Critical Inquiry* 24.2 (Winter 1998): 547–66.

———. "What Does Queer Theory Teach Us about X?" *PMLA* 110.3 (1995): 343–49.

Berle, Adolf A., and Gardiner C. Means. *The Modern Corporation and Private Property.* New York: Macmillan, 1932.

Berlin, Ira. *Many Thousands Gone: The First Two Centuries of Slavery in North America.* Cambridge: Harvard University Press, 1998.

Berman, Jacob Rama. *American Arabesque: Arabs, Islam, and the 19th-Century Imaginary.* New York: NYU Press, 2012.

Bernal, Martin. "Greece: Aryan or Mediterranean? Two Contending Historiographical Models." *Enduring Western Civilization: The Constructions of the Concept of Western Civilization and Its "Others."* Ed. Silvia Federici. Westport, CT: Praeger, 1995. 3–11.

Bernardin, Susan. "The Authenticity Game: 'Getting Real' in Contemporary American Indian Literature." *True West: Authenticity and the American West.* Ed. William R. Handley and Nathaniel Lewis. Lincoln: University of Nebraska Press, 2007. 155–78.

Berthele, Raphael. "Translating African American Vernacular English into German: The Problem of 'Jim' in Mark Twain's *Huckleberry Finn.*" *Journal of Sociolinguistics* 4.4 (2000): 588–613.

Bettie, Julie. *Women without Class: Girls, Race, and Identity.* Berkeley: University of California Press, 2003.

Bhabha, Homi K. "DissemiNation: Time, Narrative, and the Margins of the Modern Nation." *Nation and Narration.* Ed. Homi K. Bhabha. New York: Routledge, 1990a. 291–322.

———. "Introduction: Narrating the Nation." *Nation and Narration.* Ed. Homi K. Bhabha. New York: Routledge, 1990b. 1–7.

———. *The Location of Culture.* New York: Routledge, 1994.

———. "The Other Question . . . Homi K. Bhabha Reconsiders the Stereotype and Colonial Discourse." *Screen* 24.6 (1983): 18–36.

Bhagwati, Jagdish. *Free Trade Today.* Princeton: Princeton University Press, 2003.

WORKS CITED

Bhargava, Rajeev, ed. *Secularism and Its Critics*. Delhi: Oxford University Press, 1998.

Bierce, Ambrose. *Devil's Dictionary*. New York: Albert and Charles Boni, 1911.

Bijsterveld, Karin. *Mechanical Sound: Technology, Culture, and Public Problems of Noise in the Twentieth Century*. Cambridge: MIT Press, 2008.

Bilefsky, Dan. "For New Life, Blacks in City Head South." *New York Times*, June 21, 2011.

Binkey, Sam. "Governmentality and Lifestyle Studies." *Sociology Compass* 1.1 (2007): 111–26.

Birkerts, Sven. *The Gutenberg Elegies: The Fate of Reading in an Electronic Age*. New York: Fawcett Columbine, 1994.

Black, Edwin. *War against the Weak: Eugenics and America's Campaign to Create a Master Race*. Berkeley, CA: Four Walls Eight Windows, 2003.

Blackburn, Robin. *The Overthrow of Colonial Slavery*. London: Verso, 1988.

Black Hawk. *Life of Black Hawk, or Ma-ka-tai-me-she-kia-kiak: Dictated by Himself*. 1833. New York: Penguin, 2008.

Blackmon, Douglas A. *Slavery by Another Name: The Re-enslavement of Black Americans from the Civil War to World War II*. New York: Doubleday, 2008.

Blackstone, William. *Commentaries on the Laws of England*. Vol. 1: *1765–69*. Chicago: University of Chicago Press, 1979.

Blackwell, Maylei. *Chicana Power! Contested Histories of Feminism in the Chicano Movement*. Austin: University of Texas Press, 2011.

Blanc, Louis. "The Organization of Labour." 1839. Available in part at http://www.fordham.edu/halsall/mod/1840blanc.asp.

Blight, David W., and Robert Gooding-Williams. "The Strange Meaning of Being Black: Du Bois's American Tragedy." Introduction to *The Souls of Black Folk*. By W. E. B. Du Bois. Ed. David W. Blight and Robert Gooding-Williams. New York: Bedford Books, 1997. 1–30.

Blue Collar. Dir. Paul Schrader. Universal Pictures, 1978.

Blumenberg, Hans. *The Legitimacy of the Modern Age*. Trans. Robert M. Wallace. Cambridge: MIT Press, 1983.

Blumin, Stuart M. *The Emergence of the Middle Class: Social Experience in the American City, 1760–1900*. New York: Cambridge University Press, 1989.

Blyden, Edward W. *Christianity, Islam and the Negro Race*. 1887. Edinburgh: Edinburgh University Press, 1967.

Boas, Franz. *Anthropology and Modern Life*. New York: Norton, 1928.

———. *The Mind of Primitive Man*. New York: Macmillan, 1911.

———. *Race, Language, and Culture*. New York: Macmillan, 1940.

Bogdan, Robert. *Freak Show: Presenting Human Oddities for Amusement and Profit*. Chicago: University of Chicago Press, 1988.

Bogost, Ian. *Persuasive Games: The Expressive Power of Videogames*. Cambridge: MIT Press, 2007.

Bogues, Anthony. *Black Heretics, Black Prophets: Radical Political Intellectuals*. New York: Routledge, 2003.

Boime, Albert. *The Magisterial Gaze: Manifest Destiny and the American Landscape Painting, c. 1830–1865*. Washington, DC: Smithsonian Institution Press, 1991.

Bolton, Herbert Eugene. *The Spanish Borderlands: A Chronicle of Old Florida and the Southwest*. New Haven: Yale University Press, 1921.

Bonczar, Thomas P. *Prevalence of Imprisonment in the US Population, 1974–2001*. NCJ197976 . Washington, DC: U.S. Department of Justice, Bureau of Justice Statistics, 2003.

Bonilla-Silva, Eduardo. *Racism without Racists*. Lanham, MD: Rowman and Littlefield, 2003.

Bonus, Rick. *Locating Filipino Americans: Ethnicity and Cultural Politics of Space*. Philadelphia: Temple University Press, 2000.

Boon, Marcus. *In Praise of Copying*. Cambridge: Harvard University Press, 2010.

Boris, Eileen. "Beyond Dichotomy: Recent Books in North American Women's Labor History." *Journal of Women's History* 4.3 (1993): 162–79.

Bornstein, Kate. *Gender Outlaw: On Men, Women, and the Rest of Us*. New York: Routledge, 1994.

Bosniak, Linda. "The Citizenship of Aliens." *Social Text* 56 (1998): 29–35.

Boston Women's Health Book Collective. *Our Bodies, Ourselves*. New York: Simon and Schuster, 1973.

———. *Our Bodies, Ourselves*. Rev. and exp. ed. New York: Simon and Schuster, 1976.

———. *The New Our Bodies, Ourselves*. New York: Simon and Schuster, 1996.

Bourdieu, Pierre. "Cultural Reproduction and Social Reproduction." *Knowledge, Education, and Cultural Change: Papers in the Sociology of Education*. Ed. Richard K. Brown. London: Tavistock, 1973. 71–84.

———. *Distinction: A Social Critique of the Judgment of Taste*. Cambridge: Harvard University Press, 1987.

Bourne, Randolph. "Trans-national America." *Atlantic Monthly* 118 (July 1916): 86–97.

Bousquet, Marc. *How the University Works: Higher Education and the Low-Wage Nation*. New York: NYU Press, 2008.

———. "Take Your Ritalin and Shut Up." *South Atlantic Quarterly* 1084 (2009): 623–49.

Bowker, Geoffrey C., and Susan Leigh Star. *Sorting Things Out: Classification and Its Consequences*. Cambridge: MIT Press, 1999.

Bowlby, Rachel. "Domestication." *Feminism beside Itself*. Ed. Diane Elam and Robyn Wiegman. New York: Routledge, 1995. 71–92.

Boyarin, Jonathan, and Daniel Boyarin. *Powers of Diaspora: Two Essays on the Relevance of Jewish Culture*. Minneapolis: University of Minnesota Press, 2002.

Boyce Davies, Carole, and Babacar M'Bow. "Towards African Diaspora Citizenship: Politicizing an Existing Global Geography." *Black Geographies and the Politics of Place*. Ed. Katherine McKittrick and Clyde Woods. Boston: South End, 2007. 14–45.

Boydston, Jeanne. *Home and Work: Housework, Wages, and the Ideology of Labor in the Early Republic*. New York: Oxford University Press, 1990.

Boyle, James. *The Public Domain: Enclosing the Commons of the Mind*. New Haven: Yale University Press, 2010.

Brady, Erika. *A Spiral Way: How the Phonograph Changed Ethnography*. Jackson: University Press of Mississippi, 2009.

Brady, Mary Pat. *Extinct Lands, Temporal Geographies: Chicana Literature and the Urgency of Space*. Durham: Duke University Press, 2002.

———. "The Fungibility of Borders." *Nepantla: Views from South* 1.1 (2000): 171–90.

Bramen, Carrie Tirado. *The Uses of Variety: Modern Americanism and the Quest for National Distinctiveness*. Cambridge: Harvard University Press, 2001.

Branham, Robert J. "'Of Thee I Sing': Contesting 'America.'" *American Quarterly* 48.4 (December 1996): 623–52.

Bratich, Jack Z., Jeremy Packer, and Cameron McCarthy, eds. *Foucault, Cultural Studies, and Governmentality*. Albany: SUNY Press, 2003.

Braudel, Fernand. *Civilization and Capitalism*. 1981–84. 3 vols. Trans. Siân Reynold. New York: Harper and Row, 1992.

Braverman, Harry. *Labor and Monopoly Capital: The Degradation of Work in the Twentieth Century*. 1974. New York: Monthly Review Press, 1998.

Brennan, Denise. *What's Love Got to Do with It? Transnational Desires and Sex Tourism in the Dominican Republic*. Durham: Duke University Press, 2004.

Brenner, Neil. *New State Spaces: Urban Governance and the Rescaling of Statehood*. New York: Oxford University Press, 2004.

Brenner, Robert. *The Boom and the Bubble: The U.S. in the World Economy*. London: Verso, 2003.

Bridges, Khiara M. *Reproducing Race: An Ethnography of Pregnancy as a Site of Racialization*. Berkeley: University of California Press, 2011.

Briffault, Richard. "Super PACS." Columbia Public Law Research Paper WP 12-298. April 16, 2012.

Briggs, Laura. "The Race of Hysteria: 'Overcivilization' and the 'Savage' Woman in Late Nineteenth-Century Obstetrics and Gynecology." *American Quarterly* 52.2 (June 2000): 246–73.

Brisbane, Albert. "The American Associationists." *United States Magazine, and Democratic Review*, February 1846, 142.

Brodhead, Richard. *Cultures of Letters: Scenes of Reading and Writing in Nineteenth-Century America*. Chicago: University of Chicago Press, 1993.

Brodkin, Karen. *How Jews Became White Folks and What That Says about America*. New Brunswick: Rutgers University Press, 1998.

Broome, Richard. *Aboriginal Australians: A History since 1788*. 4th rev. ed. New York: Allen and Unwin, 2010.

Brown, Dona. *Inventing New England: Regional Tourism in the Nineteenth Century*. Washington, DC: Smithsonian Institution Press, 1995.

Brown, Gillian. *The Consent of the Governed: The Lockean Legacy in Early American Culture*. Cambridge: Harvard University Press, 2001.

———. *Domestic Individualism: Imagining Self in Nineteenth-Century America*. Berkeley: University of California Press, 1990.

Brown, Joshua. *Beyond the Lines: Pictorial Reporting, Everyday Life, and the Crisis of Gilded Age America*. Berkeley: University of California Press, 2002.

Brown, Kathleen M. *Good Wives, Nasty Wenches, and Anxious Patriarchs: Gender, Race, and Power in Colonial Virginia*. Chapel Hill: University of North Carolina Press, 1996.

Brown, Michelle. *The Culture of Punishment: Prison, Society, and Spectacle*. New York: NYU Press, 2009.

———. "'Setting the Conditions' for Abu Ghraib: The Prison Nation Abroad." *American Quarterly* 57.3 (September 2005): 973–94.

Brown, Wendy. *Edgework: Critical Essays on Knowledge and Politics*. Princeton: Princeton University Press, 2005.

———. "Neo-liberalism and the End of Liberal Democracy." *Theory and Event* 7.1 (2003): 1–43.

———. *States of Injury: Power and Freedom in Late Modernity*. Princeton: Princeton University Press, 1995.

Brown, William Hill. *The Power of Sympathy*. 1789. "*The Power of Sympathy*" and "*The Coquette*". New York: Penguin, 1996.

Brown, William Wells. "Lecture." 1847. *Four Fugitive Slave Narratives*. Reading, MA: Addison-Wesley, 1969. 81–98.

Browne, Simone. "Digital Epidermalization: Race, Identity and Biometrics." *Critical Sociology* 36 (January 2010): 131–50.

Bruce, Steve, and David Voas. "The Resilience of the Nation-State: Religion and Polities in the Modern Era." *Sociology* 38.5 (2004): 1025–34.

Bruce-Novoa, Juan. "Twenty Years of Transatlantic Usonianism." *The United States in Global Contexts: American Studies after 9/11 and Iraq*. Ed. Walter Grünzweig. Münster, Germany: LIT, 2004. 23.

Brueggemann, Brenda. *Deaf Subjects: Between Identities and Places*. New York: NYU Press, 2009.

Bruyneel, Kevin. *The Third Space of Sovereignty: The Postcolonial Politics of U.S.-Indigenous Relations*. Minneapolis: University of Minnesota Press, 2007.

Bryan, Dick, and Mike Rafferty. *Capitalism with Derivatives: A Political Economy of Financial Derivatives, Capital and Class*. Basingstoke, UK: Palgrave Macmillan, 2006.

Buck-Morss, Susan. "Aesthetics and Anaesthetics: Walter Benjamin's Artwork Essay Reconsidered." *October* 62 (1992): 3–41.

Buell, Lawrence. *The Environmental Imagination: Thoreau, Nature Writing, and the Formation of American Culture*. Cambridge: Harvard University Press, 1995.

Buff, Rachel Ida, ed. *Immigrant Rights in the Shadow of Citizenship*. New York: NYU Press, 2008.

Buffon, Georges-Louis Leclerc, Count de. *L'histoire naturelle, générale et particulière, avec la description du cabinet du roi*. 36 vols. Paris: L'Imprimerie Royale, 1749–89.

Buhle, Paul. *Marxism in the United States: Remapping the History of the American Left*. London: Verso, 1987.

Bullard, Robert D. "Confronting Environmental Racism in the Twenty-First Century." *The Colors of Nature: Culture, Identity, and the Natural World*. Ed. Alison H. Deming and Lauret E. Savoy. Minneapolis: Milkweed, 2002. 90–97.

Bumiller, Elisabeth. "After Cheney's Private Hunt, Others Take Their Shots." *New York Times*, December 15, 2003. http://www.nytimes.com/2003/12/15/politics/15LETT.html?smid=pl-share.

———. "Bush, Calling U.S. 'a Nation Guided by Faith,' Urges Freedom of Worship in China." *New York Times*, February 22, 2002. http://www.nytimes.com/2002/02/22/world/bush-calling-us-a-nation-guided-by-faith-urges-freedom-of-worship-in-china.html.

Burch, Susan. *Signs of Resistance: American Deaf Cultural History, 1900 to World War II*. New York: NYU Press, 2004.

Bureau of Indian Affairs. "What We Do." http://www.bia.gov/WhatWeDo/index.htm (accessed August 16, 2012).

Burgett, Bruce. "On the Mormon Question: Race, Sex, and Polygamy in the 1850s and the 1990s." *American Quarterly* 57.1 (March 2005): 75–102.

———. *Sentimental Bodies: Sex, Gender, and Citizenship in the Early Republic*. Princeton: Princeton University Press, 1998.

Burke, Edmund. *Reflections on the Revolution in France*. 1790. Oxford: Oxford University Press, 2009.

Burke, Kenneth. *The Philosophy of Literary Form*. New York: Vintage, 1957.

Burns, W. Haywood. "Law and Race in Early America." *The Politics of Law: A Progressive Critique*. Ed. David Kairys. New York: Basic Books, 1982. 279–84.

Burton, Richard Francis. *A Mission to Gelele, King of Dahome*. Vol. 2. London: Tinsley Brothers, 1864.

Bush, George W. "An Address to a Joint Session of Congress and the American People." September 20, 2001a. White House archives. http://georgewbush-whitehouse.archives.gov/news/releases/2001/09/20010920-8.html.

———. "President George W. Bush's Inaugural Address." January 21, 2001b. White House archives. http://georgewbush-whitehouse.archives.gov/news/inaugural-address.html.

———. "Remarks by the President on Goree Island, Senegal." July 8, 2003. White House archives. http://georgewbush-whitehouse.archives.gov/news/releases/2003/07/20030708-1.html.

Bushman, Richard L. *The Refinement of America: Persons, Houses, Cities*. New York: Vintage, 1992.

Butler, Judith. *Antigone's Claim*. New York: Columbia University Press, 2000.

———. *Bodies That Matter: On the Discursive Limits of "Sex."* New York: Routledge, 1993.

———. *Gender Trouble: Feminism and the Subversion of Identity*. New York: Routledge, 1990.

———. *Precarious Life: The Powers of Mourning and Violence*. London: Verso, 2004a.

———. *Undoing Gender*. New York: Routledge, 2004b.

Butler, Kim. "Defining Diaspora, Refining a Discourse." *Diaspora* 10.2 (2001): 189–219.

Byrd, Jodi A. *The Transit of Empire: Indigenous Critiques of Colonialism*. Minneapolis: University of Minnesota Press, 2011.

Cacho, Lisa M. *Social Death: Racialized Rightlessness and the Criminalization of the Unprotected*. New York: NYU Press, 2012.

Cainkar, Louise. "American Muslims at the Dawn of the 21st Century." *Muslims in the West after 9/11: Religion, Politics and Law*. Ed. Jocelyne Cesari. New York: Routledge, 2010. 176–97.

Callon, Michel. *The Laws of the Markets*. Oxford, UK: Blackwell, 1998.

Cameron, Sharon. *Choosing Not Choosing: Dickinson's Fascicles*. Chicago: University of Chicago Press, 1992.

Camp, Stephanie. *Closer to Freedom: Enslaved Women and Everyday Resistance in the Plantation South*. Chapel Hill: University of North Carolina Press, 2003.

Campbell, James. *Songs of Zion: The African Methodist Episcopal Church in the United States and South Africa*. Chapel Hill: University of North Carolina Press, 1995.

Campbell, Neil. *The Cultures of the American New West*. London: Fitzroy, 2000.

———. "Post-Westerns." *A Companion to the Literature and Culture of the American West*. Ed. Nicolas Witschi. London: Blackwell, 2011. 409–25.

———. *The Rhizomatic West: Representing the West in a Transnational, Global, Media Age*. Lincoln: University of Nebraska Press, 2008.

Canguilhem, Georges. *The Normal and the Pathological*. 1966. Trans. Carolyn R. Fawcett. New York: Zone Books, 1989.

Carby, Hazel. *Reconstructing Womanhood: The Emergence of the Afro-American Woman Novelist*. New York: Oxford University Press, 1987.

Cárdenas, Micha. *The Transreal: Political Aesthetics of Crossing Realities*. New York: Atropos, 2012.

Carey, Henry Charles. *The Past, the Present, and the Future*. New York: Augustus M. Kelley, 1967.

Carlson, Elof Axel. *The Unfit: A History of a Bad Idea*. Cold Spring Harbor, NY: Cold Spring Harbor Laboratory Press, 2001.

Carlyle, Thomas. *The History of Friedrich II of Prussia, Called Frederick the Great*. Vol. 1. London: Chapman and Hall, 1858.

Carmichael, Stokely, and Charles Hamilton. *Black Power: The Politics of Liberation in America*. New York: Vintage, 1967.

Carr-Ruffino, Norma. *Managing Diversity: People Skills for a Multicultural Workplace*. Upper Saddle River, NJ: Pearson, 1996.

Carter, Dan T. *The Politics of Rage: George Wallace, the Origins of the New Conservatism, and the Transformation of American Politics*. 1995. 2nd ed. Baton Rouge: Louisiana State University Press, 2000.

Carter, Julian B. *The Heart of Whiteness: Normal Sexuality and Race in America, 1880–1940*. Durham: Duke University Press, 2007.

Carter, Prudence. *Keepin' It Real: School Success beyond Black and White*. New York: Oxford University Press, 2005.

Casaubon, Isaac. *The Ansvvere of Master Isaac Casaubon to the Epistle of the Most Reuerend Cardinall Peron: Translated out of Latin into English*. London: Felix Kyngston, 1612.

Castells, Manuel. *The Rise of Network Society*. Oxford, UK: Blackwell, 2000.

Castiglia, Christopher. *Interior States: Institutional Consciousness and the Inner Life of Democracy in the Antebellum United States*. Durham: Duke University Press, 2008.

Castoriadis, Cornelius. "The Social Imaginary and the Institution." *The Castoriadis Reader*. Ed. David Ames Curtis. Oxford, UK: Blackwell, 1987. 196–217.

Castronovo, Russ. *Beautiful Democracy: Aesthetics and Anarchy in a Global Era*. Chicago: University of Chicago Press, 2007.

Caves, Richard E. *Creative Industries: Contracts between Arts and Commerce*. Cambridge: Harvard University Press, 2000.

Cavicchi, Daniel. *Listening and Longing: Music Lovers in the Age of Barnum*. Lebanon, NH: University Press of New England, 2011.

Centre for Contemporary Cultural Studies. *The Empire Strikes Back: Race and Racism in 70s Britain*. London: Taylor and Francis, 1982.

Chakrabarty, Dipesh. *Provincializing Europe: Postcolonial Thought and Historical Difference*. Princeton: Princeton University Press, 2000.

Chamfort, Sébastien-Roch-Nicolas. *Products of the Perfected Civilization*. Trans. W. S. Merwin. San Francisco: North Point, 1984.

Chan, Jeffrey Paul, and Frank Chin. "Racist Love." *Seeing through Schuck*. Ed. Richard Kostelanetz. New York: Ballantine, 1972. 65–79.

Chandra, Bipan. "Colonialism, Stages of Colonialism, and the Colonial State." *Journal of Contemporary South Asia* 10.3 (1980): 272–85.

Chang, Edmond Y. "Gaming as Writing, or, World of Warcraft as World of Wordcraft." *Computers and Composition Online*, August–September 2008. http://www2.bgsu.edu/departments/english/cconline/gaming_issue_2008/Chang_Gaming_as_writing/index.html.

Chang, Grace. *Disposable Domestics: Immigrant Women Workers in the Global Economy*. Boston: South End, 2000.

Chapman, Mary, and Glenn Hendler, eds. *Sentimental Men: Masculinity and the Politics of Affect in American Culture*. Berkeley: University of California Press, 1999.

Chappell, David. *A Stone of Hope: Prophetic Religion and the Death of Jim Crow*. Chapel Hill: University of North Carolina Press, 2004.

Charles, Ray. "America the Beautiful." *A Message from the People . . . by the People . . . and for the People*. Los Angeles: Tangerine Records, 1972.

Chase, Richard. *Quest for Myth*. Baton Rouge: Louisiana State University Press, 1949.

Chauncey, George. *Gay New York: Gender, Urban Culture, and the Making of the Gay Male World, 1890–1940*. New York: Basic Books, 1994.

Chavez, Leo R. *The Latino Threat: Constructing Immigrants, Citizens, and the Nation*. Stanford: Stanford University Press, 2008.

———. "Settlers and Sojourners: The Case of Mexicans in the United States." *Human Organization* 47.2 (1988): 95–108.

Chevigny, Bell Gale, and Gari Laguardia. Preface to *Reinventing the Americas: Comparative Studies of Literature of the United States and Spanish America*. Ed. Bell Gale Chevigny and Gari Laguardia. New York: Cambridge University Press, 1986. vii–xiv.

Chidester, David. *Savage Systems: Colonialism and Comparative Religion in Southern Africa*. Charlottesville: University of Virginia Press, 1996.

China Blue. Dir. Micha Peled. Teddy Bear Films, 2005.

Chomsky, Noam. "The Non-Election of 2004." *Z Magazine*, January 2005: 31–35.

Chomsky, Noam, and Edward S. Herman. *The Washington Connection and Third World Fascism*. Boston: South End, 1979.

Chomsky, Noam, and Robert W. McChesney. *Profit over People: Neoliberalism and Global Order*. New York: Seven Stories, 2011.

Christian, Barbara. "The Race for Theory." *Cultural Critique* 6 (1987): 51–63.

Christiansen, John, and Sharon Barnartt. *Deaf President Now! The 1988 Revolution at Gallaudet University*. Washington, DC: Gallaudet University Press, 2002.

Chuh, Kandice. *Imagine Otherwise: On Asian Americanist Critique*. Durham: Duke University Press, 2003.

Chun, Wendy Hui Kyong. *Control and Freedom: Power and Paranoia in the Age of Fiber Optics*. Cambridge: MIT Press, 2006.

———. *Programmed Visions: Software and Memory*. Cambridge: MIT Press, 2011.

Churchill, Ward, and John Vander Wall. *The COINTELPRO Papers: Documents from the FBI's Secret Wars against Dissent in the United States*. 1990. Boston: South End, 2001.

Clare, Eli. *Exile and Pride: Disability, Queerness, and Liberation*. Boston: South End, 1999.

Clarke, Cheryl. "The Failure to Transform: Homophobia in the Black Community." *Home Girls: A Black Feminist Anthology*. Ed. Barbara Smith. New York: Kitchen Table / Women of Color, 1983. 197–208.

Clarke, John. "After Neo-liberalism." *Cultural Studies* 24.3 (2010): 375–94.

Cleaver, Eldridge. *Soul on Ice*. New York: Laurel, 1968.

Clifford, James. "Indigenous Articulations." *Contemporary Pacific* 13.2 (2001): 468–90.

———. *Routes: Travel and Translation in the Late Twentieth Century*. Cambridge: Harvard University Press, 1997.

———. "Taking Identity Politics Seriously: 'The Contradictory, Stony Ground . . .'" *Without Guarantees: In Honour of Stuart Hall*. Ed. Paul Gilroy, Lawrence Grossberg, and Angela McRobbie. New York: Verso, 2000. 94–112.

Clifford, James, and George Marcus, eds. *Writing Culture: The Poetics and Politics of Ethnography*. Berkeley: University of California Press, 1986.

Clough, Patricia, and Jean Halley, eds. *The Affective Turn: Theorizing the Social*. Durham: Duke University Press, 2007.

Cohen, Cathy J. "Punks, Bulldaggers, and Welfare Queens: The Radical Potential of Queer Politics?" *GLQ* 3 (1997): 437–65.

Cohen, Deborah. *Braceros: Migrant Citizens and Transnational Subjects in the Postwar United States and Mexico*. Chapel Hill: University of North Carolina Press, 2011.

Cohen, Jean L. *Regulating Intimacy: A New Legal Paradigm*. Princeton: Princeton University Press, 2002.

Cohen, Jean L., and Andrew Arato. *Civil Society and Political Theory*. Cambridge: MIT Press, 1992.

Cohen, Jonathan. "The Naming of America: Fragments We've Shored against Ourselves." Jonathan Cohen's website, 2004. http://www.uhmc.sunysb.edu/surgery/america.html.

Cohen, Lizabeth. *A Consumer's Republic: The Politics of Mass Consumption in Postwar America*. New York: Knopf, 2003.

Cohen, Matt. *The Networked Wilderness: Communicating in Early New England*. Minneapolis: University of Minnesota Press, 2009.

Cohen, Patricia Cline. *A Calculating People: The Spread of Numeracy in Early America*. Chicago: University of Chicago Press, 1982.

Cohn, Deborah N. *History and Memory in the Two Souths: Recent Southern and Spanish American Fiction*. Nashville: Vanderbilt University Press, 1999.

Coiner, Constance. *Better Red: The Writing and Resistance of Tillie Olsen and Meridel Le Sueur*. Urbana: University of Illinois Press, 1995.

Collingwood, R. G. *The New Leviathan*. New York: Crowell, 1971.

Collins, Jane L., Micaela di Leonardo, and Brett Williams, eds. *New Landscapes of Inequality: Neoliberalism and the Erosion* of Democracy in America. Santa Fe, NM: School of Advanced Research Press, 2008.

Collins, John. "Terrorism." *Collateral Language: A User's Guide to America's New War.* Ed. John Collins and Ross Glover. New York: NYU Press, 2002. 155–74.

Combahee River Collective. "The Combahee River Collective Statement." *Home Girls: A Black Feminist Anthology.* Ed. Barbara Smith. New York: Kitchen Table / Women of Color, 1983. 264–74.

Comer, Krista. "Exceptionalisms, Other Wests, Critical Regionalism." *American Literary History* 23.1 (2010): 159–73.

———. "Introduction: Assessing the Postwestern." *Western American Literature* 48.1–2 (Spring–Summer 2013): 3–15.

———. *Landscapes of the New West: Gender and Geography in Contemporary Women's Writing.* Chapel Hill: University of North Carolina Press, 1999.

Commager, Henry Steele, ed. *America in Perspective: The United States through Foreign Eyes.* New York: Random House, 1947.

Comte, August. *The Positive Philosophy of August Comte.* Trans. Harriet Martineau. London: Chapman, 1858.

Condorcet, Jean-Antoine-Nicolas de Caritat de. *Esquisse d'un tableau historique des progrès de l'esprit humain.* Paris: Chez Agasse, 1795.

Cong-Huyen, Anne. "'Dark Mass,' or the Problems with Creative Cloud Labor." *E-Media Studies* 3.1 (2013). http://journals. dartmouth.edu/cgi-bin/WebObjects/Journals.woa/1/ xmlpage/4/article/427.

Conley, Dalton. *Being Black, Living in the Red: Race, Wealth, and Social Policy in America.* Berkeley: University of California Press, 1999.

Connolly, William. *Why I Am Not a Secularist.* Minneapolis: University of Minnesota Press, 2000.

Cook-Lynn, Elizabeth. *Why I Can't Read Wallace Stegner and Other Essays: A Tribal Voice.* Madison: University of Wisconsin Press, 1996.

Coombe, Rosemary. *The Cultural Life of Intellectual Properties: Authorship, Appropriation, and the Law.* Cambridge: Harvard University Press, 1998.

Coontz, Stephanie. *The Social Origins of Private Life: A History of American Families, 1600–1900.* New York: Verso, 1988.

———. *The Way We Never Were: American Families and the Nostalgia Trap.* New York: Basic Books, 1992.

———. *The Way We Really Are: Coming to Terms with America's Changing Families.* New York: Basic Books, 1998.

Corker, Mairian. "Sensing Disability." *Hypatia* 16.4 (2001): 34–52.

Costa, Robert. "Gingrich: Obama's 'Kenyan, Anti-colonial' Worldview." *National Review Online,* September 11, 2010. http://www.nationalreview.com/corner/246302/gingrich-obama-s-kenyan-anti-colonial-worldview-robert-costa.

Cott, Nancy. *Public Vows: A History of Marriage and the Nation.* Cambridge: Harvard University Press, 2000.

Crary, Jonathan. *Techniques of the Observer: On Vision and Modernity in the Nineteenth Century.* Cambridge: MIT Press, 1992.

Creed, Gerald, ed. *The Seductions of Community.* Santa Fe, NM: SAR Press, 2006.

Crenshaw, Kimberlé W. "A Black Feminist Critique of Antidiscrimination Law and Politics." *The Politics of Law: A Progressive Critique.* Ed. David Kairys. New York: Basic Books, 1990. 356–80.

———. "Mapping the Margins: Intersectionality, Identity Politics, and Violence against Women of Color." *Critical Race Theory: The Key Writings That Formed the Movement.* Ed. Kimberlé Crenshaw, Neil Gotanda, Gary Peller, and Kendall Thomas. New York: New Press, 1995. 357–83.

Crèvecoeur, J. Hector St. John de. *Letters from an American Farmer.* 1782. *"Letters from an American Farmer" and "Sketches of Eighteenth-Century America."* New York: Penguin, 1981. 35–230.

Crimp, Douglas. *Melancholia and Moralism: Essays on AIDS and Queer Politics.* Cambridge: MIT Press, 2002.

Critical Resistance and INCITE! Women of Color Against Violence. "Gender Violence and the Prison-Industrial Complex." *Color of Violence: The INCITE! Anthology.* Ed. INCITE! Women of Color Against Violence. Boston: South End. 2006. 223–26.

Cronin, Ann. *Advertising and Consumer Citizenship: Gender, Images, and Rights.* London: Routledge, 2000.

Cronon, William. "The Trouble with Wilderness; or, Getting Back to the Wrong Nature." *Uncommon Ground: Toward Reinventing Nature.* Ed. William Cronon. New York: Norton, 1995. 69–90.

Crozier, Michael, Samuel Huntington, and Joji Watanuki. *The Crisis of Democracy: Report on the Governability of Democracies to the Trilateral Commission.* New York: NYU Press, 1975.

Cruikshank, Barbara. "The Will to Empower: Technologies of Citizenship and the War on Poverty." *Socialist Review* 23.4 (1994): 29–55.

"Cultural Heritage Toolkit." Vermont Arts Council. http://www.vermontartscouncil.org/Community/ CulturalHeritageTourism/tabid/75/Default.aspx (accessed February 16, 2012).

Cumings, Bruce. *Korea's Place in the Sun: A Modern History.* New York: Norton, 2005.

Cummins, Maria Susanna. *The Lamplighter.* 1854. New Brunswick: Rutgers University Press, 1988.

Curtis, Edward E., IV. *Muslims in America: A Short History.* New York: Oxford University Press, 2009.

Cvetkovich, Ann. *An Archive of Feelings: Trauma, Sexuality, and Lesbian Public Cultures.* Durham: Duke University Press, 2003.

———. *Mixed Feelings: Feminism, Mass Culture, and Victorian Sensationalism.* New Brunswick: Rutgers University Press, 1992.

da Costa, Emilia Viotti. *Crowns of Glory, Tears of Blood: The Demerara Slave Rebellion of 1823.* New York: Columbia University Press, 1994.

Dahlberg, Lincoln. "Democracy via Cyberspace: Mapping the Rhetorics and Practices of Three Prominent Camps." *New Media and Society* 3.2 (2001): 157–77.

Dain, Bruce. *A Hideous Monster of the Mind: American Race Theory in the Early Republic.* Cambridge: Harvard University Press, 2002.

Damasio, Antonio R. *Descartes' Error: Emotion, Reason, and the Human Brain.* New York: Putnam, 1994.

Daniel, Sharon, and Erik Loyer. "Public Secrets." *Vectors* 2.2 (Winter 2007). http://vectorsjournal.org/projects/index. php?project=57.

Danielson, Florence H., and Charles B. Davenport. *The Hill Folk: Report on a Rural Community of Hereditary Defectives.* Lancaster, PA: New Era, 1912.

Danner, Mark. *Torture and Truth: America, Abu Ghraib, and the War on Terror*. New York: New York Review of Books, 2004.

Darwin, Charles. *The Voyage of the Beagle*. New York: Collier, 1909.

Das Gupta, Monisha. *Unruly Immigrants: Rights, Activism, and South Asian Politics in the United States*. Durham: Duke University Press, 2006.

Das Gupta, Tania, Carl L. James, Roger C. A. Maaka, Grace-Edward Galabuzi, and Chris Andersen, eds. *Race and Racialization: Essential Readings*. Toronto: Canadian Scholars Press, 2007.

Davidson, Cathy N. "Humanities 2.0: Promise, Perils, Predictions." *PMLA* 123.3 (May 2008): 707–17.

——. *Revolution and the Word: The Rise of the Novel in America*. 1986. Exp. ed. New York: Oxford University Press, 2004.

Davidson, Cathy N., and Jessamyn Hatcher, eds. *No More Separate Spheres!* Durham: Duke University Press, 2002.

Davies, W. D. *The Territorial Dimension of Judaism*. Berkeley: University of California Press, 1982.

Dávila, Arlene M. *Barrio Dreams: Puerto Ricans, Latinos, and the Neoliberal City*. Berkeley: University of California Press, 2004.

——. *Latinos, Inc.: The Marketing and Making of a People*. Berkeley: University of California Press, 2001.

Davis, Angela. *Are Prisons Obsolete?* New York: Seven Stories, 2003.

——. *The Meaning of Freedom and Other Difficult Dialogues*. San Francisco: City Lights Books, 2012.

——. *The Prison-Industrial Complex*. Oakland, CA: AK, 2001.

——. "Reflections on Race, Class, and Gender in the USA." Interview with Lisa Lowe. *The Politics of Culture in the Shadow of Capital*. Ed. Lisa Lowe and David Lloyd. Durham: Duke University Press, 1997. 303–23.

——. *Women, Race, and Class*. New York: Vintage, 1983.

Davis, David Brion. *The Problem of Slavery in the Age of Revolution, 1770–1823*. Ithaca: Cornell University Press, 1975.

Davis, Lennard. *Enforcing Normalcy: Disability, Deafness, and the Body*. New York: Verso, 1995.

Davis, Mike. *Buda's Wagon: A Brief History of the Car Bomb*. New York: Verso, 2007a.

——. *City of Quartz: Excavating the Future in Los Angeles*. London: Verso, 1990.

——. *Planet of Slums*. London: Verso, 2007b.

Dawson, Michael G. *Black Visions: The Roots of Contemporary African-American Political Ideologies*. Chicago: University of Chicago Press, 2001.

Dayan, Colin. *The Law Is a White Dog: How Legal Rituals Make and Unmake Persons*. Princeton: Princeton University Press, 2011.

——. *The Story of Cruel and Unusual*. Boston: Boston Review Books and MIT Press, 2007.

Dean, Mitchell. *Governmentality: Power and Rule in Modern Society*. New York: Sage, 2009.

Dean, Robert. *Imperial Brotherhood: Gender and the Making of Cold War Foreign Policy*. Amherst: University of Massachusetts Press, 2001.

Deane, Seamus. "Imperialism/Nationalism." *Critical Terms for Literary Study*. Ed. Frank Lentricchia and Thomas McLaughlin. Chicago: University of Chicago Press, 1990. 354–68.

De Genova, Nicholas. "Migrant 'Illegality' and Deportability in Everyday Life." *Annual Review of Anthropology* 31 (2002): 419–47.

——. "The 'War on Terror' as Racial Crisis: Homeland Security, Obama, and Racial (Trans)Formations." *Racial Formation in the Twenty-First Century*. Ed. Daniel Martinez HoSang, Oneka LaBennett, and Laura Pulido. Berkeley: University of California Press, 2012. 246–75.

——. *Working the Boundaries: Race, Space, and "Illegality" in Mexican Chicago*. Durham: Duke University Press, 2005.

De Genova, Nicholas, and Nathalie Mae Peutz, eds. *The Deportation Regime: Sovereignty, Space, and the Freedom of Movement*. Durham: Duke University Press, 2010.

de Kock, Leon. "Sitting for the Civilization Test: The Making(s) of a Civil Imaginary in Colonial South Africa." *Poetics Today* 22.2 (2001): 391–412.

Delany, Samuel R. *Return to Nevèrÿon*. Middletown, CT: Wesleyan University Press, 1994.

——. *Times Square Red, Times Square Blue*. Rev. ed. New York: NYU Press, 2001.

de Lauretis, Teresa. "Queer Theory: Lesbian and Gay Sexualities (an Introduction)." *differences: A Journal of Feminist Cultural Studies* 3.2 (Summer 1991): iii–xviii.

Deleuze, Gilles, and Félix Guattari. *Anti-Oedipus: Capitalism and Schizophrenia*. Minneapolis: University of Minnesota Press, 1983.

——. *A Thousand Plateaus: Capitalism and Schizophrenia*. Minneapolis: University of Minnesota Press, 1987.

Delgado, Richard, and Jean Stefancic, eds. *Critical Race Theory: The Cutting Edge*. Philadelphia: Temple University Press. 1995.

Delgado Bernal, Dolores. "Using a Chicana Feminist Epistemology in Educational Research." *Harvard Educational Review* 68.4 (1998): 555–82.

Deloria, Philip J. "American Indians, American Studies, and the ASA." *American Quarterly* 55.4 (December 2003): 669–80.

——. *Playing Indian*. New Haven: Yale University Press, 1998.

Deloria, Vine, Jr. *Custer Died for Your Sins: An Indian Manifesto*. 1969. Norman: University of Oklahoma Press, 1988.

Delphy, Christine. *The Main Enemy: A Materialist Analysis of Women's Oppression*. London: Women's Resources and Research Centre, 1977.

Delpit, Lisa. *Other People's Children: Cultural Conflict in the Classroom*. New York: New Press, 1995.

Demers, Joanna. *Steal This Book: How Intellectual Property Law Affects Musical Creativity*. Athens: University of Georgia Press, 2006.

D'Emilio, John, and Estelle Freedman. *Intimate Matters: A History of Sexuality in America*. 1988. 2nd ed. Chicago: University of Chicago Press, 1997.

Denning, Michael. *The Cultural Front: The Laboring of American Culture in the 20th Century*. London: Verso, 1997.

——. *Culture in the Age of Three Worlds*. London: Verso, 2004.

Derrida, Jacques. *Aporias*. Stanford: Stanford University Press, 1993.

——. "Plato's Pharmacy." *Dissemination*. Trans. Barbara Johnson. Chicago: University of Chicago Press, 1981. 61–119.

De Voe, Thomas. *The Market Book*. New York, 1862.

Dewey, John. *Art as Experience*. 1934. New York: Perigree, 1980.

——. *Liberalism and Social Action*. New York: Putnam, 1935.

——. *The Public and Its Problems*. New York: Holt, 1927.

Diaz, Vicente M. "Canoes of Micronesia: Navigating Tradition into the Future." *Pacific Daily News*, April 28, 1994: 38–40.

———. "Disturbing the Horizon." *Horizons: Journal of the East West Center Participants Association* 2 (1987): 100–107.

———. "Grounding Flux in Guam's Cultural History." *Work in Flux*. Ed. Emma Greenwood, Andrew Sartori, and Klaus Neumann. Melbourne: University of Melbourne, History Department, 1995. 159–71.

———. "Restless Na(rra)tives," *Inscriptions* 5 (1989): 165–75.

Diaz, Vicente M., and J. Kēhaulani Kauanui. "Native Pacific Cultural Studies on the Edge." *Contemporary Pacific* 13.2 (Fall 2001): 315–42.

Di Chiro, Giovanna. "Nature as Community: The Convergence of Environment and Social Justice." *Uncommon Ground: Rethinking the Human Place in Nature*. Ed. William Cronon. New York: Norton, 1996. 298–320.

Dickens, Charles. *American Notes, for General Circulation*. London: Chapman and Hall, 1842.

Dickinson, Laura A. *Outsourcing War and Peace: Preserving Public Values in a World of Privatized Foreign Affairs*. New Haven: Yale University Press, 2011.

Dienst, Richard. *The Bonds of Debt*. New York: Verso, 2011.

di Leonardo, Micaela. *Exotics at Home: Anthropologies, Otherness, and American Modernity*. Chicago: University of Chicago Press, 1998.

———. "Introduction: New Global and American Landscapes of Inequality." *New Landscapes of Inequality: Neoliberalism and the Erosion of Democracy in America*. Ed. Jane Collins, Micaela di Leonardo, and Brett Williams. Santa Fe, NM: School for Advanced Research Press, 2008a. 3–20.

———. "The Neoliberalization of Minds, Space and Bodies: Rising Global Inequality and the Shifting American Public Sphere." *New Landscapes of Inequality: Neoliberalism and the Erosion of Democracy in America*. Ed. Jane Collins, Micaela di Leonardo, and Brett Williams. Santa Fe, NM: School for Advanced Research Press, 2008b. 191–208.

Dillon, Elizabeth Maddock. "Sentimental Aesthetics." *American Literature* 76 (September 2004): 495–523.

Dimock, Wai Chee. *Through Other Continents: American Literature across Deep Time*. Princeton: Princeton University Press, 2006.

Dionne, E. J., Jr., ed. *Community Works*. Washington, DC: Brookings Institution Press, 1998.

Dolby, Nadine. "The Shifting Ground of Race: The Role of Taste in Youth's Production of Identities." *Race, Ethnicity, and Education* 3.1 (2000): 7–23.

Dolovich, Sharon. "Exclusion and Control in the Carceral State." *Berkeley Journal of Criminal Law* 16.2 (2011): 259–339.

Dorsey, Bruce. *Reforming Men and Women: Gender in the Antebellum City*. Ithaca: Cornell University Press, 2002.

Dossa, Parin. *Racialized Bodies, Disabling Worlds: Stories in the Lives of Immigrant Muslim Women*. Toronto: University of Toronto Press, 2009.

Douglas, Ann. *The Feminization of American Culture*. New York: Knopf, 1977.

Douglass, Frederick. *Selected Speeches and Writings*. Ed. Philip S. Foner and Yuval Taylor. Chicago: Lawrence Hill Books, 2000.

Dowd, Douglas Fitzgerald. *The Twisted Dream: Capitalist Development in the United States since 1776*. 2nd ed. Cambridge, MA: Winthrop, 1977.

Dower, John. *War without Mercy: Race and Power in the Pacific War*. New York: Pantheon, 1986.

Driscoll, Catherine. *Girls*. New York: Columbia University Press, 2002.

Drucker, Johanna. *The Century of Artists' Books*. New York: Granary, 1995.

Duboff, Richard B. *Accumulation and Power: An Economic History of the United States*. Armonk, NY: M. E. Sharpe, 1989.

Dubois, Laurent. *Avengers of the New World: The Story of the Haitian Revolution*. Cambridge: Harvard University Press, 2004.

Du Bois, W. E. B. "The African Roots of the War." *W. E. B. Du Bois: A Reader*. Ed. David Levering Lewis. New York: Holt, 1995a. 642–51.

———. *Black Reconstruction in America, 1860–1880*. 1935. New York: Free Press, 1998.

———. *The Philadelphia Negro: A Social Study*. Ed. Elijah Anderson. Philadelphia: University of Pennsylvania Press, 1995b.

———. *The Souls of Black Folk*. 1903. Ed. David W. Blight and Robert Gooding-Williams. New York: Bedford Books, 1997.

———. *The Souls of Black Folk*. 1903. *W. E. B. Du Bois: Writings*. Ed. Nathan Huggins. New York: Library of America, 1986.

———. "The Twelfth Census and the Negro Problem." 1900. *W. E. B. Du Bois: On Sociology and the Black Community*. Ed. Dan S. Green and Edwin D. Driver. Chicago: University of Chicago Press, 1978. 65–69.

DuCille, Ann. *The Coupling Convention: Sex, Text, and Tradition in Black Women's Fiction*. New York: Oxford University Press, 1993.

Duggan, Lisa. "Holy Matrimony!" *Nation Online*, February 26, 2004. http://www.thenation.com/doc.mhtml?i=20040315&c=1&s=duggan.

———. "Making It Perfectly Queer." *Socialist Review* 22 (1992): 11–31.

———. "The New Homonormativity: The Sexual Politics of Neoliberalism." *Materializing Democracy: Toward a Revitalized Cultural Politics*. Ed. Russ Castronovo and Dana D. Nelson. Durham: Duke University Press, 2002. 175–94.

———. *The Twilight of Equality: Neoliberalism, Cultural Politics, and the Attack on Democracy*. Boston: Beacon, 2003.

Dumm, Thomas. *Democracy and Punishment: Disciplinary Origins of the United States*. Madison: University of Wisconsin Press, 1987.

Dunbar, Paul Laurence. *The Collected Poetry of Paul Laurence Dunbar*. Ed. Joanne Braxton. Charlottesville: University of Virginia Press, 1993.

———. *Sport of the Gods and Other Essential Writing by Paul Laurence Dunbar*. Ed. Shelley Fisher Fishkin and David Bradley. New York: Random House / Modern Library, 2005.

Dunbar-Ortiz, Roxanne. *Red Dirt: Growing Up Okie*. Norman: University of Oklahoma Press, 2006.

Duncan, Johnny. "Afr-i-can Amer-i-can Turns Twenty-Three." *Community Audio*, January 2, 2010. Web.

Dunn, Christopher. *Brutality Garden*. Chapel Hill: University of North Carolina Press, 2001.

During, Simon, ed. *The Cultural Studies Reader*. 1993. 3rd ed. New York: Routledge, 2007.

Durkheim, Émile, and Marcel Mauss. "Note on the Notion of Civilization." 1913. Trans. Benjamin Nelson. *Social Research* 38 (1971): 808–13.

Dyer, Richard. "White." *Screen* 29.4 (1988): 44–64.

———. *White*. New York: Routledge, 1997.

Dyer-Witheford, Nick. *Cyber-Marx: Cycles and Circuits of Struggle in High-Technology Capitalism*. Urbana: University of Illinois Press, 1999.

Eade, John, ed. *Living the Global City: Globalization as a Local Process*. London: Routledge, 1997.

Eagleton, Terry. *The Idea of Culture*. Malden, MA: Blackwell, 2000.

———. *The Ideology of the Aesthetic*. Oxford, UK: Blackwell, 1990.

Eckert, Penelope. *Jocks and Burnouts: Social Categories and Identities in High School*. New York: Teachers College Press, 1989.

Edelman, Lee. *No Future: Queer Theory and the Death Drive*. Durham: Duke University Press, 2004.

Edelman, Marian Wright. "Justice Denied." Child Watch Column, Children's Defense Fund. July 14, 2013. http://www.childrensdefense.org/newsroom/child-watch-columns/child-watch-documents/justice-denied.html.

Edmondson, Locksley. "Black America as a Mobilizing Diaspora: Some International Implications." *Modern Diasporas in International Politics*. Ed. Gabriel Sheffer. London: Croom Helm, 1986. 164–211.

Edmundson, Mark. *Why Read?* New York: Bloomsbury, 2004.

Edsall, Thomas Byrne, and Mary D. Edsall. *Chain Reaction: The Impact of Race, Rights, and Taxes on American Politics*. New York: Norton, 1992.

Edwards, Brent Hayes. *The Practice of Diaspora: Literature, Translation, and the Rise of Black Internationalism*. Cambridge: Harvard University Press, 2003a.

———. "The Shadow of Shadows." *Positions* 11.1 (2003b): 11–49.

———. "The Uses of Diaspora." *Social Text* 66 (2001): 45–73.

Edwards, Brian T. "Disorienting Captivity: A Response to Gordon Sayre." *American Literary History* 22.2 (Summer 2010): 360–67.

———. *Morocco Bound: Disorienting America's Maghreb, from Casablanca to the Marrakech Express*. Durham: Duke University Press, 2005.

Eggers, Dave. *Zeitoun*. San Francisco: McSweeney's Books, 2009.

Ehrenreich, Barbara. *Nickel and Dimed: On (Not) Getting By in America*. New York: Metropolitan Books, 2001.

Eidsheim, Nina Sun. "Marian Anderson and 'Sonic Blackness' in American Opera." *Sound Clash: Listening to American Studies*. Ed. Kara Keeling and Josh Kun. Baltimore: John Hopkins University Press, 2011. 197–228.

Eisenhower, Dwight D. "Farewell Address." January 17, 1961. Transcript available at http://www.ourdocuments.gov/doc.php?doc=90&page=transcript.

Eisenman, Stephen. *The Abu Ghraib Effect*. London: Reaktion Books, 2007.

Elam, Harry Justin, and Kennell Jackson, eds. *Black Cultural Traffic: Crossroads in Global Performance and Popular Culture*. Ann Arbor: University of Michigan Press, 2005.

Elam, Michelle. *The Souls of Mixed Folk: Race, Politics, and Aesthetics in the New Millennium*. Stanford: Stanford University Press, 2011.

Elias, Norbert. *Über den Prozess der Zivilisation*. 1939. Munich: Franke Verlag Bern, 1969.

Eliot, T. S. "Notes towards the Definition of Culture." *Christianity and Culture*. New York: Harcourt, Brace and World, 1949. 79–186.

Elizondo, Virgilio. *The Future Is Mestizo: Life Where Culture Meets*. Boulder: University Press of Colorado, 2000.

Ellison, Julie. *Cato's Tears and the Making of Anglo-American Emotion*. Chicago: University of Chicago Press, 1999.

Ellison, Ralph. *Invisible Man*. 1952. New York: Vintage, 1995.

El Norte. Dir. Gregory Nava. American Playhouse / PBS, 1983.

"El Plan Espiritual de Aztlán." *El Grito del Norte* 2.9 (July 6, 1969). Reprinted in *Aztlán: An Anthology of Mexican American Literature*. Ed. Louis Valdez and Stan Steiner. New York: Vintage, 1972. 1–5.

Emerson, Ralph Waldo. "The American Scholar." 1837. *Selected Lectures and Poems*. Ed. Robert D. Richardson, Jr. New York: Bantam, 1990. 82–100.

———. "Art." *Essays and Lectures*. New York: Library of America, 1983. 429–40.

———. "Man the Reformer." 1841. *Essays and Lectures*. New York: Library of America New York, 1983. 135–50.

———. "Self-Reliance." 1841. *Selected Essays, Lectures, and Poems*. Ed. Robert D. Richardson, Jr. New York: Bantam, 1990. 148–71.

Emmanuel, Arghiri. "White-Settler Colonialism and the Myth of Investment Imperialism." *New Left Review* 73 (May–June 1972): 35–57.

Eng, David. *Racial Castration: Managing Masculinity in Asian America*. Durham: Duke University Press, 2001.

Eng, David, Judith Halberstam, and José Muñoz. "Introduction: What's Queer about Queer Studies Now?" *Social Text* 84–85 (Fall–Winter 2005): 1–17.

Eng, David, and David Kazanjian, eds. *Loss*. Berkeley: University of California Press, 2002.

Engels, Friedrich. *The Origins of the Family, Private Property, and the State*. 1884. New York: Pathfinder, 1972.

Enloe, Cynthia. *Bananas, Beaches, and Bases: Making Feminist Sense of International Politics*. Berkeley: University of California Press, 1989.

Entwistle, Joanne. *The Fashioned Body: Fashion, Dress, and Modern Social Theory*. Malden, MA: Polity, 2000.

Epstein, Steven. *Impure Science: AIDS, Activism, and the Politics of Knowledge, Medicine and Society*. Berkeley: University of California Press, 1996.

Erikson, Erik H. *Identity: Youth and Crisis*. 1944. New York: Norton, 1968.

Erlmann, Viet, ed. *Hearing Cultures: Essays on Sound, Listening, and Modernity*. Oxford, UK: Berg, 2004.

Ernst, Wolfgang. *Digital Memory and the Archive*. Minneapolis: University of Minnesota Press, 2013.

Escobar, Arturo. *Encountering Development: The Making and Unmaking of the Third World*. Princeton: Princeton University Press, 1995.

Escoffier, Jeffrey, and Allan Bérubé. "Queer/Nation." *OUT/LOOK: National Lesbian and Gay Quarterly* 11 (1991): 14–16.

Essed, Philomena, and David Theo Goldberg, eds. *Race Critical Theories*. Malden, MA: Blackwell, 2000.

Ettelbrick, Paula. "Since When Is Marriage the Path to Liberation?" *OUT/LOOK: National Lesbian and Gay Quarterly* 2 (1989): 14–16.

WORKS CITED

Etzioni, Amitai. *The Spirit of Community: Rights, Responsibilities, and the Communitarian Agenda*. New York: Crown, 1993.

Ewen, Elizabeth, and Stuart Ewen. *Typecasting: On the Arts and Sciences of Human Inequality; A History of Dominant Ideas*. New York: Seven Stories, 2006.

Fabian, Johannes. *Time and the Other: How Anthropology Makes Its Object*. New York: Columbia University Press, 2002.

Falk, Richard. "The Making of Global Citizenship." *The Condition of Citizenship*. Ed. Bart Van Steenbergen. London: Sage, 1994. 127–40.

Fanon, Frantz. *Black Skin, White Masks*. Trans. Charles Lam Markmann. New York: Grove, 1967a.

———. *A Dying Colonialism*. Trans. Haakon Chevalier. New York: Grove, 1967b.

———. *The Wretched of the Earth*. 1963. Trans. Richard Philcox. New York: Grove, 2004.

Fanuzzi, Robert. *Abolition's Public Sphere*. Minneapolis: University of Minnesota Press, 2003.

Farrow, Kenyon. "Is Gay Marriage Anti-Black?" Kenyon Farrow's blog, June 14, 2005. http://kenyonfarrow.com/2005/06/14/is-gay-marriage-anti-black/.

Fausto-Sterling, Anne. "The Five Sexes: Why Male and Female Are Not Enough." *Sciences*, March–April 1993, 20–24.

———. *Myths of Gender: Biological Theories about Women and Men*. New York: Basic Books, 1985.

———. *Sexing the Body: Gender Politics and the Construction of Sexuality*. New York: Basic Books, 2000.

Favor, Martin J. *Authentic Blackness: The Folk in the New Negro Renaissance*. Durham: Duke University Press, 1999.

Feeley, Malcolm, and Jonathan Simon. "The New Penology: Notes on the Emerging Strategy of Corrections and Its Implications." *Criminology* 30.4 (1992): 449–74.

Feenberg, Andrew. *Questioning Technology*. New York: Routledge, 1999.

Feinberg, Leslie. *Stone Butch Blues*. Ithaca, NY: Firebrand Books, 1993.

Feld, Steven. "A Rainforest Acoustemology." *The Auditory Culture Reader*. Ed. Michael Bull and Les Back. New York: Berg, 2003. 223–40.

Felski, Rita. *Doing Time: Feminist Theory and Postmodern Culture*. New York: NYU Press, 2000.

Ferguson, Roderick A. *Aberrations in Black: Toward a Queer of Color Critique*. Minneapolis: University of Minnesota Press, 2004.

———. *The Reorder of Things: On the Institutionalization of Difference*. Minneapolis: University of Minnesota Press, 2012.

———. "The Stratifications of Normativity." *Rhizomes* 10 (2005). http://www.rhizomes.net/issue10/ferguson.htm.

Fernandez, Lilia. *Brown in the Windy City: Mexicans and Puerto Ricans in Postwar Chicago*. Chicago: University of Chicago Press, 2012.

Ferreira da Silva, Denise. *Toward a Global Idea of Race*. Minneapolis: University of Minnesota Press, 2007.

Fetterley, Judith, and Marjorie Pryse. *Writing Out of Place: Regionalism, Women, and American Literary Culture*. Urbana: University of Illinois Press, 2003.

Fields, Barbara. "Slavery, Race, and Ideology in the United States of America." *New Left Review* 181 (May–June 1990): 95–118.

Fields, Barbara, and Karen E. Fields, *Racecraft: The Soul of Inequality in American Life*. London: Verso, 2012.

Filmer, Sir Robert. *Patriarcha, or, the Natural Power of Kings*. London, 1680.

Fine, Michelle. "Silencing and Nurturing Voice in an Improbable Context: Urban Adolescents in Public School." *Critical Pedagogy, the State, and Cultural Struggle*. Ed. Henry A. Giroux and Peter McLaren. New York: SUNY Press, 1989. 152–73.

Fine, Michelle, Lois Weis, Linda C. Powell, and L. Mun Wong, eds. *Off White: Readings on Race, Power, and Society*. New York: Routledge, 1997.

Fink, Bruce. *The Lacanian Subject: Between Language and Jouissance*. Princeton: Princeton University Press, 1995.

Fischer, Sibylle. *Haiti and the Cultures of Slavery in the Age of Revolution*. Durham: Duke University Press, 2003.

Fish, Stanley. "Professor Sokal's Bad Joke." *New York Times*, May 21, 1996, A23.

Fisk, Clinton B. *Plain Counsels for Freedmen: In Sixteen Brief Lectures*. Boston, 1866.

Fitzgerald, Deborah. *Every Farm a Factory: The Industrial Ideal in American Agriculture*. New Haven: Yale University Press, 2003.

Fliegelman, Jay. *Declaring Independence: Jefferson, Natural Language, and the Culture of Performance*. Stanford: Stanford University Press, 1993.

———. *Prodigals and Pilgrims: The American Revolution against Patriarchal Authority, 1750–1800*. New York: Cambridge University Press, 1982.

Flores, Juan. *From Bomba to Hip-Hop: Puerto Rican Culture and Latino Identity*. New York: Columbia University Press, 2000.

Florida, Richard. *The Rise of the Creative Class*. New York: Basic Books, 2002.

Foley, Douglas. *Learning Capitalist Culture: Deep in the Heart of Tejas*. Philadelphia: University of Pennsylvania Press, 1994.

Foner, Eric. *The Story of American Freedom*. New York: Norton, 1998.

Foote, Stephanie. "The Cultural Work of American Regionalism." *A Companion to the Regional Literatures of America*. Ed. Charles L. Crow. Malden, MA: Blackwell, 2003. 25–41.

———. *Regional Fictions: Culture and Identity in Nineteenth-Century American Literature*. Madison: University of Wisconsin Press, 2001.

Forbes, Jack D. *Africans and Native Americans: The Language of Race and the Evolution of Red-Black Peoples*. 2nd ed. Urbana: University of Illinois Press, 1992.

Fordham, Signithia. *Blacked Out: Dilemmas of Race, Identity, and Success at Capital High*. Chicago: University of Chicago Press, 1996.

Foster, John Bellamy, and Fred Magdoff. *The Great Financial Crisis: Causes and Consequences*. New York: Monthly Review Press, 2009.

Foster, Thomas. "'The Souls of Cyberfolk': Performativity, Virtual Embodiment, and Racial Histories." *Cyberspace Textualities: Computer Technology and Literary Theory*. Ed. Marie-Laure Ryan. Bloomington: Indiana University Press, 1999. 137–63.

———. *The Souls of Cyberfolk: Posthumanism as Vernacular Theory*. Minneapolis: University of Minnesota Press, 2005.

Foucault, Michel. *Abnormal: Lectures at the Collège de France, 1974–1975*. 1999. Trans. Graham Burchell. New York: Picador, 2003.

———. "Afterword: The Subject and Power." *Michel Foucault: Beyond Structuralism and Hermeneutics*. Ed. Hubert L. Dreyfus and Paul Rabinow. Chicago: University of Chicago Press, 1982. 208–26.

———. *Discipline and Punish: The Birth of the Prison*. 1975. Trans. Alan Sheridan. New York: Vintage, 1995.

———. *Essential Works of Foucault, 1954–1984*. Vol. 1: *Ethics*. New York: New Press, 2006.

———. "Governmentality." *The Foucault Effect: Studies in Governmentality*. Ed. Graham Burchell, Colin Gordon, and Peter Miller. Chicago: University of Chicago Press, 1991. 87–104.

———. *The History of Sexuality, Volume I: An Introduction*. 1976. Trans. Robert Hurley. New York: Vintage, 1990.

———. *The Order of Things: An Archaeology of the Human Sciences*. New York: Vintage, 1994.

———. *Security, Territory, Population: Lectures at the Collège de France, 1977–1978*. New York: Picador 2009.

Fowler, O. S. *Education and Self-Improvement*. New York: O. S. and L. N. Fowler, 1844.

Fox, Claire. *The Fence and the River: Culture and Politics at the U.S.-Mexico Border*. Minneapolis: University of Minnesota Press, 1999.

Fox, Richard. "The Breakdown of Culture." *Current Anthropology* 36 (1995): 1–2.

Frampton, Kenneth. "Towards a Critical Regionalism: Six Points for an Architecture of Resistance." *The Anti-Aesthetic: Essays on Postmodern Culture*. Ed. Hal Foster. Port Townsend, WA: Bay, 1983. 16–30.

Frank, Thomas. *What's the Matter with Kansas? How Conservatives Won the Heart of America*. New York: Holt, 2004.

Franke, Andre Gunder. *ReOrient: Global Economy in the Asian Age*. Berkeley: University of California Press, 1998.

Franke, Katherine M. "Becoming a Citizen: Reconstruction-Era Regulation of African-American Marriages." *Yale Journal of Law and the Humanities* 11.2 (1999): 251–309.

Frankenberg, Ruth. *White Women, Race Matters: The Social Construction of Whiteness*. Minneapolis: University of Minnesota Press, 1993.

Franklin, Benjamin. *The Autobiography of Benjamin Franklin*. Philadelphia: Henry Altemus, 1895.

———. "Sidi Mehemet Ibrahim on the Slave Trade." Letter to the *Federal Gazette*, March 23, 1790.

Franklin, H. Bruce. *The Victim as Criminal and Artist: Literature from the American Prison*. New York: Oxford University Press, 1978.

Fredrickson, George. *White Supremacy: A Comparative Study in American and South African History*. Oxford: Oxford University Press, 1981.

Freeman, Alan David. "Legitimizing Racial Discrimination through Anti-discrimination Law: A Critical Review of Supreme Court Doctrine." *Critical Race Theory: The Key Writings That Formed the Movement*. Ed. Kimberlé Crenshaw, Neil Gotanda, Garry Peller, and Kendall Thomas. New York: New Press, 1995. 29–45.

Freeman, Carla. *High Tech and High Heels in the Global Economy: Women, Work, and Pink-Collar Economies in the Caribbean*. Durham: Duke University Press, 2000.

Freeman, Elizabeth. *Time Binds: Queer Temporalities, Queer Histories*. Durham: Duke University Press, 2010.

Fregoso, Rosa Linda. *MeXicana Encounters: The Making of Social Identities on the Borderlands*. Berkeley: University of California Press, 2003.

Freyre, Gilberto. *The Masters and the Slaves: A Study in the Development of Brazilian Civilization*. 1933. Trans. Samuel Putnam. New York: Knopf, 1956.

Friedan, Betty. *The Feminine Mystique*. New York: Dell, 1963.

Friedberg, Anne. *Window Shopping: Cinema and the Postmodern*. Berkeley: University of California Press, 1993.

Friedman, Lawrence M. *American Law in the Twentieth Century*. New Haven: Yale University Press, 2002.

Friedman, Milton. *Capitalism and Freedom*. 1962. Chicago: University of Chicago Press, 2002.

Friedman, Thomas L. *The Lexus and the Olive Tree: Understanding Globalization*. New York: Farrar, Straus and Giroux, 2000.

———. *The World Is Flat: A Brief History of the Twenty-First Century*. New York: Farrar, Straus and Giroux, 2005.

Fryd, Vivien Green. *Art and Empire: The Politics of Ethnicity in the United States Capitol, 1815–1860*. New Haven: Yale University Press, 1992.

Fuchs, Christian, Matthias Schafranek, David Hakken, and Marcus Breen. "Capitalist Crisis, Communication & Culture." Special issue of *tripleC (cognition, communication, co-operation) Open Access Journal for a Global Sustainable Information Society* 8.2 (2010): 193–309.

Fujitani, Takeshi. "*Go for Broke*, the Movie: Japanese American Soldiers in U.S. National, Military, and Racial Discourses." *Perilous Memories: The Asian Pacific War(s)*. Ed. Takeshi Fujitani, Geoffrey Wright, and Lisa Yoneyama. Durham: Duke University Press, 2001. 239–66.

Fujitani, Takeshi, Geoffrey Wright, and Lisa Yoneyama, eds. *Perilous Memories: The Asian Pacific War(s)*. Durham: Duke University Press, 2001.

Fujiwara, Lynn. *Mothers without Citizenship: Asian Immigrant Families and the Consequences of Welfare Reform*. Minneapolis: University of Minnesota Press, 2008.

Fukuyama, Francis. *Trust: The Social Virtues and the Creation of Prosperity*. New York: Free Press, 1995.

Fuller, Matthew. *Media Ecologies: Materialist Energies in Art and Technoculture*. Cambridge: MIT Press, 2005.

———. *Software Studies: A Lexicon*. Cambridge: MIT Press, 2008.

Fullilove, Mindy Thompson. *Root Shock: How Tearing Up City Neighborhoods Is Ruining America and What We Can Do about It*. New York: Ballantine Books, 2004.

Gaines, Kevin K. *American Africans in Ghana: Black Expatriates and the Civil Rights Era*. Chapel Hill: University of North Carolina Press, 2006.

Galbraith, James. *Inequality and Instability: A Study of the World Economy Just before the Great Crisis*. New York: Oxford University Press, 2012.

Galloway, Alex. *Gaming: Essays on Algorithmic Culture*. Minneapolis: University of Minnesota Press, 2006.

———. *Protocol: How Control Exists after Decentralization*. Cambridge: MIT Press, 2004.

Gamber, Wendy. *The Female Economy: The Millinery and*

Dressmaking Trades, 1860-1930. Urbana: University of Illinois Press, 1997.

García, Maria Cristina. *Seeking Refuge: Central American Migration to Mexico, the United States, and Canada*. Berkeley: University of California Press, 2006.

García Bedolla, Lisa. *Latino Politics*. Malden, MA: Polity, 2009.

García Canclini, Néstor. *Diferentes, desiguales y desconectados: Mapas de la interculturalidad*. Barcelona: Gedisa, 2004.

———. *Hybrid Cultures: Strategies for Entering and Leaving Modernity*. Trans. Christopher L. Chippari and Silvia L. López. Minneapolis: University of Minnesota Press, 1995.

Gardet, L[ouis]. "Islam." *Encyclopedia of Islam*. 2nd ed. Vol. 4. Ed. E. van Donzel, B. Lewis, and Ch. Pellat. Leiden: Brill, 1978. 171-74.

Garland-Thomson, Rosemarie. "Cultural Commentary: 'Transferred to an Unknown Location . . .'" *Disability Studies Quarterly* 27.4 (2007). http://dsq-sds.org/article/view/56/56.

———. *Extraordinary Bodies: Figuring Physical Disability in American Culture and Literature*. New York: Columbia University Press, 1997.

Garroutte, Eva. *Real Indians: Identity and the Survival of Native America*. Berkeley: University of California, 2003.

Garza, Monica. *Foto-Escultura: A Mexican Photographic Tradition*. Albuquerque: University of New Mexico Art Museum, 1998.

Gates, Henry Louis, Jr. "Preface to Blackness: Text and Pretext." *Afro-American Literature: The Reconstruction of Instruction*. Ed. Dexter Fisher and Robert B. Stepto. New York: Modern Language Association, 1978. 44-69.

———. "'What's Love Got to Do with It?': Critical Theory, Integrity, and Black Idiom." *New Literary History* 18 (Winter 1987): 345-62.

Gayle, Addison, ed. *The Black Aesthetic*. New York: Doubleday, 1971.

Geertz, Clifford. "Religion as a Cultural System." 1966. *The Interpretation of Cultures: Selected Essays*. London: Fontana, 1983. 87-125.

Gelder, Ken, and Sarah Thornton, eds. *The Subcultures Reader*. London: Routledge, 1997.

Genovese, Eugene D. *From Revolution to Rebellion: Afro-American Slave Revolts in the Making of the Modern World*. Baton Rouge: Louisiana State University Press, 1979.

Georgacas, Demetrius J. "The Name *Asia* for the Continent: Its History and Origin." *Names* 17.1 (1969): 1-90.

Geronimo. *Geronimo: His Own Story: The Autobiography of a Great Patriot Warrior; as Told to S. M. Barrett*. 1905. New York: Penguin, 1996.

Giberti, Bruno. *Designing the Centennial: A History of the 1876 International Exhibition in Philadelphia*. Lexington: University Press of Kentucky, 2002.

Gibson, William. "Burning Chrome." *OMNI*, July 1982, 72-77, 102-4.

Gibson-Graham, J. K. *The End of Capitalism (as We Knew It): A Feminist Critique of Political Economy*. Cambridge, MA: Blackwell, 1996.

Gibson-Graham, J. K., Stephen Resnick, and Richard Wolff, eds. *Re/presenting Class: Essays in Postmodern Marxism*. Durham: Duke University Press, 2001.

Giddens, Anthony. *Constitution of Society: Outline of the Theory of Structuration*. Berkeley: University of California Press, 1984.

Giles, Paul. *Transatlantic Insurrections: British Culture and the Formation of American Literature, 1730-1860*. Philadelphia: University of Pennsylvania Press, 2001.

———. "Transnationalism and Classic American Literature." *PMLA* 118.1 (2003): 62-77.

Gilligan, Carol. *In a Different Voice: Psychological Theory and Women's Development*. Cambridge: Harvard University Press, 1982.

Gilman, Nils. *Mandarins of the Future: Modernization Theory in Cold War America*. Baltimore: Johns Hopkins University Press, 2003.

Gilman, Sander. "Black Bodies, White Bodies: Toward an Iconography of Female Sexuality in Late Nineteenth Century Art, Medicine, and Literature." *Race, Writing, and Difference*. Ed. Henry Louis, Jr. Chicago: University of Chicago Press, 1986. 223-61.

———. *Picturing Health and Illness: Images of Identity and Difference*. Baltimore: Johns Hopkins University Press, 1995.

Gilmore, Grant. *The Death of Contract*. Columbus: Ohio State University Press, 1974.

Gilmore, Michael T. *American Romanticism and the Marketplace*. Chicago: University of Chicago Press, 1985.

Gilmore, Ruth Wilson. "Globalisation and U.S. Prison Growth: From Military Keynesianism to Post-Keynesian Militarism." *Race and Class* 40.2-3 (1998): 171-88.

———. *Golden Gulag: Prisons, Surplus, Crisis, and Opposition in Globalizing California*. Berkeley: University of California Press, 2007.

———. "Partition." Lecture at "Decolonize the City!," Rosa Luxemburg Foundation, Berlin, Germany, September 23, 2012.

Gilroy, Paul. *Against Race: Imagining Political Culture beyond the Color Line*. Cambridge: Belknap Press of Harvard University Press, 2000.

———. *The Black Atlantic: Modernity and Double Consciousness*. Cambridge: Harvard University Press, 1993.

———. *"There Ain't No Black in the Union Jack": The Cultural Politics of Race and Nation*. Chicago: University of Chicago Press, 1987.

———. *"There Ain't No Black in the Union Jack": The Cultural Politics of Race and Nation*. Rev. ed. Chicago: University of Chicago Press, 1991.

Ginsburg, Faye T. *Contested Lives: The Abortion Debate in an American Community*. Berkeley: University of California Press, 1998.

Giroux, Henry. *Fugitive Cultures: Race, Violence, and Youth*. New York: Routledge, 1996.

Gitelman, Lisa. *Always Already New: Media, History, and the Data of Culture*. Cambridge: MIT Press, 2006.

Glazer, Nathan. *Ethnic Dilemmas, 1964-1982*. Cambridge: Harvard University Press, 1983.

Glenn, Evelyn Nakano. *Unequal Citizenship: How Race and Gender Shaped American Citizenship and Labor*. Cambridge: Harvard University Press, 2004.

Glickman, Lawrence B. *A Living Wage: American Workers and the Making of Consumer Society*. Ithaca: Cornell University Press, 1997.

Gobineau, Arthur. *The Inequality of Human Races*. 1853-55. Trans. Adrian H. Collins. New York: H. Fertig, 1967.

Goffman, Erving. *The Presentation of Self in Everyday Life*. Garden City, NY: Doubleday, 1959.

———. *Stigma: Notes on the Management of Spoiled Identity*. New York: Touchstone / Simon and Schuster, 1963.

Goldberg, David Theo. *Racist Culture: Philosophy and the Politics of Meaning*. Cambridge, MA: Blackwell, 1993.

Goldberg, David Theo, and Richard Marciano. "T-RACES: Testbed for the Redlining Archives of California's Exclusionary Spaces." *Vectors* 3.2 (Summer 2012). http://vectors.usc.edu/projects/index.php?project=93.

Goldberg, Jonathan. "The History That Will Be." *GLQ* 1.4 (1995): 385–403.

———. *Sodometries: Renaissance Texts, Modern Sexualities*. Stanford: Stanford University Press, 1992.

Goldman, Emma. *Anarchism and Other Essays*. Mineola, NY: Dover, 1969.

Goldstein, Alyosha. *Poverty in Common: The Politics of Community Action during the American Century*. Durham: Duke University Press, 2012.

Goldstein, Alyosha, and Alex Lubin. "Settler Colonialism." Special issue of *South Atlantic Quarterly* 107.4 (Fall 2008).

Goldstein, Sidney. "Migration: Dynamic of the American City." *American Quarterly* 6.4 (Winter 1954): 337–48.

Gómez, Laura E. *Manifest Destinies: The Making of the Mexican American Race*. New York: NYU Press, 2007.

Gómez-Peña, Guillermo. *Border Brujo*. Videocassette recording. Cinewest Productions, 1990.

Goodman, Audrey. *Translating the Southwest: The Making of an Anglo Literary Region*. Tucson: University of Arizona Press, 2002.

Goodman, Paul. *Of One Blood: Abolitionism and the Origins of Racial Equality*. Berkeley: University of California Press, 1998.

Goodwyn, Lawrence. *The Populist Moment: A Short History of the Agrarian Revolt in America*. Oxford: Oxford University Press, 1978.

Gopinath, Gayatri. *Impossible Desires: Queer Diasporas and South Asian Public Cultures*. Durham: Duke University Press, 2005.

———. "Queer Regions: Locating Lesbians in *Sancharram*." *A Companion to Lesbian, Gay, Bisexual, Transgender, and Queer Studies*. Ed. George E. Haggerty and Molly McGarry. Malden, MA: Blackwell, 2007. 341–54.

Gordley, James. *The Philosophical Origins of Modern Contract Doctrine*. Oxford, UK: Clarendon, 1991.

Gordon, Avery. *Ghostly Matters: Haunting and the Sociological Imagination*. Minneapolis: University of Minnesota Press, 2008.

Gordon, David M. *Fat and Mean: The Corporate Squeeze of Working Americans and the Myth of Managerial "Downsizing."* New York: Free Press, 1996.

Gordon, Edmund T. *Disparate Diasporas: Identity and Politics in an African Nicaraguan Community*. Austin: University of Texas Press, 1998.

Gotanda, Neil. "A Critique of 'Our Constitution Is Color-Blind.'" *Stanford Law Review* 44.1 (1991): 1–68.

Gould, Philip. *Barbaric Traffic: Commerce and Antislavery in the Eighteenth-Century Atlantic World*. Cambridge: Harvard University Press, 2003.

Gould, Stephen Jay. "The Hottentot Venus." *Natural History* 91.10 (1982): 20–25.

———. *The Mismeasure of Man*. New York: Norton, 1981.

Graeber, David. "The New Anarchists." *New Left Review* 13 (2002): 61–73.

Graff, Gerald. *Professing Literature: An Institutional History*. Chicago: University of Chicago Press, 1987.

Gramsci, Antonio. *Selections from the Prison Notebooks*. Ed. and trans. Quintin Hoare and Geoffrey Nowell Smith. New York: International, 1971.

Grant, Madison. *The Passing of the Great Race, or, the Racial Basis of European History*. New York: Scribner, 1916.

Green, James. *Death in the Haymarket: A Story of Chicago, the First Labor Movement, and the Bombing That Divided Gilded Age America*. New York: Random House, 2006.

Green, Nancy L. *Ready-to-Wear and Ready-to-Work: A Century of Industry and Immigrants in Paris and New York*. Durham: Duke University Press, 1997.

Green, Tara T. *From the Plantation to the Prison: African-American Confinement Literature*. Macon, GA: Mercer University Press, 2008.

Greenwald, Glenn. "NSA Collecting Phone Records of Millions of Verizon Customers Daily." *Guardian*, June 6, 2013. http://www.theguardian.com/world/2013/jun/06/nsa-phone-records-verizon-court-order.

Greeson, Jennifer. *Our South: Geographic Fantasy and the Rise of National Literature*. Cambridge: Harvard University Press, 2010.

Gregg, Melissa, and Gregory J. Seigworth, eds. *The Affect Theory Reader*. Durham: Duke University Press, 2010.

Greiman, Jennifer. *Democracy's Spectacle: Sovereignty and Public Life in Antebellum America*. New York: Fordham University Press, 2010.

Grewal, Inderpal. *Transnational America: Feminisms, Diasporas, Neoliberalisms*. Durham: Duke University Press, 2005.

———. "Transnational America: Race, Gender and Citizenship after 9/11." *Social Identities* 9.4 (December 2003): 535–61.

Griffin, Farrah Jasmine. *"Who Set You Flowin?" The African-American Migration Narrative*. New York: Oxford University Press, 1995.

Griffin, Susan. *Woman and Nature: The Roaring inside Her*. New York: Harper and Row, 1978.

Griggs, Richard. "Background on the Term 'Fourth World': An Excerpt from CWIS Occasional Paper #18, The Meaning of 'Nation' and 'State' in the Fourth World." University of Capetown, Center for World Indigenous Studies, 1992. http://cwis.org/GML/background/FourthWorld/.

Grossberg, Lawrence. *Cultural Studies in the Future Tense*. Durham: Duke University Press, 2010a.

———. "Standing on a Bridge: Rescuing Economies from Economists." *Journal of Communication Inquiry* 34.4 (2010b): 316–36.

Grossberg, Lawrence, Cary Nelson, and Paula Treichler, eds. *Cultural Studies*. London: Routledge, 1992.

Grossman, James R. *Land of Hope: Chicago, Black Southerners, and the Great Migration*. Chicago: University of Chicago Press, 1989.

Grosz, Elizabeth. *Becoming Undone: Darwinian Reflections on Life, Politics, and Art*. Durham: Duke University Press, 2011.

Gruen, Erich S. "Diaspora and Homeland." *Diasporas and Exiles: Varieties of Jewish Identity*. Ed. Howard Wettstein. Berkeley: University of California Press, 2002. 18–46.

Gruesz, Kirsten Silva. *Ambassadors of Culture: The Transamerican Origins of Latino Writing*. Princeton: Princeton University Press, 2002.

Guenther, Lisa. *Social Death and Its Afterlives: A Critical Phenomenology of Solitary Confinement*. Minneapolis: University of Minnesota Press, 2013.

Gulbenkian Commission. *Open the Social Sciences: Report of the Gulbenkian Commission on the Restructuring of the Social Sciences*. Stanford: Stanford University Press, 1996.

Gunning, Tom. "An Aesthetic of Astonishment: Early Film and the (In)Credulous Spectator." *Art and Text* 34 (Spring 1989): 31–45.

Gupta, Akhil, and James Ferguson. "Beyond 'Culture': Space, Identity and the Politics of Difference." *Cultural Anthropology* 7.1 (1992): 6–23.

Gustafson, Sandra M. *Eloquence Is Power: Oratory and Performance in Early America*. Chapel Hill: University of North Carolina Press, 2000.

——. *Imagining Deliberative Democracy in the Early American Republic*. Chicago: University of Chicago Press, 2011.

Gustafson, Sandra M., and Caroline F. Sloat. *Cultural Narratives: Textuality and Performance in American Culture before 1900*. Notre Dame: University of Notre Dame Press, 2010.

Guterson, David. *Snow Falling on Cedars: A Novel*. New York: Vintage, 1995.

Gutiérrez, David G., and Pierette Hondagneu-Sotelo. Introduction to *American Quarterly* 60.3 (2008): 503–21.

Gutiérrez, Elena R. *Fertile Matters: The Politics of Mexican-Origin Women's Reproduction*. Austin: University of Texas Press, 2008.

Gutiérrez-Jones, Carl. "Desiring B/orders." *diacritics* 25.2 (1995): 99–112.

Gutman, Herbert G. *Work, Culture, and Society in Industrializing America*. New York: Vintage, 1976.

Habermas, Jürgen. *The Philosophical Discourse of Modernity: Twelve Lectures*. Trans. Frederick Lawrence. Cambridge, UK: Polity, 1987.

——. *The Structural Transformation of the Public Sphere: An Inquiry into a Category of Bourgeois Society*. Trans. Thomas Burger. Cambridge: MIT Press, 1989.

Hacker, Jacob. *The Great Risk Shift: The Assault on American Jobs, Families, Health Care, and Retirement and How You Can Fight Back*. New York: Oxford University Press, 2006.

Hakluyt, Richard. *The Principall Navigations, Voiages, and Discoveries of the English Nation*. London: George Bishop and Ralph Newberie, deputies to Christopher Barker, 1589.

Halberstam, Judith. *Female Masculinity*. Durham: Duke University Press, 1998.

——. *In a Queer Time and Place: Transgender Bodies, Subcultural Lives*. New York: NYU Press, 2005.

——. *Skin Shows: Gothic Horror and the Technology of Monsters*. Durham: Duke University Press, 1995.

Hale, Charles R. "Between Che Guevara and the Pachamama: Mestizos, Indians, and Identity Politics in the Anti-Quincentenary Campaign." *Critique of Anthropology* 14.1 (1994): 9–39.

Hall, David D. *Cultures of Print: Essays in the History of the Book*. Amherst: University of Massachusetts Press, 1996.

Hall, Edward. *The Hidden Dimension*. Garden City, NY: Doubleday, 1969.

Hall, G. Stanley. *Adolescence: Its Psychology and Its Relation to Physiology, Anthropology, Sex, Crime, Religion, and Education*. New York: Appleton-Century-Crofts, 1904.

Hall, Gwendolyn Midlo. *Africans in Colonial Louisiana: The Development of Afro-Creole Culture in the Eighteenth Century*. Baton Rouge: Louisiana State University Press, 1992.

Hall, Stuart. "Cultural Identity and Diaspora." *Identity: Community, Culture, Difference*. Ed. Jonathan Rutherford. London: Lawrence and Wishart, 1990. 222–37.

——. "Cultural Studies and Its Theoretical Legacies." *Cultural Studies Reader*. Ed. Lawrence Grossberg, Cary Nelson, and Paula Treichler. New York: Routledge, 1991. 277–94.

——. "Cultural Studies: Two Paradigms." *Media, Culture and Society* 2.1 (January 1980): 57–72.

——. "Culture, Community, Nation." *Cultural Studies* 7.3 (1993): 349–63.

——. "Deviancy, Politics, and the Media." *Deviance and Social Control*. Ed. Paul Rock and Mary McIntosh. London: Tavistock, 1973. 261–305.

——. "Race, Articulation, and Societies Structured in Dominance." *Race Critical Theories: Text and Context*. Ed. Philomena Essed and David Theo Goldberg. Malden, MA: Blackwell, 2002. 38–68.

——. "Race, Culture and Communications: Looking Backward and Forward at Cultural Studies." *Rethinking Marxism* 5.1 (1992a): 10–18.

——. "What Is This 'Black' in Black Popular Culture?" *Black Popular Culture*. Ed. Gina Dent. Seattle: Bay, 1992b. 21–36.

Hall, Stuart, Chas Critcher, Tony Jefferson, John Clarke, and Brian Roberts. *Policing the Crisis: Mugging, the State, and Law and Order*. New York: Holmes and Meier, 1978.

Hall, Stuart, and Bram Gieben, eds. *Formations of Modernity*. Cambridge, UK: Polity, 1992a.

——. Introduction to *Formations of Modernity*. Ed. Stuart Hall and Bram Gieben. Cambridge, UK: Polity, 1992b. 1–16.

Hall, Stuart, and Tony Jefferson, eds. *Resistance through Rituals: Youth Subcultures in Post-war Britain*. London: Hutchinson / Centre for Contemporary Cultural Studies, University of Birmingham, 1976.

Halley, Janet E. *Don't: A Reader's Guide to the Military's Anti-Gay Policy*. Durham: Duke University Press, 1999.

Hamburger, Philip. *Separation of Church and State*. Cambridge: Harvard University Press, 2002.

Hames-Garcia, Michael. "How to Tell a Mestizo from an Enchirito: Colonialism and National Culture in the Borderlands." *diacritics* 30.4 (2000): 102–22.

Hammer, Michael, and James A. Champy. *Reengineering the Corporation: A Manifesto for Business Revolution*. New York: HarperCollins, 1993.

Hammonds, Evelynn. "Toward a Genealogy of Black Female Sexuality: The Problematic of Silence." *Feminist Genealogies, Colonial Legacies, Democratic Futures*. Ed. M. Jacqui Alexander and Chandra Talpade Mohanty. New York: Routledge, 1997. 170–82.

Hanchard, Michael. *Party/Politics: Horizons in Black Political Thought*. Oxford: Oxford University Press, 2006.

Haney-López, Ian F. *White by Law: The Legal Construction of Race.* New York: NYU Press, 1996.

Hannah, Matthew G. *Governmentality and the Mastery of Territory in Nineteenth-Century America.* New York: Cambridge University Press, 2000.

Hannerz, Ulf. *Cultural Complexity: Studies in the Social Organization of Meaning.* New York: Columbia University Press, 1992.

Hansen, Miriam. *Cinema and Experience: Siegfried Kracauer, Walter Benjamin, and Theodor W. Adorno.* Berkeley: University of California Press, 2011.

Hanway, Jonas. *An Historical Account of the British Trade over the Caspian Sea.* London, 1753.

Haraway, Donna. "A Cyborg Manifesto: Science, Technology, and Socialist-Feminism in the Late Twentieth Century." *Socialist Review* 80 (1985): 65–108.

———. *Simians, Cyborgs, and Women: The Re-invention of Nature.* New York: Routledge, 1991.

———. *When Species Meet.* Minneapolis: University of Minnesota Press, 2008.

Hardin, Garrett. "The Tragedy of the Commons." *Science* 162.3859 (1968): 1243–48.

Harding, Susan. *The Book of Jerry Falwell: Fundamentalist Language and Politics.* Princeton: Princeton University Press, 2001.

Hardt, Michael, and Antonio Negri. *Empire.* Cambridge: Harvard University Press, 2000.

Harkins, Anthony. *Hillbilly: A Cultural History of an American Icon.* New York: Oxford University Press, 2005.

Harkins, Gillian. *Everybody's Family Romance: Reading Incest in Neoliberal America.* Minneapolis: University of Minnesota Press, 2009.

Harlan County, U.S.A. Dir. Barbara Kopple. FirstRun Features, 1976.

Harper, Philip Brian. *Are We Not Men? Masculine Anxiety and the Problem of African-American Identity.* Oxford: Oxford University Press, 1996.

———. *Framing the Margins: The Social Logic of Postmodern Culture.* New York: Oxford University Press, 1994.

Harper, Phillip Brian, Anne McClintock, José Esteban Muñoz, and Trish Rosen. Introduction to "Queer Transexions of Race, Nation, and Gender." Ed. Phillip Brian Harper, Anne McClintock, José Estaban Muñoz, and Trish Rosen. Special issue of *Social Text* 52–53 (Fall–Winter 1997): 1–4.

Harris, Cheryl. "Whiteness as Property." *Harvard Law Review* 106 (1993): 1707–91.

Harris, Laura. "The Subjunctive Poetics of C. L. R. James's *American Civilization.*" Unpublished manuscript, 2005.

Harris, Lee. *Civilization and Its Enemies: The Next Stage of History.* New York: Free Press, 2004.

Harris, Marvin. *Cannibals and Kings: The Origins of Cultures.* New York: Random House, 1977.

Harris, Neil. *Humbug: The Art of P. T. Barnum.* Boston: Little, Brown, 1973.

Harrison, Lawrence E., and Samuel P. Huntington, eds. *Culture Matters: How Values Shape Human Progress.* New York: Basic Books, 2000.

Hart, Albert Bushnell. *The Southern South.* New York: D. Appleton, 1910.

Hart, H. L. A. *The Concept of Law.* Oxford, UK: Clarendon, 1961.

Hartigan, John, Jr. "Objectifying 'Poor Whites' and 'White Trash' in Detroit." *White Trash: Race and Class in America.* Ed. Matt Wray and Annalee Newitz. New York: Routledge, 1997. 41–56.

———. *Racial Situations: Class Predicaments of Whiteness in Detroit.* Princeton: Princeton University Press, 1999.

Hartman, Saidiya. *Scenes of Subjection: Terror, Slavery, and Self-Making in Nineteenth-Century America.* New York: Oxford University Press, 1997.

Hartz, Louis. *The Liberal Tradition in America: An Interpretation of American Political Thought since the Revolution.* New York: Harcourt Brace, 1955.

Harvey, David. *A Brief History of Neoliberalism.* New York: Oxford University Press, 2005.

———. *The Condition of Postmodernity: An Enquiry into the Origins of Cultural Change.* Oxford, UK: Blackwell, 1989.

———. *The Enigma of Capital and the Crises of Capitalism.* New York: Verso, 2010.

———. *The New Imperialism.* Oxford: Oxford University Press, 2003.

———. *Spaces of Hope.* Berkeley: University of California Press, 2000.

Haskell, Thomas L., and Richard F. Teichgraeber III, eds. *The Culture of the Market: Historical Essays.* New York: Cambridge University Press, 1996.

Hawthorne, Nathaniel. "Earth's Holocaust." *Graham's Lady's and Gentleman's Magazine,* March 1844.

———. Letter to William Ticknor, January 19, 1855. *Centenary Edition of the Works of Nathaniel Hawthorne.* Vol. 17: *The Letters, 1853–56.* Columbus: Ohio State University Press, 1987. 304.

Hay, Denys. *Europe: The Emergence of an Idea.* Edinburgh: Edinburgh University Press, 1957.

Hayek, F. A. *The Road to Serfdom.* Chicago: University of Chicago Press, 1944.

Hayles, Katherine N. *Electronic Literature: New Horizons for the Literary.* Notre Dame: University of Notre Dame Press, 2008.

———. *How We Became Posthuman: Virtual Bodies in Cybernetics, Literature, and Informatics.* Chicago: University of Chicago Press, 1999.

———. *How We Think: Digital Media and Contemporary Technogenesis.* Chicago: University of Chicago Press, 2012.

Hebdige, Dick. *Subculture: The Meaning of Style.* London: Methuen, 1979.

Hedges, Chris. *War Is a Force That Gives Us Meaning.* New York: PublicAffairs, 2002.

Hegel, G. W. F. *Hegel's Philosophy of Right.* 1821. Ed. and trans. T. M. Knox. Oxford, UK: Clarendon / Galaxy Books, 1979.

———. *The Philosophy of History.* 1837. Trans. J. Sibree. New York: Dover, 1956.

Heidegger, Martin. "The Question Concerning Technology." 1977. *Basic Writings.* Ed. David Farrell Krell. New York: Harper, 1993. 307–42.

Henderson, Bruce, and Noam Ostrander, eds. *Understanding Disability Studies and Performance Studies.* New York: Routledge, 2010.

Henderson, Mae G. "Speaking in Tongues: Dialogics and Dialectics and the Black Woman Writer's Literary Tradition." *Changing Our Own Words: Essays on Criticism, Theory, and Writing by Black Women.* Ed. Cheryl Wall. New Brunswick: Rutgers University Press, 1989.

Henderson, Stephen. *Understanding the New Black Poetry: Black Speech and Black Music as Poetic References*. New York: Morrow, 1973.

Hendler, Glenn. *Public Sentiments: Structures of Feeling in Nineteenth-Century American Literature*. Chapel Hill: University of North Carolina Press, 2001.

Henry, Patrick. "'And I Don't Care What It Is': The Tradition-History of a Civil Religion Proof-Text." *Journal of the American Academy of Religion* 49.1 (March 1981): 35–47.

Henry, Patrick. "Letter to Robert Pleasants, January 18, 1773." *Patrick Henry: Patriot in the Making*. Ed. Robert Douthat Meade. Vol. 1. Philadelphia: Lippincott, 1957.

Herbert, James D. "Visual Culture / Visual Studies." *Critical Terms for Art History*. 2nd ed. Ed. Robert S. Nelson and Richard Shiff. Chicago: University of Chicago Press, 2003. 452–64.

Herder, Johann Gottfried von. "On the Change of Taste." 1766. *Herder: Philosophical Writings*. Cambridge: Cambridge University Press, 2002. 247–56.

Herivel, Tara, and Paul Wright, eds. *Prison Nation: The Warehousing of America's Poor*. New York: Routledge, 2003.

Herman, Edward S., and Gerry O'Sullivan. *The "Terrorism" Industry: The Experts and Institutions That Shape Our View of Terror*. New York: Pantheon Books, 1989.

Herring, Scott. *Another Country: Queer Anti-urbanism*. New York: NYU Press, 2010.

Herrnstein, Richard J., and Charles Murray. *The Bell Curve: Intelligence and Class Structure in American Life*. New York: Free Press, 1994.

Hertz, Garnet. "Dead Media Research Lab." *Concept Lab*, 2009. http://www.conceptlab.com/deadmedia/.

Hietala, Thomas R. *Manifest Design: Anxious Aggrandizement in Late Jacksonian America*. Ithaca: Cornell University Press, 1985.

Higham, John. *Strangers in the Land: Patterns of American Nativism, 1860–1925*. New York: Atheneum, 1963.

Hilderbrand, Lucas. *Inherent Vice: Bootleg Histories of Videotape and Copyright*. Durham: Duke University Press, 2009.

Hilmes, Michele. "Is There a Field Called Sound Culture Studies? And Does It Matter?" *American Quarterly* 57.1 (2005): 249–59.

Hine, Darlene Clark. "Rape and the Inner Lives of Black Women in the Middle West: Preliminary Thoughts on the Culture of Dissemblance." *Signs* 14.4 (1989): 912–20.

Hine, Darlene Clark, Trica Danielle Keaton, and Stephen Small, eds. *Black Europe and the African Diaspora*. Urbana: University of Illinois Press, 2009.

Hirschkind, Charles. *The Ethical Soundscape: Cassette Sermons and Islamic Counterpublics*. New York: Columbia University Press, 2006.

Ho, Fred, ed. *Legacy to Liberation: Politics and Culture of Revolutionary Asian/Pacific America*. San Francisco: AK, 2000.

Hobsbawm, Eric. "Introduction: Inventing Tradition." *The Invention of Tradition*. Ed. Eric Hobsbawm and Terence Ranger. Cambridge: Cambridge University Press, 1983. 1–14.

Hodgson, Godfrey. *The Myth of American Exceptionalism*. New Haven: Yale University Press, 2009.

Hofmeyr, Isabel. *The Portable Bunyan: A Transnational History of "The Pilgrim's Progress."* Princeton: Princeton University Press, 2004.

Hogeland, Lisa Maria, and Mary Klages, et al., eds. *The Aunt Lute Anthology of U.S. Women Writers*. Vol. 1: *17th through 19th Centuries*. San Francisco: Aunt Lute Books, 2004.

Hollywood Shuffle. Dir. Robert Townsend. Samuel Goldwyn Company, 1987.

Holyoake, George J. *Secularism, the Philosophy of the People*. London, 1854.

Hondagneu-Sotelo, Pierette. "Beyond 'The Longer They Stay' (and Say They Will Stay): Women and Mexican Immigrant Settlement." *Qualitative Sociology* 18.1 (1995): 21–43.

Hong, Grace Kyungwon. *The Ruptures of American Capital: Women of Color Feminism and the Culture of Immigrant Labor*. Minneapolis: University of Minnesota Press, 2006.

Hong, Grace Kyungwon, and Roderick A. Ferguson. *Strange Affinities: The Gender and Sexual Politics of Comparative Racialization*. Durham: Duke University Press, 2011.

Honig, Bonnie. "Immigrant America? How Foreignness 'Solves' Democracy's Problems." *Social Text* 56 (1998): 1–27.

Hopfyl, Harro, and Martyn P. Thompson. "The History of the Contract as a Motif in Political Thought." *American Historical Review* 84.4 (1979): 919–44.

Horkheimer, Max, and Theodor W. Adorno. *Dialectic of Enlightenment: Philosophical Fragments*. 1944. Ed. Gunzelin Schmid Noerr. Trans. Edmund Jephcott. Stanford: Stanford University Press, 2002.

Horne, T. H. *Outlines for the Classification of a Library*. London: Woodfall and Court, 1825.

Horowitz, Tony. *Confederates in the Attic: Dispatches from the Unfinished Civil War*. New York: Vintage, 1999.

Horsman, Reginald. *Race and Manifest Destiny: The Origins of American Racial Anglo-Saxonism*. Cambridge: Harvard University Press, 1981.

Horwitz, Howard. "The Standard Oil Trust as Emersonian Hero." *Raritan* 6.4 (1987): 97–119.

Howard, John. *Men Like That: A Southern Queer History*. Chicago: University of Chicago Press, 2001.

Howard, June. "Introduction: Sarah Orne Jewett and the Traffic in Words." *New Essays on "The Country of the Pointed Firs."* Ed. June Howard. Cambridge: Cambridge University Press, 1994. 1–38.

———. *Publishing the Family*. Durham: Duke University Press, 2001.

———. "What Is Sentimentality?" *American Literary History* 11 (1999): 63–81.

Howe, Susan. *The Birth-mark: Unsettling the Wilderness in American Literary History*. Hanover, NH: Wesleyan University Press / University Press of New England, 1993.

Howes, David, ed. *Empire of the Senses: The Sensual Culture Reader*. Oxford, UK: Berg, 2005.

Hubbard, Ruth, Mary Sue Henifin, and Barbara Fried, eds. *Women Look at Biology Looking at Women: A Collection of Feminist Critiques*. Cambridge, MA: Schenkman, 1979.

Hughes, Langston. *Good Morning, Revolution: Uncollected Social Protest Writings*. Ed. Faith Berry. Brooklyn, NY: Lawrence Hill, 1973.

Hume, David. *The Natural History of Religion*. 1757. *"Dialogues" and "Natural History of Religion."* Oxford: Oxford University Press, 1993. 134–96.

Hunter, Tera W. *To 'Joy My Freedom: Southern Black Women's Lives and Labors after the Civil War*. Cambridge: Harvard University Press, 1997.

Huntington, Samuel P. *The Clash of Civilizations and the Remaking of World Order*. New York: Simon and Schuster, 1996.

———. "The Hispanic Challenge." *Foreign Policy*, March–April 2004a. http://www.foreignpolicy.com/articles/2004/03/01/the_hispanic_challenge.

———. *Who Are We? The Challenges to America's National Identity*. New York: Simon and Schuster, 2004b.

Hurtado, Aída. "Relating to Privilege: Seduction and Rejection in the Subordination of White Women and Women of Color." *Signs* 14.4 (1989): 833–55.

Hutcheon, Linda. *The Politics of Postmodernism*. 2nd ed. New York: Routledge, 2002.

Hutcheson, Frances. *An Essay on the Nature and Conduct of the Passions and Affections, with Illustrations on the Moral Sense*. 1742. Ed. and introd. Aaron Garrett. Indianapolis: Liberty Fund, 2003.

Ignatiev, Noel. *How the Irish Became White*. New York: Routledge, 1995.

Ihde, Don. *Technology and the Lifeworld: From Garden to Earth*. Bloomington: Indiana University Press, 1990.

Irick, Robert L. *Ch'ing Policy toward the Coolie Trade, 1847–1878*. Taipei: Chinese Materials Center, 1982.

Irvine, Janice. *Disorders of Desire: Sex and Gender in Modern American Sexology*. Philadelphia: Temple University Press, 1990.

Isambard. "Would You Describe Yourself as Queer?" Online posting. Urban75 Forums, May 22, 2004. http://www.urban75.net/vbulletin/archive/index.php/t76675.html.

Isenberg, Nancy. *Sex and Citizenship in Antebellum America*. Chapel Hill: University of North Carolina Press, 1998.

Isham, Samuel. *History of American Painting*. New York: Macmillan, 1905.

Jackson, Jonathan David. "The Social World of Voguing." *Journal for the Anthropological Study of Human Movement* 12.2 (2002): 26–42.

Jacobs, Harriet. *Incidents in the Life of a Slave Girl*. 1861. Ed. Nellie Y. McKay and Frances Smith Foster. New York: Norton, 2001.

Jacobson, Matthew Frye. *Barbarian Virtues: The United States Encounters Foreign Peoples at Home and Abroad, 1876–1917*. New York: Hill and Wang, 2000.

———. *Whiteness of a Different Color: European Immigrants and the Alchemy of Race*. Cambridge: Harvard University Press, 1998.

Jamal, Amaney, and Nadine Naber, eds., *Race and Arab Americans before and after 9/11: From Invisible Citizens to Visible Subjects*. Syracuse: Syracuse University Press, 2008.

James, C. L. R. *The Black Jacobins: Toussaint L'Ouverture and the San Domingo Revolution*. New York: Dial, 1938. Reprint, New York: Vintage 1989.

———. "Every Cook Can Govern: A Study of Democracy in Ancient Greece." *The Future in the Present: Selected Writings*. Westport, CT: Lawrence Hill, 1956. 160–74.

James, Joy. *The New Abolitionists: (Neo)Slave Narratives and Contemporary Prison Writings*. Albany: SUNY Press, 2005.

James, Lawrence. *Raj: The Making and Unmaking of British India*. New York: St. Martin's Griffin, 2000.

James, Selma, and Mariarosa Dalla Costa. *The Power of Women and the Subversion of Community: Wages for Housework*. Bristol, UK: Falling Wall, 1972.

Jameson, Fredric. "On 'Cultural Studies.'" *Social Text* 36 (1993): 17–52.

———. *Postmodernism, or, The Cultural Logic of Late Capitalism*. Durham: Duke University, 1991.

Jay, Martin. *Downcast Eyes: The Denigration of Vision in Twentieth-Century French Thought*. Berkeley: University of California Press, 1994.

Jefferson, Thomas. "Declaration of Independence." 1776. *Writings*. New York: Library of America, 1984. 19–24.

———. *Notes on the State of Virginia*. 1787. *Notes on the State of Virginia: With Related Documents*. Ed. David Waldstreicher. Boston: Bedford / St. Martin's, 2002.

———. *Notes on the State of Virginia*. 1787. *Writings*. New York: Library of America, 1984. 123–325.

Jeffords, Susan. *The Remasculinization of America: Gender and the Vietnam War*. Bloomington: Indiana University Press, 1989.

Jehlen, Myra, and Michael Warner. *The English Literatures of America, 1500–1800*. New York: Routledge, 1997.

Jenkins, Henry. *Convergence Culture: Where Old and New Media Collide*. New York: NYU Press, 2006.

Jensen, Arthur. "How Much Can We Boost IQ and Scholastic Achievement?" *Harvard Educational Review* 39 (1969): 1–123.

Johns, Elizabeth. *American Genre Painting: The Politics of Everyday Life*. New Haven: Yale University Press, 1991.

Johnson, E. Patrick. *Appropriating Blackness: Performance and the Politics of Authenticity*. Durham: Duke University Press, 2003.

———. *Sweet Tea: Black Gay Men of the South*. Chapel Hill: University of North Carolina Press, 2008.

Johnson, E. Patrick, and Mae G. Henderson. *Black Queer Studies: A Critical Anthology*. Durham: Duke University Press, 2005.

Johnson, Lyndon Baines. "Annual Message to the Congress on the State of the Union, January 8, 1964." *Public Papers of the Presidents, Lyndon Baines Johnson, 1963–64*. Vol. 1, entry 91. Washington, DC: Government Printing Office, 1965. 112–18.

Johnson, Walter. "The Pedestal and the Veil: Re-thinking the Capitalism/Slavery Question." *Journal of the Early Republic* 24 (2004): 299–308.

———. *Soul by Soul: Life inside the Antebellum Slave Market*. Cambridge: Harvard University Press, 1999.

———. "Time and Revolution in African America: Temporality and the History of Atlantic Slavery." *Rethinking American History in a Global Age*. Ed. Thomas Bender. Berkeley: University of California Press, 2002. 148–67.

Jones, Gavin. *Strange Talk: The Politics of Dialect Literature in Gilded Age America*. Berkeley: University of California Press, 1999.

Jordan, Winthrop. *White over Black: American Attitudes toward the Negro, 1550–1812*. Baltimore: Pelican Books, 1969.

Joseph, Miranda. *Against the Romance of Community*. Minneapolis: University of Minnesota Press, 2002.

———. "A Debt to Society." *The Seductions of Community*. Ed. Gerald Creed. Santa Fe, NM: SAR Press, 2006. 199–226.

Joshi, Khyati Y. "The Racialization of Hinduism, Islam, and Sikhism in the United States." *Equity and Excellence in Education* 39 (2006): 211–26.

Joyce, Joyce A. "The Black Canon: Reconstructing Black American Literary Criticism." *New Literary History* 18 (Winter 1987a): 335–44.

———. "'Who the Cap Fit': Unconsciousness and Unconscionableness in the Criticism of Houston A. Baker, Jr., and Henry Louis Gates, Jr." *New Literary History* 18 (Winter 1987b): 371–83.

Juhasz, Alexandra. *Learning from YouTube*. Cambridge: MIT Press, 2011.

Jung, Moon-Ho. *Coolies and Cane: Race, Labor, and Sugar Production in the Age of Emancipation*. Baltimore: Johns Hopkins University Press, 2006.

Justice, Daniel Heath. *Kynship: The Way of Thorn and Thunder, Book One*. Neyaashiinigmiing, Nawash First Nation: Kegedonce, 2005.

Justice, Daniel Heath, Mark Rifkin, and Bethany Schneider, eds. "Sexuality, Nationality, Indigeneity." Special issue of *GLQ* 16.1-2 (2010).

Kagan, Donald, and Frederick W. Kagan. *While America Sleeps: Self-Delusion, Military Weakness, and the Threat to Peace Today*. New York: St. Martin's, 2000.

Kallen, Horace. "Democracy versus the Melting-Pot." *Nation* 100 (February 18, 1915): 190–94, 217–20.

Kandaswamy, Priya, Mattie Eudora Richardson, and Marlon Bailey. "Is Gay Marriage Racist? A Conversation with Marlon M. Bailey, Priya Kandaswamy, and Mattie Eudora Richardson." *That's Revolting: Queer Strategies for Resisting Assimilation*. Ed. Mattilda Bernstein Sycamore. Brooklyn, NY: Soft Skull, 2006. 87–93.

Kant, Immanuel. *The Critique of Judgment*. 1790. Trans. James Creed Meredith. Oxford: Oxford University Press, 1952.

Kanter, Rosabeth Moss. *When Giants Learn to Dance*. New York: Free Press, 1990.

Kantorowicz, Ernst. *The King's Two Bodies*. Princeton: Princeton University Press, 1957.

Kaplan, Amy. *The Anarchy of Empire in the Making of U.S. Culture*. Cambridge: Harvard University Press, 2002.

———. "'Left Alone with America': The Absence of Empire in the Study of American Culture." *Cultures of United States Imperialism*. Ed. Amy Kaplan and Donald Pease. Durham: Duke University Press, 1993. 3–21.

———. "Manifest Domesticity." *American Literature* 70 (September 1998): 581–606.

———. "Nation, Region, Empire." *The Columbia History of the American Novel*. Ed. Emory Elliott. New York: Columbia University Press, 1991. 240–66.

———. "Violent Belongings and the Question of Empire Today: Presidential Address to the American Studies Association, Hartford, Connecticut, October 17, 2003." *American Quarterly* 56.1 (March 2004): 1–18.

———. "Where Is Guantanamo?" *American Quarterly* 57.3 (September 2005): 831–54.

Kaplan, Amy, and Donald E. Pease, eds. *Cultures of United States Imperialism*. Durham: Duke University Press, 1993.

Kaplan, Caren, Norma Alarcón, and Minoo Moallem, eds. *Between Women and Nation: Nationalisms, Transnational Feminisms, and the State*. Durham: Duke University Press, 1999.

Kaplan, Carla. *The Erotics of Talk: Women's Writing and Feminist Paradigms*. New York: Oxford University Press, 1996.

Kaplan, Morris. *Sexual Justice: Democratic Citizenship and the Politics of Desire*. New York: Routledge, 1997.

Karpf, Anne. *The Human Voice*. London: Bloomsbury, 2006.

Katz, Cindi. *Growing Up Global: Restructuring and Children's Everyday Lives*. Minneapolis: University of Minnesota Press, 2004.

Katz, Jonathan Ned. *The Invention of Heterosexuality*. New York: Dutton/Penguin, 1995.

Kauanui, J. Kēhaulani. "Asian American Studies and the 'Pacific Question.'" *Asian American Studies after Critical Mass*. Ed. Kent Ono. Malden, MA: Blackwell, 2004. 123–243.

———. "Diasporic Deracination and 'Off-Island' Hawaiians." *Contemporary Pacific* 19.1 (2007): 137–60.

Kazanjian, David. "Hegel, Liberia." *Diacritics* 40.1 (2012): 6–39.

———. "The Speculative Freedom of Colonial Liberia." *American Quarterly* 63.4 (2011): 863–93.

Keane, John. *Global Civil Society?* Cambridge: Cambridge University Press, 2003.

Keay, Douglas. "AIDS, Education, and the Year 2000: An Interview with Margaret Thatcher." *Woman's Own*, October 31, 1987: 8–10.

Keeling, Kara, and Josh Kun, eds. *Sound Clash: Listening to American Studies*. Baltimore: John Hopkins University Press, 2011.

Keith, Arthur. "The Evolution of the Human Races." *Journal of the Royal Anthropological Institute of Great Britain and Ireland* 58 (July–December 1928): 305–21.

Keller, Evelyn Fox. *Reflections on Gender and Science*. New Haven: Yale University Press, 1985.

Kelley, Robin D. G. *Race Rebels: Culture, Politics, and the Black Working Class*. New York: Free Press, 1994.

———. *Yo Mama's DisFUNKtional: Fighting the Culture Wars in Urban America*. Boston: Beacon, 1997.

Kempadoo, Kamala, and Jo Doezema, eds. *Global Sex Workers: Rights, Resistance, and Redefinition*. New York: Routledge, 1998.

Ken Burns's America. New York: PBS Home Video; Turner Home Entertainment, 1996.

Kennedy, John F. "Report to the American People on Civil Rights, 11 June 1963." John F. Kennedy Presidential Library and Museum. http://www.jfklibrary.org/Asset-Viewer/LH8F_0Mzvoe6Ro1yEm74Ng.aspx.

Kenny, Gale L. *Contentious Liberties: American Abolitionists in Post-Emancipation Jamaica, 1834-1866*. Athens: University of Georgia Press, 2011.

Keohane Robert O., and Joseph S. Nye, Jr. *Power and Independence*. Glenview, IL: Scott, Foresman, 1989.

Kerber, Linda K. *Women of the Republic: Intellect and Ideology in Revolutionary America*. Chapel Hill: University of North Carolina Press, 1980.

Kerber, Linda K., and Jane Sherron De Hart. *Women's America: Refocusing the Past*. 5th ed. New York: Oxford University Press, 2004.

Kernan, Alvin. *The Death of Literature*. New Haven: Yale University Press, 1990.

Kersten, Holger. "The Creative Potential of Dialect Writing in Later Nineteenth-Century America." *Nineteenth-Century Literature* 55.1 (2000): 92–117.

———. "Using the Immigrant's Voice: Humor and Pathos in Nineteenth-Century 'Dutch' Dialect Texts." *MELUS* 21.4 (1996): 3–18.

Kessler, Suzanne J. *Lessons from the Intersexed*. New Brunswick: Rutgers University Press, 1998.

Kessler, Suzanne J., and Wendy McKenna. *Gender: An Ethnomethodological Approach*. Chicago: University of Chicago Press, 1990.

Kessler-Harris, Alice. *A Woman's Wage: Historical Meanings and Social Consequence*. Lexington: University Press of Kentucky, 1990.

Keynes, John Maynard. *The General Theory of Employment, Interest and Money*. London: Macmillan, 1936.

Kilgore, DeWitt. *Afro-futurism: Science, Race, and Visions of Utopia in Space*. Philadelphia: University of Pennsylvania Press, 2003.

Kim, Ahan. "Poll Finds Many Want Restrictions on Arab Americans." *Seattle Post-Intelligencer*, September 18, 2001.

King, Martin Luther, Jr. Speech to striking sanitation workers, Memphis, Tennessee, March 18, 1968. American Federation of Teachers website. http://www.aft.org/yourwork/tools4teachers/bhm/mlkpeech031868.cfm.

Kingston, Maxine Hong. *Tripmaster Monkey: His Fake Book*. New York: Knopf, 1989.

Kipling, Rudyard. "The White Man's Burden." *McClure's Magazine*, February 1899, 240–41.

Kirschenbaum, Matthew G. *Mechanisms: New Media and the Forensic Imagination*. Cambridge: MIT Press, 2008.

Kittler, Friedrich A. *Gramophone, Film, Typewriter*. Trans. Geoffrey Winthrop-Young and Michael Wutz. Stanford: Stanford University Press, 1999.

Klein, Kerwin Lee. "Reclaiming the 'F' Word: On Being and Becoming Postwestern." *Pacific Historical Review* 65.12 (1996): 179–215.

Klein, Lisl. *The Meaning of Work: Papers on Work Organization and the Design of Jobs*. London: Karnac Books, 2008.

Klein, Naomi. *The Shock Doctrine*. New York: Metropolitan Books, 2007.

Kochhar-Lindgren, Kanta. *Hearing Difference: The Third Ear in Experimental, Deaf, and Multicultural Performance*. Washington, DC: Gallaudet University Press, 2006.

Koestenbaum, Wayne. *The Queen's Throat: Opera, Homosexuality, and the Mystery of Desire*. 1994. Cambridge, MA: Da Capo, 2001.

Kolchin, Peter. "Whiteness Studies: The New History of Race in America." *Journal of American History* 89 (2002): 154–74.

Kollin, Susan. *Postwestern Cultures: Literature, Theory, Space*. Lincoln: University of Nebraska Press, 2007.

Kolodny, Annette. *The Land before Her: Fantasy and Experience of the American Frontiers, 1630–1860*. Chapel Hill: University of North Carolina Press, 1984.

———. *The Lay of the Land: Metaphor as Experience and History in American Letters*. Chapel Hill: University of North Carolina Press, 1975.

Koselleck, Reinhart. *Futures Past: On the Semantics of Historical Time*. 1985. Trans. Keith Tribe. New York: Columbia University Press, 2004.

Kotkin, Joel, and Erika Ozuna. *The Changing Face of the San Fernando Valley*. Davenport Institute Research Report. Malibu, CA: School of Public Policy, Pepperdine University, 2002.

Kozol, Wendy. "Madonnas of the Fields: Photography, Gender, and 1930s Farm Relief." *Genders* 2 (July 1988): 1–23.

Kracauer, Siegfried. *Theory of Film: The Redemption of Physical Reality*. 1960. Princeton: Princeton University Press, 1997.

Krapp, George Philip. *The English Language in America*. 2 vols. New York: Century, 1925.

———. "The Psychology of Dialect Writing." *Bookman* 63 (1926): 522–27.

Krentz, Christopher. *Writing Deafness: The Hearing Line in Nineteenth-Century American Literature*. Chapel Hill: University of North Carolina Press, 2007.

Kroeber, Alfred Louis. "The Superorganic." *American Anthropologist* 19 (1917): 163–213.

Kroeber, Alfred Louis, and Clyde Kluckhohn. *Culture: A Critical Review of Concepts and Definitions*. New York: Vintage, 1952.

Krugman, Paul. *The Age of Diminished Expectations: U.S. Economic Policy in the 1990s*. Cambridge: MIT Press, 1997.

Krugman, Paul, and Robin Wells. *Microeconomics*. North York: Worth, 2004.

Kulick, Bruce. "Myth and Symbol in American Studies." *American Quarterly* 24 (1972): 435–50.

Kumar, Deepa. *Islamophobia and the Politics of Empire*. Chicago: Haymarket Books, 2012.

Kun, Josh. *Audiotopia: Music, Race, and America*. Berkeley: University of California Press, 2005.

Kuppers, Petra. *Disability and Contemporary Performance: Bodies on Edge*. New York: Routledge, 2003.

———. *Disability Culture and Community Performance: Find a Strange and Twisted Shape*. New York: Palgrave Macmillan, 2011.

LaBelle, Brandon. *Acoustic Territories: Sound Culture and Everyday Life*. London: Continuum, 2010.

LaBennett, Oneka. *She's Mad Real: Popular Culture and West Indian Girls in Brooklyn*. New York: NYU Press, 2011.

Lacey, Kate. *Listening Publics: The Politics and Experience of Listening in the Media Age*. Cambridge, UK: Polity, 2013.

Lacey, Nicola. "Community in Legal Theory: Idea, Ideal or Ideology." *Studies in Law, Politics and Society* 15 (1996): 105–46.

Lacey, Nicola, and Lucia Zedner. "Discourses of Community in Criminal Justice." *Journal of Law and Society* 22.3 (1995): 301–25.

Laclau, Ernesto. Introduction to *The Making of Political Identities*. Ed. Ernesto Laclau. London: Verso, 1994. 1–8.

———. *New Reflections on the Revolution of Our Time*. London: Verso, 1990.

LaFeber, Walter. *The New Empire: An Interpretation of American Expansion, 1860–1898*. Ithaca: Cornell University Press, 1963.

Lakoff, George. "Metaphor and War: The Metaphor System Used to Justify War in the Gulf." *Viet Nam Generation Journal & Newsletter* 3.3 (November 1991). http://www2.iath.virginia.edu/sixties/HTML_docs/Texts/Scholarly/Lakoff_Gulf_Metaphor_1.html.

Landry, Charles. *The Creative City: A Toolkit for Urban Innovators*. London: Earthscan, 2000.

Lanier, Jaron. *You Are Not a Gadget: A Manifesto*. New York: Vintage Books, 2010.

Laó-Montes, Agustín, and Arlene M. Dávila, eds. *Mambo Montage: The Latinization of New York*. New York: Columbia University Press, 2001.

Laqueur, Thomas. *Making Sex: Body and Gender from the Greeks to Freud*. Cambridge: Harvard University Press, 1990.

Larsen, Nella. *Passing*. New York: Knopf, 1929.

Latour, Bruno. *Science in Action: How to Follow Scientists and Engineers through Society*. Cambridge: Harvard University Press, 1987.

———. "Why Has Critique Run Out of Steam? From Matters of Fact to Matters of Concern." *Critical Inquiry* 30.2 (2004): 225-48.

Laughlin, Harry H., and John B. Trevor. *Immigration and Conquest: A Study of the United States as the Receiver of Old World Emigrants Who Become the Parents of Future-Born Americans; a Report of the Special Committee on Immigration and Naturalization of the Chamber of Commerce of the State of New York*. New York: Chamber of Commerce of the State of New York, 1939.

Lauter, Paul, ed. *The Heath Anthology of American Literature*. 2 vols. Lexington, MA: Heath, 1994.

———. "The Literatures of America: A Comparative Discipline." *Redefining American Literary History*. Ed. A. La Vonne Brown Ruoff and Jerry W. Ward, Jr. New York: Modern Language Association, 1990. 9-34.

Lavoie, Judith. *Mark Twain et la parole noire*. Montréal: Les Presses de l'Université de Montréal, 2002.

Lazo, Rodrigo. *Writing to Cuba: Filibustering and Cuban Exiles in the United States*. Chapel Hill: University of North Carolina Press, 2005.

Lazzarato, Maurizio. "Immaterial Labour." *Radical Thought in Italy: A Potential Politics*. Ed. Paolo Virno and Michael Hardt. Minneapolis: University of Minnesota Press. 132-46.

Lean, Nathan. *The Islamophobia Industry: How the Right Manufactures Fear of Muslims*. New York: Pluto, 2012.

Lears, T. J. Jackson. *No Place of Grace: Antimodernism and the Transformation of American Culture, 1880-1920*. New York: Pantheon, 1981.

Lederer, Richard M. *Colonial American English: A Glossary*. Essex, CT: Verbatim, 1985.

Lee, Anthony. *Picturing Chinatown: Art and Orientalism in San Francisco*. Berkeley: University of California Press, 2001.

Lee, Erika. *At America's Gates during the Exclusion Era*. Chapel Hill: University of North Carolina Press, 2007.

Lee, Everett S. "A Theory of Migration." *Demography* 3.1 (1966): 47-57.

Lee, James Kyung-Jin. "The Transitivity of Race and the Challenge of the Imagination." *PMLA* 123.5 (2009): 1550-56.

———. *Urban Triage: Race and the Fictions of Multiculturalism*. Minneapolis: University of Minnesota Press, 2004.

Lee, Jo-Anne, and John Lutz. "Introduction: Toward a Critical Literacy of Racisms, Anti-racisms, and Racialization." *Situating "Race" and Racisms in Space, Time, and Theory: Critical Essays for Activists and Scholars*. Ed. Jo-Anne Lee and John Lutz. Montreal: McGill-Queen's University Press, 2005. 3-29.

Lee, Stacy. *Unraveling the "Model Minority" Stereotype*. New York: Teachers College Press, 2009.

———. *Up against Whiteness: Race, School, and Immigrant Youth*. New York: Teachers College Press, 2005.

Lefebvre, Henry. *The Production of Space*. Cambridge, UK: Blackwell, 1991.

Leja, Michael. *Looking Askance: Skepticism and American Art from Eakins to Duchamp*. Berkeley: University of California Press, 2004.

Lemann, Nicholas. *The Big Test: The Secret History of the American Meritocracy*. New York: Macmillan, 2000.

LeMenager, Stephanie. *Manifest and Other Destinies: Territorial Fictions of the Nineteenth-Century United States*. Lincoln: University of Nebraska Press, 2004.

Lesko, Nancy. *Act Your Age! A Cultural Construction of Adolescence*. New York: Routledge, 2001.

Lessig, Lawrence. *The Future of Ideas: The Fate of the Commons in a Connected World*. New York: Vintage, 2002.

Levander, Caroline F., and Robert S. Levine, eds. *Hemispheric American Studies*. New Brunswick: Rutgers University Press, 2008a.

———. "Introduction: Essays beyond the Nation." *Hemispheric American Studies*. Ed. Caroline F. Levander and Robert S. Levine. New Brunswick: Rutgers University Press, 2008b. 1-17.

Levine, Lawrence. *Highbrow, Lowbrow: The Emergence of Cultural Hierarchy in America*. Cambridge: Harvard University Press, 1988.

Levine, Robert. *Martin Delany, Frederick Douglass, and the Politics of Representative Identity*. Chapel Hill: University of North Carolina Press, 1997.

Lévi-Strauss, Claude. *Cultural Anthropology*. New York: Anchor Books, 1963.

———. *The Elementary Structures of Kinship*. Boston: Beacon, 1971.

Lewis, Earl. "To Turn as on a Pivot: Writing African Americans into a History of Overlapping Diasporas." *American Historical Review* 100 (June 1995): 765-87.

Lewis, Jason E., David DeGusta, Marc R. Meyer, Janet M. Monge, Alan E. Mann, et al. "The Mismeasure of Science: Stephen Jay Gould versus Samuel George Morton on Skulls and Bias." *PLoS Biol* 9.6 (2011): e1001071. doi:10.1371/journal.pbio.1001071.

Lewis, Nathaniel. *Unsettling the Literary West: Authenticity and Authorship*. Lincoln: University of Nebraska Press, 2003.

Lewis, Oscar. *Five Families: Mexican Case Studies in the Culture of Poverty*. New York: Basic Books, 1959.

Lewis, R. W. B. *The American Adam: Innocence, Tradition, and Tragedy in the Nineteenth Century*. Chicago: University of Chicago Press, 1955.

Lewis, Victoria Ann, ed. *Beyond Victims and Villains: Contemporary Plays by Disabled Playwrights*. New York: Theatre Communications Group, 2005.

Lewis, W. David. *From Newgate to Dannemora: The Rise of the Penitentiary in New York, 1796-1848*. Ithaca: Cornell University Press, 1965.

Lichtenstein, Nelson. *State of the Union: A Century of American Labor*. Princeton: Princeton University Press 2002.

Lima, Lázaro. *The Latino Body: Crisis Identities in American Literary and Cultural Memory*. New York: NYU Press, 2007.

Limerick, Patricia Nelson. "The Trail to Santa Fe: The Unleashing of the Western Public Intellectual." *Trails: Toward a New Western History*. Ed. Patricia Nelson Limerick, Clyde A. Milner II, and Charles E. Rankin. Lawrence: University Press of Kansas, 1991. 59-80.

Limón, José. *American Encounters: Greater Mexico, the United States, and the Erotics of Culture*. Boston: Beacon, 1999.

Lincoln, Abraham. Speech at Peoria, Illinois, October 16, 1854. *The Collected Works of Abraham Lincoln*. Ed. Roy P. Basler. Vol. 2. New Brunswick: Rutgers University Press, 1953. 247–83.

Linebaugh, Peter, and Marcus Rediker. *The Many-Headed Hydra: Sailors, Slaves, Commoners, and the Hidden History of the Revolutionary Atlantic*. Boston: Beacon, 2000.

Linenthal, Edward T. *The Unfinished Bombing: Oklahoma City in American Memory*. New York: Oxford University Press, 2001.

Linnaeus, Carolus. *Systema Naturae*. Leiden, 1735.

Linton, Simi. *Claiming Disability: Knowledge and Identity*. New York: NYU Press, 1998.

Lipietz, Alain. "Post-Fordism and Democracy." *Post-Fordism: A Reader*. Ed. Ash Amin. Oxford, UK: Blackwell, 1994. 338–57.

Lipovetsky, Gilles. *The Empire of Fashion: Dressing Modern Democracy*. Princeton: Princeton University Press, 1994.

Lippmann, Walter. *The Phantom Public*. New York: Macmillan, 1927.

Lipset, Seymour. *The First New Nation: The United States in Historical and Comparative Perspective*. New York: Basic Books, 1963.

Lipsitz, George. *American Studies in a Moment of Danger*. Minneapolis: University of Minnesota Press, 2001.

———. *How Racism Takes Place*. Philadelphia: Temple University Press, 2011.

———. "Listening to Learn and Learning to Listen: Popular Culture, Cultural Theory, and American Studies." *American Quarterly* 42.4 (1990a): 615–36.

———. *The Possessive Investment in Whiteness: How White People Profit from Identity Politics*. 1998. Philadelphia: Temple University Press, 2006.

———. "The Possessive Investment in Whiteness: Racialized Social Democracy and the 'White' Problem in American Studies." *American Quarterly* 47.3 (1995): 369–87.

———. *Time Passages: Collective Memory and American Popular Culture*. Minneapolis: University of Minnesota Press, 1990b.

LiPuma, Edward, and Ben Lee. *Financial Derivatives and the Globalization of Risk*. Durham: Duke University Press, 2004.

Litman, Jessica. *Digital Copyright*. Amherst, NY: Prometheus Books, 2001.

Lloyd, David, and Paul Thomas. "Culture and Society or 'Culture and the State'?" In *Cultural Materialism: On Raymond Williams*. Ed. Christopher Prendergast. Minneapolis: University of Minnesota Press, 1995. 268–304.

———. *Culture and the State*. New York: Routledge, 1998.

Locke, John. *Second Treatise of Government*. 1690. Ed. C. B. Macpherson. Indianapolis: Hackett, 1980.

———. *Two Treatises of Government*. 1690. Ed. Peter Laslett. New York: Cambridge University Press, 1988.

London, Jack. *The People of the Abyss*. New York: Lawrence Hill, 1903.

Lone Star. Dir. John Sayles. Columbia Pictures Corporation / Rio Dulce, 1996.

Longmore, Paul. *Why I Burned My Book and Other Essays on Disability*. Philadelphia: Temple University Press, 2003.

Longmore, Paul, and Lauri Umansky, eds. *The New Disability History: American Perspectives*. New York: NYU Press, 2001.

Loomba, Ania. *Colonialism/Postcolonialism*. 2nd ed. London and New York: Routledge, 2005.

Loraux, Nicole. *Mothers in Mourning*. Ithaca: Cornell University Press, 1998.

Lorde, Audre. "Age, Race, Class, and Sex: Women Redefining Difference." *Sister Outsider: Essays and Speeches*. Trumansburg, NY: Crossing, 1984a. 114–23.

———. "Poetry Is Not a Luxury." *Sister Outsider: Essays and Speeches*. Trumansburg, NY: Crossing, 1984b. 36–39.

Losh, Elizabeth. "Hacktivism and the Humanities: Programming Protest in the Era of the Digital University." *Debates in the Digital Humanities*. Ed. Matthew K. Gold. Minneapolis: University of Minnesota Press, 2012. 161–86.

Lothian, Alexis, and Amanda Phillips. "Can Digital Humanities Mean Transformative Critique?" *E-Media Studies* 3.1 (2013). http://journals.dartmouth.edu/cgi-bin/WebObjects/Journals.woa/1/xmlpage/4/article/425.

Lott, Eric. "Back Door Man: Howlin' Wolf and the Sound of Jim Crow." *Sound Clash: Listening to American Studies*. Ed. Kara Keeling and Josh Kun. Baltimore: Johns Hopkins University Press, 2011. 253–66.

———. *Love and Theft: Blackface Minstrelsy and the American Working Class*. New York: Oxford University Press, 1993.

Loughran, Trish. *The Republic in Print: Print Culture in the Age of U.S. Nation Building, 1770–1870*. New York: Columbia University Press, 2007.

Louie, Miriam Ching Yoon. *Sweatshop Warriors: Immigrant Women Workers Take on the Global Factory*. Cambridge, MA: South End, 2001.

Love, Heather. *Feeling Backward: Loss and the Politics of Queer History*. Cambridge: Harvard University Press, 2007.

Loveman, Mara. "Is 'Race' Essential?" *American Sociological Review* 64 (1999): 891–98.

Lowe, Lisa. "Autobiography out of Empire." *small axe* 28 (2009): 98–111.

———. *Immigrant Acts: On Asian American Cultural Politics*. Durham: Duke University Press, 1996.

———. "The Intimacies of Four Continents." *Haunted by Empire: Geographies of Intimacy in North American History*. Ed. Ann Laura Stoler. Durham: Duke University Press, 2006. 191–212.

Lowe, Lisa, and David Lloyd, eds. *The Politics of Culture in the Shadow of Capital*. Durham: Duke University Press, 1997.

Loyd, Virgil. "Statement of a Louisiana Freedman." 1865. *Freedom: A Documentary History of Emancipation, 1861–1867*. Ser. 1, vol. 3: *The Wartime Genesis of Free Labor: The Lower South*. Ed. Ira Berlin, Steven F. Miller, Joseph P. Reidy, and Leslie S. Rowland. New York: Cambridge University Press, 1990. 614–16.

Luce, Henry R. "The American Century." *Life*, February 17, 1941: 61–65.

Luibhéid, Eithne. *Entry Denied: Controlling Sexuality at the Border*. Minneapolis: University of Minnesota Press, 2002.

Luibhéid, Eithne, and Lionel Cantú, eds. *Queer Migrations: Sexuality, U.S. Citizenship, and Border Crossings*. Minneapolis: University of Minnesota Press, 2005.

Lye, Colleen. *America's Asia: Racial Forms and American Literature, 1893–1945*. Princeton: Princeton University Press, 2004.

Lyman, Stanford M. *Civilization: Contents, Discontents, Malcontents, and Other Essays in Social Theory*. Fayetteville: University of Arkansas Press, 1990.

MacLean, Nancy. *Freedom Is Not Enough: The Opening of the American Workplace*. Cambridge: Harvard University Press, 2006.

Macpherson, C. B. *The Political Theory of Possessive Individualism: Hobbes to Locke*. New York: Oxford University Press, 1962.

Mactavish, Andrew, and Geoffrey Rockwell. "Multimedia Education in the Arts and Humanities." *Mind Technologies: Humanities Computing and the Canadian Academic Community*. Ed. Raymond Siemens and David Moorman. Calgary: University of Calgary Press, 2006. 225–43.

Maddox, Lucy. *Citizen Indians: Native American Intellectuals, Race, and Reform*. Ithaca: Cornell University Press, 2005.

———. *Removals: Nineteenth-Century American Literature and the Politics of Indian Affairs*. New York: Oxford University Press, 1991.

Maira, Sunaina. *Desis in the House: Indian American Youth Culture in New York City*. Philadelphia: Temple University Press, 2002.

Maira, Sunaina, and Elisabeth Soep. *Youthscapes: The Popular, the National, the Global*. Philadelphia: University of Pennsylvania Press, 2005.

Makdisi, Ussama S. *Artillery of Heaven: American Missionaries and the Failed Conversion of the Middle East*. Ithaca: Cornell University Press, 2007.

Mamdani, Mahmood. *Good Muslim, Bad Muslim: America, the Cold War, and the Roots of Terror*. 2004. New York: Three Rivers, 2005.

Manalansan, Martin F. *Global Divas: Filipino Gay Men in the Diaspora*. Durham: Duke University Press, 2003.

———. "Queer Intersections: Gender and Sexuality in Migration Studies." *International Migration Review* 40.1 (Spring 2006): 224–49.

Mandel, Ernest. *Late Capitalism*. Rev. ed. New York: Schocken Books, 1976.

———. "Marx's Labor Theory of Value." 1974. Available at http://www.internationalviewpoint.org/spip.php?article284.

Manovich, Lev. *The Language of New Media*. Cambridge: MIT Press, 2001.

Manuel, George, and Michael Posluns. *The Fourth World: An Indian Reality*. New York: Free Press, 1974.

Marable, Manning. "Introduction: Black Studies and the Racial Mountain." *Dispatches from the Ebony Tower: Intellectuals Confront the African American Experience*. Ed. Manning Marable. New York: Columbia University Press, 2000. 1–30.

Marchand, Ronald. *Creating the Corporate Soul: The Rise of Public Relations and Corporate Imagery in American Big Business*. Berkeley: University of California Press, 1998.

Marcus, George E. *The Sentimental Citizen: Emotion in Democratic Politics*. University Park: Pennsylvania State University Press, 2002.

Marcus, George E., and Michael Fischer. *Anthropology as Cultural Critique: An Experimental Moment in the Human Sciences*. Chicago: University of Chicago Press, 1986.

Marcuse, Herbert. *One-Dimensional Man: Studies in the Ideology of Advanced Industrial Society*. 1964. New York: Routledge, 2002.

Marinetti, F. T. "The Foundation and Manifesto of Futurism." 1909. *Critical Writings: F. T. Marinetti*. Ed. Günter Berghaus. New York: Farrar, Straus and Giroux, 2006. 11–17.

Mariscal, George. *Brown-Eyed Children of the Sun: Lessons from the Chicano Movement, 1965–1975*. Albuquerque: University of New Mexico Press, 2005.

Marr, Timothy. *The Cultural Roots of American Islamicism*. New York: Cambridge University Press, 2006.

Marsden, George. *Fundamentalism and American Culture: The Shaping of Twentieth-Century Evangelicalism, 1879–1925*. New York: Oxford University Press, 1980.

Marsh, Margaret. *Suburban Lives*. New Brunswick: Rutgers University Press, 1990.

Marshall, T. H. *Class, Citizenship, and Social Development*. New York: Doubleday Anchor, 1965.

Martí, José. "Our America." 1891. *Selected Writings*. New York: Penguin, 2002. 288–95.

Martin, Biddy, and Chandra Mohanty. "Feminist Politics: What's Home Got to Do with It?" *Feminist Studies, Critical Studies*. Ed. Teresa de Lauretis. Bloomington: Indiana University Press, 1986. 191–212.

Martin, David. *A General Theory of Secularization*. New York: Harper and Row, 1978.

———. *The Religious and the Secular*. London: RK, 1969.

Martin, Randy. *Financialization of Daily Life*. Philadelphia: Temple University Press, 2002.

———. "The Good, the Bad and the Ugly: Economies of Parable." *Cultural Studies* 24.3 (2010): 418–30.

———. *Under New Management: Universities, Administrative Labor, and the Professional Turn*. Philadelphia: Temple University Press, 2011.

Martineau, Harriet. *Society in America*. London: Sanders and Otley, 1837.

Marx, Karl. *Capital*. 1867–94. 3 vols. Trans. Ben Fowkes and David Fernbach. New York: Vintage, 1976–81.

———. *The Eighteenth Brumaire of Louis Bonaparte*. 1852. Moscow: Progress, 1954.

———. "Estranged Labour." 1844. *Economic and Philosophical Manuscripts of 1844*. Available at http://www.marxists.org/archive/marx/works/1844/manuscripts/labour.htm.

———. *Grundrisse: Foundations of the Critique of Political Economy*. 1858. New York: Penguin, 1993.

———. "On the Jewish Question." 1844. *The Marx-Engels Reader*. 2nd ed. Ed. Robert Tucker. New York: Norton, 1978. 26–52.

Marx, Karl, and Friedrich Engels. *The German Ideology*. 1845–46. Ed. C. J. Arthur. New York: International, 1972.

———. *The Holy Family*. 1845. *Collected Works*. Vol. 4. New York: International, 1975. 5–211.

———. *Manifesto of the Communist Party*. 1848. *Collected Works*. Vol. 6. New York: International, 1976. 477–519.

Marx, Leo. *The Machine in the Garden: Technology and the Pastoral Ideal in America*. 1964. New York: Oxford University Press, 2000.

Massad, Joseph. *Desiring Arabs*. Chicago: University of Chicago Press, 2007.

———. *The Persistence of the Palestinian Question: Essays on Zionism and the Palestinians*. New York: Routledge, 2006.

Massey, Doreen. *Space, Place, and Gender*. Minneapolis: University of Minnesota Press, 1994.

Massumi, Brian. "Navigating Moments." *Hope: New Philosophies for Change*. Ed. Mary Zournazi. New York: Routledge, 2002a. 210–43.

———. *Parables for the Virtual: Movement, Affect, Sensation*. Durham: Duke University Press, 2002b.

Mather, Cotton. *Magnalia Christi Americana*. 1702. New York: Russell and Russell, 1967.

Mathias, Charles M., Jr. "Ethnic Groups and Foreign Policy." *Foreign Affairs* 59.5 (1981): 975–98.

Matory, J. Lorand. "The English Professors of Brazil: On the Diasporic Roots of the Yorùbá Nation." *Comparative Studies in Social History* 41.1 (1999): 72–103.

Matthews, Glenna. *"Just a Housewife": The Rise and Fall of Domesticity in America*. New York: Oxford University Press, 1987.

Matthiessen, F. O. *American Renaissance: Art and Expression in the Age of Emerson and Whitman*. New York: Oxford University Press, 1941.

Maxwell, William. *New Negro, Old Left*. New York: Columbia University Press, 1999.

May, Elaine Tyler. *Homeward Bound: American Families in the Cold War Era*. New York: Basic Books, 1988.

May, Henry F. *The Enlightenment in America*. New York: Oxford Hutchinson University Press, 1976.

Mayer, Margit. "Post-Fordist City Politics." *Post-Fordism: A Reader*. Ed. Ash Amin. Oxford, UK: Blackwell, 1994. 316–37.

McAlister, Melani. *Epic Encounters: Culture, Media, and U.S. Interests in the Middle East, 1945–2000*. Berkeley: University of California Press, 2001.

———. *Epic Encounters: Culture, Media, and U.S. Interests in the Middle East, 1945–2000; Updated Edition, with a Post-9/11 Chapter*. Berkeley: University of California Press, 2005.

McCarthy, Cormac. *All the Pretty Horses*. New York: Vintage, 1992.

McCarthy, Kevin F., Elizabeth H. Ondaatje, Laura Zakaras, and Arthur C. Brooks. *Gifts of the Muse: Reframing the Debate about the Benefits of the Arts*. Santa Monica, CA: Rand, 2005.

McClintock, Anne. "Family Feuds: Gender, Nationalism and the Family." *Feminist Review* 44 (1993): 61–80.

———. *Imperial Leather: Race and Gender in the Colonial Contest*. Durham: Duke University Press, 1995.

McCullough, Kate. *Regions of Identity: The Construction of America in Women's Fiction, 1885–1914*. Stanford: Stanford University Press, 1999.

McGann, Jerome. *Radiant Textuality: Literature after the World Wide Web*. New York: Palgrave Macmillan, 2001.

McGill, Meredith L. *American Literature and the Culture of Reprinting, 1834–1853*. Philadelphia: University of Pennsylvania Press, 2003.

McGrory, Kathleen. "At Florida's Capitol, Dream Defenders Are Determined to Make a Difference." *Miami Herald*, July 19, 2013. http://www.miamiherald.com/2013/07/19/3509975/at-flori-das-capitol-dream-defenders.html.

McKenzie, Evan. *Privatopia: Homeowner Associations and the Rise of Residential Private Government*. New Haven: Yale University Press, 1994.

McLeod, Kembrew. *Freedom of Expression: Resistance and Repression in the Age of Intellectual Property*. Minneapolis: University of Minnesota Press, 2007.

McLeod, Kembrew, and Peter DiCola. *Creative License: The Law and Art of Digital Sampling*. Durham: Duke University Press, 2011.

McLuhan, Marshall. *Understanding Media: The Extensions of Man*. 1964. Ed. W. Terrence Gordon. Corte Madera, CA: Gingko, 2003.

McPherson, Tara. "Media Studies and the Digital Humanities." *Cinema Journal* 48.2 (Winter 2009): 119–23.

———. *Reconstructing Dixie: Race, Gender, and Nostalgia in the Imagined South*. Durham: Duke University Press, 2003.

———. "U.S. Operating Systems at Mid-century: The Intertwining of Race and UNIX." *Race after the Internet*. Ed. Lisa Nakamura, Peter Chow-White, and Alondra Nelson. New York: Routledge, 2012a. 21–37.

———. "Why Are the Digital Humanities So White? or Thinking the Histories of Race and Computation." *Debates in the Digital Humanities*. Ed. Matthew K. Gold. Minneapolis: University of Minneapolis Press, 2012b. 139–60.

McRobbie, Angela. *British Fashion Design: Rag Trade or Image Industry?* London: Routledge, 1988.

McRobbie, Angela, and Jenny Garber. "Girls and Subcultures: An Exploration." *Resistance through Rituals: Youth Subcultures in Post-war Britain*. Ed. Stuart Hall and Tony Jefferson. London: Hutchinson / Centre for Contemporary Cultural Studies, University of Birmingham, 1976. 209–22.

McRuer, Robert. *Crip Theory: Cultural Signs of Queerness and Disability*. New York: NYU Press, 2006.

McRuer, Robert, and Anna Mollow, eds. *Sex and Disability*. Durham: Duke University Press, 2012.

McRuer, Robert, and Abby L. Wilkerson, eds. "Desiring Disability: Queer Theory Meets Disability Studies." Special issue of *GLQ: A Journal of Lesbian and Gay Studies* 9.1–2 (2003): 1–23.

Mead, Margaret. *And Keep Your Powder Dry: An Anthropologist Looks at America*. 1942. New York: Morrow Quill, 1965.

———. *Coming of Age in Samoa*. 1928. New York: William Morrow, 1961.

———. *Cooperation and Competition among Primitive Peoples*. New York: McGraw-Hill, 1937.

Mehta, Uday Singh. *Liberalism and Empire: A Study in Nineteenth-Century British Liberal Thought*. Chicago: University of Chicago Press, 1999.

Meier, August, and Elliott Rudwick. *From Plantation to Ghetto*. 3rd ed. New York: Hill and Wang, 1976.

Meister, Robert. "Debt and Taxes: Can the Financial Industry Save Public Higher Education?" *Representations* 116 (2011): 128–47.

Melamed, Jodi. *Represent and Destroy: Rationalizing Violence in the New Racial Capitalism*. Minneapolis: University of Minnesota Press, 2011.

Melville, Herman. *Moby-Dick; or, The Whale*. 1851. Ed. Harrison Hayford, Hershel Parker, and G. Thomas Tanselle. Evanston, IL: Northwestern University Press; Chicago: Newberry Library, 1971.

Mensch, Elizabeth. "The History of Mainstream Legal Thought." *The Politics of Law: A Progressive Critique*. Ed. David Kairys. New York: Basic Books, 1982. 23–53.

Meranze, Michael. *Laboratories of Virtue: Punishment, Revolution, and Authority in Philadelphia, 1760–1835*. Chapel Hill: University of North Carolina Press, 1996.

Mercer, Kobena. *Welcome to the Jungle: New Positions in Black Cultural Studies*. New York: Routledge, 1994.

Merish, Lori. *Sentimental Materialism: Gender, Commodity Culture, and Nineteenth-Century American Literature*. Durham: Duke University Press, 2000.

Meriwether, James H. *Proudly We Can Be Africans: Black Americans and Africa, 1935-1961*. Chapel Hill: University of North Carolina Press, 2002.

Michaels, Walter Benn. "Corporate Fiction." *The Gold Standard and the Logic of Naturalism: American Literature at the Turn of the Century*. Berkeley: University of California Press, 1987. 181-213.

———. "The Vanishing American." *American Literary History* 2.2 (1990): 220-41.

Mignolo, Walter. *The Idea of Latin America*. Malden, MA: Blackwell, 2005.

Migrant Rights International. Home page. http://www.migrantwatch.org/ (accessed 2012).

Migration Policy Institute. "About MPI." http://www.migrationpolicy.org/about/index.php (accessed 2012).

Miles, Robert, and Rudy Torres. "Does 'Race' Matter? Transatlantic Perspectives on Racism after 'Race Relations.'" *Race and Racialization: Essential Readings*. Ed. Tania Das Gupta, Carl E. James, Roger C. A. Maaka, Grace-Edward Galabuzi, and Chris Andersen. Toronto: Canadian Scholars' Press, 2007. 65-73.

Mill, John Stuart. *On Liberty*. 1859. London: Longman, Roberts, & Green, 1869; New York: Bartleby.com, 1999.

———. *The Subjection of Women*. 1869. *Three Essays*. New York: Oxford University Press, 1976.

Miller, Perry. *Errand into the Wilderness*. Cambridge: Harvard University Press, 1960.

Miller, Toby. "Introducing . . . Cultural Citizenship." *Social Text* 19.4 (2001): 1-5.

———. *The Well-Tempered Self: Citizenship, Culture, and the Postmodern Subject*. Baltimore: Johns Hopkins University Press, 1993.

Miller, Toby, Nitin Govil, John McMurria, and Richard Maxwell. *Global Hollywood*. London: British Film Institute, 2001.

Mills, Charles. *The Racial Contract*. Ithaca: Cornell University Press, 1997.

Mindt, Mark L. *Koda the Warrior*. Harvey, ND: Pony Gulch, 2005.

Mintz, Sidney. *Sweetness and Power: The Place of Sugar in Modern History*. New York: Viking, 1985.

Mirabeau, Victor de Riqueti, Marquis de. *L'ami des hommes: ou, Traité de la population*. 1756-58. 2 vols. Aalen, Germany: Scientia, 1970.

Mirzoeff, Nicholas. *Introduction to Visual Culture*. London and New York: Routledge, 1999.

Mises, Ludwig von. *Human Action*. New Haven: Yale University Press, 1949.

Mishel, Lawrence R., John Bivens, Elise Gould, and Heidi Shierholz. *The State of Working America*. 12th ed. Ithaca, NY: ILR, 2012.

Mishra, Vijay. "The Diasporic Imaginary: Theorizing the Indian Diaspora." *Textual Practice* 10.3 (1996): 421-47.

Mitchell, David T., and Sharon Snyder, eds. *The Body and Physical Difference: Discourses of Disability*. Ann Arbor: University of Michigan Press, 1997.

———. *Narrative Prosthesis: Disability and the Dependencies of Discourse*. Ann Arbor: University of Michigan Press, 2001.

Mitchell, Lee Clark. *Westerns: Making the Man in Fiction and Film*. Chicago: University of Chicago Press, 1996.

Mitchell, Timothy. "Economists and the Economy in the Twentieth Century." *The Politics of Method in the Human Sciences: Positivism and Its Epistemological Others*. Ed. George Steinmetz. Durham: Duke University Press, 2005. 126-41.

———. *Rule of Experts: Egypt, Techno-Politics, Modernity*. Berkeley: University of California Press, 2002.

———. "The Stage of Modernity." *Questions of Modernity*. Ed. Timothy Mitchell. Minneapolis: University of Minnesota Press, 2000. 1-34.

Mitchell, W. J. T. *Cloning Terror: The War of Images, 9/11 to the Present*. Chicago: University of Chicago Press, 2011.

———. *Picture Theory: Essays on Verbal and Visual Representation*. Chicago: University of Chicago Press, 1994.

Miyoshi, M. "A Borderless World? From Colonialism to Transnationalism and the Decline of the Nation State." *Critical Inquiry* 19.4 (1993): 726-51.

Mizen, Phillip. "Putting the Politics Back into Youth Studies: Keynesianism, Monetarism, and the Changing State of Youth." *Journal of Youth Studies* 5.1(2002): 5-20.

Mnookin, Jennifer. "The Image of Truth: Photographic Evidence and the Power of Analogy." *Yale Journal of Law and the Humanities* 10.1 (1998): 1-74.

Moallem, Minoo. *Between Warrior Brother and Veiled Sister: Islamic Fundamentalism and the Cultural Politics of Patriarchy in Iran*. Berkeley: University of California Press, 2005.

Mogul, Joey L., Andrea J. Ritchie, and Kay Whitlock. *Queer (In) Justice: The Criminalization of LGBT People in the United States*. Boston: Beacon, 2011.

Mohanty, Chandra Talpade. *Feminism without Borders: Decolonizing Theory, Practicing Solidarity*. Durham: Duke University Press, 2003.

Mohanty, Chandra Talpade, Anna Russo, and Lourdes Torres. *Third World Women and the Politics of Feminism*. Bloomington: Indiana University Press, 1991.

Momaday, N. Scott. *House Made of Dawn*. New York: Harper and Row, 1968.

Money, John, and Anke Ehrhardt. *Man and Woman, Boy and Girl: The Differentiation and Dimorphism of Gender Identity from Conception to Maturity*. Baltimore: Johns Hopkins University Press, 1972.

Montagu, Ashley. *Man's Most Dangerous Myth: The Fallacy of Race*. New York: Columbia University Press, 1942.

Montesquieu, Charles de Secondat, Baron de. *De l'esprit des lois*. Amsterdam: Chez Chatelain, 1748.

Montgomery, David. *The Fall of the House of Labor*. Cambridge: Cambridge University Press, 1987.

Moraga, Cherríe. *Loving in the War Years: Lo que nunca pasó por sus labios*. Boston: South End, 1983.

Moraga, Cherríe, and Gloria Anzaldúa. *This Bridge Called My Back: Writings by Radical Women of Color*. Watertown, MA: Persephone, 1981.

———. *This Bridge Called My Back: Writings by Radical Women of Color*. 2nd ed. New York: Kitchen Table / Women of Color, 1983.

Morais, Herbert M. *Deism in Eighteenth-Century America*. New York: Columbia University Press, 1934.

Moreton, Bethany. *To Serve God and Wal-Mart: The Making of Christian Free Enterprise*. Cambridge: Harvard University Press, 2009.

Morgan, Edmund S. *American Slavery, American Freedom: The Ordeal of Colonial Virginia*. New York: Norton, 1975.

Morgan, Jennifer L. *Laboring Women: Reproduction and Gender in New World Slavery*. Philadelphia: University of Pennsylvania Press, 2004.

Morgan, Jo-Ann. *"Uncle Tom's Cabin" as Visual Culture*. Columbia: University of Missouri Press, 2007.

Morgan, William. *Questionable Charity: Gender, Humanitarianism, and Complicity in U.S. Literary Realism*. Hanover, NH: University Press of New England, 2004.

Morgenson, Scott Lauria. *Spaces between Us: Queer Settler Colonialism and Indigenous Decolonization*. Minneapolis: University of Minnesota Press, 2011.

Morone, James A. *Hellfire Nation: The Politics of Sin in American History*. New Haven: Yale University Press, 2003.

Morrison, Toni. *Beloved*. New York: Knopf, 1987.

———. *Playing in the Dark: Whiteness in the Literary Imagination*. New York: Random House, 1993.

Moses, Wilson J. *Afrotopia: The Roots of Popular African American History*. Cambridge: Cambridge University Press, 1998.

Moten, Fred. *In the Break: The Aesthetics of the Black Radical Tradition*. Minneapolis: University of Minnesota Press, 2003.

Motorcycle Diaries, The. Dir. Walter Salles. FilmFour, 2004.

Mouffe, Chantal. "Citizenship." *The Encyclopedia of Democracy*. Ed. Seymour Martin Lipset. Vol. 1. Washington, DC: Congressional Quarterly, 1995. 217–21.

———. "Democratic Citizenship and the Political Community." *Dimensions of Radical Democracy: Pluralism, Citizenship and Community*. Ed. Chantal Mouffe. London: Verso, 1992. 225–39.

Moynihan, Daniel Patrick. *The Negro Family: The Case for National Action*. Washington, DC: U.S. Department of Labor, 1965.

Mumford, Kevin. *Interzones: Black/White Sex Districts in Chicago and New York in the Early Twentieth Century*. New York: Columbia University Press, 1997.

Mumford, Lewis. *Brown Decades: A Study of the Arts in America, 1865–1895*. New York: Harcourt, Brace, 1931.

Muñoz, José Esteban. *Cruising Utopia: The Then and There of Queer Futurity*. New York: NYU Press, 2009.

———. *Disidentifications: Queers of Color and the Performance of Politics*. Minneapolis: University of Minnesota Press, 1999.

Murphree, Daniel. "Race and Religion on the Periphery: Disappointment and Missionization in the Spanish Floridas, 1566–1763." *Race, Nation, and Religion in the Americas*. Ed. Henry Goldschmidt and Elizabeth McAlister. New York: Oxford University Press, 2004. 35–59.

Myrdal, Gunnar. *An American Dilemma: The Negro Problem and Modern Democracy*. New York: Harper, 1944.

Nakamura, Lisa. *Cybertypes: Race, Ethnicity, and Identity on the Internet*. New York: Routledge, 2002.

———. *Digitizing Race: Visual Cultures of the Internet*. Minneapolis: Minnesota University Press, 2008.

Nakamura, Lisa, and Peter A. Chow-White, eds. *Race after the Internet*. New York: Routledge, 2012.

Nance, Susan. *How the Arabian Nights Inspired the American Dream, 1790–1935*. Chapel Hill: University of North Carolina Press, 2009.

Nandy, Ashis. "Dialogue and the Diaspora: Conversation with Nikos Papastergiadis." *Third Text* 11 (1990): 99–108.

Nash, Gary B. *Race, Class, and Politics: Essays on Colonial and Revolutionary Society*. Urbana: University of Illinois Press, 1986.

Nash, Roderick. *Wilderness and the American Mind*. 3rd ed. New Haven: Yale University Press, 1982.

National Endowment for the Humanities. "NEH Launches Initiative to Develop 10 Regional Humanities Centers throughout the Nation." Press release, May 10, 1999. http://www.neh.gov/news/press-release/1999-05-10.

Negt, Oskar, and Alexander Kluge. *Public Sphere and Experience: Toward an Analysis of the Bourgeois and Proletarian Public Sphere*. Trans. Peter Labanyi, Jamie Owen Daniel, and Assenka Oksiloff. Minneapolis: University of Minnesota Press, 1993.

Nel, Philip, and Lissa Paul. *Keywords for Children's Literature*. New York: NYU Press, 2011.

Nelson, Benjamin. "Civilizational Complexes and Intercivilizational Encounters." *Sociological Analysis* 34 (1973): 79–105.

Nelson, Cary, ed. *Will Work for Food: Academic Labor in Crisis*. Minneapolis: University of Minnesota Press, 1997.

Nelson, Dana. *National Manhood: Capitalist Citizenship and the Imagined Fraternity of White Men*. Durham: Duke University Press, 1998.

———. *The Word in Black and White: Reading "Race" in American Literature, 1638–1867*. Oxford: Oxford University Press, 1992.

Nelson, Jennifer. *Women of Color and the Reproductive Rights Movement*. New York: NYU Press, 2003.

Nelson, Lowry. "The American Rural Heritage." *American Quarterly* 1.3 (Autumn 1949): 225–34.

Nesbitt, Nick. "Négritude." *Africana: The Encyclopedia of the African and African American Experience*. Ed. Kwame Anthony Appiah and Henry Louis Gates, Jr. New York: Basic Books, 1999.

Nevins, Joseph. *Operation Gatekeeper: The Rise of the Illegal Alien and the Making of the U.S.-Mexico Boundary*. New York: Routledge, 2002.

Newfield, Christopher. "Corporate Culture Wars." *Corporate Futures: The Diffusion of the Culturally Sensitive Corporate Form*. Ed. George E. Marcus. Chicago: University of Chicago Press, 1998. 23–62.

———. *Unmaking the Public University: The Forty-Year Assault on the Middle Class*. Cambridge: Harvard University Press, 2008.

Newman, Louise. *White Women's Rights: The Racial Origins of Feminism in the United States*. New York: Oxford University Press, 1999.

New Social History Project. *Who Built America?* 2 vols. New York: Pantheon, 1989–92.

Newton, Esther. *Mother Camp: Female Impersonators in America*. Chicago: University of Chicago Press, 1972.

Ngai, Mae. *Impossible Subjects: Illegal Aliens and the Making of Modern America*. Princeton: Princeton University Press, 2004.

Ngai, Sianne. *Ugly Feelings*. Cambridge: Harvard University Press, 2005.

Ngũgĩ wa Thiong'o. *Penpoints, Gunpoints, and Dreams: Towards a Critical Theory of the Arts and the State in Africa*. Oxford: Oxford University Press, 1998.

Nguyen, Mimi T. *The Gift of Freedom: War, Debt, and Other Refugee Passages*. Durham: Duke University Press, 2012.

Noble, David F. *America by Design: Science, Technology, and the Rise of Corporate Capitalism*. New York: Knopf, 1977.

———. *Progress without People: New Technology, Unemployment, and the Message of Resistance*. Toronto: Between the Lines, 1995.

Noble, David W. *Death of a Nation*. Minneapolis: University of Minnesota Press, 2002.

Noiriel, Gérárd. *La tyrannie du national*. Paris: Calmann Levy, 1991.

Noriega, Chon, and Chela Sandoval, eds. *The Chicano Studies Reader: An Anthology of Aztlán, 1970–2010*. Los Angeles: UCLA Chicano Studies Research Center Press, 2011.

Norman, Donald A. *The Invisible Computer: Why Good Products Can Fail, the Personal Computer Is So Complex, and Information Appliances Are the Solution*. Cambridge: MIT Press, 1998.

Norquist, Grover. Interview. *Morning Edition*, National Public Radio, May 25, 2001.

North, Michael. *The Dialect of Modernism: Race, Language, and Twentieth-Century Literature*. New York: Oxford University Press, 1994.

Norton, Mary Beth. *Founding Mothers and Fathers: Gendered Power and the Formation of American Society*. New York: Knopf, 1996.

Novick, Peter. *That Noble Dream: The "Objectivity Question" and the American Historical Profession*. Cambridge: Cambridge University Press, 1988.

Nunberg, Geoffrey. "The -Ism Schism: How Much Wallop Can a Simple Word Pack?" *New York Times*, July 11, 2004.

Nwankwo, Ifeoma Kiddoe. *Black Cosmopolitanism: Racial Consciousness and Transnational Identity in the Nineteenth-Century Americas*. Philadelphia: University of Pennsylvania Press, 2005.

Oakes, James. "The Peculiar Fate of the Bourgeois Critique of Slavery." *Slavery and the American South*. Ed. Winthrop Jordan. Jackson: University Press of Mississippi, 2003. 29–48.

O'Brien, Jean M. *Firsting and Lasting: Writing Indians out of Existence in New England*. Minneapolis: University of Minnesota Press, 2010.

———. "Why Here? Scholarly Locations for American Indian Studies." *American Quarterly* 55.4 (December 2003): 689–96.

O'Brien, Ruth. *Crippled Justice: The History of Modern Disability Policy in the Workplace*. Chicago: University of Chicago Press, 2001.

Office of Diversity and Inclusion, World Bank. 2013. http://web.worldbank.org/WBSITE/EXTERNAL/EXTSTAFF/EXTHR/0,,contentMDK:22305779~menuPK:7257707~pagePK:64233720~piPK:444052~theSitePK:444049,00.html.

O'Gorman, Edmundo. *The Invention of America: An Inquiry into the Historical Nature of the New World and the Meaning of its History*. Bloomington: Indiana University Press, 1961.

Okihiro, Gary Y. *Margins and Mainstreams: Asians in American History and Culture*. Seattle: University of Washington Press, 1994.

Oliver, Melvin, and Thomas Shapiro. *Black Wealth, White Wealth: A New Perspective on Racial Inequality*. New York: Routledge, 1995.

Omi, Michael, and Howard Winant. *Racial Formation in the United States: From the 1960s to the 1980s*. 1986. New York: Routledge, 1994.

Ong, Aihwa. "Cultural Citizenship as Subject Making: Immigrants Negotiate Racial and Cultural Boundaries in the United States." *Current Anthropology* 37.5 (1996): 737–62.

———. *Neoliberalism as Exception: Mutations in Citizenship and Sovereignty*. Durham: Duke University Press, 2006.

Ongiri, Amy Abugo. *Spectacular Blackness: The Cultural Politics of the Black Power Movement and the Search for a Black Aesthetic*. Charlottesville: University of Virginia Press, 2010.

Ordover, Nancy. *American Eugenics: Race, Queer Anatomy, and the Science of Nationalism*. Minneapolis: University of Minnesota Press, 2003.

Ortiz, Fernando. *El engaño de las razas*. Havana: Editorial Páginas, 1946.

Ortiz, Paul. *Emancipation Betrayed: The Hidden History of Black Organizing and White Violence in Florida from Reconstruction to the Bloody Election of 1920*. Berkeley: University of California Press, 2005.

Orwell, George. "You and the Atom Bomb." *Tribune* (London), October 19, 1945.

Osborne, Peter. *The Politics of Time: Modernity and Avant-Garde*. New York: Verso, 1995.

Oshinsky, David M. *Worse than Slavery: Parchman Farm and the Ordeal of Jim Crow Justice*. New York: Simon and Schuster, 2008.

Ospina, William. *Mestizo America: The Country of the Future*. New York: Villegas Editores, 2000.

O'Sullivan, John L. "Annexation." *Democratic Review*, July–August 1845: 5–10.

Otiono, Nduka. "Tracking Skilled Diasporas: Globalization, Brain Drain, and the Postcolonial Condition of Nigeria." *Transfers* 1.3 (Winter 2011): 5–23.

Paine, Thomas. *Common Sense*. 1776. *Common Sense and Other Political Writings*. Indianapolis: Bobbs-Merrill, 1953.

———. *Common Sense*. 1776. *Common Sense and Other Writings*. Ed. Joyce Appleby. New York: Barnes and Noble Classics, 2005.

———. *Rights of Man*. 1791. Minneola, NY: Dover, 1999.

Painter, Nell Irvin. *The History of White People*. New York: Norton, 2010.

Paranjape, Makarand. "Theorising Postcolonial Difference: Culture, Nation, Civilization." *SPAN: Journal of the South Pacific Association for Commonwealth Literature and Language Studies* 47 (1998): 1–17.

Paredes, Américo. *George Washington Gómez: A Mexicotexan Novel*. Houston: Arte Público, 1990.

———. *With His Pistol in His Hand: A Border Ballad and Its Hero*. Austin: University of Texas Press, 1958.

Parédez, Deborah. *Selenidad: Selena, Latinos, and the Performance of Memory*. Durham: Duke University Press, 2009.

Parenti, Christian. *Lockdown America: Police and Prisons in the Age of Crisis*. London: Verso, 1999.

Paris Is Burning. Dir. Jennie Livingston. Miramax, 1991.

Park, Robert Ezra. *Human Communities: The City and Human Ecology*. Glencoe, IL: Free Press, 1952.

———. *Race and Culture: The Collected Papers of Robert Ezra Park*. Ed. Everett C. Hughes, Charles S. Johnson, Jitsuichi Masuoka, Robert Redfield, and Louis Wirth. Glencoe, IL: Free Press, 1950.

Parker, Andrew, Mary Russo, Doris Sommer, and Patricia Yaeger. *Nationalisms and Sexualities*. New York: Routledge, 1992.

Parker, Theodore. *Sermons on War.* 1863. Ed. Frances P. Cobbe. New York: Garland, 1973.

Parlapiano, Alice. "(Not) Spreading the Wealth." *Washington Post* June 18, 2011. http://www.washingtonpost.com/wp-srv/special/business/income-inequality/.

Parreñas, Rhacel Salazar. *Servants of Globalization: Women, Migration, and Domestic Work.* Stanford: Stanford University Press, 2001.

Parsons, Lucy. *Freedom, Equality and Solidarity: Writings and Speeches, 1878–1937.* Ed. Gale Ahrens. Chicago: Charles H. Kerr, 2004.

Pateman, Carole. *The Sexual Contract.* Stanford: Stanford University Press, 1988.

Patterson, Orlando. *Slavery and Social Death: A Comparative Study.* Cambridge: Harvard University Press, 1982.

Patton, Cindy. *Fatal Advice: How Safe-Sex Education Went Wrong.* Durham: Duke University Press, 1996.

———. *Sex and Germs: The Politics of AIDS.* Boston: South End, 1985.

Paulicelli, Eugenia, and Hazel Clark. *The Fabric of Cultures: Fashion, Identity, and Globalization.* New York: Routledge, 2009.

Payne, Daniel G. *Voices in the Wilderness: American Nature Writing and Environmental Politics.* Hanover, NH: University Press of New England, 1996.

Pease, Donald E. *The New American Exceptionalism.* Minneapolis: University of Minnesota Press, 2009a.

———. "New Perspectives on U.S. Culture and Imperialism." *Cultures of United States Imperialism.* Ed. Amy Kaplan and Donald E. Pease. Durham: Duke University Press, 1993. 22–37.

———. "Re-thinking American Studies after US Exceptionalism." *American Literary History* 21.1 (Spring 2009b): 19–27.

Peck, Jamie, and Adam Tickell. "Searching for a New Institutional Fix: The After-Fordist Crisis and the Global-Local Disorder." *Post-Fordism: A Reader.* Ed. Ash Amin. Oxford, UK: Blackwell, 1995. 280–315.

Pedersen, Susan, and Caroline Elkins, eds. *Settler Colonialism in the Twentieth Century.* New York: Routledge, 2005.

Peiss, Kathy. *Cheap Amusements: Working Women and Leisure in Turn-of-the-Century New York.* Philadelphia: Temple University Press, 1986.

Pérez, Laura Elisa. *Chicana Art: The Politics of Spiritual and Aesthetic Altarities.* Durham: Duke University Press, 2007.

Perry, Pamela. *Shades of White: White Kids and Racial Identities in High School.* Durham: Duke University Press, 2002.

Perry, Pamela, and Alexis Shotwell. "Relational Understanding and White Antiracist Praxis." *Sociological Theory* 27.1 (March 2009): 33–50.

Philip, Cynthia Owen, ed. *Imprisoned in America: Prison Communications, 1776 to Attica.* New York: Harper and Row, 1973.

Phillips, Kevin. *Wealth and Democracy: A Political History of the American Rich.* New York: Broadway Books, 2002.

Piore, Michael, and Charles F. Sabel. *The Second Industrial Divide: Possibilities for Prosperity.* New York: Basic Books, 1984.

Plummer, Brenda Gayle. *Rising Wind: Black Americans and Foreign Affairs, 1935–1960.* Chapel Hill: University of North Carolina Press, 1996.

Polanyi, Karl. *The Great Transformation.* New York: Farrar and Rinehart, 1944. Reprint, Boston: Beacon, 2001.

Pollin, Robert. *Contours of Descent: U.S. Economic Fractures and the Landscape of Global Austerity.* London: Verso, 2003.

Poovey, Mary. *Genres of the Credit Economy: Mediating Value in Eighteenth- and Nineteenth-Century Britain.* Chicago: University of Chicago Press, 2008.

———. *A History of the Modern Fact: Problems of Knowledge in the Sciences of Wealth and Society.* Chicago: University of Chicago Press, 1998.

Porter, James I. Foreword to *The Body and Physical Difference: Discourses of Disability in the Humanities.* Ed. David T. Mitchell and Sharon Snyder. Ann Arbor: University of Michigan Press, 1997. xiii–xiv.

Poster, Mark. "CyberDemocracy: Internet and the Public Sphere." Home page. 1999. http://www.hnet.uci.edu/mposter/writings/democ.html.

Postman, Neil. *Technopoly: The Surrender of Culture to Technology.* New York: Vintage, 1993.

Povinelli, Elizabeth A. *Economies of Abandonment: Social Belonging and Endurance in Late Liberalism.* Durham: Duke University Press, 2011.

———. *The Empire of Love: Toward a Theory of Intimacy, Genealogy, and Carnality.* Durham: Duke University Press, 2006.

Povinelli, Elizabeth A., and George Chauncey. "Thinking Sexuality Transnationally: An Introduction." *GLQ* 5.4 (1999): 439–50.

powell, john a. "New Property Disaggregated: A Model to Address Employment Discrimination." *University of San Francisco Law Review* 24 (Winter 1990): 363–83.

Prakash, Gyan. *Another Reason: Science and the Imagination of Modern India.* Princeton: Princeton University Press, 1999.

Prashad, Vijay. *Everybody Was Kung Fu Fighting: Afro-Asian Connections and the Myth of Cultural Purity.* Boston: Beacon, 2001.

———. *Karma of Brown Folk.* Minneapolis: University of Minnesota Press, 2000.

———. "Orientalism." *Keywords for American Cultural Studies.* Ed. Bruce Burgett and Glenn Hendler. New York: NYU Press, 2007. 174–77.

Pratt, Lloyd. *Archives of American Time: Literature and Modernity in the Nineteenth Century.* Philadelphia: University of Pennsylvania Press, 2010.

Prescott, William. *History of the Conquest of Mexico.* New York: Harper, 1843.

Price, Richard. Letter to Thomas Jefferson, July 2, 1785. *The Papers of Thomas Jefferson.* Ed. Julian Boyd. Vol. 8. Princeton: Princeton University Press, 1953.

Prince, Mary. *The History of Mary Prince.* 1831. Ed. Sara Salih. New York: Penguin, 2000.

Prosser, Jay. *Second Skins: The Body Narratives of Transsexuality.* New York: Columbia University Press, 1998.

Puar, Jasbir K. "On Torture: Abu Ghraib." *Radical History Review* 93 (Fall 2005): 13–38.

———. *Terrorist Assemblages: Homonationalism in Queer Times.* Durham: Duke University Press, 2007.

Pulido, Laura. *Environmentalism and Economic Justice.* Tucson: University of Arizona Press, 1996.

Putnam, Robert D. *Bowling Alone: The Collapse and Revival of American Community.* New York: Simon and Schuster, 2000.

———. "The Prosperous Community." *American Prospect* 13 (1993): 35–42.

Quadagno, Jill. *The Color of Welfare: How Racism Undermined the War on Poverty.* Oxford: Oxford University Press, 1994.

Queers for Economic Justice. "A Military Job Is Not Economic Justice." 2010. http://q4ej.org/military-job-is-not-economic-justice-qej-statement-on-dadt.

Quetelet, Adolphe. *Sur l'homme et le développement de ses facultés, ou Essai de physique sociale.* Paris: Bachiliers, 1835.

Quiroga, José. *Tropics of Desire: Interventions from Queer Latino America.* New York: NYU Press, 2000.

Rabaka, Reiland. *Forms of Fanonism: Fanon's Critical Theory and the Dialectics of Decolonization.* Lanham, MD: Lexington Books, 2010.

Rabinowitz, Paula. *Labor and Desire: Women's Revolutionary Fiction in Depression America.* Chapel Hill: University of North Carolina Press, 1991.

Raboteau, Albert. *Slave Religion: The "Invisible Institution" in the Antebellum South.* New York: Oxford University Press, 1978.

Radano, Ronald, and Philip V. Bohlman. *Music and the Racial Imagination.* Chicago: University of Chicago Press, 2000.

Radway, Jan. "What's in a Name?" *The Futures of American Studies.* Ed. Donald Pease and Robyn Wiegman. Durham: Duke University Press, 2002. 45–75.

Rafael, Vicente. *Contracting Colonialism: Translation and Christian Conversion in Tagalog Society under Early Spanish Rule.* Ithaca: Cornell University Press, 1988.

Rajshekar, V. T. *Dalit: The Black Untouchables of India.* Atlanta: Clarity, 2009.

Rana, Junaid. *Terrifying Muslims: Race and Labor in the South Asian Diaspora.* Durham: Duke University Press, 2011.

Rancière, Jacques. *Disagreement: Politics and Philosophy.* Minneapolis: University of Minnesota Press, 1998.

———. *Dissensus: On Politics and Aesthetics.* London: Continuum, 2010.

Ransby, Barbara. *Ella Baker and the Black Freedom Movement: A Radical Democratic Vision.* Chapel Hill: University of North Carolina Press, 2003.

Ransom, John Crowe. "Forms and Citizens." *The World's Body.* Baton Rouge: Louisiana State University Press, 1965. 29–54.

Raphael, Ray. *A People's History of the American Revolution.* New York: New Press, 2001.

Ratto, Matt. "Critical Making: Conceptual and Material Studies in Technology and Social Life." *Information Society* 27.4 (2011): 252–60.

Ravenstein, Ernest George. "The Laws of Migration." *Journal of the Statistical Society of London* 48.2 (June 1885): 167–235.

Raz, Joseph. "The Rule of Law and Its Virtue." *Law Quarterly Review* 93 (1977): 195–211.

Razack, Sherene. "'We Didn't Kill 'Em, We Didn't Cut Their Head Off': Abu Ghraib Revisited." *Racial Formation in the Twenty-First Century.* Ed. Daniel Martinez HoSang, Oneka LaBennett, and Laura Pulido. Berkeley: University of California Press, 2012. 217–45.

Reagan, Ronald. "Remarks at the Annual Convention of the National Association of Evangelicals in Orlando, Florida." March 8, 1983. Ronald Reagan Presidential Library and Museum. http://www.reaganlibrary.gov/major-speeches-index/31-archives/speeches/1983/2177-30883b.

———. "Remarks on East-West Relations at the Brandenburg Gate in West Berlin." June 12, 1987. Ronald Reagan Presidential Library. http://www.reagan.utexas.edu/archives/speeches/1987/061287d.htm.

———. "Second Inaugural Address of Ronald Reagan." January 21, 1985. Avalon Project: Documents in Law, History, & Diplomacy, Yale Law School. http://avalon.law.yale.edu/20th_century/reagan2.asp.

Reddy, Chandan. *Freedom with Violence: Race, Sexuality, and the US State.* Durham: Duke University Press, 2011.

Reed, T. V. *The Art of Protest: Culture and Activism from the Civil Rights Movement to the Streets of Seattle.* Minneapolis: University of Minnesota Press, 2005.

———. "Theory and Method in American/Cultural Studies: A Bibliographic Essay." 1999. http://xroads.virginia.edu/~DRBR/TVReed/bib.html.

Reich, Robert B. "Secession of the Successful." *New York Times,* January 20, 1991. http://www.nytimes.com/1991/01/20/magazine/secession-of-the-successful.html.

Renan, Ernest. "What Is a Nation?" 1882. *Nation and Narration.* Ed. Homi K. Bhabha. London: Routledge, 1990. 8–22.

Renda, Mary A. *Taking Haiti: Military Occupation and the Culture of U.S. Imperialism, 1915–1940.* Chapel Hill: University of North Carolina Press, 2001.

Resnick, Stephen A., and Richard D. Wolff. *Knowledge and Class: A Marxian Critique of Political Economy.* Chicago: University of Chicago Press, 1987.

Reverby, Susan. *Examining Tuskegee: The Infamous Syphilis Study and Its Legacy.* Chapel Hill: University of North Carolina Press, 2009.

Reynolds, David S. *Beneath the American Renaissance: The Subversive Imagination in the Age of Emerson and Melville.* Cambridge: Harvard University Press, 1989.

Rhodes, Lorna A. *Total Confinement: Madness and Reason in the Maximum Security Prison.* Berkeley: University of California Press, 2004.

Ricardo, David. *On the Principles of Political Economy and Taxation.* London: Murray, 1817. Available at http://www.econlib.org/library/Ricardo/ricP.html.

Rich, Adrienne. "Compulsory Heterosexuality and Lesbian Existence." 1980. *Powers of Desire: The Politics of Sexuality.* Ed. Ann Snitow, Christine Stansell, and Sharon Thompson. New York: Monthly Review Press, 1983. 177–205.

———. "Sources: IV." *Your Native Land, Your Life.* New York: Norton, 1986.

Richie, Beth E., Dana-Ain Davis, and LaTosha Traylor. "Feminist Politics, Racialized Imagery, and Social Control." *Souls: A Critical Journal of Black Politics, Culture and Society* 14.1–2 (2012): 54–66.

Ridge, John Rollin. *Life and Adventures of Joaquin Murieta: Celebrated California Bandit*. 1854. Norman: University of Oklahoma Press, 1977.

Rifkin, Jeremy. *The Age of Access: The New Culture of Hypercapitalism, Where All of Life Is a Paid-For Experience*. New York: Jeremy P. Tarcher / Putnam, 2000.

Robbins, Bruce. "Introduction: The Public as Phantom." *The Phantom Public Sphere*. Ed. Bruce Robbins. Minneapolis: University of Minnesota Press, 1993. vii–xxvi.

Roberts, Dorothy E. *Killing the Black Body: Race, Reproduction, and the Meaning of Liberty*. New York: Vintage, 1998.

———. "Racism and Patriarchy in the Meaning of Motherhood." *American University Journal of Gender and Law* 1 (1993): 1–38.

Robespierre, Maximilien. *Slavoj Žižek Presents Robespierre: Virtue and Terror*. 1794. Ed. Slavoj Žižek. New York: Verso, 2007.

Robinson, Cedric J. *Black Marxism: The Making of the Black Radical Tradition*. 1983. Chapel Hill: University of North Carolina Press, 2000.

Robinson, Forrest G. "Clio Bereft of Calliope: Literature and the New Western History." *The New Western History: The Territory Ahead*. Ed. Forrest G. Robinson. Tucson: University of Arizona Press, 1997. 61–98.

Rodgers, Tara. *Pink Noises: Women on Electronic Music and Sound*. Durham: Duke University Press, 2010.

Rodríguez, Clara E. *Changing Race: Latinos, the Census, and the History of Ethnicity in the United States*. New York: NYU Press, 2000.

Rodríguez, Dylan. *Forced Passages: Imprisoned Radical Intellectuals and the U.S. Prison Regime*. Minneapolis: University of Minnesota Press, 2006.

Rodríguez, Juana María. *Queer Latinidad: Identity Practices, Discursive Spaces*. New York: NYU Press, 2003.

Rodríguez, Richard T. *Next of Kin: The Family in Chicano/a Cultural Politics*. Durham: Duke University Press, 2009.

Rodríguez-Silva, Ileana M. "*Libertos* and *Libertas* in the Construction of the Free Worker in Postemancipation Puerto Rico." *Gender and Slave Emancipation in the Atlantic World*. Ed. Pamela Scully and Diana Paton. Durham: Duke University Press, 2005. 199–222.

Roediger, David R. *Towards the Abolition of Whiteness: Essays on Race, Politics, and Working-Class History*. London: Verso, 1994.

———. *The Wages of Whiteness: Race and the Making of the American Working Class*. London: Verso, 1991.

———. *The Wages of Whiteness: Race and the Making of the American Working Class*. Rev. ed. London: Verso, 1999.

Rogin, Michael. *Black Face, White Noise: Jewish Immigrants in the Hollywood Melting Pot*. Berkeley: University of California Press, 1996.

———. *Ronald Reagan, the Movie, and Other Episodes in Political Demonology*. Berkeley: University of California Press, 1987.

Rohy, Valerie. *Anachronism and Its Others: Sexuality, Race, Temporality*. Albany: SUNY Press, 2009.

Román, Miriam Jiménez, and Juan Flores, eds. *The Afro-Latin@ Reader: History and Culture in the United States*. Durham: Duke University Press, 2010.

Romero, Lora. *Home Fronts: Domesticity and Its Critics in the Antebellum United States*. Durham: Duke University Press, 1997.

Romero, Mary. *Maid in the U.S.A.* New York: Routledge, 1992.

Roosevelt, Theodore. Fourth Annual Message to Congress, December 6, 1904. *A Compilation of the Messages and Papers of the Presidents: 1789–1908*. Vol. 10. Ed. James D. Richardson. Washington, DC: Bureau of National Literature and Art, 1908. 802–38.

———. *Report of the Country Life Commission*. Washington, DC: Government Printing Office, 1909.

———. "True Americanism." *Forum*, April 1894, 15–31.

Root, Regina A. *Couture and Consensus: Fashion and Politics in Postcolonial Argentina*. Minneapolis: University of Minnesota Press, 2010.

Rosa, Andrew Juan. "El que no tiene dingo, tiene mandingo: The Inadequacy of the 'Mestizo' as a Theoretical Construct in the Field of Latin American Studies—the Problem and Solution." *Journal of Black Studies* 27.2 (1996): 278–91.

Rosaldo, Michelle Z. "Toward an Anthropology of Self and Feeling." *Culture Theory: Essays on Mind, Self and Emotion*. Ed. Richard A. Shweder and Robert A. LeVine. New York: Cambridge University Press, 1984. 137–57.

Rosaldo, Renato. "Cultural Citizenship, Inequality, and Multiculturalism." *Race, Identity, and Citizenship: A Reader*. Ed. Rodolfo D. Torres, Louis F. Miron, and Jonathan Xavier Inda. Oxford, UK: Blackwell, 1999. 253–61.

Rosales, Francisco A. *Chicano! The History of the Mexican American Civil Rights Movement*. 2nd rev. ed. Houston: Arte Público, 1997.

Rosas, Gilberto. "The Thickening Borderlands: Diffused Exceptionality and 'Immigrant' Social Struggles during the 'War on Terror.'" *Cultural Dynamics* 18.3 (2006): 335–49.

Rose, Mark. *Authors and Owners: The Invention of Copyright*. Cambridge: Harvard University Press, 1995.

Rose, Nikolas. *The Powers of Freedom*. Cambridge: Cambridge University Press, 1999.

Rose, Nikolas, and Peter Miller. *Governing the Present: Administering Economic, Social, and Personal Life*. Malden, MA: Polity, 2008.

Rose, Tricia. *Black Noise: Rap Music and Black Culture in Contemporary America*. Hanover, NH: Wesleyan University Press, 1994.

Rosenberg, Samuel. *American Economic Development since 1945*. New York: Palgrave, 2003.

Ross, Andrew. "Hacking Away at the Counterculture." *Postmodern Culture* 1.1 (September 1990). http://pmc.iath.virginia.edu/text-only/issue.990/ross-1.990 and http://pmc.iath.virginia.edu/text-only/issue.990/ross-2.990.

———. *Nice Work If You Can Get It: Life and Labor in Precarious Times*. New York: NYU Press, 2009.

———. *No Collar: The Humane Workplace and Its Hidden Costs*. Philadelphia: Temple University Press, 2004.

———. *No Sweat: Fashion, Free Trade, and the Rights of Garment Workers*. New York: Verso, 1997.

Rossi, Alice S., ed. *The Feminist Papers: From Adams to de Beauvoir*. New York: Columbia University Press, 1973.

Rothenberg, Winifred Barr. *From Market-Places to a Market Economy: The Transformation of Rural Massachusetts, 1750–1850*. Chicago: University of Chicago Press, 1992.

Rothman, David. *The Discovery of the Asylum: Social Order and Disorder in the New Republic*. Boston: Little, Brown, 1971.

Rousseau, Jean-Jacques. *A Discourse on Inequality*. 1754. Trans. Maurice Cranston. New York: Penguin, 1984.

———. *The Social Contract*. 1762. Trans. Maurice Cranston. London: Penguin, 1968.

Rowe, John Carlos, ed. *Post-nationalist American Studies*. Berkeley: University of California Press, 2000.

Roy, William G. *Socializing Capital: The Rise of the Large Industrial Corporation in America*. Princeton: Princeton University Press, 1997.

Ruben, Matthew. "Suburbanization and Urban Poverty under Neoliberalism." *The New Poverty Studies: The Ethnography of Power, Politics, and Impoverished People in the United States*. Ed. Judith G. Goode and Jeff Maskovsky. New York: NYU Press, 2002. 434–69.

Rubin, Gayle. "Studying Sexual Subcultures: Excavating the Ethnography of Gay Communities in Urban North America." *Out in Theory: The Emergence of Lesbian and Gay Anthropology*. Ed. Ellen Lewin and William L. Leap. Urbana: University of Illinois Press, 2002. 17–67.

———. "Thinking Sex: Notes for a Radical Theory of the Politics of Sexuality." *Pleasure and Danger: Exploring Female Sexuality*. Ed. Carole S. Vance. Boston: Routledge and Kegan Paul, 1984. 267–319.

———. "The Traffic in Women: Notes on the 'Political Economy' of Sex." *Toward an Anthropology of Women*. Ed. Rayna R. Reiter. New York: Monthly Review Press, 1975. 157–210.

Ruccio, David F. "Globalization and Imperialism." *Rethinking Marxism* 15 (2003): 75–94.

Ruccio, David F., and J. K. Gibson-Graham. "'After' Development: Reimagining Economy and Class." *Re/presenting Class: Essays in Postmodern Political Economy*. Ed. J. K. Gibson-Graham, Stephen Resnick, and Richard Wolff. Durham: Duke University Press, 2001. 158–81.

Rugemer, Edward Bartlett. *The Problem of Emancipation: The Caribbean Roots of the American Civil War*. Baton Rouge: Louisiana State University Press, 2008.

Russ, Joanna. "Speculations: The Subjunctivity of Science Fiction." *To Write Like a Woman: Essays in Feminism and Science Fiction*. Bloomington: Indiana University Press, 1995. 15–25.

Ryan, Mary P. *Cradle of the Middle Class: The Family in Oneida County, New York, 1790–1865*. New York: Cambridge University Press, 1981.

———. *Womanhood in American from Colonial Times to the Present*. New York: New Viewpoints, 1975.

Ryan, Susan M. *The Grammar of Good Intentions: Race and the Antebellum Culture of Benevolence*. Ithaca: Cornell University Press, 2003.

Rybczynski, Witold. *Home: A Short History of an Idea*. London: Longman, 1988.

Sabol, William J., and Heather Couture. *Prisoners at Midyear 2007*. NCJ221944. Washington, DC: U.S. Department of Justice, Bureau of Justice Statistics, 2008.

Safran, William. "Diasporas in Modern Societies: Myths of Homeland and Return." *Diaspora* 1.1 (1991): 83–99.

Said, Edward W. *Covering Islam: How the Media and the Experts Determine How We See the Rest of the World*. New York: Vintage, 1981.

———. *Culture and Imperialism*. New York: Random House, 1993.

———. *Orientalism*. New York: Vintage, 1978.

Saint-Simon, Henri de. *Mémoire sur la science de l'homme*. 1813. *La physiologie sociale*. Ed. G. Gurwitch. Paris: Presses Universitaires de France, 1965.

Saito, Leland. *The Politics of Exclusion: The Failure of Race-Neutral Policies in Urban America*. Stanford: Stanford University Press, 2009.

Sakai, Naoki. "'You Asians': On the Historical Role of the West and Asia Binary." *South Atlantic Quarterly* 99.4 (2000): 789–817.

Sakai, Naoki, and Meaghan Morris. "The West." *New Keywords: A Revised Vocabulary of Culture and Society*. Ed. Tony Bennett, Lawrence Grossberg, and Meaghan Morris. London: Blackwell, 2005.

Saks, Eva. "Representing Miscegenation Law." *Raritan* 8 (1988): 39–69.

Salazar, James B. *Bodies of Reform: The Rhetoric of Character in Gilded Age America*. New York: NYU Press, 2010.

Saldaña-Portillo, María Josefina. *The Revolutionary Imagination in the Americas and the Age of Development*. Durham: Duke University Press, 2003.

———. "Who's the Indian in Aztlán? Re-writing Mestizaje, Indianism, and Chicanismo from the Lacandón." *Latin American Subaltern Studies Reader*. Ed. Ileana Rodríguez. Durham: Duke University Press, 2001. 402–23.

Saldívar, José David. "Américo Paredes and Decolonization." *Cultures of United States Imperialism*. Ed. Amy Kaplan and Donald Pease. Durham: Duke University Press, 1993. 292–311.

———. *Border Matters: Remapping American Cultural Studies*. Berkeley: University of California Press, 1997.

Saldívar-Hull, Sonia. *Feminism on the Border: Chicana Gender Politics and Literature*. Berkeley: University of California Press, 2000.

Salter, Mark. "The Global Visa Regime and the Political Technologies of the International Self: Borders, Bodies, Biopolitics." *Alternatives* 31 (2006): 167–89.

Samuels, Ellen. "Critical Divides: Judith Butler's Body Theory and the Question of Disability." *NWSA Journal* 14.3 (2002): 58–76.

Samuels, Shirley, ed. *The Culture of Sentiment: Race, Gender, and Sentimentality in Nineteenth-Century America*. New York: Oxford University Press, 1992.

Samuelson, Paul A., and William D. Nordhaus. *Economics*. 18th ed. New York: McGraw-Hill / Irwin, 2004.

Sánchez, María Carla. *Reforming the World: Social Activism and the Problem of Fiction in Nineteenth-Century America*. Iowa City: University of Iowa Press, 2008.

Sánchez-Eppler, Karen. *Touching Liberty: Abolition, Feminism, and the Politics of the Body*. Berkeley: University of California Press, 1993.

Sandahl, Carrie, and Philip Auslander, eds. *Bodies in Commotion: Disability and Performance*. Ann Arbor: University of Michigan Press, 2005.

Sanders, Bernie. "What If There Were 83 Women Senators?" Bernie Sanders's Senate website. March 1, 2012. http://www.sanders.senate.gov/newsroom/news/?id=17e5beaf-4b3f-4db5-ad70-d7bead096937.

Sandoval, Tomás F. Summers, Jr. "Disobedient Bodies: Racialization, Resistance, and the Mass (Re)Articulation of the Mexican Immigrant Body." *American Behavioral Scientist* 52.4 (December 2008): 580–97.

Sandvig, Christian. "Connection at Eqiiaapaayp Mountain: Indigenous Internet Infrastructure." *Race after the Internet*. Ed. Lisa Nakamura, Peter Chow-White, and Alondra Nelson. New York: Routledge, 2012. 168–200.

Sanger, Margaret. *Family Limitation*. New York, 1914.

Santiago, Silviano. *Latin American Literature: The Space in Between*. 1971. Trans. Stephen Moscov. Buffalo: Council on International Studies, SUNY Buffalo, 1973.

Sarachild, Kathie. "Consciousness Raising: A Radical Weapon." *Feminist Revolution*. Ed. Redstockings of the Women's Liberation Movement. New York: Random House, 1978. 144–50. An adaptation of the program for "Radical Feminist Consciousness-Raising" presented at First National Women's Liberation Conference, outside Chicago, November 27, 1968. Available from "Documents from the Women's Liberation Movement: An On-line Archival Collection," Duke University Special Collections, http://library.duke.edu/rubenstein/scriptorium/wlm/fem/sarachild.html.

Sarat, Austin. "Going to Court: Access, Autonomy, and the Contradictions of Liberal Legality." *The Politics of Law: A Progressive Critique*. Ed. David Kairys. New York: Basic Books, 1982. 97–114.

Sarmiento, Domingo Faustino. *Facundo: Civilization and Barbarism*. 1845. Trans. Kathleen Ross. Berkeley: University of California Press, 2004.

Sassen, Saskia. *The Global City*. Princeton: Princeton University Press, 1991.

———. *Globalization and Its Discontents: Essays on the New Mobility of People and Money*. New York: New Press, 1998.

———. "Incompleteness and the Possibility of Making: Towards Denationalized Citizenship?" *Cultural Dynamics* 21 (2009): 227–54.

———. "Why Migration?" *Report on the Americas* 26.1 (1992): 14–19.

Sawyer, Suzana. *Crude Chronicles: Indigenous Politics, Multinational Oil, and Neoliberalism in Ecuador*. Durham: Duke University Press, 2004.

Saxton, Alexander. *The Rise and Fall of the White Republic*. New York: Verso, 1990.

Sayers, Jentery. "Tinker-centric Pedagogy in Literature and Language Classrooms." *Collaborative Approaches to the Digital in English Studies*. Ed. Laura McGrath. Logan: Utah State University Press, 2011. 279–300.

Sayre, Gordon. "Renegades from Barbary: The Transnational Turn in Captivity Studies." *American Literary History* 22.2 (2010): 347–59.

Scarry, Elaine. *The Body in Pain: The Making and Unmaking of the World*. New York: Oxford University Press, 1985.

———. *On Beauty and Being Just*. Princeton: Princeton University Press, 2001.

Schafer, R. Murray. *The Soundscape: Our Sonic Environment and the Tuning of the World*. New York: Knopf, 1977.

Schiebinger, Londa. *The Mind Has No Sex? Women in the Origins of Modern Science*. Cambridge: Harvard University Press, 1989.

Schiller, Friedrich. *On the Aesthetic Education of Man in a Series of Letters*. 1794. Trans. Reginald Snell. New Haven: Yale University Press, 1954.

———. *On the Aesthetic Education of Man in a Series of Letters*. 1794. Ed. and trans. Elizabeth M. Wilkinson and L. A. Willoughby. Oxford, UK: Clarendon; New York: Oxford University Press, 1982.

Schivelbusch, Wolfgang. *The Railway Journey: The Industrialization of Time and Space in the 19th Century*. 1977. Berkeley: University of California Press, 1986.

Schlesinger, Arthur M., Jr. *The Age of Jackson*. Boston: Little, Brown, 1945.

———. *The Disuniting of America: Reflections on a Multicultural Society*. Rev. ed. New York: Norton, 1998.

Schlund-Vials, Cathy, Linda Vo, and K. Scott Wong. *Keywords for Asian American Studies*. New York: NYU Press, forthcoming.

Schmidt, Leigh Eric. *Hearing Things: Religion, Illusion, and the American Enlightenment*. Cambridge: Cambridge University Press, 2000.

Schmidt Camacho, Alicia. "Hailing the Twelve Million: U.S. Immigration Policy, Deportation, and the Imaginary of Lawful Violence." *Social Text* 28.4 105 (2010): 1–24.

———. *Migrant Imaginaries: Latino Cultural Politics and the Mexico-U.S. Borderlands*. New York: NYU Press, 2008.

Schmitt, Carl. *The Crisis of Parliamentary Democracy*. 1923. Trans. Ellen Kennedy. Cambridge: MIT Press, 1985.

———. *Four Chapters on the Concept of Sovereignty*. Trans. George Schwab. Cambridge: MIT Press, 1986.

Schwartz, Nelson D. "Corporate Profits Soar as Worker Income Limps." *New York Times*, March 3, 2013. http://www.nytimes.com/2013/03/04/business/economy/corporate-profits-soar-as-worker-income-limps.html.

Schwarz, Roberto. "Culture and Politics in Brazil, 1964–1969." 1970. *Misplaced Ideas: Essays on Brazilian Culture*. London: Verso, 1992.

Schweik, Susan. *The Ugly Laws: Disability in Public*. New York: NYU Press, 2009.

Scott, David. "Colonial Governmentality." *Social Text* 43 (Autumn 1995): 191–220.

Scott, Pamela. "'This Vast Empire': The Iconography of the Mall, 1791–1848." *The Mall in Washington, 1791–1991*. Ed. Richard Longstreth. Washington, DC: National Gallery of Art; New Haven: Yale University Press, 2002. 37–60.

Sears, John F. *Sacred Places: American Tourist Attractions in the Nineteenth Century*. Amherst: University of Massachusetts Press, 1989.

Sedgwick, Eve Kosofsky. *Epistemology of the Closet*. Berkeley: University of California Press, 1990.

———. "Queer and Now." *Tendencies*. Durham: Duke University Press, 1993.

———. *Touching Feeling*. Durham: Duke University Press, 2003.

Sedgwick, Eve Kosofsky, and Adam Frank, eds. *Shame and Its Sisters: A Silvan Tompkins Reader*. Durham: Duke University Press, 1995.

Segura, Denise, and Patricia Zavella, eds. *Women and Migration in the U.S.-Mexico Borderlands*. Durham: Duke University Press, 2007.

Sekula, Allan. "The Body and the Archive." *OCTOBER* 39 (Winter 1986): 3–64.

Sellers, Charles. *The Market Revolution: Jacksonian America, 1815–1846.* New York: Oxford University Press, 1991.

Sen, Amartya. *Development as Freedom.* New York: Random House, 1999.

Senghor, Léopold Sedar. *Négritude et huminisme.* Paris: Editions du Seuil, 1964.

Senna, Danzy. *Caucasia: A Novel.* New York: Riverhead, 1999.

———. *Where Did You Sleep Last Night? A Personal History.* New York: Picador, 2010.

Sernett, Milton C. *Bound for the Promised Land: African American Religion and the Great Migration.* Durham: Duke University Press, 1997.

Sewall, Samuel. *Phaemonena quaedam Apocalyptica ad aspectum Novi Orbis configurata; or, Some Few Lines towards a Description of the New Heaven.* 1697. Ed. Rainer Slominski. University of Nebraska–Lincoln Electronic Texts in American Studies, 1997. http://digitalcommons.unl.edu/etas/25.

Shah, Nayan. *Contagious Divides: Epidemics and Race in San Francisco's Chinatown.* Berkeley: University of California Press, 2001.

———. *Stranger Intimacy: Contesting Race, Sexuality, and the Law in the North American West.* Berkeley: University of California Press, 2012.

Shaheen, Jack G. *Reel Bad Arabs: How Hollywood Vilifies a People.* New York: Olive Branch, 2001.

Shain, Yossi. "Ethnic Diaspora and U.S. Foreign Policy." *Political Science Quarterly* 109.5 (1994–95): 811–42.

Shane. Dir. George Stevens. Paramount, 1953.

Shanley, Kathryn W. "The Indians America Loves to Love and Read: American Indian Identity and Cultural Appropriation." *American Indian Quarterly* 21.4 (1997): 675–702.

Sharpe, Jenny. "Is the United States Postcolonial? Transnationalism, Immigration, and Race." *Diaspora* 4.2 (1995): 181–99.

Sheehi, Stephen. *Islamophobia: The Ideological Campaign against Muslims.* Atlanta: Clarity, 2011.

Shell, Marc, ed. *American Babel: Literatures of the United States from Abnaki to Zuni.* Cambridge: Harvard University Press, 2002.

Shiekh, Irum. *Muslims' Stories of Detention and Deportation in America after 9/11.* New York: Palgrave Macmillan, 2011.

Shigematsu, Setsu, and Keith Camacho, eds. *Militarized Currents: Toward a Decolonized Future in Asia and the Pacific.* Minneapolis: University of Minnesota Press, 2010.

Shohat, Ella. "Notes on the 'Post-Colonial.'" *Social Text* 31–32 (1992): 99–113.

Sidbury, James. *Ploughshares into Swords: Race, Rebellion, and Identity in Gabriel's Virginia, 1730–1810.* Cambridge: Cambridge University Press, 1997.

Siebers, Tobin. "Disability as Masquerade." *Literature and Medicine* 23.1 (2004): 1–22.

Silko, Leslie Marmon. *Almanac of the Dead: A Novel.* New York: Simon and Schuster, 1991.

Silvers, Anita. *Disability, Difference, Discrimination.* New York: Rowman and Littlefield, 1998.

Simmel, Georg. "Fashion." *American Journal of Sociology* 62.6 (May 1957): 541–58.

Simon, Jonathan. *Governing through Crime: How the War on Crime Transformed American Democracy and Created a Culture of Fear.* New York: Oxford University Press, 2007.

Sinclair, Upton. *The Jungle.* 1906. Introd. James Barrett. Urbana: University of Illinois Press, 1988.

Singer, Peter W. *Corporate Warriors: The Rise of the Privatized Military Industry* Ithaca: Cornell University Press, 2003.

Singh, Nikhil Pal. *Black Is a Country: Race and the Unfinished Struggle for Democracy.* Cambridge: Harvard University Press, 2004.

———. "Racial Formation in the Age of Permanent War." *Racial Formation in the Twenty-First Century.* Ed. Daniel Martinez HoSang, Oneka LaBennett, and Laura Pulido. Berkeley: University of California Press, 2012. 276–301.

Sinha, Mrinalinhi. *Colonial Masculinity: The "Manly Englishman" and the "Effeminate Bengali" in the Late Nineteenth Century.* Manchester: Manchester University Press, 1995.

Sjoberg, Laura, and Sandra E. Via. *Gender, War, and Militarism: Feminist Perspectives.* Santa Barbara, CA: Praeger, 2010.

Skelton, Tracey, and Gill Valentine, eds. *Cool Places: Geographies of Youth Cultures.* London: Routledge, 1998.

Skinner, Quentin. *Foundations of Modern Political Thought.* 2 vols. Cambridge: Cambridge University Press, 1978.

Sklair, Leslie. *Sociology of the Global System.* Hertfordshire, UK: Harvester Wheatsheaf, 1991.

Slotkin, Richard. *The Fatal Environment: The Myth of the Frontier in the Age of Industrialization, 1800–1890.* Middletown, CT: Wesleyan University Press, 1985.

———. *Gunfighter Nation: The Myth of the Frontier in Twentieth-Century America.* New York: Atheneum, 1992.

———. *Regeneration through Violence: The Mythology of the American Frontier, 1600–1860.* Middletown, CT: Wesleyan University Press, 1973.

Smallwood, Stephanie. "Commodified Freedom: Interrogating the Limits of Anti-slavery Ideology in the Early Republic." *Journal of the Early Republic* 24 (2004): 289–98.

Smiley, Jane. *A Thousand Acres.* New York: Knopf, 1991.

Smith, Adam. *An Inquiry into the Nature and Causes of the Wealth of Nations.* 1776. Ed. Edwin Canaan. New York: Modern Library, 1937.

———. *The Theory of Moral Sentiments.* 1759. New York: Augustus M. Kelley, 1966.

Smith, Adam C. "No Telling If Voter Rolls Are Ready for 2004." *St. Petersburg Times,* December 21, 2003. http://www.sptimes.com/2003/12/21/State/No_telling_if_voter_r.shtml.

Smith, Andrea. *Conquest: Sexual Violence and American Indian Genocide.* Boston: South End, 2005.

———. "Indigeneity, Settler Colonialism, White Supremacy." *Global Dialogue* 12.2 (Summer–Autumn 2010). http://worlddialogue.org/issue.php?id=44.

Smith, Barbara. "Toward a Black Feminist Criticism." *All the Women Are White, All the Blacks Are Men, but Some of Us Are Brave: Black Women's Studies.* Ed. Gloria T. Hull, Patricia Bell Scott, and Barbara Smith. New York: Feminist Press, 1982. 157–75.

Smith, Caleb. *The Prison and the American Imagination*. New Haven: Yale University Press, 2009.

Smith, David L. "Huck, Jim and American Racial Discourse." *Satire or Evasion? Black Perspectives on "Huckleberry Finn."* Ed. James S. Leonard, Thomas A. Tenney, and Thadious M. Davis. Durham: Duke University Press, 1991. 103-20.

Smith, Henry Nash. *Popular Culture and Industrialism, 1865–1890*. Garden City, NY: Anchor Books, 1967.

———. *Virgin Land: The American West as Symbol and Myth*. Cambridge: Harvard University Press, 1950.

Smith, Jon, and Deborah N. Cohn. *Look Away! The U.S. South in New World Studies*. Durham: Duke University Press, 2004.

Smith, Mark M. "Listening to the Heard Worlds of Antebellum America." *Journal of the Historical Society* 1 (June 2000): 63-97.

———. *Mastered by the Clock: Time, Slavery, and Freedom in the American South*. Chapel Hill: University of North Carolina Press, 1997.

Smith, Martha Nell. "Dickinson's Manuscripts." *The Emily Dickinson Handbook*. Ed. Gudrun Grabher, Roland Hagenbüchle, and Cristanne Miller. Amherst: University of Massachusetts Press, 1998. 113-37.

Smith, Neil. *The Endgame of Globalization*. New York: Routledge, 2004.

———. *Uneven Development: Nature, Capital, and the Production of Space*. Athens: University of Georgia Press, 1983.

Smith, Paul Chaat, and Robert Warrior. *Like a Hurricane: The Indian Movement from Alcatraz to Wounded Knee*. New York: New Press, 1996.

Smith, Rogers M. *Civic Ideals: Conflicting Visions of Citizenship in U.S. History*. New Haven: Yale University Press, 1997.

Smith, Shawn Michelle. *American Archives: Gender, Race, and Class in Visual Culture*. Princeton: Princeton University Press, 1999.

Smith, Valerie. *Not Just Race, Not Just Gender: Black Feminist Readings*. New York: Routledge, 1998.

Smith, Wilfred Cantwell. *The Meaning and End of Religion*. New York: New American Library, 1964.

Smith-Rosenberg, Carroll. *This Violent Empire: The Birth of an American National Identity*. Chapel Hill: University of North Carolina Press, 2010.

Snyder, Sharon L., and David T. Mitchell. *Cultural Locations of Disability*. Chicago: University of Chicago Press, 2006.

———. "Re-engaging the Body: Disability Studies and the Resistance to Embodiment." *Public Culture* 13.3 (2001): 367-89.

Soja, Edward. *Postmodern Geographies: The Reassertion of Space in Postmodern Geographies*. London: Verso, 1989.

Sokal, Alan. "A Physicist Experiments with Cultural Studies." *Lingua Franca* 6.4 (1996a): 62-64.

———. "Transgressing the Boundaries: Toward a Transformative Hermeneutics of Quantum Gravity." *Social Text* 46-47 (1996b): 217-52.

Solanas, Valerie. *The SCUM Manifesto*. 1968. Introd. Avital Ronell. New York: Verso, 2004.

Sollors, Werner. *Beyond Ethnicity: Consent and Descent in American Culture*. New York: Oxford University Press, 1986.

———, ed. *Multilingual America: Transnationalism, Ethnicity, and the Languages of American Literature*. New York: NYU Press, 1998.

Somerville, Siobhan B. *Queering the Color Line: Race and the Invention of Homosexuality in American Culture*. Durham: Duke University Press, 2000.

Sone, Monica. *Nisei Daughter*. 1953. Seattle: University of Washington Press, 1979.

Sonnenschein, William. *The Diversity Toolkit: How You Can Build and Benefit from a Diverse Workforce*. New York: McGraw-Hill, 1999.

Sontag, Susan. *Regarding the Pain of Others*. New York: Farrar, Straus and Giroux, 2003.

Soto, Sandra K. *Reading Chican@ Like a Queer: The De-mastery of Desire*. Austin: University of Texas Press, 2010.

Spade, Dean. *Normal Life: Administrative Violence, Critical Trans Politics, and the Limits of Law*. Cambridge, MA: South End, 2011.

Spade, Dean, and Craig Willse. "Confronting the Limits of Gay Hate Crimes Activism: A Radical Critique." *UCLA Chicano-Latino Law Review* 21 (2000): 38-52.

Spencer, Herbert. *Principles of Sociology*. Vol. 1. London and Edinburgh: Williams and Norgate, 1874-75.

Spillers, Hortense. *Black, White, and in Color: Essays on American Literature and Culture*. Chicago: University of Chicago Press, 2003.

———. "Mama's Baby, Papa's Maybe: An American Grammar Book." *Diacritics* 17 (Summer 1987): 65-81.

Spivak, Gayatri Chakravorty. "Can the Subaltern Speak?" *Marxism and the Interpretation of Culture*. Ed. Cary Nelson and Lawrence Grossberg. Urbana: University of Illinois Press, 1988. 271-313.

———. *A Critique of Postcolonial Reason: Toward a History of the Vanishing Present*. Cambridge: Harvard University Press, 1999.

———. *The Post-colonial Critic: Interviews, Strategies, Dialogues*. Ed. Sarah Harasym. New York: Routledge, 1990.

———. "Scattered Speculations on the Question of Cultural Studies." *Outside in the Teaching Machine*. New York: Routledge, 1993. 255-84.

Spivak, Gayatri Chakravorty, and Judith Butler. *Who Sings the Nation-State? Language, Politics, Belonging*. London: Seagull Books, 2007.

Stacey, Judith. *Brave New Families: Stories of Domestic Upheaval in Late-Twentieth-Century America*. New York: Basic Books, 1990.

Stack, Carol B. *Call to Home: African-Americans Reclaim the Rural South*. New York: Basic Books, 1996.

Stadler, Gustavus. "Introduction: Breaking Sound Barriers." *Social Text* 28.1 102 (2010): 1-12.

Staiger, Janet, Ann Cvetkovich, and Ann Reynolds, eds. *Political Emotions*. New York: Routledge, 2010.

Stallybrass, Peter, and Allon White. *The Politics and Poetics of Transgression*. Ithaca: Cornell University Press, 1986.

Stange, Maren. *Symbols of Ideal Life: Social Documentary Photography in America, 1890–1950*. New York: Cambridge University Press, 1989.

Stanley, Amy Dru. *From Bondage to Contract: Wage Labor, Marriage, and the Market in the Age of Slave Emancipation*. New York: Cambridge University Press, 1998.

———. "Home Life and the Morality of the Market." *The Market Revolution in America: Social, Political, and Religious Expressions, 1800–1880*. Ed. Melvyn Stokes and Stephen Conway. Charlottesville: University of Virginia Press, 1996. 74-96.

Stanley, Sara G. "What, to the Toiling Millions There, Is This

Boasted Liberty?" 1860. *Lift Every Voice: African American Oratory, 1787-1900.* Ed. Philip Foner and Robert James Branham. Tuscaloosa: University of Alabama Press, 1997. 284-87.

Stannard, David. *American Holocaust: The Conquest of the New World.* Oxford: Oxford University Press, 1992.

Stansell, Christine. *City of Women: Sex and Class in New York, 1789-1860.* New York: Knopf, 1986.

Stanton, Elizabeth Cady. "Marriages and Mistresses." *Revolution,* October 15, 1868a.

———. "Miss Becker on the Difference in Sex." *Revolution,* September 24, 1868b.

Stark, Rodney, and Roger Finke. *Acts of Faith: Explaining the Human Side of Religion.* Berkeley: University of California Press, 2000.

———. *The Churching of America, 1776-1990: Winners and Losers in Our Religious Economy.* New Brunswick: Rutgers University Press, 1992.

Starobinski, Jean. *1789: The Emblems of Reason.* Cambridge: MIT Press, 1988.

Stauffer, John. *The Black Hearts of Men: Radical Abolition and the Transformation of Race.* Cambridge: Harvard University Press, 2004.

Stecopoulos, Harilaos. *Reconstructing the World: Southern Fictions and U.S. Imperialisms, 1898-1976.* Ithaca: Cornell University Press, 2008.

Stegner, Wallace. *Where the Bluebird Sings to the Lemonade Springs: Living and Writing in the West.* New York: Random House, 1992.

Stein, Gertrude. *The Making of Americans: Being a History of a Family's Progress.* 1925. Normal, IL: Dalkey Archive, 1995.

Stephen, Lynn. *Transborder Lives: Indigenous Oaxacans in Mexico, California, and Oregon.* Durham: Duke University Press, 2007.

Sterling, Dorothy, ed. *The Trouble They Seen: The Story of Reconstruction in the Words of African Americans.* Garden City, NY: Doubleday, 1976.

Stern, Alexandra Minna. "Buildings, Boundaries and Blood: Medicalization and Nation-Building on the U.S.-Mexico Border, 1910-1930." *Hispanic American Historical Review* 79.1 (1999a): 41-82.

———. "Secrets under the Skin: New Historical Perspectives on Disease, Deviation, and Citizenship." *Comparative Studies in Society and History* 41.3 (July 1999b): 589-96.

Sterne, Jonathan. *The Audible Past: Cultural Origins of Sound Reproduction.* Durham: Duke University Press, 2003.

Stevens, Jacqueline. "The Politics of LGBTQ Scholarship." *GLQ* 10.2 (2004): 220-26.

———. *Reproducing the State.* Princeton: Princeton University Press, 1999.

Stewart, Kathleen. *Ordinary Affects.* Durham: Duke University Press, 2007.

———. *A Space at the Side of the Road: Cultural Poetics in an "Other" America.* Princeton: Princeton University Press, 1996.

Stiglitz, Joseph E. *Globalization and Its Discontents.* New York: Norton, 2002.

———. *The Price of Inequality: How Today's Divided Society Endangers Our Future.* New York: Norton, 2013.

Stiglitz, Joseph E., and Carl E. Walsh. *Economics.* 3rd ed. New York: Norton, 2002.

Stoever-Ackerman, Jennifer. "Splicing the Sonic Color-Line: Tony Schwartz Remixes Postwar Nueva York." *Social Text* 28.1 102 (2010): 59-85.

Stokoe, William C., Dorothy C. Casterline, and Carl G. Croneberg. *A Dictionary of American Sign Languages on Linguistic Principles.* Washington, DC: Gallaudet College Press, 1965.

Stolberg, Sheryl Gay. "A Pregnant Pause." *New York Times,* November 29, 2009. http://query.nytimes.com/gst/fullpage.html?res=9903E3DE1E31F93AA15752C1A96F9C8B63&ref=sherylgaystolberg.

Stoler, Ann Laura. *Carnal Knowledge and Imperial Power: Race and the Intimate in Colonial Rule.* Berkeley: University of California Press, 2010.

———, ed. *Haunted by Empire: Geographies of Intimacy in North American History.* Durham: Duke University Press, 2006.

———. *Race and the Education of Desire: Foucault's History of Sexuality and the Colonial Order of Things.* Durham: Duke University Press, 1995.

Stone, Allucquère Rosanne. *The War of Desire and Technology at the Close of the Mechanical Age.* Cambridge: MIT Press, 1996.

Stone, Deborah A. *The Disabled State.* Philadelphia: Temple University Press, 1984.

Stone, Sandy. "The 'Empire' Strikes Back: A Posttranssexual Manifesto." *Body Guards: The Cultural Politics of Gender Ambiguity.* Ed. Kristina Straub and Julia Epstein. New York: Routledge, 1991. 280-304.

Stowe, Harriet Beecher. *Uncle Tom's Cabin, or, Life among the Lowly.* 1852. New York: Penguin, 1981.

Strachey, William. "A True Reportory of the Wreck and Redemption of Sir Thomas Gates, Knight." 1610. *A Voyage to Virginia in 1609: Two Narratives.* Ed. Louis B. Wright. Charlottesville: University of Virginia Press, 1964. 1-102.

Streeby, Shelley. *American Sensations: Class, Empire, and the Production of Popular Culture.* Berkeley: University of California Press, 2002.

———. *Radical Sensations: World Movements, Violence, and Visual Culture.* Durham: Duke University Press, 2013.

Stryker, Susan. *Transgender History.* Berkeley, CA: Seal, 2008.

Stuckey, Sterling. *Slave Culture: Nationalism and the Foundations of Black America.* New York: Oxford University Press, 1987.

Sturken, Marita, and Lisa Cartwright. *Practices of Looking: An Introduction to Visual Culture.* New York: Oxford University Press, 2009.

Sturm, Circe. *Blood Politics: Race, Culture, and Identity in the Cherokee Nation of Oklahoma.* Berkeley: University of California Press, 2003.

Suárez-Orozco, Marcelo, Carola Suárez-Orozco, and Carolyn Sattin-Bajaj. "Making Migration Work." *Peabody Journal of Education,* October 2010.

Sudarkasa, Niara. "Interpreting the African Heritage in AfroAmerican Family Organization." *Black Families.* Ed. Harriett P. McAdoo. Beverly Hills, CA: Sage, 1988. 37-53.

Sudbury, Julia. *"Other Kinds of Dreams": Black Women's Organisations and the Politics of Transformation.* London: Routledge, 1998.

Suisman, David, and Susan Strasser, eds. *Sound in the Age of Mechanical Reproduction.* Philadelphia: University of Pennsylvania Press, 2009.

Susman, Warren I. *Culture as History: The Transformation of American Society in the Twentieth Century*. New York: Pantheon, 1984.

Sutherland, William. *Britain's Glory; or, Ship-Building Unvail'd, Being a General Director, for Building and Compleating the Said Machines*. London, 1717.

Swatos, William H., Jr., and Daniel V. A. Olson, eds. *The Secularization Debate*. Lanham, MD: Rowman and Littlefield, 2000.

Sweet, John. *Bodies Politic: Renegotiating Race in the American North, 1730–1830*. Baltimore: Johns Hopkins University Press, 2003.

Swinth, Kirsten. "Review: Strangers, Neighbors, Aliens in a New America: Migration Stories for the Twenty-First Century." *American Quarterly* 57.2 (June 2005): 507–21.

Sylvia Rivera Law Project. "SRLP Opposes the Matthew Shepard and James Byrd, Jr. Hate Crimes Prevention Act." 2009. http://srlp.org/fedhatecrimelaw.

Sylvia Rivera Law Project, FIERCE, Queers for Economic Justice, Peter Cicchino Youth Project, and the Audre Lorde Project. "SRLP Announces Non-Support of the Gender Employment Non-Discrimination Act." 2009. http://srlp.org/genda.

Szwed, John. *Space Is the Place: The Lives and Times of Sun Ra*. New York: Da Capo, 1998.

Tagg, John. *The Burden of Representation: Essays on Photographies and Histories*. Minneapolis: University of Minnesota Press, 1988.

Tahmahkera, Dustin. "'An Indian in a White Man's Camp': Johnny Cash's Indian Country Music." *Sound Clash: Listening to American Studies*. Ed. Kara Keeling and Josh Kun. Baltimore: Johns Hopkins University Press, 2011. 147–74.

Takaki, Ronald. *A Different Mirror: A History of Multicultural America*. Boston: Little, Brown, 1993.

———. *Strangers from a Different Shore: A History of Asian Americans*. Boston: Little, Brown, 1989.

Tarter, Jim. "Some Live More Downstream than Others: Cancer, Gender, and Environmental Justice." *The Environmental Justice Reader: Politics, Poetics, and Pedagogy*. Ed. Joni Adamson, Mei Mei Evans, and Rachel Stein. Tucson: University of Arizona Press, 2002. 213–28.

Tate, Claudia. *Domestic Allegories of Political Desire: The Black Heroine's Text at the Turn of the Century*. New York: Oxford University Press, 1992.

Tatum, Stephen. "The Problem of the 'Popular' in the New Western History." *The New Western History: The Territory Ahead*. Ed. Forrest G. Robinson. Tucson: University of Arizona Press, 1997. 153–90.

———. "Spectrality and the Postregional Interface." *Postwestern Horizons: Literature, Theory, Space*. Ed. Susan Kollin. Lincoln: University of Nebraska Press, 2007. 3–30.

Taub, Nadine, and Elizabeth M. Schneider. "Women's Subordination and the Role of Law." *The Politics of Law: A Progressive Critique*. Ed. David Kairys. New York: Basic Books, 1982. 328–55.

Taylor, Charles. *Modern Social Imaginaries*. Durham: Duke University Press, 2004.

———. *Multiculturalism and "The Politics of Recognition."* Princeton: Princeton University Press, 1992.

———. *Varieties of Religion Today*. Cambridge: Harvard University Press, 2002.

Taylor, Frederick Winslow. *The Principles of Scientific Management*. 1911. New York: Cosimo, 2010.

Taylor, Peter J. *Modernities: A Geohistorical Interpretation*. Minneapolis: University of Minnesota Press, 1999.

Teaiwa, Teresia K. "Native Thoughts: A Pacific Studies Take on Cultural Studies and Diaspora." *Indigenous Diasporas and Dislocations*. Ed. Graham Harvey and Charles D. Thompson. London: Ashgate, 2005. 15–35.

———. "Yaqona/Yagona: Roots and Routes of a Displaced Native." Ed. Stephen Muecke and Meaghan Morris. *UTS Review* (University of Technology at Sydney) 4.2 (1998): 92–106.

Ten Commandments, The. Dir. Cecil B. DeMille. Paramount Pictures / Motion Picture Associates, 1956.

Terry, Jennifer. *An American Obsession: Science, Medicine, and Homosexuality in Modern Society*. Chicago: University of Chicago Press, 1999.

Thomas, Deborah A., and Kamari Maxine Clarke. "Introduction: Globalization and the Transformations of Race." *Globalization and Race: Transformations in the Cultural Production of Blackness*. Ed. Kamari Maxine Clarke and Deborah A. Thomas. Durham: Duke University Press, 2006. 1–34.

Thomas, Paul. "Modalities of Consent." *Beyond Nationalism?* Ed. Fred Dallmayr and José Maria Rosales. Lanham, MD: Lexington Books, 2001. 3–18.

Thomas, William I., and Florian Znanieki. *The Polish Peasant in Europe and America*. 5 vols. Boston: Gorham, 1918–20.

Thompson, E. P. "The Long Revolution (Part I)." *New Left Review* 9 (1961a): 24–33.

———. "The Long Revolution (Part II)." *New Left Review* 10 (1961b): 34–39.

———. *The Making of the English Working Class*. New York: Vintage, 1963.

———. "Time, Work-Discipline, and Industrial Capitalism." *Past and Present* 38 (1967): 56–97.

Thompson, Emily. *The Soundscape of Modernity: Architectural Acoustics and the Culture of Listening in America, 1900–1933*. Cambridge: MIT Press, 2004.

Thoreau, Henry David. Letter to Thomas Cholmondeley, November 8, 1855. *The Correspondence of Henry David Thoreau*. Ed. W. Harding and C. Bode. New York: NYU Press, 1958. 398.

———. "On Civil Disobedience." 1849. *Walden and Civil Disobedience*. Ed. Owen Thomas. New York: Norton, 1966. 276–300.

———. *Walden; or, Life in the Woods*. 1854. *Walden and Civil Disobedience*. Ed. Owen Thomas. New York: Norton, 1966. 2–275.

———. "A Week on the Concord River and Merrimack." 1849. *A Week, Walden, Maine Woods, Cape Cod*. New York: Library of America, 1985. 1–320.

Thrift, Nigel. *Non-representational Theory: Space, Politics, Affect*. New York: Routledge, 2008.

Tinker, Hugh. *A New System of Slavery: The Export of Indian Labour Overseas, 1830–1920*. Oxford: Oxford University Press, 1974.

Tocqueville, Alexis de. *Democracy in America*. 1835. Trans. Arthur Goldhammer. New York: Library of America, 2004.

Todd, Janet. *Sensibility: An Introduction.* New York: Methuen, 1986.

Tölölyan, Khachig. "Rethinking Diaspora(s): Stateless Power in the Transnational Moment." *Diaspora* 5.1 (1996): 3-36.

Tompkins, Jane. *Sensational Designs: The Cultural Work of American Fiction, 1790-1860.* New York: Oxford University Press, 1985.

Tongson, Karen. *Relocations: Queer Suburban Imaginaries.* New York: NYU Press, 2011.

Toomer, Jean. *Cane.* 1923. New York: Liveright, 1969.

Torpey, John. *The Invention of the Passport.* Cambridge: Cambridge University Press, 2000.

Toynbee, Arnold J. *The Study of History.* 12 vols. Oxford: Oxford University Press, 1934-1961.

Trachtenberg, Alan. *Brooklyn Bridge: Fact and Symbol.* Chicago: University of Chicago Press, 1979.

———. *The Incorporation of America: Culture and Society in the Gilded Age.* New York: Farrar, Straus and Giroux, 1982.

Traffic. Dir. Steven Soderbergh. Bedford Falls Productions, 2000.

Treichler, Paula A. *How to Have Theory in an Epidemic: Cultural Chronicles of AIDS.* Durham: Duke University Press, 1999.

Trent, James W., Jr. *Inventing the Feeble Mind: A History of Mental Retardation in the United States.* Berkeley: University of California Press, 1994.

Tribe, Keith. *Land, Labour and Economic Discourse.* London: Routledge and Kegan Paul, 1978.

Triumph of the Will. Dir. Leni Riefenstahl. Leni Riefenstahl-Produktion/Reichspropagandaleitung der NSDAP, 1935.

Trouillot, Michel-Rolph. *Silencing the Past: Power and the Production of History.* Boston: Beacon, 1995.

Truax, Barry. *Acoustic Communication.* Norwood, NJ: Ablex, 1984.

Truettner, William, and Roger B. Stein, eds. *Picturing Old New England: Image and Memory.* Washington, DC: National Museum of American Art, Smithsonian Institution; New Haven: Yale University Press, 1999.

Tsing, Anna. *Friction: An Ethnography of Global Connection.* Princeton: Princeton University Press, 2011.

Tu, Thuy Linh Nguyen. *The Beautiful Generation: Asian Americans and the Cultural Economy of Fashion.* Durham: Duke University Press, 2011.

Tuan, Yi-fu. *Space and Place: The Perspective of Experience.* Minneapolis: University of Minnesota Press, 1977.

Tucker, Kenneth H., Jr. *Workers of the World Enjoy! Aesthetic Politics from Revolutionary Syndicalism to the Global Justice Movement.* Philadelphia: Temple University Press, 2010.

Turner, Bryan S. *Citizenship and Social Theory.* London: Sage, 1993.

Turner, Frederick Jackson. *The Frontier in American History.* 1893. New York: Holt, 1920.

Turner, Victor. *The Ritual Process: Structure and Anti-structure.* Chicago: Aldine, 1969.

Tuveson, Ernest Lee. *Redeemer Nation: The Idea of America's Millennial Role.* Chicago: University of Chicago Press, 1968.

Twain, Mark. *Adventures of Huckleberry Finn.* 1885. Berkeley: University of California Press, 1985.

———. "A True Story, Repeated Word for Word as I Heard It." *Atlantic Monthly,* November 1874, 591-94.

Tyler, Royall. *The Algerine Captive; or, the Life and Adventures of Doctor Updike Underhill: Six Years a Prisoner among the Algerines.* Walpole, NH: David Carlisle, 1797.

Tylor, Edward Burnett. *Primitive Culture: Researches into the Development of Mythology, Philosophy, Religion, Art, and Custom.* London: J. Murray, 1871.

Tyrell, Ian. "American Exceptionalism in an Age of International History." *American Historical Review* 96 (1991): 1031-55.

United Nations. "Declaration on the Rights of Indigenous Peoples." Adopted by General Assembly Resolution 61/295. September 13, 2007. http://daccess-dds-ny.un.org/doc/UNDOC/GEN/N06/512/07/PDF/N0651207.pdf?OpenElement.

———. Fact sheet produced by the UN Permanent Forum on the Rights of Indigenous Peoples. 2005.

———. *State of the World's Indigenous Peoples.* Department of Economic and Social Affairs, Division of Social Policy and Development, Secretariat of the Permanent Forum on Indigenous Issues. New York: United Nations, 2009.

U.S. Bureau of Labor Statistics. "2010 Union Members Summary." January 21, 2011. http://www.bls.gov/news.release/union2.nro.htm.

U.S. News and World Report. "Success Story of One Minority Group in the United States." December 26, 1966. Reprinted in *Asian American Studies: A Reader.* Ed. Jean Yu-Wen Shen Wu and Min Song. New Brunswick: Rutgers University Press, 2004. 158-63.

Vaid, Urvashi. *Virtual Equality: The Mainstreaming of Gay and Lesbian Liberation.* New York: Anchor Books, 1996.

Vaidhyanathan, Siva. *Copyrights and Copywrongs: The Rise of Intellectual Property and How It Threatens Creativity.* New York: NYU Press, 2001.

———. *The Googlization of Everything (and Why We Should Worry).* Berkeley: University of California Press, 2011.

Vaillant, Derek W. "Sounds of Whiteness: Local Radio, Racial Formation, and Public Culture in Chicago, 1921-1935." *American Quarterly* 54.1 (2002): 25-66.

Valdez, Luis. "La Plebe." *Aztlán: An Anthology of Mexican American Literature.* Ed. Luis Valdez and Stan Steiner. New York: Vintage, 1972.

Valentine, David. *Imagining Transgender: An Ethnography of a Category.* Durham: Duke University Press, 2007.

Valenzuela, Angela. *Subtractive Schooling: U.S.-Mexican Youth and the Politics of Caring.* Albany: SUNY Press, 1999.

Valverde, Mariana. "Genealogies of European States: Foucauldian Reflections." *Economy and Society* 36 (2007): 159-78.

van Wyck, Peter C. *Primitives in the Wilderness: Deep Ecology and the Missing Human Subject.* Albany: SUNY Press, 1997.

Vargas, Deborah R. *Dissonant Divas in Chicana Music: The Limits of La Onda.* Minneapolis: University of Minnesota Press, 2012.

Vasconcelos, José. *The Cosmic Race.* 1925. Trans. Didier T. Jaén. Baltimore: Johns Hopkins University Press, 1997.

Veblen, Thorstein. *The Theory of the Leisure Class.* 1899. New York: Dover, 1994.

Vento, Arnoldo Carlos. *Mestizo: The History, Culture, and Politics of the Mexican and the Chicano, the Emerging Mestizo-Americans.* New York: University Press of America, 2002.

Venturelli, Shalini. *From the Information Economy to the Creative Economy: Moving Culture to the Center of International Public Policy.* Washington, DC: Center for Arts and Culture, 2001.

Vera, Hernán, and Andrew Gordon. *Screen Saviors: Hollywood Fictions of Whiteness.* New York: Rowman and Littlefield, 2003.

Vidal, Gore. "State of the Union, 2004." *Nation*, September 13, 2004.

Villa, Pablo. *Ethnography at the Border*. Minneapolis: University of Minnesota Press, 2003.

Villa, Raul. *Barriologos*. Austin: University of Texas Press, 2000.

Virno, Paolo. "The Soviets of the Multitude: On Collectivity and Collective Work." Interview by Alexei Penzin. *Mediations* 25 (Fall 2010). http://www.mediationsjournal.org/articles/the-soviets-of-the-multitude.

Vizenor, Gerald, and A. Robert Lee. *Postindian Conversations*. Lincoln: University of Nebraska Press, 1999.

Vo, Linda Trinh. *Mobilizing an Asian American Community*. Philadelphia: Temple University Press, 2004.

Von Eschen, Penny. *Race against Empire: Black Americans and Anticolonialism, 1937-1957*. Ithaca: Cornell University Press, 1997.

———. *Satchmo Blows Up the World: Jazz Ambassadors Play the Cold War*. Cambridge: Harvard University Press, 2004.

Wacquant, Loïc. "From Slavery to Mass Incarceration: Rethinking the 'Race Question' in the U.S." *New Left Review* 13 (2002): 41–60.

———. *Punishing the Poor: The Neoliberal Government of Social Insecurity*. Durham: Duke University Press, 2009.

Wajcman, Judy. *Feminism Confronts Technology*. Cambridge, UK: Polity, 1991.

Walcott, Rinaldo, ed. *Rude: Contemporary Black Canadian Cultural Criticism*. Toronto: Insomniac, 2000.

Wald, Priscilla. *Constituting Americans: Cultural Anxiety and Narrative Form*. Durham: Duke University Press, 1995.

Waldstreicher, David. *Slavery's Constitution: From Revolution to Ratification*. New York: Hill and Wang, 2010.

Waligora-Davis, Nicole. *Sanctuary: African Americans and Empire*. New York: Oxford University Press, 2011.

Walker, Alice. *The Color Purple: A Novel*. New York: Harcourt, Brace, Jovanovich, 1982.

Walker, David. *David Walker's Appeal, in Four Articles, Together with a Preamble, to the Coloured Citizens of the World, but in Particular, and Very Expressly, to Those of the United States of America*. 1829. New York: Hill and Wang, 1995.

Walker, Rebecca. *Black, White, and Jewish: Autobiography of a Shifting Self*. New York: River Trade, 2002.

Wallerstein, Immanuel. *The Modern World-System*. New York: Academic, 1976.

———. *Unthinking Social Science: The Limits of Nineteenth-Century Paradigms*. 2nd ed. Philadelphia: Temple University Press, 2001.

———. *World-Systems Theory: An Introduction*. Durham: Duke University Press, 2004.

Wallis, Brian. "Black Bodies, White Science: Louis Agassiz's Slave Daguerreotypes." *American Art* 9.2 (Summer 1995): 38–61.

Walzer, Michael, ed. *Toward a Global Civil Society*. New York: Berghahn Books, 1995.

Wardrip-Fruin, Noah, and Nick Montfort. *The New Media Reader*. Cambridge: MIT Press, 2003.

Wark, McKenzie. *A Hacker Manifesto*. Cambridge: Harvard University Press, 2004.

Warner, Michael. *The Letters of the Republic: Publication and the Public Sphere in Eighteenth-Century America*. Cambridge: Harvard University Press, 1990.

———. "Publics and Counter-Publics." *Public Culture* 14.1 (2002): 49–90.

———. *The Trouble with Normal: Sex, Politics, and the Ethics of Queer Life*. New York: Free Press, 1999.

Warner, Susan. *The Wide Wide World*. 1850. New York: Feminist Press, 1993.

Warner, W. Lloyd, and Leo Srole. *The Social Systems of American Ethnic Groups*. Chicago: University of Chicago, 1945.

Warren, Kenneth W. "Appeals for (Mis)recognition: Theorizing the Diaspora." *Cultures of United States Imperialism*. Ed. Amy Kaplan and Donald E. Pease. Durham: Duke University Press, 1993. 392–406.

Warrior, Robert Allen. "A Room of One's Own at the ASA: An Indigenous Provocation." *American Quarterly* 55.4 (December 2003): 681–87.

Watkins, Evan. *Everyday Exchanges: Marketwork and Capitalist Common Sense*. Stanford: Stanford University Press, 1998.

Wayne, Michael. "Post-Fordism, Monopoly Capitalism, and Hollywood's Media Industrial Complex." *International Journal of Cultural Studies* 6.1 (2003): 82–103.

Webb, Walter Prescott. *The Great Plains*. 1931. Lincoln: University of Nebraska Press, 1981.

Weber, Max. *Economy and Society: An Outline of Interpretive Sociology*. New York: Bedminster, 1968.

———. *Max Weber on Capitalism, Bureaucracy, and Religion: A Selection of Texts*. Ed. Stanislav Andreski. London: Allen and Unwin, 1983.

———. *The Protestant Ethic and the Spirit of Capitalism*. 1905. Trans. Talcott Parsons. New York: Scribner's, 1958.

Weinbaum, Alys Eve. *Wayward Reproductions: Genealogies of Race and Nation in Transatlantic Modern Thought*. Durham: Duke University Press, 2004.

Weiser, Mark. "The Computer for the 21st Century." *Scientific American*, September 1991, 78–89.

Welke, Barbara Young. *Law and the Borders of Belonging in the Long Nineteenth Century United States*. New York: Cambridge University Press, 2010.

West, Cornel. *Race Matters*. New York: Vintage Books, 1994.

Wettstein, Howard. Introduction to *Diasporas and Exiles: Varieties of Jewish Identity*. Ed. Howard Wettstein. Berkeley: University of California Press, 2002. 1–17.

Wexler, Laura. *Tender Violence: Domestic Visions in an Age of U.S. Imperialism*. Chapel Hill: University of North Carolina Press, 2000.

Wheatley, Phillis. "To His Excellency General Washington." 1775. *Phillis Wheatley: Complete Writings*. New York: Penguin, 2001. 88–99.

Whelchel, Toshio. *From Pearl Harbor to Saigon: Japanese American Soldiers and the Vietnam War*. London: Verso, 1999.

White, G. Edward. "From Legal Realism to Critical Legal Studies: A Truncated Intellectual History." *Southwestern Law Journal* 4 (1986): 819–43.

White, Hayden. "The Politics of Historical Interpretation: Discipline and De-sublimation." *Critical Inquiry* 9 (1982): 113–37.

Whitlock, Katherine. *In a Time of Broken Bones: A Call to Dialogue on Hate Violence and the Limitations of Hate Crime Laws*. Philadelphia: American Friends Service Committee, 2001.

Whitman, James Q. *Harsh Justice: Criminal Punishment and the Widening Divide between America and Europe.* Oxford: Oxford University Press, 2003.

Whitman, Walt. *Leaves of Grass.* 1855. Ed. Harold W. Blodgett and Sculley Bradley. New York: NYU Press, 1965.

———. "Whitman's Preface to *Leaves of Grass.*" 1855. *Selected Poems, 1855–1892: A New Edition.* Ed. Gary Schmidgall. New York: St. Martin's, 1999. 3–14.

Widmer, Edward L. *Young America: The Flowering of Democracy in New York City.* New York: Oxford University Press, 1999.

Wiegman, Robyn. *American Anatomies.* Durham: Duke University Press, 1997.

Wilentz, Sean. "Against Exceptionalism: Class Consciousness and the American Labor Movement." *International labor and Working Class History* 26 (1984a): 1–24.

———. *Chants Democratic: New York City and the Rise of the American Working Class, 1788–1850.* New York: Oxford University Press, 1984b.

Wilkins, David E., and Heidi Kiiwetinepinesiik Stark. *American Indian Politics and the American Political System.* 3rd ed. Lanham, MD: Rowman and Littlefield, 2011.

Williams, Eric. *Capitalism and Slavery.* 1944. Chapel Hill: University of North Carolina Press, 1994.

Williams, Linda. *Playing the Race Card: Melodramas of Black and White from Uncle Tom to O. J. Simpson.* Princeton: Princeton University Press, 2002.

Williams, Randall. *The Divided World: Human Rights and Its Violence.* Minneapolis: University of Minnesota Press, 2010.

Williams, Raymond. *The Country and the City.* New York: Oxford University Press, 1973.

———. *Culture and Society, 1780–1950.* New York: Columbia University Press, 1958.

———. *Keywords: A Vocabulary of Culture and Society.* 1976. London: Fontana; New York: Oxford University Press, 1983.

———. *Marxism and Literature.* 1977. Oxford: Oxford University Press, 1997.

———. *The Sociology of Culture.* New York: Schocken Books, 1982.

Williams, Robert A., Jr. *Like a Loaded Weapon: The Rehnquist Court, Indian Rights, and the Legal History of Racism in America.* Minneapolis: University of Minnesota Press, 2005.

Williams, Sherley Anne. *Dessa Rose.* New York: William Morrow, 1986.

Williams, William Appleman. "The Frontier Thesis and American Foreign Policy." *A William Appleman Williams Reader.* Ed. Henry W. Berger. Chicago: Ivan R. Dee, 1992. 89–104.

Willis, Paul. *Learning to Labor: How Working-Class Kids Get Working-Class Jobs.* New York: Columbia University Press, 1977.

Wilson, Bryan. "Secularization: The Inherited Model." *Religion in American History: A Reader.* Ed. Jon Butler and Harry S. Stout. New York: Oxford University Press, 1998. 335–44.

Wilson, Elizabeth. *Adorned in Dreams: Fashion and Modernity.* 1985. New Brunswick: Rutgers University Press, 2003.

———. *Psychosomatic: Feminism and the Neurological Body.* Durham: Duke University Press, 2004.

Wilson, George. *What Is Technology? An Inaugural Lecture Delivered in the University of Edinburgh.* Edinburgh: Sutherland and Knox, 1855.

Wilson, Harriet. *Our Nig; or, Sketches from the Life of a Free Black.* 1859. New York: Vintage, 1983.

Wilson, Rob. *Reimagining the American Pacific: From "South Pacific" to Bamboo Ridge and Beyond.* Durham: Duke University Press, 2000.

Wilson, Woodrow. "Address to a Joint Session of Congress Requesting a Declaration of War against Germany, April 2, 1917." American Presidency Project. http://www.presidency.ucsb.edu/ws/index.php?pid=65366&st=safe+for+democracy&st1= (accessed April 27, 2014).

Winant, Howard. *Racial Conditions: Politics, Theory, Comparisons.* Minneapolis: University of Minnesota Press, 1994.

———. *The World Is a Ghetto: Race and Democracy since World War II.* New York: Basic Books, 2001.

Winthrop, John. "A Modell of Christian Charity." 1630. *Collections of the Massachusetts Historical Society.* 3rd ser., vol. 7. Boston: Charles C. Little and James Brown, 1838. 31–48.

Wirtén, Eva Hemmungs. *Terms of Use: Negotiating the Jungle of the Intellectual Commons.* Toronto: University of Toronto Press, 2008.

Wolf, Eric. *Europe and the People without History.* Berkeley: University of California Press, 1982.

Wolfe, Patrick. "Settler Colonialism and the Elimination of the Native." *Journal of Genocide Research* 8 (2006): 387–410.

Wollstonecraft, Mary. *"A Vindication of the Rights of Woman" and "A Vindication of the Rights of Men."* 1790; 1792. Oxford: Oxford University Press, 2009.

Womack, Craig S. *Red on Red: Native American Literary Separatism.* Minneapolis: University of Minnesota Press, 1999.

Women Who Rock. *Women Who Rock: Making Scenes, Building Communities.* University of Washington Libraries, Seattle, 2012. http://womenwhorockcommunity.org/.

"Women Working, 1800–1930" (digital archive). Harvard University Library Open Collections Program. http://ocp.hul.harvard.edu/ww/mills.html.

Wood, Gordon S. *The Radicalism of the American Revolution.* New York: Knopf, 1992.

Woodmansee, Martha, and Peter Jaszi, eds. *The Construction of Authorship: Textual Appropriation in Law and Literature.* Durham: Duke University Press, 1994.

Woodward, C. Vann. *The Strange Career of Jim Crow.* New York: Oxford University Press, 1955.

Woolf, Virginia. "Mr. Bennett and Mrs. Brown." 1924. *The Essays of Virginia Woolf.* Vol. 3: *1919–1924.* Ed. Andrew McNeillie. San Diego, CA: Harcourt Brace, 1989. 384–89.

Woolsey, Theodore Dwight. *Political Science; or, the State Theoretically and Practically Considered.* Vol. 1. New York: Scribner, Armstrong, 1878.

Wray, Matt. *Not Quite White: White Trash and the Boundaries of Whiteness.* Durham: Duke University Press, 2006.

Wright, Erik Olin. *Classes.* London: Verso, 1985.

Wright, Melissa W. "The Dialectics of Still Life: Murder, Women and the Maquiladoras." *Public Culture* 11 (1999): 453–74.

Wright, Michelle. *Becoming Black: Creating Identity in the African Diaspora.* Durham: Duke University Press, 2004.

Wright, Richard. *The Color Curtain: A Report on the Bandung Conference.* 1956. Jackson, MS: Banner Books, 1995.

Yeh, Chiou-ling. *Making an American Festival: Chinese New Year in San Francisco's Chinatown*. Berkeley: University of California Press, 2008.

Yelvington, Kevin. "The Anthropology of Afro-Latin America and the Caribbean: Diasporic Dimensions." *Annual Review of Anthropology* 30 (2001): 227–60.

Yoneyama, Lisa. "Liberation under Siege: U.S. Military Occupation and Japanese Women's Enfranchisement." *American Quarterly* 57.3 (2005): 885–910.

Young, Alex Trimble. "Settler Sovereignty and the Rhizomatic West, or, the Significance of the Frontier in Postwestern Studies." *Western American Literature* 48.1–2 (Spring–Summer 2013): 115–40.

Young, Alfred F. *The American Revolution: Explorations in the History of American Radicalism*. DeKalb: Northern Illinois University Press, 1976.

———. *Beyond the American Revolution: Explorations in the History of American Radicalism*. DeKalb: Northern Illinois University Press, 1993.

Young, Iris Marion. *Inclusion and Democracy*. New York: Oxford University Press, 2000.

———. *Justice and the Politics of Difference*. Princeton: Princeton University Press, 1990.

Young, Jock. *The Drugtakers: The Social Meaning of Drug Use*. London: Paladin, 1971.

Yu, Henry. *Thinking Orientals: Migration, Contact, and Exoticism in Modern America*. New York: Oxford University Press, 2001.

Yúdice, George. *The Expediency of Culture: Uses of Culture in the Global Era*. Durham: Duke University Press, 2003.

Yuval-Davis, Nira. *Gender and Nation*. London: Sage, 1997.

Yuval-Davis, Nira, and Floya Anthias, eds. *Women–Nation–State*. London: Macmillan, 1989.

Zagarri, Rosemarie. *Revolutionary Backlash: Women and Politics in the Early American Republic*. Philadelphia: University of Pennsylvania Press, 2007.

Zakaria, Fareed. *The Post-American World*. New York: Norton, 2008.

Zavella, Patricia. *I'm Neither Here nor There*. Durham: Duke University Press, 2011.

Zimmermann, Eberhard August Wilhelm von. *A Political Survey of the Present State of Europe*. London, 1787.

Zinn, Howard. *A People's History of the United States*. New York: Harper and Row, 1980.

Žižek, Slavoj. "How to Begin from the Beginning." *The Idea of Communism*. Ed. Costas Douzinas and Slavoj Žižek. London: Verso, 2010. 209–26.

———. *The Ticklish Subject: The Absent Centre of Political Ontology*. London: Verso, 1999.

Zukin, Sharon, *Naked City: The Death and Life of Authentic Urban Places*. New York: Oxford University Press, 2010.

Zunshine, Lisa. *Why We Read Fiction: Theory of Mind and the Novel*. Columbus: Ohio State University Press, 2006.

About the Contributors

Lauren Berlant is George M. Pullman Distinguished Professor of English at the University of Chicago. Her work on citizenship includes *The Anatomy of National Fantasy, The Queen of America Goes to Washington City, The Female Complaint,* and *Cruel Optimism.* Her most recent book is, with Lee Edelman, *Sex, or the Unbearable.*

Marc Bousquet is Associate Professor of English at Emory University. He is the author of *How the University Works: Higher Education and the Low-Wage Nation.*

Mary Pat Brady is Associate Professor in the Department of English and Director of the Latino Studies Program at Cornell University. She is the author of *Extinct Lands, Temporal Geographies: Chicana Literature and the Urgency of Space.*

Bruce Burgett is Dean and Professor in the School of Interdisciplinary Arts and Sciences at the University of Washington, Bothell, graduate faculty in the Department of English at the University of Washington, Seattle, and Codirector of the UW graduate Certificate in Public Scholarship. He is the author of *Sentimental Bodies: Sex, Gender, and Citizenship in the Early Republic.*

Kandice Chuh is a Professor in the PhD program in English at the CUNY Graduate Center, where she is also affiliated with the Mellon Committee on Globalization and Social Change and the American Studies program. Her current research brings together aesthetic philosophies and theories, minority discourse,

and analysis of globalization's impact on modern sociopolitical subjectivity.

Ann Cvetkovich is Ellen Clayton Garwood Centennial Professor of English and Professor of Women's and Gender Studies at the University of Texas at Austin. Her most recent book is *Depression: A Public Feeling.*

Lisa Duggan is Professor of Social and Cultural Analysis at New York University and the author most recently of *Twilight of Equality? Neoliberalism, Cultural Politics, and the Attack on Democracy.*

Brent Hayes Edwards is Professor in the Department of English and Comparative Literature at Columbia University and the author of *The Practice of Diaspora,* among other works. His current book projects include a cultural history of the "loft jazz" scene in downtown Manhattan in the 1970s and a translation of Michel Leiris's anthropological classic *L'Afrique fantôme.*

Brian T. Edwards is Associate Professor of English, Comparative Literary Studies, and American Studies at Northwestern University, where he is also Director of the Program in Middle East and North African Studies. He is the author of *Morocco Bound: Disorienting America's Maghreb, from Casablanca to the Marrakech Express* and coeditor, with Dilip Gaonkar, of *Globalizing American Studies.* He is completing a book called *After the American Century: Ends of Circulation in Cairo, Casablanca, and Tehran.*

Roderick A. Ferguson is Professor of Race and Critical Theory in the Department of American Studies at the University of Minnesota. He is coeditor with Grace Hong of *Strange Affinities: The Gender and Sexual Politics of Comparative Racialization* and the author of *Aberrations in Black: Toward a Queer of Color Critique* and *The Reorder of Things: The University and Its Pedagogies of Minority Difference*.

Elizabeth Freeman is Professor of English at the University of California–Davis and coeditor of *GLQ: A Journal of Lesbian and Gay Studies*. She is the author of *Time Binds: Queer Temporalities, Queer Histories* and *The Wedding Complex: Forms of Belonging in Modern American Culture*, as well as guest editor of a special issue of *GLQ*, "Queer Temporalities."

Kevin K. Gaines is Robert Hayden Collegiate Professor of History and Afroamerican and African Studies at the University of Michigan. He is the author of *American Africans in Ghana: Black Expatriates and the Civil Rights Era*.

Alyshia Gálvez is Associate Professor and Director of the CUNY Institute of Mexican Studies at Lehman College. She is the author of *Guadalupe in New York: Devotion and the Struggle for Citizenship Rights among Mexican Immigrants* and *Patient Citizens, Immigrant Mothers: Mexican Women, Public Prenatal Care, and the Birth Weight Paradox*, which was awarded the 2012 Book Award by the Association of Latino and Latin American Anthropologists.

Rosemary Marangoly George was Associate Professor in the Department of Literature at the University of California–San Diego. She was the author of *The Politics of Home: Postcolonial Relocations and Twentieth-Century Literature*. She passed away in October 2013.

Kirsten Silva Gruesz is Professor of Literature at the University of California–Santa Cruz. She is the author of *Ambassadors of Culture: The Transamerican Origins of Latino Writing*.

Sandra M. Gustafson is Professor of English, Concurrent Professor of American Studies, and Faculty Fellow at the Kroc Institute of International Peace Studies at the University of Notre Dame. Her most recent book is *Imagining Deliberative Democracy in the Early American Republic*.

Jack Halberstam is Professor of American Studies and Ethnicity at the University of Southern California. When not trying to compress an entire cultural history into one keyword, Halberstam works on subcultures, queer epistemologies, music, and visual media. Halberstam's most recent books are *The Queer Art of Failure* and *Gaga Feminism*, and Halberstam's next book will be a cultural appraisal of queer anarchy titled *The Wild*.

Glenn Hendler is Associate Professor and Chair in the English Department at Fordham University, where he also teaches in the American Studies Program. He is the author of *Public Sentiments: Structures of Feeling in Nineteenth-Century American Literature*.

Scott Herring is Associate Professor of English at Indiana University–Bloomington. He is the author of three books: *Queering the Underworld*, *Another Country*, and *The Hoarders*.

Daniel Martinez HoSang is Associate Professor of Ethnic Studies and Political Science at the University of Oregon. He is the author of *Racial Propositions: Ballot Initiatives and the Making of Postwar California*.

Janet R. Jakobsen is Ann Whitney Olin Professor of Women's Gender and Sexuality Studies and Director of the Center for Research on Women at Barnard College. She is the author of *Working Alliances and the Politics of Difference: Diversity and Feminist Ethics* and coeditor of *Love the Sin: Sexual Regulation and the Limits of Religious Tolerance* as well as of *Secularisms* and *Interventions: Academics and Activists Respond to Violence.*

E. Patrick Johnson is the Carlos Montezuma Professor of Performance Studies and African American Studies at Northwestern University. He is the author of *Appropriating Blackness: Performance and the Politics of Authenticity* and *Sweet Tea: Black Gay Men of the South— An Oral History.*

Walter Johnson is Professor of History and African and African American Studies at Harvard University. He is the author of *River of Dark Dreams: Slavery and Empire in the Cotton Kingdom.*

Miranda Joseph is Associate Professor of Gender and Women's Studies at the University of Arizona. She is the author of *Against the Romance of Community* and *Debt to Society: Accounting for Life under Capitalism.*

J. Kēhaulani Kauanui is Associate Professor in the Departments of American Studies and Anthropology at Wesleyan University. She is the author of *Hawaiian Blood: Colonialism and the Politics of Sovereignty and Indigeneity.*

David Kazanjian is Associate Professor of English and Comparative Literature and Literary Theory at the University of Pennsylvania. He is the author of *The Colonizing Trick: National Culture and Imperial Citizenship in Early America* and *The Brink of Freedom: Improvising Life in the Nineteenth-Century Atlantic World.*

Kanta Kochhar-Lindgren is Associate Professor in the Theater and Dance Department at Macalester College. Her current art projects—"We Carry the Water," "Water Theatres," and "Pier Windows"—focus on the relationships between memory, water, and urban experience. Her written scholarship addresses topics such as water and performance, translation and embodiment, disability and performance, and transnational avant-garde Asian performance histories.

Oneka LaBennett is Associate Professor of Africana Studies and American Studies at Cornell University. She is coeditor of *Racial Formation in the Twenty-First Century*, along with Daniel Martinez HoSang and Laura Pulido, and the author of *She's Mad Real: Popular Culture and West Indian Girls in Brooklyn.*

George Lipsitz is Professor of Black Studies and Sociology at the University of California–Santa Barbara. His books include *How Racism Takes Place, American Studies in a Moment of Danger, The Possessive Investment in Whiteness,* and *Time Passages.* He served as coeditor of the American Crossroads series at the University of California Press and is editor of the Critical American Studies series at the University of Minnesota Press.

Eric Lott is Professor of English at the University of Virginia. His most recent book is *Black Mirror: The Cultural Contradictions of American Racism.*

Lisa Lowe is Professor of English and American Studies at Tufts University. She is the author of books on race, immigration, and globalization, including the forthcoming *The Intimacies of Four Continents.*

Eithne Luibhéid is Associate Professor of Gender and Women's Studies at the University of Arizona. She is the author of *Pregnant on Arrival: Making the "Illegal" Immigrant* and *Entry Denied: Controlling Sexuality at the Border* and coeditor of *A Global History of Sexuality* and *Queer Migration: Sexuality, U.S. Citizenship, and Border Crossings.*

Sunaina Maira is Professor of Asian American Studies at the University of California–Davis. She is the author of *Desis in the House: Indian American Youth Culture in New York City, Missing: Youth, Citizenship, and Empire after 9/11*, and *Jil [Generation] Oslo: Palestinian Hip Hop, Youth Culture, and the Youth Movement*. She coedited *Youthscapes: The Popular, the National, and the Global*.

Susan Manning is Professor of English, Theatre, and Performance Studies at Northwestern University. She is the author of *Modern Dance, Negro Dance: Race in Motion*.

Randy Martin is Professor and Chair of Art and Public Policy and Director of the graduate program in Arts Politics at New York University. He is the author of numerous books on financialization, including the forthcoming *Knowledge, LTD: Toward a Social Logic of the Derivative*.

Kembrew McLeod is Professor of Communication Studies at the University of Iowa. He has published and produced several books and documentaries about music and popular culture, and his writings have appeared in the *New York Times*, *Slate*, and *Rolling Stone*. His book *Freedom of Expression*® received an American Library Association book award, and his documentary *Copyright Criminals* aired on PBS.

Tara McPherson is Associate Professor in the Critical Studies and Media Arts + Practice Divisions in the University of Southern California's School of Cinematic Arts. Her coedited collection, *Transmedia Frictions*, and monograph, *Designing for Difference*, are forthcoming.

Robert McRuer is Professor of English and Chair of the Department of English at The George Washington University. He is the author of *Crip Theory: Cultural Signs of Queerness and Disability* and coeditor, with Anna

Mollow, of *Sex and Disability*. He is completing a book tentatively titled *Cripping Austerity*.

Leerom Medovoi is Professor and Department Head of English at the University of Arizona. He was the founding director of the Portland Center for Public Humanities. He is the author of *Rebels: Youth and the Cold War Origins of Identity*. He is at work on a book titled *The Second Axis of Race: Biopolitics of the Dogma Line*.

Jodi Melamed is Associate Professor of English and Africana Studies at Marquette University. She is the author of *Represent and Destroy: Rationalizing Violence in the New Racial Capitalism*.

Timothy Mitchell is Professor in the Department of Middle Eastern, South Asian, and African Studies at Columbia University. His most recent book is *Carbon Democracy: Political Power in the Age of Oil*.

Fred Moten is Professor of English at the University of California–Riverside. He is the author of *In the Break: The Aesthetics of the Black Radical Tradition* and coauthor, with Stefano Harney, of *The Undercommons: Fugitive Planning and Black Study*.

Lisa Nakamura is Professor of Screen Arts and Cultures and American Cultures at the University of Michigan, Ann Arbor. She is the author of *Digitizing Race: Visual Cultures of the Internet*, which won the Asian American Studies Association 2010 book award in cultural studies, and *Cybertypes: Race, Ethnicity, and Identity on the Internet* and is coeditor of *Race in Cyberspace* and *Race after the Internet*.

Christopher Newfield is Professor of American Studies at the University of California–Santa Barbara. His most recent book is *Unmaking the Public University: The Forty-Year Assault on the Middle Class*.

Tavia Nyong'o is Associate Professor of Performance Studies at New York University, where he teaches courses on African American art and culture, queer studies, and popular music. The author of *The Amalgamation Waltz: Race, Performance, and the Ruses of Memory*, he is completing a manuscript titled "Dark Days: Race against Time in Black Art, Cinema, and Performance since the Sixties." He is coeditor of the journal *Social Text*.

Vijay Prashad is Professor of International Studies and George and Martha Kellner Chair in South Asian History at Trinity College. His most recent books include *The Poorer Nations: A Possible History of the Global South* and *Uncle Swami: South Asians in America Today*.

Junaid Rana is Associate Professor of Asian American Studies at the University of Illinois at Urbana-Champaign. He is the author of *Terrifying Muslims: Race and Labor in the South Asian Diaspora*.

Chandan Reddy is Associate Professor of English and Gender, Women and Sexuality Studies at the University of Washington–Seattle. He is the author of *Freedom with Violence: Race, Sexuality, and the U.S. State*, which won awards from the Modern Language Association and the Asian American Studies Association. He is currently at work on a new book, *Burials of Globalization: Race, Rights, and the Failures of Culture*.

Bruce Robbins is Old Dominion Foundation Professor in the Humanities in the Department of English and Comparative Literature at Columbia University. His most recent book is *Perpetual War: Cosmopolitanism from the Viewpoint of Violence*. He is also the director of the documentary film *Some of My Best Friends Are Zionists*.

Juana María Rodríguez is Professor of Gender and Women's Studies at the University of California–Berkeley.

Her most recent book is *Sexual Futures, Queer Gestures, and Other Latina Longings*.

Valerie Rohy is Professor of English at the University of Vermont. Her most recent book is *Anachronism and Its Others: Sexuality, Race, Temporality*.

David F. Ruccio is Professor of Economics at the University of Notre Dame and a former editor of the journal *Rethinking Marxism*. Among his recent books is *Development and Globalization: A Marxian Class Analysis*.

Jentery Sayers is Assistant Professor of English and Director of the Maker Lab in the Humanities at the University of Victoria. His work has appeared in *American Literature, Digital Studies, e-Media Studies, Computational Culture, The New Work of Composing*, the *International Journal of Learning and Media, Victorian Review*, and *Kairos: Rhetoric, Technology, and Pedagogy*, among others.

Nikhil Pal Singh is Associate Professor of Social and Cultural Analysis and History at New York University. He is the author of *Black Is a Country: Race and the Unfinished Struggle for Democracy* and editor of *Climbin' Jacob's Ladder: The Black Freedom Movement Writings of Jack O'Dell*.

Stephanie Smallwood is Dio Richardson Professor and Associate Professor in the Department of History at the University of Washington–Seattle. She is the author of *Saltwater Slavery: A Middle Passage from Africa to American Diaspora*.

Caleb Smith is Professor of English and American Studies at Yale University. He is working on an edition of a nineteenth-century prison narrative, "The Life and Adventures of a Haunted Convict."

Siobhan B. Somerville is Associate Professor of English and Gender and Women's Studies at the University of Illinois at Urbana-Champaign and an affiliated faculty member in the Department of African American Studies and the Unit for Criticism and Interpretive Theory. She is the author of *Queering the Color Line: Race and the Invention of Homosexuality in American Culture* and coeditor of several special issues of journals, most recently "Queering the Middle: Race, Region, and Sexual Diasporas," a special issue of *GLQ*.

Dean Spade is Associate Professor at the Seattle University School of Law. He is the author of *Normal Life: Administrative Violence, Critical Trans Politics, and the Limits of Law*.

Amy Dru Stanley is Professor of History at the University of Chicago. She is the author of *From Bondage to Contract: Wage Labor, Marriage, and the Market in the Age of Slave Emancipation*. Her current book project explores human rights in the age of slave emancipation.

Shelley Streeby is Professor in the Departments of Literature and Ethnic Studies at the University of California–San Diego. Her most recent book is *Radical Sensations: World Movements, Violence, and Visual Culture*.

John Kuo Wei Tchen is founding director of the Asian/Pacific/American Studies Institute and Program at New York University. He is cofounder of the Museum of Chinese in America (MOCA). He is coeditor of *Yellow Peril! An Archive of Anti-Asian Fear* and chief historian for a New-York Historical Society traveling exhibition on the origins and legacy of the Chinese Exclusion Act (1882).

Thuy Linh Tu is Associate Professor of Social and Cultural Analysis at New York University. She is the author of *The Beautiful Generation: Asian Americans and the Cultural Economy of Fashion* (2011) and is currently working on a new project about the multinational cosmetics industry, "The Landscapes of Hope: Beauty, Bodies, and Buildings."

Michael Warner is Seymour H. Knox Professor of English Literature and American Studies at Yale University. He is the author of *Publics and Counterpublics* and coeditor of *Varieties of Secularism in a Secular Age*.

Robert Warrior is a member of the Osage Nation and Founding President of the Native American and Indigenous Studies Association. He is Professor of American Indian Studies, English, and History at the University of Illinois at Urbana-Champaign.

Alys Eve Weinbaum is Associate Professor of English at the University of Washington–Seattle. She is the author of *Wayward Reproductions: Genealogies of Race and Nation in Transatlantic Modern Thought* and is completing a book titled *The Afterlife of Slavery: Human Reproduction in Biocapitalism*.

Henry Yu is Associate Professor of History and Principal of St. John's College at the University of British Columbia. He is the author of *Thinking Orientals: Race, Migration, and Contact in Modern America*.

George Yúdice is Professor and Chair of Modern Languages and Literatures and Latin American Studies at the University of Miami, where he is also Director of the Miami Observatory on Communication and Creative Industries. He is the author of *Cultural Policy*, *The Expediency of Culture: Uses of Culture in the Global Era*, *Nuevas tecnologías, música y experiencia*, and *Culturas emergentes en el mundo hispano de Estados Unidos*.

CPSIA information can be obtained
at www.ICGtesting.com
Printed in the USA
LVOW03s1559030816

498915LV00015B/563/P